Continuum Glossary of Religious Terms

Continuum Glossary of Religious Terms

Ron Geaves

continuum
LONDON · NEW YORK

Continuum
The Tower Building, 11 York Road, London SE1 7NX
370 Lexington Avenue, New York, NY 10017-6503

First published 2002

© Ron Geaves 2002

British Library Cataloguing-in-Publication Data
A catalogue record for this book is available from the British Library.

ISBN 0-8264-4881-X (hardback)
0-8264-4882-8 (paperback)

Library of Congress Cataloging-in-Publication Data
Geaves, Ron.
    Continuum glossary of religious terms / Ron Geaves.
        p. cm.
    ISBN 0-8264-4881-X — ISBN 0-8264-4882-8 (pbk.)
    1. Religions—Terminology. I. Title: Glossary of religious terms. II. Title.

BL82 .G43 2001
200′.3—dc21

00-047570

Typeset by CentraServe Ltd, Saffron Walden, Essex
Printed and bound in Great Britain by
CPD, Ebbw Vale

Contents

Preface

Over ten years ago I was working as an associate tutor for the Open University, teaching their course 'The Religious Quest', which introduced six religions through distance learning. Many of the students told me that they found the mastering of religious terminology in so many unknown languages and involving unfamiliar concepts to be the most daunting part of the module. Later, as a full-time lecturer in Religious Studies at the University of Wolverhampton, the same sentiments were expressed to me by undergraduates. It was then that I decided to create a glossary of religious terminology of the six religions taught in British schools and also add Jainism. The glossary had a humble beginning. I intended to produce a small booklet that could be reproduced internally for my students with simple but clear one-line definitions. However, that was four years ago. The completed glossary contains over 2,500 entries. The project grew as I added term after term and then realized that I had gone past my personal brief. Even now the glossary's completion is arbitrary, as each religion covered is a conceptual framework for viewing the world that commands a vast vocabulary. However, I have decided to stop adding new terms in the interests of maintaining a single volume. My choice of terms has been determined by school and undergraduate curricula, and the length of each definition has been dictated by the fact that this is a glossary and not a specialist religious dictionary. Inevitably, however, some concepts and persons needed more than a short passage in order to clarify their significance and highlight their importance within the world of their respective religion.

Several of the religions included have spread across the globe and have therefore developed terminologies in several languages. For example, Islam naturally has a vast number of terms in Arabic but it also has a religious language in Urdu. Buddhism is expressed in both Sanskrit and Pali, and also has religious terms unique to Japan and Tibet. Where a term is employed that is not in the main language of the religion, an abbreviation indicates the language. Therefore Muslim terminology is from the Arabic unless indicated otherwise. The code for the languages is:

Ch	Chinese	Sin	Sinhalese
J	Japanese	T	Tibetan
P	Pali	U	Urdu
S	Sanskrit		

Finally, I would like to thank Catherine Barnes, whose patience and support has been remarkable over the last four years, and Janet Joyce, who provided the opportunity for this project to grow from its inception to completion.

Aaron *Judaism* The brother of MOSES, who was chosen by God to be the prophet's spokesperson to the Egyptians. It was Aaron who smote the Red Sea so that it opened and allowed the freed slaves to cross and thus escape the Egyptian forces. It is said that Moses was not able to do this himself as he once had enjoyed the hospitality of Egypt. (*See also* EXODUS)

Ab *Judaism* The categorization in the Bible of thirty-nine kinds of labour that are forbidden to Jews on the SHABBAT. These were further developed by rabbinical commentators, since the categories reflect the period in which they were written down in the scripture: for example, sowing, weaving, planting, building. (*See also* TOLADOT)

Abbasid *Islam* A dynasty of caliphs who ruled from Baghdad and were descendants of an uncle of Muhammad, Muttalib Ibn Hashim. The Abbasids joined with the followers of Ali, the Prophet's son-in-law, who had a stronger claim to the leadership of the Muslims than the ruling UMAYYADS. Under the leadership of Abu al-Abbas, promising a return to religious orthodoxy combined with theocracy and the support of non-Arab Muslims and the SHI'A, they ousted the Umayyads in 750. Their dynasty ruled until 1258 when it was destroyed by the Mongols. In this period there was an extraordinary flowering of Muslim culture and the development of the mystical path of the SUFIS.

Abbess *Christianity* The title given to the heads of certain orders of nuns, particularly those of the BENEDICTINE rule. The Benedictines make life appointments but other orders, such as the FRANCISCANS, hold regular elections and circulate the position amongst the sisters of the institution. There is also a marked difference in degrees of authority between the various orders. (*See also* ABBOT)

Abbot *Christianity* The title given to the heads of certain orders of monks, particularly those of the BENEDICTINE rule. An abbot has far-reaching powers over the maintenance and control of his community. He is perceived as the father of his community and generally elected for life by his brothers. Other orders who appoint an abbot may be more democratic. (*See also* ABBESS)

Abd *(slave, servant)* Islam   A term used to denote the status of a Muslim who is obedient to the will of Allah by following His commandments as laid down for all humanity in the QUR'AN. It follows on from Islam, which means 'surrender'. The highest ideal of Islam is to be the servant or slave of God, entirely submitted to His will.

Abduh, Muhammad (1845–1905)   Islam   A Muslim reformer influenced by Jamal al-Din AFGHANI. Although a traditionally trained scholar of Islam, he argued that revelation and science were not incompatible, as faith and reason operated in independent spheres and were therefore not in conflict. He argued that reason and faith had to work hand in hand with each other to benefit humankind. He enjoined Muslims to maintain their traditional faith but to develop their knowledge in other spheres of learning. He has influenced contemporary Muslims by his powerful argument that Islam was the only religion that actively calls upon human beings to investigate nature and utilize reason. (*See also* KHAN, SAYYID AHMAD)

Abhaya dana *(no-fear giving)* Jainism   One of the four ways of providing charity (DANA), which is one of the six daily duties practised by devout lay Jains. 'No-fear' refers to the development of the inner qualities required to live in such a way as not to cause any anxiety or fear in other living beings. This quality is regarded very highly by Jains because it is part of the code of AHIMSA.

Abhidhamma (P) / Abhidharma (S)   *Buddhism*   The philosophy and psychology of Buddhism presented in an abstract systematic form as a 'higher' or 'further' exposition of the Buddha's teachings. The Abhidhamma literature consists of commentaries and interpretations of the earliest SUTRAS and provides a systematic analysis of the Buddha's discourses. (*See also* ABHIDHAMMA PITAKA)

Abhidhamma Pitaka (P) / Abhidharma Pitaka (S) *(basket of higher teachings)*   Buddhism   The third section of the canon of scripture in the THERAVADA tradition, consisting of seven texts arranged by the Buddha's early followers. It is an abstract and impersonal philosophical treatise concerned with psychical and mental phenomena which was extracted and systematized from the basic teachings of the Buddha. The texts function as a series of commentaries. (*See also* TIPITAKA)

Abhiseka *Hinduism*   The rite of bathing the MURTI, a central part of temple

2

worship. Each day the *murti* is woken, bathed in various sacred substances such as sesame oil or curd, and then adorned in new clothes, jewellery and a sacred thread. (*See also* PUJA)

Abinu Malkenu *Judaism* A group of forty-five supplication prayers recited on specific occasions such as the ten days of penitence, fast days or the Jewish New Year.

Abjuration *Christianity* The act of renouncing a previously held conviction or loyalty to a person or institution, sometimes required when Christians move from one denomination to another. (*See* APOSTASY)

Ablutions *Christianity* The ritual washing of the fingers in holy water by the priest before the EUCHARIST. (*See also* MASS)

Abot di Rabbi Nathan *Judaism* A large treatise of Jewish ethics and commentaries that is separate from the MISHNAH and attributed to Rabbi NATHAN.

Abraham *Judaism* The father of the Jewish people, who entered the first covenant with God after demonstrating his obedience by offering to sacrifice his son ISAAC. It is said in the Bible that he was originally a native of the city of Ur in Chaldea but after travelling with his family, he settled near Hebron. The practising Jew looks to Abraham as the ideal of faithfulness, longing for the True God and generosity of spirit.

Abrahma *(unchaste)* *Jainism* A variety of actions that should be avoided by the vow of BRAHMACARYA, adapted for the use of lay Jains. Usually it refers to various immoral sexual activities, such as adultery, fornication, sexually explicit language and using pornography, but there are also prescriptions on finding one's own marriage partner or passing time in the company of the opposite sex without a third person being present.

Absolution *Christianity* The formal forgiveness of SINS, pronounced by a priest in the name of Christ and given to those who are penitent. Absolution is required before participating in the MASS or EUCHARIST. Although Roman Catholics still perform personal confession, in which the individual asks for forgiveness after acknowledging specific sins directly to a priest separated by a grid or curtain, it is now more common for all the congregants at the Mass or Eucharist to make a communal liturgical confession and receive communal forgiveness. (*See also* PENANCE)

3

Abstinence *Christianity*   Usually associated with not eating certain kinds of food on various feast days. Traditionally Roman Catholics did not eat meat on Fridays. In the Eastern churches there are around 150 days of abstinence in the calendar. (*See* GOOD FRIDAY)

Abu Bakr *Islam*   The first caliph of Islam, who succeeded the Prophet in the leadership of the Muslim community after his death in 632 and ruled until his own death in 634. Abu Bakr was the Prophet's father-in-law and one of the first three or four to accept him and the message of Islam. He was known for his piety and is believed to have compiled the first QUR'AN by collecting all the verses and placing them in one book. The NAQSHBANDI Sufi TARIQAH regards Abu Bakr as the founder of their line of SHAIKHS. The caliphate of Abu Bakr was riven by war between the tribes that had accepted Islam and those that had not. However, Muslim historians believe that the wars were fought against tribes that had already offered their oath of allegiance to the Prophet but later seceded and followed false prophets and gods. (*See also* AL-KHALIFA-UR-RASHIDUN)

Abu Hanifa (d.767) *Islam*   The founder of the HANAFI school of jurisprudence that developed in Iraq and went on to become the largest in the Muslim world. It was accepted as the official law school of the Ottoman empire and still remains the dominant one in the Indian subcontinent. Abu Hanifa was a merchant by trade but became the most influential of the Muslim jurists. He taught orally, and his work was collected by one of his followers, Abu Yusef. Abu Hanifa emphasized the role of QIYAS or analogical deduction, but also acknowledged the role of independent reasoning in deducing law from the revelation. (*See also* FIQH; IJTIHAD)

Acaradasa *Jainism*   One of a group of seven SUTRAS (scriptures) known as CHEDA SUTRAS. The *Acaradasa* deals with transgressions against the ascetic life and lists the perfect qualities of a senior monk. It also provides the eleven stages of spiritual development that allow lay Jains to progress towards liberation. (*See also* PRATIMA)

Acaranga Sutra *Jainism*   One of the eleven primary canons (ANGAS) and amongst the oldest Jain scriptures (fourth to fifth century), it tells of the conduct and ascetic life of MAHAVIR, the historic founder of Jainism. It also lists the rules of behaviour for a monk, the major transgressions that can be committed by Jains and botanical and zoological explanations for the world. (*See also* AGAMA)

Acarya *Jainism*   A title conferred on a senior monk who is given leadership responsibility or administrative duties over a group of other monks. Also used as a title of respect for the ascetic-scholars in Jain history. (*See also* SADHU)

Acarya / Acharya *(one who teaches by example)* *Hinduism* Title given to a prominent or exemplary spiritual teacher or a religious scholar who teaches correct conduct based on observance of DHARMA. Traditionally it was necessary to be able to expound the UPANISHADS, the BRAHMA SUTRAS and the BHAGAVAD GITA in order to receive the title of *acarya*. One of the four orders of renunciates established by SHANKARA.

Acaurya *(non-stealing)* *Jainism* One of the five vows of Jainism that are binding on both ascetic and lay Jains. Non-stealing or theft means taking anything that is not given freely. The vow of non-stealing for lay Jains applies to tax evasion, overcharging, adulterating food and drink or any form of dishonesty. Jain monks interpret this vow to mean renouncing any possessions that are not permitted by their vows and given freely by the SANGHA. They are even fed by the community. (*See also* ANUVRATAS; MAHAVRATAS)

Acelakka *(nudity)* *Jainism* Believed to have been practised by all Jain ascetics originally, it is now confined to the DIGAMBARA monks. The traditional explanation for the founding of the two main sects of Jainism states that after a famine in Bihar, some monks travelled south. When they returned they discovered that the monks who stayed behind had taken to wearing a white cloth to cover their nakedness. (*See also* SVETAMBARA)

Acts of the Apostles *Christianity* The fifth book of the New Testament, which is a valuable source of information on the early church after the death and resurrection of Jesus Christ. It was probably written by Luke, Paul's physician and fellow traveller, who accompanied the apostle on evangelical journeys. The overall tone and themes of the writing suggest that one intention was to convince the Roman authorities that Christianity was not a threat to imperial order. The book begins with Jesus' ascension and the receiving of the Holy Spirit at Pentecost which transformed the demoralized apostles. It then goes on to record the development of the church in Jerusalem, the martyrdom of Stephen, early missionary work to the Jewish communities around the Mediterranean and the first contact with GENTILES. The book details the events that led to the conversion of Paul and the final section deals with his missionary journeys, culminating in his house arrest in Rome.

Actual sin *Christianity* A SIN which results from a free decision of the will to perform an ungodly act, as opposed to ORIGINAL SIN.

AD *Christianity* The abbreviated form of *Anno Domini* (Latin: in the year of our Lord), used in the Christian calendar, which begins from the approximate date of the birth of Jesus Christ. (*See* BCE; CE)

Adab *Islam*   The term refers to ideal behaviour or habits and to the practice of modelling an ideal Muslim life on the behaviour and habits of the Prophet. It is used by SUFIS to describe the practice of followers modelling themselves on the behaviour of their particular SHAIKH and to describe spiritual or ritual practices unique to the TARIQAH. *Adab* may involve wearing the same style of clothing or even carrying the same kind of stick as the *shaikh*. It is hoped that by imitating the habits of the holy man, his piety and closeness to Allah will also be absorbed.

Adam *Christianity*   In Christian theology Adam is the first human being, whose fall from the state of grace is inherited by all succeeding generations until the intercession of Christ. Adam appears most frequently in the letters of St Paul, where he is contrasted with Jesus Christ. Christ is sometimes likened to Adam before the fall and is called the 'second Adam'. The victory of Christ over death at the resurrection counteracts the punishment for Adam's original disobedience and allows the possibility for human beings to be reconciled with God as they were meant to be in the garden of EDEN before the fall. (*See also* EVE)

Adam *Islam*   The father of the human race and the first prophet of Allah. Unlike mainstream Christianity, Islam has no concept of original sin and the fall. Although Adam and Eve disobey God, they are both later reconciled after begging for forgiveness. The moment of reconciliation is believed to have taken place on a hill near MAKKAH, an event which Muslims re-enact ritually in the annual pilgrimage to Makkah known as the HAJJ.

Adana-niksepa samiti *(carefulness in picking and placing)* *Jainism*   One of the five 'carefulnesses' or precautions practised vigilantly by Jain ascetics to ensure that they do not accidentally cause harm to small creatures, such as insects, when putting down or picking up possessions. (*See* SAMITI)

Adat *Islam*   The local customs of a particular culture that has been converted to Islam. In the SHARI'A legal system, local customs are recognized as legitimate practices unless they directly contradict the precepts of Islamic law. A whole body of law exists that deals especially with local custom. (*See also* URF)

Adattadana-viramana *(refraining from stealing)* *Jainism*   One of the principal virtues or rules of right conduct laid down in Jain scripture. It is binding upon both lay Jains and monks. (*See* ACAURYA; PRATIMA)

Adawiya, Rabi'a al- (d.801) *Islam*   A famous female mystic born in Basra, who was sold into slavery but released after demonstrating her piety and asceticism. She did not marry and stories abound of her single-minded love for Allah. It is said that even in spring she refused to open her shutters in case she was distracted from her contemplation. Rabi'a has come to epitomize loving devotion in the SUFI tradition.

Adha   *Islam*   The need to cling to God for protection and take refuge in the shelter of His revelation. It also carries with it the need to escape from the clutches of Satan and ensure one's safety in the afterlife. In various forms of folk religion *adha* is associated with the practice of providing TA'WIDHS or amulets for protection from disease or evil spirits.

Adhan / Azhan (U)   *Islam*   The prayer-call which is recited aloud from the mosque five times a day to usher Muslims to prayer. It is said to have originated in a revelation from Allah after Muhammad had deliberated on the best way to remind human beings of their obligation to God in prayer. The Christians used bells and the Jews used the ram's horn. It was eventually decided that the human voice was the best means. The first caller of the prayer was a black companion of the Prophet named BILAL. In Britain, the prayer-call is usually made inside the mosque so as not to disturb the surrounding non-Muslim community.

In translation the prayer-call is as follows:
Allah is Great (four times)
I testify that there is no god but Allah (twice)
I testify that Muhammad is Allah's messenger (twice)
Come to prayer (twice)
Come to success (twice)
Prayer has begun (twice)
Allah is Great (twice)
There is no god but Allah (once).
(*See also* ALLAHU AKBAR; SALAH)

Adi Granth *(first book)*   *Sikhism*   The principal scripture of the Sikh religion. It is usually known by its title GURU GRANTH SAHIB. Adi Granth refers to the scripture before it became the last and eternal Guru of the Sikhs after the death of GURU GOBIND SINGH. The Adi Granth was originally compiled by the fifth Guru, GURU ARJAN DEV, who, according to Sikh tradition, dictated it to his devotee, Bhai Gur Das (d.1629). There have been later additions by Guru Arjan's successors but the final version was put together by Guru Gobind Singh, the tenth and last of the Sikh human Gurus.

Adi Guru *(the primal teacher)*   *Sikhism*   Used to describe the first GURU. The first human Guru was GURU NANAK, who received his commission to teach from God, the primal Guru. The term *Adi Guru* is usually associated with the revelationary aspect of God rather than the human Gurus. (*See also* SATGURU)

Adivasis *Hinduism*   The numerous tribes of indigenous people whose culture can be traced back over half a million years. Their practices and beliefs have influenced popular Hinduism and may reflect the original religion of the Indian subcontinent.

Adonai *(Lord)* *Judaism*   The name most often used to call upon God and to replace YHWH whenever it appears, as it cannot be pronounced. *Adonai* reflects the relationship of master and servants but also indicates that the God of Israel is a personal Lord. (*See also* EHYEH ASHER EHYEH; YAHWEH)

Advaita Vedanta *Hinduism*   The non-dualistic system of VEDANTA taught by SHANKARA, based on his monistic interpretation of the famous pronouncement of the CHANDOGYA UPANISHAD: TAT TVAM ASI ('You are that'). Shankara argued that this referred to complete identity of BRAHMAN, ATMAN and the world. Any form of perception that does not recognize the reality of this monistic unity is under the sway of MAYA or illusion.

Advent *(coming)* *Christianity*   The time set aside for spiritual preparation for CHRISTMAS that originated in the merging of Gallician and Roman traditions. It begins on the fourth Sunday before Christmas, except in the Eastern churches, which start forty days before. Traditionally it used to be a time of periodic preparatory fasting known as St Martin's Lent. Today, many people maintain an Advent calendar, which provides a day-to-day run-in to the festival period of Christmas. Church sermons in the period of Advent tend to focus on calls to repentance.

Adventists *Christianity*   Various Christian communities who believe that the second coming of Christ is imminent. The movement was established by William Miller (1782–1849), a Baptist farmer from New York, who declared that Christ would come again in 1843/4. Despite the failure of the predictions, a variety of Adventist movements continue to exist. (*See* JEHOVAH'S WITNESSES; SEVENTH DAY ADVENTISTS)

Afghani, Jamal al-Din (1839–97) *Islam*   An influential nineteenth-century reformer who cautioned Muslims to unite against the dominance of Western power and culture, he also argued that there was nothing in Islam that was opposed to the discoveries of science and technology. He urged them to discard a medieval mindset and begin to address the demands of modern society. (*See* ABDUH, MUHAMMAD; KHAN, SAYYID AHMAD)

Afikomen *Judaism*   The portion of MATZAH which is eaten near the end of the SEDER (Passover) and commemorates the occasion when the feast culminated with eating the paschal lamb that had been sacrificed in the Temple.

Agadah / Aggadah   *Judaism*   Part of the Jewish oral tradition contained in the TALMUD which deals with ethics and moral values based on rabbinical interpretation of the TORAH. The teachings were derived from searching every book of the BIBLE for material on ethics, morality, values, theology and the history of the Jewish people. The canon of moral and ethical laws derived from this process pertained to both the individual and the Jewish nation. The Agadah differs from HALAKHAH in that it contains non-legal material, such as folklore, exemplary behaviour of pious Jews and legends, which can be used to provide examples or support for the laws and regulations. (*See also* MIDRASH)

Agam Mandirs   *Jainism*   Jain temples that are dedicated to the AGAMA texts. They are generally found in Gujarat and Maharashtra.

Agama   *Buddhism*   *See* NIKAYA.

Agama   *Hinduism*   The collection of scriptures acknowledged as the sacred canon of the SHAIVITE tradition and believed to have been uttered by SHIVA or PARVATI himself or herself. They provide the authority for most of the rituals and doctrines of specific Shaivite and Tantric sects. (*See also* TANTRA)

Agama *(tradition)*   *Jainism*   The collection of Jain scriptures that is divided into three categories: pre-canons (PURVAS), primary canons (ANGAS) and secondary canons (UPANGAS). Jain scriptures are not believed to be of divine origin but contain the teachings of human beings who have obtained omniscience. The DIGAMBARA sect maintains that the primary canons were forgotten before the scriptures could be written down.

Agape   *Christianity*   The Greek term for divine love as opposed to worldly love, it can be directed towards God, Christ or fellow Christians. The term is also used in the New Testament for the communal meal partaken by the early Christians that developed into the EUCHARIST.

Agenda   *Christianity*   A liturgical term used to describe matters of religious practice as opposed to doctrine, particularly the prescribed forms of service. (*See* LITURGY; EUCHARIST)

Aggadah   *Judaism*   *See* AGADAH.

Aghatiya Karma / Aghati Karma   *Jainism*   The four types of nonharmful KARMA that do not lead to ignorance or lack of knowledge of the essential nature of the self. They are lifespan-determining karma (*ayu*), body-producing karma (NAMA), status-determining karma (*gotra*) and feeling-producing karma (*vedaniya*). (*See also* GHATI KARMA)

Aghori   *Hinduism*   A SHAIVITE sect of SADHUS who live at cremation grounds, drink and eat from human skulls and offer polluting substances such as blood, meat, alcohol and sexual fluids to the deities they propitiate. The intention is to obtain powers through practising taboos. This type of asceticism has virtually died out in India but is maintained by the Aghoris in VARANASI.

Agni   *Hinduism*   The Vedic god of fire who mediates between gods and humans. He is the principal god invoked in the sacrifice, along with SOMA. Agni is the ultimate priest, who brings men and gods together by consuming the sacrifice offered by the BRAHMINS. (*See also* VEDA)

Agra puja   *Jainism*   A common Jain form of worship that takes place in the temple either as a ritual in its own right or as the final stage of the longer ASTA-PRAKARI PUJA (the eightfold worship). The devotees approach the inner shrine of the temple and stand in front of the image of the JINA, where they burn incense and wave a tray of lighted ghee candles. (*See also* ARTI)

Agunah   *Judaism*   A woman whose husband has disappeared. In orthodox Judaism, where there is no evidence of death, the woman is not allowed to remarry. (*See also* HALAKHAH)

Ahamkara / Ahankara   *Hinduism*   The sense of ego or 'I'-ness. The awareness of individual being that can be transcended by the experience of the self's true identity. (*See* YOGA)

Ahampratyaya   *Jainism*   The Jain doctrine of self-awareness or knowledge of the self or soul. Once one knows the reality of the soul and the universe, then it is essential to apply that knowledge to spiritual progress.

Ahankar *(self-conceit, pride or ego)*   *Sikhism*   One of the conditions of ignorance that separate human beings from God. *Ahankar* can arise from attachment to wealth, beauty, physical strength or intellectual prowess, all of which may inflate the ego and lead to self-consciousness (HAUMAI) rather than God-consciousness. The only antidote to *ahankar* is humility.

Ahara   *Buddhism*   The condition or cause that maintains an object's existence. Materially it means nourishment, but the concept refers to four causes or conditions essential for the existence and continuity of beings. (*See* KAHALINKAR-AHARA; MANOSANCETANAHARA; PASSAHARA; VINNANAHARA)

Aharonim *(The Later Ones)* *Judaism*   The rabbinic authorities who emerged after the writing down of the SHULHAN ARUKH, the authoritative code of Orthodox Jewish law written in the sixteenth century CE. Usually these later authorities had to acknowledge as precedent the earlier legal decisions of those who came before the writing of the *Shulhan Arukh*. (*See also* RISHONIM)

Ahimsa *Buddhism*   *Ahimsa*, or harmlessness, is a central aspect of right livelihood in Buddhism, one of the aspects of the noble eightfold path that leads to eventual freedom from SAMSARA. A practising Buddhist will refrain from anything that may cause harm to other living beings, a consideration that should influence the choice of occupation. (*See also* SAMMA AJIVA)

Ahimsa *Hinduism*   Non-violence, harmlessness or respect for the sanctity of life. In Hinduism it has been popularized by the figure of Gandhi in his campaign of SATYAGRAHA ('holding on to the truth') against the British raj. *Ahimsa* had long been one of the essential stages of the discipline of YOGA and had developed as the central doctrine of Jainism.

Ahimsa *(harmlessness)* *Jainism*   The central doctrine and one of the three principles of Jainism that insists upon non-violence to all creatures and the avoidance of causing suffering. Reverence for all life is paramount, and can be achieved by taking care not to inflict mental, verbal or physical injury. Avoidance of violence also includes restricting others' freedom of thought and speech. Jainism believes that *ahimsa* is the highest principle of religion and in many ways it has become synonymous with Jain tradition. (*See* ANEKANTAVADA APARIGRAHA)

Ahl al-Bait *Islam*   The household of the Prophet, in particular ALI and FATIMA, the daughter of the Prophet, and his two grandsons, HUSAIN and HASAN. Although held in very high regard by all Muslims, the SHI'A hold the immediate family and their descendants in deep reverence. They believe that the bloodline of the Prophet is endowed with spiritual power that gives them some of the authority of the Prophet himself. Ali and Husain are particularly revered.

Ahl al-Hadith *Islam*   A nineteenth-century reform movement founded by Sayyid Nazir Hussein (d.1902), who studied with Muhammad Ishaq, the grand-son of the famous Indian theologian and mystic, Shah WALIALLAH. The Ahl al-Hadith is extremely conservative and opposed to all Muslim mysticism. Most of its members are from the higher classes and it has never become as successful as

11

DEOBAND, the other great school founded by successors of Shah Waliallah. Birmingham is the central headquarters of the Ahl al-Hadith in Britain. In recent times it has allied itself with the Middle Eastern movement known as the SALAFI.

Ahl al-Kitab *(The People of the Book)* *Islam* Used to refer to Jews and Christians, who are regarded as special communities that have been chosen by Allah as recipients of a prophet and a revealed scripture. There are several references in the QUR'AN to the status of Jews and Christians. For example:

Those who believe in the Qur'an, those who follow the Jewish scriptures, and the Sabians and the Christians, and who believe in Allah and the Last Day, and work righteousness, on them shall be no fear, nor shall they grieve (5:69)

In Muslim societies, the People of the Book were given privileged status and according to Muslim law (SHARI'A), it is permissible to marry a Christian or a Jew. In India, it was decided that the ancient scriptures of the Hindus, such as the UPANISHADS, were monotheistic in content and therefore allowed for a pragmatic tolerance to exist towards the majority Hindu population.

Ahl as-Sunna wa Jamaat / Ahl-li Sunnat wa-Jamaat *Islam* The majority of traditional SUNNI Muslims as opposed to the SHI'A. However, in the contemporary Muslim world there is a fierce debate about who can be considered a real Sunni. The WAHHABIS claim that they are the true Sunnis, but traditional Muslims who have always regarded the SUFIS with honour and used the Prophet for his intercession, believing that he has special powers to know the unseen, are beginning to rally behind the title of Ahl as-Sunna wa Jamaat. (*See also* ISTIGHATHA)

Ahmadiya / Ahmadiyya *Islam* A movement founded in the subcontinent by Mirza Ghulam Ahmad (1835–1908), whose members believed him to be the promised MAHDI. The movement divided, as some followers took a more eclectic line and associated their founder with Jesus and Krishna. The division is usually known as Qadiani. The belief in the pre-eminence of Mirza Ghulam Ahmad has resulted in the Ahmadiya being declared non-Muslim by several states including Pakistan. Through migration they have become an international movement and are known for their organizational ability.

Ahwal *Islam* The states of being on the path of internal purification that lead to loss of the NAFS (ego) and absorption into God (FANA) as practised by Sufis. The states of being are contrasted to the stages through which a disciple is guided by a SHAIKH (teacher), although they are linked to them. The stages are achieved by human effort, but the states of being are given by the grace of Allah. (*See also* TARIQAH)

Aisha / Aishah   *Islam*   The most beloved of Muhammad's wives and the daughter of his trusted companion, ABU BAKR. She married the Prophet at the end of his life whilst she was still a young woman. After his death she became known as the 'mother of the believers' and played a prominent public role in the early years of the Muslim community, and many HADITH are attributed to her. After ALI was appointed as caliph, she led an army against him, as she did not support his claim to the caliphate. However, she was defeated and captured. Ali treated her with great honour but confined her to MADINAH. Her dislike of Ali may have arisen from an incident that occurred when the Prophet was still alive. She had been left behind without a companion when travelling in a caravan and had been rescued by a male Muslim. Ali had suggested that her virtue could no longer be trusted, as she had been alone with a male stranger. (*See also* KHADIJAH)

Aisle   *Christianity*   Traditionally used to describe an extension of the nave or main part of the church where the congregation are seated. However, today it is more commonly used to denote the walkway up the centre of the nave that divides the main body of the church and leads up to the SANCTUARY and ALTAR.

Ajal   *Islam*   The concept that the lifespan of all creatures is predetermined by God. Frequently mentioned in several passages in the QUR'AN, it is used as a warning to remind people that the time to turn towards God should not be delayed, as no one knows when their allotted days will end. Pre-Islamic Arab tribes were extremely fatalistic and believed that time itself functioned in the same way to predetermine the term of life. The message of Islam replaced time with an absolute omniscient, omnipotent God. (*See* AMR)

Ajapa Jap   *Sikhism*   The continuous remembrance of the name of God, which the Sikh gurus taught was possible to maintain without the aid of external rituals or aids. It is described as the final stage of meditation where inner devotion or awareness of the presence of God is automatic and not dependent on special events, actions, places or times. (*See* SATGURU; SATNAM)

Ajiva   *Jainism*   All the components of the universe with the exception of the soul. *Ajiva* is everlasting but constantly changing, and consists of matter, motion, inertia, space and time. (*See* JIVA)

Ajna vicaya   *Jainism*   One of the four types of virtuous meditation practised by Jains. It refers to reflection on the teachings of the JINAS accompanied by an inner attitude of complete faith. This meditation usually consists of close study of scripture. (*See also* VICAYA)

Akal Bungga *(Pavilion of Immortality)*   *Sikhism*   Built by the sixth Guru of

Sikhism, GURU HARGOBIND, opposite the entrance to the Golden Temple in Amritsar. It is used for the AMRIT PAHUL initiation rite into the KHALSA. (*See also* HARMANDIR)

Akal Purakh / Akal Purukh *(The Eternal One)* *Sikhism*   *Akal* means not subject to death. It was one of the titles for God used by GURU NANAK, the founder of Sikhism.

Akal Takht / Akal Takhat *(Throne of the Immortal One)* *Sikhism*   There are five *takhts* or seats of religious authority in Sikhism. The Akal Takht, which faces the entrance to the Golden Temple in Amritsar, is the oldest and most important. The administrative or temporal headquarters of Sikhism, it was built by GURU HARGOBIND in 1608. The present building, although severely damaged by the Indian army in 1984, was built in the eighteenth century during the reign of Maharaja RANJIT SINGH. The Akal Takht is managed by the General Committee of the SGPC, the Shiromani Gurdwara Prabandhak Committee, and is the ultimate authority in all religious decisions. Disobedience to the decisions made in the Akal Takht can lead to excommunication. The GURU GRANTH SAHIB rests in the Akal Takht at night, from where it is taken to the Golden Temple in procession every morning. The Akal Takht represents the MIRI/PIRI authority of the guru. (*See also* HARMANDIR; PANJ TAKHT; SGPC)

Akal Ustat *(Praise of the Eternal One)* *Sikhism*   A poetic composition of the tenth GURU GOBIND SINGH. In 272 verses, the Guru praises various aspects of God and maintains the teachings of earlier GURUS on the universality of humankind and the pointlessness of ritual in obtaining realization of God.

Akali Dal *Sikhism*   A political party within Sikhism, founded in 1920, which has promoted the ideal of an autonomous state or homeland for the Sikhs in the Punjab, based on the separate identity of the Sikh community and the adoption of GURMUKHI as the state language.

Akalis *(The Immortals)* *Sikhism*   A sect of warrior ascetics who have been active since the end of the seventeenth century. The Akalis are distinctive in their blue-chequered robes, yellow turbans and displays of traditional weaponry, which include steel quoits in their turbans. They pride themselves on maintaining the traditions of Sikhism but are unusual in their strict vegetarianism and vows of celibacy. (*See* NIHANG)

Akash Bani / Akash Vani *(The Word of God)* *Sikhism*   The command or will of God expressed to a person in a high state of spiritual awareness. It can also refer to the thoughts which arise in the mind of a spiritually inspired person.

Consequently, it can allude to either revelation or inspiration from the divine. (*See* SABAD)

Akedah *Judaism* The sacrifice of ISAAC by his father ABRAHAM which represents surrender to God, as described in Genesis 22: 1–19.

Akhand Path *Sikhism* The continuous reading of the complete GURU GRANTH SAHIB by a succession of readers. The full rendering of the scripture will normally take forty-eight hours. The reading can take place on a special occasion like a festival or as requested by a Sikh family or individual to mark success or sorrow. In many GURDWARAS in Britain, it has become automatic to hold Akhand Paths from Friday to Sunday. (*See also* GRANTHI)

Akharas *Hinduism* Orders of SHAIVITE warrior ascetics that developed from the ninth to the eighteenth centuries in response to the Muslim invasions of India. They were six in number and are called Ananda, Niranjani, Juna, Avahan, Atal and Nirvani. (*See also* SADHU)

Akhlaq *(conduct, character)* *Islam* This refers to a person's attitudes and ethical code. The highest exemplary behaviour is that of Muhammad. Pious Muslims try to maintain *akhlaq-I Muhammadi*, or the imitation of the character and ethics of the Prophet. This has been particularly marked in the SUFI tradition, where the imitation of the Prophet is part of the TARIQAH or spiritual discipline.

Akusala (P) *(unwholesome)* *Buddhism* Used to describe actions that bring about bad KARMA and consequently lead to bad rebirth. Philosophically it is used to describe desires which are accompanied by greed, hatred or delusion. (*See also* KUSALA)

Al-Adil *(The Giver of Justice)* *Islam* One of the descriptions of Allah that emphasizes justice as a central attribute of God. Although Allah is the ultimate judge of all creation, it is also beholden on a Muslim to behave justly and dispense justice. To judge correctly is considered a religious action, but ideal Muslim governments do not exist to create laws that provide social justice, but to maintain the laws of God already laid down in the SHARI'A. The role of Muhammad and the prophets is to spread justice as well as interpret the divine will. (*See also* QADI)

Al-Aman *(The Trustworthy)* *Islam* A title that was used to describe the character of Muhammad by those around him even before he began to receive the revelation from Allah. It is probably derived from AMIN (Amen), which is translated as 'so be it'. Essentially, once someone has given his or her word about a matter it is always fulfilled.

Al-Azhar *Islam*   The most famous college in the Muslim world for the study of Islam. Throughout centuries many clerics have travelled to Cairo in order to study religion at the college. It is known for its conservatism, and many Muslims look to its scholars for decisions about points of law. (*See* DAR AL-ULUM; MADRASA; SHARI'A)

Al-Fatiha *(The Opener)* *Islam*   The first SURA of the Qur'an that is described as the essence of the revelation and is recited at least seventeen times during SALAH, the daily prayers. Fatiha is essential to the prayer-rite and is obligatory for the IMAM and the congregation. BUKHARI, the most eminent of the HADITH collectors, stated that the Prophet had said: 'he who does not recite the Fatiha has not performed the prayer-rite'. In the liturgy of prayer, the Fatiha is always followed by the repetition of AMIN by the congregation. In some ways, it can be compared with the PATERNOSTER in Christianity. The Fatiha has an important role amongst Muslim mystics, who have endowed it with great sanctity and believe that its repetition is an acceptable offering to God. It is also believed that it has the power to fulfil the desires of the worshipper. However, this has led to abuses, in which the prayer has been used for magical purposes. (*See also* SUFI)

Al-hamdu-li-Llah *(All praise belongs to Allah)* *Islam*   Commonly used by Muslims as an expression of thanks or gratitude to Allah.

Al Hanissim *Judaism*   A paragraph inserted into the AMIDAH and the Grace recited before meals that proclaims divine deliverance from enemies.

Al-Kafi *Islam*   The SHI'A collection of HADITH compiled by Muhammad ibn-Yaqub Koleini (d.939) in the ninth century that provides the distinctive legal doctrines of the Twelve Shi'as. These Hadith collections have the same functions for the Shi'a as the four collections of Hadith in the SUNNI tradition.

Al-Khalifa-ur-Rashidun / Al-Khulafa-ur-Rashidun *(The Rightly Guided Caliphs)* *Islam*   The first four successors to the leadership of the Muslim community after the death of Muhammad, who had been amongst his early companions and some of his staunchest followers. After the death of ALI, the leadership of the Muslim community went to the UMAYYAD leader, Mu'awiyah, who had not been a companion. Muslims hold these first four caliphs in high regard and believe that they kept to the right path as demonstrated by the Prophet and the revelation contained in the QUR'AN. They are ABU BAKR, UMAR, UTHMAN and Ali.

al-Madinah *Islam*   *See* MADINAH.

Alaya-vijnana *Buddhism*   A store of past KARMA maintained in the field of consciousness that is carried on to the next birth. This store contains the pure seeds of karma that will eventually awaken the desire to achieve enlightenment. (*See also* KUSALA)

Albigenses *Christianity*   Heretical movement, also known as Cathars, which was widespread in twelfth- and thirteenth-century southern France, particularly in the Languedoc. They originated in Germany, but the name Cathars derived from several sects in the Patristic period. Gnostic in many of their beliefs, they were violently suppressed by Pope Innocent III.

Aleinu / Alenu *Judaism*   An important prayer which comes at the end of all services. The first part proclaims God as the Lord of Israel and the finale looks to the time when all humanity will recognize the glory of God and renounce all idolatry. The prayer was spoken on the occasion of ROSH HASHANAH but is now part of all Jewish liturgy in recognition of its sublime message.

Ali ibn Talib *Islam*   One of the Prophet's foremost companions and his cousin by birth and son-in-law by marriage to FATIMA. He was one of the first to accept Islam and the father of the Prophet's grandchildren: HASAN, HUSAIN, and Zainab. He became the fourth caliph of the Muslim community after the death of UTHMAN in 656. Ali is regarded as the last of the AL-KHALIFA-UR-RASHIDUN and was known for his great piety and valour. Unfortunately his caliphate was marred by dissent that led to several civil wars. AISHA, the youngest wife of the Prophet, sided against him and supported his rivals to the leadership. Although she was defeated and exiled in Madinah, other forces opposed him, notably the KHARIJITES and the UMAYYAD leader, Mu'awiyah. He was assassinated by a Kharijite in 661. SHI'A Muslims believe he is the rightful successor of the Prophet Muhammad and the first IMAM, and is endowed with sinlessness and infallibility. All Muslims regard him as the epitome of nobility and chivalry. All Sufi orders (TARIQAHS) except the NAQSHBANDIS believe that they originate from him.

Alim *Islam*   Singular of ULAMA, a learned man, usually used to describe a religious scholar or graduate of a MADRASA.

Alima *Islam*   The feminine equivalent of ALIM. It is unusual in traditional Islam to find women trained as religious scholars, although Muslim law does not prohibit it. There have been great women scholars in the past and some of the new Islamic revivalist movements are asserting that women should be trained as well as men. (*See also* ULAMA)

Aliyah *(to ascend)* *Judaism*   A term used either to refer to the migration of Jews to Israel or being called to read the SEFER TORAH in the synagogue. Originally every person was given this task, but in order not to cause embarrassment for the unlearned, experts in reading scripture were appointed. The first three readers are traditionally a Cohen, Levi and Yisrael, to represent the historic temple priests, their assistants and the remainder of the tribes of Israel. (*See also* LEVITES)

All Saints' Day *Christianity*   The feast day celebrating the community of all Christian SAINTS; part of the Christian liturgical calendar. It is observed on 1 November in the West but on the first Sunday after PENTECOST in the Eastern churches.

All Souls' Day *Christianity*   A day in the Christian liturgical calendar, held on 2 November in the West, immediately following ALL SAINTS' DAY. It is the day of commemoration for all the faithful who have already departed from this world.

Allah *Islam*   The one supreme, sovereign creator-God who is also the same God as worshipped by the Christians and Jews. The Arabic term 'Allah' has no grammatical plural and points to the overriding urgency of the proclamation and affirmation of God's oneness. The pre-Muslim Arabs were not unaware of the one God but they gave precedence to idols. Above all, Islam is a message to turn only to Allah for mercy and blessing and to give up all other religious allegiance to false deities. God and idolatry are incompatible. (*See* SHIRK; TAUHID; WAHY)

Allahu Akbar *(God is great)* *Islam*   Known as *takbir*, this exclamation of the supremacy of Allah is used by Muslims on numerous occasions in worship and to celebrate success or victory. It acknowledges that Allah is the source of all successful endeavour and is preferred to applause by clapping by devout Muslims. (*See* ADHAN)

Alleluia *(Praise to God)* *Christianity*   An expression of joy used in praise of God that occurs in the Bible and was adopted into Christian liturgical use. In the Middle Ages various musical forms were adopted for the chanting of alleluia.

Almoner *Christianity*   A priest who traditionally had the duty of distributing alms to the needy. (*See* DEACON)

Altar *Christianity*   A table used to celebrate the EUCHARIST or Communion usually situated at the front of the church at its eastern end. Traditionally it stands between the SANCTUARY and the nave. The practice of celebrating the

Eucharist on an altar table goes back to the early custom of observing the rite on the graves of the faithful departed.

Alvars   *Hinduism*   The twelve Tamil Vaishnavite poet-saints who lived between the seventh and tenth centuries and travelled from temple to temple singing the praise of VISHNU. (*See also* VAISHNAVA)

Amen *(verily)*   *Christianity*   Used to indicate agreement at the end of prayers.

Amida (J) / Amitabha (S)   *Buddhism*   The transcendent Buddha of Infinite Light or the Buddha of the Pure Realm; the personification of mercy, wisdom, love and compassion found in Chinese and Japanese Buddhism. The MAHAYANA belief that there were Buddhas who were teaching in other realms known as the Pure Land gave rise to the east Asian schools of Buddhism known as Pure Land sects. The unique feature of these movements was the aspiration to attain rebirth in the Pure Land by the repetition of the name of the Amida Buddha. The Chinese BODHISATTVA DHARMAKARA became the Japanese Amida Buddha central to the worship of the JODO school.

Amidah   *Judaism*   The standing prayer also known as shemoneh esre. It is a series of eighteen blessings divided into three parts. The first part consists of three blessings that proclaim the greatness and goodness of God, His promise to the patriarchs and His merciful relations with humankind. The middle section contains twelve blessings, some of which predate the destruction of the Temple. The blessings are mostly concerned with messianic hopes for the restoration of the lineage of David in a restored Jerusalem and the return of the scattered Jewish nation to Israel. The final three blessings contain prayers for a life lived in peace and obedience to God's will manifested in the affairs of daily life. The prayer lies at the heart of Jewish worship, and although the full version is only recited on weekdays, the six benedictions that form the beginning and end are recited at all services.

Amin *(so be it)*   *Islam*   The Muslim equivalent of 'Amen' exclaimed by the congregation at the finale of AL-FATIHA and other prayers. It is the only time that the congregants speak at the same time as the IMAM rather than following his lead.

Amir   *Islam*   A traditional title that was given to a military commander, governor or prince. In religious parlance, it is used by the Muslim organization, JAMAAT-I ISLAMI, as the title for their elected leader.

Amitabha (S)   *Buddhism*   *See* AMIDA.

Amoraim *(The Interpreters)* Judaism   The term refers to the Talmudic teachers who lived after the editing of the MISHNAH in 200 CE. (*See also* SAVORAIM; TALMUD; TANNAIM)

Amos Judaism   One of the books of the BIBLE that describes the activities and words of the prophet, Amos. A shepherd in the reign of Jeroboam II, Amos was chosen by God to warn the people not to oppress the poor, practise idolatry or live immoral lives. He told the Jewish people that they would be punished more severely if they transgressed God's law, since they had been chosen as God's people.

Amr Islam   An affair or command of God. This is an important concept in that it refers to a God who works and intervenes in human history. The QUR'AN acknowledges that certain incidents would have developed differently and changed the face of human history if God had not directly intervened. Examples include the destruction of Sodom and Gomorrah and the saving of a remnant at the time of the flood. (*See also* AJAL; NOAH)

Amrit *(nectar of immortality)* Hinduism   Originally churned by the gods and demons from the cosmic ocean of milk at the beginning of the world. *Amrit* is believed to be present in the human body at the *talu-chakra* (the uvula) and can be drunk by YOGIS through a special technique. This is particularly associated with NATH YOGIS. (*See also* CHAKRA)

Amrit *(Nectar)* Sikhism   One of the key terms used in the sacred imagery of the Sikh GURUS. Their poems and songs refer to it as the intoxication resulting from the bliss of God experienced in union. It is also the term used to describe the holy water made by dissolving sugar crystals which is used in KHALSA initiation and Sikh naming ceremonies. (*See also* AMRIT PAHUL)

Amrit Pahul Sikhism   The initiation ceremony into membership of the KHALSA brotherhood which imitates the original initiation of the PANJ PIARE by GURU GOBIND SINGH in 1699 when he established the Khalsa. The ceremony takes place in front of the GURU GRANTH SAHIB and requires seven people including the candidate. Five Khalsa Sikhs represent the original Panj Piare. The remaining member is the GRANTHI. The AMRIT is prepared in the traditional way and poured into the hands of each initiate to be drunk. It is also rubbed into the hair and eyes.

Amritdhari Sikhism   A Sikh man or woman who has undertaken the initiation ceremony and undergone a form of baptism in AMRIT to become a full member of the KHALSA. (*See also* AMRIT PAHUL)

Amritpan karna   *Sikhism*   Another name for the KHALSA initiation ceremony. (*See also* AMRIT PAHUL)

Amritsar *(Pool of Nectar)*   *Sikhism*   Although spiritually it refers to the inner pool of nectar which lies within the human consciousness, it is more often used to refer to the town of the same name founded by GURU RAM DAS in 1576. It was GURU ARJAN DEV who constructed the Golden Temple in the middle of the lake constructed by his father for ritual bathing. The temple was completed in 1601. The city became the religious, social, commercial and political centre of the Punjab and remains the foremost shrine and administrative centre of Sikhism. (*See also* AKAL TAKHT; AMRIT; HARMANDIR)

Anaba *(repentance)*   *Islam*   In Islam there is no concept of original sin and although Adam and Eve, the father and mother of the human race, committed an error before God by disobeying His injunctions, it is believed that they 'turned back' to Him. This idea of turning back is central to the relationship between Allah and His creatures. The revelation, in a sense, provides right guidance in order that repentance can take place. It is the prophet's task to ask people to turn back towards God. The penitent should return with wholeheartedness and sincerity. (*See* DA'WA)

Anabaptists   *Christianity*   Various Protestant groups who refused to allow their children to be baptized, as they believed that the participant should make a public and personal proclamation of faith before undergoing BAPTISM. In addition, they rejected participation in warfare and maintained communal ownership of property. They were persecuted by both Roman Catholics and mainstream Protestants who followed Luther, Calvin or Zwingli. Some works of scholarship refer to them as 'radical Protestants' or the 'left wing of the REFORMATION'.

Anagara-dharma   *Jainism*   The discipline of an ascetic monk that leads to complete renunciation of the world with the sole objective of obtaining liberation. The intention is to stop the inflow of KARMA and to get rid of previously collected karma. Monks therefore live a life focused on ascetic precepts, austerities, study and meditation whilst following detailed rules of conduct. (*See also* SADHU)

Anamnesis   *Christianity*   The liturgical commemoration of the passion, resurrection and ascension of Christ contained in certain prayers recited at the EUCHARIST. It takes place when the bread and cup are accepted in remembrance of Christ's death and offered in thanksgiving. (*See also* ANAPHORA)

Anand *(bliss)* *Sikhism*   The bliss of union with God which is experienced by the devotee or liberated Sikh. The term is also used to describe the joy of marriage, which is regarded as the union of two souls and is therefore analogous to the union between God and the individual, the ultimate goal of Sikhism. (*See* ANAND KARAJ)

Anand karaj / Anand sanskar *(The Ceremony of Bliss)* *Sikhism*   The term used for a Sikh wedding. Although Sikhs originally followed the customary Hindu rites, since the time of GURU AMAR DAS, Sikhs have developed their own wedding rituals. The essential difference is that Sikhs circumambulate their holy book, the GURU GRANTH SAHIB, and utilize various set passages from it for recitation. In 1909, the Sikh marriage ceremony was given legal recognition in the Anand Marriage Act. (*See also* RAHIT MARYADA)

Ananda *(bliss)* *Hinduism*   One of the three qualities of BRAHMAN in VEDANTA philosophy. The other two are SAT and CHIT. These three qualities give rise to the name of SATCHITANANDA to describe the ultimate reality.

Anandpur Sahib *(The City of Bliss)* *Sikhism*   Founded by GURU TEGH BAHADUR in 1664, it is believed to be the site where GURU GOBIND SINGH founded the KHALSA brotherhood in 1699. Guru Gobind Singh spent twenty-five years of his life in the city and it contains many important shrines of Sikhism. At the time of Holi, in March, thousands of Sikhs visit Anandpur to partake in a variety of religious ceremonies.

Ananta-sukha *Jainism*   The infinite bliss achieved by those who have become liberated souls by shedding all KARMA from their being. The soul does not return through rebirth but dwells in a state of perfect bliss at the summit of the universe. (*See also* KEVALAJNANA; KEVALIN)

Anapanasati (P) / Anapanasmrti (S) *(awareness of the in-and-out breathing)* *Buddhism*   Mindfulness of or meditation on the breath, which is one of the most common forms of Buddhist meditation. Always practised in the seated position, or at least with an erect spine, it is usually associated with fostering concentration and calm. It is important in developing VIPASSANA.

Anaphora *Christianity*   The central prayers recited at the EUCHARIST, also known as Eucharistic prayers, and which contain the CONSECRATION, the ANAMNESIS and the Communion.

Anarthadanda Vratas *(vow of avoidable activities)* *Jainism*   These are vows undertaken by devout lay Jains which prohibit certain states of mind, such as hateful or sorrowful thoughts, and certain kinds of activity, such as trades or professions that may harm other living beings. Immoral activities should also be avoided. (*See* APADHYANA; VRATAS)

Anasakti *Hinduism* The doctrine of selfless action. Gandhi believed that it was the central message of the BHAGAVAD GITA. (*See also* KARMA)

Anasana / Anashana *Jainism* The generic term for all forms of Jain fasting. Fasting is an important aspect of Jain spiritual discipline and there are many examples, from the short *navakasi* or 48-minute fast undertaken after sunrise when the adherent has fasted the previous day, to the much longer *masaksamana* or thirty-day fast. Whilst fasting, Jains should meditate, read scriptures or engage in religious recitation. Water is taken only after it has been filtered, boiled and then cooled.

Anastikaya *(to exist as a body)* *Jainism* In the Jain categorization of the cosmos, every created entity, with the exception of time, has both existence and a form or body. (*See* PARAMANU; PUDGALA)

Anatta (P) / Anatman (S) *Buddhism* The concept that there is no permanent self or ego and that everything in SAMSARA is in a condition of insubstantiality or impermanence. The denial of a permanent self or soul is unique to Buddhism amongst religions of Indian origin, and debates have taken place as to whether or not Buddha denied the existence of a permanent self. What is not in doubt is the fact that the self described by the Buddha was formed of various aggregates that would eventually separate into their various components. However, when asked by his disciple Ananda whether the self was permanent or impermanent, he is recorded as refusing to answer on the grounds that he did not wish to enter into doctrinal disputes. Certainly, according to traditional Buddhist teaching, it is one of the three signs of illusionary being, and the belief that there is a permanent ego or soul will ensure that suffering continues as a characteristic of transitory existence. (*See also* ANICCA; ATMAN; DUKKHA)

Anbiya *Islam* The plural of NABI, prophet. (*See also* RASUL)

Andhara *(to warn)* *Islam* The function of all prophets is to warn human beings of the dangers of turning away from God and to emphasize the rewards that come to those who turn in His direction. (*See* NADHIR)

Andrew, St *Christianity* One of the original twelve APOSTLES of Jesus Christ. Formerly a follower of JOHN THE BAPTIST, who introduced him to Jesus, Andrew then introduced his brother, Peter, to Christ. The two were fishermen from the town of Bethsaida on the banks of the Sea of Galilee. He is last mentioned as being with the disciples at the ASCENSION and is believed to have been crucified at Achaia. He is the patron saint of Scotland. (*See also* PETER, ST)

Anekantavada / Anekanta   *Jainism*   The third principle of Jainism, known as many-sidedness or manifold aspects, which asserts that objects of knowledge are seen from many changing modes of perception. It is only in the state of omniscience that the human being can see things as they truly are. Everyone else possesses only partial knowledge of reality. This doctrine is best expressed in the famous story of the elephant and the seven blind men, who are unable to describe the totality of the elephant. (*See* AHIMSA; APARIGRAHA)

Anga puja   *Jainism*   A form of Jain worship carried out in a temple often as part of the more complex ASTA-PRAKARI PUJA. With their faces covered by a white cotton mask to ensure that small organisms are protected from harm, devotees approach the image, where they clear away the old offerings of flowers and sandalwood paste with a fine brush and damp cloth. (*See also* PUJA)

Angabahyas   *Jainism*   Jain scriptures which elaborate on the doctrine of AHIMSA. These are texts which are not included amongst the ANGAS, or primary canon, but are part of the SVETAMBARA scriptural tradition.

Angas *(limbs)*   *Jainism*   The twelve earliest canonical scriptures of Jainism. There are now only eleven as one was lost. They can be arranged into five categories: rules for ascetics, stories, accounts of erroneous views, doctrine and other matters. (*See* ACARANGA SUTRA; ANTAKRIDDASA; ANUTTARA UPAPATIKA-DASA; BHAGAVATI SUTRA; UPASAKADASA; VIPAKA SUTRA)

Angel   *Christianity*   In the Jewish and Christian scriptures, a multitude of heavenly beings who act as messengers between God and human beings. They also form part of the divine court around the throne of God. Usually represented as God's spokesmen or personal agents, angels are also mentioned as agents of destruction and judgement, protection and deliverance, and sometimes as warners. (*See* ARCHANGELS; GABRIEL)

Anglican communion   *Christianity*   The large variety of denominations around the world which acknowledge the leadership of the Archbishop of Canterbury and whose origins are linked with the CHURCH OF ENGLAND. For two hundred and fifty years after the Reformation, the Church of England was restricted to the State Church of England and the Episcopal Church in Scotland. At the end of the eighteenth century, an Act of Parliament was passed allowing the consecration of bishops to serve abroad. Bishoprics were gradually established throughout the British empire and colonies, beginning with the Protestant Episcopal Church of the USA.

Anglicanism *Christianity* The system of doctrine and practice maintained by the denominations that form part of the ANGLICAN COMMUNION. Although rejecting the authority of the Pope in Rome, Anglicanism maintained the episcopal authority but refused to recognize its divine origin. Ecclesiastical tradition was acknowledged during the first four centuries of Christian tradition but was limited by the right of direct appeal to scripture. (*See also* CHURCH OF ENGLAND)

Anglo-Catholic *Christianity* See HIGH CHURCH.

Anhad / Anhad Nad / Anhat Bani *(unstruck sound)* *Sikhism* One of the key terms used in the poetry of the Sikh Gurus to describe their inner experience of the divine, it refers to an inner audible life-current that is unending. Sikhs tend to use it to describe the bliss experienced when listening to the GURBANI.

Anicca (P) / Anitya (S) *Buddhism* The second of the three signs of being which constitute the continuation of SAMSARA. *Anicca* is the continuing flux of all matter, states of mind or consciousness and describes the important doctrine of the impermanence of all things. (*See also* ANATTA; DUKKHA)

Aninut *Judaism* The period from death to burial in which the mourner is considered traumatized by the loss. Since it is accepted that the mourner may lose faith in God's justice, they should not be expected to participate in normal religious activity, as this would be hypocritical. Normal daily activities should be suspended so that all attention may be given to the funeral arrangements. During this period it is considered unacceptable to offer consolation, and the mourner is allowed to be consumed by grief. The funeral itself acts as the catharsis. (*See* AVELUT; KADDISH; SHELOSHIM; SHIVA)

Anitya (S) *Buddhism* See ANICCA.

Anitya *(impermanence)* *Jainism* One of the twelve reflections practised by ascetics in order to maintain a correct religious attitude. *Anitya* refers to the belief that everything is transitory except for the soul. (*See* ANUPREKSAS)

Anrta *Hinduism* The Vedic concept of chaos believed to pre-exist RTA or cosmic order. *Rta* also indicates social order, and when this breaks down there is a return to social and cosmic chaos. (*See also* DHARMA)

Ansar *(supporters)* *Islam* The term used to distinguish the Muslims of MADINAH from the original followers who joined with Muhammad in MAKKAH. The Madinan Muslims accepted, helped and supported the first followers of Islam who had migrated from Makkah to escape from the persecution of the ruling merchants of the QURAYSH. (*See also* HIJRA; MUHARJIHUN)

Ant Kal *Sikhism* The last few moments before a person's death. The Sikh Gurus taught that a person on the moment of death should immerse his/her minds in the remembrance of God's true name. (*See* SATNAM)

Antakriddasa *(stories of liberated ones)* *Jainism* The eighth canon of Jain scripture that deals with liberated souls and their qualities. It explores the various austerities undertaken by ascetics and relates the life stories of those who achieved liberation and some of the early TIRTHANKARAS. (*See also* ANGAS)

Antaraya *(will-obstructing karma)* *Jainism* One of the four kinds of harmful KARMA that prevent the soul from attaining liberation. This type of karma prevents spiritual progress by negating the individual's pleasurable experience of giving charity and enjoying wealth, food and possessions. It weakens the ability to manifest one's will and decreases spiritual energy. (*See also* GHATI KARMA)

Antardvipa *Jainism* The collective name for the fifty-six celestial realms of pleasure enjoyed by those souls who have accrued good KARMA through the performance of virtuous deeds. Even TIRTHANKARAS might pass aeons in such a realm before returning in a human rebirth to complete their journey towards liberation. (*See also* BHOGABHUMI)

Antaryamin *Hinduism* According to RAMANUJA, the inner controller or the soul within the soul, which is the form of VISHNU manifested in the world in the heart of all beings. (*See also* VISHISHTADVAITA)

Antichrist *Christianity* The term *antichristos* only appears once in the New Testament, in the letters of St John. The epistle refers to the enemy or denier of Christ, who will appear as a personification of the forces of darkness in the last days. He will be finally defeated by the return of Christ in glory. However, the same epistle also seems to refer to a general atmosphere or mood of antichrist, in which society denies Christ and becomes unrighteous. Amongst contemporary Christians, some perceive the antichrist to be a force of evil, whilst others believe him to be a historical person who will materialize prior to Christ's second coming.

Antinominianism *Christianity* The view that Christians are released from the need to observe any moral law by the intervention of GRACE. It was maintained by several early Gnostic groups and appeared in a variety of heretical sects such as the Beguines and Beghards in the fourteenth century. In its extreme forms it asserts that none of the externals of religion have to be followed, including sacramental grace and good works. It was partially reasserted by the Protestant reformers, including Luther. (*See also* JUSTIFICATION)

Antiphon   *Christianity*   Sentences generally taken from scripture that are recited before and after the Psalms in VESPERS. In the Eastern Church it refers to various chants that are sung by two choirs using alternate voices.

Antitrinitarianism   *Christianity*   A variety of Christian positions that deny the validity of the doctrine of the TRINITY. They include the declared heresies of ARIANISM, EBIONITES, Modalists and, in the present day, Unitarians. (*See also* UNITARIANISM)

Anukampa   *Jainism*   The Jain doctrine of compassion towards all beings which arises from the awareness that all life is equal. The term is also used for gifts of charity given to those in need, including animal welfare and care of the environment. (*See* AHIMSA)

Anumati tyaga pratima   *Jainism*   One of the higher vows undertaken by a lay Jain when he/she is very close to renouncing the world and becoming a monk. Although part of the household, they remain completely uninvolved in its activities. (*See* ARAMBHA SAMARAMBA TYAGA PRATIMA; BRAHMACARYA PRATIMA; DARSHANA PRATIMA; PARIGRAHA TYAGA PRATIMA; PRATIMA; PROSADHOPAVASA PRATIMA; RATRI BHOJANA TYAGA PRATIMA; SACCITTA TYAGA PRATIMA; SAMAYIKA PRATIMA; UDDISTA TYAGA PRATIMA; VRATA PRATIMA)

Anupassana   *Buddhism*   The attention or observation required by the practitioner in meditation to attain mindfulness or awareness. (*See* VIPASSANA)

Anupreksas   *Jainism*   The twelve reflections that should be meditated upon by ascetics in order to arrive at the correct religious attitude to cultivate right knowledge. Also referred to as Bhavana, they are transitoriness, non-surrender, the cycle of worldly existence, solitariness, separateness, impurity, influx, stoppage, shedding, the universe, the rarity of spirituality and religion. (*See* ANITYA; ANYATVA; ASARANA; ASRAVA; ASUCI; BODHI DURLABHA; DHARMA; EKATVA; LOKA; NIRJARA; SAMSARA; SAMVARA)

Anuttara Upapatikadasa   *(stories of those who rise to the topmost heavens)*   *Jainism*   The ANGAS which deals with specific forms of reincarnation and how they arise. It also recounts the lives of those who achieved rebirth as heavenly beings.

Anuvratas *(the lesser vows)* *Jainism* The five vows of AHIMSA, SATYA, ACAURYA, APARIGRAHA and BRAHMACHARYA required of lay Jains which enable them to live their lives in moderation and progress on the path to liberation. The vows are the same for ascetics but have been adapted to lay circumstances. (*See also* MAHAVRATAS; SRAVAKA)

Anviksiki *Hinduism* The intellectual analysis of Vedic knowledge utilizing logic that is taught within the six orthodox schools of philosophy. (*See* ASTIKA; DARSHAN SHASTRAS)

Anyatva *(separateness)* *Jainism* One of the twelve reflections practised by ascetics in order to maintain a correct religious attitude. Anyatva refers to the belief that everything, including one's own body, is external to the soul. The soul alone constitutes one's real self. (*See also* ANUPREKSAS; JIVA)

Apadhyana *Jainism* Sorrowful or hateful thoughts that should be avoided in order to progress on the path to liberation. This avoidance is part of the vows of 'avoidable activities' undertaken by devout lay Jains as part of their ethical code. (*See* ANARTHADANDA VRATAS; GUNAVRATAS)

Aparigraha *(non-possession)* *Jainism* One of the three principles of Jainism which involves developing the attitude of non-attachment to material possessions and mental attitudes. Whilst ascetics maintain a strict non-possession, this is adapted for lay Jains, who ideally observe a vow of limited possession. Once the limit is achieved the rest should be utilized for charitable works. (*See* AHIMSA; ANEKANTAVADA)

Apasmara *Hinduism* The dwarf that represents ignorance and is danced upon by SHIVA in the form of NATARAJA, the Lord of the Dance.

Apaurusya *Hinduism* The belief that the VEDAS do not have human authorship but represent a timeless revelation that contains all human and divine knowledge. It is this belief that marks the Vedas out as SHRUTI and leads many contemporary Hindus to describe them as a revelation of God. However, this idea may have developed after the influence of Islam.

Apaya vicaya *Jainism* One of the four types of virtuous meditation practised by Jain ascetics, in which they focus on dissolving the harmful passions of anger, greed, deceit and pride. This meditation consists of deep reflection upon the effect of the passions on the soul. (*See* VICAYA)

Apocalyptic literature   *Christianity*   Christian sacred texts which claim to reveal things that are normally hidden, or to foretell the future. The most important apocalyptic text is the book of Revelation, the final book in the NEW TESTAMENT. Early Christianity was influenced by the tradition of apocalyptic literature in the Jewish sacred writings, which believed that the age when the fulfilment of prophecy would take place was yet to come. These types of literature were also part of the tradition of messianic expectations. Both Jesus and the early Christian writers were influenced by apocalyptic thought, but the New Testament modifies it to the extent that fulfilment has already begun through the birth and death of Jesus Christ. God's redemptive work has already started with the incarnation of Jesus Christ and will extend to the final days. All Christians are therefore living in an apocalyptic time. (*See also* REVELATION, BOOK OF)

Apocrypha   *Judaism*   Certain works written after the period of the Second Temple which were excluded by the Jews as part of their biblical canon but were added by the Christians to their canon of scripture, the OLD TESTAMENT. These include Ecclesiasticus, The Wisdom of Solomon, Macabees I and II, Tobit and Judith. (*See also* TANAKH)

Apocryphal New Testament   *Christianity*   A relatively modern title describing a variety of early Christian epistles and gospels that were not included in the canon of scripture. The most important are the Acts of Peter, Paul, John, Andrew and Thomas, probably written in the second century CE. They are partly derived from oral tradition, popular curiosity to know more about the life of Christ and the views of various heretical Gnostic movements. (*See* APOCRYPHA)

Apologetics   *Christianity*   The defence and explanation of the Christian faith by intellectual reasoning. The persecution of Christians gave rise to a variety of texts written from the second century onwards. The period from 130 to 180 is known as the age of the APOLOGIST.

Apologist   *Christianity*   The title given to early Christian writers (*c.* 120–220) who first began the task of defending and explaining their faith to outsiders through the application of reason. Foremost amongst them are Quadratus, Aristides, Justin Martyr and Theophilus of Antioch. Although they were highly valued amongst Christians, there is no evidence to suggest that they influenced non-Christian opinion or the Roman authorities. (*See* APOLOGETICS)

Apostasy   *Christianity*   In Christian scripture, apostasy is defined as rebellion

29

against God incited by SATAN. In the early church, apostasy was seen as a great threat and was taken to be the act of falling away or giving up the faith. From that period to the present day it is regarded as defection from the Christian faith. The Roman Catholic Church uses the term to describe someone who publicly leaves the tradition.

Apostle   *Christianity*   In the New Testament 'apostle' is used to describe both Jesus Christ, as one sent by God, and those who were dispatched as missionaries in the early church. The title is usually given to the most prominent twelve disciples of Christ who were selected and taught by him and who were sent out to preach the gospel with the power to heal and exorcize. They were witnesses to the RESURRECTION and, with the exception of JUDAS ISCARIOT who betrayed Jesus and then hanged himself in remorse, formed the backbone of the development of the early church.

Apostles' Creed   *Christianity*   A usual statement of faith used by the Western churches and repeated in church services. Falling into three main sections, it provides the essence of Christian belief concerning God, Jesus and the Holy Spirit. It also contains brief information on the essential beliefs concerning judgement, resurrection and the church. It was universally introduced in the West during the reign of Charlemagne (d.814). (*See* CREED)

Apostolic see   *Christianity*   *See* VATICAN.

Apostolic succession   *Christianity*   The belief that the priesthood of the Roman Catholic and Anglican churches is a direct succession from the original APOSTLES through an unbroken line of bishops, and that it maintains its authority on this basis. Most Protestants deny the validity of the Apostolic succession, which is replaced with the ideal of the priesthood of all believers. It was commonly called upon by opponents of female ordination in the CHURCH OF ENGLAND as a justification for their position that women cannot be called to the priesthood. (*See also* PRIEST)

Apramana (S) / Appamana (P)   *Buddhism*   A form of meditation known as the four sublime states, in which the practitioner tries to achieve unlimited universal love for all beings, compassion for everything that is suffering, sympathetic joy for others' happiness and success, and equanimity in all the ups and downs of existence. These states are also known as BRAHMA VIHARAS. (*See also* KARUNA; METTA; MUDITA; UPEKKHA)

Apsaras   *Hinduism*   In Hindu cosmology, the universe is inhabited by various kinds of beings in different realms. It is possible for souls to be reborn into any of these worlds depending upon KARMA. The *apsaras* are heavenly nymphs.

Apurva *Hinduism*   Similar to the theory of KARMA, *apurva* is the sacred power that provides the result for the devotee who successfully performs the Brahmanic ritual sacrifice. *Apurva* will ensure that the performer of the sacrifice will eventually receive their reward in heaven after death, but it cannot bring MOKSHA or liberation from SAMSARA. The theory of *apurva* is particularly associated with the MIMANSA school of philosophy. (*See also* ASTIKA)

Aqida *Islam*   The body of belief embodied in the QUR'AN, HADITH and the four schools of law by which Muslims live their lives. With the fragmentation of the Muslim community into various movements, *aqida* has become associated with the particular interpretation maintained by distinct religious positions. (*See also* HANAFI; HANBALI; MALIKI; SHAFI'I; SUFI; WAHHABI)

Aql *(reason)* *Islam*   There has always been a certain tension within Islam between reason denoting humanity's investigations of truth and the revelation of God that delivers the truth. Early in Islam's history, the ASHARITES determined that theological and metaphysical issues belonged to reason, but law and ethics were under the control of the revelation. The divide between reason and revelation has led to some mystics and philosophers arguing the extreme position that the revelation was for the ordinary or uneducated masses. The ULAMA closed the doors of independent use of reason to interpret revelation in the medieval period; however, some Muslim revivalist movements have insisted that these doors remain open. In recent history influential reformers have attempted to restore the balance between reason and revelation by asserting that they have different spheres of influence. (*See also* ABDUH, MUHAMMAD; WAHY, IJTIHAD;)

Aquinas, St Thomas (1225–74)   *Christianity*   A Dominican monk, eminent theologian and philosopher who was one of the key thinkers of medieval Christianity. His main works were *Summa Contra Gentiles*, in which he developed arguments for missionaries to use against Muslims and Jews, and *Summa Theologica*, in which he developed aspects of Christian theology such as the 'Five ways' arguments for the rational proof of God, his discussion of the relationship between faith and reason and his use of analogy, which allowed God to be known through creation. (*See* SCHOLASTICISM; THOMISM)

Arabi, Muhiy'ud-Din ibn (1165–1240)   *Islam*   Considered to be one of the greatest Muslim mystics. Born in Spain, he was a prolific writer, visionary, mystic and philosopher. His influence on the development of Sufism, the Muslim mystical tradition, is immense. He is attributed with the authorship of over six hundred books, but the most widely known is the Seals of Wisdom. He made no secret of his contempt for the lack of spiritual understanding and general ignorance of orthodox religious scholars. (*See* SUFI)

Arabic *Islam* The language in which the QUR'AN was delivered to Muhammad. As the language of the final and complete revelation from God to human beings, it is regarded as sacred. The actual words of the Qur'an provide a blessing over and above the meaning of the message. As they were spoken by God to the angel, the words of the language of the Qur'an are immersed in the sacred presence of the divine. The liturgy of prayer is also conducted in Arabic. Most Muslim children will at least learn to read the Qur'an even if they cannot understand it. (*See also* SALAH)

Arafat *Islam* A plain situated 13 miles outside MAKKAH below the Mount of Mercy. On the ninth day of the HAJJ, Muslim pilgrims gather there from noon to sunset to pray and ask for forgiveness whilst a number of sermons are delivered. This is considered to be the culmination of the pilgrimage. Muslims believe that this is the site of the reconciliation of ADAM and EVE with God.

Arahunt (P) *Buddhism* *See* ARHANT.

Arambha samaramba tyaga pratima *Jainism* One of the eleven pratimas or vows that can be taken by a lay Jain in order to achieve liberation. This is the eighth PRATIMA and is only undertaken when the lay Jain is close to becoming a monk. Having already undertaken celibacy, the lay Jain withdraws from any paid occupation and undertakes to study scripture and engage in spiritual practices. (*See also* ANUMATI TYAGA PRATIMA; BRAHMACARYA PRATIMA; DARSHANA PRATIMA; PARIGRAHA TYAGA PRATIMA; PROSADHOPAVASA PRATIMA; RATRI BHOJANA TYAGA PRATIMA; SACCITTA TYAGA PRATIMA; SAMAYIKA PRATIMA; UDDISTA TYAGA PRATIMA; VRATA PRATIMA)

Arambhaja-himsa *Jainism* The Jain doctrine of AHIMSA categorizes violence into intentional or accidental or unintentional violence. *Arambhaja-himsa* refers to the latter. Unintentional violence is always involved in everyday activities such as washing, cooking, bathing and travelling. It is also used to describe the violence that results from a sanctioned occupation such as medicine and farming.

Aranyakas *(belonging to the forest)* *Hinduism* The SHRUTI texts attached to the BRAHMANAS (1000–600 BCE) which were composed by sages in the forests. They move away from the ritual dimension of the VEDAS to a more speculative introversion that seeks the answers to the meaning of existence. They form part of the Vedic canon and provide the ideas developed by the UPANISHADS.

Arba Kanfot *Judaism*   A garment worn by Orthodox men and given in childhood, also known as *tallith katan*. Worn underneath one's daily clothing, it is a small TALLIT containing the obligatory fringes or TZIZIT.

Arba Minim *Judaism*   The festive bouquet of four aromatic plants that have to be ritually arranged as a thanksgiving during the festival of SUKKOT (Harvest). The plants are the branch and fruit of the citron (*etrog*); the branch of the date palm (LULAV); three branches of the myrtle (*hadassim*); willow branches (*aravot*). The plants symbolize a human society or even the various parts of the single individual. Together they form the whole.

Arba'in *Islam*   Collections of forty HADITH considered by the authors to be the most important or to contain the essentials of Islamic teaching. They were often decorated with wonderful calligraphy and considered to be blessed, as they carried Muhammad's sayings. The number 'forty' is also associated with patience, suffering, steadfastness and preparation, such as in the forty days that Jesus spent in the desert before beginning his mission, or the forty years passed by the tribes of Israel in the wilderness. Many mystics of the SUFI tradition have participated in forty-day spiritual retreats that are also known as *arba'in* or *chilla*. (*See also* SUNNA)

Archangels *Christianity*   The highest level in the hierarchy of ANGELS and the only ones to be given names. Some sources maintain there are four, whilst others state that there are seven. The most commonly mentioned and well known are GABRIEL and Michael.

Archbishop *Christianity*   A BISHOP who has authority over an ecclesiastical province which is made up of several DIOCESES. The highest cleric in the CHURCH OF ENGLAND is the Archbishop of Canterbury. (*See also* ARCHDIOCESE)

Archdeacon *Christianity*   A priest in the ANGLICAN COMMUNION who has diocesan administrative duties delegated to him by the BISHOP. (*See also* DIOCESE)

Archdiocese *Christianity*   The DIOCESE or ecclesiastical territory under the jurisdiction of an ARCHBISHOP. It contains several dioceses under the control of bishops, which in turn are made up of parishes under the jurisdiction of a parish priest.

Archimandrite *Christianity*   A title of honour reserved for a member of the monastic clergy in the Eastern Orthodox churches, it was formerly used to describe the head of a religious order or group of monasteries.

Ardas *Sikhism*   The formal prayer recited in most Sikh religious ceremonies and by individual Sikhs before any important undertaking, it consists of four parts. The first part invokes the blessings of God and the nine human GURUS prior to GURU GOBIND SINGH. The second part recounts the achievements of Guru Gobind Singh and subsequent Sikh history. The third part is personal and deals with the purpose of reciting the prayer, whilst the final part consists of supplication and prayers for the benefit of humanity.

Arhant / Arahunt (P) / Arhat (S) *Buddhism*   An enlightened disciple or one who has attained enlightenment. The *arhant* is believed to be free from all craving and desire for rebirth and has attained the state of NIRVANA. It is the ideal goal in the THERAVADA tradition of Buddhism and used to describe the Buddha and the highest level of his disciples. In the MAHAYANA tradition, it describes one who enters nirvana but selfishly does not remain in the BODHI-SATTVA condition.

Arianism *Christianity*   An influential doctrine branded as heresy which was not resolved until Constantine convened the Council of NICAEA in 325 to deal with disputes in the empire. The doctrine denied that Christ was eternal or divine and asserted that he was only the principal or foremost of God's creatures, although unlike any other creature. He was created by the Father and therefore not God by nature. The doctrine was asserted by Arius (250–336), a priest of Alexandria, who as a strict monotheist, emphasized the total transcendence and inaccessibility of God to all creatures, including the Son. He was excommunicated at the Council of Alexandria and further condemned at Nicaea.

Ariyatthangikamagga *Buddhism*   The noble eightfold path taught by the Buddha as the skilful means or middle way to obtain release from suffering. It consists of right understanding, right thought, right speech, right action, right livelihood, right effort, right mindfulness and right concentration. (*See* SAMMA AJIVA; SAMMA DITTHI; SAMMA KAMMANTA; SAMMA SAMADHI; SAMMA SANKAPPA; SAMMA SATI; SAMMA VACA; SAMMA VAYAMA)

Arjuna *Hinduism*   The third of the five PANDAVAS brothers, the sons of King Pandu. Their struggle to reclaim their kingdom forms the central plot of the Hindu epic, the MAHABHARATA. Arjuna's dialogue with KRISHNA provides the setting and the subject matter for the BHAGAVAD GITA.

Armageddon *Christianity*   The site of the great battle that will be fought during the last days according to the book of Revelation. It is the apocalyptic assembly point for the final struggle between the forces of good and the forces of evil. It is speculated that the geographical location is the plateau of Megiddo in Israel, the site of many battles throughout history. (*See* PAROUSIA; REVELATION, BOOK OF)

Aron Hakodesh *Judaism* The holy ark used in biblical times to transport the TORAH. Originally the term was used to describe the golden ark that transported the two tablets of stone containing the ten commandments given to MOSES. In contemporary Judaism, the ark is a cabinet built into the east wall of a SYNAGOGUE where the scrolls of the Torah are still kept. It is the focal point in the synagogue and its eastern position provides the direction of prayer towards Jerusalem. However, if for some reason it cannot be placed in the east wall, the congregation will still face the ark. A curtain is usually hung over the front of the ark and some synagogues place two tablets of stone above it to represent the original commandments given to Moses. (*See also* PAROKHET)

Arsala *(the message)* *Islam* This refers to the message that God sends to human beings through a chosen messenger or prophet: in other words, the revelation which lies at the heart of Islam. (*See* WAHY; RASUL)

Artha *Hinduism* Worldly or material success usually associated with wealth. Although shunned by the renunciate, *artha* is a legitimate goal of the lay Hindu and Jain, along with DHARMA (duty), KAMA (sexual pleasure) and MOKSHA (liberation). Some Hindus consider all four to be the gift of God bestowed upon the righteous person.

Arti *Hinduism* A ceremony in which lighted ghee lamps and incense are swung on a tray in offering to the deity or a guru whilst singing verses of praise. *Arti* forms a vital constituent of both temple and home worship. (*See* PUJA)

Arti *Jainism* A ceremony in Jainism that is very similar to that performed in Hinduism and known by the same name. The distinctive difference is that Jains will light ghee lamps and wave them in front of images of the JINAS, who are venerated for their pursuit of liberation rather than as part of a pantheon of deities.

Arti *Sikhism* In Sikhism, *arti* is sung on auspicious occasions and is made up of special songs chosen from hymns of adoration selected from the GURU GRANTH SAHIB. Unlike Hindus, Sikhs do not utilize candles or lamps on trays, or any other externals, although sometimes flowers may be offered to the Guru Granth Sahib in the GURDWARA.

Arupadhatu *Buddhism*   The domain of formless, superhuman activity and one of three layers or realms of existence that make up the world system in Buddhist cosmology. It refers to the highest meditative world which is achieved by the Buddhas before final enlightenment and NIRVANA, and gives rise to the MAHAYANA doctrines of Pure Land, or realms where the Buddhas teach. (*See also* AMIDA; AVACARA; KAMADHATU; RUPADHATU)

Arya Samaj *Hinduism*   A Hindu reform movement founded by Swami DAYANANDA in 1875. The movement is opposed to folk Hinduism based on the teachings of the PURANAS and attempts to restore Hinduism as taught in the VEDAS. The movement was important in counteracting the criticisms of Hinduism made by Christian missionaries and has influenced the revival of Hindu nationalism prevalent in India today. The organization has founded schools, Vedic training institutions and has generally involved itself in political and cultural activities, with the aim of promoting Vedic culture. (*See also* BRAHMO SAMAJ)

Aryan *Hinduism*   Although sometimes used to indicate those who know the spiritual values of life, it usually refers to the Aryan people believed to have invaded north India and conquered the DRAVIDIAN settlements that extended from Sind to Bihar. The term derived from *arya* ('noble') used by the authors of the VEDAS.

Aryika *Jainism*   The name given to female DIGAMBARA ascetics. There are probably only around 300 nuns in the Digambara sect, although female lay Jains are also able to take a vow of celibacy (BRAHMACHARINI). Nuns in the other Jainist sects are more common and outnumber the male monks by two to one. (*See also* BRAHMACARI; SADHVI)

As-Salamu-Alaykum *(Peace of God be upon you)* *Islam*   A well-known Muslim greeting, sometimes known as salaam. The response is *wa'alaykum salaam* ('and upon you peace'). The greeting of peace is also used at the completion of the prayer-rite when Muslims turn their heads to the right and then to the left, each time offering the greeting to the two angels who accompany all human beings throughout their mortal life. However, it also carries with it the connotation of greeting God, the Prophet and all believers. (*See also* SALAH)

Asana *Hinduism*   Various postures that are considered beneficial when practising meditation. The science of HATHA YOGA has developed a system of complex postures which when combined with breathing exercises are believed to lead to liberation.

Asarana *(non-surrender)* *Jainism*   One of the twelve reflections practised by ascetics in order to maintain a correct religious attitude. It is the belief that since KARMA alone influences destiny, no human or divine agency can alter the human beings' position. The practice of the Jain discipline to destroy karma can have the required effect on the destiny of the soul. (*See also* ANUPREKSAS)

Asavas *Buddhism*   The four mental defilements which delude the mind and prevent enlightenment. (*See* AVIJJA; BHAVA; DITTHI; KAMA)

Asbab an-nuzul *(the occasions of the revelation)* *Islam*   Early Muslim scholars needed to resolve the relationship between the eternality of God's final revelation through the pre-existent QUR'AN and the fact that the individual revelations relate to specific localized events that occurred in the lifetime of Muhammad. It is believed that these events do not undermine the universality of the Qur'an, as God predetermines all actions and knew such events would take place from the beginning of time. The occasions merely provided the vehicle for the revelations. (*See also* WAHY)

Ascension *Christianity*   The transporting of the risen Christ to heaven as witnessed by the APOSTLES forty days after the RESURRECTION and recorded in the Gospel of Luke and the Acts of the Apostles. Although there are contemporary objections that heaven does not exist in a temporal direction, it is central to Christian belief that the physical manifestation of Christ departed from this world avoiding the normal human processes associated with death. Jesus moves to a heavenly state and the HOLY SPIRIT replaces his presence on earth until the second coming, when Christ will return to the earth in glory. (*See also* CRUCIFIXION)

Ash Wednesday *Christianity*   The first day of LENT, which begins the forty days of abstention leading up to EASTER. A popular custom was to place ashes on the heads of the clergy and the congregation. Protestants ceased the practice after the Reformation, although it remains a part of the Roman Catholic missal.

Ashari, Abu'l Hasan al- (d.913)   *Islam*   The founder of the ASHARITE viewpoint that was to prevail over other theological stances and claim the position of Muslim orthodoxy. Originally educated at the MU'TAZILA college in Basra, he experienced a change of heart and adopted the anti-rationalist position of Ibn Hanbal. Al-Ashari opposed the entry of Greek thought into Islam. (*See also* MURJI'ITE)

Asharite *Islam*   A system of dogma that finally won over all resistance and became mainstream thought for most schools of Sunni Islam. It was founded by

Abu'l Hasan al-Ashari (d.913). The Asharite view tried to resolve contradictions and argument between rationalist approaches to revelation and tradition. (*See also* ASHARI, ABU'L HASAN AL-; MURJI'ITE; MU'TAZILA)

Ashkenazim *Judaism*   The term used to refer to Jews of Central or East European descent. Originally used to describe German Jews, today it is commonly employed to differentiate between all Jews of Western as opposed to Eastern descent (SEPHARDIM). This division has existed for least a thousand years, and in Israel, their own Chief Rabbi represents both groups.

Ashoka (S) / *Buddhism*   *See* ASOKA.

Ashraf *Islam*   The position of those who can claim ancestry to Muhammad through ALI and FATIMA. They occupy a prestigious place in the Muslim world and it is felt that some of the Prophet's power to bless remains with them in a diluted form. The family name most associated with this status is Sayyid or Said. Many Muslim mystics from the SUFI tradition have claimed descent from the Prophet. In the subcontinent it is used by well-born Muslims to claim ancestry to the original Arab/central Asian invaders and refers to someone who lives a particular lifestyle associated with high culture deriving from the court of Moguls. (*See also* HASAN; HUSAIN)

Ashram *(shelter)* *Hinduism*   A place of retreat or hermitage used for spiritual development and often the centre of teaching for a particular GURU or sect.

Ashrama *Hinduism*   The four stages of life considered as the ideal for all Hindus and part of VARNASHRAMDHARMA. These are: (1) BRAHMACHARYA (celibate student). Traditionally a BRAHMIN boy would pass twelve years with a religious teacher after the UPANAYANA (sacred thread) ceremony held between the ages of eight and twelve. (2) GRIHASTHA (householder). After studenthood the boy marries and devotes his time to the acquisition of wealth, the procreation of children and the observation of DHARMA. (3) VANAPRASTHA (withdrawal). After the children reach adulthood the couple begin to withdraw from worldly activities. Traditionally they would move from the village to the forest nearby and dedicate themselves to religious activities. (4) SANNYASIN (complete renunciation). The last years of life are spent in the pursuit of MOKSHA as a homeless and possessionless mendicant.

Today very few Hindus observe the last two stages.

Asoka (P) / Ashoka (S) *Buddhism*   The ruler of the kingdom of Magadha in northern India (273–232 BCE). He embraced Buddhism after his conquest of the kingdom of Kalinga, for which he experienced deep remorse at the level of bloodshed. Although he met with many monks, tradition states that his conversion took place after meeting the monk Nigodha. Asoka adopted AHIMSA or non-violence and based his administration on Buddhist DHAMMA. He was highly influential in the spread of Buddhist teachings throughout his dominions in India and southeast Asia.

Asr / Salat-al'Asr *Islam* The third of the five obligatory prayers to be performed by all Muslims. It is carried out either individually or communally in the mosque and may be performed from late afternoon until a short while before sunset. (*See* FAJR; ISHA; MAGHRIB; SALAH; ZUHR)

Asrava *(influx)* *Jainism* One of the twelve reflections practised by ascetics in order to maintain a correct religious attitude. *Asrava* refers to the small particles of KARMA that Jains believe adhere to the JIVA and hold it down in the endless round of suffering caused by continuous rebirth into worldly existence. Karma itself is created by the passions of anger, greed, deceit and fear. (*See also* ANUPREKSAS)

Asta-prakari puja *(eightfold worship)* *Jainism* A well-known Jain temple worship that incorporates several PUJAS. (*See also* AGRA PUJA; ANGA PUJA; BHAVA PUJA; CAITYA VANDANA; CANDANA PUJA)

Astika *Hinduism* The Hindu orthodox who accept the Vedic revelation. They usually belong to one of the six orthodox schools of Hindu philosophy. Astika excludes Buddhists, Jains and Sikhs. (*See* NASTIKA)

Astikaya *Jainism* In Jain cosmology all substance falls into two categories. With the exception of time, everything else is *astikaya*, or a substance that exists and has a body. (*See* AJIVA; ANASTIKAYA)

Asuci *(impurity)* *Jainism* One of the twelve reflections practised by ascetics in order to maintain a correct religious attitude. *Asuci* refers to the belief that the body is inferior to the soul, as it is subject to death, old age and disease. Therefore the ascetic should give it no more attention than is necessary to maintain good health. The soul's liberation should dominate the ascetic's activity. (*See* ANUPREKSAS)

Asuras *Hinduism* This term was originally used to describe the supreme gods but is now applied to the demons and anti-gods of the Vedic hymns who were the enemies of the ARYAN gods. According to the BRAHMANAS, both the DEVAS and the *asuras* were created by PRAJAPATI, the creator-god. The *asuras* made offerings to themselves and the *devas* made offerings to each other. This developed into a divine hierarchy in which the *devas* accepted offerings and provided reciprocal rewards, whilst the *asuras* were essentially selfish.

Athalta de-geulah *Judaism* The beginning of the age of redemption that will culminate in the coming of the Messiah. Some Jews believe that this time has already begun, as the return of the promised land of ISRAEL to the Jewish people is a sign of its advent. (*See also* MASSIACH)

Athanasian creed *Christianity* A profession of faith once used in the Western churches but now only employed on certain special occasions by the Roman Catholic Church and rarely in Anglican churches. It contains the doctrines of the TRINITY and the INCARNATION and adds the most important events in Jesus' life. (*See also* CREED)

Atharva Veda *Hinduism* The fourth of the VEDAS, recognized as SHRUTI at a later date, which is famous for its magical incantations and spells. Many of these may have been passed on from pre-ARYAN religious traditions, as there is little emphasis on the sacrificial rite that dominates the other three Vedas.

Atithi samvibhaga *Jainism* A part of the ethical code for lay Jains that insists upon hospitality or sharing with a guest. In its simplest form it is expressed by refraining from eating until the food has been offered to others. (*See* SIKSAVRATAS)

Atma *Sikhism* In Sikhism, it refers to the individual self which partakes of the nature of the divine or supreme soul and therefore desires to reunite with its source. This may be achieved by NAM SIMRAN, good deeds and keeping the company of holy persons, but also requires the grace and mercy of God. (*See also* SATSANG)

Atman (S) *Buddhism* See ATTA.

Atman *Hinduism* The soul, the real self or the principle of life. In the UPANISHADS, atman is used instead of BRAHMAN when referring to the eternal or ultimate power within the individual rather than the cosmos. The Upanishads posit the unique metaphysical idea that atman and Brahman are one entity. The difference is only one of perspective. Atman is microcosmic, whereas Brahman is macrocosmic.

Atonement *Christianity* The reconciliation or propitiation between God and human beings through the death and RESURRECTION of Jesus Christ, which atoned for the ORIGINAL SIN of ADAM. The Jewish scriptures tell of the fall from

GRACE of the first human beings, Adam and EVE and their expulsion from the garden of EDEN. Consequently, the human race is unable to deal with sin and the separation from God. The essential message of the NEW TESTAMENT is that the sacrificial act of CRUCIFIXION by Jesus Christ atoned for the fallen condition of humanity. (*See also* SIN)

Atta (P) / Atman (S) *Buddhism*   The self or soul, which in Buddhist teaching refers to the illusory ego or self-identity. Belief in its permanence is responsible for bondage to SAMSARA. Buddhist doctrine teaches that there is no permanent self, in contrast to the eternal and unchanging doctrine of the ATMAN found in Hindu teaching. (*See also* ANATTA)

Attarah *Judaism*   The dark band on the prayer shawl that enables one of the four sides to be differentiated. When the shawl is worn the band should always appear on the outside and the top. (*See* TALLIT)

Augustine of Hippo, St (354–430) *Christianity*   The most influential Christian theologian and bishop of Hippo from 395. At the age of thirty-two he underwent a sudden conversion after reading St Paul's Epistle to the Romans. His writings are substantial, especially his detailed expositions of St Paul, and were to form the basis of Christian theology in the early medieval period. He is most famously known for his formulation of the doctrine of ORIGINAL SIN and PREDESTINATION, but also provided key contributions to the theological areas of the SACRAMENTS and the doctrines of GRACE and the TRINITY. It can be argued that Augustine was the forerunner of the academic study of theology. (*See also* PAUL, ST)

Aum / Om *Hinduism*   The most sacred spoken MANTRA, virtually the religious symbol that represent Hinduism, is also known as *pranava*, the seed mantra. It is used as a symbol to represent the ultimate divine. All religious recitations begin and end with Aum, and it is printed at the front and back of all religious books. It is also engraved on the walls and doors of religious buildings. The three sounds 'A', 'U' and 'M' represent the essence of all spoken speech or the root of all creation. Aum, literally the supreme in the form of the spoken word, is regarded as the most powerful seed mantra as it does not associate the devotee who repeats it with any particular deity. It is therefore perceived as the sound of BRAHMAN, the absolute being. (*See also* SABDA BRAHMAN)

Authorized Version *Christianity*   The 1611 English edition of the Bible authorized by King James I and often known as the 'King James' version. It replaced the GENEVA BIBLE published in Switzerland by Protestant exiles from the reign of the Catholic Queen Mary. For generations it remained the official bible for the English-speaking world and is still used by many Protestant sects.

Avacara *Buddhism* One of the three spheres of existence, KAMA, RUPA and ARUPADHATU, in which all beings exist.

Avalokiteshwara *Buddhism* A title used in MAHAYANA tradition for one of the greatest BODHISATTVAS. He is 'the *lord who is seen*', or '*the lord who lowers his gaze towards humanity in mercy and compassion and the wish to help*'. In China worshipped as the feminine Kwan Yin or KWANNON in Japan.

Avarsarpini *Jainism* Jain cosmology divides time into cycles that consist of several epochs. Every cycle is divided into two halves, each marked by the advent of a TIRTHANKARA. The *avarsarpini* is the descending half-cycle characterized by a decline in spirituality. The round of cycles is endless, as creation is regarded as eternal. (*See also* UTSARPINI)

Avasyikas *Jainism* The six obligatory duties required of a Jain nun or monk and also recommended for the laity. They are *samayika*, the practice of meditation to create equanimity; CATURVISANTI STAVA, the praise of the twenty-four TIR-THANKARAS; *vandana*, the praise of mendicant teachers; PRATIKRAMANA, confession and expiation of wrongdoing; *kayotsarga*, standing or sitting motionless for periods of time; PRATYAKHYANA, renunciation of certain and actions for a specified period of time. (*See also* PRATIMA; SAMAYIKA PRATIMA)

Avatamsaka Sutra *Buddhism* MAHAYANA scripture which presents the doctrine of cosmic identity and forms the basis of the teachings of the HUA-YEN school. The idea of cosmic identity advocates that everything interpenetrates everything else so that ultimate truth may be perceived in a grain of dust.

Avatar *(a descent)* *Hinduism* The Vaishnavite tradition of Hinduism is shaped by its belief in the incarnation of VISHNU into ten forms. However, other traditions suggest that incarnations of *Vishnu* are countless. The most famous are the human incarnations, RAMA and KRISHNA. However, popular Hinduism also acknowledges that SHIVA and the Goddess have taken various human forms. The belief in avatars predisposes Hindu disciples to regard their respective GURUS as incarnations of the divine.

Avelut *Judaism* The period of mourning that follows a Jewish funeral. The mourning period is regarded as a time of healing and it follows several stages. The first is SHIVA, which lasts for seven days after the burial. This is followed by a further period of thirty days known as SHELOSHIM, which is extended to one year in the case of the death of a parent. Both periods of mourning are cancelled if a major festival occurs. (*See also* ANINUT; KADDISH)

Avidya *Hinduism* The condition of ignorance or lack of vision that is the plight of those not liberated from the cycle of rebirth. In ADVAITA VEDANTA it arises from the influence of MAYA and is destroyed by the knowledge that BRAHMAN and ATMAN are identical.

Avijja (P) / Avidya (S) *(Not knowing or ignorance)* *Buddhism* Ignorance of the true nature of existence and the primary root of being trapped in the wheel of SAMSARA. It is the root of evil, the cause of desire and the first NIDANA or link in the causal chain of existence. Is is also one of the four ASAVAS that create attachment. (*See also* KARUNA; METTA; MUDITA; UPEKKHA)

Avinu Malkinu *(our Father, our King)* *Judaism* A litany that calls on God as father to reflect the close personal relationship between the Jew and the creator of the universe and also to acknowledge God as ruler and judge of the creation. It is God the King who entered into a covenant with Israel as His chosen and obedient nation. The litany is used in the major Jewish festivals such as YOM KIPPUR and ROSH HASHANAH. (*See also* BERIT)

Avodah *Judaism* The term is taken from the sacrificial rite performed at the Temple by the high priest on YOM KIPPUR. The instructions for the performance of the original *avodah* are laid out in Leviticus 16, and are still read out in traditional or Orthodox synagogues on Yom Kippur. The *avodah* functioned to purify the sanctuary ritually and as an expiation of the people's sins. In the original ceremony a goat was released and sacrificed as a representative of the community's sin. It is this occasion that gave rise to the idea of the 'scapegoat'. Contemporary Orthodox communities use the recitation of the *avodah* service in its original form as described in Leviticus as the purging and forgiveness of the community's sin. The founders of the modern state of Israel used the word '*avodah*' to mean labour or work in order to indicate that building the new Jewish state was a contemporary form of sacrifice.

Awliya *Islam* Plural of WALI.

Ayah *Islam* A verse within a chapter of the QUR'AN. (*See also* SURA)

Ayat *Islam* Plural of AYAH.

Ayatollah *(sign of God)* *Islam* The highest rank of SHI'A religious scholar and cleric. It is believed that certain scholars are of high enough rank to carry out IJTIHAD, or personal interpretation of the revelation. Amongst these scholars there are those who are believed to be in spiritual contact with the Hidden IMAM and therefore his agents or viceroys on earth. These are known as ayatollahs and are able to interpret the mind of the Hidden Imam. At various times in history there has been one ayatollah who has risen above all others to become the leader of the Shi'a community. (*See also* KHOMEINI, AYATOLLAH)

Ayn Sof *Judaism* The kabbalistic doctrine of the Godhead, or the idea that behind the successive emanations or SEFIROTH of the divine, there is an absolute, impersonal, incomprehensible being devoid of all qualities known to creation. This being is referred to as *ayin* ('nothingness'). The emanations or *sefiroth* contain the divine qualities such as mercy, compassion and justice. (*See also* KABBALAH)

Ayodhya *Hinduism* A city in northern India believed to be the birthplace of RAMA and therefore one of the important TIRTHAS or pilgrimage sites for Hindus. In recent years Ayodhya has been the centre of activity for Hindu communalism and anti-Muslim feeling gathered around the issue of the Babri mosque that was built on the site of an older Hindu temple. (*See also* RAMAYANA)

Ayogi kevalin *Jainism* Someone in the brief but final fourteenth stage before disembodied liberation. In this stage the soul ceases to perform any kind of action and awaits death in perfect bliss and tranquillity. All forms of KARMA have been shed. (*See also* KEVALAJNANA; SAYOGAKEVALIN; SIDDHA)

Ayurveda *Hinduism* Medical science derived from the Vedic teachings. *Ayurveda* is essentially a system of medicine derived from herbs. However, the science of *ayurveda* is concerned with all aspects of health, including longevity and fertility. It also includes complex purification practices.

Azhan (U) *Islam* See ADHAN.

Azraqites *Islam* One of the sects of KHARIJITES that developed shortly after the death of Muhammad. All the Kharijite groups believed that the leadership of the Muslims should be invested in the community and that leaders should be elected and removed by majority opinion. The Azraqites believed that it was not sufficient merely to hold to correct belief but that it was also a mark of disbelief to remain at home and not join them in active JIHAD. Such disbelief was punishable by death.

B

Baal Shem Tov *(Master of the Good Name)* *Judaism*   The title given to the eighteenth-century mystic and founder of the HASIDIM. Born Israel ben Eliezer in southern Poland, he travelled in Eastern Europe and Russia, where he is believed to have performed many miracles whilst instructing followers in the teachings and practices of KABBALAH.

Badr *Islam*   A battle fought by Muhammad and the first Muslims in March 624, where three hundred Muslims defeated a much larger force of Meccans. This victory, following close on Muhammad's new position of leadership in Madinah, provided the impetus for a theological change to take place. The doctrine of 'Manifest Success', which links divine approval to worldly success, became the norm for SUNNI Muslims. This established a pattern, in which religious revival was linked to social, political or economic failure as Muslims responded to decline as a mark of Allah's disapproval. (*See also* UHUD)

Bai'a / Bai'at *Islam*   The traditional oath of allegiance made to a SHAIKH on commencing discipleship or joining a TARIQAH. A traditional *bai'a* might consist of a reaffirmation of the SHAHADAH. In the subcontinent, some *bai'as* involve the new disciple holding one end of an unravelled turban whilst the shaikh holds the other, imitating a wedding ceremony and demonstrating the importance of the shaikh/MURID (master/disciple) relationship. The new disciple is initiated into the level of practice suitable for his/her stage of awareness. (*See also* SUFI)

Baiga / Bhopa *Hinduism*   A village priest who serves a local deity or GRAM DEVATA. A *baiga* does not have to belong to the BRAHMIN caste, nor is his religious activity associated with sacrifice or propitiation of the high gods. Most of his religious work will involve the exorcism of evil spirits, curses and perceived supernatural causes of disease, infertility and misfortune. (*See also* BHUT)

Baikunth   *Sikhsm*   *See* VAIKUNTH.

Baisakhi / Vaisakhi   *Sikhism*   The Sikh festival celebrated in April which commemorates the establishment of the KHALSA by GURU GOBIND SINGH in 1699.

Bait al-Mal / Bait ul-Mal *(house of wealth)*   *Islam*   A term used for the public treasury in Muslim nations or for the post of treasurer in some Muslim organizations.

Bala tapa *(childish austerities)*   *Jainism*   TAPAS or austerities are a very important part of Jain spirituality. *Bala tapas* refers to austerities that are carried out for the wrong reasons, such as worldly desire.

Balkafiyya   *Islam*   Those who maintain the position of BI-LA KAYF.

Bandha   *Jainism*   The condition of being bound by KARMA. This is a central doctrine of Jainism that proclaims that all beings are kept in the cycle of transmigration by the bondage of karma.

Bangla Sahib   *Sikhism*   The name of the GURDWARA in the centre of New Delhi which is dedicated to the memory of GURU HAR KRISHAN, the eighth Guru of Sikhism. Har Krishan became the Guru as a young child. He visited Delhi at the time of a cholera and smallpox epidemic, and is believed to have cured people with the water from the bungalow where he stayed. Shortly after, he contracted smallpox and died. Sikh devotees still visit Bangla Sahib, because they believe that the water has curative properties.

Bani *(word or speech)*   *Sikhism*   The hymns or poems of the Gurus and other devotees acknowledged by Sikhism which are contained in the GURU GRANTH SAHIB.

Banna, Hasan al- (1906–49)   *Islam*   The founder of the neo-revivalist movement, the Muslim Brotherhood, in Egypt. Like Maulana MAWDUDI in Pakistan, Hasan al-Banna was committed to Islamic revolution through political and social action. His aim was to create a society of like-minded, highly committed Muslims who would transform society on Islamic principles and eventually establish an Islamic state based upon full implementation of Islamic law. In 1928, he established the Jamaat al-Ikhwan al-Muslimin (the Muslim Brotherhood) as the tool to fulfil his vision of an Islamic society in Egypt. The organization engaged in moral and social programmes such as religious education and publications, youth work, the building of schools and hospitals and various other social welfare activities. Islam was perceived as an all-embracing ideology that could provide the solution to all aspects of religious, political, social and personal life. (*See also* JAMAAT-I ISLAMI)

Banns *Christianity* The traditional custom of announcing coming marriages during church services, normally on the three Sundays before the actual wedding. (*See* SACRAMENT)

Baoli Sahib *Sikhism* A deep well or spring made for the use of the public. The most famous *baolis* of Sikhism were constructed by the Gurus and are still visited by thousands of Sikh devotees. The most important is the well built by GURU AMAR DAS, the third Guru, in GOINDWAL. It consists of a GURDWARA and eighty-four steps which lead down to the water level. Sikh pilgrims perform JAPJI on each step believing that it will liberate them from transmigration.

Baptism *Christianity* The sacramental rite of initiation into Christianity which involves immersion into, or sprinkling with, water. The rite is regarded as purification by washing away past sins and as regenerative, as one enters the Christian communion reborn in the life of the spirit. The custom goes back to the mission of JOHN THE BAPTIST and the baptism of Jesus. The earliest converts to the new faith were baptized and Paul acknowledges that baptism was the initiation rite for the first Christians. There have been strenuous debates in Christianity concerning infant baptism. Although there are no direct references to the practice in the NEW TESTAMENT, there are passages indicating that entire households were baptized. The more that baptism is perceived as an expression of faith, the more likely it is that the Christian denomination or movement will oppose infant baptism. However, if baptism is seen as an expression of grace and forgiveness of ORIGINAL SIN, then infant baptism becomes justifiable. Where infant baptism is practised, there is a CONFIRMATION rite at puberty, which allows the initiate to make a conscious statement of faith. In many Christian nations baptism is sought by parents as a rite of passage and naming ceremony for newborn children without any meaningful consideration of the religious implication. (*See also* ANABAPTISTS; BAPTISTS; BELIEVER'S BAPTISM)

Baptistry *Christianity* A building or a pool used for BAPTISM or a place in a church where baptism takes place. The spread of the popularity of infant baptism led to the establishment of FONTS traditionally placed at the west end of the church or at the opposite end of the NAVE to the SANCTUARY.

Baptists *Christianity* A Protestant denomination founded in the sixteenth century and influenced by the ideas of the ANABAPTISTS, they are widespread in the USA. Their name derives from the conviction of an early founder, John Smyth (1570–1612), who established the English Baptists, that the APOSTLES admitted new members to the Christian community through BAPTISM involving profession of repentance and acceptance of Jesus Christ. This conviction that baptism should be the rite of initiation for believers only meant that they opposed infant baptism. Consequently only adults were baptized by the means of total immersion into water. (*See also* BELIEVER'S BAPTISM)

Bar Mitzvah *(Son of Commandment)* *Judaism* A rite of passage that marks a boy's coming of age at thirteen and is held on the SHABBAT of the week of his birthday. He is then able to form part of the quorum necessary for the performance of public worship and to take responsibility for legal decisions. It acknowledges that the boy has reached religious maturity and is no longer the responsibility of his father's religious practice but is able to follow God's commandments himself. The boy will be required to read the law at the ceremony in the SYNAGOGUE. The occasion is an important ceremony in contemporary Jewish communities and even non-practising Jews usually observe it. (*See also* BAT MITZVAH)

Barabbas *Christianity* A robber or bandit who had been involved in some kind of homicidal incident (possibly linked with Jewish political aspirations), who was released instead of Christ by Pontius Pilate. As was the custom on the feast of Passover, Pilate had offered the Jews the choice of freeing one prisoner, in this case either Jesus Christ or Barabbas. (*See* CRUCIFIXION)

Barah wafat *Islam* The twelfth night of the third lunar month, Rabi' al-awwal, which is remembered as both the day of Muhammad's birth and the night of his death. It is a major celebration throughout the Muslim world but is better known as MAULID. Indian Muslims still acknowledge Muhammad's death on this day of general festivity by spending the night in the mosque praying and listening to sermons.

Baraka / Barakat *(Blessing)* *Islam* This has to be understood as a special power that radiates from certain objects, holy men and women and, of course, the words of the QUR'AN, as they are in touch with the hidden or mystical power of the divine world. Many rural Muslims or SUFIS believe it is the power to bless, inherent in a saint, his tomb and his relics. It also applies to anything that has belonged to Muhammad. *Baraka* is usually received through physical contact, but it is also existent in the Qur'an and the words of the revelation. (*See also* SUFI; SHAIKH)

Bardo *Buddhism* In Tibetan Buddhism, a series of intermediate states of being between death and rebirth where the consciousness-continuum faces powerful and sometimes terrifying apparitions according to the level of understanding and progress achieved in the former life. Rebirth is determined by the ability to deal with these phenomena. The precise nature of the *bardo* experiences is laid out in the Tibetan Book of the Dead. (*See* KARMA)

Barelwi   *Islam*   A nineteenth-century movement founded by Ahmed Riza Khan Barelwi in order to counter the criticisms originating from DEOBAND and other reform movements. The Barelwis did not desire to change religious practice, but adhered to custom-laden styles of Sufism and closely allied themselves to the teachings of the medieval PIRS. They defended vigorously any custom that raised the status of Muhammad and the saints. (*See also* AHL AS-SUNNA WA JAMAAT; SUFI; WALI)

Barnabas, St   *Christianity*   One of the earliest disciples in Jerusalem amongst those converted after the death of Jesus Christ. He is mentioned for selling his property for the good of the church, and Paul describes him as an apostle. After Paul's conversion experience on the road to Damascus, Barnabas introduced him to the APOSTLES in Jerusalem and later travelled with him on some of his missionary journeys. He was active in the debates that took place between Paul and the church in Jerusalem regarding Jewish customs being applicable to Gentile converts. Barnabas is regarded as the founder of the Church of Cyprus. (*See also* PAUL, ST)

Bartholomew, St   *Christianity*   One of the original twelve APOSTLES who were chosen by Jesus Christ as his companions and missionaries. Although mentioned in all the NEW TESTAMENT lists of the original twelve, nothing further is said about him.

Barzakh   *Islam*   The term used to define the role of Muhammad as the intermediary between the creation and the divine world. Ibn ARABI, the great SUFI teacher, elaborated a theosophy in which Muhammad becomes the manifesting principle of the divine and the bridge between the numinon and the phenomenon. The term is also applied to other kinds of intermediary worlds between this one and the next, such as the stay in the grave until the Day of Judgement. (*See also* BHIDHR; NUR I MUHAMMADI)

Basadi   *Jainism*   The name given to a Jain temple complex in south India.

Bashar *(a human being)*   *Islam*   In Islam, human beings are created from clay, enthused with the spirit of God and given the privilege of being God's KHALIFA or representatives on earth. The central role of all human beings is submission to the sovereignty of Allah and therefore God selects chosen human beings as His messengers and recipients of revelation. This closeness to Allah resulted in the

ANGELS being asked to prostrate themselves before the first human, ADAM. IBLIS refused out of pride, as he was created from fire not clay, and was expelled to become the tempter of human beings.

Basilica *Christianity* An early church design based on Roman architecture. In Roman Catholicism, the title of basilica is given as a sign of privilege by the Pope to certain churches. (*See* CHURCH)

Basmalla *Islam* See BISMILLAH-IR-RAHMAN-IR-RAHIM.

Basri, Hasan al- (d.728) *Islam* Regarded as the epitome of Madinan piety and asceticism in the early years of the UMAYYAD empire, he opposed the doctrine of predestination and argued that human beings are responsible for their own actions. Many SUFI orders (TARIQAH) include him as an early member of their chain of master that goes back to the Prophet. He is regarded as one of the great forerunners of the mystical tradition. (*See also* SILSILA)

Bat Mitzvah / Bat Chayil *(Daughter of Commandment)* *Judaism* The coming-of-age ceremony for girls, originally designed by Jacob Ettliner in the nineteenth century, involving a banquet and the recitation of a benediction. The emphasis on this rite of passage changes from community to community, but it has become widely accepted in the USA since Mordecai Kaplan devised a SYNAGOGUE ceremony in the early twentieth century. In non-Orthodox communities, the ceremony is virtually identical to the BAR MITZVAH, whereas Orthodox synagogues have a more restricted ceremony; however, the girl may be called to read the Torah at a gathering of women. Outside the USA, the practice is less common in Orthodox communities.

Bawa *Sikhism* The title given to the male descendants of the first three GURUS of the Sikhs.

BC The term used in the Christian calendar to refer to the period of history that precedes the birth of Jesus Christ. (*See* AD; CE)

BCE Before the Common Era. (*See* CE).

Be-pir (U) *(Without a pir/shaikh)* *Islam* An expression used to describe someone who is cruel or heartless. The linking of a heartless person to an individual who is without the guidance of a SHAIKH or spiritual master indicates the importance of the SUFI tradition of personal guidance in the subcontinent forms of Islam. (*See also* MURID)

Beatific vision *Christianity* The state of union with, or the vision of, God in paradise which is regarded as the final destination of the saved. It is the ultimate goal of human existence and some denominations believe that it can be bestowed on exceptional individuals for brief moments in their lives. (*See also* HEAVEN; SAINT)

Beatification *Christianity* A Roman Catholic practice whereby the Pope allows public veneration of a faithful Catholic after his/her death. It is the required stage before CANONIZATION, or the conferring of sainthood. The beatified person is given the title of 'blessed'. (*See also* SAINT)

Beatitudes *Christianity* The qualities of perfection as described by Christ at the SERMON ON THE MOUNT and the foundation of Christian ethics. They are described in Matthew's Gospel (5:3–10) as a series of blessings as follows:
Blessed are the poor in spirit, for theirs is the kingdom of heaven.
Blessed are those who mourn, for they will be comforted.
Blessed are the meek for they will inherit the earth.
Blessed are those who hunger and thirst for righteousness, for they will be filled.
Blessed are the merciful, for they will be shown mercy.
Blessed are the pure in heart, for they will see God.
Blessed are the peacemakers, for they will be called sons of God.
Blessed are those who are persecuted because of righteousness, for theirs is the kingdom of heaven.

Bedikat Hometz *Judaism* The symbolic search for traces of leavened food that takes place in the home on the night before PESACH (Passover). It is symbolic, since all leavened food has been removed several days before the festival. Traditionally, the head of the household will search with a candle for a few remaining crumbs, which are then burned the following morning. The search for leavened bread is very popular with children.

Beelzebub *Christianity* In the OLD TESTAMENT, Beelzebub (Baal-Zabub) is the name given to an Ekron deity supplicated by Ahaziah, a king of Israel, as he lay dying from an incurable illness. However, in the NEW TESTAMENT, the name is given to the prince of devils and associated with SATAN.

Beit ha Knesset Shul *Judaism* See BET HA KNESSET.

Bektashi *Islam* A SUFI order (TARIQAH) founded by Hajji Bektash of Khurusan (d.1338) that is strongly influenced by SHI'A. The order was extremely successful in Anatolia and spread down into the Balkans. In its heyday under the

Ottoman sultans, it became a kind of guild for the Janisseries, the special elite chosen by the ruler from amongst Christians in order to ensure personal loyalty. The Bektashis have therefore also been influenced by Christian doctrines and practice.

Believer's baptism *Christianity*   The term used to refer to the BAPTISM of adults who are old enough to experience and understand the Christian commitment involved, as opposed to the baptism of children. (*See* ANABAPTISTS; BAPTISTS)

Benares *Hinduism*   *See* VARANASI.

Benedicamus *Christianity*   A formula meaning 'let us bless the Lord' used in the conclusion of some of the offices. (*See* OFFICES, DIVINE; VESPERS)

Benedict, St (480–550) *Christianity*   Known as Benedict of Nursia and the founder of the BENEDICTINE monastic rule, he withdrew from the world to live as a hermit in a cave near Subiaco in Italy. However, he attracted followers and organized them into small communities around him. He established twelve monasteries, each with twelve MONKS under the authority of an ABBOT. Benedict moved to Monte Cassino, between Rome and Naples, where he founded the monastery upon which the Benedictine order is based.

Benedictine *Christianity*   The monastic order founded by St Benedict based upon his *Rule*. Arguably the most influential of the monastic orders, it provided the norm for Western monastic traditions. There is great stress placed upon scholarship and learning, and the *Rule* itself is noted for its detail. Benedict's vision of monastic life was of a self-supporting community dedicated to following Christ. The basis of the community was made up of the lifetime members, who were committed to celibacy and non-ownership. The head of the community is an ABBOT, who must be obeyed. The principal activities of the MONKS include communal praise of God through the divine office, manual labour in the monastery and meditative study of the scripture. The order grew slowly in spite of the patronage of Pope Gregory the Great, but by the Middle Ages, its monasteries were the most important learning centres in Europe. (*See also* BENEDICT, ST; RELIGIOUS)

Benediction *Christianity*   A blessing that offers to the individual or the congregation the favour of God. It is given by a PRIEST and conferred at various points in Christian liturgy, most notably at the blessing of the elements at CONSECRATION. It is customary to provide a blessing at the end of worship.

Benedictus   *Christianity*   A song of thanksgiving taken from the Gospel of Luke (1:68–79) originally attributed to ZECHARIAH on the birth of his son, JOHN THE BAPTIST. In the Western Church it is sung in MATINS.

Berakhah *(blessing)*   *Judaism*   There are set blessings in Judaism for every aspect of life. These fixed spoken blessings help the practising Jew to develop attunement, a sense of wonder and awe with creation and a never-ending communion with God. (*See* KAVANAH)

Berit *(covenant)*   *Judaism*   The reciprocal bond made between God and His chosen people. Three such covenants are made in the BIBLE. The first covenant was made with NOAH after the flood and is binding on all humanity. The second was with ABRAHAM, the first Jew and the father of the people, and for this reason male circumcision is regarded as a covenant. The third covenant was made specifically with the Jewish tribes at Sinai when the law was revealed to MOSES and is eternally binding on all Jews. Jews believe that this covenant makes them God's chosen people with the responsibility to uphold His will and to love God. The covenant brings with it reciprocal duties – the Jewish people are God's treasured possession and function as his priests and holy people. This covenant is expressed in the affirmation of the faith or SHEMA taken from the book of Deuteronomy 6:5–9, which begins: 'Hear O Israel: the Lord our God, the Lord is One!' (*See also* BERIT MILAH)

Berit milah / Brit milah / Bris *(The covenant of circumcision)*   *Judaism*   All male children are circumcised when they are eight days old. The circumcised male organ is regarded as the seal of the covenant with God undertaken first by ABRAHAM. ISAAC, his second son, was circumcised on the eighth day of his life. The preparations for circumcision begin at birth and the main responsibility for the ceremony lies with the father. The parents select two godparents who are honoured with carrying the child to the ceremony and holding him during the act of circumcision. They take on the role of the child's life advisers. The circumcision is performed by a religious specialist known as a MOHEL and the ceremony consists of three parts: *Milah*, the actual cutting of the foreskin from the penis; *P'riah*, another cut that ensures that the remaining skin does not grow back; *Metzitah*, the wiping of the blood. The ceremony is performed in the SYNAGOGUE or at home. (*See also* BERIT)

Bet Din *(House of Justice)*   *Judaism*   The traditional court of three RABBIS that has the authority to pronounce on matters of Jewish law. The laws of the court are given in the book of Deuteronomy. Many large Jewish communities have a Bet Din and often Jews prefer to use its justice rather than go to non-Jewish secular court.

Bet ha Knesset / Beit ha Knesset Shul *(House of Study)*   *Judaism*   An alternative title for the SYNAGOGUE and also the name given to the parliament of the modern state of ISRAEL. (*See also* BET HA MIDRASH; BET HA TEFILLAH)

Bet ha Midrash *(The House of Study)*   *Judaism*   An alternative name for the SYNAGOGUE. (*See also* BET HA KNESSET; BET HA TEFILLAH)

Bet ha Mikdash   *Judaism*   The first Temple was built by Solomon in YERUSALEM in the tenth century BCE and became the first permanent structure to hold the ark of the covenant. It served as the central site for prayer and the place of daily communal sacrifices. At Passover, all families were obliged to attend for the paschal sacrifice. In the sixth century BCE, the first Temple was destroyed by the Assyrians when they invaded ISRAEL. On the return of the Jews at the end of the century, permission was granted to rebuild the Temple and this site was maintained until its destruction by the Romans in 70 CE. The only surviving part of the Temple is the wall that backs on to the Muslim mosque of Al Aqsa in Jerusalem and is known as the Wailing Wall. This is a famous site of Jewish prayer in the old quarter of the city. Although the SYNAGOGUE was introduced by the Jews who were in captivity at the time of the destruction of the first Temple, and is now the mainstay of Jewish congregational prayers, most traditional Jews still hope for the restoration of the Temple in Jerusalem when the Messiah returns. (*See also* ARON HAKODESH; MASSIACH)

Bet ha Tefillah *(House of Prayer)*   *Judaism*   An alternative name for the SYNAGOGUE. (*See also* BET HA KNESSET; BET HA MIDRASH)

Bethlehem   *Christianity*   The reputed birthplace of Jesus Christ 5 miles south of JERUSALEM, that is associated in Jewish prophecy with the birthplace of the MESSIAH, as it was also the native city of David and the home of his ancestors. The city is famous for the pilgrimage that takes place at CHRISTMAS when Christians gather at the Church of the Nativity erected by Helena in the reign of Constantine and proclaimed to be the birthplace of Jesus Christ.

Bhabhut   *Hinduism*   The ashes from a fire offering, *bhabut* can be used in a variety of ways. It is sometimes placed on the forehead but some ascetics cover their entire bodies in fire ash. In some popular traditions, *bhabut* is used to remove possession by evil or malevolent forces. (*See* BHUT; HAVAN)

Bhagat *(devotee)*   *Sikhism*   In Sikhism it generally refers to the SANTS and SUFIS whose poetry is included in the GURU GRANTH SAHIB because their teachings are the same as the Sikh Gurus'.

Bhagavad Gita *(The Song of the Lord)* *Hinduism* The most famous and popular of all Hindu scriptures. It consists of a dialogue between KRISHNA and the warrior ARJUNA. It is the eighteenth chapter of the epic, the MAHABHARATA, and was probably written somewhere in the first millennium BCE. It is regarded so highly that many Hindus consider it to be an UPANISHAD or part of the SHRUTI canon. The Bhagavad Gita's authorship is attributed to the sage, VYASA. The narrative develops around a dialogue in which Krishna reveals himself as the AVATAR to his friend Arjuna in the middle of a battlefield. The dialogue begins in response to Arjuna's dilemma as he faces the possibility of fighting against his friends, relatives and teachers in the battle. Krishna quickly moves the discussion past the immediate crisis to a syncretistic exposition of the ways to discover the absolute. The Bhagavad Gita is particularly important to BHAKTI movements, as Krishna finally indicates the superiority of the devotional path over and above all others.

Bhagavati Sutra / Vyakhya Prajnapti *Jainism* The fifth and largest canon (ANGAS) of scripture that details the teachings of MAHAVIR in a question-and-answer format between the TIRTHANKARA and his chief disciple, Gautama. There are 36,000 questions.

Bhagvan / Bhagwan / Bhagavan *Hinduism* Generally speaking, *bhagvan* is used (as distinct from the impersonal BRAHMAN) as the most common appellation for the personal God or ISVARA. *Bhagwan* is the term used by Hindu theists to describe a supreme being who creates, maintains and destroys the cosmos but who also intervenes in human life to save devotees by the power of grace. The most common forms of *bhagvan* are the various manifestations of VISHNU and SHIVA.

Bhai *(brother)* *Sikhism* The term is normally restricted to the title of outstanding devotees in Sikh religious history. Used by GURU NANAK as a title for his followers, it is sometimes employed today as a title of respect for Sikhs who have made a deep study of the GURU GRANTH SAHIB. (*See also* GRANTHI)

Bhai Buddha *Sikhism* A famous devotee of GURU NANAK who was given the task of anointing the successors of the first Guru. It is believed that he was appointed the first GRANTHI of the Golden Temple in AMRITSAR. (*See also* HARMANDIR)

Bhai Khanaya *Sikhism* A Sikh devotee who was praised by GURU GOBIND SINGH for giving water to the wounded Muslims who had fought against the Sikhs.

Bhai Lalo *Sikhism*   A poor carpenter and devotee who offered hospitality to GURU NANAK. His food was preferred by the Guru to a local rich merchant's. It is believed that the Guru held Lalo's food in one hand and the merchant's in the other, and squeezed them both. While Lalo's food poured out as milk and honey, the merchant's flowed as the blood of the people he had exploited.

Bhajan *Hinduism*   A devotional song often used in communal temple worship. Many of them were written by the poet-saints of the medieval BHAKTI/SANT tradition and describe their intense experience of close intimate relationship with God as either a formless reality or an AVATAR. The most common *bhajans* are those of the female mystic, MIRABAI. (*See also* NIRGUNA; SAGUNA)

Bhakta *Hinduism*   A devotee or one who practises devotion (BHAKTI). Devotion may be given to the personal God or ISVARA, both with and without form. Most *bhaktas* fall into the two categories of Vaishnavite or SHAIVITE, that is devotees of the various forms of VISHNU and SHIVA. However, there are countless manifestations of goddess worship. (*See also* VAISHNAVA)

Bhakti *Hinduism*   The path of devotion or love or the attitude of loving adoration towards the divine. Most forms of *bhakti* posit the possibility of close proximity or even union with the divine through ecstatic love and service. *Bhakti* may be expressed towards an ISVARA or a human GURU often believed to be a manifestation of the divine. Devotion is praised by KRISHNA in the BHAGAVAD GITA and many Hindus consider it to be the easiest and most enjoyable way to worship God. *Bhakti* has entered the popular expression of Hinduism and can be regarded in its multivarious forms as the most prevalent manifestation of the religion. Although it reached out to the people through the popular saint cults of the medieval period that criticized the brahminical grip on access to the divine, the thread of *bhakti* can be picked up in the earlier classical periods of Hindu history. (*See also* BHAKTI YOGA; RAMAYANA; SANT; SHIVA; VISHNU)

Bhakti Yoga *Hinduism*   The path to loving devotion and the way to achieve the pure love of God. The BHAGAVAD GITA expounds the doctrine that there are various routes to discover God. These are primarily the three YOGAS. Bhakti Yoga is clearly indicated by KRISHNA as the easiest and most enjoyable path that is available to all human beings, including outcastes and women. This provided a revolutionary inspiration against the hegemony of the BRAHMINS and their belief that only the twice-born castes could achieve liberation through renunciation. Bhakti Yoga introduces the idea of loving service to a personal Lord, who bestows his grace on human beings and allows the possibility of a close bond of love between the human and the divine. (*See also* BHAKTI; JNANA YOGA; KARMA MARGA; MARGA; SANT)

Bhaktivedanta Prabhupada, Swami (1896–1977)   *Hinduism*   The founder of the ISKCON (International Society for Krishna Consciousness) movement popularly known as HARE KRISHNA in the West. Prabhupada represented a fifteenth-century tradition of ecstatic KRISHNA worship known as GAUDIYA VAISHNAVISM, that was founded in Bengal by CAITANYA MAHAPRABHU. Caitanya himself is regarded as an AVATAR of Krishna and RADHA in one body. In 1965, Prabhupada travelled to North America to fulfil the instructions of his guru to spread Krishna consciousness throughout the world. Since then, the ISKCON movement has successfully established itself throughout the world and has become arguably the most successful form of Hinduism outside India. Although originally a movement followed only by hippies in North America and Western Europe, it is now successfully integrated into the diaspora Hindu communities that have been created by migration. Prabhupada was also a prominent commentator on the BHAGAVAD GITA and SRIMAD BHAGAVATUM.

Bharat Mata *(Mother India)*   *Hinduism*   Hindus generally refer to India as *Bharat*, or the holy land. In this respect, Hinduism is a geographical religion, in which the divine is manifested in countless ways on *Bharat*'s sacred space. The whole of India is a complicated network of local and national shrines that present the full complexity of Hinduism. The concept of *Bharat Mata* was picked up by the Hindu nationalist movements in their successful attempt to create a common Indian identity and remove the British from India.

Bhasa samiti   *Jainism*   One of the SAMITIS (carefulnesses) that are part of the ascetic's discipline. It refers to observing carefulness in speech to avoid hurting the feelings of others.

Bhatra   *Sikhism*   An important caste whose members are mostly Sikh in the PUNJAB. Many *Bhatras* migrated to Britain and were instrumental in establishing the first GURDWARAS. They are famous for their practice of palmistry.

Bhattaraka   *Jainism*   A kind of semi-ascetic somewhere between the monks and laity of Jainism. First introduced in the medieval period in north India, they are now highly respected figures who act as spiritual advisers and perform rituals in both homes and temples.

Bhava *(becoming and rebecoming)*   *Buddhism*   The longing for life that is the normal state of all living beings confined to SAMSARA. It is one of the four ASAVAS that sustains a human being in a condition of attachment, and a link in the chain which preserves a being in the wheel of samsara and maintains the cycle of rebirth. In the causal chain of existence *bhava* arises from UPADANA, or clinging to existence. (*See also* JATI; NIDANAS)

Bhava *(attributes or qualities)* *Jainism* One of the four aspects of matter contained within the PARAMANU (smallest unit of matter). *Bhava* refers to the qualities contained within a particular unit of matter that will determine the unique characteristics of any particular phenomenon within the created universe.

Bhava puja *Jainism* *See* CAITYA VANDANA.

Bhava sravaka *Jainism* Those who consciously follow the Jain path, whether as ascetics or lay practitioners. They have right faith and follow the teachings of MAHAVIR. (*See also* DRAVYA SRAVAKA)

Bhavana *Buddhism* The path of development which is divided into ordinary and transcendent attainments: ordinary attainment is the mastery of calm, but the transcendent path involves complete loss of attachment, including even the fruits of meditation. (*See* VIPASSANA)

Bhavana *(contemplations)* *Jainism* An alternative term for ANUPREKSAS.

Bhavanga *Buddhism* The mind that has achieved a state of rest, in which it is free from the process of sense perception and reaction to sense perception. (*See* BHAVANA)

Bhedabhedavada *Hinduism* The doctrine of identity in difference expounded by RAMANUJA in opposition to SHANKARA's monistic idea of complete identity of ATMAN and BRAHMAN. Ramanuja perceived Brahman to be both the same and different from atman. The individual self (JIVA) is distinct from Brahman but cannot exist without God as the inner controller and essence of being (atman). There is therefore inseparability but not identity between God and the self. (*See also* ADVAITA VEDANTA; VISHISHTADVAITA VEDANTA)

Bheru *Hinduism* The ferocious aspect of SHIVA usually represented as a stone painted with lead oxide which often resembles the Shiva LINGAM. This form of Shiva traditionally functions as the guardian of wells and is more commonly found in rural Hinduism.

Bhidhr *(seed)* *Islam* The mystical conception that Muhammad pre-existed ADAM as the first creation of God and is therefore the archetypal perfect man or seed of the human race. This theosophy is depicted in songs and poetry throughout the Muslim world. (*See also* BARZAKH; NUR I MUHAMMADI; SUFI)

Bhikku (P) / Bhikshu (S) *(one who begs food)* *Buddhism* Although probably used at the time of the Buddha to describe all mendicants, he used it specifically as the title for a member of the Order of the SANGHA or a fully ordained Buddhist monk. Today it is used only to describe Buddhist monks rather than mendicants in general. (*See also* BHIKKUNI)

Bhikkuni (P) / Bhikshuni (S)   *Buddhism*   A fully ordained Buddhist nun. Although the Buddha ordained women into the Order of the SANGHA, it is believed that he insisted that they were always subordinate to a male monk regardless of age or duration in the Sangha. In most Buddhist countries the order of nuns has declined or even disappeared, although there have been attempts to revitalize it. (*See also* BHIKKU)

Bhima   *Hinduism*   One of the PANDAVAS, or sons of King Pandu, who were robbed of their kingdom by their cousins, the Kauravas. The conflict between the two groups is recorded in the MAHABHARATA. Bhima is the second eldest of the brothers and his character is marked by gluttony and violence. (*See also* ARJUNA)

Bhindranwale, Jarnail Singh (d.1984)   *Sikhism*   The head priest of the Damdami Taksal religious teaching college famous for his vigorous preaching to promote KHALSA membership. He occupied the AKAL TAKHT with heavily armed followers and supported the movement to create a separate Sikh state in the PUNJAB. On 3 June 1984, the Indian army occupied the Golden Temple. After five days of fighting Bhindranwale and his followers were killed. He is considered a martyr by those Sikhs who still wish to establish their own independent state free from India. (*See also* HARMANDIR; KHALISTAN)

Bhishma   *Hinduism*   The common grandfather to both the PANDAVAS and the Kauravas in the MAHABHARATA. Bhishma aligned himself for reasons of DHARMA with the Kauravas in the battle of KURUKSHETRA and he contributed to ARJUNA's unease about the righteousness of fighting for his rights. At the end of the battle, YUDHISHTHIRA, the eldest Pandava, asks KRISHNA to teach him the path of *dharma*. Krishna declines and instructs Yudhishthira to seek advice from Bhishma on his deathbed.

Bhogabhumi   *Jainism*   A land of pleasure where everyone is reborn as a couple. All desires are fulfilled by a wish-fulfilling tree. There are fifty-six such realms in Jainism, and even TIRTHANKARAS may be reborn there for a time in order to reap the rewards of their good actions. However, such heavens are transitory. (*See also* KARMABHUMI)

Bhopa   *Hinduism*   See BAIGA.

Bhut   *Hinduism*   Supernatural beings or the ghosts of human beings who are envious of the living and haunt them. Many of the religious practices of popular rural Hinduism are concerned with protection from or exorcism of these beings. (*See* BAIGA)

Bi-la kayf   *Islam*   The doctrine that deals with the anthropomorphic passages in the QUR'AN such as 'the hand of God', 'the face of God' or 'the throne of God'. Since anthropomorphism presented the believer with an intellectual challenge to Islam's uncompromising monotheism, one solution was to interpret these passages as belonging to God's own understanding of His nature and not try to investigate the meaning either literally or metaphorically. This is still a current debate between SALAFI and WAHHABI movements, who maintain the first position, and traditional Muslims, who maintain that metaphorical interpretation is permissible. (*See also* SUFI; TAUHID)

Bible   *Christianity*   The Christian collection of sacred writings consisting of the OLD TESTAMENT and NEW TESTAMENT that are considered to be canonical. The Old Testament consists of the Jewish scriptures, while the New Testament contains the GOSPELS, which recount the birth, life, death and teachings of Jesus Christ, and the books that describe the development of the early church. (*See also* EPISTLES)

Bible   *Judaism*   *See* TANAKH.

Bid'a   *Islam*   An illegal innovation in religion. In a religion that is based on revelation of divine law and maintains a central relationship to God through obedience, it is important to know what is permissible or correct. Islam has cultivated a sophisticated approach to defining correct practice and belief throughout its history, but many sects and movements have developed their own interpretation or modification of practice. The issue of *bid'a*, therefore, becomes a thorny debate between scholars as to whether a particular innovation is legal or illegal. All parties will attempt to defend their position from tradition. (*See* HADITH; IJMA; IJTIHAD; QIYAS)

Bilal   (d.641)   *Islam*   A black Ethiopian companion of Muhammad who tradition asserts was the first MU'ADHIN appointed by the Prophet to call the prayer. Bilal had adopted Islam very early in the career of Muhammad whilst still a slave. Tortured by his owner because of his allegiance to the new faith, he was purchased from slavery by ABU BAKR. In popular tradition he has become the symbol of black people who have embraced Islam and is regarded as the exemplar of Islam's creed that recognizes no differentiation of races. Contemporary black Muslim movements acknowledge him as a kind of patron saint and some have even adopted the term 'Bilalian' to describe themselves. (*See also* ADHAN)

Bimah   *Judaism*   A raised platform or pulpit in the SYNAGOGUE from which the TORAH is read. It corresponds to the sanctuary in the Temple and contains an eternal flame kept in a simple lamp that symbolizes how the light of the Torah will never die and that the synagogue is always ready to receive worshippers and religious scholars. The pulpit is situated in the centre of the synagogue so that the people can gather around the Torah.

Binah   *Judaism*   One of the ten SEFIROTH or emanations of the AYN SOF or Godhead. *Binah* refers to the spelling out of the details of creation in the divine mind. (*See also* KABBALAH)

Binitarianism   *Christianity*   The doctrine that opposes the orthodox theology of the TRINITY and asserts that there are only two persons in the Godhead, the Father and the Son. (*See also* UNITARIANISM)

Birkat ha-Mozon   *Judaism*   The four benedictions recited as a grace after meals. The first benediction is an expression of gratitude to God for providing the food; the second thanks God for the gift of the TORAH and the promised land; the third is a prayer of redemption and a request for the return of JERUSALEM; and the last is a prayer of general thanksgiving.

Bishop   *Christianity*   The highest order of ministers or priests in the Episcopalian churches. Although the origin of bishops has been disputed, certainly by the second century they seem to have been in control of all the main centres of Christianity and remained unchallenged until the Reformation. The authority of Roman Catholic and Anglican bishops is based upon APOSTOLIC SUCCESSION, although some Protestant churches have retained bishops without subscribing to this doctrine. Today, the principal duties of a bishop are the performance of SACRAMENTS and the administration of a DIOCESE or ecclesiastical territory consisting of several parishes. In Catholicism, bishops are distinguished from other priests in that they confer holy orders and administer CONFIRMATION. (*See also* ORDINATION)

Bismillah-ir-Rahman-ir-Rahim   *(In the name of Allah, the all-gracious and all-merciful)*   *Islam*   Known as the *Basmalla*, it is the preface to all the SURAS of the QUR'AN except for the ninth. Unlike the Jews, who decided that the name of God was too sacred to be uttered, Muslims sanctify all activities by its repetition. It is usually recited before eating food or commencing any action such as entering a room or a building, opening a book, before drinking, after yawning or going to bed. The formula is traditionally included at the beginning of a book, and many Muslims will not read a text that omits it. The sacred formula contains BARAKA, a blessing, and can be used to ward off evil or misfortune or protect against the supernatural. (*See also* DHIKR)

Bistami, Abu Yazid (d.874)   *Islam*   A well-known SUFI mystic who is attributed with being the first to express the idea of FANA or annihilation of the lower self and absorption into the divine attributes. Bistami is accredited with uttering various statements when ecstatic that seem to indicate complete unity between himself and Allah. These were explained as divine intoxication and the person was not held responsible as they were not considered to be in a normal state of consciousness.

Black Theology   *Christianity*   A movement established in the 1960s in the USA to ensure that black Christians and their experience of Christian life was represented in theology. Originally arising out of the civil rights movement and as a reaction against white domination in Western Christianity, it began in the black Protestant communities of North America and stressed the importance of liberation. This focus on liberation and suffering led to a wider identification with LIBERATION THEOLOGY and the development of black-led churches.

Blackfriars   *Christianity*   A popular name for the MONKS of the DOMINICAN order which arises from the black cowls they wear over their white habits.

Blessed Sacrament   *Christianity*   A name sometimes used for the EUCHARIST rite, but more commonly applied to the bread and wine which has been consecrated for the Eucharist sacrament.

Blessed Virgin Mary   *Christianity*   See MARY, THE BLESSED VIRGIN.

Bodh-Gaya   *Buddhism*   A town in the northern state of Bihar where the Buddha achieved enlightenment. It is named after the BODHI TREE where the Buddha sat whilst meditating before entering SAMADHI. It is now an important international Buddhist pilgrimage site containing temples built by Buddhist communities throughout the world. (*See also* BODHI)

Bodhi   *Buddhism*   Enlightenment or awakening. The spiritual condition of a BUDDHA, BODHISATTVA or an ARHANT, which involves an understanding of the processes of suffering, the cause of suffering and the cessation of suffering through the application of the noble eightfold path. Various forms of Buddhism teach both gradual and sudden awakening. (*See also* NIRVANA; SAMADHI; SATORI)

Bodhi Durlabha *(the rarity of spirituality)*   *Jainism*   One of the twelve reflections practised by ascetics in order to maintain a correct religious attitude.

Bodhi durlabha refers to the belief that the correct religious position necessary to obtain liberation is hard to discover and accomplish. Human life is an uncommon rebirth, but amongst human beings few will seek to discover the path to liberation. (*See* ANUPREKSAS)

Bodhi Tree *(Ficus religiosa)* *Buddhism*   The tree under which the Buddha meditated and achieved enlightenment, also known as the Tree of Wisdom. The original Bodhi tree is believed to be in BODH-GAYA, but offshoots were transplanted in Sri Lanka and Sarnath, the site of the Buddha's first sermon near VARANASI. All three are now major pilgrimage sites.

Bodhicitta *Buddhism*   The wisdom-filled heart of the BODHISATTVA that creates the motivation to seek rebirth in order to relieve the suffering of all sentient beings who remain trapped in SAMSARA.

Bodhidharma *Buddhism*   The legendary Indian Buddhist monk who is believed to have founded the CH'AN school in China in the fifth or sixth century CE. Bodhidharma emphasized the teachings of the Lankavatara Sutra, which centres on reaching the 'emptiness' beyond all forms of conceptual thought. The Buddha-nature within all beings is realized by sudden awakening. According to tradition, he transported Ch'an from China to Japan in about 520 CE, where it became ZEN.

Bodhisattva (S) / Bodhisatta (P) *Buddhism*   A term used in MAHAYANA tradition for someone destined to become a Buddha through the development of BODHICITTA, but who renounces entry to NIRVANA in order to help other beings through compassion or empathy with their suffering. This compassion creates a deep resolve to assist others to become free from the wheel of SAMSARA. Thus the Bodhisattvas postpone their own final entry into nirvana in order to help others towards their spiritual goal. Many Bodhisattvas are regarded as living in pure realms as supernatural beings, where they teach and assist sentient beings towards enlightenment. Mahayana Buddhists perform PUJA or veneration towards them in the hope of spiritual reward. Other Bodhisattvas are human beings of great spiritual attainment. (*See also* AVALOKITESHWARA; DALAI LAMA)

Bodhisattva Pitaka *Buddhism*   An important MAHAYANA SUTRA that provides a detailed map of the stages required to become a BODHISATTVA.

Bodiya *Jainism*   A term used to describe nakedness as a spiritual austerity in Jainism. Some of the Jain TIRTHANKARAS are represented as naked. Jain monks were believed to have been naked until the DIGAMBARA and SVETAMBARA split in the tradition. In contemporary Jainism only Digambara monks remain naked.

Bompu Zen *Buddhism*   The first of the five types of ZEN known as 'Ordinary' Zen, as opposed to the other four, which are thought to be special and only suitable for particular types of individual or specialized intentions. (*See also* DAIJO ZEN; GEDO ZEN; SAIJOJO; SHOJO)

Brahma *Hinduism*   The first part of the TRIMURTI, this refers to the creator-god or the creative aspect of BRAHMAN. He is depicted as having four heads and four arms. In each arm he holds a drinking vessel, a bow, a sceptre and a book. His VAHANA is a swan. In the PURANAS, he is described as the source of all scriptures, but it is generally believed in popular mythology that he appeared from the lotus that emerged from VISHNU's heart at the birth of creation. Brahma then manifests the universe. At the end of the universe, Brahma withdraws back into the lotus and Vishnu enters a deep sleep. The cycle is known as the day and night of Brahman. In spite of Brahma's high status as the creator-god, he has never been as popular as Vishnu or SHIVA, and there are only two temples to the deity in India.

Brahma Sutras *Hinduism*   A collection of aphorisms attributed to the sage Badarayana concerning BRAHMAN, which, along with the UPANISHADS, forms the basis of VEDANTA philosophy. MADHVA, RAMANUJA and SHANKARA all wrote commentaries on the Brahma Sutras that develop their various schools of Vedanta.

Brahma Viharas *Buddhism*   The four sublime states of loving kindness, compassion, sympathetic joy and evenness of mind achieved by the practice of BHAVANA. (*See also* KARUNA; METTA; MUDITA; UPEKKHA)

Brahmabhuta *(to become Brahman) Hinduism*   This is the goal of Hindu religious aspirations. It is in this state that the being attains complete liberation from SAMSARA and its consequent suffering. The essence of the message of the UPANISHADS is to become BRAHMAN or, more accurately, to realize that one always was and is Brahman. (*See also* MOKSHA)

Brahmacari (m) / brahmacarini (f) *Jainism*   One who has taken the vow of celibacy. Celibacy is important in Jainism, as passion runs the risk of bondage to KARMA. All monks are celibate, but lay Jains can also take a vow of celibacy. (*See also* ARYIKA)

Brahmacarya *Jainism*   Generally the term used to describe a condition of celibacy that is obligatory for monks but voluntary for lay Jains, who only take such a vow in special circumstances. However, *brahmacharya* is also one of the major vows that is observed by all pious Jains. Although the Jain monk maintains complete celibacy, the lay Jain is also forbidden to have any kind of sexual relationship outside of marriage and to refrain from any activity that may increase sexual desire. (*See* ABRAHMA; ANUVRATAS; BRAHMACARI; MAHAVRATAS)

Brahmacarya pratima   *Jainism*   The seventh of the eleven stages of spiritual progress that direct the lay Jain progressively towards liberation. At this stage, the lay Jain observes complete celibacy, in common with the Jain ascetics. Any decorative clothing, ornaments or jewellery that might attract sexual desire are removed. (*See* BRAHMACARYA; PRATIMA)

Brahmacharin / Brahmacarin   *Hinduism*   A celibate student in the first stage of life who maintains chastity, sexual abstinence or a life of spiritual discipline whilst studying with a teacher. Any person who maintains celibacy for religious reasons. (*See* ASHRAMA; BRAHMACHARYA)

Brahmacharya / Brahmacariya   *Hinduism*   The first of the four stages of life or ASHRAMAS, in which a 'twice-born' boy lives as a celibate student under the guidance of a teacher in order to study the VEDAS. According to tradition he can remain there for a period of nine to thirty-six years. *Brahmacharya* is also used to describe anyone who maintains the state of celibacy in order to sublimate their sexual energy for religious purposes.

Brahman   *Hinduism*   The power present in the whole universe or the ultimate reality behind the creation. Although indescribable, Brahman has the three qualities of SAT, CHIT and ANANDA. There is nothing beyond Brahman, who is the ultimate being who both transcends and pervades the universe. The enlightened sage or YOGI discovers their oneness with that supreme being by purifying individual consciousness so that it can flow back into the universal ocean of pure awareness that is Brahman. This state is known as MOKSHA or eternal freedom from the phenomenal world. In this state the endless round of rebirth comes to an end. (*See also* ATMAN; SAMSARA; VEDANTA)

Brahmanas   *Hinduism*   One of the four sets of scriptures in the SHRUTI category that form the VEDAS. These scriptures interpret the sacred formulas of the Vedas and provide the precise rules and regulations for performance of ritual. They also contain the original myths that were developed in later centuries.

Brahmin   *Hinduism*   The highest class or VARNA, from which the priests are drawn. They are the custodians of both the sacred text of the VEDAS and the rituals believed to be essential for the correct ordering of society. The authority of the brahmins is originally described in the oldest Hindu creation myth depicted in the RIG VEDA. In this myth human beings are created from the cosmic sacrifice of the PURUSHA. The brahmin caste is said to have sprung forth from *purusha*'s head.

Brahmo Samaj *Hinduism*   A nineteenth-century reform Hindu sect founded by RAM MOHAN ROY in 1827. Roy attempted to establish a Hinduism based on ethical and moral teachings that moved away from the popular polytheistic Hinduism of the masses. Roy was strictly monotheistic and claimed that true Hinduism was incorporated in the UPANISHADS. His movement had little mass appeal but found support amongst the newly emerging merchant middle classes. The Brahmo Samaj can be interpreted as a reaction to European colonial domination and an early attempt to establish a Hindu national identity. (*See also* ARYA SAMAJ)

Breviary *Christianity*   A liturgical book which contains the psalms, hymns and lessons used by the Roman Catholic Church for divine offices. However, since VATICAN COUNCIL II, offices are no longer a daily requirement for priests and are mostly confined to monastic orders. (*See also* OFFICES, DIVINE)

Brhadaranyaka Upanishad / Brihadaranyaka Upanished *(the great forest)* *Hinduism*   One of the earliest UPANISHADS, written between 600 and 300 BCE, in which the idea that all the gods are manifestations of one supreme being is proclaimed for the first time.

Bris *Judaism*   *See* BERIT MILAH.

Brit Milah *Judaism*   *See* BERIT MILAH.

Buddha *Buddhism*   A title meaning the enlightened or awakened one given to SIDDATTHA GOTTAMA after his enlightenment. The MAHAYANA tradition recognizes more than one Buddha, as it believes that countless Buddhas have manifested out of the life principle throughout aeons of time. On the other hand, the THERAVADA tradition focuses on the historical Siddattha Gottama. Although the condition of a Buddha is also considered to have been achieved by his closest disciples and other ARHANTS throughout Buddhist history, it is the Buddhas who receive the veneration of Buddhists throughout the world. (*See also* BODHI; BODHISATTVA)

Buddha *Hinduism*   Although the Buddha criticized aspects of the brahminical tradition, asserting that the only true BRAHMIN is a person of outstanding spiritual and moral character rather than someone born into a particular VARNA, he has been incorporated into the Hindu pantheon of deities. Buddha is regarded in Hinduism as the ninth incarnation or AVATAR of VISHNU.

Buddha nature   *Buddhism*   *See* TATHAGATA.

Buddha Pratima / Buddha Rupa   *Buddhism*   An image or statue of the Buddha, it usually represents the Buddha as seated, standing or lying on his right side. There are many versions used throughout the Buddhist world especially in the MAHAYANA tradition. (*See also* PUJA)

Buddhaghosha   *Buddhism*   A monk sent from Bodh-gaya in the fourth century CE to Sri Lanka to bring the vast PALI CANON and its commentaries back to India.

Buddhavatara *(The age of the Buddha)*   *Hinduism*   BRAHMIN priests in India begin their daily oblations with the prayer, 'in this age of the Buddha I offer my oblation', in spite of BUDDHA's powerful critique of their practices.

Buddhi   *Hinduism*   The first manifestation of PRAKRITI, *buddhi* is the intellect or 'higher mind'. It is from the *buddhi* that the ego or AHAMKARA arises, from there emerge the mind (MANAS), the five senses of perception, the five organs of action and the five gross elements that form creation. This hierarchical cosmology was first fully developed in the SAMKHYA school of philosophy but now pervades most Hindu metaphysics in some form. It is given universality by the BHAGAVAD GITA, which describes KRISHNA's nature as consisting of the same categories.

Bukhari, Muhammad ibn Ishmael al- (810–70)   *Islam*   The most authoritative collector of HADITH, whose collection is known as the greatest authority in Islam after the QUR'AN. During the ninth century various scholars took on the massive task of travelling the Muslim world to collect together the sayings and deeds of the Prophet. By this time there were many spurious ones that needed to be sifted out. Al-Bukhari was particularly strict and reduced hundreds of thousands of these to only a few thousand. (*See also* SAHIH AL-BUKHARI)

Buraq   *Islam*   The heavenly steed brought by an angel to Muhammad to take him on his mystical night journey. It is described by poets as being smaller than a horse with a woman's head and a peacock tail. Its depiction is regarded as giving protection to believers and it is possible to find wonderful paintings of Buraq on trucks in Pakistan and Afghanistan. There is also a genre of miniature paintings that depict the mythical creature. (*See* MI'RAJ)

Burda   *Islam*   *See* KHIRQA-I SHARIF.

Burqa *Islam*   The veil worn by women in order to conform to the QUR'AN's dress codes regarding modesty for both men and women. The *burqa* is usually associated with the strictest kind of veiling, where a cloak is worn over the clothes and covers the head, body and legs with often only a slit for the eyes. (*See* HIJAB)

Cabala *Judaism*   *See* KABBALAH.

Caiaphas *Christianity*   The Jewish high priest from 18 to 36 CE who presided over the trial of Jesus Christ and the persecutions of the early Christians described in the ACTS OF THE APOSTLES. (*See also* CRUCIFIXION)

Caitanya Mahaprabhu / Chaitanya Mahaprabhu (1486–1533)   *Hinduism*   A Bengali Vaishnavite reformer whose ecstatic devotion was focused on KRISHNA. He followed the philosophy of a thirteenth-century Bengali Vaishnavite named Nimbarka which posited that God was both the same as, but different from, individual souls. Caitanya preached devotion to Krishna expressed through ecstatic singing of KIRTAN. He is believed by many Hindus to be an incarnation of Krishna. ISKCON devotees believe him to be the combined incarnation of Krishna, RADHA and their original founder. (*See also* BHAKTIVEDANTA PRABHU-PADA, SWAMI; VAISHNAVA)

Caitya vandana / Bhava Puja *Jainism*   Temple worship in which songs of praise, adoration and devotion are recited together with penances and meditation. The majority of prayers are in praise and veneration of the TIRTHAN-KARAS. There are also prayers of forgiveness if any harm has been caused to a living being.

Caliph *Islam*   *See* KHALIFA.

Calvary *Christianity*   The reputed place of Christ's CRUCIFIXION, described in the Gospels as being outside JERUSALEM near a garden containing a tomb. Today there are two locations believed to be the site of Calvary, also known as Golgotha (the place of skulls). One is the Church of the HOLY SEPULCHRE and the other is the Garden Tomb, also known as Gordon's Calvary.

Calvin, John (1509–64)   *Christianity*   A French Protestant reformer who broke with the Roman Catholic Church after receiving a vision in which he believed that God instructed him to restore the church to its original purity. In 1541, he returned to Geneva, where he had initially fled on breaking with Rome, and established a theocratic state which placed the government in the hands of the clergy. The state inflicted harsh penalties for breaches of religious discipline and all opposition was overcome by force. (*See also* CALVINISM)

Calvinism   *Christianity*   The Protestant theological system developed by John CALVIN. Calvinism differs from Lutheranism in that it did not intend to challenge the doctrine of the church but only to change worship and moral laws to conform to scripture. However, Calvinism emphasizes PREDESTINATION, ELEC-TION and ORIGINAL SIN. Aspects of Calvinism are accepted by BAPTISTS, PRESBY-TERIANS and the REFORMED CHURCHES of France, Switzerland and Holland. Since other thinkers besides Calvin influenced the developments of these traditions, they prefer to be known as Reformed Christianity. (*See also* PURITANS)

Candan puja   *Jainism*   A form of ritual temple worship performed by Jains consisting of anointing the image of a JINA with sandalwood paste on the feet, legs, arms, shoulders, chest, navel, neck and head. Flowers and garlands are offered to the feet of the image with appropriate prayers. *Candan puja* is sometimes a part of the longer ASTA-PRAKARI PUJA. (*See also* PUJA)

Candlemas   *Christianity*   A feast day in the Christian liturgical calendar celebrated on 2 February, which celebrates the purification of the Virgin Mary and Christ's presentation at the Temple. It is known as Candlemas because of the Roman Catholic tradition of processing with lighted candles.

Canon   *Christianity*   The title given to members of the clergy who are on the staff of a CATHEDRAL or collegiate church, either as full-time salaried staff responsible for the maintenance of its ecclesiastical functions or as unsalaried volunteers.

Canon law   *Christianity*   The complete collection of ecclesiastical rules which govern matters of doctrine, morality and discipline. The main body of canon law has been derived from the decisions made at a number of COUNCILS throughout the history of Christianity.

Canon of scripture   *Christianity*   The authoritative collection of Christian scripture made up from the accepted books of the OLD TESTAMENT and NEW TESTAMENT. The main texts were fixed in the PATRISTIC period, but they vary from denomination to denomination. Although there was discussion over the

Epistle to the Hebrews, Revelations and the Epistles of Peter, John and Jude, the final canon of scripture was agreed by the beginning of the fifth century. (*See also* APOCRYPHA; BIBLE)

Canonization   *Christianity*   The conferral of sainthood on a dead member of the church, declared by the POPE in Roman Catholicism or a synod of BISHOPS in Eastern Orthodoxy. Originally the declaration of sainthood was made at diocesan level, but the problems brought about by the lack of central control led to papal intervention. (*See also* SAINT)

Canterbury   *Christianity*   Since the fourteenth century Canterbury cathedral has been the foremost SEE in England, and after the Reformation continued in the same function for the ANGLICAN COMMUNION. The first church was established by St Augustine of Canterbury, who was sent from Rome to England as a missionary in 597. The Archbishop of Canterbury is the Primate of all England and effective leader of the state church. (*See also* CHURCH OF ENGLAND)

Canticle   *Christianity*   A song or prayer derived from the BIBLE which is used in Christian worship. The most important are the MAGNIFICAT, NUNC DIMITTIS and the BENEDICTUS, which are used in the daily divine offices. (*See also* OFFICES, DIVINE)

Capel   *Judaism*   See KIPPAH.

Capernaum   *Christianity*   A town on the northwest shore of the Sea of GALILEE close to the River JORDAN which became the headquarters of Christ during his Galilean ministry. The house of the disciple Peter was also situated in Capernaum, and there are accounts of it being visited by pilgrims up until the fourth century. By the sixth century it had been replaced by a basilica. (*See also* PETER, ST)

Capuchins   *Christianity*   An important religious order founded in Italy in the sixteenth century by Matteo de Bascio (1495–1552) and three companions. They were all FRANCISCANS determined to restore the order to its original intention by following to the letter the *Rule* of St Francis. The Capuchins are known for their distinctive coarse habit and four-pointed hood (capuchio) from which they derive their name. (*See also* FRANCIS OF ASSISI, ST)

Cardinal   *Christianity*   The title conferred on PRIESTS, usually with the rank of BISHOP, who form the college of immediate counsellors to the POPE. Their function is essentially administrative and they reside in the VATICAN unless of a foreign DIOCESE. Since 1179 they have held the privilege of electing the Pope. (*See also* COLLEGE; ROMAN CATHOLIC)

Caritra Mohaniya *Jainism*   Conduct-deluding KARMA that overcomes right conduct by creating the four passions of anger, greed, deceit and pride. There are twenty-five types of conduct-deluding karma that are generally categorized on the severity and length of time that they affect the soul. (*See also* MOHANIYA KARMA)

Carmelites *Christianity*   A mendicant order, properly called the Order of Friars of the Blessed Virgin Mary of Mount Carmel but also known as the White Friars, that was founded in 1154 by Berthold of Calabria, who established a community of hermits renowned for their extreme asceticism and mysticism. In 1238, they left the Holy Land for Europe and ceased to be hermits, organizing themselves in urban cloisters. The monks and nuns are renowned for their ardent devotion to the Virgin Mary. (*See also* DOMINICANS; FRANCISCANS; FRIAR; RELIGIOUS)

Caro, Joseph (1488–1575)   *Judaism*   A famous RABBI and mystic who wrote the SHULHAN ARUKH, the definitive codification used by traditional Jews in order to interpret the laws of the TORAH and maintain Jewish life.

Carol *Christianity*   A song of joy that celebrates the nativity or birth of Jesus Christ and is usually sung at the festival of CHRISTMAS.

Carthusians *Christianity*   A silent order of solitary contemplative monks founded by St Bruno of Cologne. Having withdrawn from the world to join a number of hermits near Grenoble, in 1084 he founded a monastery that attempted to combine monastic and hermit lifestyles. The monks lived as hermits undertaking vows of silence, but came together for worship and mealtimes. (*See* RELIGIOUS)

Cassock *Christianity*   The long gown, usually black, which is the standard wear of Christian clergy. In the Roman Catholic Church BISHOPS wear purple, CARDINALS wear red and only the POPE is garbed in white. (*See also* VESTMENTS)

Caste *Hinduism*   *See* JATI.

Catacombs *Christianity*   Underground burial places used by early Christians as places of refuge during persecution. Since Roman law regarded cemeteries as sacrosanct, Christians could use them for hiding and the performance of the

EUCHARIST with little possibility of discovery. The most extensive catacombs are in Rome. (*See also* MARTYR)

Catechism *Christianity*   The manual of Christian doctrine in a question-and-answer format generally associated with the teaching of those who are preparing for CONFIRMATION.

Catechumens *Christianity*   The name given in the early church to those awaiting BAPTISM and undergoing the necessary preparations. The Roman Catholic Church restored the Catechumate in 1972 for adult baptisms.

Cathedra *Christianity*   The throne of a BISHOP maintained in his respective CATHEDRAL, which both demonstrates his ecclesiastical authority in the DIOCESE and symbolizes his position in the lineage of APOSTOLIC SUCCESSION.

Cathedral *Christianity*   A church containing the BISHOP's throne, usually larger and more splendid than a normal parish church. The activities of the DIOCESE, extending over several parishes, will be coordinated by the cathedral staff.

Catholic *Christianity*   First and foremost, it refers to the full or universal Christian community regardless of any denominational loyalty. It is also used as a popular abbreviation for the Roman Catholic Church. More uncommonly it refers to Christianity before the schism into Eastern and Western churches. (*See* ROMAN CATHOLIC)

Cattari Ariyasaccani *Buddhism*   The four noble truths and the heart of Buddhist teaching concerning suffering taught by the Buddha in his first sermon at VARANASI after he had achieved enlightenment. It was delivered to the ascetics who had deserted him after he had given up practising austerities. (*See also* DUKKHA; MAGGA; NIRODHA; SAMUDAYA)

Caturmas *Jainism*   A four-month period of fasting, spiritual discipline and retreat that usually takes place in the monsoon season.

Caturvarna *(four classes)* *Hinduism*   The name for the orthodox Hindu social system that divides humanity into four classes or VARNAS, namely BRAHMIN, KSHATRIYA, VAISHYA and SUDRA.

Caturvisanti stava *Jainism*   The veneration of all twenty-four TIRTHANKARAS of this age and one of the six daily duties required of all devout lay Jains.

It may be carried out alone or as part of temple worship. (*See also* CAITYA VANDANA; PUJA)

CE   Abbreviation for Common Era. The term used to replace AD (Anno Domini) in order to provide a more neutral terminology for dating that does not offend members of non-Christian religious communities. The period before Jesus Christ's birth (BC) is replaced by BCE.

Celtic Church   *Christianity*   The church that already existed in Britain before the arrival of Roman Christianity in 597. There are accounts of BISHOPS representing British Christianity at the Council of Arles in 314. After the invasion of the Saxons, British Christians took shelter in Wales, Scotland and Cornwall. These communities, together with Irish Christianity, became known as Celtic. Celtic Christianity had a very strong monastic and hermit tradition and pursued a particularly zealous missionary role. There were theological, political and organizational differences between the Celtic and the Roman Church. At the Council of Whitby in 664, the two traditions presented their views, but King Oswy declared loyalty to Rome when he learned that the Pope in Rome was the direct successor of the apostle Peter. In the latter part of the twentieth century there was a concerted attempt to revive the spirituality of Celtic Christianity in Britain.

Cetana *(consciousness)*   *Jainism*   This is an aspect of the soul that expresses itself as DARSHANA (perception) and JNANA (knowledge). Consciousness is manifested in empirical experience that arises out of the contact between the senses and their respective objects of perception. (*See also* UPAYOGA)

Cettana   *Buddhism*   Volition or the will to live, to continue which functions as the root of existence that leads to rebirth by driving human beings towards good and bad actions. (*See* MANOSANCETANAHARA)

Chaitanya Mahaprabhu   *Hinduism*   *See* CAITANYA MAHAPRABHU.

Chakra   *Hinduism*   The belief prevalent in YOGA philosophy that the body contains centres or wheels of energy connected by three central channels of life-force (PRANA). There are believed to be six or seven CHAKRAS located at the perineum, genitals, solar plexus, heart, throat, between the eyes and at the top of the head. Some yoga techniques attempt to raise the KUNDALINI (serpent power) up the central channel to the thousand-petalled lotus at the crown of the head, where it is believed the bliss of liberation is experienced by the practitioner.

Chakravartin *(one who is at the centre of the wheel)*   *Hinduism*   The ruler of the universe or universal monarch. Kingship has performed an important role in ancient Hindu DHARMA. The king was believed to play an intermediary role between his subjects and the divine. The qualities of deities were often given to kings, and many of them were also AVATARS, such as KRISHNA and RAMA. A king aspired to be the ruler of the universe or CHAKRAVARTIN. Buddha's birth was heralded by the prophecy that he would either be a CHAKRAVARTIN or a world-renouncer.

Chalcedonian Declaration *Christianity*   The declaration made at the fourth ecumenical council in 451 that confirmed the decisions of the Council of NICAEA concerning the divinity and humanity of Jesus Christ. The declaration stated that Jesus was both fully human and fully divine. (*See also* ARIANISM; CHRISTOLOGY)

Chalice *Christianity*   A long-stemmed cup, usually silver, although early versions were made of glass, which contains the wine for use in the EUCHARIST.

Challah *Judaism*   See HALLAH.

Ch'an *Buddhism*   The Chinese pronunciation of DHYANA or JNANA, the Ch'an school is focused around direct experience in meditation and simple activity. It is opposed to discursive thinking, which it considers to be a hindrance on the path to awakening. Its origin is attributed to BODHIDHARMA, but it acknowledges a lineage of masters each enlightened by direct transmission. The lineage began with MAHAKASYAPA, who according to legend achieved enlightenment when he saw the Buddha silently holding a flower. The tradition believes in a sudden awakening that recognizes the existence of the Buddha nature within. (*See also* ZEN)

Chancel *Christianity*   The area of a church that used to be known as the SANCTUARY but now also includes the area reserved for the choir and the priest, as well as the area surrounding the ALTAR.

Chanda *Hinduism*   See VEDANGAS.

Chandni / Chanani *Sikhism*   A canopy placed over the GURU GRANTH SAHIB in the GURDWARA as a mark of respect. In some gurdwaras it takes the form of a wood or stone dome.

Chandogya Upanishad *Hinduism*   One of the oldest UPANISHADS that deals in detail with the nature of the relationship between BRAHMAN and ATMAN. It is an important text for the VEDANTA schools, which have argued over the meaning of its pronouncement, TAT TVAM ASI (You are that).

Chantry   *Christianity*   A chapel in a church which is reserved for prayers for the soul of the founder, and for his friends or family to celebrate MASS. Chantries were as common as independent CHAPELS until the REFORMATION and the chantry priest often acted in the capacity of local schoolteacher.

Chanukiah   *Judaism*   *See* MENORAH.

Chanukkah   *Judaism*   *See* HANUKKAH.

Chapel   *Christianity*   A smaller place of worship contained within a church or CATHEDRAL, or a small room or hall used for prayer in a school, hospital, college or private home. It is also used to describe the places of worship which belong to dissenting Protestant denominations separate from the Church of England. (*See also* NON-CONFORMISTS)

Chaplain   *Christianity*   A member of the clergy who does not have parish duties but works in public institutions such as hospitals, universities, prisons and schools taking care of the pastoral needs of the residents.

Chapter   *Christianity*   The members of the governing body responsible for an ecclesiastical institution such as a CATHEDRAL. (*See also* CANON)

Charan Pahul / Charan Amrit   *Sikhism*   The form of ritual initiation used to demonstrate allegiance to the Sikh Gurus until changed by GURU GOBIND SINGH when he inaugurated the KHALSA. It consists of drinking water that has been touched by the foot or the toe of the right foot of the Guru.

Charismatic   *Christianity*   A contemporary movement influenced by evangelicalism and particularly Pentecostalism which has spread across denominations. Charismatics place particular emphasis on the presence and experience of the HOLY SPIRIT. Although conservative in its theology and interpretation of scripture, it is spontaneous in its forms of worship. Charismatics emphasize religious experience such as being 'born again in the spirit', healing or speaking in tongues. (*See also* EVANGELICAL; PENTECOSTALISTS)

Chasidim   *Judaism*   *See* HASIDIM.

Chaur / Chauri   *Sikhism*   *See* CHOWRI.

Chazan   *Judaism*   *See* HAZZAN.

Chazanut   *Judaism*   *See* HAZANUT.

Cheda Sutras *Jainism*   A category of Jain scripture that deals with disciplinary matters mainly concerning ascetics. There were originally seven texts but one was lost. One of the texts includes the important eleven-stage categorization of spiritual progress towards liberation for lay Jains. The most revered text of the SVETAMBARA Jains, the KALPA SUTRA, which deals with the lives of the TIRTHAN-KARAS and their principal disciples, has been created from the third chapter of one of the Cheda Sutras. (*See also* ACARADASA; AGAMA; PRATIMA)

Chela *Hinduism*   A village exorcist. One who is skilled in the art of overcoming the effects of sorcery through the use of MANTRAS.

Chilla *Islam*   *See* ARBA'IN.

Chinmoyananda, Swami (b.1931)   *Hinduism*   One of the Hindu teachers who came to the West in the 1960s. He was a disciple of the VEDANTA teacher Sivananda of Rishikesh, who became popular amongst young truth-seekers from the USA and Europe who visited India to study yoga in the early 1960s. Shri Chinmoy, as he is often called, established centres throughout the world and attracted publicity when the rock band Santana became his followers.

Chishti / Chishtiya / Chishtiyya *Islam*   The largest SUFI order, or TARIQAH, founded in the subcontinent by Mu'inuddin Chishti of Ajmer. The Sufis of the Chishti order are famous for their use of QAWWALIS, ecstatic music sung in devotion to Allah. The *Chishtis* are sometimes accused of adopting Hindu practices, and there is no doubt that they have influenced more eclectic forms of universal Sufism through such teachers as Hazrat Inayat Khan, who taught in Europe and the USA in the first half of the twentieth century. The shrine centre at Ajmer where Mu'inuddin Chishti lived and was buried is famous throughout India and is visited by millions of pilgrims, including Hindus and Sikhs. (*See also* CHISHTI, MU'INUDDIN)

Chishti, Mu'inuddin (1142–1236)   *Islam*   The historical founder of the CHISHTI TARIQAH, which is very popular in the Indian subcontinent. Mu'inuddin Chishti, also known as Hazrat Gharib Nawaz (the Helper of the Poor) studied the traditional Islamic subjects of the QUR'AN and HADITH in central Asia but was not satisfied and began to pursue a spiritual quest that took him into discipleship under Khwaja Uthman Herwani, a Chishti master from Persia. Mu'inuddin Chishti travelled and studied with his master for over twenty years, but after a visit to MAKKAH and MADINAH he received instructions to promote Islam in India. After a forty-day retreat at the tomb of Shaikh Hujwiri in Lahore, he made his way to Ajmer in Rajasthan. He lived a very pious and simple life and quickly began to attract converts and disciples. It is said that he personally brought 40,000 families into the fold of Islam. Today, his shrine is one of the most famous in all India.

Chit / Cit *(consciousness)*   *Hinduism*   The second of the three qualities of BRAHMAN and ATMAN, as in SATCHITANANDA (truth, consciousness and bliss). Truth is unalloyed consciousness existing in its own pure state rather than having become identified with the world and the body through the vehicle of the senses. The idea that the supreme being is best expressed as *Satchitananda* is expounded fully by SHANKARA.

Chola   *Sikhism*   A long shirt worn by the Gurus or a Sikh spiritual leader. It is also used for the outer covering of cloth that is bound around the Sikh flag that is always displayed outside a GURDWARA. (*See also* NISHAN SAHIB)

Chowri / Chauri / Chaur   *Sikhism*   A fan traditionally made of yak's hair which is waved over the GURU GRANTH SAHIB. A symbol of royalty, it demonstrates the MIRI/PIRI authority of the Guru.

Chrism   *Christianity*   A mixture of olive oil and balsam used for anointing (chrismation) in the SACRAMENTS of BAPTISM, CONFIRMATION, ORDINATION and the dedication of sacred buildings within the Greek Orthodox and Roman Catholic churches. It is usually consecrated on Maundy Thursday by either a bishop or a patriarch. It is kept in a container known as the chrismata.

Chrismata   *Christianity*   See CHRISM.

Chrismation   *Christianity*   See CHRISM.

Christ *(the anointed one)*   *Christianity*   The Greek translation of the Jewish word for MESSIAH. The Jewish tradition expected a leader who would herald God's salvation. The disciples of Jesus gave him the title especially after his resurrection, and it has come to refer to the divine nature of the resurrected figure as opposed to the human figure of Jesus of Nazareth. (*See also* CHRISTIAN; JESUS CHRIST)

Christian   *Christianity*   The name given to the followers of JESUS CHRIST, regardless of denominational loyalty, which is also used in a nominal sense to describe the indigenous populations of secular nations that are historically Christian. The book of Acts in the NEW TESTAMENT places the first use of the term Christian as a self-ascription to the followers of Christ in Antioch. However, it is likely that the term was first used as a nickname by outsiders to describe the followers of the new religion and then became adopted by the followers themselves. (*See also* CHRIST)

Christmas *Christianity* The festival which celebrates the nativity of Christ and is held in the Western churches on 25 December. It is not actually known when Jesus Christ was born, and it is speculated that the festival, which was certainly held on this date as early as 331, was originally the pagan solstice festival. At midnight on Christmas Eve there is a traditional candlelit EUCHARIST. The twelve days of the Christmas period also contain the holy days of Saint Stephen (26 December), St John (27 December), Holy Innocents (28 December), The Circumcision of Our Lord (1 January) and EPIPHANY (6 January). In the Christian world, New Year is marked on 1 January. (*See also* NICHOLAS, ST)

Christology *Christianity* Christian theology which deals with the significance, identity and nature of Christ. Much of the debate takes place around theories concerning the relationship between Christ and God and the nature of the balance between the human and divine nature of Jesus Christ. (*See* ARIANISM; CHALCEDONIAN DECLARATION; DOCETISM; EBIONITES; NICAEA, COUNCIL OF)

Chronicles *Judaism* The two books of Chronicles are counted as one work and together constitute one of the twelve books of the Hebrew scriptures that are known as Jewish Holy Writings. It consists of a survey of history, but particularly focuses on the role of the priesthood and the forms of worship in the Temple in Jerusalem. (*See also* KETUVIM; TANAKH)

Chuppah *Judaism* See HUPPAH.

Church *Christianity* A term used variously to describe the community consisting of all Christians, a particular DENOMINATION of Christianity and an individual Christian place of worship. The word is derived from the Greek 'the Lord's House' but the NEW TESTAMENT uses the word 'ekklesia', which means a community or local congregation of Christian worshippers and has no connotation of a building. However, the New Testament also refers to the church as the new society created by Christ as the participant of the new covenant to replace Israel. The Roman Catholic Church focuses attention on participation in the SACRAMENTS as defining the church, but Protestant groups have changed the emphasis to participation in the word of God. Questions of Christian unity have led to a distinction between the visible church, which is a human manifestation prone to error and correction, and the invisible church, which is the body of the saved known only to God. (*See also* CATHEDRAL; CHAPEL)

Church of England *Christianity* That part of the ANGLICAN COMMUNION which formally exists as the state religion of Britain. It came into existence during the REFORMATION when Henry VIII split from Rome after the Pope had refused to annul his marriage. Henry was acknowledged as the supreme head on earth of the Church of England, since when it has recognized the reigning monarch as its temporal leader. Although it does not acknowledge the POPE, many aspects of the Church of England remain essentially Catholic, including EPISCOPACY and belief in the authority of tradition as well as scripture and acknowledgement of the APOSTOLIC SUCCESSION. The Catholic wing of the church was rejuvenated by the OXFORD MOVEMENT, and the church today perceives itself as a broad and tolerant alliance of HIGH CHURCH and LOW CHURCH, Anglo-Catholics, EVANGEL-ICALS and CHARISMATICS. Since the second half of the twentieth century it has become more autonomous from the state and the issue of disestablishment is prominent. (*See also* CANTERBURY; COMMON PRAYER, THE BOOK OF; THIRTY-NINE ARTICLES)

Church Militant, The   *Christianity*   The body of Christians who still remain living on earth as human beings rather than those already departed to PURGATORY or HEAVEN. The term suggests that they are still engaged in the struggle between the forces of good and evil. (*See also* SATAN; SIN)

Churchwardens   *Christianity*   In the CHURCH OF ENGLAND they are members of the laity elected to be responsible for the objects and furniture in the church building.

Churchyard   *Christianity*   The land in which a CHURCH stands but which is often used to describe the burial ground maintained in the precincts of a church.

Cistercians   *Christianity*   The monastic order founded in France in 1098 by Robert, abbot of the monastery at Molesme, and a small band of companions. They established a new monastery at Citeaux, also known as Cistercium, based on a life of great strictness. It originated as an attempt to reform the BENEDICTI-NES on the basis of strictness and simplicity and return to the original observance of the Benedictine rule. The monks are known as 'White Monks' because of their simple garb of undyed wool. The order spread under the influence of St Bernard of Clairvaux (1090–1153) during the twelfth century.

Cit   *Hinduism*   *See* CHIT.

Citta *(consciousness)*   *Buddhism*   The experience of being aware of something. However, in Buddhism, consciousness is an aggregate of associated mental factors such as contact, feeling, recognition, volition, single-mindedness and bringing to mind. Each combination that arises lasts for a short moment and is conscious of just one thing. Thus consciousness cannot be seen as the ground of our being or a constant, as is the case in most Hindu philosophy. (*See* CHIT)

Cittakaggata (P) / Cittakagrata (S) *Buddhism*   One of the two forms of meditation that can lead to single-mindedness and can be achieved by a variety of techniques and methods depending on the school or teacher. The Buddha taught that they pre-existed his life and therefore are not explicitly Buddhist. The other form of meditation is uniquely Buddhist. (*See* VIPASSANA)

Cittamatra *Buddhism*   The aspect of NIRVANA as nothing-but-thought as taught by the YOGACARA school. The proposition is that one can only know an experience of something with the mind.

Clare, St (1194–1253) *Christianity*   A friend and disciple of St FRANCIS OF ASSISI who joined him in 1212 and was established with a few companions in the monastery founded by St Francis in the church of St Damian in the city. She developed it into the women's branch of the FRANCISCAN order, which is called the POOR CLARES after her.

Cloister *Christianity*   The enclosed space at the centre of a MONASTERY or other religious building. It is sometimes used to describe a monastery itself or the life of a RELIGIOUS enclosed within one of the monastic orders.

Coenobite *Christianity*   A monk or a nun who lives in a monastic community as opposed to the solitary life of a hermit. (*See also* RELIGIOUS)

Collation *Christianity*   A term used for either a light meal allowed on a day of fasting or readings that take place in MONASTERIES and focus on the lives of the church fathers.

Collect *Christianity*   Short prayers used in the EUCHARIST which consist of an invocation and petition in Christ's name.

College *Christianity*   The assembly of CARDINALS in Roman Catholicism which acts as an advisory body to the POPE and gathers after his death to select a new pontiff. (*See also* CONCLAVE)

Colossians, Epistle to the *Christianity*   A short EPISTLE attributed to Paul contained in the NEW TESTAMENT but whose authorship has been challenged on linguistic and doctrinal grounds. It was written to the Christian community in Colossae after Paul had received news that they were under threat from false teachers who were leading people away from the message preached by Christ.

The author does not refute the heresies but lays out a clear position of correct Christian teaching. (*See also* PAUL, ST)

Comforter   *Christianity*   *See* HOLY SPIRIT.

Common Prayer, The Book of   *Christianity*   The official service book of the CHURCH OF ENGLAND compiled in 1549 by Archbishop Cranmer and which contains the order of service for morning and evening prayer and the SACRAMENTS. The Book of Common Prayer has gone through many revisions outside England but the Church of England has generally maintained the original 1662 version. However, new books of alternative services were produced in the twentieth century.

Communion   *Christianity*   *See* EUCHARIST.

Communion table   *Christianity*   *See* ALTAR.

Compline   *Christianity*   In the Western Church, the final office said before sleeping. It consists of a hymn, psalms and the NUNC DIMITTIS. Although maintained in monastic communities, in the Anglican churches, it has been combined with VESPERS and incorporated into EVENSONG. (*See also* OFFICES, DIVINE)

Comprecation   *Christianity*   The intercession of the SAINTS made to God on behalf of all other Christians. Rejected by Protestant traditions, it remains an important part of Roman Catholic belief and common practice.

Conclave   *Christianity*   The gathering of Roman Catholic CARDINALS that takes place within an enclosed room at the VATICAN, known as the Conclave, in order to select a new POPE from amongst their number after the death of the present incumbent.

Confession   *Christianity*   The term confession is used in three different ways in Christianity. The first simply implies an admission of SIN by a Christian. However, several denominations provide the possibility for personal confession to a PRIEST as well as the general confessional prayer that appears at the beginning of the EUCHARIST. Where confession is heard before a priest (confessor) in confidence and various PENANCES are given for ATONEMENT, the rite is considered to be one of the seven SACRAMENTS. Finally, confession is used to describe an official statement of faith concerned with doctrinal correctness. For example, during the REFORMATION, an emphasis was placed on 'confessions' meaning declarations of denominational loyalty through allegiance to statements of beliefs. These are known as confessions. (*See also* REDEMPTION; ROSARY)

Confessor *Christianity*   See CONFESSION.

Confirmation *Christianity*   The rite of passage and one of the seven SACRAMENTS which facilitates full entry into the Christian community and allows the person to share in the Communion. It usually takes the form of the laying on of hands, which is performed by a BISHOP, close to the onset of puberty. Confirmation completes the process begun at BAPTISM. The justifications for the rite come from a New Testament source that indicates how bishops were required to baptize in the HOLY SPIRIT after the initial water baptism carried out by DEACONS. However, the rite is first mentioned in 450 and may have come about as infant baptisms increased in order to provide a strengthening of Christian commitment in new adulthood.

Congregationalist *Christianity*   A form of PURITAN Protestant dissent originating from the beliefs of Robert Browne (1550–1633) which developed from the idea that each local church should have autonomy and independence as practised in the early church. The Congregationalist movement was influential in the English Civil War and was prominent in the army of Oliver Cromwell. The 1662 Act of Uniformity forced them to declare their position as NON-CONFORMISTS and resulted in their final break with the CHURCH OF ENGLAND. In 1972, the majority of the Congregationalists joined with the English PRESBYTERIANS to form the United Reformed Church.

Congruism *Christianity*   The doctrine that GRACE is given by God according to the performance of good works and the circumstances in which it will be put to use. (*See* JUSTIFICATION)

Consecration *Christianity*   The term used to describe either the ritual which sanctifies churches and altars or the rite in which the bread and wine literally become, or are associated with, the body and blood of Christ. It takes place in the EUCHARIST after the offering of the elements to the altar and before the congregation participates in the Communion. The culmination of the consecration is the lifting up of the elements by the priest in view of the entire congregation and the solemn ringing of the sanctus bell. (*See also* HOST)

Constantine (274–337) *Christianity*   The Roman emperor who made Christianity the faith of the empire by giving his imperial favour to the religion after winning the battle of Milvian Bridge. He united the church to the state and in 325 summoned the various bishops to the Council of NICAEA to resolve the issue of Arian CHRISTOLOGY and other disputes between Christians. In 330, he moved the capital of his empire from Rome to Constantinople, which became the new capital of Eastern Christianity. (*See also* ARIANISM)

Consubstantiation   *Christianity*   The belief that after CONSECRATION, the substances of the bread and wine and the body and blood of Christ exist in union with each other. Consubstantiation is particularly associated with Martin LUTHER and the Protestant traditions. Luther believed that both the bread and wine and the body of Christ are present in the EUCHARIST but that there is no change of substance. The important point is to believe that Christ is present at the Eucharist. (*See also* TRANSUBSTANTIATION)

Convent   *Christianity*   Although historically referring to the dwelling of a religious monastic community or the community itself, contemporary usage only applies to a community of NUNS or the building where they reside. (*See also* MONK; ORDER; RELIGIOUS)

Cope   *Christianity*   A semi-circular cloak worn by priests at the EUCHARIST. Its use in the CHURCH OF ENGLAND was revived in the nineteenth century under the influence of the OXFORD MOVEMENT. (*See also* VESTMENTS)

Corinthians, Epistles to the   *Christianity*   Two New Testament EPISTLES written by Paul to the Christian community at Corinth around 51–55. These are part of the undisputed letters whose authorship is attributed to Paul. The apostle himself had helped establish the church in Corinth and maintained close links with it. The letters were written to help the church deal with errors of belief arising from the influence of GNOSTICISM, misunderstandings of Paul's own teaching and perhaps to bring the church up to date with changes taking place in Paul's own thinking. The church had split into factions under several leaders and a number of Christians had written to Paul asking him to resolve various questions. The letters to the Corinthians are his response to all of the above factors. (*See also* PAUL, ST)

Council   *Christianity*   An assembly of BISHOPS and church leaders brought together from all over the Christian world in order to maintain discipline and unity by settling disputes over doctrine or to effect major changes in church organization or liturgy. Notable examples are the Councils of NICAEA in 325 and VATICAN COUNCIL II from 1962 to 1965. (*See also* VATICAN COUNCIL I)

Credence   *Christianity*   A small side table placed near the altar to hold the elements or the bread, wine and water that have been consecrated and used at the EUCHARIST.

Creed *Christianity*   A formal statement of religious belief that can be used to maintain orthodox doctrine and is held in common by all Christian believers. The most important are the APOSTLES' CREED and the NICENE CREED.

Crib *Christianity*   A custom of the Western Church in which a representation of the crib or manger in which the newly born Christ was laid is placed in a CHURCH on Christmas Eve. It depicts the child Christ surrounded by the holy family, shepherds and the three MAGI or wise men. (*See also* CHRISTMAS)

Crosier *Christianity*   The staff shaped like a shepherd's crook carried by a BISHOP and sometimes an ABBOT or ABBESS of a monastic community. The shepherd's crook is symbolic of Christ's role as the Good Shepherd or custodian of the Christian community.

Crucifix *Christianity*   A model of the cross which contains the form of the crucified Christ. They are often worn around the neck on chains or appear on the end of rosaries. Most Roman Catholic churches contain statues or models of the crucified Christ above the ALTAR in the SANCTUARY. The plain cross without the crucified Christ is preferred in Protestant churches to emphasize the resurrected Christ. (*See also* CRUCIFIXION)

Crucifixion *Christianity*   A common Roman punishment whereby a criminal or slave was put to death by being nailed or bound to a cross. The crucifixion of Jesus Christ was witnessed by the writers of all four gospels, but they do not supply the details of Jesus' physical suffering other than to indicate that he refused to accept any aid. They are more concerned with the cosmic and soteriological significance of the event. The word 'cross' came to exemplify the gospel message that Jesus Christ, the Son of God, had died for human salvation through the ATONEMENT of all human sin. The cross has become a universal symbol of Christianity, and Christian discipleship is often perceived as cross-bearing or walking in the footsteps of Christ. (*See also* CRUCIFIX; REDEMPTION)

Crusades *Christianity*   A series of holy wars that took place between 1095 and 1464 ostensibly to reclaim the Holy Land from the Muslims. Although there were a number of economic reasons for taking part in the Crusades, and many probably participated for the material rewards of plunder and land and the spiritual rewards of forgiveness of sins, there were also religious reasons for the pious. The Crusader's life was perceived as an imitation of monastic life and a way of embarking on the road to spiritual perfection.

Curail *Hinduism*   A female ghost that often possesses young women in pregnancy. It is believed that the *curail* is either a woman who has died in childbirth or without children, and is thus envious of women who are bearing children. These kinds of village beliefs are dealt with by special practitioners who are proficient in exorcism.

Curate *Christianity* A member of the clergy appointed to assist the parish PRIEST in the performance of his/her duties.

Curia *Christianity* The papal court which administers the Roman Catholic Church from the Vatican City. The term is also used for the officials of the CHAPTER who assist a diocesan BISHOP. (*See also* DIOCESE)

Daijo Zen *Buddhism*   The fourth of the five types of ZEN known as MAHAYANA or 'Great Vehicle' Zen. The central teaching involves seeing into one's essential nature and realizing the way in your daily actions.

Dakini *Buddhism*   A powerful female deity associated with Tantric traditions. She has the power of flight and almost certainly was borrowed from pre-ARYAN folklore. (*See also* TANTRA)

Dakshina *Hinduism*   The fee paid to a BRAHMIN or other religious officiate for performing a religious ceremony. It can also be a financial offering to a temple or a GURU.

Dakshineshwar *Hinduism*   The nineteenth-century temple complex dedicated to KALI built 4 miles outside Calcutta. In 1852, a young BRAHMIN was appointed assistant priest and went on to become one of Hinduism's most important influences in the twentieth century. Renamed RAMAKRISHNA on initiation by a wandering ADVAITA monk, he is considered by many Hindus to be a contemporary AVATAR. Consequently Dakshineshwar is now an important pilgrimage centre. (*See also* VIVEKANANDA)

Dal Khalsa *(Army of the Pure)* *Sikhism*   The Sikh military was known by this term from at least 1734. Due to the difficult political situation which the Sikhs faced from their MOGUL rulers, it became necessary to maintain a strong military force from early in their history. The army consisted of cavalry who found their own horses and received prize money. Under the leadership of Maharaja RANJIT SINGH, the Sikhs developed formidable infantry battalions.

Dalai Lama *Buddhism*   The head of Tibetan Buddhism and the spiritual and temporal leader of the Tibetan people. As the head of the Yellow Hat monks, he is regarded as the reincarnation of the Bodhisattva Chenresi. The reincarnation of the deceased Dalai Lama is recognized and selected in childhood. The chosen child is then trained to occupy the position that he held in the past life. The present Dalai Lama resides in Dharamsala since the occupation of Tibet by China.

Dala'il *(Proofs)* *Islam*   A form of literature that praises Muhammad. The *dala'il* collections are essentially biographies that are complemented by miracle stories. They detail his genealogy and noble qualities, along with a variety of miracle stories in which men and women were able to recognize his special status as God's final messenger. Famous collections were composed by Abu Nu'aim al-Isfahani (d.1037) and al-Baihaqi (d.1066). (*See* SIRA)

Dalits *Hinduism*   The self-chosen name for the members of the 'scheduled castes' or 'untouchables'. *Dalit* means oppressed, and in recent times this group have managed to organize themselves into a powerful political force to resist the economic and social injustices they have suffered because of their position in the Hindu caste system. (*See* HARIJANS)

Damdama Sahib *(a mound)* *Sikhism*   The term refers to a monument erected in memory of the Sikh Gurus. Some historic GURDWARAS which were visited by the Gurus are known as *Damdama Sahib*.

Damnation *Christianity*   The Christian belief in the possibility of punishment for SIN by passing an eternity in HELL. In the latter half of the twentieth century there were several theological challenges to the belief in a literal location for the damned soul. Others have questioned how a God of love could damn souls for ever based on sins committed in a short human lifespan. Many now perceive damnation as a state of alienation from the presence of God rather than an eternity in hell. (*See also* PURGATORY; SATAN)

Dan *Hinduism*   Body or physical resources. Usually used in association with MAN and *tan* (mind and wealth) to indicate the commitment considered essential on the path of BHAKTI. Surrender to the will of the deity in order to be the recipient of grace is fundamental to the *bhakti* path. This is practically possible through the commitment of a proportion of one's physical, mental and material resources to the path of devotion.

Dana *(generosity, liberal giving, a gift)* *Buddhism*   One of the six PARAMIS, or perfections, whose constant practice over lifetimes leads to enlightenment. The second precept of good conduct advises against taking things that are not given as gifts. Thus BHIKKUS (monks) should only accept that which is offered to them as *dana* by the laity, who, in turn, have the opportunity to provide for the SANGHA through their offering.

Dana *Jainism*   The giving of charity. This is one of the most important duties of the lay Jain. There are several ways in which the lay Jain can give charity. The first and foremost is through supporting the monks, as without charity the order could not be maintained. However, donations can also be given to the poor and needy and to relieve the suffering of animals. (*See* ABHAYA DANA; ANUKAMPA; JNANA DANA)

Danda *(a stick)* *Hinduism*   *Danda* can refer to the fear that is instilled in all beings by divine order to ensure that they do not wander away from the ideals of DHARMA. It is also used for the stick or staff carried by wandering holy men, particularly those of the SHAIVITE tradition. There may be a connotation here that the stick can be used to reprimand religious recalcitrants and bring them back to the way of dharma.

Daniel *Judaism*   A book of the BIBLE that describes a time when Judaism was in danger of extinction after conquest and persecution by the Greeks under Antiochus. The book describes the persecution of the prophet, Daniel, and the divine intervention that saved him during the earlier period of conquest and slavery under the Persians. It thus provides an example of courage, forbearance and faithfulness in the new apparently hopeless situation.

Dar / Dargah *Islam*   A shrine to a Muslim holy man and a place of pilgrimage. Often the *dars* are the place where a SUFI or pious man spent his life in remembrance of Allah and teaching. After death, the tomb becomes a place of veneration. Pilgrims will come to receive the saint's blessings and use him for prayers of intercession. The poor and the destitute are usually allowed to stay in the *dar* for periods of time, and some may manage communal kitchens to feed the poor and travellers. Generally, there is an attached mosque for worship where special gatherings take place for DHIKR (the remembrance of God). The place may remain a centre of teaching under the direction of the Sufi's spiritual descendants. (*See also* MAZAR; TARIQAH)

Dar al-Amn *(abode of peace)* *Islam*   Used to describe territory that is not under Islamic law but where Muslims can live in peace and harmony without interference in their practice of Islam. (*See* DAR AL-HARB; DAR AL-ISLAM)

Dar al-Harb *(abode of war)* *Islam*   Territory that is not under the jurisdiction of Islamic law or geographical areas that are not under the control of Islam. The distinction between *dar al-harb* and DAR AL-ISLAM has been crucial in Muslim thought and action. *Dar al-harb* remains territory that can be brought into submission to God's will by active proselytizing, or if threatening to the *dar al-Islam*, can be overcome by JIHAD. (*See also* DA'WA)

Dar al-Islam *(abode of Islam)* *Islam*   Territory that is under Islamic law or the geographical domain of Muslim faith and practice. In spite of the encroachment of national loyalties, there is still a strong sense of an overriding Muslim identity or membership of the UMMA (community), and Islam remains a religion committed to bringing the world under the dominion of Allah. (*See also* DAR AL-HARB, JIHAD, DA'WA)

Dar al-ulum / Dar al-uloom / Dar ul-ulum *(abode of sciences)* *Islam* Higher institutions for the study of Islamic religious education. (*See also* MADRASA)

Darban (U) *Islam*   The doorkeeper who guards the entrance to a shrine, protecting the sacred space from unwelcome intrusion, and maintains some control on the influx of devotees waiting to enter. (*See* DAR; MAZAR)

Darbar Sahib *Sikhism*   The common or popular name for the Golden Temple at AMRITSAR. (*See also* HARMANDIR)

Dargah *Islam*   *See* DAR.

Dars i Nizami *Islam*   Islamic curriculum devised in the eighteenth century by Farangi Mahal, a college in Lucknow, that still forms the basis for religious education in the MADRASAS of the subcontinent. The curriculum was divided into two parts: MANQULAT, which consisted of the study of QUR'AN and HADITH; and MA'QULAT, which involved the study of law, logic and philosophy. The emphasis was originally on the latter, but most modern *madrasas* have placed *manqulat* at the centre of the curriculum and many will not teach philosophy.

Darshan *Hinduism*   *Darshan* is a vital part of the Hindu religious experience and forms the *raison d'être* of pilgrimage and temple worship. *Darshan* means the vision of the deity and it is believed that when the worshippers or devotees come before the MURTI or a GURU, they are blessed with a vision of the divine. Rituals are carried out at the installation of a *murti* in order to invite the presence of God to inhabit the deity. Thus the *murti* is brought to life and becomes the embodiment of the god that it represents. When Hindus visit the temple they enter the presence of the divine, so *darshan* carries the connotation of both being seen and seeing the divine.

Darshan Shastras *Hinduism* The six systems of orthodox Hindu philosophy. By the medieval period the various intellectual traditions that had developed from a range of commentaries on Vedic and Sutric literature had been codified into six schools of orthodoxy. These are not rigid systems and there will be many opinions within one school; indeed, the ideas of the various schools are interwoven into the blanket of everyday Hinduism. (*See* ASTIKA; MIMANSA; NASTIKA; NYAYA; SAMKHYA; VAISESHIKA; VEDANTA; YOGA)

Darshana *Jainism* The faculty of intuition or perception. It is one of the aspects of conscious activity (UPAYOGA), the basic characteristic of the soul. The other is JNANA or knowledge. (*See also* CETANA)

Darshana Mohaniya *Jainism* Deluding KARMA that creates false ideas or delusions concerning the teachings of the JINAS. In its milder forms it produces doubt concerning right belief, or clouds right belief with erroneous views. (*See also* MOHANIYA KARMA)

Darshana Pratima *Jainism* The first of the eleven stages of spiritual progress that provide the lay Jain with a progressive path towards liberation. This is the stage of right faith, in which the Jain devotee is required to develop a reasoned faith in the tradition based on sound doctrine and its application. (*See* PRATIMA; SAMYAK DARSHANA)

Darshanavaraniya *(faith-obscuring karma)* *Jainism* This is one of the four types of KARMA that is harmful to the progress of the soul towards liberation. This type of karma leads to delusion through false perceptions of reality obtained through the senses. (*See also* GHATI KARMA)

Dasam Granth *(Book of the Tenth)* *Sikhism* The Sikh scripture which consists of compositions attributed to GURU GOBIND SINGH, the tenth and final human Guru, and to four scribes in his service. As well as hymns, the scripture contains remarkable mythological passages concerning the past lives of Guru Gobind Singh. There are also many passages which link Sikhism to the mythology of Hinduism.

Dasanamis *Hinduism* Ten orders of SHAIVITE ascetics believed to have been founded by SHANKARA in the ninth century. They are known for their scholarship and pursuit of the absolute.

Dasaratha *Hinduism* The legendary king of AYODHYA and the father of RAMA. The king died of heartbreak after being tricked by the jealousy of his second wife, KAIKEYI, who made him promise to banish Rama from the kingdom in favour of her son, Bharat. These incidents triggered the saga of Rama described in the RAMAYANA.

Dassera / Dassehra / Vijay Dashmi   *Hinduism*   The ten-day festival associated with the victory of RAMA over RAVANA. However, most Gujarati Hindus celebrate it as the festival of DURGA, also called Amba in Gujarat, known as NAVARATRI (Nine Nights). At the end of this period the festival of DURGA PUJA takes place alongside the celebration of Rama's victory. It is held between September and October.

Daswand   *Sikhism*   The religious obligation on Sikhs to donate one-tenth of their earnings either to a religious or to a charitable concern. It is believed to have originated in the commands of the GURUS. KHALSA Sikhs have to promise to give *daswand* at their initiation ceremony.

Dat   *Judaism*   The Hebrew word used to express religion. Its meaning is nearer to law rather than an expression of belief.

David (c. 970 BCE)   *Christianity*   The first king of the Judean dynasty and the second king of Israel. His importance in Christianity is affirmed in the NEW TESTAMENT, which states that Jesus was born of the lineage of David. He is perceived as a foreshadower of Jesus Christ, who is sometimes called 'the son of David'. Jesus himself is attributed with the words, 'I am the root and the offspring of David' (Revelations 22:16). This is important, as OLD TESTAMENT prophecies stated that the MESSIAH would be born in the lineage of David. The Psalms, which are used extensively in Christian liturgy, are also traditionally attributed to David. (*See also* DAVID)

David   *Judaism*   The King of Israel after Saul who united the two kingdoms of Judah and Ephraim and established his capital at Jerusalem. David was believed to have been 'anointed' or chosen by God, and various biblical verses state that the descendants of David will rule over the kingdom of Israel for ever. After the division of the land and subsequent defeat and conquest by the Greeks and the Romans, the belief in a messiah from the house of David became a part of Jewish tradition. David is also believed to be the originator of the physical format of the Jewish prayer. (*See* MASSIACH)

Da'wa / Da'wah (*call*)   *Islam*   The promotion of Islam to both Muslims and non-Muslims that is considered to be a central duty for all Muslims. *Da'wa* can be achieved either by preaching or by exemplary good actions. The majority of twentieth-century *da'wa* movements were engaged in preaching activities inside the Muslim community in an attempt to bring back lapsed Muslims to the practice of their faith. However, Islam remains a proselytizing religion and attracts converts wherever it is established. Since the twentieth century there has been a huge increase in the use of tracts, leaflets and pamphlets to promote various aspects of the religion. (*See* TABLIGH-I JAMAAT)

Dawud   *Islam*   The Muslim name for David, believed to be the Prophet of Allah to whom the book of Psalms (ZABUR) was revealed. (*See also* NABI; RASUL)

Dayananda, Swami (1824–83)   *Hinduism*   The founder of the Hindu reform movement, ARYA SAMAJ. After running away from home in order to avoid an arranged marriage, he met with a guru who advised him to commit himself to the correct interpretation of the VEDAS. He went on to become a considerable Sanskrit scholar. In 1875 he founded the Arya Samaj in Bombay. He attacked the corruptions that he perceived existing in nineteenth-century Hinduism, but unlike other Hindu reform movements such as the BRAHMO SAMAJ, he was not influenced by Christianity. He preached a message of return to the religion of the Vedas based upon his own interpretation.

Dayyan   *Judaism*   A RABBI who acts as a judge in a religious court to make decisions on matters of Jewish religious law. The ultimate judge is God. (*See also* BET DIN; HALAKHAH)

Deacon   *Christianity*   From the Greek word *diakonia* (a servant or waiter at tables), the NEW TESTAMENT usually associates the function with pastoral or preaching activities. In the early church, the function became more specialized as deacons were appointed to serve the poor and take care of the distribution of alms (Acts 6:1–6). They came below the BISHOP and the PRIEST in the episcopal hierarchy and exercised an administrative and social responsibility. In most Western Episcopal churches the term is now used for the stage of preparation for priesthood and until recently defined the limit of female participation in the clergy. In the Eastern Church and many Protestant denominations, deacons function to care for the poor and the sick or administer alms. (*See also* DEACONESS)

Deaconess   *Christianity*   The duties of a deacon carried out by a woman probably goes back to the New Testament period, where Phoebe is identified as the *diakonos* of the church at Cenchreae. Certainly, the Episcopal churches have never denied women access to the deaconate in the way that they have with the priesthood. (*See* DEACON)

Dead Sea Scrolls   *Christianity*   A library of Hebrew and Aramaic scrolls discovered on the northwest shore of the Dead Sea at QUMRAN in 1947 that provide insight into the political, religious and social organization of Hebrew life in the century before and after the life of Jesus Christ. In particular, they give considerable information on a semi-ascetic Jewish religious community known as the ESSENES, from whom they are believed to have originated.

Dean   *Christianity*   The title given to the PRIEST in the Episcopal churches who manages and administers the affairs of a CATHEDRAL. (*See also* ARCHBISHOP; BISHOP)

Deborah   *Judaism*   A woman who achieved the status of a judge and war leader, as described in the book of Judges.

Decalogue   *Christianity*   The Ten Commandments given by God to MOSES on Mount Sinai and also accepted by Christians. However, generally they differ from Jewish understanding of the law given by Moses, in that the relationship of acceptance is based not on obedience but intuitional or inner understanding of the relationship of love that exists between God and humans and between humans. Some have argued (for example, William Blake) that Christians are not bound to obey Jewish law but should rely on their intuitional awareness of love, thus following in the footsteps of Jesus Christ, who overruled the law when the occasion demanded mercy or compassion. (*See also* TORAH)

Deen   *Islam*   *See* DIN.

Deg   *(a large cooking pot)*   *Sikhism*   *Deg* is symbolic of the institution of LANGAR or free kitchen. *Tegh* (sword) and *deg* were inscribed on Sikh coins and have also been found on seals. Sikh legends state that Bhai Buddha, the last remaining devotee of GURU NANAK, prophesied to the wife of GURU ARJAN DEV that she would give birth to a child who would be the master of *tegh* and *deg*. The two categories correspond to the MIRI/PIRI authority of the Gurus.

Deism   *Christianity*   A movement that became increasingly popular in France and Germany after the seventeenth century and rejected the idea that God is still involved in the creation, although it did accept that he was the creator. Some individuals also rejected the idea of divine rewards, punishments and providence. Although never widely accepted in England, a system of natural religion was developed by a few prominent philosophers in the eighteenth century that was known by the same name.

Denominations   *Christianity*   The term used to describe Christian movements or churches that are accepted as orthodox by the WORLD COUNCIL OF CHURCHES. Denominationalism represents a move away from the church/sect model which promoted the view that one movement contained the doctrinal truth and others were merely breakaway heresies. Christian denominations accept their differences and acknowledge their unity, striving towards an ecumenical relationship with each other. (*See also* ECUMENISM)

Deoband *Islam*   A famous Muslim college founded in 1867 in northern India in a small town of the same name. The founders had all fought against the British in 1857 and realized that there was no longer any hope of defeating the invader by a call for JIHAD. Their vision was to maintain the integrity of Muslim belief and practice through education and to close ranks in the community to protect it from the non-Muslim population. The aim of the founders was to train ULAMA who would be committed to a conservative reform of Islam based on their interpretation of HADITH. The school went on to become a powerful and influential reform movement, essentially anti-mystic but without the political dimension of the twentieth-century revivalist movements. It remains influential throughout the subcontinent and wherever subcontinent Muslims have established migrant communities. There are around 10,000 Deobandi colleges in the subcontinent. (*See also* BARELWI; TABLIGH-I JAMAAT)

Dera Sahib *Sikhism*   The historic GURDWARA built on the site of GURU ARJAN DEV's martyrdom in 1606 on the banks of the River Ravi. A large festival takes place here annually in June, attracting Sikhs from all over the world.

Derek Eretz *Judaism*   A term used for good manners, it is also the title of a book on ethics and right conduct.

Deuteronomy *Judaism*   The fifth book of the SEFER TORAH which contains the words of MOSES and the Book of the Covenant. (*See also* BERIT; PENTATEUCH; TORAH)

Deva *Buddhism*   Devas are regarded as superhuman spiritual beings or the shining ones, and their realms deemed one of the six destinations into which it is possible to be reborn. In Buddhist cosmology the gods reside in a paradise of delights where every kind of pleasure and luxury is available. Although their lives are very long, eventually they will die and re-enter the cycle of SAMSARA. Consequently, even the gods envy and respect the human practitioner of the DHAMMA.

Deva *Hinduism*   Usually one of the major gods or deities of the Hindu pantheon. While Hindus choose from the pantheon of gods the one that they feel most drawn to worship, this does not negate worship of other deities on special occasions. There may be a tradition of worshipping a particular god within a family or caste group, but it is important to remember that most Hindus believe the gods to be aspects of one supreme being, so worship of one deity does not exclude the worship of others. (*See* DEVI)

Devata *Hinduism* A minor divinity or demi-god usually associated with a DEVA. They are not malevolent and usually appear in the minor mythological texts. Particular *devatas* may be worshipped regionally or within particular sub-castes. (*See also* GRAM DEVATA)

Devekut *Judaism* The intimate, single-minded and enduring contemplation of God that is the goal of the mystic's endeavour as described in the KABBALAH.

Devi *Hinduism* A female deity, usually of the higher pantheon. Most of the male deities have a female partner: for example, LAKSHMI or PARVATI. However, KALI and DURGA are goddesses in their own right and have a considerable following amongst Hindus. (*See also* DEVA)

Devil *Christianity* See SATAN.

Dhajjal, al- *Islam* The antichrist figure who in Muslim eschatological traditions will appear on the earth just prior to the return of ISA (Jesus) and the MAHDI, when he will be overthrown by Isa, and the world will embrace the religion of God before the final Day of Judgement.

Dhamma (P) / Dharma (S) *Buddhism* The term has a variety of meanings (right, law, truth, justice, doctrine), but is usually understood as the BUDDHA's teachings and their application. As such, *Dhamma* is a universal law or ultimate truth. When written without a capital 'D' it refers to the 'phenomena' or 'things' that make up all the constituents of the conditioned realm or SAMSARA. (*See also* DHAMMAKAYA; NIRVANA)

Dhamma-cakkhu (P) *(the eye of Dhamma)* *Buddhism* The experiential insight or understanding of the Buddha's teachings which is accompanied by a spiritual transition. It is also known as 'stream-entry'. The first person to experience this transition was Kondanna, one of the ascetics who listened to the first sermon of the Buddha. (*See* DHAMMACHAKKA)

Dhammachakka (P) / Dharmachakra (S) *(the wheel of Dhamma)* *Buddhism* The term used to describe how Buddha's teachings set in motion an era of spiritual influence that began with the first sermon on the four noble truths delivered at VARANASI. The SUTRA of the first sermon is known as *Dhamma-cakka-pavattana* or 'setting in motion of the *Dhamma* wheel'. (*See also* DHAMMA)

Dhammakaya (P) / Dharmakaya (S) *(the body of the law)* *Buddhism*   In the MAHAYANA tradition the Buddha is perceived as the personification of the truth. He is beyond all dualities and conception and one with the eternal DHAMMA. Consequently, everyone shares in the Buddha nature or principle of Buddhahood found within. In the THERAVADA tradition *Dhammakaya* refers to the totality of the Buddha's teachings. (*See also* NIRMANAKAYA; SAMBHOGAKAYA; TATHAGATA)

Dhammapada (P) / Dharmapada (S) *(the path or way of the Dhamma)* *Buddhism*   An important book in the second basket (SUTTA PITAKA) of the PALI CANON, consisting of 423 verses which are attributed to the Buddha. (*See also* NIKAYA)

Dhammavicaya (P) *Buddhism*   Conquest by piety as opposed to the use of force. The Buddhist ideal of *Dhammavicaya* is the kingdom of ASOKA after his conversion.

Dhammavijaya (P) *Buddhism*   The search for truth or the longing to end the suffering caused by existence in the endless wheel of SAMSARA. The Buddha's quest for enlightenment is the ideal of the search for truth. (*See also* DHAMMA)

Dhammavinaya (P) *Buddhism*   A term used in early Buddhism to refer to the doctrine or discipline that provided the basis for the community's religious life. (*See* DHAMMA; SANGHA)

Dharam *(religious duty)* *Sikhism*   The Sikh equivalent of Hindu DHARMA. GURU NANAK, the founder of Sikhism, essentially perceived *dharam* as actions that bring someone closer to God and away from ego and selfishness. In essence, the Sikh *dharam* consists of remembrance of NAM, the giving of charity (DAN), physical and mental purity (*ishnan*), supporting oneself through honest labour (KIRAT KARNA), sharing food (*wand-chakna*) and associating with holy company (SATSANG). *Dharam* is usually considered to be the KHALSA code by orthodox Sikhs. The VARNASHRAMDHARMA of Hinduism is rejected by Sikhs. (*See also* SATNAM)

Dharam Khand *Sikhism*   According to the teachings of GURU NANAK, the first of the five stages or realms which the human being has to pass through to achieve liberation. It is the stage of religious duty, the recognition of God's law, which is beholden on all people simply through their birth into a human body. Obedience to religious duty brings merit, which leads the person on to higher stages or realms. (*See also* GYAN KHAND; KARAM KHAND; SAC KHAND; SARAM KHAND)

Dharam-Yudh *Sikhism* A war of righteousness which is fought against oppression or tyranny. GURU HARGOBIND was the first Sikh Guru to raise an army against Moghul oppression. GURU GOBIND SINGH provided a code of warfare.

Dharamsala *Hinduism* A religious hospice or guest-house used to accommodate travellers and pilgrims. Also the name of a town in the Himalayas famous as the home-in-exile of the DALAI LAMA and the Tibetan community that has accompanied him.

Dharamsala *Sikhism* A place of worship and temporary accommodation for travellers and pilgrims. Originally Sikh places of worship, they were superseded by the GURDWARAS, which were first established at the time of GURU HARGOBIND. The *dharamsalas* were used as places of worship and for the singing of KIRTAN.

Dharana *Buddhism* The beginning of meditation, which consists of fixing the mind on one single object or thought. (*See* BHAVANA; CITTAKAGGATA; VIPASSANA)

Dharana *Hinduism* Used in a similar way to Buddhist terminology to describe one-pointed concentration on a single object, often a MANTRA or an ISVARA. The term is most commonly used by the YOGA school.

Dharani *Buddhism* Long sequences of syllables from scriptural passages used in Tantric Buddhism as spells or incantations and believed to provide special powers to invoke a god or goddess, generate good KARMA or help fix the concentration of a meditator. (*See also* TANTRA)

Dharma (S) *Buddhism* *See* DHAMMA.

Dharma *Hinduism* A cosmic principle variously translated as righteousness, right conduct, duty and way of life or religion. The source of dharmic obligations is the VEDAS, which subscribe certain ritual actions to the BRAHMINS to maintain both social and cosmic order. The reward for the performance of these rituals is heaven, but dharma is carried out for its own sake and failure to do so results in sin (PAP). However, dharma is usually regarded as context and caste specific. Most Hindus would consider themselves bound to perform the dharmic actions that are required according to their status in society. For those who belong to BHAKTI or other religious movements, dharma is usually associated with religious activity that will bring liberation closer. The association with religion has become the common definition of dharma and many Indians use the term in the context of a particular religious identity and practice such as Sikh dharma, Jain dharma etc. Dharma is often linked with caste or VARNA as it has also come to mean the correct ritual, social or ethical action associated with a particular subgroup. (*See also* JATI; KARMA; VARNASHRAMDHARMA)

Dharma *Jainism* Jains are similar to Buddhists in their use of dharma to refer to spiritual teachings that lead to liberation. Generally these are the teachings of MAHAVIR, even though Jainism considers itself to be an eternal religion. Dharma also refers to the ten virtues that need to be developed in order to overcome the four passions of anger, pride, greed and dishonesty. These virtues are humility, contentment, naturalness, forgiveness, austerity, renunciation, self-restraint, truthfulness, chastity and non-possession.

Dharma Sastras *Hinduism* A branch of SMRITI literature written around 300–600 that deals with the precise code of behaviour for high-caste lay Hindus. They are also a source for jurisprudence and have been used by assemblies of BRAHMINS to determine Hindu law and legislation. They contain the important LAWS OF MANU *(manusmriti)*.

Dharma-tirtha *Jainism* The more accurate terminology for Jain DHARMA. It is the path to liberation as set out by the JINAS or TIRTHANKARAS, especially Mahavir.

Dharmachakra (S) *Buddhism* See DHAMMACHAKKA.

Dharmakara *Buddhism* The BODHISATTVA who promises to build a 'pure land' in which the DHARMA can be practised freely. He presides over this blissful world as the AMIDA Buddha, where he is joined by those human beings who have been devoted to him. The schools of Buddhism which followed the tradition of devotion or faith in the Amida Buddha became known as 'Pure Land'. (*See also* JODO)

Dharmakaya (S) *Buddhism* See DHAMMAKAYA.

Dharmapada (S) *Buddhism* See DHAMMAKAYA.

Dhikr / Zhikr *Islam* The essential message of the QUR'AN to remember Allah. Although the Qur'an extols prayer as a central means of remembrance, it praises those who remember Allah in all walks and arenas of life. Consequently, the SUFI mystics developed methods to remember Allah at all times. The most common is the distinctive repetitive and rhythmic recollection of the names of Allah in various formulas. Each Sufi TARIQAH has its own unique form of *dhikr* as practised by its great exponents and believed to date back to the founder of the order. A MURID (follower) will be initiated into both individual and communal *dhikr* on entry to the order. The most common form of *dhikr* is the repetition of LA ILAHA ILLA ALLAH, the first clause of the SHAHADAH, either aloud or in silence. *Dhikr* is also used to describe the reading of sections of the Qur'an or remembering Allah in the heart. (*See also* SHAIKH)

Dhikra   Islam   One of the main activities of a prophet of God to remind the people to remember Allah and offer submission to the one true God. *Dhikra* goes hand in hand with the prophet's obligation to warn of the penalties of disobedience. (*See* ARSALA; NABI; NADHIR; RASUL)

Dhimmi / Zimmi   Islam   Non-Muslims belonging to one of the revealed religions, such as Christians and Jews, who live in Muslim territory and therefore have protected status as People of the Book. They are subject to a special tax in lieu of ZAKAH. (*See also* AHL AL-KITAB)

Dhul-Hijjah   Islam   The last month of the Muslim lunar calendar and the time of the pilgrimage to MAKKAH known as the HAJJ.

Dhu'l-nun (796–861)   Islam   An influential SUFI, who was born in Upper Egypt and travelled extensively in Syria and Arabia. He was one of the first to talk about a mystical union based on the relationship of lover and beloved. Before conversion to Islam he was an alchemist, and there is some speculation that he was influenced by Egyptian Hermeticism. He was arrested in 829 in Baghdad for heresy but was released on the caliph's orders and allowed to return to Cairo. His tombstone remains in the city and is a site of veneration.

Dhyana   Buddhism   Although sometimes used as a generic term for meditation, its more specific meaning applies to advanced meditation where intense or ecstatic concentration is attained by the practitioner leading to SAMADHI. (*See also* CH'AN; VIPASSANA)

Dhyana   Hinduism   A common term used to describe the vast variety of meditational practices available within Hinduism. Generally, the term is used to describe practices that lead to SAMADHI or union with the eternal life-principle.

Dhyana   Jainism   Meditation is an important part of the Jain tradition. The objective is control of the mind and senses to help the soul retain mastership over the body. Meditation is believed to provide benefits for the physical body such as relaxation, mental steadiness, relief from tension and freedom from inner turmoil; however, it can also affect the subtle body by depleting karmic particles and helping towards purification of the soul.

Diaconicon *Christianity* The area to the south of the sanctuary in an Eastern Orthodox church which is under the domain of the DEACON and where the VESTMENTS, prayer-books and sacred vessels used in the LITURGY are kept. (*See also* VESTRY)

Diaspora *Judaism* The term used to describe the dispersion of the Jewish people throughout the world after the fall of Jerusalem and the destruction of the Temple in 70 CE, also known as Galut (exile). The Jewish people have suffered various exiles, all of which are associated with the loss of the promised land or ISRAEL. Exile has become associated with messianic expectations in Jewish belief, where the return of the people to the promised land would occur simultaneously with the coming of the Messiah. (*See also* MASSIACH)

Digambara *(the sky-clad) Jainism* The branch of Jains whose monks do not wear any clothing. Stronger in southern India, the Digambara believe they maintain the original doctrines and practices of Jainism and include far fewer scriptures than the SVETAMBARAS in their canon. They do not believe that women can attain liberation without rebirth as a male. Traditionally, it is believed that the Digambara sect arose after a famine in the first century CE devastated Bihar. One group of monks left Bihar for southern India. When they returned they found that the remaining monks had taken to wearing a simple white cloth and that they had also set up a council to determine the canon of Jain scripture. The returning monks disagreed with both of these innovations and subsequently became known as the Digambara. They form the major schism in Jain tradition. (*See also* STHANAKAVASI; TERAPANTHIS)

Diksa / Diksha *Jainism* The ceremony or initiation undertaken in order to become a monk or nun. It takes place before the community and the initiates take a vow to pursue equanimity throughout their lives and renounce all sinful activities. The initiate is also given a new name to mark the break with their past life. (*See* SADHU; SANGHA)

Diksha *Hinduism* An initiation ceremony usually associated with becoming a SANNYASIN or renunciate. It is also used to describe any initiation where a devotee is accepted by a GURU. Various sects founded by a guru and maintained by a lineage will also usually have an initiation ceremony on entry. (*See also* SAMPRADAYA)

Din / Deen *(a way of life)* *Islam*   The Arabic term used for religion and its practices, although it conveys far more than the usual Western concept of religion. It is usually used to convey the idea of a primordial religion that exists within God and appears to human beings as an unchanging or eternal revelation. Individual revealed religions are expressions of the *din*; although the core or essence will remain the same, unique expressions will appear according to time and culture. Islam is the final *din* and closest to the primordial *din*. The term conveys the idea that religion is all-encompassing and influences every aspect of human existence. *Din* is not confined to private individual devotion but is an overarching, all-comprehensive view which permeates the whole of society. (*See* DIN AL-FITRAH; FITRAH; WAHY)

Din *Judaism*   The act of justice or a judgement made on a specific law in the religious court. It can also be used to describe the law in general. (*See* BET DIN; DAYYAN; HALAKHAH)

Din al-Fitrah *Islam*   A term used to describe Islam as the natural way of life for all human beings to live. It is founded on the idea that there is a natural religion or way of life which is innate to human nature before contact with society. All the world's religions are believed to have arisen from contact with this innate capacity for righteousness, but Islam is the ideal expression of FITRAH. (*See also* DIN)

Diocese *Christianity*   The territorial unit of administration under the control of a BISHOP usually divided into parishes. In the Eastern Church it describes the territory under the control of a PATRIARCH.

Dirge *Christianity*   The traditional name for the Office for the Dead. (*See* UNCTION)

Disciples *Christianity*   The term used to describe all those associated with Jesus and who responded to his message, particularly those who accompanied him on his travels. It can also be used to refer to the twelve men who gave him exclusive loyalty. (*See* APOSTLE)

Dissenters *Christianity*   Those who separate themselves from the communion of the Established Church, in particular, the CHURCH OF ENGLAND. After the Restoration of the monarchy in 1660, the Act of Uniformity was passed in 1662 which forbade the use of any other service than that authorized by the revised Prayer Book. Effectively, this move barred PURITANS from the church, and they were forced out of the establishment and became known as Dissenters. (*See also* NON-CONFORMIST)

Ditthi *Buddhism*   One of the four ASAVAS that delude the mind and prevent progress on the path to enlightenment. *Ditthi* refers to erroneous views concerning the nature of existence. For example, the belief that the soul is eternal.

Divali / Diwali *Hinduism*   One of the major Hindu festivals that takes place at the end of the year around October and lasts for five days. It is known as the Festival of Lights, as lamps are ceremoniously lit and presents exchanged. Traditionally, there are often large firework displays. The festival celebrates particular events in the life of VISHNU and one day is given over to worship of his consort, LAKSHMI, the goddess of wealth. The last day is usually celebrated as sisters' day.

Divali *Sikhism*   Held between October and November, Sikhs celebrate Divali as a commemoration of the day that GURU HARGOBIND was released from imprisonment in Gwalior Fort. A major celebration takes place over three days at the Golden Temple in AMRITSAR, and includes a large fair.

Diwan *(royal court)* *Sikhism*   An act of public or communal worship usually performed in the GURDWARA.

Djinn *Islam*   *See* JINN.

Docetism *Christianity*   An early form of CHRISTOLOGY declared to be HERESY which maintained that the humanity and suffering of Christ was apparent rather than real. Christ was perceived to be a divine being and not human. Some forms of Docetism even maintained that Christ escaped the CRUCIFIXION. The criticism of Docetism is based on the view that if Christ is not human, then he loses any point of contact with those he came to save. His exemplary role becomes insignificant if performed by someone who is not fully human. (*See also* IMITATION OF CHRIST; NESTORIAN)

Doctrine *Christianity*   A body of teaching used as a standard of orthodoxy. In the NEW TESTAMENT it refers to a body of teaching given to those who respond to the call of the disciples to become followers of Christ. Over the centuries correct Christian doctrine was established by a series of councils and used to define HERESY. (*See also* DOGMA)

Dogen (1200–54) *Buddhism*   The founder of the SOTO division of ZEN who, after visiting China to find the true expression of the Buddha's teachings, transferred the teaching of Ts'ao-tung Ch'an to Japan, where it became known as Soto Zen.

Dogma   *Christianity*   A religious truth that is first established by divine revelation and laid down in scripture and then defined or interpreted by the church. (*See* DOCTRINE; HERESY)

Dokusan   *Buddhism*   A term used in ZEN Buddhism for a formal private meeting with the master in his teaching chamber.

Dom   *Christianity*   The abbreviation of *dominus* (master) given as a title to monks of the BENEDICTINE order.

Dominic, St (1170–1221)   *Christianity*   Born Dominic de Guzman near Castile in Spain, he entered the Augustinian order. In 1206, he visited Languedoc, where he was surprised to discover the strength of the Cathars and the general feeling of contempt for the Cistercian order amongst the local populace. He believed that the solution was a reform of the monastic orders so that they emulated the Cathars' strength of piety, asceticism and zeal in preaching. As a result he established the DOMINICAN order after visiting Rome for the Fourth Lateran Council.

Dominicans   *Christianity*   An order of friars founded by St Dominic in the thirteenth century which was devoted to study and preaching. They were partly created as a reaction to the heretical Cathars and Waldensians by providing preachers of equal devotion and asceticism. The order grew rapidly and by the fourteenth century contained over 600 houses throughout Europe, including several nunneries. The nuns of the order were enclosed and were renowned for their lives of poor humility. Their emphasis on study created an environment of learning and service in addition to evangelizing. The Dominicans were asked by Gregory IX in 1232 to form and staff the INQUISITION. (*See also* DOMINIC, ST)

Dosa *(hatred, anger, ill-will)*   *Buddhism*   One of the three fires that have to be extinguished in order to achieve enlightenment. (*See* MOHA; RAGAS)

Dove   *Christianity*   A well-known Christian symbol that denotes peace and reconciliation, the church and the soul that has been saved through the rite of BAPTISM. It is also used to represent the HOLY SPIRIT. The symbol primarily derives from the incident in which a dove appeared over the head of Jesus Christ at his baptism by JOHN THE BAPTIST as a manifestation of the Holy Spirit. It may also refer to the dove that appeared on the receding waters and made NOAH aware that the survivors of the human race were reconciled to God.

Dravidian   *Hinduism*   The ancient culture of south India that is believed to predate the ARYAN invasion. Many aspects of Dravidian culture have survived and south Indian Hinduism contains many features not present in the north.

Dravya *Jainism*   Substance, or one of the four properties of material entities or events along with area, time and attribute. (*See* BHAVA; KALAH; PARAMANU)

Dravya sravaka *Jainism*   The term used to describe those who are born Jains but do not necessarily live a Jain life according to the teachings of MAHAVIR.

Dravyasrava *Jainism*   The inflow of karmic particles into the soul. The sole objective of Jain discipline is first to prevent this karmic input and then remove any existing KARMA that has come from previous lives.

Du'a *Islam*   Free prayer as opposed to the five daily ritual prayers that are obligatory for all Muslims. *Du'a* consists of varying forms of personal prayer often containing supplication and pleading for intercession, sometimes made through Muhammad. *Du'a* prayers do not follow any prescribed pattern or ritual and the petitioners may use their own words, derivations from the Qur'an or other sources. (*See* SALAH)

Dukkha (P) / Duhka (S) *(suffering, misery, pain)* *Buddhism*   The essence of the Buddha's teaching that the nature of existence and the condition of all beings, except for the enlightened, is suffering or dissatisfaction. The Buddha presented the essence of his teaching on *dukkha* in the four noble truths of his first sermon at Sarnath near VARANASI. The eightfold path practised by Buddhists is the vehicle to end the suffering caused by conditioned existence. (*See also* SAMMA; SAMUDAYA)

Durga *Hinduism*   A principal manifestation of the goddess, who is depicted as riding on a tiger and carrying many weapons. In spite of being a war goddess and associated with killing demons, Durga assumes a feminine and benign aspect in popular iconography. The more fierce aspect of the goddess is KALI. Both are associated as forms of the consort of SHIVA known as PARVATI. However, although goddess worship is closely aligned with *Saivism*, Durga is worshipped in her own right and has become one of the major deities of contemporary Hinduism, particularly in Bengal. (*See also* SHAIVITE; SHAKTI)

Durga Puja *Hinduism*   The festival in honour of DURGA that takes place within the larger festival of DASSERA held between August and September to mark the end of the monsoon. The ninth day is traditionally used to worship Durga. The festival is popularly celebrated in Bengal, where there is a strong tradition of Durga worship.

Durud-i Sharif *Islam* Popular prayers that bless Muhammad, the Prophet of God, often sung by the faithful to the accompaniment of beautiful tunes. They were introduced throughout the Muslim world by travelling SUFIS, who venerated the Prophet highly. (*See also* BHIDHR)

Dvaita Vedanta *Hinduism* A theistic form of VEDANTA taught by MADHVA (1238–1317). Madhva's doctrine of dualism posits that the selves and the universe are both distinct from BRAHMAN. Each self is also different from Brahman and remains individual even when liberated. It is even possible that some selves may never be liberated. This is a unique perspective in Hindu doctrine. In other respects, Madhva's doctrines are similar to RAMANUJA.

Dvapara Yuga / Dwapara Yuga *Hinduism* Hinduism deals with vast expanses of time based on the day and night of BRAHMA. According to the PURANAS, each day of Brahma consists of one thousand *manvantaras*. Each of these periods is further divided into four YUGAS or ages of decreasing righteousness. *Dvapara* is the third age and lasts for 864,000 years. Since all of these ages are cyclical, the cosmos has no beginning or end in Hindu cosmology.

Dvarka / Dwarka *Hinduism* A famous pilgrimage site on the northwest coast of India associated with KRISHNA. One of the seven most sacred sites of pilgrimage, Dvarka is believed to be Krishna's capital. Recent excavations have found a large city, now submerged in the Arabian Sea, that dates back to *c.*1600 BCE. (*See also* TIRTHA)

Dvija *(twice-born)* *Hinduism* The term is applied to the three highest VARNAS (BRAHMINS, KSHATRIYAS and VAISHYAS) who are allowed to study the VEDAS and receive the sacred thread at puberty.

Dwapara Yuga *Hinduism* See DVAPARA YUGA.

Dwarka *Hinduism* See DVARKA.

Easter *Christianity*   The oldest and most important festival celebrating the RESURRECTION of Jesus Christ from the dead. The dates of Easter usually fall between the third week of March and the fourth week of April, depending on the date of the full moon. However, Eastern Orthodox churches do not observe Easter until the Jewish Passover is completed. Traditionally, Easter was a time which the early church set aside for the BAPTISM of initiates. The holiday is preceded by the forty days of traditional abstinence known as LENT, culminating in MAUNDY THURSDAY, which remembers the last supper of Christ and his disciples before the vigil in the garden of GETHSEMANE. Good Friday commemorates the CRUCIFIXION. The festival culminates with the triumphant celebration of Easter Sunday when the resurrection is remembered.

Ebionites *Christianity*   An ascetic sect of Jewish Christians from the early years of the development of Christianity. They emphasized the importance of the Mosaic law and played down the idea of the divinity of Jesus. It has come to be associated with any kind of heretical position in which Jesus Christ is treated merely as an enlightened human being and thus essentially the same as those he came to redeem. (*See* DOCETISM; HERESY)

Ecclesiastes *Judaism*   A book included in the Hebrew scriptures after many years of debate. It contains the words of Solomon and teaches the ultimate vanity of all worldly activities. The debate amongst rabbis was not concerned with its message but whether the words were inspired by God or simply Solomon's own sayings. (*See also* APOCRYPHA; TANAKH)

Ecclesiology *Christianity*   An aspect of theology that deals with the theory or doctrine of the church and attempts to provide justification for the institutional developments that have taken place throughout its history, often as a result of social and political change. (*See* COUNCIL)

Ectene *Christianity*   A short prayer performed in the Eastern Church consisting of petitions recited by the DEACON and responded to by the choir or congregation. (*See also* LITURGY; ORTHODOX CHURCH)

Ecumenism *Christianity*   The movement within the church to reconcile and promote understanding between the denominations in the hope of restoring unity. Although the drive towards ecumenism was a prominent feature in the twentieth-century development of Christianity, it has roots in various historical developments that extend as far back as the sixteenth century. Various factors, such as cooperation in missionary work, youth work, education, liturgical developments, common ethical actions and attempts to deal with doctrinal differences, have all contributed to the development of ecumenism. One of the great momentums for the ecumenical drive was the creation of the WORLD COUNCIL OF CHURCHES in 1948.

Eden *Christianity*   The original home of the first human beings, ADAM and EVE, before their fall into sin and consequent expulsion, and therefore a powerful symbol of the return of human beings to a state of grace brought about by the 'second Adam', a title given to Jesus in the NEW TESTAMENT. (*See also* ORIGINAL SIN)

Ehyeh Asher Ehyeh *(I am who I am)*   *Judaism*   The description that God provides for Himself when MOSES asked for a name that he could reveal to the people. In ancient cultures, knowledge of a name was often perceived as providing power over the name's owner. God's refusal to give His name indicates that the Jewish people could exert no such power over Him, as His power was eternal and unlimited. God's name is regarded as ineffable and may not be pronounced. It consists of the unpronounceable letters YHWH rendered as Jehovah. (*See also* ADONAI)

Eid *Islam*   *See* ID.

Eid al-Adha *Islam*   *See* ID AL-ADHA.

Eid al-Fitr *Islam*   *See* IDAL-FITR.

Eid Mubarak / Id Mubarak *Islam*   A greeting and also blessing exchanged between Muslims at the two festivals of Id. (*See* ID AL-ADHA; ID AL-FITR)

Ekasringa *Hinduism*   An early animal form or AVATAR of VISHNU who manifested as a unicorn to save the first man, MANU, from the great flood which destroyed the rest of humankind.

Ekatva *Jainism*   One of the two aspects of perception available to the Jain practitioner. Besides being aware of the transient multiplicity of reality (*anekatva*), the Jain can also be aware of the unity of all substance (*ekatva*). The enlightened Jain would be simultaneously aware of both aspects of reality. The complexity of reality in which there is both unity and multiplicity finds expression in the Jain doctrine of ANEKANTAVADA. (*See also* ANUPREKSAS; KEVALAJNANA)

Ekendriya / Nigoda *Jainism*   In the Jain categorization of beings, the simplest forms of life or those that possess only the sense of touch. These include plants, earth, minerals, water and air.

Elders *Christianity*   A title given to officers in the PRESBYTERIAN churches. They are either teaching elders, whose duties are pastoral, or ruling elders, who are responsible under the pastor for administration. The term is probably derived from the Old Testament, where it is described in the book of Exodus that the tribes of Israel were led by seventy elders possessed by the Spirit of God who assisted Moses in the governance of the people.

Election *Christianity*   The theological term describing an act of the divine will which chooses to save some of humankind from the moment of creation, whilst condemning others to eternal damnation. It is particularly associated with CALVINISM and PREDESTINATION. However, the OLD TESTAMENT is important, in that it maintains that the Jewish tribes are the elect of God and chosen recipients of His covenant. The NEW TESTAMENT proclaims the extension of this covenant of salvation to the Gentile world. It replaces the elect of the people of Israel with an elect who become the true Israel through faith in Jesus Christ. (*See also* BERIT)

Elevation *Christianity*   The lifting of the bread and wine by the priest after CONSECRATION in the Eucharistic rite introduced in 1200 in the Western Church. It is followed by the words 'behold the Lamb of God who taketh away the sins of the world' and the ringing of the sanctus bells. In some churches, particularly Roman Catholic, the incense is directed towards the elevated host. (*See also* CHALICE; EUCHARIST)

Elijah *Judaism*   The prophet who is believed to come again as a forerunner to the Messiah. He is regarded as the guardian of ISRAEL and according to the Bible never died, as he was taken up to heaven in a fiery chariot (II Kings 2:11–12). It is believed that he will return at the end of time to tell the world that the Messiah is here. As the protector of Israel and the covenant, his name is invoked on important religious occasions such as the Passover and circumcision. He is also called upon to protect Jews in the coming week at the finale of the Sabbath. (*See also* BERIT MILAH; MASSIACH; PESACH; SHABBAT)

Ellul *Judaism*   The Jewish month that runs from 8 August to 6 September that is used to prepare for some of the most important religious occasions in the Jewish calendar, known as the Days of Awe. (*See* ROSH HASHANAH; YOM KIPPUR)

Emunah *(faith)* *Judaism*   The foundation of the Jewish tradition, it essentially refers to trust in God and reliance on Him to guide the people perfectly. If a person trusts in God completely, everything else will fall into place.

Enarxis *Christianity*   A series of litanies or prayers recited in the Byzantine LITURGY and accompanied by ANTIPHONS from the choir.

Encyclical *Christianity*   A circular letter sent out by the POPE to all the churches in order to provide new direction or doctrine. (*See also* INFALLIBILITY)

Enthronization *Christianity*   The ceremony in which an ARCHBISHOP or a BISHOP is placed in possession of his throne in a CATHEDRAL and granted ecclesiastical authority over a DIOCESE.

Ephesians, Epistle to the *Christianity*   One of the books of the New Testament apparently written to the early church in Ephesus by St Paul when he was in prison. This has been questioned by some scholars, on the grounds that both the language and the content differ from other letters written by Paul. The letter makes no attempt to address controversies or to involve itself in the pastoral concerns of the early Christian communities. Instead, it focuses on the eternal purposes of God and the manifestion of Christ in the church. (*See* EPISTLES; PAUL, ST)

Epiphany *Christianity*   The twelfth and final day of CHRISTMAS in the Christian liturgical year and maintained on 6 January. Traditionally, it celebrates the MAGI'S bestowing of gifts on the newborn Christ. This is considered to be a symbol of the acknowledgement of Christ by the GENTILES, as the magi were the first non-Jews to recognize and venerate Christ. The Epiphany is also associated with Christ's baptism and the first miracle in Cana, when Jesus turned water into wine at a wedding feast.

Episcopacy *Christianity*   A system of church government by BISHOPS, who maintain a hierarchy of bishops, priests and laity most familiarly associated with Roman Catholicism. The authority for the episcopalian leadership rests in the APOSTOLIC SUCCESSION, which asserts an unbroken line of male priestly authority from the original APOSTLES through the leaders of the early church to the bishops of today. Although episcopalian authority was challenged at the Protestant Reformation, it is still maintained by some Protestant groups known as the

Episcopal churches. They include the ANGLICAN COMMUNION and METHODISM. (*See also* CHURCH OF ENGLAND)

Epistles *(Greek: letter)* *Christianity*   Several letters circulated from the first leaders of the Christian community to the various churches that were beginning to spring up around the Mediterranean Greek world and included in the New Testament. There are twenty-one in total, of which most are attributed to Paul and include letters to the ROMANS, COLOSSIANS, EPHESIANS, PHILIPPIANS, CORIN-THIANS, GALATIANS and THESSALONIANS, along with the personal letters to TIMOTHY AND TITUS and PHILEMON. The remaining epistles are attributed to John, JUDE, James and Peter. (*See also* JAMES, EPISTLE OF; JOHN, EPISTLE OF; PETER, EPISTLE OF ST)

Erev Shabbat *Judaism*   Friday, the eve of the Sabbath, which is used to prepare for the holiest day of the week. On this day, Jews should try to create an atmosphere of holiness that will prepare them for the day of rest that follows. The Sabbath food is prepared, the family dress for the occasion and the table is set. Traditionally, the Sabbath is said to begin when the mother lights the two candles on the table and gives the blessing. In the SYNAGOGUE, the Sabbath is welcomed and the congregation recites Psalms 95–9. They then face towards the door of the synagogue to welcome the Sabbath whilst singing a hymn composed by Rabbi Solomon Halevi Alkabetz (sixteenth century). Afterwards, normal prayer resumes and the worship ends with the KIDDUSH and wine. The congregation depart for their homes after greeting each other with 'Shabbat Shalom'. Once home, the father will bless his wife and the parents their children, after which the Sabbath meal is taken. The father recites the Kiddush and speaks of the Genesis verses in which God sanctified time by appointing the Sabbath as holy. Each member of the family will partake of the wine from the Kiddush cup. A blessing is spoken over the HALLAH bread, which is then partaken of by each member of the family. Grace and Psalm 126 complete the celebration. (*See also* SHABBAT)

Erub *Judaism*   A device that was used in traditional Jewish communities to mitigate the severity of the Sabbath codes regarding the carrying of objects. A section of the streets in a town was separated off by fixing a wire supported by two poles. The street was then considered to be fenced off and its status changed from public to private property. No longer regarded as a public thoroughfare, it then became a place where people were allowed to carry objects. (*See also* ERUB TEHUHIM; SHABBAT)

Erub Tehuhim *Judaism*   A device to mitigate the severity of the Sabbath laws in regard to the distance that a person is allowed to walk. The Bible states that one should not leave his or her 'place' on the Sabbath. Oral law interprets place as the distance of 2,000 cubits (just over half a mile) on either side of the town of residence in which one can walk purely for pleasure. (*See* ERUB; SHABBAT)

Esana samiti *(carefulness in eating)*   *Jainism*   One of the five 'carefulnesses' or precautions undertaken by Jain ascetics in order to avoid causing accidental harm to small or unseen living creatures. Jain monks will only eat food that is given to them by Jain laity, who make sure that it observes scrupulous dietary requirements. (*See* SAMITI)

Esau   *Judaism*   The son of ISAAC and twin brother of JACOB, who, as recounted in Genesis, loses his birthright on the death of his father after being tricked by their mother.

Essenes   *Christianity*   The Jewish ascetic community most commonly associated with the DEAD SEA SCROLLS. They probably existed from the second century BCE to the second century CE. They established a community at Qumran where the Dead Sea Scrolls were discovered. They were highly organized and communalistic. Some scholars have suggested that John the Baptist was a former member of the community and there has been considerable speculation about the influence of the Essenes on the teachings of Jesus.

Esther   *Judaism*   The ward of a Jewish sage named Mordecai, whose legendary story is told in the Book of Esther in the Bible. She was chosen to be the new bride of the Persian King Ahasverus, who did not know that she was a Jew. Her father saved the king's life by revealing a palace plot to his daughter. Later, the king appointed a new viceroy, who was enraged by Mordecai's refusal to bow to him and therefore plotted to have all the Jews killed. Esther intervened to save her people and bring down the viceroy, who was hanged on the gallows that he had built for Mordecai. Her father was appointed viceroy in his place. The story is used as early example of anti-Semitism, as the Book of Esther elaborates on the reasons cited by the viceroy to persuade the king that the Jews should be destroyed. They eerily echo the reasons that have been used for the persecution of the Jews throughout their history in DIASPORA. The story of Esther is celebrated in the Feast of PURIM.

Eternal life   *Christianity*   The term used in the Gospel of St John to describe the special quality of life enjoyed by the followers of Jesus Christ. Although often used by Christians to refer to an eternal duration in Paradise after death, it can also refer to the possession of the here and now through joining with God's eternal being. (*See* HEAVEN; REDEMPTION)

Eucharist *(Greek: thanksgiving)*   *Christianity*   One of the several terms, including Lord's Supper, Mass and Holy Communion, used to name the central act of worship in the Christian tradition. It is derived from the LAST SUPPER or Passover meal which Jesus Christ celebrated with his disciples. On that occasion, immediately prior to his death, he broke bread and drank wine with the disciples and asked them to follow the practice in remembrance of him. The Eucharist, therefore, celebrates the sacrificial death and RESURRECTION of Jesus Christ by using the elements of bread and wine as an offering. The Christian Church is divided over the significance of what takes place at the Eucharist. The basic division is between those who believe that the elements are changed into the substance of the body of Christ and those who prefer to make the lesser claim that they are powerful symbols or reminders of the origins of the Christian faith. (*See also* CONSUBSTANTIATION; TRANSUBSTANTIATION)

Euchologian *Christianity* The book which contains the LITURGY of the three Eucharistic rites and the prayers to be used in the SACRAMENTS still utilized by the Eastern ORTHODOX CHURCH. (*See also* EUCHARIST)

Evangelical *Christianity* A group or church which places particular emphasis on the scriptures as the only authority in matters of faith and conduct. It was first used in the sixteenth century to refer to Catholic writers who wished to place more emphasis on the authority of scripture than medieval church tradition, but is now used to describe any group of Christians across the denominations who place particular emphasis on the use of the BIBLE in Christian life. Most EVANGELISTS subscribe to four assumptions concerning the reality of being a Christian, which includes the fundamental tenet of following the authority of scripture. The other three are the uniqueness of REDEMPTION through the CRUCIFIXION and RESURRECTION of Jesus Christ, the need for a personal redemptive experience and the urgent necessity of preaching the gospel. (*See also* CHARISMATIC; FUNDAMENTALISM)

Evangelist *Christianity* Used in the New Testament to denote someone who 'announces news' and usually translated as 'preach the gospel'. The scripture utilizes the term for the work of God, Jesus Christ, the APOSTLES and even ordinary members of the fledgling church. It is now used to describe anyone who commits his or her life to spreading the Christian message. More specifically it is used to describe any of the writers of one of the four GOSPELS. (*See also* EVANGELICAL)

Eve *Christianity* The first woman and the partner of ADAM. The ORIGINAL SIN and fall of humankind from the grace of God is attributed to Eve succumbing to the temptation of SATAN and eating the forbidden fruit of the tree of knowledge. (*See also* EDEN)

Evensong *Christianity*   The common name given to the CHURCH OF ENGLAND and Anglican evening prayer service which has conflated the two divine offices of VESPERS and COMPLINE. It consists of PSALMS, a lesson from the OLD TESTAMENT, the MAGNIFICAT, a lesson from the NEW TESTAMENT, the NUNC DIMITTIS, the APOSTLES' CREED and various prayers.

Excommunication *Christianity*   The term used to describe exclusion from the communion of the faithful of any member who, having committed a serious offence, has failed to be corrected by educative means or the application of church discipline. The gradual progression to the final exclusion consists of private and then witnessed remonstrance. If this repeatedly fails, the offender should be dealt with by officials of the church. Excommunication is primarily intended to invoke repentance but it is also designed to protect other church members from contamination. In the Roman Catholic Church, while it denies the possibility of administering or receiving the SACRAMENTS, the offender may still attend the preaching of the Word. Although it is now rarely applied, historically it has generally been used to control doctrinal HERESY.

Exodus *Judaism*   The second book of the SEFER TORAH, which contains the account of the liberation of the Israelites from slavery in Egypt and the revelation of the TORAH to MOSES on Mount Sinai. The Passover festival traditionally celebrates the occasion when Moses led his people to freedom. (*See also* PENTATEUCH; PESACH)

Expiation *Christianity*   A theological term generally applied to the sacrifice of Jesus Christ on the Cross, by which act he made amends for the inherited sin of mankind which began with the fall of ADAM and EVE. (*See also* CRUCIFIXION; RANSOM; REDEMPTION)

Ezekiel *Judaism*   A prophet and a book of the Hebrew scriptures named after him. He rebuked the people for accepting the Egyptian practice of worshipping the sun. The source of the Jewish prayer for the dead can be found in the book of Ezekiel. (*See* KADDISH)

Ezra *Judaism*   Ezra was a scribe who led a group of Jews back from exile in Babylon. There is a book of the Hebrew scriptures named after him in the section known as Holy Writings. Ezra is believed to have been a religious leader of the Jewish people soon after their release from captivity by the Babylonians in the sixth century BCE. Ezra led a religious revival and restored the TORAH to its place of prominence in Jewish life. It is believed that he also instituted the reading of the Torah on the afternoon of the SHABBAT. (*See also* KETUVIM; NEHEMIAH; TANAKH)

Faith *Christianity*   In Christianity faith means more than a commitment to belief without any empirical evidence. It is, first of all, a body of truth as propounded in doctrine which accepts as true the articles of the faith as summarized in the CREEDS. However, it was Martin LUTHER who made the point that faith is fundamental to Christian salvation. He asserted that faith is the human response to the truth claim of Christian doctrine and is the right relationship to have with God. Lost at the fall and resurrected by the INCARNATION of Jesus Christ, it is, therefore, regarded as a supernatural act of will and a higher faculty than reason. (*See also* JUSTIFICATION)

Fajr / Salat al-Fajr) *Islam*   The first of the five daily obligatory prayers or dawn prayer which can be performed from dawn until just before sunrise. (*See also* SALAH; RAK'AH)

Fakir *Islam*   *See* FAQIR.

Falah *Islam*   The Muslim prayer-call summons the faithful to *falah* (the good) as well as SALAH (prayer). This central concept of Islam moves the religion away from personal piety to a communal thrust built on social welfare and prosperity. Islam is fulfilled in this social order in which well-being can be achieved in the Muslim environment. Religion is thus about behaviour as well as belief and individual piety. (*See also* ADHAN; UMMA)

Falasifa *Islam*   Muslims who became interested in Greek thought and utilized philosophy to develop, substantiate and modify orthodox Islamic doctrine. This led to the development of KALAM, or Muslim theology. From 800 to 1100, many Muslim thinkers adopted Greek ideas, particularly Neoplatonism, but the Falasifa movement went into decline after the challenge from al-Ghazali (d.1111). Greek thought survived, but only if it was completely assimilated or submerged into Muslim doctrine. (*See also* GHAZALI, AHMAD AL-)

Fana *Islam* A term used in Sufism to describe the complete loss of self or annihilation caused by the experience of the unity of Allah. In some SUFI traditions there is a progression of degrees of *fana*, beginning with annihilation of the self through complete identity with the SHAIKH. However, as the shaikh is believed to have submerged his own identity into the Prophet Muhammad, he will lead the MURID (disciple) towards *fana f'ir rasul* (annihilation into the Prophet). The Prophet will then lead the *murid* to the final annihilation into Allah. (*See also* ADAB)

Faqir (U) / Fakir *Islam* A wandering SUFI mendicant who lives only for God in a vow of poverty. (*See* QALANDARI)

Fard *Islam* One of the five categories of Islamic law. An obligatory duty imposed by the revelation, its omission is punishable by God (for example, the five pillars of Islam). (*See* HALAL; HARAM; SHARI'A)

Fateh Nama *(letter of victory)* *Sikhism* A poetic composition written in admonition to the Emperor Aurangzeb by GURU GOBIND SINGH, the last and tenth human Guru.

Fatehgarh Sahib *Sikhism* A small town in the Punjab sacred to the memory of the two younger sons of GURU GOBIND SINGH, who were both martyred by being bricked up alive for refusing to accept Islam. Their anniversary is held on 27 December, when thousands of Sikhs gather in the town and visit its historic GURDWARAS.

Fatihah / Fatiha *Islam* See AL-FATIHA.

Fatima / al-Zahrah *Islam* Known as *al-Zahrah* (the luminous). The only one of Muhammad's four daughters to outlive him. She was married to ALI and was the mother of HASAN, HUSAIN and Zainab, the grandchildren of the Prophet. A legendary figure who is surrounded by miracle stories, she is highly respected in SHI'A as the mother of the Prophet's bloodline. It is said that light surrounded her birth and that she never menstruated. She was honoured with the title of 'virgin'. In Shi'a tradition Muhammad, Ali, Fatima and their two sons are known as the Panjtan (the Five People). It is said that Muhammad took them under his cloak to show their unity with him. (*See also* AHL AL-BAIT)

Fatimids *Islam* A Muslim dynasty that began in Tunisia but took control of Egypt in 969 and established the city of Cairo as its capital. They ruled in Egypt until 1169. During their rule they founded the university of AL-AZHAR, which eventually became a SUNNI institution and the most authoritative body in the

Muslim world. The Fatimids were followers of a form of SHI'A known as the ISHMAELIS or Seveners.

Fatwa *Islam*   The legal opinion or religious decision made by a Muslim scholar on the basis of an interpretation required to demonstrate correct observance in novel situations. It is the application of the SHARI'A (Islamic law) to a particular case or situation to determine a precedent. While a *fatwa* can be issued by a member of the ULAMA, it may be contradicted by the scholars of a different tradition within the religion. There is no central authority for issuing a *fatwa*. (*See also* IJMA; IJTIHAD; QIYAS)

Feretory *Christianity*   A shrine where a SAINT's bones are kept and venerated. (*See also* RELICS; RELIQUARY)

Filioque *Christianity*   The addition of the words 'and from the son' to the sentence which states that the Holy Ghost 'proceedeth from the Father', as contained in the NICENE CREED and normative in the Western Church. The Eastern Church disagreed and argued that both the Son and the HOLY SPIRIT proceed from the Father. They believed that the Father must be not be compromised as the sole source of divinity. It was, therefore, one of the principal causes of doctrinal dispute between the Eastern and Western churches and contributed to the division between them.

Fiqh *(understanding)* *Islam*   The personal understanding of a scholar organized into a disciplined body of knowledge achieved by deduction. This once personal activity developed into a structured discipline of Islamic jurisprudence that utilized Islamic methodology. It comprises the legal order of Islam according to the four authoritative schools of law in the SUNNI tradition and one from the SHI'A tradition. Decisions concerning precedents that require a legal ruling are usually taken from the body of *fiqh* rather than direct from the scriptural source. While *fiqh* has traditionally been the preserve of the ULAMA, recent twentieth-century revivalist movements sometimes insisted that instead scholars can go direct to the QUR'AN and HADITH for clarity and understanding. (*See also* HANAFI; HANBALI; IJMA; IJTIHAD; MALIKI; QIYAS; SHAFI'I)

Fish *Christianity*   A symbol for Christ used in Christian iconography, which originated at the time of the early church from the fact that the letters of the Greek word ICHTHYS (fish) the initials of Iesous Christos Theou Hyios Soter (Jesus Christ, of God the Son, Saviour). However, the NEW TESTAMENT contains many references to fish, arising from the exploits of Jesus around GALILEE and from the fact that several of his first followers were fishermen.

Fitna / Fitnah   *Islam*   A term originally employed to describe the persecution suffered by Muslims in the name of religion, but later used for sedition or conspiracy against an Islamic state.

Fitrah   *Islam*   The idea of an innate nature which contains a blueprint of the original form of the divine law. For this reason a human being may be propelled towards God and the good even without the aid of revelation. Because of *fitrah* it is believed that every child is born into natural Islam or submission to God. However, without the aid of revelation, *fitrah* and is overcome by social conditioning and the temptations of SHAITAN. In the mystical tradition, a person should follow their heart, as it is perceived to be the seat of *fitrah* and will lead them towards God. Islam is believed to be the religion that most closely corresponds to *fitrah*. (*See also* DIN AL-FITRAH)

Font   *Christianity*   Receptacle, usually made of stone, which stands at the west end of the nave and holds the water used for the sacrament of BAPTISM. The ceremony at the font consists of procession, renunciation of SATAN, profession of faith, immersion in water and sometimes anointing with oil.

Form Criticism   *Christianity*   A method of analysis which attempts to discover the origin of particular passages in the Old and New Testaments through exploring the variety of structural forms. The aim is to ascertain the earliest forms of the texts, possibly in the oral tradition, and then establish the historical context in which they develop later written forms.

Formal Sin   *Christianity*   *See* SIN.

Forty-Two Articles   *Christianity*   The statements of correct Anglican doctrine devised in 1553 by Archbishop Cranmer and signed by Edward VI. Although Protestant in tone they were designed to offset ANABAPTIST doctrines as well as Roman Catholicism. Their number was revised to thirty-nine in 1563 during the reign of Elizabeth I. (*See also* THIRTY-NINE ARTICLES)

Fraction   *Christianity*   The ritual breaking of bread by the PRIEST which takes place in all Eucharistic LITURGIES before the act of Communion. (*See also* CONSECRATION; EUCHARIST; OFFERTORY)

Francis of Assisi, St (1181–1226)   *Christianity*   Born Giovanni Bernardone in the central Italian city of Assisi, he was the founder of the FRANCISCAN order. Although worldly as a young man, he gradually turned to religion as a result of experiences arising from illness and participating in warfare. He began to rebuild churches in the area of Assisi after a vision in which God commanded him to 'rebuild my church'. In 1208, aware that he had received the same call as the APOSTLES, he began to preach repentance. Francis lived in complete poverty and modelled his life on the imitation of Christ. His humility, devotion, love of nature and compassion make him one of the most loved saints in Christianity.

Franciscans *Christianity*   The order of FRIARS founded by St Francis of Assisi in 1210 and licensed to preach by Pope Innocent III. Living a life of absolute poverty and renunciation of worldly pleasure, they preach the gospel and take care of the needy and the sick. The organization of the order is similar to that of the DOMINICANS and they also have a female order known as the POOR CLARES. The growth of the order was rapid, especially in the cities, where they were successful in strengthening religion amongst the laity. The Franciscans have a tertiary order open to pious inviduals, who are allowed to live a semi-monastic life of fasting, prayer and good deeds. (*See also* FRANCIS OF ASSISI, ST)

Free Churches *Christianity*   NON-CONFORMIST Protestant denominations free from state control.

Friar *Christianity*   A member of one of the mendicant orders founded in the Middle Ages. They were not allowed to maintain or own property and moved around begging or working for their living. They were exempt from the control of the diocesan bishop and passed their time in preaching and receiving confession. (*See* FRANCISCANS)

Friends, Society of *Christianity*   See RELIGIOUS SOCIETY OF FRIENDS.

Fundamentalism *Christianity*   American EVANGELICAL movements created out of opposition to secularization in the second half of the twentieth century. Fundamentalism is characterized by its literalness in scriptural interpretation and animosity to any form of biblical criticism. It asserts the imminent return of Christ before the end of time.

Furqan, al- *Islam*   A name for the QUR'AN that refers to its function to provide correct guidance or act as the source of discrimination between truth and falsehood for believers.

G

Gabriel *(man of God or strength of God)* *Christianity*   One of the four ARCHANGELS with special responsibility over paradise and a functionary of the LAST JUDGEMENT. In the New Testament, Gabriel is sent to announce the birth of JOHN THE BAPTIST to his father, ZECHARIAH, and the conception of Jesus Christ to MARY. (*See also* JIBRIL)

Galatians, Epistle to the *Christianity*   One of the earliest of the books in the New Testament. It was written by Paul, somewhere between 49 and 53 CE, to the Christian community in Galatia in order to clarify the relationship between faith in Christ and obedience to the Jewish law. Paul affirms his authority as coming directly from Christ and warns against the dangers of mixing the Christian message of salvation for all with Jewish legalism. (*See* PAUL, ST; EPISTLES)

Galilee *Christianity*   The district between the coastal strip of the Mediterranean and the River JORDAN in the north of Israel which contains the town of NAZARETH, where Jesus grew to adulthood. Jesus spent most of his life and ministry in Galilee and the first disciples came from the region. The Sea of Galilee is a lake in the region also known as Gennesaret or the Sea of Tiberias. The shores of the lake contain the towns of Bethsaida and CAPERNAUM, where much of Christ's ministry took place.

Galut *(exile)* *Judaism*   See DIASPORA.

Ganapati *Hinduism*   See GANESH.

Gandharas *Jainism*   The immediate disciples of MAHAVIR, who are believed to be endowed with perfect knowledge and who attained liberation at the end of their human lives. It is thought that they compiled the oldest Jain scriptures containing the teachings of Mahavir. (*See also* KEVALAJNANA)

Gandharva Veda *Hinduism* A sacred text that deals with the art of music and dance. Although known as a VEDA, it is, in fact, an UPAVEDA, texts that deal with lesser knowledge rather than the higher transcendent knowledge of the Vedas.

Gandhava *Hinduism* Semi-divine musicians who occupy one of the heavenly realms. Hindu cosmology contains countless different worlds that are populated by heavenly and demonic beings. However, all these realms are impermanent and the occupants will eventually die and be reborn elsewhere. (*See* SAMSARA)

Gandhi, Mahatma (1869–1948) *Hinduism* A Hindu reformer who stressed the doctrine of AHIMSA (non-violence) and inspired the movement to free India from British rule. He was born in the state of Gujarat and travelled to London, where he studied law. Whilst in Britain, he was influenced by the spiritual teachings of the BHAGAVAD GITA and the SERMON ON THE MOUNT. After his studies he departed for South Africa, where he lived for twenty-one years. Deeply shocked by his experience of apartheid, he began to develop his ideas to free people from political oppression whilst maintaining a deep commitment to non-violence. On his return to India, he inspired Indians to free themselves from British rule through the application of passive resistance based on the principle of *ahimsa*. His political and religious philosophy became known as SATYAGRAHA. Gandhi's tolerant attitude towards all of India's religious communities resulted in his assassination in 1948 by a militant nationalist Hindu.

Ganesh / Ganupati / Ganapati *Hinduism* The god of wisdom, prudence and salvation, whose name is derived from *Ga* meaning 'knowledge' and *Na* meaning 'salvation'. He is one of the most widely worshipped deities in Hinduism and easily recognizable by his elephant head. Ganesh is depicted as a short, large-bellied man with an elephant head that has only one tusk. He is usually seated cross-legged and his skin is yellow. His four arms hold a conch shell, a discus, a club and a lotus flower. He is usually shown with a small bowl of the Indian sweet known as the *ladoo* to represent prosperity. He is also accompanied by a rat, which is his vehicle (VAHANA), to symbolize the union of the large with the small. Since he is regarded as the deity who removes obstacles, he is often placed in a position in the temple where he will be the first deity to be seen by worshippers, who use his DARSHAN to pray that the god will remove the obstacles from devotees so that they can approach the other deities. Hindu rituals usually begin with an invocation to Ganesh, and many Hindus begin their daily activities with a short prayer that invokes the god's name. According to the PURANAS, Ganesh is the younger son of SHIVA and PARVATI, but he is not mentioned in Hindu scriptures before 500 CE and only became popular in the later medieval period. The Shiva Purana recounts the legend of his elephant's head by explaining that when Shiva was away for thousands of years practising austerities, Parvati appointed her son to guard her door whilst bathing. When Shiva returned, Ganesh, who did not know his father, refused him entry to the house. The irate father cut off his son's head but, when confronted with his error by the inconsolable Parvati, restored his son to life with the head of a young elephant.

Ganga / Ganges *Hinduism*   Ganga is the Indian name for the Ganges, the most sacred of India's rivers. Commonly known as Ganga Mai, or Mother Ganga, the river is believed to be a goddess, whose descent to earth was controlled by flowing through SHIVA's matted locks. Many towns on the Ganga are sacred sites and several of them constitute some of Hinduism's most renowned places of pilgrimage. The most famous is VARANASI. Millions of pilgrims bathe in the Ganga and may perform the SHRADDHA ceremony on its banks (an annual homage to a departed ancestor). Most Hindus will want to drink Ganga water immediately before dying. (*See also* HARDWAR)

Gangotri *Hinduism*   The source of the GANGA in the Himalayas and a famous pilgrimage site.

Ganupati *Hinduism*   *See* GANESH.

Garbha-griha *(womb-house)* *Hinduism*   The innermost sanctum of a Hindu temple where the MURTI or image of the god is installed. This structure will usually be located at the back of the temple. In traditional temple design the shrine room is topped by a tapering ornate tower that can be seen from the outside of the temple. (*See also* MANDIR; SHIKHARA)

Garuda *Hinduism*   The king of the birds and the mount of VISHNU, usually depicted as an eagle.

Gatha *Buddhism*   A hymn or set of verses composed by monks in a state of spiritual insight. There are thousands of such inspired compositions from around the various parts of the Buddhist world.

Gaudapada *Hinduism*   The guru of SHANKARA's guru, whom Shankara describes as his supreme guru. Gaudapada's teachings seem to be influenced by Buddhism, even though Shankara himself vehemently opposed Buddhist doctrine. (*See also* ADVAITA VEDANTA)

Gaudiya Vaishnavism *Hinduism*   This form of Vaishnavism developed in early medieval Bengal and expressed the ideal of ecstatic devotion to KRISHNA. The ideal of devotional love is expressed in the relationship between RADHA and

Krishna. The devotee longs for Krishna with the same emotional intensity that Radha exhibits for her absent Lord. The greatest exponent of this tradition was CAITANYA MAHAPRABHU (1486–1533), who is often regarded as an AVATAR of Krishna and Radha in one being. The goal of liberation is attained by the Gaudiya followers in this world by maintaining an ecstatic experience of divine love. This is often expressed through singing and dancing. The Gaudiya tradition is best known in the West through the activities of ISKCON or the HARE KRISHNA movement.

Gautama (S) *Buddhism*   See SIDDATTHA GOTTAMA.

Gayatri Mantra *Hinduism*   A famous Sanskrit MANTRA from the RIG VEDA used in daily worship by many Hindus. It is also ritually repeated by a 'twice-born' male youth at the sacred thread ceremony. The mantra is as follows: *om bhur bhuvah swahah om tat savitur varenyam bhargo devasya dhimahi* ('we concentrate our minds upon the most radiant light of the supreme god, who sustains the earth, the interspace and the heavens. May this god activate our thoughts'). Traditionally the mantra is recited in praise of the sun-god, but most contemporary Hindus would direct it towards the supreme being, BRAHMAN.

Gedo Zen *Buddhism*   The second of five types of ZEN Buddhism taught in Japan and known as 'the outside way'. It implies that the school acknowledges or utilizes teachings derived from other non-Buddhist sources, such as Hindu YOGA, Confucian practices or the contemplative teachings of Christianity.

Gehenna / Gehinnon / Sheol *Judaism*   The place of burning or torment which is the equivalent of hell as described in Jewish apocryphal literature. It is not regarded as eternal punishment but a place where the wicked are punished until the Day of Resurrection when all will be judged. Not all Jews share the same beliefs regarding hell and punishment, and many have interpreted hell as a figurative state of existence where the soul is separated from God.

Gemara / Gemarah *(completion)* *Judaism*   The commentary on the MISHNAH contained in the TALMUD, in which the AMORAIM (early rabbinical scholars) expound and develop the oral law in order to reach an accurate interpretation of a scriptural command. The commentary is written in Aramaic and deals primarily with festivals, ceremonies, legal matters, social conduct and education.

Gematria *Judaism*   The art of using numerology to search for links between the names of God and the words of the Bible, possibly introduced by the mystic Abu Aaron in the ninth century. It has become part of the KABBALAH tradition.

General *Christianity*   The head of a religious order. The head of the FRANCISCANS is known as the Minister-General, while the head of the DOMINI-CANS is called the Master-General. (*See also* BENEDICTINE; JESUIT)

Genesis *Judaism*   The first of the five books of the Hebrew scriptures that form the PENTATEUCH, the heart of the TORAH. The book tells of the creation of the world and the human race and gives an account of the relationship between God and NOAH, ABRAHAM, ISAAC and JACOB, the patriarchs of the Jewish people. The final chapters tell the story of Joseph and his rise to power in Egypt.

Geneva Bible *Christianity*   The English Bible published in Geneva in 1560 by the Protestant exiles from the reign of the Catholic queen Mary Tudor and widely used for fifty years until the publication of the AUTHORIZED VERSION in 1611.

Genizah *Judaism*   A storage place in the SYNAGOGUE used for damaged religious texts.

Gentiles *Christianity*   The term used in the New Testament to describe non-Jews. Israel had developed a sense of itself as a distinct nation chosen by God after the revelation of the covenant to MOSES. By the time of Jesus, an exclusive attitude to other nations had developed as a result of efforts to maintain Judaism's freedom from other cultural accretion. Jewish prophecies had always indicated that the expected MESSIAH would restore righteousness throughout the world. Therefore, the stage was set for the Jewish disciples of Jesus to consider the possibility that his message was also for non-Jews. The conversion of Cornelius and the mission of Paul to bring the Gentiles to Christ's salvation initially created misgivings and much soul-searching amongst the Jewish followers of Jesus, but the growing church quickly adapted to the idea of the equality of all people before God. (*See also* BERIT; EXODUS; PAUL, ST; TORAH)

Genuflexion *Christianity*   A movement down on to one knee and then up to the standing position again. It is commonly used in the Western Church to show reverence when passing before the reserved SACRAMENT or on other ritual occasions.

Geonim *Judaism*   The heads of the important Talmudic academies of the Middle East responsible for developing the teachings of the TALMUD and spreading them throughout the Jewish world. They were particularly skilled in codifying Jewish law and developed RESPONSA literature, in which queries were addressed through the format of questions and answers. The period of the *Geonim* is known as the Gaonic, and it ended in the eleventh century CE when the centre of scholarship shifted to Spain and north Africa. (*See also* SAVORAIM; SHEELOT U-TESHUVOT)

Ger *Judaism* A Jewish proselyte. Conversion to Judaism has always been allowed but has passed through several stages. Up until the period of the Roman empire, conversion was encouraged and the new convert entered fully into Jewish life and received a new name. During the Roman empire, Jewish missionary activity was widespread, but when Christianity became the state religion of the empire, conversion to Judaism was punishable by death. This may have led to the Orthodox reluctance about conversion that exists in the present. During the period of the Second Temple it was established that the convert should be motivated only by religious conviction, but today converts are accepted on the grounds of mixed marriage. A long period of instruction is required in Orthodoxy but the REFORM tradition makes conversion easier.

Gershom, Rabbi (940–1028) *Judaism* Known as the 'Light of the Exile' and a famous writer of 'responsa literature', which is a series of questions and answers dealing with queries on matters of Jewish law. He issued a decree banning polygamy in 1000. Originally followed only by the Ashkenazi nations, this is now observed by all Jews throughout the world. He also stated that a woman could not be divorced against her will.

Gersonides (1288–1344) *Judaism* A Jewish philosopher and writer of scriptural commentary. The medieval period saw a flowering of Jewish philosophy as they got to grips with Aristotle and Plato. Gersonides moved more towards Neoplatonism. (*See* MAIMONIDES)

Get *Judaism* A Bill of Divorce issued by a Jewish court that can dissolve the KETUBAH (marriage contract). The *get* must be accepted freely by all parties and each one is written individually and signed by two witnesses. It has thirteen lines and must not contain any errors or corrections. The *get* is placed into the hands of the woman, who is then divorced. She returns it to the presiding rabbi, who files it, and after ninety-two days she is free to remarry. A man who remarries without a *get* is considered to have committed polygamy; a woman commits adultery.

Gethsemane *Christianity* The garden just outside the walls of Jerusalem near the Mount of Olives to the east of the city. The garden was frequently used by Jesus and his disciples as a place of retreat, and it is here that Jesus passed the night in prayer with his disciples before betrayal by JUDAS ISCARIOT and his arrest. The descriptions of Christ's vigil of prayer in St Mark's Gospel have given rise to the practice of kneeling in prayer which is customary amongst Christians. (*See also* CRUCIFIXION; MAUNDY THURSDAY; PASSION)

Gevurah *(power)* *Judaism*   One of the ten SEFIROTH or emanations of the AYN SOF that represent the aspects of God working in creation. *Gevurah* is the power or judgement that prevents the love of God (HESED) overwhelming all creatures and instilling them with a longing to merge back into Him. A balance of power and love is required for the world to exist. (*See also* KABBALAH)

Gharib al-Hadith *Islam*   The study of the HADITH in order to ascertain the meaning of difficult words based on their linguistic origin. The most famous work is that of the twelfth-century scholar, al-Zamakshari.

Ghat *Hinduism*   A flight of steps leading down to a river usually associated with assisting pilgrims to bathe. A daily bath is a prescribed ritual for Hindus. Many will take their ritual bath in a river. Some *ghats* are also used for cremation. The most famous are located in VARANASI. (*See also* TIRTHA)

Ghati Karma / Ghatiya Karma *Jainism*   The four types of KARMA that are harmful to the soul. They are knowledge-obscuring karma, faith-obscuring karma, deluding karma and will-obstructing karma. The other four kinds of karma are referred to as non-destructive. (*See also* AGHATIYA KARMA; ANTARAYA; DARSHANAVARANIYA; JNANAVARANIYA; MOHANIYA KARMA)

Ghazali, Ahmad al- (d.1111)   *Islam*   Arguably the greatest of all Muslim scholars and said to be the foremost Muslim after the Prophet. As a theologian and a mystic, al-Ghazali succeeded in refuting the ideas of Muslim philosophers who had borrowed heavily from Greek thought, but he also resolved the tensions between orthodoxy and Sufism by bringing the two closer together. In order to achieve this he challenged the extreme mystical claims of union, incarnation and absorption by asserting that God could only be related to, or known, to the degree that He chose to reveal Himself to human beings. This revelation is contained in the divine names, which can be penetrated through mysticism. Al-Ghazali's own journey was that of a spiritual seeker. He had originally rejected orthodox Muslim theology on the grounds that it was too formalistic and exoteric. However, after a thorough study, Greek philosophy was also rejected as being far removed from Islamic thought and having no grounds for certainty. He finally concluded that certainty could only be found in the experiential dimension of Sufism but that Islamic mysticism had to be rooted in the Qur'anic revelation. (*See* FALASIFA; KALAM; SUFI)

Ghee / Ghi *Hinduism*   Clarified butter considered propitious as it is a product of the cow and used by Hindus for cooking and sacrificial purposes. The oil is used to make the small candles that are placed on a tray and swung in veneration of the gods. Ghee is also used for cremation. (*See* ARTI)

Ghusl   *Islam*   The formal washing of the entire body prior to worship, otherwise known as the greater ablution. It is required in certain circumstances such as sexual activity before the prayer, when the normal WUDU is not sufficient.

Giani / Gyani   *Sikhism*   A person who has studied and is knowledgeable of the traditional interpretation of Sikh scripture. They usually preach in the GURDWARA.

Giarvin Sharif   *Islam*   The celebration of SUFI teachings that usually takes place on a Thursday evening amongst the followers of a Sufi order and is often associated with Abdul Qadir Gilani, the founder of the QADIRIYA TARIQAH. The event takes place after the evening prayer and consists of DHIKR, DU'A and blessings given to Muhammad and well-known Sufis.

Gilani, Abdul Qadir   *Islam*   The founder of the QADIRIYA Sufi order (TARIQAH) but considered to be the archetypal Sufi and the *al-Qutb al-Azam*, the summit of sainthood and the spiritual ruler of the world who is the perfect man who inherits the spiritual perfection of Muhammad. As such he is acknowledged by all the Sufi orders and many of them maintain Thursday night as a time of worship in his honour. He was born in 1077 in Iran and went to study in Baghdad. After a long period of retreat in the desert he began to preach in the city. The vast amount of hagiographical material concerning miracle stories makes it very difficult to establish Gilani's biography with any accuracy, but there is no doubting the veneration in which he is held by pious traditional Muslims throughout the Islamic world. (*See also* QUTB)

Gita Govinda   *Hinduism*   A famous poem about the love of KRISHNA and RADHA composed by Jayadeva, a court poet who wrote under the patronage of the Bengali king, Lakshmanasena (1179–1209). Its themes are union, separation and the longing for reunion. It is therefore regarded as symbolic of the love of the devotee for the Lord. (*See also* BHAKTI; GOPIS)

Glossolalia   *Christianity*   Known as 'speaking in tongues', it describes a religious phenomenon where the person is possessed by the HOLY SPIRIT and speaks in an unknown language. It was first recorded in the New Testament (Acts 2:4) when the APOSTLES preached on the feast of PENTECOST and were understood by people as speaking many different languages. Contemporary manifestations of glossolalia include the utterance of an unknown tongue rather than the ability to speak and be understood in several languages. The gift of glossolalia also requires the ability to interpret the word of the Spirit for the congregation. This may be a result of Paul's criticism that it was more important to preach the gospel than speak in unknown languages (Corinthians 14:19). However, Paul did not denigrate glossolalia and it is widely considered to be a gift from the Holy Spirit, featuring in several Christian revival movements, particularly the Pentecostalist movement. (*See also* PENTECOSTALISTS)

Gnosticism   *Christianity*   Derived from the Greek word *gnosis* meaning knowledge, it is an umbrella term used to describe a host of movements, both Christian and non-Christian, who believed in a special knowledge of God which leads to enlightenment or redemption. Some of the movements were very strong at the time of the early church but were opposed because they minimized the role of faith in salvation and maintained heretical positions regarding the status of Christ. The common feature of all the Gnostic movements was a dualistic cosmology based on the belief that the created world was evil and completely separate from the perfect world of the spirit. Matter was not created by God but by a lesser spirit known as the demiurge. Gnosis, or knowledge, allows the recipient to liberate the soul from the bondage of matter usually through the intervention of a redeemer who descends from the spiritual world. The Gnostic quest is therefore redemption through discovery of the soul as one's real identity. The early church fathers fought against Gnostic influences in Christianity and regarded it as a perversion of Christ's teaching.

Goindwal   *Sikhism*   A small village established by GURU AMAR DAS as the centre of Sikhism. It remained the centre until GURU ARJAN DEV moved to AMRITSAR after the completion of HARMANDIR. The most important shrine is BAOLI SAHIB, built by Guru Amar Das.

Golem   *Judaism*   A legendary monster created out of clay by the Maharal of Prague, a kabbalist. Given life by means of the magical use of the names of God, it was created to protect the Jews of Prague against persecution. (*See* KABBALAH)

Gompa (T)   *Buddhism*   The term used in Tibetan Buddhism to describe a monastery or a place of meditation.

Good Friday   *Christianity*   The Friday of Holy Week, which precedes Easter Sunday. It commemorates the CRUCIFIXION of Jesus Christ. Normally the liturgy of Good Friday does not feature the celebration of the EUCHARIST, but in Roman Catholicism there is a service known as the Veneration of the Cross that developed in the third and fourth centuries, in which the clergy and the congregation solemnly venerate a cross close to the SANCTUARY area. Good Friday is normally a time of fasting, penance and abstinence. (*See also* EASTER)

Gopis *Hinduism*   The childhood playmates of KRISHNA when he lived in exile in Gokula, identified as VRINDAVAN by CAITANYA MAHAPRABHU. Ancient stories depict the amorous adventures of Krishna with the cowherd girls. In later Vaishnavite traditions (from the twelfth century onwards) the love between the *gopis* and Krishna becomes the symbol of the all-embracing love of the devotee for the supreme Lord – the ultimate goal of BHAKTI. This passionate play of love, reciprocated by the Lord himself, is encapsulated in the love that existed between Krishna and his favourite *gopi*, RADHA. (*See also* GAUDIYA VAISHNAVISM)

Gorakhnath *Hinduism*   A famous medieval SHAIVITE YOGI who taught in northwest India and is the reputed founder of several ascetic movements usually defined as NATH YOGIS or KANPHATA. Gorakhnath has been deified in popular tradition and is considered to be a miraculous offspring of SHIVA. There are countless legends of his birth and the miracles that he performed in his lifetime. He is considered to be the founder of the HATHA YOGA system and is also held in high regard by Tibetan Buddhists. Matsyendranath was his guru, and there are countless stories symbolizing the relationship of guru and disciple associated with them. The Naths became famous for their supposed mastery of psychic and miraculous powers achieved through their austerity and practice of yoga, and were later criticized by GURU NANAK, the founder of Sikhism, on the grounds that such practices promoted ego rather than humble surrender to the will of God.

Gospel *(Old English: the good news)*   *Christianity*   The message of salvation through Jesus Christ proclaimed through Christian mission, especially in the apostolic period. The term came to be used for the written accounts of Jesus Christ that form the first four books of the New Testament. The Gospels contain Jesus' message that the time appointed for the kingdom of God had arrived as a fulfilment of the prophecies communicated through the Jewish prophets. This message is reinforced by parables and examples of teaching sessions with the disciples and confrontation with Jewish religious leaders. The Gospels also contain Jesus' actions, in particular accounts of his miracles. However, the dominant emphasis is on the events leading to the CRUCIFIXION and RESURREC-TION. The Gospels can be dated to somewhere between 60 and 100, and although there has been debate concerning their authorship, it is generally acknowledged that St John's Gospel is uniquely different to the other three SYNOPTIC GOSPELS. (*See also* JOHN, GOSPEL OF; LUKE, GOSPEL OF; MARK, GOSPEL OF; MATTHEW, GOSPEL OF)

Goswamis   *Hinduism*   The six close disciples of CAITANYA MAHAPRABHU (1486–1533), the ecstatic Bengali devotee of KRISHNA. The goswamis developed the theology of intense devotional love as manifested through the erotic tales of Krishna and RADHA. They travelled to VRINDAVAN with Caitanya and helped develop that city as one of the great centres of Krishna devotion. There are temples in Vrindavan associated with all six goswamis, and many of the SAMPRADAYAS (sectarian traditions) in the city claim to have originated from one of them.

Gotama (P)   *Buddhism*   See SIDDATTHA GOTTAMA.

Gotra   *Hinduism*   Exogamous group within a caste or JATI. It is the *gotra* membership that controls marriage partners. Generally, in rural India it will extend over several neighbouring villages.

Grace   *Christianity*   The freely given and unmerited favour of God's love, which breaks the hold of SIN on the human being. Christian doctrine asserts that humankind does not have the essential qualities required for its own salvation, as the human will was corrupted by sin. Humans can never enter a relationship with God as a result of their own efforts; the process of salvation can only be initiated by God through the birth, death and resurrection of Jesus Christ. Grace is also a term for a prayer of thanksgiving normally made before a meal. (*See also* REDEMPTION)

Gram devata   *Hinduism*   A village deity or godling whose powers are confined to the locality. In thousands of Indian villages, these lesser manifestations of the divine are worshipped every day by Hindus, who consider the great gods of Hinduism too remote or unconcerned with their daily affairs. Many of the *gram devatas* are female. (*See* BHUT; MATA; OJHA)

Granth *(a book)*   *Sikhism*   A term used to describe scripture. The two most important are the GURU GRANTH SAHIB and the DASAM GRANTH.

Granthi   *Sikhism*   The custodian and reader of the GURU GRANTH SAHIB who officiates at weddings and religious ceremonies such as the KHALSA initiation. Large GURDWARAS may have several *granthis*, who are generally appointed by the management committees. They should not be confused with priests, as the idea of priesthood is alien to Sikhs.

Grihastha / Gristhi / Grhastha   *Hinduism*   A householder, the second and most emphasized of the four stages of life that ideally should be followed by a Hindu. On completion of the student period, traditionally passed under the tutelage of a BRAHMIN guru, the male Hindu should marry and raise a family. Certain religious commitments are expected during this stage of life: an ideal householder should restrain the senses, practise non-violence and maintain equanimity and detachment. The difference between a householder and a renunciate is one of scale. While the householder should aspire to the renunciate's ideal, he has ritual obligations, whereas the renunciate has none. (*See also* VARNASHRAMDHARMA)

Gun   *Hinduism*   A quality or attribute that arrives as a gift from God rather than being an innate quality of the personality. It is believed that such spiritual or virtuous attributes are bestowed by God on those who follow the path of intense devotion. (*See* BHAKTI)

Guna   *Hinduism*   One of three forces or qualities that make up all inner or outer nature. Everything which is created is an interplay of these three *gunas*: SATTVA (harmony), RAJAS (activity) and TAMAS (inertia). They intermix in infinite varieties to create the quality of a being or entity. Hindu philosophy has developed classifications defined according to these three qualities. For example, food can be *sattvic*, such as fresh vegetables, fruit or the products of the cow; these will promote spiritual development. On the other hand, *rajasic* food (meat) promotes energy, activity, anger or lust, whilst *tamasic* food (decayed) will promote sloth or inertia. Many of these classifications are based on Krishna's discourse to Arjuna in the BHAGAVAD GITA, although the theory of the *gunas* is older and was used in SAMKHYA philosophy.

Gunas   *Jainism*   The eternal qualities that attach to the substance of material objects and affect our perceptions of the world. They are described as existence, substantiveness, knowability, endurability and the quality of possessing form.

Gunavratas   *Jainism*   The restraints on behaviour imposed by the three 'multiplicative vows' that can be undertaken by lay Jains in addition to the minor vows (ANUVRATAS). They are as follows: the directional vow, which restricts unnecessary movement so as to avoid injury to living beings; the vow of limitation of a real movement, which restricts moving between villages in order to prepare the lay Jain for a future life as an ascetic; the vow of avoidable activities, which prohibits the lay Jain from certain professions and trades that may lead to morally harmful activities. (*See also* APADHYANA; VRATAS)

Gupti   *Jainism*   The three types of 'guard' or protection for the soul observed by Jain ascetics to ensure that KARMA is not accruing to their being. The guards protect the soul from the influx of karma through the mind, body and speech. The mind is observed to guard against impure thoughts; the actions of the body are regulated so as to perform only spiritual activities; speech is guarded by only talking when it is considered to be essential. The major priority is to avoid any activity in mind, body or speech that will harm one's own soul or other living beings. (*See also* SADHU; KEVALIN)

Gur Darshan *Sikhism* The beliefs and practices of Sikhism as laid down by the ten GURUS and discovered in the GURU GRANTH SAHIB. Through following them completely, it is possible for a human being to achieve release from the cycle of birth and death.

Gurbani / Gurvani *Sikhism* The divine word revealed by the Gurus. Its full expression is believed to be contained in the GURU GRANTH SAHIB. Sikhs believe that wherever a congregation gathers to hear the *gurbani*, God is present. (*See also* BANI)

Gurdwara / Gurudwara *(the doorway to the guru)* *Sikhism* The Sikh place of worship, which must contain the GURU GRANTH SAHIB. There are famous historical gurdwaras associated with the activities of the ten human Gurus which function as places of pilgrimage. A gurdwara is a centre of congregational worship, although Sikhs visit individually to offer their respects to the Guru Granth Sahib and pray. It is open to all castes, as everyone is considered equal in the House of God. This equality is demonstrated practically by the presence of a LANGAR in all gurdwaras. Devotees cover their heads and remove their shoes inside the temple, and tobacco, alcohol and narcotics are forbidden within its precincts.

Gurmat *(the guru's guidance)* *Sikhism* Strictly speaking, this is the correct title for the path that has become known as Sikhism. It is a way of life based on the collective teachings of ten human GURUS which are now enshrined in the GURU GRANTH SAHIB. Fundamentally, *gurmat* teaches that mankind is divine in origin but remains separated from God by ego. *Gurmat* shows how to remove that separation and end the cycle of continuous rebirth.

Gurmata *(the guru's decision)* *Sikhism* An institution initiated by GURU GOBIND SINGH to ensure that all major decisions affecting the community reflected the communal will of the GURU PANTH. Resolutions are passed by Grand Conventions of representatives of the Panth. Although discontinued by Maharaja RANJIT SINGH, they were brought back by the Shiromani Gurdwara Prabandhak Committee (SGPC) in 1920 and still make the major decisions in contemporary Sikhism.

Gurmukh *(the mouth of the guru)* *Sikhism* The goal of the Sikh is to live by the Guru's teachings rather than the desires and dictates of his/her own mind. Someone who has achieved this state is known as a *gurmukh*. (*See* HAUMAI; MANMUKH)

Gurmukhi *(proceeding from the mouth of the guru)* Sikhism   Gurmukhi is the script of the GURU GRANTH SAHIB. In the time of GURU ANGAD DEV, the second guru, Lahnda was the only language used in the Punjab to write the vernacular language. It was a confusing language to read, as it did not have any characters for vowel sounds. It is said that the Guru, realizing this, created a new script by borrowing vowel signs from the Devanagari alphabet. The Guru's intention was to provide an alphabet in which the scripture could be read without confusion.

Gurparb / Gurpurb Sikhism   The anniversary of a Guru's birth or death. The most widely celebrated are the birthdays of GURU NANAK and GURU GOBIND SINGH and the martyrdoms of GURU ARJAN DEV and GURU TEGH BAHADUR. It is sometimes used for the anniversaries of other key events in Sikh history. Generally, a *gurparb* is celebrated by AKHAND PATHS, KIRTAN, religious discourses, processions and free food distributed from the LANGAR.

Guru *(darkness to light)* Hinduism   A teacher or preceptor, guru refers to someone who becomes a spiritual instructor. The disciple/teacher relationship lies at the heart of traditional Hindu culture. There are many different kinds of guru: one could have a music guru, for example. However, it is in the realm of religion that the term is most popularly used. While a guru could be a family priest or one who teaches the rituals of Hindu tradition, in Hinduism, the guru is often associated with the divine. In the Shaivite tradition, it is believed that the guru is the physical form of SHIVA sent to save souls from the cycle of birth and rebirth. Similarly, the role of the guru is considered essential in Vaishnavism, where some later developments claimed that the guru was more important than God, as he held the key to salvation. The true guru should be able to impart spiritual knowledge, be completely free from selfish motives and considerate of the spiritual welfare of all other human beings. Many such gurus have taught paths to God or self-realization that have created countless sects or SAMPRADAYAS. Although many Hindu gurus have functioned within the caste system, there have been famous examples who have challenged its supremacy in Hindu society and attracted disciples from all sectors. Contemporary gurus are often claimed to be divine by their followers, but they tend to be universal in that they frequently allow anyone to become a follower regardless of caste, gender or nationality. Many have travelled to the West to extend the range of their teachings. (*See also* DIKSA; SATGURU)

Guru *(a teacher or one who removes ignorance)* Sikhism   In Sikhism the title is reserved for God, who was the Guru of Nanak, the first of the line of human Gurus, the nine human Gurus who succeeded him and, finally, the GURU GRANTH SAHIB, which contains the BANI, or collective teachings of the Gurus. The term 'guru' is used only to refer to a universal guide who teaches the way to salvation through reunion with the divine. The teaching of the true Guru is given to all human beings regardless of caste, nationality, gender or creed. The essence of the message is that the Lord dwells in the human heart and can be discovered there through the devotee's thirst and remembrance of His name. (*See also* GURU AMAR DAS; GURU ANGAD DEV; GURU ARJAN DEV; GURU GOBIND SINGH; GURU HAR KRISHAN; GURU HAR RAI; GURU HARGOBIND; GURU NANAK; GURU RAM DAS; GURU TEGH BAHADUR)

Guru Amar Das (1552–74)   *Sikhism*   The third Guru, he succeeded GURU ANGAD DEV at the age of sixty-two after being his disciple for eleven years. He helped to rationalize the new faith by organizing the growing communities into twenty-two MANJIS under the direction of leaders called SANGATIAS. He began the process of providing the Sikhs with a separate identity from Hinduism by inviting them to visit him at GOINDWAL on the two Hindu festivals of BAISAKHI and DIVALI, rather than celebrating in the traditional manner in their own villages. He moved the centre of Sikhism from KARTARPUR to Goindwal, where he constructed the famous BAOLI SAHIB with eighty-four steps as a place of pilgrimage for Sikhs. It is significant in the development of Sikhism that he was the first Guru to have never met or had any contact with GURU NANAK.

Guru Angad Dev (1539–52)   *Sikhism*   The second Guru, who succeeded GURU NANAK. His importance lies in his success in consolidating the work begun by Guru Nanak. Traditionally, he is believed to have collected all the hymns of Guru Nanak and thus begun the process of compiling the ADI GRANTH. He is also associated with the invention of the GURMUKHI alphabet used in the scripture. The collection of hymns was used to promote the correct teachings of the gurus to Sikhs who were scattered in remote communities.

Guru Arjan Dev (1582–1606)   *Sikhism*   The fifth Guru and first martyr. He was the first Guru to be born a Sikh and was chosen by his father, who perceived qualities of guruship in his son. Guru Arjan embarked on several missionary journeys and the influx of JATS into Sikhism began under his influence. Under his guruship, Sikhism flourished. The Guru enjoyed the patronage of the Emperor Akbar and was a considerable temporal and spiritual leader in his own right. He was known as the *sacha padshah* (the true emperor) and created four new towns in the Punjab. In the city of Amritsar, founded by his father, he built HARMANDIR and turned the city into a pilgrimage centre for Sikhs. The ADI GRANTH was produced in its authoritative edition and placed in Harmandir where, it is said,

Guru Arjan prostrated before it. After the death of Akbar, Guru Arjan did not enjoy the same relationship with his son Jahangir. It is believed that he supported the attempt by Khusrau to overthrow Jahangir. Whatever the truth, he was killed while held in captivity by the Muslims and became the first Sikh martyr.

Guru Gobind Singh / Guru Govind Singh (1675–1708)   *Sikhism*   The tenth and final human Guru. He succeeded his father, at the age of eight, after his death at the hands of the Muslim authorities in Delhi. Guru Gobind Singh's time as Guru was marked by increasing hostility between the Sikhs and the Moghul rulers. He is regarded by Sikhs as the most important of the Gurus after their founder, GURU NANAK. In terms of the religious development of Sikhism, he was instrumental in changing the direction of the PANTH. In 1699 he created the KHALSA by baptizing five followers and giving them the five symbolic emblems which are still the outward signs of a Khalsa Sikh. On his deathbed, he announced that there would be no more human Gurus and henceforth, the GURU GRANTH SAHIB would be the eternal guide of the Sikh community. (*See also* GURU TEGH BAHADUR)

Guru Granth Sahib   *Sikhism*   The Sikh sacred text. Although the hymns of GURU NANAK had been collected by his successor, GURU ANGAD DEV, it was GURU ARJAN DEV who compiled the definitive version of the scripture and installed it in HARMANDIR, where it was known as the ADI GRANTH. The final version was produced by GURU GOBIND SINGH, who added the poems of his father, GURU TEGH BAHADUR. It consists of a collection of hymns composed by the Gurus and other well-known SUFIS and SANTS of northern India whose teachings reflected that of the Gurus. After the death of Guru Gobind Singh, the GURU GRANTH SAHIB became the final and eternal Guru of the Sikhs.

Guru Har Krishan / Guru Harkrishan (1661–4)   *Sikhism*   The eighth Guru. Succeeding his father, GURU HAR RAI, at the age of five, he was taken to Delhi while the Muslim ruler decided who was the rightful leader of the Sikhs. While in the city, he contracted smallpox and died on the site now occupied by BANGLA SAHIB. He nominated his great-uncle, GURU TEGH BAHADUR, as his successor.

Guru Har Rai (1644–61)   *Sikhism*   The seventh Guru. Guru Har Rai succeeded his father, GURU HARGOBIND, at the age of fourteen. He inherited a difficult political situation and continued to maintain a Sikh army. He was summoned to Delhi by the Emperor Aurangzeb and eventually died in the city of smallpox. He is usually depicted as a compassionate man who was passionately concerned with the needs of the poor and sick. Stories of miraculous healings are associated with his time in Delhi, and during his preaching tours of the Punjab, a LANGAR constantly travelled with him to feed the poor. (*See also* BANGLA SAHIB)

Guru Hargobind / Guru Har Govind / Guru Hargovind (1606–44)
Sikhism   The sixth Guru. The main religious contribution of Guru Hargobind to Sikhism was the concept of MIRI/PIRI, representing the temporal and spiritual authority of the Guru. Hargobind was criticized for placing too much emphasis on the *miri* aspect of his guruship. The Sikh flag, or NISHAN SAHIB, was first used by the Guru as the pennant of his troops.

Guru Nanak (1469–1539)   *Sikhism*   The first Guru and founder of Sikhism. Sikhism has a vast number of hagiographical accounts which indicate the spirituality of Nanak in his childhood and youth. His experience of enlightenment is described in the JANAM SAKHI accounts when he disappeared into the river for three days after going there to bathe. On his return, he announced that he had been taken to the court of God, where he had been given the command to preach the Name of God and had bestowed upon him the divine guruship. Nanak went on several important preaching tours before settling in the community of disciples named KARTARPUR. He was a prolific writer and singer of inspired poetry and the majority of poems found in the GURU GRANTH SAHIB are attributed to him. Guru Nanak was an ardent iconoclast who cast considerable doubt on the ability of the externals of religion to provide salvation. In essence, he taught that only the remembrance of the true name of God could purify the heart so that God's presence may be found within. This purification can only take place through obedience to the Guru's teachings. A variety of reform groups have emerged within Sikhism that are critical of the rites and rituals that have appeared in Sikhism, and which they consider to have departed from Guru Nanak's teachings. (*See also* NANAK; PANTHIS; SATNAM)

Guru Panth   *Sikhism*   The community that follows the teachings of the GURU. It is believed that the spirit of the Guru is present wherever Sikhs are gathered together in the presence of the GURU GRANTH SAHIB. On his deathbed, GURU GOBIND SINGH had announced that the Guru would henceforth be present in the Guru Granth Sahib and the Guru Panth. At the time of Maharaja RANJIT SINGH, the emphasis was placed on the guruship of the Guru Granth Sahib.

Guru Ram Das (1574–81)   *Sikhism*   The fourth Guru. He is remembered as the founder of the city of AMRITSAR, which he built as the new centre of Sikhism. Located on the trade routes to Delhi, the town flourished and provided an impetus for the development of the Sikh community. Guru Ram Das also initiated several reforms which helped to provide the Sikhs with a separate identity. He forbade the Hindu custom of *suttee* (burning widows) and the Muslim custom of PURDAH (isolation or veiling of women). He also composed the wedding-hymn which is used to distinguish Sikh weddings. (*See also* GURU ARJAN DEV)

Guru Tegh Bahadur / Guru Teg Bahadur (1664–75)   *Sikhism*   The ninth Guru. The martyred father of GURU GOBIND SINGH had little opportunity to live peacefully. His guruship was marked by dissent within the Sikh community and oppression from the Moghul rulers. Aurangzeb's reign as emperor was noted for its policy of Islamization. Guru Tegh Bahadur rallied the resistance of Sikhs and Hindus. He was imprisoned in Delhi and martyred after refusing to convert to Islam. His death is seen by Sikhs as representing the struggle for religious freedom against oppression.

Guru Vandana   *Jainism*   One of the six daily duties required of all devout lay Jains. It consists of the veneration of ascetics by providing for their physical needs. A ritual prayer is also offered in veneration of Jain ascetics that enables the lay Jain to cultivate humility and devotion. (*See* DANA; SADHU)

Gurudwara   *Sikhism*   See GURDWARA.

Gurukula   *Hinduism*   Traditional forest universities believed to have been maintained by sages in ancient Vedic culture. The idea of the *gurukula* was re-established in the late nineteenth century by the conservative wing of the ARYA SAMAJ, a Hindu reform movement. The schools were established to promote Hindu unity and ARYAN culture. Children entered as young as eight years old and underwent sixteen years of training in Sanskrit and Vedic culture. The period of training was meant to coincide with the traditional BRAHMACHARYA phase of VARNASHRAMDHARMA. (*See also* DAYANANDA, SWAMI)

Gyan Khand   *Sikhism*   The second of the five stages or realms taught by GURU NANAK which are experienced on the path to final liberation. This is the stage or realm of attainment of spiritual knowledge or awareness of what is hidden within the creation. In this stage, the devotee passes beyond the earth-bound realm of duty to a new vision of reality. (*See also* DHARAM KHAND; KARAM KHAND; KHAND; SAC KHAND; SARAM KHAND)

Gyana   *Hinduism*   Spiritual knowledge. Sometimes it is understood that such knowledge can be learned by the study of scriptures, but it is also used to describe knowledge that arises from direct experience of God (BRAHMAN) or realization of the self (ATMAN). The relationship between these two informs different theories concerning spiritual knowledge. (*See also* JNANA; VEDANTA)

Gyani   *Sikhism*   See GIANI.

H

Habit *Christianity* The distinctive outer garb of a male or female member of a religious order. (*See* FRIAR; MONK; NUN)

Habukkuk *Judaism* A prophet and a book of the same name that is included in the Jewish scriptures. Habukkuk was probably a contemporary of JEREMIAH. The book is concerned with the question of divine justice, and the prophet asks why should a non-believing nation such as the Chaldeans be chosen to carry out God's punishment of the tribes of Israel, as they will kill both the just and the wicked. (*See also* NEVIIM; TANAKH)

Hadhrat (U) / Hazrat *(dignity, nearness)* *Islam* A title given to an eminent SUFI or a companion of Muhammad. It is very often used in the subcontinent CHISHTI TARIQAH as a title for the shaikhs of the order.

Hadith *Islam* The extensive collections of sayings attributed to Muhammad which form the second most authoritative scriptural source for Muslim belief and practice after the QUR'AN. They differ from the Qur'an in that they were inspired by Muhammad's own initiative rather than by Allah. In the eighth and ninth centuries, various scholars began the process of collecting and collating the Hadith from all over the Muslim world on the basis of their reliability. Six collections came to be regarded as reliable and authoritative. The two most eminent are BUKHARI and Muslim. Although some Western scholars have challenged the view that the Hadith genuinely represent the views and actions of the Prophet, Muslim scholars use them as the secondary source for establishing precedent based on the SUNNA of the Prophet. Each Hadith is divided into parts, isnad and *matn*. Whereas *matn* provides the main body of text of the Hadith itself, it is *isnad* that demonstrates the degree of reliability. (*See also* HADITH QUDSI)

Hadith Qudsi *Islam* A special kind of HADITH that are believed to have been voiced by Muhammad but whose meaning and content were inspired by Allah. Any Hadith which has been deemed to be *Hadith al-Qudsi* is regarded as more authoritative and accepted by most Muslims.

Hafiz   *Islam*   A person who has learned to recite the complete QUR'AN by memory. It has always been an important concern of Muslims that the Qur'an should be passed on without error orally as well as in written form. Most children are taught to recite from the Qur'an from an early age and some go on to complete the full Qur'an. Hafiz have a special status in the community and are also called upon to provide recitations on religious or civil occasions. (*See also* MADRASA)

Haftarah   *Judaism*   A passage from one of the books of the Prophets read in the SYNAGOGUE either on the Sabbath or at the major festivals. It is used as a supplement to the TORAH reading, but will be selected to coincide with the message contained in the Torah scrolls on that day's reading. The reading will take place prior to the reading from the SEFER TORAH. (*See also* NEVIIM; TANAKH)

Hagadah / Haggadah *(telling)*   *Judaism*   The prayer-book used on the eve of the Passover for the SEDER ritual that contains the narrative or storytelling that goes with the meal. The *New Hagadah* was produced in 1942 and contains references to the plight of the Jews in Nazi Germany. (*See also* PESACH)

Haggai   *Judaism*   A prophet and a book of the same name included in the Jewish scriptures. He began his mission in 520 BCE amongst the returned exiles who had been released by Cyrus in 538 BCE. Haggai encouraged the returning Jews to begin building the Second Temple in spite of opposition from the SAMARITANS. (*See also* BET HA MIKDASH; NEVIIM; TANAKH)

Haiku (J)   *Buddhism*   A Japanese verse form introduced in the seventeenth century by Basho. It consists of seventeen syllables arranged in three lines of five, seven and five syllables respectively. The content was much influenced by ZEN and attempts to capture the moment or eternal present.

Hajar   *Islam*   The wife of the Prophet IBRAHIM (Abraham) and mother of the Prophet ISHMAEL. According to the Islamic view of history, Hajar and her son were cast out because of the jealousy of Abraham's first wife, Sara. They wandered in the desert until reaching the area where MAKKAH is now situated. They were both dying of thirst but, through a miracle, water sprung forth from the ground underneath the feet of the small child. The pair remained in this place and were visited by Ibrahim, who built the altar known as the KA'ABA for the worship of the one God. (*See also* ZAMZAM)

Hajj *Islam*   The annual pilgrimage to MAKKAH and the fifth of the five pillars of Islam. A religious duty that all Muslims must complete at least once in their life provided they are in good health and can afford to go. However, it is possible to have the hajj undertaken on your behalf by proxy. Muslims who have completed the hajj are entitled to be called hajji (male) and hajjah (female). The pilgrimage takes place in the month of Dhu'l-Hijjah, and before departure the pilgrim enters a consecrated state symbolized by wearing a simple cotton cloth thrown across the body that leaves one shoulder and arm bare. It is forbidden to shave or wash, apart from ritual ablutions performed at various stages of the pilgrimage. Sexual relations are also forbidden. On arrival in Makkah, the pilgrim first makes seven circumambulations of the KA'ABA and if possible kisses the Black Stone in the wall of the shrine. After this, the pilgrim runs back and forth between two small hills just outside the mosque to commemorate HAJAR's desperate search for water. After listening to preaching in the mosque, the pilgrim sets out for MINA and ARAFAT. On the ninth day, the pilgrim must stand in the sun from noon to sunset in Mina, 5 miles from Makkah in the desert, and listen to sermons. On the following day, the ritual stoning of Shaitan takes place, which symbolizes the victory of IBRAHIM when the devil tempted him to disobey God's command to sacrifice ISHMAEL. After the stoning, a sheep is sacrificed and the pilgrims shave their heads. The pilgrims then return to Makkah, where they circumambulate the Ka'aba again and then pass three days in rest and relaxation. After a farewell visit to the Great Mosque, the pilgrims return home.

Halakhah / Halacha *Judaism*   Jewish law as contained in the TALMUD, comprising rabbinical debates and discussions on rules and regulations derived from interpretation of the TORAH. It is used as a guide for every aspect of life. (*See also* AGADAH)

Halal *Islam*   A term used to describe any action that is permitted or lawful for a Muslim, and which does not contradict the laws of God. It is more often used for Muslim dietary laws concerning the slaughter of permitted animals in such a way as to drain them of blood. The Qur'an also forbids the eating of pig, carrion, birds of prey, blood, animals that died of sickness or through being killed by a carnivore or that were slaughtered as a sacrifice to an idol. (*See* HARAM)

Hallah / Challah *Judaism*   The two loaves of white bread used during festivals and on the Sabbath over which the blessings and the grace before meals are recited. The loaves are covered with a cloth and symbolize the manna on which the Jews miraculously survived whilst wandering in the wilderness after release from Egypt. It is said in the book of Exodus that the manna fell in a double portion before the Sabbath. (*See* SEDER; SHABBAT)

Hallaj, Mansur al- (858–922)   *Islam*   A famous mystic from Persia who was murdered by the orthodox for uttering 'ana'l Haqq' ('I am the Truth'). Al-Hallaj had been a follower of several prominent SUFIS and his own poetry resounds with ecstatic and intoxicated divine love. Amongst contemporary Sufis, his reputation is untarnished and he is considered one of the greatest amongst the lovers of God. However, it is acknowledged that he may have gone too far in expressing his intoxication. (*See also* FANA)

Hallel   *Judaism*   The repetition of Psalms 113–18 that takes place in the Morning Prayer liturgy on special occasions, such as the three festivals, but is forbidden on the high holy days of YOM KIPPUR and ROSH HASHANAH. (*See also* PESACH; SHAVUOT; SUKKOT; TEFILLAH)

Halo   *Christianity*   A circle of light that appears around the head of Jesus Christ, the Virgin Mary and the saints in traditional Christian iconography and represents the presence of God or divinity.

Hamd   *Islam*   Thankful praise of Allah expressed through various phrases in Arabic, the most common being HAMDU LILLAH. A devout Muslim would try to thank God even in situations of distress or crisis. The Qur'an states: 'if you give thanks, I will give you increase' (14:7). While gratitude is believed to bring with it spiritual joy, its absence runs the risk of loss of grace. This uttering of thankful praise is a solitary activity unlike the obligatory SALAH. (*See also* DU'A)

Hamdu lillah *(praise be to God)*   *Islam*   The first line of the first sura of the Qur'an and the most commonly repeated thankful praise of Allah expressed by Muslims. (*See* HAMD)

Hanafi   *Islam*   A school of Islamic jurisprudence founded by ABU HANIFA (d.767) in Baghdad. Although the largest school of law in the Muslim world, it is also the dominant school in western Asia, lower Egypt and the subcontinent. (*See also* FIQH; HANBALI; MADHHAB; MALIKI; SHAFI'I)

Hanbali   *Islam*   One of the four schools of SUNNI Islamic jurisprudence founded by Ahmad Ibn Hanbal (d.855). Ibn Hanbal was a traditionalist who supported the use of HADITH to create Islamic law. He had opposed the rationalist views of the Mutazilites and passed a period in prison for refusing to acknowledge that the Qur'an was not eternal. His teachings were organized by his followers after his death into one of the four schools of law. The dominant school in northern and Central Asia, its teachings were revived by the eighteenth century WAHHABI movement in Arabia. (*See also* HANAFI; MALIKI; SHAFI'I; SHARI'A)

Hanif *Islam*   A God-seeker. Islam recognizes that there were pious, faithful worshippers of the one God prior to its advent even outside the ranks of Jews and Christians. These monotheists, who before the coming of Islam maintained monotheism amongst the pagan Arab tribes, are generally ascribed the title of *hanif*. Usually they are associated with various individuals who tried to maintain the worship of one God at the KA'ABA stone in MAKKAH and opposed the installation of idols at the shrine.

Hansa *Hinduism*   A mythological swan that can separate milk and water. The swan is used as a symbol for the soul that is able to discriminate the real from the unreal. *Hansa* is therefore sometimes used as a title for an enlightened GURU who possesses the same quality of discrimination. (*See also* VIVEKA)

Hanukiah *Judaism*   *See* MENORAH.

Hanukkah / Chanukkah *Judaism*   The Feast of Dedication, also known as the Feast of Lights from the use of the MENORAH during the eight days of the festival. It is celebrated in the month of Kislev (5 November to 3 December). On the first day, one branch of the candle is lit, a process that is repeated each day until the whole candelabra is lit. It commemorates the victory of Judas Maccabeus over Antiochus V Epiphanes, which led to the rededicating of the Temple in Jerusalem in 165 BCE. The festival is a minor one in the Jewish religious year, as the winter festivals are considered to be man-made, unlike the summer festivals, which are divine ordinances in the TORAH; despite this, however, it has become very popular.

Hanuman *Hinduism*   The monkey warrior-chief and son of the wind-god, VAYU, who faithfully served RAMA and SITA as recounted in the great epic, the RAMAYANA. Although possessing supernatural strength and other extraordinary powers, it is for his personal devotion and service to the AVATAR, Ram, that Hanuman is best loved. In the BHAKTI tradition, he is regarded as the personification of devotion. In TULSIDAS' Hindi version of the Ramayana, Ram offers Hanuman the traditional Hindu life-goals of wealth, pleasure, DHARMA and spiritual liberation as rewards for his service. Hanuman refuses them all and asks instead for devotion. In Hindu temples that contain the MURTIS of Ram and Sita, he is usually present as a kneeling monkey with hands folded in adoration at their feet. Very often he is placed at the door to Hindu temples as the guardian deity, but there are also specific Hanuman temples dedicated to him. He is also the patron deity of wrestlers. (*See also* RAMACHARITAMANASA)

Haqiqa *Islam*   The inner reality or the truth where the presence of God is found in the human heart after inner purification. In Sufism, *haqiqa* becomes the goal, but most *Sufis* have acknowledged that *haqiqa* (the internal reality) and SHARI'A (the external law) should accompany the ideal Muslim life. Sufism has developed extensive practices for the purification of the ego (NAFS) so that the state of *haqiqa* can be revealed or discovered. These mostly consist of the remembrance (DHIKR) of Allah's divine names. (*See also* HAQQ)

Haqiqa Muhammadiya   *Islam*   The way of imitation of the Prophet Muhammad much loved by the practitioners of Muslim mysticism, the Sufis. Muhammad is regarded as both the exemplar of the Muslim revelation and the primal mystic who is fully surrendered to the will of Allah. Practitioners of the Sufi path attempt to model themselves on the Prophet's example and even physical appearance. The intention is to achieve his spiritual relationship of surrender, not to imitate his relationship of prophethood. (*See also* ADAB; SHAIKH; TARIQAH)

Haqq *(the truth)*   *Islam*   The divine reality that is behind and within all created phenomenon. It is one of the ninety-nine names or attributes of Allah and is used by SUFIS in their recitation. It is Allah's presence as truth that allows the mystic to discover reality as an indwelling presence found in the purified heart. (*See also* HAQIQA; QALB)

Haram   *Islam*   The fifth of the five categories of action that constitute the SHARI'A (Islamic law). *Haram* refers to actions that are unlawful or forbidden and are subject to punishment if performed. The general principle of Islam is that all things are deemed to be lawful unless expressly prohibited in the QUR'AN. It is therefore God who has decreed what is forbidden in His revelation, rather than the decisions of human executive bodies or governments. (*See also* FARD)

Haram Sharif   *Islam*   The grand mosque in MAKKAH that contains the KA'ABA, the well of ZAMZAM and the hills of Marwah and SAFA. It is the foremost mosque in the Islamic world and the centre of the rites that take place on the annual pilgrimage. (*See also* HAJJ)

Harappa   *Hinduism*   One of the two principal cities of the old Indus Valley civilization excavated in the 1920s. The Harappa civilization is believed to have reached its peak somewhere around 2500–2000 BCE and had disappeared a thousand years later. The Indus Valley civilization was vast and covered nearly one million square miles of territory including most of northern India, Pakistan and extending down into Gujarat. Although little is known about their religion, there is some speculation, arising from excavated figurines and seals, that the people may have worshipped a variety of goddesses and a proto-SHIVA figure who sits in a yogic-type posture. (*See also* ARYAN; DRAVIDIAN)

Hardwar / Haridwar *Hinduism* A famous pan-Indian pilgrimage town that is one of the seven sacred sites revered by all Hindus. Hardwar is built on the banks of the GANGA in the Himalayan foothills in the state of Uttar Pradesh. It is one of the sites for the KUMBHA MELA, the three-yearly Hindu festival in which millions gather to bathe in the Ganga and co-exist for several days with gatherings of SADHUS and holy men and women from all over India.

Hare Krishna *Hinduism* The popular name for the ISKCON movement derived from the first two words of the MANTRA that is chanted by the devotees and believed to contain the real name of God that can save devotees in the KALI YUGA (age of darkness). The mantra is *Hare Krishna, Hare Krishna, Krishna, Krishna, Hare, Hare. Hare Rama, Hare Rama, Rama, Rama, Hare, Hare.*

Hari *Hinduism* An affectionate name used by the devotees of VISHNU to describe the personal Lord, especially his human AVATARS, RAMA and KRISHNA. (*See also* VAISHNAVA)

Hari-Hara *Hinduism* The fusing of VISHNU and SHIVA into one composite being containing the form and qualities of both.

Harijans *(sons of Hari)* *Hinduism* Gandhi used this term to describe untouchables, as he perceived them to be the blessed of God. Although discrimination on the grounds of untouchability is outlawed by the Indian Constitution, it remains prevalent, especially in rural India. Untouchables have organized themselves effectively into social and political movements, but they prefer to call themselves DALITS.

Hariva-msa *Hinduism* A scripture that supplements the great epic, the MAHABHARATA. It recounts tales of KRISHNA's early life, whereas the Mahabharata is only concerned with his involvement in the politics of the great battle when he is already king of Dvarka.

Harmandir *Sikhism* Commonly known as the Golden Temple in AMRITSAR, it is more affectionately called DARBAR SAHIB by Sikhs. The temple was built by GURU ARJAN DEV in the middle of the lake constructed by his father in Amritsar. The famous gold leaf was added to the temple by Maharaja RANJIT SINGH. It is said that the foundation stone was laid by the famous SUFI saint, MIAN MIR, which indicates the eclectic or universal nature of Sikh tradition. The GURDWARA has become the foremost place of pilgrimage and the spiritual centre of Sikhism. (*See also* GURU RAM DAS)

Haroset *Judaism* One of the foods partaken in the ritual meal at the

Passover. It consists of a mixture of apples, nuts, cinnamon and sometimes a little wine blended into a creamy sauce. (*See* SEDER; PESACH)

Harvest Thanksgiving   *Christianity*   An unofficial festival of thanksgiving for the produce of the earth celebrated in Britain usually in September or October. The festival is marked by the bringing of produce to the church and replaces the older pagan Harvest Home festivals.

Hasan   *Islam*   The grandson of Muhammad, son of ALI and FATIMA and brother of HUSAIN. He is regarded by SHI'A Muslims as the second IMAM and the third rightful leader of the Muslim community. The Shi'a believe that when MU'AWIYAH assumed the leadership of the Muslim community and established the UMAYYAD dynasty, he promised that on his death he would return the leadership of the community to Ali's children, Hasan and Husain. It is believed that Mu'awiyah bribed Hasan to live in Madinah and make no attempt to establish his claim. He died in mysterious circumstances in Madinah and Shi'a Muslims believe that he was poisoned on Mu'awiyah's instructions. (*See also* KARBALA)

Hashgahah   *Judaism*   A central belief in Judaism that God is the controller and guide of the entire universe. All events are therefore ultimately preordained and there is a good providence operating everywhere throughout the creation. This benevolent providence operates both generally throughout creation and in special events that take place in the life of an individual. It is believed that nothing takes place by accident.

Hasidim / Chasidim   *Judaism*   A religious movement founded by Rabbi Israel ben Eliezer (1700–60), better known as BAAL SHEM TOV, in the middle of the eighteenth century in Eastern Europe. The movement rapidly gained popularity and won thousands of members throughout Poland, Russia, Lithuania, Hungary and Romania. It stressed piety and joyful worship over the intellectual study of the TALMUD. There are two basic beliefs that make Hasidism unique. The first is the idea of DEVEKUT or attachment to God. Since all things are pervaded by God and the only true reality is God, God should therefore be remembered in everything that we do. Consequently, the Hasidim should always be filled with the joy of God's presence (*simhah*) and be humble before that presence (*shiflut*). Those who achieve this state of *devekut, simhah* and *shiflut* are regarded as holy men fit to teach or lead others. This resulted in a new kind of REBBE or leader who attracted disciples, as opposed to the traditional rabbis who were versed in law. In time dynasties developed from the various great rebbes and formed religious subgroups within the movement, such as the LUBAVITCH, Sotmar, Ger, Beltz and Vishnitz. The Hasidim are also distinctive in their dress.

They wear a long cloak (*kapote*), a fur hat made of sable with thirteen tails (*streimel*) and a special belt when in prayer (*gartle*). They are also recognizable from their long curled beards. Hasidic prayer is accompanied by melody, and from time to time individuals will break out into an ecstatic dance in which one leg is always kept off the ground. (*See also* ZADDIKIM)

Haskalah *(enlightenment)* *Judaism*   Usually used to describe the eighteenth-century movement led by Moses Mendelssohn which emphasized education and the study of scripture within a modern framework. He translated the PENTA-TEUCH into German so that it would become available to Jews in their own spoken language. The movement encouraged Jews to abandon medieval ways of life and thought. It spread from Prussia to Austria and then into Russia. (*See also* REFORM)

Hatan Torah *(The Groom of the Torah)* *Judaism*   The last reader of the TORAH in the joyful celebration of SIMCHAT TORAH. He is called to read the final portion of the Torah which marks the culmination of the religious year. He will walk to the BIMAH escorted by children. It is deemed a special privilege and usually reserved for an elder person known for their piety and goodness.

Hatha Yoga *Hinduism*   Although best known in the West as a system of physical postures used in some yogic disciplines and practised for reasons of health, hatha yoga was, in fact, the system of postures and breathing exercises developed by the NATH YOGIS, a well-known SHAIVITE renunciate order, as a specific path to spiritual liberation. (*See also* GORAKHNATH)

Haumai *Sikhism*   The term refers to self-centredness or ego, which is the source of anger, doubt and suffering. The intention of the Guru's teaching was to show how it could be replaced by God-centredness. It is essential to remove *haumai* before salvation can be achieved. (*See* GURMUKH; MANMUKH)

Havan *Hinduism*   The sacrificial ceremony, also known as Hom or Homa, in which GHEE and grains are offered into fire. Performed by a BRAHMIN priest, it is the main ritual associated with many life-cycle rituals and Hindu ceremonies. (*See also* YAJNA)

Havan Kund *Hinduism*   The container in which the HAVAN fire is burned.

Havdalah *Judaism*   The service at the end of the Sabbath which is celebrated at home and in the SYNAGOGUE. It requires a KIDDUSH cup, a plate on which the cup is set, a spice box filled with sweet-smelling spices and a twisted candle. The wine is blessed, and the spice box is passed round for everyone to smell as a symbol of the last fragrance of the Sabbath. The candle is then lifted up whilst a blessing is recited. The leader drinks the wine and then passes it around to the members partaking in the ceremony. The candle is traditionally extinguished in the wine that has overflowed onto the plate to mark the end of the Sabbath. (*See also* SHABBAT)

Hawa *Islam*   The enemy within described in the Qur'an as the 'self urgent to evil' (12:53). This inclination to waywardness arising out of human imperfection or weakness has to be fought against and mastered. The directions of the Qur'an and the life of Muhammad provide the two great inspirations and guides for self-mastery and submission to God. (*See* DHIKR; NAFS)

Hazanut / Chazanut *Judaism*   The art of singing or chanting scripture in the correct manner in the services held in the SYNAGOGUE. This is the responsibility of the cantor, who learns and performs the required melodies and cadences. (*See also* HAZZAN)

Hazrat *Islam*   *See* HADHRAT.

Hazur Sahib *Sikhism*   The shrine on the banks of the Godavari River in Maharashtra which is sacred to the memory of GURU GOBIND SINGH. It marks the place of his death and according to tradition is the spot where he bowed before the GURU GRANTH SAHIB and made it the guru of Sikhs in perpetuity. The shrine is one of the five *takhts* or seats of authority for Sikhism.

Hazzan / Chazan *Judaism*   The cantor who leads the congregation in the singing and chanting of scripture and prayer in the services of the SYNAGOGUE. In early Jewish literature the cantor is known as 'the deputy of the congregation', reflecting the fact that he is the one chosen to speak to God on behalf of the congregation. In the SHULHAN ARUKH, it is written that the cantor must have the following qualifications: a good voice, an impeccable character and be accepted by the congregation. (*See also* HAZANUT)

Heaven *Christianity*   The dwelling place of God and the ANGELS, also known as Paradise, and the place or state of being in which redeemed souls or SAINTS will be united with God after death. Heaven is also used in an eschatological sense to indicate the final and perfect condition of creation after the second coming of Christ, when all things will fully express the will of God. This is expressed in the line of the LORD'S PRAYER which states 'Thy Kingdom come on Earth as it is in Heaven'. (*See also* PAROUSIA)

Hebrew *Judaism*   *See* IVRIT.

Hebrews, Epistle to the *Christianity* One of the books of the New Testament attributed to Paul, although very few modern scholars would acknowledge Pauline authorship. The EPISTLE was probably written to Jewish Christians to warn them of the dangers of returning to Judaism, or it may have been an attempt to convince Jewish Christians of the new universal context to the faith. The author addresses the issue of the new covenant of God given through Jesus Christ which replaces the old covenant given to the people of Israel.

Hell *Christianity* The place or state of being for unredeemed souls after death. It is the place reserved for unrepentant sinners and is the consequence of removal from the presence of God. The New Testament is unequivocal regarding hell and states that its fires are unquenchable and eternal. Jesus Christ warns of the undoubted reality of God's punishment for evil-doers in the afterlife. There has been debate as to whether a merciful and loving God could consign all sinners to eternal punishment with no hope of salvation. In recent times this debate has extended to incorporate the idea that hell is a state of being rather than a location. (*See* PURGATORY)

Heresy *(Greek: choice)* *Christianity* The denial of orthodox doctrine or the belief in a doctrine that has been officially declared unorthodox and heretical. The word refers to those who choose to follow their own way or to form their own group. Although the New Testament use of heresy to mean doctrinal error only occurs in one of the letters of Peter, that became the general meaning throughout the history of Christianity. Major schisms have resulted over interpretations of Christ's identity and often Christian COUNCILS were called to resolve doctrinal divisions by asserting orthodoxy and declaring divergent opinions as heresy. Once Christianity became a state religion, heresy was likely to be punished as a crime. (*See also* ARIANISM; CHRISTOLOGY; EBIONITES; INQUISITION)

Herod the Great *Christianity* The king of the Jews who governed over Judea at the time of the birth of Christ. He is mentioned in Matthew's Gospel as responsible for the massacre of first-born male children in Bethlehem after the MAGI had told him that they had come to see the newly born 'King of the Jews'. He is not to be confused with Herod the Tetrarch, the younger son of Herod the Great, who was involved with the imprisonment and murder of JOHN THE BAPTIST and to whom Jesus was sent by PONTIUS PILATE during the events that led up his trial and death. (*See also* CRUCIFIXION)

Hesed *(loving kindness)* *Judaism* According to the tradition of the KABBALAH, the fifth of the ten SEFIROTH, that emanate from the AYN SOF. Second on the right-hand branch of the Tree of Life underneath HOKHMAH, it is the love that

God has for His creatures and is controlled by the GEVURAH, the power of discrimination or judgement.

Hevrah Kabranim   *Judaism*   The traditional organization that existed in every Jewish community and received the bodies of dead Jews at the graveyard. They were responsible for the digging of the grave, the placing of the body in the grave and the final filling in with soil. In the past, it was traditional that all funeral services were not paid for. (*See* HEVRAH KADISHAH)

Hevrah Kadishah   *Judaism*   The traditional organization that existed in every Jewish community to provide the services required for the dead. The members of the organization would be called to sit with the dying person throughout the day and night, making sure that they confessed and uttered the SHEMA on their dying breath. After death had been confirmed, they took the body away to be prepared for the funeral. They washed and dressed the deceased, prepared the coffin and took the body to the cemetery, where it became the responsibility of the gravediggers. (*See also* HEVRAH KABRANIM; TAHARAH; TUMAH)

Hidaya / Hidayah   *Islam*   Legal textbook brought to India by Maulana Buhari-uddin from central Asia in the thirteenth century. It has remained the basis for Muslim law in the subcontinent.

Hifz   *Islam*   The traditional method of learning to recite the QUR'AN in Arabic. (*See also* HAFIZ)

High Altar   *Christianity*   The main ALTAR of a church that traditionally stands at the entrance to the SANCTUARY at the east end of the NAVE.

High Church   *Christianity*   The group within the CHURCH OF ENGLAND that emphasizes its continuity with Catholic Christianity and places the same emphasis on the seven SACRAMENTS and the importance of the episcopate as Roman Catholicism. This wing of the Church of England, also known as Anglo-Catholic, has existed since the Tudor period but declined during the seventeenth and eighteenth centuries. It was revived under the influence of the OXFORD MOVEMENT in the nineteenth century. (*See also* TRACTARIANISM)

Hijab *(a veil)*   *Islam*   Usually employed to describe the head covering worn by women to maintain modesty, it was originally used to describe the curtain placed between the mosque and the Prophet's living quarters to protect privacy. Sufis also use the term to mean the veil that stands between Allah and his worshippers. (*See* HIJAB AL-AZAMAH)

Hijab al-Azamah   *Islam*   The veil that stands between Allah and His creation that prevents human beings from seeing Him. It is believed by Muslims that Muhammad was taken right to the presence of God on his mystical Night Journey and therefore surpassed the experience of Moses, who was denied the privilege of going past the veil. It is a common concept used in Sufism, which regards Muhammad as the ultimate mystic in his capacity as the final prophet of God. SUFI mystics themselves have modelled their lives on the Prophet in the hope of God being gracious enough to lift the veil that obscures His presence. (*See also* MI'RAJ)

Hijra *(emigration)*   *Islam*   Muhammad left the troubled environment of MAKKAH and travelled to MADINAH, arriving in September 622. Most of the loyal followers of the Prophet had made the journey ahead of him. The Islamic calendar begins from this event, starting in June 622 and continuing through a lunar year based on 354 days. The idea of hijra, or flight from a non-Muslim environment in order to seek a more conducive place to practise the religion, is recommended in the SHARI'A.

Hillel, Rabbi   *Judaism*   A famous first-century CE RABBI who founded the school of Hillel. There is a well-known story that he was asked by a would-be convert to teach him the entire TORAH in the period that he was able to stand on one leg. It is said that Hillel replied, 'Do unto others as you would be done by'. He claimed that this was the essence of the Torah and all the rest was commentary. This is known as the 'golden rule'.

Himsa   *Jainism*   Actions that bring harm to other living creatures, whether intentional or unintentional. In Jainism, violence also includes thoughts and speech. Included in the category of violence are actions that cause pain to any living creature even for nourishment. Jains are strict vegetarians and are also not allowed to eat eggs, honey, alcohol, butter, root vegetables and vegetables containing many seeds. Exploitation or overwork of humans and animals is also considered to be *himsa*. (*See* AHIMSA)

Hinayana   *Buddhism*   A term used by MAHAYANA tradition to indicate the doctrine of the THERAVADA school. It literally means 'Lesser Vehicle'. Originally, there were eighteen schools but only the Theravada, which was strong in south India and Sri Lanka, survived and flourished, gradually spreading eastwards into southeast Asia. The school is very strict and believes that it represents the purest form of the Buddha's teachings. It is certainly the earliest school of Buddhism still surviving today.

Hira   *Islam*   The name of the place outside MAKKAH where Muhammad went to pray and find solitude in a cave. The appearance of the angel JIBRIL and the first revelation of the Qur'an are believed to have taken place there. The cave remains an important site for Muslim pilgrims.

Hiranya Kasipu *Hinduism*   The wicked demon and tyrannical father of PRAHLADA, the child-devotee of VISHNU. Hiranya Kasipu was destroyed by NARASIMHA, the half-man, half-lion incarnation of Vishnu. Hiranya Kasipu had practised intense austerities to be granted the wish of virtual immortality. He could not be killed by a human or an animal, either in the daytime or at night. Thus Vishnu had to manifest a unique AVATAR to destroy him and save the persecuted Prahlada. This event is celebrated in the Hindu festival of HOLI.

Hirz *(stronghold)* *Islam*   A word used in prayer to describe Allah as the shelter of the worshipper. It is also used in popular folk traditions to describe amulets containing verses of the Qur'an that are used to ward off evil. (*See* HIZB; TA'WIDH)

Hitopadesh *Hinduism*   A collection of moral tales often involving animals, similar to Aesop's fables.

Hizb *Islam*   A division of the Qur'an usually associated with one-sixtieth of the content. It consists of petitions and prayers of the heart, arranged for recital and memorization. Alternatively known as wird, particular ones are adopted by individual SUFI orders as part of their own liturgy of worship. However, they have also been used in folk tradition as formulas for magical protection or to control either natural or supernatural hostile forces. (*See also* HIRZ)

Hod *(splendour)* *Judaism*   According to the tradition of the KABBALAH, the seventh of the ten SEFIROTH that emanate from the AYN SOF. It is the third on the left-hand side of the Tree of Life and, along with NETZAH, is one of the two supports for the *sefiroth*.

Hokhmah *(wisdom)* *Judaism*   According to the tradition of the KABBALAH, the third of the ten SEFIROTH that emanate from the AYN SOF. It is the first on the right-hand side of the Tree of Life and is the 'point', the first flash of an idea, in which the whole of creation is spelled out in the divine mind.

Hol ha-Moed *Judaism*   The intermediate days of the festivals of PESACH and SUKKOT that are distinguished from the named sacred days and observed as semi-holy days. Essential work is allowed and in the SYNAGOGUE, HALLEL and MUSAPH are read in addition to the TORAH. (*See also* HOSHANA RABBA)

Hola Muhalla   *Sikhism*   A Sikh spring festival which takes place around the time of the Hindu festival of HOLI. The first Hola Muhalla was celebrated in 1700, the year after the formation of the KHALSA. The most important celebration takes place at ANANDPUR SAHIB in the Punjab, which is an important pilgrimage centre associated with GURU GOBIND SINGH and his father, GURU TEGH BAHADUR.

Holi   *Hinduism*   The Hindu festival of colours celebrated in Phalguna (March–February). Traditionally, this is a time when everyone throws coloured powder dyes on each other. There are also bonfires and street processions. The festival is associated with disorder and anarchy. In some parts of India normal authority relations are overturned for the day, and wives will be seen beating their husbands in the street. Religiously, the festival is associated with the manifestation of NARASIMHA, the man-lion AVATAR of VISHNU, to protect his devotee, PRAHLADA, from his demon-king father. (*See* HIRANYA KASIPU)

Holy Communion   *Christianity*   See EUCHARIST.

Holy Orders   *Christianity*   The membership of the priesthood, either as BISHOP, PRIEST or DEACON.

Holy See   *Christianity*   The spiritual and temporal domain of the POPE. (*See also* ROMAN CATHOLIC; SEE; VATICAN)

Holy Sepulchre   *Christianity*   The church in Jerusalem, which is supposedly built over the cave where Jesus Christ is believed to have been buried after the CRUCIFIXION and prior to his RESURRECTION. The first church on the site was built in 335. The present church contains several chapels which represent those main strands of Christianity that maintain a historical presence in Jerusalem. (*See also* CALVARY)

Holy Spirit / Holy Ghost / Paraclete   *Christianity*   The third person of the Holy Trinity, sometimes referred to as the Comforter, is the Spirit of God. The OLD TESTAMENT utilizes images of wind and breath (*ruach*) to indicate the life-giving and refreshing properties of God's presence in creation. However, both the Old and NEW TESTAMENT refer to the function of the Spirit in filling an individual with God's presence, which then acts as a guide, inspiration or motivator and possibly the provider of divine gifts such as healing or prophecy. It is believed that after the ascension of Christ, the Holy Spirit continued the redemptive work of God in the world and came down upon the APOSTLES at the Feast of PENTECOST. It is therefore active as God's presence in the world and some Christian groups, such as Pentecostalists and CHARISMATICS, place their emphasis on this aspect of divinity. (*See also* GLOSSOLALIA; TRINITY)

Holy Water   *Christianity*   Water that has been blessed for religious purposes and used for blessings, exorcisms and ritual purification of a church. It is not to be confused with the water used at BAPTISM.

Holy Week   *Christianity*   The week that culminates in EASTER and is observed by Christians in remembrance of Christ's last week on earth.

Homa / Hom   *Hinduism*   *See* HAVAN.

Homoiousios *(of one substance)*   *Christianity*   The term used in the NICENE CREED to indicate the orthodox Christological relationship between the Father and the Son which asserts that Jesus Christ was of the same substance as God. The doctrine was in opposition to the Arian heresy that Christ was a similar substance, not the same. (*See also* ARIANISM; CHRISTOLOGY; NICAEA, COUNCIL OF; TRINITARIAN; TRINITY)

Honen (1133–1212)   *Buddhism*   An influential Japanese teacher who popularized Amidism or AMIDA Buddhism and who believed, after many years of searching, that only the repetition of the name of the Amida Buddha could provide release from suffering. A monk at the age of nine, he went on to found the JODO sect or 'Pure Land' school.

Hope   *Christianity*   One of the three theological virtues along with FAITH and LOVE as taught by Paul. Paul uses hope in a special sense, describing pagans or non-Christians as a people without hope, as they were without God. In its widest sense, it can be used to celebrate the possibility of finding the highest good that is one's ultimate end in God, but in Christian terms it also refers to the faith in a living God who intervenes in human history and individuals' lives to fulfil His promise of salvation. Paul links hope with faith and love, and states that they are the fundamental features of Christian life.

Hosanna   *Christianity*   A celebratory term employed in Christian liturgy that was first used by the crowds that celebrated Jesus' triumphal entry into Jerusalem on PALM SUNDAY. It is difficult to ascertain whether this was spontaneous or a traditional greeting with palms that originated in the Jewish feast of SUKKOT.

Hosea   *Judaism*   A prophet and a book of the same name included in the Jewish scriptures. A contemporary of ISAIAH, he warned against the evil-doing and injustice that he saw in the reign of Jeroboam II in the middle of the eighth century BCE. Speaking of the relationship between God and His chosen people in terms of the intimate relationship between a husband and a wife, he preaches that if only the unfaithful wife would repent her sins, then the faithful husband would forgive her. (*See also* NEVIIM; TANAKH)

Hoshana Rabba   *Judaism*   The last of the intermediate days of the festival of SUKKOT that falls on the seventh day. In the time of the Temple it used to be known as the 'day of the willow branch' after the custom in which the priests circled the altar seven times beating the floor with willow branches. Today, seven circuits are made around the TORAH scrolls whilst reciting HOSANNA prayers. In the past, the day was also associated with prayers for rain but is now regarded as the day when divine judgement will be handed out. Pious Jews will pass the night in the SYNAGOGUE reading the Torah. The association with judgement makes the day a solemn occasion. (*See also* HOL HA-MOED)

Hospitallers   *Christianity*   The Knights of St John, who were founded in Jerusalem by Raymond du Poys (1120–60), the grand master of the hospital named after John the Baptist. He turned the foundation into a military order similar to that of the TEMPLARS, although it was committed to maintaining its medical work. The order successfully resisted the Turks and Moors from the Mediterranean islands of Rhodes and Malta. (*See also* CRUSADES)

Host   *Christianity*   The consecrated bread considered to be the sacrificed body of Christ. (*See* EUCHARIST; TRANSUBSTANTIATION)

Hua-Yen *(flower garden)* *Buddhism*   The school based on the doctrines of the Mahayanan text, AVATAMSAKA SUTRA. The Hua-Yen developed in China as a fully fledged system, which regarded itself as the pinnacle of the Buddha's teaching. It was founded by five patriarchs, but Fa-tsangh (seventh century) was the great systemizer of the tradition. Hua-Yen focuses on visionary experience and magic rather than philosophical speculation, and the patriarchs were known for their miracles and healing abilities. Like CH'AN, Hua-Yen believes in sudden awakening to the ever-present Buddha nature already existing within. Later the school was transferred to Japan, where it is known as KEGON.

Huda *(guidance)* *Islam*   One of the titles of respect given to the QUR'AN that describes the function of the revelation to provide correct guidance to human beings. Human reason or conscience are not considered to be reliable tools for knowing the correct path through life, and thus humanity requires the direct guidance and intervention of God.

Huguenots   *Christianity*   The name given to Calvinist French Protestants who, in their desire to convert, caused France to be divided by a series of religious wars between the Catholic majority and the Protestant minority in the sixteenth century. Following their decline after the massacre of St Bartholomew's Day and a period of persecution during the sixteenth century, they finally won the right to freedom of worship in 1593. (*See also* CALVINISM)

Hukam *(command)* *Sikhism*   It refers to the will of God which controls the universe and is the cause of creation. God acts as He pleases and is not subject to any control. The duty of all human beings is to submit to the divine will. The Sikh GURUS were completely submitted to the divine will.

Hukam Nama *Sikhism*   A proclamation or order relating to the Sikh faith which is binding on all Sikhs. Originally they were made by the Gurus to their followers, but are now issued from AMRITSAR. Failure to obey a proclamation of this kind can result in excommunication from the community.

Hukam / Vak / Vaak *Sikhism*   The term used when a Sikh individual or family consult the GURU GRANTH SAHIB to receive guidance on particular problems. The answer is perceived to emanate from the divine will. Usually they will visit the GURDWARA to receive a random reading of the Guru Granth Sahib that will offer them specific guidance.

Huldah *Judaism*   A prophetess and an example of a pious woman, who lived in Jerusalem and was sought out by the leaders of the people after the discovery of the TORAH in the damaged Temple. She advised the King of Judah to continue in obedience and humility (II Kings 22:14–20).

Humanae Vitae *Christianity*   The ENCYCLICAL issued by the Pope in 1968 which affirmed the traditional opposition of the Roman Catholic Church to abortion and all contraception except for the rhythm method. It came after the more liberalizing influence of the changes brought about in VATICAN COUNCIL II and in spite of a special commission that had advocated a change of position. As a result, thousands left the priesthood and religious orders.

Humility *Christianity*   Humility is perceived as being an aspect of God's nature, in that being all-powerful he still partakes in creation. The greatest act of humility in Christianity is God incarnating as Jesus Christ and suffering the humiliation of CRUCIFIXION. Paul suggests that humility was practised by Jesus Christ and culminated in his eventual victory over death and ascension to the right hand of God. There is a sense throughout both the OLD and NEW TESTAMENTS that tribulations or trials are sent to provide the opportunity to develop humility. As a virtue it is considered essential for progress in spiritual life, and Paul warns Christians to look out for those who put on false humility. (*See also* SEVEN VIRTUES)

Huppah / Chuppah   *Judaism*   The canopy that forms a sacred space under which the bride and groom stand surrounded by both parents and the rabbi during a Jewish wedding. The basic form of the *huppah* is a canopy supported on four poles. Some are very simple, while others can be highly decorated. (*See* KETUBAH; YIHUD)

Husain (d.680)   *Islam*   The grandson of Muhammad, son of ALI and FATIMA and brother of HASAN. He is regarded by SHI'A Muslims as the third Imam and the fourth rightful leader of the Muslim community. The Shi'a believe that when Mu'awiyah achieved the leadership of the Muslim community and established the UMAYYAD dynasty, he promised that on his death he would return the leadership of the community to Ali's children, Hasan and Husain. When Yazid succeeded to his father's throne, Husain led around 600 loyal followers to Damascus to claim the rightful leadership of the Muslim community. They were met by Yazid's army at Kerbala in Iraq and slaughtered. The martyrdom of the grandson of Muhammad is commemorated on the annual occasion of MOHAR-RAM. Husain is regarded as the greatest of martyrs and has a redemptive role in Shi'a theology.

Hymns   *Christianity*   The Greek word *hymnos* is used for any song that praises a god or hero, but in Christianity it has come to denote religious poetry set to music that forms a key part of communal worship. However, the practice is an ancient one, and the New Testament records examples of the first Christians singing as an expression of spontaneous joy in their experience of salvation. (*See* PSALMS)

I

Ibadah   *Islam*   Muslim acts of worship or permissible actions performed with the intention to please Allah, as they form part of His divine law. The ideal of *ibadah* would be to obey Allah's will in all realms of life. The word is derived from ABD (servant, slave) and denotes one whose attitude towards Allah is that of a servant or slave, maintained through worship.

Iblis   *Islam*   The JINN (sometimes described as an angel) who disobeyed Allah by refusing to bow to Adam after his creation. He later becomes the tempter of all human beings until the final Day of Judgement. Iblis also exemplifies the dangers of the sin of pride.

Ibrahim   *Islam*   The Arabic form of Abraham. He is regarded as the exemplary Muslim and a prophet of God. Muhammad presented his early Muslim followers with a religion that was regarded as a return to the pure monotheism of Ibrahim, and thus disassociated the fledgling community from the Jews or Christians. The Qur'an describes Ibrahim as an UMMA (Godly community) by himself, as Allah made a covenant with him as an individual rather than a religious community. He is believed to be the father of three religions, which were granted as a reward for the surrender and piety he exemplified in his willingness to sacrifice his son ISHMAEL. He is also believed to be the founder of the KA'ABA in MAKKAH. (*See also* HAJAR; HAJJ)

Ichthys *(Greek: fish)*   *Christianity*   In Greek, the letters of the word for fish are the initials of Jesus Christ, Son of God, Saviour. In the early church, the fish was used as a symbol of Christianity, sometimes even as a secret communication of belonging for Christians who were being persecuted. (*See* FISH)

Icon   *Christianity*   One-dimensional paintings and mosaics of Jesus Christ, Mary or the Christian saints used in the Eastern Orthodox churches as an aid for devotion or a window to the divine. Believed to contain the presence of the divine, they are used at all the important events of human life or rites of passage. (*See* ICONOSTASIS)

Iconostasis *Christianity*   A screen covered in icons and containing two doors used to separate the ALTAR from the NAVE in Eastern churches. The screen functions to divide the PRIESTS from the laity during the LITURGY or celebration of Communion.

Id / Eid *Islam*   The two religious festivals or feasts to thank Allah. The two Ids are celebrated at the end of RAMADAN and near the completion of the HAJJ. (*See* ID AL-ADHA; ID AL-FITR)

Id al-Adha / Eid al-Adha / Id al-Kabir *(The Feast of Sacrifice)*   *Islam*   It is observed near to the completion of the HAJJ on the day when pilgrims to MAKKAH offer their sacrifice of goats in the valley of MINA. The sacrifice remembers IBRAHIM's willingness to offer his son ISHMAEL to Allah. It is sometimes known as the greater Id.

Id al-Fitr / Eid al-Fitr / Id al-Saghir *Islam*   The festival that marks the completion of the RAMADAN month of fasting. It is celebrated on the first day of the Muslim month Shawal, the tenth month of the year, and begins with the first sighting of the new moon. It is also known as the lesser Id, although it is celebrated with more verve than the ID AL-ADHA. It is a joyous occasion after a long fast, and gifts and cards are exchanged. It has sometimes been known as Bairam, after the practice of giving away sweetmeats to fellow Muslims and family members.

Id Mubarak *Islam*   See EID MUBARAK.

Ihram *Islam*   The state or condition of purity required to perform the HAJJ, when many actions normally permitted to Muslims are no longer allowed. It is also used to describe the two pieces of plain cotton cloth that are worn by male pilgrims to indicate the state of purity and equality that they share with each other. Women are expected to wear their normal modest clothing.

Ihsan *Islam*   The ideal condition of a Muslim in prayer. It is explained in a HADITH attributed to Muhammad that a Muslim in prayer should exhibit a mental state that reflects the condition that the supplicant would experience if God was to appear before him. If such a condition is not possible, the Muslim should at least be aware that God sees the supplicant in front of Him. (*See also* TAQWA)

Ijma *Islam* The consensus of the community on a matter of law or practice. It is one of the four ways of arriving at a correct judgement concerning application of the revelation to new matters. The decision is arrived at by a consensus of scholars. After the death of Muhammad, a vast body of material was published relating to the QUR'AN and the practice of the Prophet. When the UMAYYAD rulers assigned the task of legislation to acknowledged religious leaders, they realized that there was already in existence a large body of agreed practice. This was drawn upon in subsequent attempts at analogical reasoning to interpret correct practice in new situations. *Ijma* was perceived to be authoritative, and even infallible, to the degree that it actually defined right interpretation of the Qur'an and the SUNNA of the Prophet. This was based on a saying attributed to the Prophet: 'my community will never agree on an error'. (*See also* IJTIHAD; QIYAS; SHARI'A)

Ijtihad *Islam* An individual initiative by a qualified scholar to develop a response to a new situation by going directly to the QUR'AN and HADITH rather than to the existent body of law or FIQH. Although practised in the early years after the death of Muhammad, *ijtihad* was considered to be defunct or unreliable after the establishment of a body of law (*fiqh*) created largely on the authority of IJMA and QIYAS. The orthodox ULAMA declared the door of *ijtihad* to be closed. A limited form of *ijtihad* was allowed, in that scholars could interpret laws already existing in their own school. Some rare scholars, such as Ibn Taimiyya and Shah WALIALLAH, maintained the right of *ijtihad*. In the contemporary Muslim world there is considerable debate over *ijtihad*, as a variety of modernist and revivalist thinkers have declared their right to perform the task. (*See also* SHARI'A)

Ijtihad-nabawi *Islam* The capacity of Muhammad to resolve problems that were not discussed in the Qur'an. It is believed by Muslims that the prophetic intelligence is endowed with wisdom and is of a greater capacity than ordinary human intelligence. (*See* IJTIHAD)

Ik *(One)* *Sikhism* It usually symbolizes the oneness of God or the one supreme reality which exists in all things. (*See* IK ONKAR)

Ik Onkar / Ik Omkar *(One Being Is)* *Sikhism* The opening line of the MOOL MANTAR attributed to GURU NANAK, the founder of Sikhism, and first line of the GURU GRANTH SAHIB. It is an affirmation that 'God is One' and is often used as a symbol to decorate religious objects.

Ikhwan, al-Muslimun *Islam* Popularly known as the Muslim Brotherhood, Ikhwan was founded in Egypt in 1928 by Hasan al-Banna. The movement was created to implement al-Banna's analysis of the situation of Muslims in Egypt. Al-Banna believed that the problems facing Egyptian society were caused by: i) the failure of the ULAMA to provide guidance for Muslims that offered a viable alternative to Western values; ii) the corruption of the divided political establishment and their nominal allegiance to Islam; iii) the encroachment on the Muslim world that was not only materialistic but also led to a subsequent loss of spiritual values. The movement was dedicated to the creation of an Islamic state, providing an example of true Muslim morality and creating a broad-based welfare programme as an alternative to the government in the areas of education, health and social services. (*See also* BANNA, HASAN AL-; JAMAAT-I ISLAMI; MAWDUDI, MAULANA)

Imago Dei *(Latin: image of God) Christianity*   The doctrine that human beings are created in the image of God as recounted in Genesis. The early church fathers tended to interpret this as the potential of human beings, through reason and grace, to stand above the rest of creation in their relationship to God.

Imam   *Islam*   In the SUNNI tradition of Islam, the title simply refers to one who leads the public prayers in the mosque. Such a person is usually an ALIM who has completed full religious education in a MADRASA, but in the absence of a qualified *imam*, the eldest or most pious member of the community is called upon. Sometimes the title is conferred upon the founders of the four schools of law as an honorific. However, in the SHI'A tradition, the title of *imam* carries far more mystical and temporal weight, as it is given to the Prophet's successors through the line of ALI and FATIMA, who are the spiritual leaders of the Shi'a community. They are believed to share in the Prophet's knowledge of the Unseen and to be the only correct interpreters of the inner meaning of the QUR'AN. There are two main branches of Shi'a. The larger are the Ithna'ashariyya, who acknowledge twelve *imams*, while the smaller group is the ISHMAELIS, who acknowledge seven. The final *imam* in each group is believed to have been taken to a special place by Allah until the final Day of Judgement and is represented in Shi'a by AYATOLLAHS. (*See also* HASAN; HUSAIN)

Imam khatib   *Islam*   The title used to differentiate an IMAM, who leads the prayers, from one who is a qualified ALIM. (*See also* IMAM RHATIB)

Imam rhatib   *Islam*   A qualified IMAM who is able to preach and instruct as well as lead the prayers. He will be an ALIM who has completed an eight-year course in a MADRASA. (*See also* IMAM KHATIB)

Imamah   *Islam*   The office and function of the IMAM in the SHI'A tradition.

Iman *(faith)* *Islam*   An essential component of being a MU'MIN (believer). It refers also to the activity of belief which is necessary to follow the DIN or the path of revelation. Muslim theologians identified three aspects of *iman*: the heart had to accept the articles of the faith; the lips must utter the SHAHADAH and give vocal witness to the faith; and the limbs should perform the activities of the faith, such as the five-times obligatory prayer. (*See also* ISLAM; SHIRK)

Imitation of Christ *Christianity*   The doctrine that Jesus Christ was not only the means of salvation through his death and resurrection but also the perfect exemplar of, or paradigm for, the redeemed life. The medieval writer and mystic Thomas à Kempis' work *Imitation of Christ* provides an example of the view that the Christian should use Christ as an example of the ideal relationship between a human being and God.

Immaculate Conception *Christianity*   The doctrine that MARY, the mother of Jesus, was free from sin at her conception and remained so throughout her life. It was championed by Duns Scotus (1265–1308) and had become the dominant doctrine by the end of the Middle Ages. The position is still maintained by Roman Catholicism but was discarded by the Protestant reformers. (*See also* VIRGIN BIRTH)

Immersion *Christianity*   A method of BAPTISM where the candidate is partially or completely immersed in water and in which water is poured over the head. Generally, this form of baptism takes place in Protestant denominations that insist upon a method of adult baptism that resembles as closely as possible the method employed by JOHN THE BAPTIST with Jesus. Eastern Orthodox traditions also immerse babies. (*See also* BAPTISTS; INFANT BAPTISM)

Impediment *Christianity*   A legal or moral obstacle standing in the way of Christian marriage. Normally, the priest will ask the guests attending the wedding if they know of any just cause as to why the union of the man and woman cannot take place. (*See* CANON LAW)

Incarnation *Christianity*   The doctrine that God became human in the form of Jesus Christ. Although the theological term 'incarnation' does not appear in the Bible, several of the NEW TESTAMENT writers indicate that the belief in Christ as the incarnate Son of God was already developed. For example, St Paul argues that God sent His Son 'in the likeness of sinful flesh' (Romans 8:3). Although the New Testament is clear that the birth, life and death of Jesus were entirely human events, in some way God never ceased to be God although fully manifested as a human being. Thus, Christian orthodoxy asserts that the historical Jesus is at once fully human and fully divine. (*See also* ATONEMENT; CHRISTOLOGY; LOGOS)

Incumbent *Christianity*   The term used in the Church of England for the member of the clergy in charge of a PARISH. (*See also* VICAR)

Indra *Hinduism*   The sky- and storm-god of the early Vedic period and the most important of the old Vedic gods, he later declined in importance. However, by the time of the RIG VEDA he had become the great warrior-god of the ARYAN civilization. He is closely associated with SOMA, the unknown drug of Vedic ritual. Indra is the ideal of the fighting hero, the KSHATRIYA, and a king by virtue of his might of conquest. Although king of the gods in the Rig Veda period, he has now declined in importance to the position of god of rain and his place in the Hindu pantheon has been supplanted by VISHNU.

Indulgences / Pardon *Christianity*   The authority of the Roman Catholic Church to provide remission of the temporal punishment for SINS either in this life or PURGATORY. There has been much controversy over the practice of selling indulgences and this was one of the causes of LUTHER's dissatisfaction with the Roman Catholic Church. While it is certainly the case that donations were originally given to good causes by grateful pentitents, the system was also open to abuse, allowing penitents to believe that they could buy indulgence from their sins and therefore avoid divine punishment. (*See also* ABSOLUTION; CONFESSION)

Infallibility *Christianity*   The Roman Catholic doctrine that in certain situations the church or the POPE cannot make errors in teaching revealed truth. Since 1870, the Pope has been considered infallible when defining a doctrine on faith or morality. (*See also* VATICAN COUNCIL I)

Infant baptism *Christianity*   Although not clearly mentioned in the New Testament, there is also no condemnation of the practice. Since at least the third century, children of Christians have been baptized in infancy. However, although the practice was widespread, there was opposition: for example, from Tertullian, who argued that the new Christian should be old enough to know Christ. Counter-arguments stated that redemption must be available for all, including children. It is also possible that it replaced the Jewish ritual of circumcision as a rite of passage for young Christians. There is still controversy over infant baptism. The main arguments for the practice state that it remits the guilt of ORIGINAL SIN and provides affirmation of membership of the Christian community, which is built upon a covenant between God and His church. The main argument against the practice was strengthened after the Reformation and maintains that BAPTISM should only occur after recognition has taken place that redemption is required through the grace and mercy of Jesus Christ. (*See also* CONFIRMATION; IMMERSION)

Injil *Islam*   The term used in the QUR'AN for the Gospels or the book of revelation given to the Prophet (Jesus). However, it is believed that an original book was given to Jesus as revelation in the same manner as the Qur'an was given to Muhammad. This book has been lost and the four gospels of the Christian New Testament are, at best, attempts to re-create it. Since they have been reinterpreted by human inspiration rather than the direct words of God, they are not to be completely trusted. (*See also* ISA)

Inquisition *Christianity*   A permanent institution established for the persecution of HERESY by specially convened ecclesiastical courts. It was introduced in 1232 by Pope Gregory IX and finally suppressed in 1820. The task of rooting out heresy and trying the heretics was entrusted to the DOMINICAN order, who set up their own courts virtually independent from any local church authority, the proceedings of which were shrouded in secrecy. Those heretics who recanted were given a PENANCE to perform, while those who refused to admit their guilt were handed over to the secular authorities, where they were usually burned to death at the stake.

Insan al-kamil *(the perfect man)* *Islam*   Ibn Arabi developed the theosophy of the perfect man as embodied in the figure of Muhammad. The Prophet becomes the original creation which God uses as a mirror in order to admire Himself. This is achieved by the purity and sinlessness of the Prophet's heart. Muhammad is the bridge between the divine world and creation, and the divine attributes and names of Allah are reflected perfectly in his being and actions. In this role, the Prophet becomes the perfect model for Muslims, particularly in the SUFI tradition, where devout adherents use Muhammad as the role model of the perfect mystic. (*See also* ARABI, MUHIY'UD-DIN IBN; HAQIQA MUHAMMADIYA)

Iqama / Iqamah *Islam*   The call given in the mosque by the IMAM that instructs the gathered congregation to stand up for SALAH or the five-times daily communal prayer.

Iqra *(recite or read)* *Islam*   The first commandment of the angel JIBRIL to Muhammad, thus beginning the revelation of the QUR'AN. The important point here is that the Qur'an was revealed and recited by the Prophet rather than written by him. Tradition states that Muhammad replied, 'I do not read' or according to the translation, 'What shall I recite?'

Irya samiti *Jainism*   Care in walking observed by Jain monks to ensure that they do no harm to living creatures. This would involve taking steps to avoid small insects and damaging living plants. It is one of the five 'carefulnesses' (SAMITI) that help Jain monks avoid an influx of KARMA. (*See also* AHIMSA)

Isa *Islam*   The Arabic form of the name of Jesus, who is highly regarded as a prophet of Allah, who immediately preceded Muhammad and who the Qur'an describes as a Sign of Allah. Such an appellation is only given to Isa and the creation. It is considered that just as creation is able to remind the discerning of the existence and glory of Allah, so Isa, in his life, speech and presence, had a similar impact on those who met him. It is believed that Isa brought the revelation to the Jewish people to remind them of their chosenness and to restore the heart to the law of Moses that was by then corrupted and dry. In the SUFI tradition, Isa has great status as a mystic and a practitioner of the TARIQAH. Muslims believe in the virgin birth but do not accept that the Prophet of God would have endured such an ignominious death as crucifixion, believing instead that a semblance was crucified through God's intervention. (*See also* RASUL)

Isaac *Judaism*   One of the first Jewish patriarchs and the son of ABRAHAM, who according to the Hebrew scriptures was offered to God in sacrifice as a test of his father's submission. Isaac is seen as the ideal of Judaism, in that he was willing to offer himself as a sacrifice. The binding of Isaac (AKEDAH), as described in Genesis 22:1–15, is celebrated by Jews on the eve of the feast of ROSH HASHANAH.

Isaiah *Judaism*   One of the most important prophets and a book of the same name in the Hebrew scriptures. He may have been a member of the royal family and prophesied during the reigns of Jotham, Ahaz and Hezekiah. It is believed by the biblical authorities in Judaism that the utterances of Isaiah were written down and edited by Hezekiah and his scribes. Isaiah's prophecies outspokenly criticized the people for their religious hypocrisy, poor moral standards, oppression of the poor and corruption amongst their leaders. He warns of divine punishment, but indicates that a remnant of the people will uphold the truth. (*See* NEVIIM)

Isha / Salat al-'Isha *Islam*   The evening prayer, and the last of the five obligatory prayers that constitute SALAH, which may be performed from just over an hour after sunset up until midnight. (*See also* ASR; FAJR; MAGHRIB; ZUHR)

Isha Upanishad *Hinduism*   One of the collections of UPANISHADS and famous for its statement that the whole world is pervaded by BRAHMAN. The Isha Upanishad was a great favourite of Mahatma GANDHI, who claimed that he based his life on its first verse: 'All this whatsoever moves on earth, is pervaded by the Lord. When you have renounced this, then you may enjoy. Do not covet the wealth of anyone.'

Ishmael / Isma'il / Isamail *Islam*   The son of IBRAHIM and HAJAR and a prophet of Allah. He is believed to be the father of the Arab people and was miraculously shown the site of the ZAMZAM spring when stranded in the desert with his mother. He is therefore attributed with founding the city of MAKKAH. According to the Qur'an, he helped his father build the KA'ABA and placed the black stone within it. Muslims believe that it was Ishmael, not ISAAC, who was prepared for sacrifice by Ibrahim.

Ishmaeli / Ishmaili / Ishma'ili *Islam*   A branch of SHI'A sometimes known as the Seveners because they believe that the seventh IMAM was the last and the greatest. The Ishmaelis were the first major division of Shi'a concerned with a difference over leadership. The main group accepted Musa, the son of the sixth imam, Ja'far (d.765), while a breakaway group disputed the new leadership and supported the elder son, Ishmael, who was alleged to have drunk wine. It is Ishmael who, it is believed, will one day return as the MAHDI. From the ninth to the eleventh century, the Ishmaelis were strong throughout the Muslim world and established the FATIMID dynasty in Egypt. Nowadays, they are found predominantly in the Indian subcontinent and central Asia. The Ishmaelis combine traditional Shi'a belief and practice with a theosophy based on esoteric interpretation of the Qur'an which is highly influenced by emanationist theories deriving from Neoplatonism. The Ishmaelis also differ from SUNNI and other Shi'a Muslims in that they do not accept the finality of Muhammad as a prophet. The Ishmaelis are divided into two: the Musta'lis, led by Muhammad Burhan al-Din in Bombay, and the Nizaris, led by the Aga Khan.

Ishvara *Hinduism*   See ISVARA.

ISKCON *Hinduism*   The International Society for Krishna Consciousness, founded by Swami Bhaktivedanta Prabhupada in the late 1960s. Although first perceived as a bizarre hippy cult, the HARE KRISHNA movement, as it is more popularly known, has now achieved worldwide respectability in the Hindu community. The movement, although comprising predominantly white converts, has its roots in GAUDIYA VAISHNAVISM, a medieval Krishna BHAKTI movement established in Bengal. The most famous proponent and claimed founder of the movement is CAITANYA MAHAPRABHU. Today ISKCON is a respected part of Hindu tradition and supported by thousands of Hindu migrants, who respect the way of life of the devotees and their strict adherence to Vedic ritual ceremonies. Although ISKCON devotees remain a presence on the streets of British cities, singing KIRTAN and selling their publications, they are now accepted as part of contemporary Western culture and rarely attract the attention of the anti-cult movements or the media. Today the ISKCON movement is a prolific publisher and closely involved in educational activities to promote Hinduism.

Islah *(reform)* *Islam*   A concept often drawn upon by revivalist movements in the twentieth century and a term used in the Qur'an to describe the preaching of prophets who warn people of the need to return to God's ways. *Islah* is defined as the effort to maintain the purity of the faith by increasing the righteousness of the people through various activities. (*See* DA'WA; TAJDID)

Islam *Islam*   The religious teaching, practice, faith and obedience to Allah based on the revelation of the QUR'AN and exemplified in the character and behaviour of the final Prophet Muhammad. Islam also means the state of submission or surrender to the divine best achieved through practice of the above, although it conceded in the historical tradition founded under Muhammad that there were always individuals who had attained to the state of Islam prior to the final revelation. The epitome of this state of surrender would have been the prophet IBRAHIM. (*See also* AHL AL-KITAB; HANIF)

Isma *Islam*   The doctrine that Muhammad was protected from sin and error. Although not found in the earliest records of the faith or reflected in the HADITH, where the Prophet is often recorded as praying for the forgiveness of his sins, later Muslim commentators began to develop the theology of sinlessness. It is generally accepted that absolute obedience to the Prophet can only be viable if Muhammad was free from any faults himself and thus able to provide an immaculate model. (*See also* INSAN AL-KAMIL)

Isma'il *Islam*   See ISHMAEL.

Isnad *Islam*   The important chain of transmission that authenticates the HADITH by tracing them back through a line of authorities who heard the saying to a companion of the Prophet who would have heard it from Muhammad himself. The shorter the chain, the more authentic the Hadith. In the eighth and ninth centuries, it became essential to authenticate the millions of sayings that existed in the Muslim world. Various scholars collected and collated the Hadith and attributed a chain to each one. Indisputable chains are considered the mark of authenticity. Each Hadith is written with its chain.

Israel / Yisreal *(one who struggles with God)* *Judaism*   It refers to the worldwide community of Jews or the land of Israel. It is also the name of the modern Jewish state that was founded in 1948. The worldwide community of Jews represents the totality of Israel, and it is to this people that the TORAH, or law of God, was given in the covenant accepted by MOSES and the Jewish people. The land of Israel was promised to Moses and his people and is regarded as the Holy Land. The site of the Temple, it is the land where all the prophets and patriarchs lived and taught and the location of Jerusalem. Whenever the Jewish

people have lost land through conquest or invasion, they have regarded themselves as exiles and developed religious traditions and practices to maintain the
ideal of Israel in their hearts and minds. They have always prayed for a return to
the land and the messianic ideal of Judaism is bound up with the return of Israel.
Even after the destruction of the Second Temple by the Romans and the
consequent dispersion of the people, some Jews always remained in Jerusalem,
while the city of Safat in GALILEE was a great centre of KABBALAH. During the
persecution of Jews in Eastern Europe and Germany, the Zionist movement
campaigned for and finally achieved the return of Israel. The return of the Holy
Land to the Jews has been a source of conflict ever since with the Muslim world,
and is further complicated by the fact that Jerusalem is holy to three world
religions: Judaism, Christianity and Islam. Tensions also exist within the Jewish
community amongst the orthodox movements, as many of them do not accept
the idea of a modern secular state of Israel but look to a return of the religious
state and the coming of the Messiah. (*See also* BERIT; MASSIACH; ZIONISM)

Isru Chag *(to bind the festival)* *Judaism*   The day that follows directly after the
feasts of PESACH, SHAVUOT and SUKKOT.

Ista devata *Hinduism*   The personal god picked by the individual from the
Hindu pantheon as his/her chosen deity. Individual worship will be offered to
this deity daily and the devout lay Hindu would repeat the name of this deity
each morning before uttering any other word. (*See* MURTI)

Istafta *Islam*   Legal queries concerned with problems that involve a decision
being made on a point of religious law. These are made by members of the
ULAMA on the basis of their knowledge of FIQH (jurisprudence). Some Muslims
have claimed the right to independent reasoning, but this remains rare. (*See also*
IJTIHAD; MUJTAHID)

Istighatha *Islam*   A form of TAWASSUL where the Muslim supplicant seeks
assistance from the Prophet usually by calling for his intercession. (*See also* DU'A;
SHAFA'A)

Istihsan *Islam*   A category of independent reasoning (IJTIHAD) in which the
MUJTAHID considered a certain course of action to be good and therefore
permissible. (*See also* FIQH; ISTISHAB; ISTISLAH)

Istishab *Islam*   A category of independent reasoning (IJTIHAD) in which the
MUJTAHID considered a certain course of action to be permissible by the use of
analogy that linked it back to a provision in the QUR'AN or HADITH. (*See also*
FIQH; ISTIHSAN; ISTISLAH)

Istislah *Islam* A category of independent reasoning (IJTIHAD) in which the MUJTAHID considered a certain course of action to be permissible by deeming that it was beneficial for the public good. (*See also* FIQH; ISTIHSAN; ISTISHAB)

Istisqa *Islam* A special prayer for rain in times of drought used particularly by oriental Muslim nations in the subcontinent. It is believed that Muhammad himself was the first to pray successfully for rain and the prayer is thought to be the same one that he used. (*See* DU'A)

Isvara / Ishvara / Iswara *Hinduism* Usually translated as the Lord or master, *isvara* refers to the various personal forms of God worshipped by a devotee in the BHAKTI tradition as opposed to the impersonal BRAHMAN. SHANKARA, the founder of ADVAITA VEDANTA, considered the *isvara* to be a manifestation of the cosmic impersonal Brahman who creates, sustains and destroys the universe. It is this god who is worshipped by the devotee through ritual action but who, at the end of creation, returns into the formless Brahman. This emanationist theory of *isvara* is denied by RAMANUJA, the great proponent of VAISHNAVA, who claims that *isvara* and Brahman are one and the same being. In some Vaishnavite traditions, the form of the personal *isvara* is the ultimate being. The formless God exists as an emanation of the ultimate form. This position reveres that of Shankara.

Itihasa Purana *Hinduism* The two great epics, the MAHABHARATA and the RAMAYANA, are collectively known as Itihasa Purana. It can be argued that these two SMRITI texts have had far more influence on popular Hinduism than the Vedic texts.

Itikaf *Islam* A retreat maintained by the pious in the mosque during the last ten days of RAMADAN. It consists of a small tent-like enclosure of white sheeting wrapped around four poles. The individual Muslim performing the retreat will enter usually with a copy of the Qur'an and remain there until re-emerging to join the congregation for the five ritual prayers. The most auspicious place to perform *itikaf* is the first mosque in MADINAH established by Muhammad.

Ivrit / Lashon ha-kodesh *Judaism* The Hebrew language in which the scriptures are written, it is used in the Orthodox synagogue services and Jewish prayer. Traditionally, young Jews would study Hebrew in order to understand their religion. While the language has been restored to everyday use in ISRAEL, many religious Jews will still only use it for sacred purposes.

Izzat (U) *Islam*   The concept of honour or family pride. *Izzat* functions as an eclectic mixture of Islamic codes and local customs which the family members are expected to observe. Non-observance leads to disgrace for the individual and the family.

Jabr *(predestination)*   Islam   There was considerable debate among various groups after Muhammad's death concerning the issue of predestination and free will. The overriding mood in Islam is towards predestination, as it is difficult to promote free will alongside Allah's omnipotence and omniscience. However, the early Muslims were aware of the tension between God's omnipotence and human moral responsibility. Al-Ashari resolved the issue by declaring that while the power to act belonged to God, the specific choice of action belonged to human beings. (*See* ASHARI, ABU'L HASAN AL-; QADAR)

Jacob   *Judaism*   One of the first Jewish patriarchs, the son of ISAAC and the father of JONAH, who had been forced to flee from his brother ESAU. Jacob represents the balance between mercy and judgement.

Jagannath / Jagannatha / Jagganath   *Hinduism*   A form of KRISHNA worshipped in the famous temple in Puri, Orissa. Every year Jagannath is paraded in a huge processional carriage around the town. The MURTI is accompanied by elephants, holy men and horses as it is taken through the streets. Although a regional festival, it has become famous throughout the whole of India.

Jagat   *Hinduism*   The cosmos of moving beings or creatures engaged in action. It is usually used to refer to the world of human beings, but actually includes the wider universe incorporated in the concept of SAMSARA.

Jahiliya / Jahiliyya / Jahiliyah / Jahiliyyah *(a time of ignorance)*   Islam
The time of ignorance first used to describe pre-Islamic Arabia, especially the pagan culture of the tribes and the greed of the polytheistic merchants in MAKKAH. The concept of *jahiliya* as an infidel, godless society is sometimes extended to describe the non-Muslim world. Used by various modern revivalist movements to describe the West, it provides a justification for JIHAD and DA'WA activities.

Jaina *Jainism* One who follows the teachings of a JINA, or liberated being, in order to achieve liberation of the soul from its bondage to matter. It particularly refers to the follower of the teachings of MAHAVIR and is therefore the correct appellation for a Jain.

Jalal *(majesty)* *Islam* One of the two complementary aspects or attributes of Allah and one of the ninety-nine divine names. The other is JAMAL (beauty). It is the interplay of these two that keeps the universe in motion and maintains the flow of created life. Muhammad is believed by many traditional Muslims to have been endowed with both *Jalal* and *Jamal*. *Jalal* has been compared with Rudolf Otto's idea of the *tremendum* aspect of the divine.

Jamaat / Jami'at / Jamiyat *(The Party of God)* *Islam* An Islamic group committed to DA'WA activities to promote the correct practice of Islam in the Muslim world. In this respect, the term has a modern usage, but originally was used by Muhammad to describe the complete body of Muslims *(jamaat al-Muslimin)* or the totality of the body politic. (*See also* IKHWAN, AL-MUSLIMUN; JAMAAT-I ISLAMI; TABLIGH-I JAMAAT)

Jamaat-i Islami *Islam* A movement founded in 1941 by Maulana MAWDUDI (1904–80) to provide youth with instruction in Islam. The Jamaat-i Islami was created to establish Mawdudi's vision of an Islamic state in Pakistan. Although it never achieved mass support, especially in rural areas, its organizational ability and attraction of the urban middle classes provided it with enough influence to impact on various governments. The Jamaat-i Islami is essentially anti-clerical and recruits extensively from the universities of the subcontinent. They provide a similar model of organization and ideological belief to the IKHWAN in Egypt founded by Hasan al-Banna. (*See also* BANNA, HASAN AL-)

Jamaat-khana *Islam* A gathering of disciples meeting with their SHAIKH to perform DHIKR (remembrance of Allah) or listening to him preach. It would usually take place inside the dwelling place of the shaikh and his family. (*See also* DAR; TARIQAH)

Jamadut *Sikhism* A term used for the angels or receivers of the dead. Sikhism accepted the wheel of transmigration, but it was also influenced by Islam. The idea of angels of death instead of the Hindu concept of Dharmraj, or judge of KARMA, may have come from Islam.

Jamal *(beauty)* *Islam* One of the two complementary aspects or attributes of Allah and one of the ninety-nine divine names. The other is JALAL (majesty). It is the interplay of these two that keeps the universe in motion and maintains the flow of created life. Muhammad is believed by many traditional Muslims to have been endowed with both *Jalal* and *Jamal*. *Jamal* has been compared with Rudolf Otto's idea of the *fascinans* aspect of the divine.

Jamapuri   *Sikhism*   The city of the dead or the place where souls are taken while awaiting rebirth. Sikhism does not place the same emphasis on rebirth as Hinduism, as it focuses on salvation or liberation through the teachings of the gurus. However, popular or village Sikhism has many beliefs or superstitions concerning the afterlife.

James, Epistle of   *Christianity*   A book of the New Testament written as a letter to the churches concerning moral matters. Traditionally, its authorship, although disputed, is ascribed to JAMES, the brother of Jesus, who was the leader of the early church in Jerusalem. With the emphasis on moral and ethical matters, the author seems to be asserting the doctrine of JUSTIFICATION through works rather than the Pauline position of justification through faith. This has led to the epistle being used as part of the doctrinal struggle between Roman Catholicism and Protestantism. LUTHER, for example, devalued the writings, whereas Roman Catholicism has always used the contents to support justification by works, personal confession and the sacrament of unction.

James, St   *Christianity*   The brother of Jesus Christ and the first leader of the Jewish Christian church in Jerusalem. It is generally believed that he did not accept Jesus' authority until receiving a vision of the risen Christ after the RESURRECTION. James presided over the Council of Jerusalem, which debated with PAUL the issue of allowing GENTILES to become Christians. He worked to maintain unity with Paul and was finally martyred by stoning in 61 CE. (*See also* JAMES, ST (THE GREAT); JAMES, ST (THE LESS))

James, St (the Great)   *Christianity*   One of the original twelve APOSTLES chosen by Jesus Christ as companions and missionaries. He was the elder brother of St John and the son of Zebedee, a Galilean fisherman. The two brothers were nicknamed 'sons of thunder' by Jesus and, along with Peter, formed the privileged band allowed to witness the TRANSFIGURATION and the agony of Jesus in the garden of GETHSEMANE. (*See also* JAMES, ST; JAMES, ST (THE LESS); JOHN, ST; PETER, ST)

James, St (the Less)   *Christianity*   Also known as the 'younger'. One of the original twelve APOSTLES who were chosen by Jesus Christ as his companions and missionaries. He is known as 'the Less' to distinguish him from James, the brother of John. St Mark's Gospel indicates that he was the son of Alphaeus. (*See also* JAMES, ST; JAMES, ST (THE GREAT))

Jami'at / Jamiyat *Islam*   *See* JAMAAT.

Jamuna *Hinduism*   *See* YAMUNA)

Janak *Hinduism*   The famous king of Videha. Named as the father of SITA in the RAMAYANA, he also appears in the BRHADARANYAKA UPANISHAD as an enlightened monarch who questions the sage YAJNAVALKYA about the reality of BRAHMAN. In Indian popular religious stories he often represents perfect detachment from the world although living in its midst.

Janam Sakhi / Janamsakhi *(birth stories)* *Sikhism*   The hagiographic collection of stories of the lives of the gurus, particularly GURU NANAK. Written at various times after Guru Nanak's death, they recount a large number of supernatural occurrences and miracle stories. Sikhs themselves acknowledge that some Janam Sakhis are more reliable than others, although the scholar of Sikhism, McLeod, claimed that they tell us more about the condition of Sikhism at the time of their compilation than historic events in the life of Guru Nanak. According to Sikhs, the two most reliable accounts are the Janam Sakhi of Bhai Bala and Sewa Das.

Janeu *Hinduism*   The sacred thread that goes over one shoulder and across the chest. It is invested at the UPANAYANA ceremony, in which young males of the three highest VARNAS, believed to be 'twice-born', are initiated into adulthood and Hindu society. Recently a number of female activists have begun to initiate girls, claiming that this was the practice in early Vedic culture.

Janmashtami *Hinduism*   The festival that celebrates the birthday of KRISHNA.

Jap *Sikhism*   The silent remembrance of the name of God sometimes accompanied by counting beads on a rosary. The Sikh Gurus taught that remembrance of the name of God was the only way to salvation. (*See* SATNAM)

Japa *Hinduism*   The repetition of the name of God or a MANTRA (sacred formula) as a means to spiritual experience or as a devotional exercise. It can also be performed in silence as a meditation technique. (*See also* NAMAJAPA)

Japji *Sikhism*   The opening hymn or first chapter of the GURU GRANTH SAHIB, composed by GURU NANAK, which contains his basic teachings. The first lines of the *Japji* are the MOOL MANTAR, which contains the essence of the Guru's teaching. It has almost become the central creed of Sikhism. The *Japji* is used by Sikhs as their morning prayer to begin the day.

Jaramarana *Buddhism* Old age and death. The final link in the causal chain of existence which arises from JATI or birth. The Buddha left his palace to search for enlightenment after experiencing the shock of seeing old age, sickness and death. (*See also* NIDANAS; SAMSARA; SIDDATTHA GOTTAMA)

Jat *Sikhism* Although Sikhism is open to all, membership is made up of predominantly Jat Sikhs. First recruited by GURU RAM DAS, their numbers increased under the subsequent Gurus. The Jats were small landowners and peasants with a martial tradition whose strongholds were located in the Shivalik Hills in the northern Punjab. It has been suggested that the influx of Jats contributed to the martial ethos which developed under the later Gurus.

Jataka *(birth stories)* *Buddhism* A collection of 550 stories which form part of the THERAVADA canon of scripture. They consist of accounts of the previous lives of the Buddha and provide a heritage of both moral teaching and mythology.

Jathedar *Sikhism* The head of one of the five *takhts* who is authorized to issue religious edicts that are binding upon all Sikhs. (*See* HUKAM NAMA)

Jati *Buddhism* Birth and rebirth. The fate of all sentient beings caught in the cycle of SAMSARA. The Buddhist doctrine of rebirth differs from that of Hinduism, as there is no belief in an eternal ATMAN which reincarnates again and again in different bodies. It is KAMMA itself which drives the wheel. In the causal chain of existence, *jati* arises from BHAVA and leads to the final link of old age and death, or JARAMARANA. (*See also* KARMA; NIDANAS)

Jati *(birth)* *Hinduism* The complex hierarchical structure of Hindu society based on caste. Whereas Vedic society categorizes everybody into four VARNAS, the caste system further subdivides the Hindu population into countless *jatis* based on occupational purity and impurity. Although the system is based upon occupation, it is hereditary and maintained by endogamy and commensality. It is believed that the Hindu's caste status is actually a property of the body itself and received through KARMA and rebirth. Every Indian village will maintain several castes living in close proximity but separate, ranging from the BRAHMIN at the top to the untouchables at the bottom. (*See also* HARIJANS)

Jatra *Hinduism* Annual fairs or festivals to village deities, during which people make offerings and mark their foreheads with the holy ash kept near the shrine. The occasion is classed as a holiday, and includes wrestling competitions, magicians, fortune-tellers and the dramatization of well-known folk stories.

Jehovah's Witnesses *Christianity* A sect founded in the USA by Charles

T. Russell (1852–1916), also known as the Watch Tower Bible and Tract Society. They are best known for their door-to-door ministry and their beliefs concerning the near end of the world and the millennium, when it was believed that only an elect chosen from amongst the witnesses would become members of the messianic kingdom established after the physical resurrection of the dead. (*See* ADVENTISTS)

Jeremiah *Judaism*   An important prophet and book of the same name in the Hebrew scriptures. He was born near Jerusalem and prophesied in the reign of King Josiah until after the arrival of the Assyrians in 586 BCE and the destruction of the First Temple in Jerusalem. He was frequently imprisoned for condemning the priests for their idolatry and hypocrisy. He prophesied for over forty years and his utterances were maintained by his scribe, Baruch. (*See* NEVIIM)

Jerusalem *Christianity*   The ancient and modern capital of Israel and the location of the final short period of Christ's ministry and his subsequent arrest, trial, CRUCIFIXION and RESURRECTION. It was also the place where the disciples lived and taught immediately after the death of Christ and became the centre of the Jewish/Christian church under the leadership of James, the brother of Jesus Christ. The city was visited by St Helena, the wife of the Roman emperor, Constantine, in 326. She is believed to have identified all the places associated with Jesus' life and death by miraculous means. Since that time the city has been a famous Christian centre of pilgrimage. (*See also* JAMES, ST)

Jerusalem *Judaism*   See YERUSALEM.

Jesuit *Christianity*   The Society of Jesus founded by St Ignatius Loyola in 1534. Its intentions were to reform the Roman Catholic Church to answer Protestant criticisms and engage in missionary work in the recently discovered parts of the world. Members of the order take a vow of absolute obedience to the POPE. The order is famous for its intellectualism and missionary endeavours. Ignatius himself established missions in India, Japan, China, Ethiopia, Malaysia and Brazil. Although suppressed in Latin Europe during the eighteenth century, they were restored in 1814. Members of the order do not wear a distinctive habit and are exempt from reciting the office communally. (*See* LOYOLA, IGNATIUS; OFFICES, DIVINE)

Jesus Christ *Christianity*   The central figure of faith and devotion for all Christians, who was born shortly before the death of HEROD THE GREAT in 4 BCE and met his death by crucifixion somewhere close to 33 CE. Little is known about Jesus' life other than the accounts written in the four GOSPELS, which are generally concerned to present the Jesus of faith and focus on miracle stories, the events of his death and RESURRECTION and some teachings. The Gospels provide details of Jesus' birth and childhood, the beginning of his public ministry, including his baptism by JOHN THE BAPTIST, his temptation by SATAN whilst in retreat in the Judean desert and his move to GALILEE and recruiting of his first disciples. They then describe his teachings, miracles and his disputes with the Jewish religious leaders over the issue of traditional authority. Much of the Gospel narratives are concerned with the events leading up to the CRUCIFIXION in Jerusalem. Whatever the historical reality of the life and death of Jesus, he is regarded by the early followers of his message to be the incarnation of God, and this doctrine remains the bedrock upon which most Christian denominations found their faith. It is central to Christian belief that Jesus Christ was born as a divine sacrifice in order to provide the possibility of salvation to all human beings through his death and resurrection. He restores humanity from the fallen state induced by the ORIGINAL SIN of Adam and Eve. (*See also* CHRISTOLOGY)

Jesus Movement   *Christianity*   A collection of EVANGELICAL groups that emerged out of the spontaneity of alternative youth culture of the 1960s, especially in California. Sometimes known as 'Jesus People', they are known for their fervour, which combines spontaneity of worship and lifestyle with traditional morality and literalist interpretation of scripture. They are usually millenarian, influenced by Pentecostalism and distrustful of organized or institutional Christianity. They believe they are returning to the structures and faith of the first-generation Christians, who practised and built the church after the death of Christ. (*See also* PENTECOSTALISTS)

Jesus Prayer   *Christianity*   'Lord Jesus Christ, Son of the living God, have mercy upon me, a sinner'. A meditative prayer chanted in the Eastern Orthodox Church, sometimes in rhythm with the breath, and used as a mystical technique to achieve greater closeness to God. (*See* ORTHODOX)

Jethro   *Judaism*   The father-in-law of MOSES and priest of Midian, with whom Moses stayed whilst hiding in exile from Egypt after killing an Egyptian officer who had been mistreating some Jewish slaves.

Jew   *Judaism*   See YEHUDIM.

Jhana (P)   *Buddhism*   See DHYANA.

Jhatka *(a blow)*   *Sikhism*   Meat that is approved for Sikhs to eat. GURU GOBIND SINGH approved the eating of meat that had been killed by a single blow from a sword. HALAL meat, in which the animal has been slaughtered according to Muslim law, is forbidden to KHALSA Sikhs.

Jiania *Sikhism* The soul of human beings. Caught in delusion and unaware of its true nature as part of the divine, the human soul is under the influence of HAUMAI or false self-identity and needs to be purified by discovering the reality of God within the human heart. Through single-minded devotion and remembrance of God's true name, the Grace of God can lead it to the state of liberation through reunion. (*See also* JIVAN MUKT; SATGURU; SATNAM)

Jibril / Jibreel *(Gabriel)* *Islam* The angel who always appears to Allah's chosen prophets as the messenger of God. The revelation of the QU'RAN to Muhammad came through Jibril, and Miriam (Mary) received a visitation when told that she was about to give birth to ISA (Jesus).

Jihad *(striving)* *Islam* The term refers to the duty imposed upon every Muslim in the Qur'an to struggle against evil whilst walking the path of Allah. It is both the inner struggle against the manifestations of sin in oneself and the outer struggle to promote Islam and protect the faith against its enemies. In this latter context, jihad has often been interpreted as 'holy war' either against polytheists or Christians and Jews that threaten the security of Islam. A genuine jihad has to be defined carefully by criteria laid down in the SHARI'A and led by an IMAM or Muslim head of state. The main criteria are that it must be fought only to protect the faith and cannot be used for any lesser temporal motive. After returning from battle, Muhammad famously told his companions that 'this was the lesser jihad, I will now show you the greater jihad'. It was explained that the latter jihad constituted the battle against carnal desire and the purification of the inner being. The emphasis on the inner jihad has been mostly followed by the SUFIS. Some twentieth-century revivalist movements declared jihad to be the sixth pillar of Islam, usually emphasizing the duty of Muslims to struggle to promote their faith amongst lapsed members of the community and the apparent threat to Islamic values from the globalization of Western values. (*See also* JAHILIY; SHAHID)

Jijnasa *Hinduism* The constant search for spiritual knowledge (JNANA). *Jijnasa* is best expressed as the search for illumination or direct apprehension of ultimate reality.

Jina *(conqueror)* *Jainism* Someone who has achieved an exemplary spiritual victory over the conditions of existence. One who has conquered the self. Jains do not worship a creator God but meditate on the virtues of the *jinas* who have obtained liberation. *Jina* images are the main focus for Jain temple worship. The *jinas* are seen as an example of a human being who has attained perfection rather than as a divinity. They are always represented as meditating in either a sitting or standing position, while DIGAMBARA *jinas* are depicted as naked. By the first century CE, the Jain pantheon included twenty-four *jinas*, of which the most

177

commonly known are RISABHDEVA, Shantinatha, NEMINATHA, PARSHVANATHA and MAHAVIR. The lives of these *jinas* are told in the KALPA SUTRA, written around the third century BCE. (*See also* KEVALIN; TIRTHANKARA)

Jinakalpin *Jainism* A monk who faithfully follows the pattern of behaviour ascribed to MAHAVIR in order to achieve liberation. The term can also be used for the monk who adheres to nudity. These are rarely found outside of the DIGAMBARA sect.

Jinn / Djinn *Islam* A supernatural life-form that Allah created from fire, as opposed to humankind, who were created from earth. Tradition states that Muhammad was sent to preach to them, after which some became Muslims. It is even stated that Muhammad first believed that he was under attack by *jinn* when he received the first revelations of the QUR'AN. Many IMAMS are taught how to exorcize bad *jinns* during their training at the DAR AL-ULUM or religious schools. In village traditions, *jinn* are often blamed for mental and physical illnesses and misfortune.

Jiriki *('self' or 'own power')* *Buddhism* A term used by Pure Land sects to describe ZEN as the way to salvation using self-power or self-effort, as opposed to TARIKI or salvation through the intervention of an outside agency. The Pure Land schools of Buddhism believe that this age is so corrupt that it is impossible to achieve enlightenment without the assistance of the AMIDA Buddha.

Jiva *Jainism* A non-material and spiritual entity that has eternal existence either bound in matter through KARMA or liberated. The soul is always individual even after liberation, where it dwells in eternal freedom and bliss at the summit of the universe. The soul can be experienced by direct perception achieved through meditation and purification. The Jain tradition exists as a method to free the soul from its bondage to matter by purifying it of karma and preventing the karmic influx. In this way, the soul is returned to its original pure state and liberated. (*See also* KEVALIN)

Jiva-daya *Jainism* Mercy and compassion towards all living creatures, particularly expressed through animal welfare. Jain scriptures provide many teachings on the welfare of plants and animals as part of the all-encompassing doctrine of AHIMSA. Consequently, contemporary Jains manage animal sanctuaries throughout India and are foremost in ecological and environmental issues.

Jiva mukti *Hinduism* The state of having attained liberation whilst still alive. There is debate amongst various Hindu SAMPRADAYAS (sects) concerning whether this is actually possible, what is achieved and how it differs from liberation after death. Most later medieval BHAKTI and SANT traditions emphasized the attainment of *jiva mukti*. (*See also* MUKTI)

Jivan Mukt / Jivan Mukht   *Sikhism*   A spiritually enlightened person who is free from worldly attachment and identification with the ego. This is the ideal of Sikhism, which can only be achieved by grace and following the teachings of the guru.

Jivanamukti   *Jainism*   Liberation in this life. In Jainism it is possible to obtain omniscience whilst still in human form once all GHATI KARMA (obscuring or destructive karma) has been removed from the soul. Jain development of the soul is made up of fourteen stages, the last two being stages of omniscience, in which the soul is liberated from karmic influx. In the thirteenth stage the soul remains in human form engaged in activities that usually assist others in the pursuit of happiness and to lessen suffering. These souls are regarded as being liberated in this life even though the fourteenth and final stage will only occur after disembodiment. The final liberation of the soul takes place at death. (*See also* JINA; JIVA; KEVALIN; SIDDHA)

Jivatman   *Hinduism*   The individual self or soul that separates from the body at death but continues to exist through endless rebirths until liberation or union with BRAHMAN is achieved. *Jivatman* differs from ATMAN in that it contains elements of individual personality carried over by KARMA into rebirth. (*See also* MOKSHA)

Jizya   *Islam*   Islamic law indicates that a reasonable tax should be levied on *dhimmi* or 'people of the Book' within a Muslim nation in order to pay for defence and the administration of the state. Non-Muslims are required to pay ZAKAH and should be given complete religious, political and administrative freedom. (*See also* AHL AL-KITAB)

Jnana   *Hinduism*   Generally used to describe the knowledge or wisdom that comes from direct insight or experience of the divine or ultimate reality. However, the search for reality has developed into several sophisticated philosophies concerning the relationship between ATMAN, BRAHMAN and the world. *Jnana* is often used to describe the intellectual knowledge and understanding that arises from studying such systems. (*See also* JNANA YOGA)

Jnana   *Jainism*   Spiritual knowledge. This can be knowledge of the scriptures achieved through study, or direct perception of the soul achieved through meditation and asceticism.

Jnana dana   *Jainism*   One of the forms of giving (DANA). It refers to imparting spiritual knowledge that helps others on the path of liberation. It can be achieved through disseminating Jain teachings by preaching, writing books and articles or financing the publication of Jain religious materials. (*See also* ABHAYA DANA; ANUKAMPA; SUPATRA DANA)

Jnana-sambhara   *Buddhism*   An aspect of the accumulation of merit gathered by a BODHISATTVA to achieve enlightenment. It is the perfection of wisdom brought about by the practice of the sixth PARAMI. (*See also* PRAJNA)

Jnana Yoga   *Hinduism*   One of the three major ways to salvation mentioned by KRISHNA in the BHAGAVAD GITA and concerned with developing methods to achieve the intuitive knowledge of the absolute BRAHMAN as the ultimate reality. However, Hindus call anyone who pursues a path to the knowledge of reality through intellectual disciplines and philosophical discourse, rather than the practices of BHAKTI (devotion), a practitioner of jnana yoga. (*See also* BHAKTI YOGA; JNANA; KARMA MARGA)

Jnana Yoga   *Jainism*   YOGA is central to Jain spirituality and the way to liberation. *Jnana yoga* refers to 'knowledge-activity'. There are three types of such yoga: meditation on objects such as images of TIRTHANKARAS, exegesis of scriptural passages and deep contemplation or direct experience of the soul. (*See also* DHYANA)

Jnanadeva   *Hinduism*   A thirteenth-century Maharashtrian BHAKTI poet inspired by his own personal experience of God. He wrote in Marathi and composed over one thousand devotional songs. He also wrote commentaries on the BHAGAVAD GITA and the UPANISHADS.

Jnanaprasthana   *Buddhism*   A text that forms the central part of the ABHIDHAMMA PITAKA written by the ARHANT Katyayaniputra around 200 BCE.

Jnanavaraniya *(knowledge-obscuring karma)*   *Jainism*   One of the four types of KARMA that are harmful to the soul and prevent progress on the path to liberation. This type of karma obscures all forms of knowledge so that the individual cannot understand the nature of the world or the reality of living beings. (*See also* GHATI KARMA)

Job   *Judaism*   A righteous man who suffered badly and questioned God as to the reason why. The problems of Job provide a dialogue with which to consider the human situation and suffering. The conclusion is that a human being must have complete faith in God and endure everything patiently. One of the books of the Hebrew scriptures is named after him and focuses on his trials. Some Jewish commentators have suggested that the Book of Job was written by Moses. The book is included in the part of the Bible known as Holy Writings. (*See* EMUNAH; KETUVIM)

Jodo *Buddhism*   A Japanese sect of Pure Land Buddhism which proclaims devotion to the Buddha of Infinite Light and Great Compassion. Founded by HONEN, the disciple of Bencho, it is marked by the belief in salvation through faith in the AMIDA Buddha. (*See also* TARIKI)

Joel *Judaism*   One of the twelve minor prophets and a short book of the same name in the Hebrew scriptures, although the twelve books are treated as one because of their brevity. It is not known when Joel prophesied: some argue that he is one of the oldest prophets, whilst others believe that he is associated with the return from exile in Assyria. Joel called upon the nation of Israel to repent their sins and turn to God, and he is famous for the destruction of Judah by a plague of locusts. (*See* NEVIIM)

John, Epistles of *Christianity*   Three books of the New Testament tradition-ally ascribed to John, the apostle of Jesus, but probably written by the unknown author of St John's Gospel. The first epistle was written in response to the activities of certain leaders who had separated themselves from the early church and were promoting a form of GNOSTICISM. The other two epistles are real letters, the first of which deals with similar themes to John 1, while the other is concerned with the correct behaviour of a Christian community leader and his lack of hospitality to travelling missionaries and preachers. (*See also* JOHN, ST; JOHN, GOSPEL OF; REVELATION, BOOK OF)

John, Gospel of *Christianity*   The fourth gospel, traditionally ascribed to St John the Apostle, although the actual authorship is not certain. Written later than the three SYNOPTIC GOSPELS, the emphasis is not on the popular teachings of Jesus Christ but on higher doctrinal matters concerning the revelation that Jesus Christ is the Son of God or an incarnation of the divine. The famous first chapter does not begin with the birth story of Jesus but the proclamation that Jesus is the pre-existent LOGOS who shares in the glory of the Father and demonstrates that glory to the world. The gospel is very selective of the events in Jesus' life and sets most of the action in Jerusalem rather than Galilee. Scholarship has usually argued the gospel is influenced by Greek ideas and mystery religions, although recently there have been attempts to reclaim its Jewish background. It is, however, more contemplative and mystical than the other gospels and has been used as inspiration by contemplatives and mystics of all traditions, not only Christian. (*See also* JOHN, ST)

John, St   *Christianity*   One of the twelve original APOSTLES chosen by Jesus Christ as companions and missionaries. He was a son of Zebedee, a Galilean fisherman, and together with his brother, James, and Peter, he belonged to an inner group of disciples chosen to witness the raising of Jairus' daughter and the TRANSFIGURATION. John is certainly the disciple referred to as 'the disciple who Jesus loved' and who was entrusted with the care of MARY after the death of Jesus. He was the first to understand the significance of the missing body when he visited the tomb with Peter on Easter morning. It is, however, uncertain that he was the author of the fourth gospel which carries his name. (*See also* JAMES, ST; JOHN, GOSPEL OF)

John the Baptist   *Christianity*   The son of ZECHARIAH and Elizabeth, whose birth was foretold by the angel GABRIEL. He lived as an ascetic in the Judean desert and preached and baptized at the River JORDAN, where he called upon people to repent. He saw his prophetic mission as preparing the way for the coming of the MESSIAH. Recently he has been associated with the ESSENE community in QUMRAN but if this is correct, his solitude and new individual mission suggest that he subsequently parted company with the Jewish sect. Christ chose to be baptized by him and, according to the New Testament, was hailed as the expected Messiah; however, later, whilst in prison, John seems to have been unaware of this when told of Jesus' activities. John attracted the animosity of Herod Antipas, who suspected him of being the leader of a rebellious mass movement. He was also unpopular with Herod's wife Herodius, as he had denounced their marriage as illicit. John was subsequently imprisoned and killed. In Christianity he is important as the forerunner of Christ and the last of the Jewish prophetic tradition.

Jonah   *Judaism*   One of the twelve minor prophets and a short book of the same name in the Hebrew scriptures, although the twelve books are treated as one because of their brevity. It is not known when the prophet lived, but some Jewish commentators have identified him with Jonah, the son of Amittai, who prophesied in the reign of King Jeroboam II. Although Jonah's story of his flight from God after being called to bring the people of Ninevah to righteousness and his subsequent sojourn in the belly of a whale is well known, he is regarded in Judaism as the epitome of the futility of humans trying to escape their obligations to the creator. (*See* NEVIIM)

Jordan   *Christianity*   The river which flows from the Sea of Galilee to the Dead Sea in Israel. The river is mentioned throughout the Jewish scriptures and has become a symbol of purity for Christians. JOHN THE BAPTIST preached and baptized in the Jordan prior to the mission of Jesus, and it is here that he baptized Jesus and heralded the coming of the MESSIAH.

Joseph *Christianity*   The husband of MARY (the mother of Jesus Christ) and a carpenter by profession. The gospel writers depict Joseph as a pious Jew and Matthew claims that he was descended from the House of David. Although Jesus was raised by him in NAZARETH and Joseph acted as a father, both Matthew and Luke make it clear that Jesus was conceived by the HOLY SPIRIT when Joseph and Mary were only betrothed and she was still a virgin. The Gospels refer to other children belonging to the couple and it is natural to assume that they were born after Jesus; however, Roman Catholicism insists that Mary died a virgin. (*See also* JAMES, ST)

Joseph of Arimathea *Christianity*   A pious Jew who was searching for the kingdom of God and met with Jesus. It is believed that he was a secret Christian and a member of the SANHEDRIN, the Jewish council that voted to kill Jesus. After Jesus' crucifixion, Joseph offered his tomb for the burial and it was from here that Christ arose from the dead. In Britain, a legend states that he founded the first Christian community in Glastonbury in 63 CE. Other legends claim that he brought Jesus to Britain as a child. (*See also* RESURRECTION)

Joshua *Judaism*   A leader of the people of Israel and a book of the Hebrew scriptures included amongst the early prophets. Joshua led the people in the conquest of the land of Canaan after the death of MOSES. It is Joshua who leads the people across the banks of the River JORDAN into the promised land of ISRAEL. The book of Joshua tells of the miraculous events at the fall of the city of Jericho when the sun stood still in the sky and the walls of the city fell to allow the armies of Joshua to be victorious.

Juba *Islam*   A cloak of wool traditionally given by a PIR or SHAIKH in the SUFI tradition to his successor or KHALIFA. (*See also* SILSILA)

Judah ha-Nasi *Judaism*   A second-century CE Palestinian rabbi, otherwise known as Judah the Prince, whose great achievement was to arrange the material of the TALMUD into a concise, clearly arranged text covering the whole of Jewish life known as the MISHNAH. This work was essential after the destruction of the Second Temple in 70 CE by the Romans and the dispersion of the Jewish people from the land of ISRAEL.

Judaism *Judaism*   See YAHADUT.

Judas Iscariot *Christianity*   One of the original twelve APOSTLES chosen by Jesus Christ as companions and missionaries and infamous as the betrayer of Jesus' whereabouts to the Jewish authorities which led to the events of the trial and CRUCIFIXION of Jesus. Judas was the treasurer for the bands of disciples, and the gospel writers generally depict him as dishonest or full of avarice. Not only does he betray Christ for thirty pieces of silver to the Jewish high priests but he also objects to Mary anointing the feet of Christ with perfumed ointment, on the grounds that the ointment was expensive. The secret that Judas apparently gave away to the Jewish authorities was the whereabouts of Jesus in the garden of GETHSEMANE after the gathering together of Jesus and the apostles to celebrate the Passover meal. The narrative accounts of the New Testament indicate that he committed suicide on the land that he purchased with the reward for his betrayal. It is difficult to establish why Judas betrayed Christ, but he may have been disappointed in his expectations of Jesus as the Jewish MESSIAH who would lead a successful uprising against Rome and restore ISRAEL to greatness.

Jude, St *Christianity*   One of the original twelve APOSTLES chosen by Jesus Christ as his companions and missionaries. He is usually identified with the writer of the Epistle of St Jude. Here, the writer identifies himself as the brother of James and, therefore, may have been one of the brothers of Jesus Christ. In Roman Catholicism he is regarded as the saint to be invoked in times of great adversity. (*See also* JAMES, ST)

Judges *Judaism*   One of the books of the Hebrew scriptures included in the section known as the Prophets. The book of Judges is regarded as belonging to the early period of prophecy. The lives of the prophets SAMUEL, NATHAN, ELIJAH and Elisha are introduced, but the teachings focus primarily on the issue of kingship and obedience to God. The judges were inspired leaders of the nation who were chosen for their qualities of justice, selflessness and heroism to liberate the people of Israel from their enemies. They included DEBORAH, Gideon and Samson. (*See also* NEVIIM)

Julus (U) *Islam*   A procession of Muslims traditionally held to celebrate Muhammad's birthday. This is an event usually associated with the SUFI tradition and is often led by SHAIKHS accompanied by their MURIDS (followers). It has been associated with sacralizing space and is often carried out in cities in Britain where there are strong subcontinent communities of Muslims. (*See also* BARELWI; MAULID)

Juma / Jumu'ah / Salat al-jumu'ah / Juma Namaz (U) *Islam*   The weekly communal prayer and attendance at the KHUTBA (sermon) held on Friday shortly after midday and completed by 2pm. Traditionally this is the minimum attendance that is required at the mosque for those who pray at work or in the home.

Junayd (d.910) *Islam*   Imam Junayd al-Baghdadi was born in Persia but went on to become the chief judge of Baghdad after studying law in the city. He was a famous SUFI who taught that inner striving should be undertaken to return to one's source, which is Allah. Many Sufi orders trace their lineage through him and he is reported to have said: 'If I had known any science greater than Sufism, I would have gone to it even on my hands and knees'. Junayd's most famous disciple was Mansur al-Hallaj, who was executed for blasphemy. It was Junayd who signed his death warrant as the chief judge of Baghdad. (*See also* HALLAJ, MANSUR AL-)

Justification *Christianity*   The process by which a person passes from a state of sin to being declared saved by entering into a relationship with God. In Christianity, the debate was concerned with what an individual had to do in order to be saved. In Protestant theology justification is achieved by repentance and faith in Jesus Christ. In Roman Catholic theology there is more emphasis on grace mediated through the sacraments. St Paul made justification the central plank of his soteriology. He defines justification as 'God's act of remitting the sins of guilty men, and accounting them righteous, freely, by His grace, through faith in Christ, on the ground, not of their own works, but of the representative law-keeping and redemptive blood-shedding of the Lord Jesus Christ on their behalf'. Debate has taken place between Roman Catholic and Protestant theologians as to whether the emphasis of salvation should lie in justification by faith or justification by works. (*See* JAMES, ST; PAUL, ST)

Jyotisa *Hinduism*   Vedic explanatory literature that introduces the BRAHMIN student to the astronomical calculations needed to determine the correct time for rituals. (*See also* VEDA; VEDANGAS)

K

Ka'aba / Ka'bah   *Islam*   A cube-shaped structure in MAKKAH and the geographical focal point for Muslim communal prayer. It is believed to be the first house built for the worship of the one God constructed by IBRAHIM and ISHMAEL. Muhammad, as a part of his prophetic role, restored the ancient place of worship to the one God and threw out the idols installed inside. The Ka'aba is 12 metres long, 11 metres wide and 15 metres high. The cube itself is covered by a black cloth interwoven with the SHAHADAH, which is renewed every year. The black stone, probably a meteorite, is set in the east corner of the Ka'aba and is circumambulated by pilgrims at the time of the HAJJ. (*See also* SALAH)

Kabbalah / Cabala / Kabbala   *Judaism*   Jewish mystics have long believed that it is possible to have so close an intimacy or relationship with God that His presence can be seen with the eye of the Spirit. Studies that penetrated the TORAH in the light of such wisdom were carried out by Jewish sages. Such figures occur in the TALMUD, but ORTHODOX JUDAISM always had a tense relationship with these mystical teachings, which were on one hand respected but on the other seen to be fraught with danger. A vast literature known as *Hekhalot* refers to the heavenly halls or stages through which the mystic travels on the inner journey of the soul. In the twelfth century CE, there was an increase in Jewish mysticism, which drew upon these ancient traditions but began to develop a systematic and coherent theosophy that is now known as Kabbalah. The tradition is passed down from master to disciple, and the corpus of work known as the ZOHAR contains the kabbalistic interpretation of the five books of Moses. The city of Safat in GALILEE became the great centre for the study of Kabbalah and was famous for the piety and devotion of its mystical rabbis. They practised their mystical disciplines, led ascetic existences, studied the Torah unceasingly, gave to charity and maintained strict control over their mental and emotional moods to avoid lust or anger. This simple mysticism, based on the love of God and the longing to seek closeness with Him, has been complicated by arcane studies of numerology and sometimes far-fetched secret interpretations of the Torah. (*See also* AYN SOF; SEFIROTH)

Kabir (1398–1448)   *Hinduism*   A NIRGUNA BHAKTI SANT famous for his uncompromising poems which preach the message that without direct experience of God within, all the externals of religion are pointless. He was extremely critical of the outer forms of religion but was equally revered by Hindus and Muslims for his uncompromising attacks on hypocrisy, caste, idolatry and empty rituals. Five hundred and forty-one of his poems are included in the GURU GRANTH SAHIB, the scripture of the Sikhs. Some Hindus believe that he influenced GURU NANAK, the historical founder of Sikhism, and others have even suggested that he was Nanak's guru. However, this is unlikely, as Nanak was not born until 1469. Kabir was born in Benares to a weaver family who had converted to Islam. Tradition insists that he was a disciple of RAMANANDA, a Vaishnavite BRAHMIN teacher in direct lineage from RAMANUJA. Kabir, however, promoted the teaching that God is imminent in all beings, including low caste. The sect that has developed from the teachings of Kabir is called the KABIRPANTHI, and their most famous temple, dedicated to the saint, is situated in the heart of Varanasi.

Kabirpanthi   *Hinduism*   The Hindu sect that developed from the teachings of KABIR, the medieval SANT master of NIRGUNA BHAKTI. The Kabirpanthi is the Hindu sect that aspires to follow his teachings by not worshipping any Hindu deity or observing any rites or rituals common to Hindus, although in all other respects it conforms to a VAISHNAVA sect.

Kaccha / Kachera   *Sikhism*   One of the five symbols of the KHALSA initiated by GURU GOBIND SINGH in 1699, the term refers to the traditional baggy underpants worn by Khalsa Sikhs which should not restrict quick movement. It is said that they were worn in this style so as not to hinder a Sikh's martial prowess. They are also symbolic of sexual restraint and moral purity. (*See also* PANJ KAKKE)

Kaddish   *Judaism*   A very special prayer recited in Aramaic that expresses the hope of eternal peace in God and affirms God's holiness. It was written in Aramaic, as that was the language used by Jews after the Babylonian exile. The prayer is used in the SYNAGOGUE to mark the completion of a section of the service, such as the AMIDAH or the culmination of the service, but the most famous Kaddish is the mourner's prayer recited for eleven months after the death of a parent (although it can be used for other close relatives). The Kaddish is also recited after completion of a period of study of the Torah. (*See also* SHELOSHIM)

Kadosh *(set apart)*   *Judaism*   The idea that the Jew sets himself apart from the world in order to join with God. It would be expressed through maintenance of the laws and commandments and the concept of a chosen people. (*See* BERIT; KAVANAH)

Kafir *Islam*   *See* KUFR.

Kahalinkarahara *(material food or sustenance)* *Buddhism*   One of the four AHARAS, or conditions, which enable a sentient being to exist. (*See also* MANOSAN-CETANAHARA; PASSAHARA; VINNANAHARA)

Kaikeyi *Hinduism*   The mother of RAMA's elder half-brother, Bharat. Kaikeyi was jealous of Rama and used her seductive wiles on her husband, the king of AYODHYA, named DASARATHA, to ensure that her son became ruler of the kingdom. The king succumbed and agreed to exile Rama into the jungle, but Bharat refused to rule his brother's kingdom. These events set the scene for the stories that appear in the great epic, the RAMAYANA.

Kakka *Sikhism*   The Punjabi letter 'K' used to describe the five symbols of the KHALSA. (*See also* PANJ KAKKE)

Kalachakra *Buddhism*   A form of public initiation of empowerment given by the DALAI LAMA at BODH-GAYA and in the West. Thousands have attended the initiation as a way of receiving a blessing.

Kalah *Jainism*   Time. One of the subdivisions of matter. In Jain scriptures time is cyclical and moves in a clockwise direction. The cycle is divided into two equal parts. One is the descending cycle, in which the world experiences spiritual decline and the deterioration of material things. The second cycle is marked by spiritual progress. Each cycle is divided into six epochs which are characterised by either joy or misery. We are now about 2,500 years into the fifth epoch of a descending cycle that will last for 21,000 years. Time is eternal and the cycles will continue endlessly. (*See* AVARSARPINI; UTSARPINI)

Kalam *Islam*   Classical Muslim theology that developed in the first centuries after Muhammad, as various factions debated issues raised by the message of the QUR'AN and the prevailing political situation. The major concerns of *kalam* were predestination, free will, the nature of good and evil, the unity of God and His attributes and the eternality of the Qur'an. The major schools were the MURJI'ITES, MU'TAZILA and the ASHARITES.

Kali *Hinduism*   The best-known form of the malevolent or dark aspect of the Goddess (SHAKTI), usually depicted as a young naked woman dressed only in a garland and short skirt made from skulls and bloody severed heads. Her hair is long and wild and her tongue protrudes red and bloody from her mouth. She is four-armed: two arms carry a sword and a severed head; the other two generally show her hands in MUDRAS (positions) of blessing. Kali, however, is not considered terrifying to her devotees, in spite of her appearance. She dances upon the prone form of her consort, SHIVA, and thus represents the relationship of Shakti and Shiva or PRAKRITI and PURUSHA. Shakti dances the eternal manifestations of creation upon the supine motionless absolute. She therefore represents the endless motion containing, and barely controlling, chaos, disorder, death, decay and disruption. Her votaries seek protection from these aspects of existence. As in the SHAIVITE tradition, there is a Tantric form of Kali worship, whose followers seek to subvert the usual Hindu categories of pollution and purity by seeking salvation through copulation and the consumption of meat and alcohol. The tradition of Kali worship is known throughout India, but is particularly strong in the state of Bengal. (*See also* KUNDALINI; TANTRA)

Kali Yuga *Hinduism* The fourth of the four ages that compose a cycle of time. The Kali Yuga lasts for 432,000 years and is associated with darkness and ignorance. It is believed that we are at present in the Kali Yuga and that it will finally end with the coming of the tenth AVATAR of VISHNU named KALKI. However, TULSIDAS believed that the Kali Yuga is the age when salvation is most easily achieved through the remembrance of the name of God. (*See also* KALPA)

Kalika Purana *Hinduism* One of the PURANAS that deals with legends of the Goddess and practices of her worship. It tries to make a cohesive system of all the various forms of the Goddess that are worshipped in Hinduism by differentiating them as parts of the body of the one Goddess. There are also descriptions of how to perform human sacrifice. While this is not a part of contemporary Hindu Goddess worship, occasionally stories do emerge of isolated incidents. (*See also* KALI; SHAKTI)

Kalima / Kalimah *Islam* See SHAHADAH.

Kalki *Hinduism* The tenth AVATAR of VISHNU, who will appear at the end of the present KALI YUGA and re-establish an age of righteousness. It is believed that he will appear on a white horse.

Kalpa *Hinduism* Hindu belief has a cyclic view of creation and time. The universe passes endlessly through alternate periods of activity and repose, each one known as a *kalpa* and 8,649 million years in duration. Each period of activity and repose is known as a day and night of BRAHMA.

Kalpa Sutra   *Jainism*   A three-part anthology of scriptures highly revered by SVETAMBARA Jains. Although not as ancient as the primary and secondary canons, it is more widely used in ritual and popular devotion. The three parts deal respectively with strictures for ascetics, disciplic lines of succession and biographies of TIRTHANKARAS. (*See also* ACARADASA)

Kalyanakas   *Jainism*   The five most auspicious occasions in the life of a TIRTHANKARA that are celebrated in the Jain religious calendar. They are conception, birth, renunciation, omniscience and liberation. These occasions are usually marked by religious activities and fasting.

Kam *(lust)*   *Sikhism*   One of the five enemies of the soul and an aspect of HAUMAI (ego) that prevents salvation through creating attachment to the world. The true Sikh should cultivate the love of God and longing for the remembrance of God's name. In this way lust will be contained. It is important to remember that Sikhism is not a world-renouncing religion which encourages celibacy but that it insists that sexual relations should be contained within marriage.

Kama   *Buddhism*   Sensual pleasure or desire, especially sexual, which is regarded as the main obstacle to spiritual progress. It is one of the four ASAVAS, or mental defilements, and the elimination of *kama* is essential to achieve liberation from rebirth.

Kama   *Hinduism*   The Hindu god of sensual love. Originally he had a form, but lost it after tempting SHIVA out of a long period of meditation. The gods had approached Kama to end the great ascetic's SAMADHI, so that he would fulfil destiny and marry PARVATI, his eternal consort. Although Kama succeeded in tempting Shiva, he was blasted by a ray of pure energy from the third eye of the angry god. *Kama* (sensual satisfaction) is also one of the four aims of life that can be fulfilled by a lay Hindu as long as it is regulated by DHARMA. (*See also* ARTHA)

Kama Sutra   *Hinduism*   A well-known manual of sexual conduct, seduction and positions for lovemaking that needs to be read in the context of overall Hindu society. KAMA, or pleasure, is one of the legitimate aims of lay Hindu life, as long as it is practised within the rules of DHARMA. Indulging in sex for its own sake is, however, usually considered to be an obstacle to the spiritual path.

Kamadhatu   *Buddhism*   In Buddhist cosmology our world-system is made up of three interlocking layers of existence. *Kamadhatu* is the plane of existence for beings immersed in material desire or passion. This plane is inhabited by DEVAS and humans. (*See also* ARUPADHATU; RUPADHATU)

Kamandalu *Jainism*   A gourd or wooden pot for carrying boiled drinking water. It is one of the only three possessions allowed to a DIGAMBARA monk. The other two are a brush made of peacock feathers and scriptures.

Kamma (P) / Karma (S) *Buddhism*   Action in this and future lives performed by body, speech or mind creating a reaction of suffering or pleasure which affects one's circumstances in equal measure to the action. The Buddha's insistence that the effect depends on volition defines the distinction between Buddhist and Hindu understanding of KARMA. It is *kamma* that drives the wheel of SAMSARA rather than an omniscient creator deity. (*See also* JATI)

Kamma-phala / Kamma-vipaka *Buddhism*   The fruit or result of an action that creates KARMA. (*See also* KAMMA; KUSALA)

Kangha / Kanga *Sikhism*   One of the five symbols of the KHALSA initiated by GURU GOBIND SINGH in 1699. The small wooden comb worn in the hair is obligatory for all Khalsa Sikhs. The hair is left uncut but worn in a topknot, which is held in place by the *kangha*. Some Sikhs believe that it symbolizes cleanliness of mind and body. (*See also* PANJ KAKKE)

Kanphata *Hinduism*   A term used to describe the renunciate followers of GORAKHNATH. These YOGIS of the SHAIVITE tradition are also known as Gorakhnathi and Darsani but are more commonly called NATH YOGIS in the Punjab and the Himalayan regions. *Kanphata* literally means 'split-eared' and refers to their practice of splitting the cartilage of their ears in order to wear the huge earrings that are one of their unique characteristics. (*See also* HATHA YOGA)

Kapila *Hinduism*   A sixth-century BCE sage who is reputed to be the founder of the SAMKHYA school of philosophy. Kapila is difficult to establish historically, as he is semi-legendary and believed to be an incarnation of VISHNU in some Hindu traditions. In the MAHABHARATA he is described as the son of BRAHMA, the creator-god.

Kapilavastu *Buddhism*   The capital of the Sakya kingdom where the Buddha passed his childhood as a prince. It is near LUMBINI, the birthplace of the Buddha. (*See also* SIDDATTHA GOTTAMA)

Kapparot *Judaism*   A custom practised only by some Orthodox Jewish communities and regarded as superstition by many rabbis. It is based on the ancient idea of ransom, in which one life can be sacrificed to preserve another. A cockerel is selected for a male or a hen for a female; it is taken by the head of the household to a group of men and whirled three times around the heads of the group. Sacred words are recited, requesting that the life of the bird should be taken as a ransom for the life of the person. The bird is then killed. It is essential that this act should not be confused with the sacrifice at the Temple, which ceased after the expulsion of the Jews from ISRAEL in 70 CE when the Temple was destroyed.

Kara *Sikhism* One of the five symbols of the KHALSA initiated by GURU GOBIND SINGH in 1699. Although almost all Sikhs wear the steel bracelet on the right wrist, it is only obligatory for Khalsa members. It is said to remind them of their AMRIT vows. Other Sikhs claim that the bracelet is symbolic of the oneness of God. Originally it functioned as a protection for the sword arm whilst in combat. (*See also* PANJ KAKKE)

Karad Bhet *Sikhism* The tradition of touching the KARAH PARSHAD with the tip of a KIRPAN before distributing it to the congregation. The custom originated in the practice of GURU GOBIND SINGH, who touched the *karah parshad* with the tip of an arrow.

Karah parshad / Karah prasad *Sikhism* The traditional PRASAD given out to all the worshippers in the GURDWARA. It is made of flour, sugar, clarified butter and water by a Sikh repeating the JAPJI.

Karam Khand *Sikhism* The fourth of the five stages or realms that are traversed on the path to salvation, according to the teachings of GURU NANAK. This is the stage, which transcends human effort, where grace transforms human beings and directs their lives towards wisdom and beauty. (*See also* DHARAM KHAND; GYAN KHAND; KHAND; SAC KHAND; SARAM KHAND)

Karama / Karamat *Islam* The supernatural power from Allah that is given to a prophet or a WALI (Sufi saint) that enables him to perform miracles. (*See also* BARAKA)

Karbala *Islam* An important SHI'A shrine situated in Iraq. It was the site of the martyrdom of HUSAIN, the grandson of the Prophet and the third IMAM. He had marched with a small number of followers to overthrow the UMAYYAD dynasty after the death of Mu'awiyah. This event is marked every year in the festival of MOHARRAM.

Karma (S) *Buddhism* See KAMMA.

Karma *Hinduism* Derived from the Sanskrit root *kr* (to act or create), it refers to the immutable law of cause and effect which controls rebirth. Karma generally refers to all human activity and its consequences. It is a cosmic law that governs SAMSARA and ensures that all good and bad deeds bring their precise result. It is karma that governs rebirth. The accumulated karma of past actions has ensured the life that all living beings currently hold, and the actions performed in this life ensure the next rebirth. Generally, rebirth is seen in terms of caste. A better rebirth would be into a higher caste, but it is possible to be reborn in an animal form as a consequence of actions performed in previous lives. It is also possible to be reborn as a god (DEVA) in a supernatural paradise. Hindus believe there are 8,400,000 species of life that the soul can be reborn into as a result of karma. (*See also* DHARMA; MUKTI)

Karma *Jainism* All living beings have been attached to karma since eternity. It is the cause of suffering, birth, death, illusionary perception of reality and the pursuit of temporary pleasures. Karma is carried over from previous lives and is further increased by all our actions, whether good or bad. On death, the soul leaves the body but takes its accrued karma with it. Liberation can only be obtained once all karma has been discarded and no new karma is allowed to accrue. This law applies also to karmic merit as well as the result of bad actions. Jainism is unique amongst Indian traditions in that it believes karma to be part of matter and made of subatomic particles that are able to penetrate the soul and cover its qualities of bliss, omniscience and freedom. (*See* AGHATIYA KARMA; GHATI KARMA; KEVALAJNANA)

Karma Marga / Karma Yoga *Hinduism* One of the three great paths to liberation along with BHAKTI and JNANA. *Karma marga* is the path to salvation through action. It is sometimes known as Karma Yoga. The BHAGAVAD GITA teaches that it is achieved through selfless action, or not being attached to the fruit of action. However, in the MIMANSA school of philosophy it is associated with correct performance of brahminic ritual. (*See also* NISHKAM KARMA)

Karmabhumi *Jainism* In Jain cosmology, the *karmabhumi* are the thirty-five worlds of action where the law of karmic retribution holds sway. Fifteen of these worlds are occupied by various species of human being, and in these liberation of the soul can be achieved. (*See* BHOGABHUMI; KEVALAJNANA; MANUSHYA)

Kartar *(Creator)* *Sikhism* A term used by GURU NANAK; the founder of Sikhism, to describe the supreme being or God. (*See also* KARTARPUR)

Kartarpur *(The Place of the Creator)* *Sikhism* The community of devotees established as a small town by GURU NANAK in 1521. After many years of travelling on preaching journeys the Guru settled at Kartarpur with his devotees.

There is also a town by the same name in the Jullandhar district of the PUNJAB, which was founded by GURU ARJAN DEV in 1593. It is famous for its GURDWARAS and a copy of the GURU GRANTH SAHIB written by Bhai Gurdas at the time of Guru Arjan Dev.

Kartikeya *Hinduism*   One of the two sons of SHIVA and his consort, Parvati. The other son is the elephant-headed god known as GANESH. Kartikeya is depicted with six heads and riding upon a peacock. He is often identified with the old Vedic war-god SKANDA and is known in south India as SUBRAMANIYAM.

Karuna *(compassion)* *Buddhism*   Along with wisdom, compassion is essential for the human being who hopes to attain enlightenment, and it is one of the two pillars of MAHAYANA Buddhism. Compassion is required for all beings who are suffering or caught in the wheel of SAMSARA, and consists of love, charity, kindness and tolerance. (*See also* BODHISATTVA; BRAHMA VIHARAS; PRAJNA)

Kasaya *Jainism*   There are four passions that Jains must aspire to be free from in order to attain liberation. These are anger, pride, deceit and greed. Karmic bondage depends upon the degree of passion, and each one is further subdivided into intense, great, moderate and mild. Some texts ascribed to female ascetics add laughter, pleasure, pain, grief, fear, hatred and three forms of lust. Intensity of passion causes lack of self-control, harm to other living beings and clouds the discrimination and intellect.

Kasher *Judaism*   See KOSHER.

Kashf *Islam*   Discovery or knowledge that comes through illumination rather than reason, and forms the basis of the mystical path or Sufism. In this form of knowing, the meaning of faith and truth is given in experiential immediacy direct to the soul without going first to the intellect. Al-Ghazali defended *kashf* as the most certain form of knowledge. (*See* GHAZALI, AHMAD AL-; SUFI)

Kashrut *Judaism*   The term that is used to denote Jewish dietary laws worked out by rabbinical interpretation of the food restrictions implied by the ordinances in the TORAH. The Bible forbids eating any four-footed, cloven-hooved animal that does not chew the cud, fish that do not have fins and scales and all birds of prey and members of the crow family. Insects, reptiles and shellfish are also forbidden, along with any animal that has not been killed according to the Jewish rules of slaughter and drained of blood, or found to be diseased after correct slaughter. Correct observance of KOSHER would require the meat to have been slaughtered by an expert, checked for disease and apportioned in the correct way. Soaking the meat in water or covering it in salt can help reinforce the prohibition on blood, and this can be done in the home. There is also a prohibition on consuming milk and meat together, and to this end utensils used for cooking meat are kept apart from those used for dairy products. (*See also* SHECHITA)

Katha *Hinduism*   A reading of scripture by a BRAHMIN priest that is sponsored by an individual Hindu or a family. It can take place either in the home or in a temple. The sponsor will pay the priest to carry out the reading either to fulfil a vow or to bring blessings to an occasion such as marriage or a new business venture.

Katha Upanishad *Hinduism*   One of the principal UPANISHADS that contains the famous dialogue between the young BRAHMIN, Natchiketas, and Death on the means to escape death and rebirth. This Upanishad also emphasizes the doctrine of grace as a prerequisite for salvation and thus introduces one of the most important elements of BHAKTI, the Hindu devotional tradition.

Kaur *(princess)* *Sikhism*   The name given to all female Sikhs by GURU GOBIND SINGH at the inauguration of the KHALSA in 1699. Traditionally, it was a common name of women of the Rajput (ruling) caste, but is now given to all female initiates into the Khalsa.

Kavanah *(attunement)* *Judaism*   Intention is an important concept in Judaism and it is necessary that any law be performed with the right intent. A pious Jew should examine his/her motives and the reasons behind the existence of the law to ensure that the law does not become merely a dry performance bereft of meaning. Ideally, it is necessary for the Jew to arrive at a place of attunement to the will of God, from where all the laws will be obeyed in an atmosphere of sanctification. (*See* MITZVAH)

Kaya *Buddhism*   The body or the material component of human beings and other living creatures. It can also be used to describe the 'body of the Law'. (*See* DHAMMAKAYA)

Kedushah *(sanctification)* *Judaism*   An especially sacred prayer that is offered in the SYNAGOGUE service during the repetition of the AMIDAH that proclaims the holiness, glory and sovereignty of God. The prayer is as follows: 'Holy, Holy, Holy is the Lord of Host; the whole earth is full of His Glory'.

Kegon (J) *Buddhism*   The Japanese version of the HUA-YEN school introduced from China by Ryonin (1072–1132). (*See also* AVATAMSAKA SUTRA)

Kerygma *(Greek: preaching)* *Christianity*   The proclamation of the good news concerning the offer of salvation brought about by the life, death and resurrection of Jesus Christ which was proclaimed by the early Christians. (*See also* GOSPEL)

Kes / Kesh *Sikhism* One of the five symbols of the KHALSA initiated by GURU GOBIND SINGH in 1699. It is forbidden for Khalsa initiates to cut their hair, which is usually tied up in a knot and held by the KANGHA. Guru Gobind Singh's idea of asking Khalsa Sikhs to grow their hair suggested that they were saints/warriors, as both SADHUS and Rajputs kept their hair unshorn. Some Sikhs argue that all the gurus kept their hair long and that to do so follows their tradition and blesses the Sikh with their appearance. (*See also* PANJ KAKKE)

Kesa (J) *Buddhism* The robe worn over the shoulder by a monk, nun or priest in the ZEN school. (*See also* KOROMO)

Kesdharis / Keshdharis *Sikhism* Sikhs who keep their hair uncut. Normally this would apply to KHALSA initiates, but not all Sikhs who keep their hair unshorn are initiates of the AMRIT ceremony. Khalsa Sikhs tend to regard Kesdharis as in preparation for the vows of initiation. The term is usually used to distinguish Sikhs who cut their hair from those who leave it uncut. (*See also* SAHAJDHARI)

Kesgarh Sahib *(The Fort of Hair)* *Sikhism* The shrine in the PUNJAB where GURU GOBIND SINGH created the KHALSA. The site contains a magnificent GURDWARA and several relics of Guru Gobind Singh.

Kesh *Sikhism* See KES.

Ketubah / Ketubbah *Judaism* A traditional marriage contract made out by the groom which lists the financial rights of the bride. Today, Jews use whatever legal requirements are available in the civil laws of the country of citizenship, but there is still a customary reading of the contract by the rabbi after the exchange of the ring. The contract is signed by the witnesses and left in a safe place. Orthodox rabbis read the entire contract, which may become a crucial document in the event of divorce. (*See also* GET)

Ketuvim *(Holy Writings)* *Judaism* The third section of the TANAKH, the Jewish scripture that consists of the remaining books that are not included in the first five books of Moses or amongst the books attributed to the prophets. These are the twelve books of PSALMS, JOB, Song of Songs, RUTH, LAMENTATIONS, ECCLESIASTES, ESTHER, DANIEL, EZRA, NEHEMIAH and CHRONICLES. (*See also* NEVIIM; TORAH)

Kevalajnana *Jainism* Knowledge of all things; omniscience. The attainment of omniscience is the goal of Jainism and the prerequisite for liberation. Omniscience is not a function of the mind but an eternal quality of the soul that is uncovered once all KARMA has been removed and the karmic influx has ceased. The soul is then able to apprehend the entire cosmos in its experience. Omniscients in Jainism are believed to possess infinite faith, knowledge and energy and their conduct is deemed perfect. Those who have attained omniscience remain in this world often as teachers, but on death attain liberation. (*See also* AYOGI KEVALIN; JINA; SIDDHA; TIRTHANKARA)

Kevalin *Jainism* The person who has achieved KEVALAJNANA. Some, like the TIRTHANKARAS, show the way to liberation to other human beings through example and teaching. Others, such as AYOGI KEVALINS, have no specific activity associated with their state. DIGAMBARA Jains believe that *kevalins* possess supernatural powers and do not need to eat, for example. SVETAMBARA Jains generally believe that *kevalins* function as other human beings but with extraordinary compassion and virtue.

Khadijah *Islam* The first wife of the Prophet and mother of his daughter FATIMA. Khadijah was a widow who had inherited her deceased husband's business as a merchant. Muhammad, who was known for his trustworthiness, managed caravans for her. She was the first to accept the revelation of the QUR'AN and the prophethood of Muhammad and subsequently supported him in the first years in MAKKAH when the fledgling community faced many difficulties. Tradition states that the Prophet was initially terrified by the revelation of the Qur'an and the presence of the angel JIBRIL. He ran from his place of retreat and hid and trembled in Khadijah's skirts. She died before the HIJRA to Madinah. (*See also* AISHA)

Khalifa / Khalifah / Caliph *Islam* The successors to the Prophet. They do not inherit the mantle of prophethood but lead the Muslim community. The first khalifa was ABU BAKR, and he and the three khalifas who followed are known as the four righteous ones. After the death of ALI, the UMAYYAD caliphate came into existence and transferred the capital of the empire to Damascus. It was superseded by the ABBASID caliphate in 750, whose caliphs ruled from Baghdad until 1258. After the invasion of the Mongols and the collapse of the Muslim empires into sultanates, there was no effective caliphate, although the succession was maintained and disputed in various parts of the Muslim world. In 1517, the Ottomans removed the caliphate to Istanbul, from where it was finally abolished by Mustapha Kemal (Ataturk) in 1924. Today, there are small movements who wish a return to a caliphate and a decline in the prominence of nation over UMMA. The term can also be used to signify the position of humankind as the viceregent of Allah in the world. It is the God-given role of human beings to maintain Allah's rule over creation. (*See also* AL-KHALIFA-UR-RASHIDUN; ALI IBN TALIB; UMAR IBN UL-KHATTAB; UTHMAN)

Khalistan *(Land of the Khalsa)* *Sikhism* The name for the separate Sikh state in the Punjab, independent from India, which was proposed and struggled for by Sikh separatists throughout the 1980s. The idea of a Sikh state draws upon narratives in Sikh religious history that assert both the temporal and spiritual power of the later Sikh Gurus. An independent state of the Punjab was achieved during the reign of RANJIT SINGH (1780–1839) but was lost to the British in the nineteenth century. While it is unlikely that this kingdom was a Sikh theocracy, the contemporary movement is driven by ultra-orthodox KHALSA movements who would like to create an independent state based upon the rule of the Khalsa. (*See also* MIRI/PIRI; GURU HARGOBIND; GURU GOBIND SINGH)

Khalsa *(the pure)* *Sikhism* The brotherhood founded by GURU GOBIND SINGH in 1699, in which he initiated five Sikhs known as the PANJ PIARES by inviting them to partake in the first AMRIT PAHUL ceremony. They, in turn, initiated the Guru. The initiates were instructed to maintain the PANJ KAKKE or five Ks. Today, Khalsa Sikhs form the orthodox section within the wider Sikh community and compose approximately 20 per cent of the total Sikh population.

Khan, Sayyid Ahmad (1817–96) *Islam* A Muslim modernist who, after the 1857 mutiny against the British in India, opposed the futility of militant opposition. Sayyid Ahmad Khan chose instead to focus on encouraging Indian Muslims to close ranks by overcoming ethnic and regional differences and to cooperate with the British rulers. Concerned to modernize Muslim education in line with Western education, he founded the famous Aligarh University. In a break with traditional Islam, he advocated that the QUR'AN be reinterpreted to remove all apparent contradictions with scientific truths. He believed that any passages that conflicted with demonstrative truth should be regarded as metaphorical. While his ideas were not received well by traditionalists, he is still revered as one of the first exponents of Muslim nationalism. His loyalty to the British won him a knighthood, which has not endeared him to contemporary Muslim revivalist movements. (*See also* ABDUH, MUHAMMAD; AFGHANI, JAMAL AL-DIN; MAWDUDI, MAULANA)

Khand *Sikhism* The five stages or realms described by GURU NANAK in the JAPJI which refer to the levels of consciousness which the soul has to pass on its way towards oneness with God. (*See also* DHARAM KHAND; GYAN KHAND; KARAM KHAND; SAC KHAND; SARAM KHAND)

Khanda *Sikhism* The supreme insignia of the KHALSA. The double-edged sword symbolizing spiritual authority (*piri*) and temporal authority (*miri*) first worn by GURU HARGOBIND. Representing the ideal of the saint/warrior, it is used in the Khalsa initiation ceremony to stir the AMRIT. It is also a symbol of Sikhism and can be seen on the Sikh flag, where it is contained in five concentric circles. (*See also* MIRI/PIRI; NISHAN SAHIB)

Khandha *Buddhism* The five elements or aggregates that make up human nature (form, feeling, perception, mental formation and consciousness). As they are aggregates and will eventually dissolve into their constituent parts, they cause suffering when creatures cling to them as reality. (*See* SKANDA)

Khanqah *Islam* A place where a SUFI establishes a centre around his group of disciples. (*See also* DAR)

Khanti *(patience or forbearance)* *Buddhism* One of the ten PARAMITAS and an important virtue to be cultivated as one follows the DHAMMA. A story goes that the Buddha described patience as the most important virtue for the BHIKKU to achieve, as patience was required to wait for all the other fruits of the *dhamma* to arrive.

Kharijite *Islam* A number of Muslim sectarian movements that developed during the time of the third and fourth caliphs but that flourished during the regime of Mu'awiyah, the first UMAYYAD caliph. Opposed to the wealth and irreligious lifestyles of the Umayyad rulers, they withdrew from the wider Muslim community and pursued a lifestyle which they believed was based on Muhammad and his companions. The main difference between them and other Muslims centred on the issue of leadership. The SUNNI community had placed the leadership in the hands of a succession of caliphs, who had become, in effect, monarchs, while the SHI'A community believed that leadership belonged to a mystical understanding of the Prophet's bloodline. In contrast, the Kharijite movements believed that the community should appoint the leader on the basis of piety. He could also be removed by the community if felt to be inadequate. Their major contribution was their belief that Muslims who are disobedient to the revelation were apostates and guilty of treason against the community. They argued that all true believers were obliged to wage JIHAD against nominal or self-styled Muslims. (*See also* AZRAQITES)

Khatam al-anbiya *(The Seal of the Prophets)* *Islam* The important and central doctrine that Muhammad is the last of the messengers of God who has received the final complete revelation for all human beings contained in the QUR'AN. This is a qualitative as well as quantitative distinction, because the final prophet manifests the complete and perfected character of all the prophets. (*See also* NABI; RASUL)

Khatib   *Islam*   A religious specialist who is appointed to a large mosque as the deliverer of the Friday sermon. Such preachers have an important role in bringing the text of the QUR'AN and the sayings of the HADITH to everyday life. Most mosques would not be able to support an independent *khatib* and his function will be performed by the IMAM. (*See also* KHUTBA)

Khilafa (T)   *Islam*   The institution of the caliphate. (*See* KHALIFA)

Khima *(forgiveness)*   *Sikhism*   Seen as a great virtue in Sikhism and linked with patience. It implies an attitude of tolerance and acceptance of human weakness and helps to reduce ego. It promotes peace of mind in both the forgiver and the forgiven.

Khirqa-i Sharif   *Islam*   Supposedly the cloak (burda) of Muhammad found as a holy relic in several mosques around the Muslim world, including Kandahar in Afghanistan, Kuldabad in India and, most famously, in the Topkapi Museum in Istanbul.

Khojah   *Islam*   A trading community of Hindu converts found mainly in the state of Sind in Pakistan or Gujarat in India. Mainly ISHMAELIS, some of them have moved into Twelver SHI'A, as practised in Iran. Migration from Gujarat to East Africa and other parts of the world has resulted in small Khojah communities in Britain, Canada and the USA.

Khomeini, Ayatollah (d.1989)   *Islam*   The SHI'A cleric who was the architect of the Islamic revolution in Iran. Exiled to France in the 1960s by the Shah, he returned in triumph in 1979 and was appointed the leader of the new Iranian Islamic republic. He condemned Western imperialism and the globalization of Western culture, which he saw as a threat to Islamic identity. He proposed an Islamic state opposed to all Western forms of governance over Muslim nations, including monarchy. He affirmed the unity of Islam and politics and proposed that the Shi'a Muslim clerics should participate in government. Islamic polity must be based on the rule of the SHARI'A, and therefore the best ruler would be one most qualified in interpreting Islamic jurisprudence. After an initial struggle, Khomeini and his followers prevailed, the Shah was overthrown and Iran was declared an Islamic state. (*See also* AYATOLLAH)

Khota   *Hinduism*   The displeasure of a village deity or GRAM DEVATA which can bring misfortune to the recipient. Continuous misfortune is often perceived to originate from the displeasure of a local deity. In such circumstances a specialist exorcist might be called in to help. (*See also* OJHA)

Khums *Islam* A donation to charity or to a Muslim state treasury which is in addition to ZAKAH. SUNNI Muslims consider that it is only payable on booty gathered in warfare or as a percentage of income gained from natural resources; whereas SHI'A Muslims regard it as an extra payment of one-fifth of a person's surplus annual income. (*See also* SADAQAH)

Khutba / Khutbah / Qutbah *Islam* The sermon delivered at the JUMA prayers on Friday or at the ID celebrations. The sermon generally follows a set pattern and is exhortatory in tone. It rarely analyses or even provides exegesis. The general assumption is that believers know what is required but forget to do it. Many mosque preachers follow a set theme based on the time of the year and traditionally may have commented on political and state affairs. Today, this will vary from Muslim state to state depending on the relationship that exists between religion and state. There are also published collections of sermons. (*See also* IMAM; KHATIB)

Kiddush *Judaism* A prayer used to sanctify the Sabbath and other holy days. The prayer is recited before the meal on the Friday evening and consists of the recitation of the passages describing the beginning of creation in Genesis 1:1–3. A short benediction is also given. The prayer is recited over a cup of wine and the Sabbath bread. (*See* HALLAH; SHABBAT)

Kilesa (P) / Klesa (S) *Buddhism* Mental defilement such as greed, hatred or ignorance which must be eliminated by following the discipline of the noble eightfold path in order to attain enlightenment. (*See* BODHI)

Kingdom of God *Christianity* Jesus' teachings concerning the kingdom of God are based on the Jewish idea of a God that rules eternally in heaven but does not yet have full control on earth. Consequently, the disciples saw Jesus as the fulfilment of the prophecy that God's kingdom would be established on earth. However, Jesus modified the teaching to stress the ethical and spiritual qualities that were demanded to enter the kingdom of God rather than tangible rewards. The church has developed a doctrine of an imminent and full manifestation of the kingdom of God that is linked with the second coming of Christ.

Kippah / Capel *Judaism* The small skullcap worn by all Orthodox male Jews at all times but by non-Orthodox only during prayers. Two reasons have been given for the wearing of the skullcap. The first is the awareness of the immanence of God in creation through the presence of the SHEKHINA, and therefore the cap is worn out of awe and respect. The second reason concerns the ancient idea that an uncovered head denoted freedom. Jews acknowledge their submission to God through covering their heads. (*See also* YAMULKAH)

Kirat Karna *Sikhism* One of the key doctrines of Sikhism believed to have been taught by GURU NANAK, the founder of Sikhism, it stresses the requirement of earning an honest living. This effectively indicates that renunciation is forbidden in Sikhism, although, in practice, it does exist.

Kirk *Christianity* The term used for a church in Presbyterianism and the lowest level of authority at which a PRESBYTERIAN council will function. (*See also* PRESBYTER)

Kirpa *(grace)* *Sikhism* The Gurus taught that salvation was not possible without grace, which is sought through devotion and service. No amount of human effort is sufficient unless divine grace is showered on the devotee. The GURU GRANTH SAHIB uses several other terms for grace including *Daya, bakshshish, karam,* and *nadar.*

Kirpan *Sikhism* One of the five symbols of the KHALSA initiated by GURU GOBIND SINGH in 1699. The short curved knife worn by Khalsa members is seen as a symbol of their fight against evil and oppression. It is only to be used in defence and for the protection of the weak and oppressed. It is believed to be a symbol of courage and of the inner struggle against evil. (*See also* PANJ KAKKE)

Kirtan / Samkirtana *Hinduism* Congregational devotional singing that has become the popular medium of Hindu temple worship. It is likely that *kirtan* was introduced into popular Hinduism through medieval devotional movements, who used it as a means to achieve ecstatic union with the divine and to promote their teachings. Today, it forms a widespread part of Hindu practice. Most visitors to a Hindu temple in the West would observe *kirtan* taking place wherever Hindus gather for congregational worship. (*See also* BHAKTI)

Kirtan *(singing the praises of the Lord)* *Sikhism* Congregational singing of the compositions in the GURU GRANTH SAHIB, which were composed by the Sikh gurus using classical *ragas* and folk tunes. The gurus taught that *kirtan* was the easiest way to lift the soul up towards God and experience devotion. GURU NANAK, the founder of Sikhism, is believed to have been the first exponent of *kirtan,* as he composed and sang spiritual songs along with his companion MARDANA. (*See also* KIRTAN MARYADA; RAGAS)

Kirtan Maryada *Sikhism* The traditional schedule of a KIRTAN session when a Sikh congregation are gathered together for a formal sacred event. After the *kirtan*, the Anand Sahib, a political composition of GURU AMAR DAS, is recited that celebrates the state of permanent joy and bliss, followed by ARDAS and HUKAM. The session ends with the distribution of KARAH PARSHAD.

Kirtan Sohila *Sikhism* The prayer recited by devout Sikhs before they sleep. It is a collection of five hymns from the GURU GRANTH SAHIB found on pages 12 and 13. It is also used at cremation or when putting the Guru Granth Sahib to rest in the SAC KHAND.

Kiss of Peace *Christianity* The greeting in the EUCHARIST, also known as Pax, where the participants express their mutual love and unity by a kiss, an embrace or the more formal shaking of hands.

Kitab *(a book)* *Islam* Although the term is used to describe any book, Islam is a religion of the book and has a deep respect for the written word. Revelation from God comes in its highest form as a divine book passed to a messenger, who embodies its teachings. There are four such respected and revered books in Islam – TAWRAH, INJIL, ZABUR and QUR'AN. The first three (Torah, Psalms and the Gospels) are believed to have been corrupted by human error, and only the Qur'an is regarded as perfect and complete. (*See also* AHL AL-KITAB)

Klesa (S) *Buddhism* See KILESA.

Knesset *Judaism* See BET HA KNESSET.

Knox, John (1513–72) *Christianity* A Scottish Protestant reformer who fled England during the Catholic reign of Queen Mary. He passed his exile in Geneva, where he was influenced by CALVINISM. After returning to Scotland in 1559 he established committees which abolished the authority of the Pope and forbade attendance at Mass. He is the founder of Scottish Presbyterianism. (*See also* CALVIN, JOHN; PRESBYTERIAN; REFORMATION)

Koan (J) *Buddhism* Used in RINZAI Zen as a technique to create sudden awakening or to develop intuition. A master will give the disciple a problem or riddle which cannot be solved by the intellect. When the intellect is short-circuited, awakening can take place. The most famous koan is the question, 'What is the sound of one hand clapping?' (*See also* KUNG-AN; ZEN)

Kol Nidrei / Kol Nidre *(all the vows)* *Judaism* These special prayers are recited on the evening of YOM KIPPUR with deep sincerity and solemnity. God is asked to forgive the petitioners for any promises that were made to Him but not fulfilled. On this special occasion male Jews in the congregation wear the TALLIT (prayer shawl) which is normally worn during morning prayers.

Korach *Judaism* The name of the leader of the LEVITES who defied MOSES in the wilderness after the release of the Jews from captivity in Egypt. The challenge of the Levites is described in the book of NUMBERS and arose from the tensions created between the ideal that all the Jews are a sacred people and the new appointment of a special group of priests chosen from the Levites. The laity objected to the priesthood, but Korach tried to demand an even more privileged position for the Levites and was corrected by the appearance of the divine presence. (*See also* SHEKHINA)

Kornvoschinian *Christianity* A knotted cord used by the Eastern Orthodox Church that has the same function as a ROSARY.

Koromo (J) *Buddhism* The black or dark blue robe worn by a Japanese monk or priest. (*See* KESA)

Kosher / Kasher *Judaism* Food that is allowed by Jewish dietary laws. (*See* KASHRUT)

Krishna *Hinduism* The eighth AVATAR of VISHNU, who is considered by many Vaishnavites to be the fullest manifestation of the deity. Krishna means 'dark' or 'black' and he is worshipped in a variety of forms throughout India. Famous deities such as JAGANNATH and Behari are perceived as forms of Krishna, and the cities of PURI and VRINDAVAN are associated with their worship. Many of the cities that play a part in the Krishna legend are famous pilgrimage places. The legend states that Krishna was the son of Vasudeva and Devaki but also the nephew of the tyrannical ruler, Kamsa. It had been prophesied that Kamsa would be slain by a nephew, so the king ordered them all to be slain at birth. Krishna and his brother were saved and adopted by the cowherd Nanda, and Krishna's subsequent amorous adventures with the cowherd girls are famous symbols of divine love. These stories are perceived as the LILA (play) of the manifest Lord and have constituted the central teachings of several Vaishnavite sects. Krishna is eventually restored to his kingdom after slaying Kamsa. During this period he becomes involved in the feud between the PANDAVAS and the Kauravas that culminates in the battle of KURUKSHETRA. These events are told in the great epic, the MAHABHARATA. Other main sources for the life of Krishna are found in the PURANAS, especially the SRIMAD BHAGAVATUM. One of the chapters of the Mahabharata is the famous BHAGAVAD GITA, in which Krishna expounds his teachings on liberation to ARJUNA, one of the Pandava princes. In the Bhagavad Gita Krishna is identified with the supreme being. Along with RAMA, he is the most popular deity worshipped by British Hindus and has become well known throughout the Western world through the preaching activities of the ISKCON movement. (*See also* GAUDIYA VAISHNAVISM; VASUDEVA)

Krishnamurti (1895–1986)   *Hinduism*   A famous writer and lecturer on spirituality who has consistently refused to be acknowledged as a guru. However, his books represent a significant contribution to the extension of Hindu spiritual ideas to the West. Krishnamurti was brought up by the founder of THEOSOPHY, Annie Besant, to be the AVATAR of the twentieth century. However, he refused to take part in the event organized by the Theosophists to announce him to the world. Completely independent, he has contributed to the development of a universal world spirituality.

Kriyas   *Jainism*   Physical action. The term is usually applied in the context of meditation. The spiritual path to liberation is known as YOGA and consists of several types of meditation. Two of these are known as *kriyas*, as they consist of physical rather than knowledge activity. The first is the yoga of posture; the second is the yoga of the spoken word or the rituals and activities that take place in temple worship. (*See also* JNANA YOGA)

Krodh *(anger)*   *Sikhism*   According to the teachings of the gurus, one of the five enemies of the soul that prevents salvation. Anger is the result of attachment to the world and is one of the impurities that covers the divinity of the soul and prevents reunion with God. It is a manifestation of HAUMAI or self-centredness and can only be removed through obedience to the guru's teachings.

Krodha   *Hinduism*   The vice of anger, which, along with LOBHA (greed) and MOHA (delusion), is considered to be at the heart of human failure to achieve progress on the path to liberation.

Krta Yuga / Sat Yuga   *Hinduism*   One of the four ages. This is the only one of the cycles of Hindu time where DHARMA is not corrupted to any degree. No disease exists and an individual human lifespan lasts for four hundred years. (*See also* DVAPARA YUGA; KALI YUGA; KALPA; TRETA YUGA; YUGA)

Kshama   *Jainism*   The virtue of forgiveness essential for spiritual progress. Forgiveness is a feature of AHIMSA, as its opposite would lead to harmfulness to living beings. At SAMASVATSARI, the holiest day of the Jain year, forgiveness is asked for from all living creatures that one has harmed, either knowingly or unknowingly.

Kshanti   *Jainism*   The virtue of forbearance. One of the ten DHARMAS or virtues that need to be cultivated in order to offset the four KARMA-producing passions of anger, greed, deceit and pride. (*See also* KASAYA)

Kshatriya   *Hinduism*   The second of the four VARNAS after the BRAHMINS, they compose the warrior class whose duty it is to rule and protect righteousness (DHARMA). The duty of the warrior was to protect the citizens through physical prowess and courage. The ultimate Kshatriya would be the just and enlightened king, who in the Vedic period was often perceived as a deity. The duties of the just king are laid out in the epic scriptures, particularly the RAMAYANA and the MAHABHARATA. Many such kings were seen as enlightened beings: for example, Raja JANAK. The human AVATARS of VISHNU, RAMA and KRISHNA were also born into the Kshatriya varna and ruled as kings.

Kshayika-samyak-darshana   *Jainism*   True insight into the real nature of the cosmos which arises as the result of the destruction of KARMA. Increasing in direct proportion to the elimination of karma, it becomes total at the state of omniscience when all karmic influx is stopped. (*See also* KEVALAJNANA)

Kufr / Kafir   *Islam*   Someone who rejects revelation and has disbelief in God and his signs. Along with SHIRK (worshipping something other than God), it is the ultimate sin. There has been considerable debate over who should be declared *kufr*. Most generally, it is used as a term to describe non-Muslims, but this is problematic as the QUR'AN gives special status to Christians and Jews as People of the Book. Various factions within Islam have labelled each other as *kufr* based on their acceptance of certain beliefs that divide the various movements. (*See also* AHL AL-KITAB; KHARIJITES)

Kumbha Mela   *Hinduism*   Probably the largest religious gathering in the world, the festival is held every three years at the rotating sites of Hardwar, Ujjain, Nasik and, finally, Allahabad, where the Jamuna and GANGA rivers meet. It is estimated that between twelve and twenty million pilgrims attended the Kumbha Mela held in Allahabad in 1989. But this was surpassed by the festival held in 2001, where it was estimated that attendance could have been as high as fifty million. The festival celebrates the spilling of the jar of nectar of immortality at the creation of the universe. Too precious to be given over to the demons, it was transported to the realm of the gods by VISHNU. During the twelve-year journey four drops of the nectar were spilled onto the four sites of the pilgrimage. One of the famous features of the festival is the procession of all the major sects of Hinduism.

Kun *(Be!)*   *Islam*   The mystic word that reflects how God gives birth to creation. The divine imperative calls everything into existence and maintains it until the command is withdrawn. Thus the command to existence is not in the past tense, denoting an event that took place in history, but is the agency of creation in this present moment.

Kundalini *(serpent power)*   *Hinduism*   A Tantric concept that maintains there are six CHAKRAS or concentrations of psychic power in the human body situated between the base of the spine and the top of the head. The *kundalini* energy is normally quiescent in the chakra at the base of the spine. When awakened through certain practices, it rises up like a serpent, undulating through the chakras inside the SUSHUMNA (a psychic canal that parallels the spinal cord) to the thousand-petalled lotus chakra at the top of the head. Once the *kundalini* energy reaches this point, it is believed that SAMADHI takes place and liberation from SAMSARA can be achieved. (*See also* KKUNDALINI YOGA; TANTRA)

Kundalini yoga   *Hinduism*   A Tantric system of yoga that provides various MANTRAS, postures and breathing exercises believed to raise the KUNDALINI energy from its quiescent position at the base of the spine. *Kundalini* yoga attempts to unite the power of SHAKTI, manifested as *kundalini*, with SHIVA present as the ultimate existence in the lotus chakra at the top of the head. The union of the two spiritual powers brings about a loss of duality and thus leads to liberation. As well as leading to liberation, it is believed that the awakened *kundalini* power can result in supernatural prescience and a variety of miraculous powers. (*See also* SIDDHI; TANTRA)

Kung-an (Ch)   *Buddhism*   In the CH'AN school, the *kung-an* is a dialogue between an awakened master and a disciple that leads to the disciple's sudden awakening. The dialogue usually consists of paradoxes that prevent reliance on the intellect. When Ch'an was introduced into Japan as ZEN, the *kung-an* was adapted into the KOAN of the RINZAI school.

Kurma   *Hinduism*   The AVATAR (manifestation) of VISHNU as a tortoise at the beginning of creation when the gods and demons churned the ocean of life. The divine tortoise appeared to churn the ocean to discover its secret treasures, such as the urn containing the nectar of immortality and the goddess, LAKSHMI.

Kurma Purana   *Hinduism*   The PURANA or popular SMRITI scripture that relates the legend of the manifestation of VISHNU as KURMA, the tortoise-AVATAR.

Kuruhit   *Sikhism*   Items such as intoxicants, which are prohibited. All GURDWARAS exhibit a sign at the entrance forbidding tobacco, narcotics and alcohol from the premises. The RAHIT NAMA lays down specific prescriptions for KHALSA Sikhs.

Kurukshetra *Hinduism*   The battle between the PANDAVAS and the Kauravas which is the subject matter of the MAHABHARATA. It is the famous location for the discourse between KRISHNA and ARJUNA that is recorded in the BHAGAVAD GITA.

Kusala *Buddhism*   Good KAMMA which produces good effects and leads to more happiness or a better rebirth; that which is profitable or good.

Kvater *Judaism*   The Yiddish term for the godmother who is appointed by the parents at the time of circumcision and remains with the child throughout its life as a guide and counsellor. (*See* KVATERIN; SANDEK)

Kvaterin *Judaism*   The Yiddish term for the godfather who is appointed by the parents at the time of circumcision and remains with the child throughout its life as a guide and counsellor. (*See* KVATER; SANDEK)

Kwannon (J) / Kwan Yin (Ch) *Buddhism*   The feminine aspect of the Bodhisattva AVALOKITESHWARA, known as the BODHISATTVA of Great Mercy. Represented by a female figure, sometimes with a child, she is revered throughout China and Japan.

Kyotsarga *Jainism*   One of the six daily duties required of all devout lay Jains. It refers to the practice of meditation in a relaxed position, which is performed either standing or sitting silently with the intention of forgetting about the body and its needs. The object is contemplation of the soul.

Kyrie *(Greek: O Lord)* *Christianity*   A title addressed to Jesus in prayer and the diminutive for the KYRIE ELEISON.

Kyrie Eleison *(Greek: Lord, have mercy)* *Christianity*   A liturgical prayer addressed to Christ and chanted by the congregation near the beginning of the MASS in response to a series of prayer bids known as the LITANY.

La ilaha illa Allah *(There is no god but God)*   *Islam*   The first part of the SHAHADAH or the witnessing that defines someone as a Muslim. It is also the most common form of DHIKR (remembrance of Allah) repeated rhythmically by the followers of SUFI TARIQAHS as a means of purification and emotional expression of their love. Although a simple statement of monotheism, it has been modified by diverse movements in the Muslim world to express their own tradition of belief and practice. Maulana MAWDUDI, for example, provided an exegesis of sovereignty, which becomes a political statement opposing ideologies such as nationalism or secular democracy that do not acknowledge the mood of Islam to offer allegiance only to God's law. Sufi traditions, on the other hand, are more likely to perceive the statement in mystical terms as a tool for transformation. Here the mood of interpretation is more inclined towards monism – nothing exists except God.

Labbaika *(Here I am before you)*   *Islam*   The greeting, known as the Talbiya, uttered by Muslims on their arrival in MAKKAH for the HAJJ after they have donned their white garment and entered the sanctified state of the pilgrim. It is repeated throughout the pilgrimage.

Ladino   *Judaism*   A language that was used by Sephardic Jews in the period of the DIASPORA. (*See also* SEPHARDIM)

Lady, Our   *Christianity*   A common title used by Roman Catholics for MARY, the mother of Jesus.

Lady Chapel   *Christianity*   A CHAPEL dedicated to MARY often found at the side of the NAVE in an Anglican or Roman Catholic church.

Lady Day   *Christianity*   The feast held on 25 March known as the Annunciation of MARY. It celebrates the announcement by the angel GABRIEL of the birth of Jesus and his conception in his mother's womb. Christianity has traditionally believed that Jesus died on the same day that he was conceived, as these two events are the most important in the salvation of the world. (*See also* CHRISTMAS; EASTER; IMMACULATE CONCEPTION)

Lag Ba'Omer   *Judaism*   A feast day that occurs in the month of Iyyar between the two festivals of PESACH and SHAVUOT. The festival is a day of celebration, in spite of the fact that Iyyar is associated with sadness and no joyous occasions, such as weddings, are held during this period. The feast day is a popular occasion in Israel, where thousands of people make their way to the city of Safat to visit the tomb of Rabbi Simeon ben Yochai who defied the decree of the Roman emperor, Hadrian, and continued to teach the TORAH.

Lahina   *Sikhism*   A devotee of GURU NANAK who subsequently became the second Guru and was renamed Angad (a limb). There are several accounts in the various JANAM SAKHI of Lahina's singular devotion and faith towards Guru Nanak. The most famous tells of how he was prepared to eat a corpse in order to obey the instructions of his Guru. (*See also* GURU ANGAD DEV)

Laity   *Christianity*   Members of the church who are neither clergy nor ordained into the priesthood. Most members of monastic orders are laity and those Protestant denominations who do not accept the EPISCOPACY have no priesthood. Their MINISTERS are therefore technically laity. (*See also* BISHOP; PRIEST)

Laksana   *Buddhism*   The generic term for the three conditions that bind all beings in SAMSARA. They are ANICCA, DUKKHA and ANATTA, or impermanence, suffering and devoid of essence. Understanding these three is seeing the world as it is and forms the Buddhist worldview.

Lakshman   *Hinduism*   The loyal and dedicated brother of RAMA who accompanies the AVATAR of VISHNU into exile along with Rama's wife, SITA. The two brothers spend fourteen years in exile in the forest and after Sita's kidnapping by the demon-king, RAVANA, Lakshman went on to perform many great deeds of heroism. He is represented in Hindu temples as a young warrior armed with a bow standing next to the enthroned Rama and his consort. (*See also* RAMAYANA)

Lakshmi   *Hinduism*   The consort of VISHNU who incarnates with his AVATARS. As a result, the consorts of RAMA and KRISHNA, namely SITA and RADHA, are considered to be her manifestations and she is also the primordial guru, the merciful form of the Goddess known as SRI. Usually depicted as the loving and loyal consort of Vishnu in his temples, she also appears in her own right as the goddess of wealth and fortune. Her image is often found in shops, places of business, offices and schools. Her festival is the well-known DIVALI or festival of lights which is celebrated throughout India in October and November when business people balance their books hoping for her blessings. Lakshmi is usually represented as a four-armed woman dressed in a red sari standing on a lotus surrounded by water. Two of her arms hold lotus flowers, while another showers gold coins.

Lama (T) *(teacher, or one who is revered)* *Buddhism*   A term used to describe a guru in Tibetan Buddhism. His guidance is essential to the progress of the adherent on the Way, particularly on the Tantric path. In Tibetan Buddhism the disciple regards the Lama as highly as the Buddha himself.

Lamb of God *Christianity*   An expression used in the New Testament and first attributed to JOHN THE BAPTIST, who described Jesus Christ as the Lamb of God when he came for baptism. The term 'lamb' probably refers to the paschal lamb, which Jews offered as a sacrifice to the temple, and which therefore symbolizes the sacrificial role and the removal of sins associated with Jesus Christ in Christian doctrine. (*See also* CRUCIFIXION; REDEMPTION; SIN)

Lamentations *Judaism*   One of the books of the Jewish scriptures that belongs to the section known as the Holy Writings. Traditionally, the elegiac text is attributed to the prophet Jeremiah, writing after the destruction of the Temple in JERUSALEM. The complete book is usually read in the SYNAGOGUE during the fast that takes place on the ninth day of the month of Av. The day of fast is held primarily to mourn the loss of the Temple. (*See also* JEREMIAH; KETUVIM)

Langar *Sikhism*   Sometimes called *Guru ka langar* (the Guru's kitchen). It is obligatory for every GURDWARA to contain a kitchen which provides a communal meal for the congregation after worship or for any visitors. The Gurus introduced the *langar* to break down the Hindu caste system by ensuring commensality. It is also a manifestation of hospitality and the Sikh regard for humanity. It provides a major means by which Sikhs can fulfil the necessity for service in their spiritual path. While Sikhs believe that GURU NANAK first established the idea in his community at KARTARPUR, certainly the *langar* was made an instititional part of Sikh practice by GURU AMAR DAS, the third Guru.

Lashon ha-kodesh *(a holy tongue)* *Judaism*   See IVRIT.

Last Judgement *Christianity*   Christianity, like Judaism, has a strong belief in a personal, merciful God who actively intervenes in human history, with both compassion and wrath, to deliver human beings and punish evil. The NEW TESTAMENT focuses on a future and final judgement that will manifest at the end of time with the triumphant Christ returning to separate the saved from the damned. (*See also* JUSTIFICATION; ORIGINAL SIN; REDEMPTION; RESURRECTION; SIN)

Last Supper *Christianity* The final meal taken by Christ with his disciples before the CRUCIFIXION described in the Gospels. It is believed to have been held on the Jewish feast of the Passover, as it reproduces many of the elements of the Passover meal. During the meal Jesus announced that he would be betrayed by one of the people present in the room. He then performed the action of breaking bread and tasting the wine from a cup and then passing them around the table, stating that they were his body and blood and should be partaken in remembrance of him. Thus the meal is the important precursor for the sacrament of the EUCHARIST.

Lauds *Christianity* The traditional morning prayer and the first of the divine offices recited by members of the religious orders. Named after the recitation of the Laudate psalms (148–50), it includes psalms, hymns, Benedictus and prayers of supplication. (*See* EVENSONG; MATINS; OFFICES, DIVINE; VESPERS)

Laukika *Buddhism* The term used to describe the 'worldly' or 'unliberated' as opposed to *lokottara*, those who are beyond this world. (*See* NIRVANA; SAMSARA)

Lavan *Sikhism* The name given to four verses in the GURU GRANTH SAHIB, composed by GURU RAM DAS, which are used as a wedding song at Sikh marriages. They are sung twice as the couple circumambulates the Guru Granth Sahib. (*See also* ANAND)

Laws of Manu *Hinduism* The translation of Manusmriti, the famous text of BRAHMIN orthodoxy that focuses on the social prescriptions of DHARMA and outlines the duties of the ideal representative of each VARNA. Written somewhere between 300 BCE and 100 CE, it is the first text to insist that varna ascription is determined by birth. (*See also* MANU)

Laya yoga *Hinduism* A system of YOGA that concentrates on techniques that achieve the dissolution of the self through absorption back into the absolute. The practices are usually similar to TANTRA.

Laylat ul-Qadr *(The Night of Power)* *Islam* The night when the first revelation of the QUR'AN was given to Muhammad in the cave above MAKKAH, where he used to go regularly for retreat. Muslims believe it to be one of the last ten days of RAMADAN and it is considered one of the most sacred days of the fast.

This is the day when, in a sense, God came down to earth and intervened in human history by revealing his final prophet and rewarding him with the last revelation. Traditionally, Muslims believe that the day in which this event is celebrated is distinguished by a loosening of the boundaries between the world and the divine. The angels are still thought to descend to the holy places of Islam and many believe that it is easier to experience the transcendent on this day than any other. (*See also* JIBRIL)

Lazarus *Christianity*   A resident of Bethany and the brother of the two sisters Martha and Mary who were friends of Jesus Christ. The New Testament does not tell us anything about Lazarus' background, other than to describe the events of the miracle in which Jesus brought him back to life after he had been pronounced dead for three days. Some commentators have interpreted the story as Jesus foretelling his power over death before his own CRUCIFIXION and RESURRECTION.

Leah *Judaism*   The sister of RACHEL who was given to JACOB in marriage by her cunning father, Laban. Laban hid Leah's face with a veil so that Jacob was tricked into believing that he was marrying Rachel, the woman he loved and to win whose hand he had served her father for seven years. It is still the custom in Jewish weddings that the groom lifts the veil of his bride in private just before the public ceremony in order that the same error is not made. (*See also* KETUBAH)

Lectern *Christianity*   A stand in a church which supports the Bible and is used for the reading of the LESSON in the various services. Traditionally it is often in the shape of an eagle.

Lectionary *Christianity*   A book containing the list of set scriptural passages and sometimes their extracts which are read throughout the Christian liturgical year in evensong, morning prayer and the EUCHARIST. (*See also* LESSON)

Legate, Papal *Christianity*   A personal representative of the POPE entrusted with his authority and given important missions on the behalf of the VATICAN. They often function as ambassadors to secular nations. (*See also* NUNCIO)

Lekhah Dodi *Judaism*   The hymn composed by Solomon Alkabetz of Safat, a RABBI of the KABBALAH tradition, to celebrate the arrival of the Sabbath. In the city of Safat in Galilee, the great centre of Jewish mystical practice, it was the tradition to welcome the Sabbath as a bride by dressing in white on the Sabbath eve and going out into the fields to rejoice. The hymn begins 'Come, my beloved, to meet the Bride' and is now sung in all synagogues on the Sabbath eve. (*See also* EREV SHABBAT; SHABBAT)

Lent *Christianity*   The forty days leading up to EASTER in the Christian cycle of the liturgical year which begin on Ash Wednesday and end on Easter Eve. The forty days are supposed to be a time of penance and are traditionally observed by fasting or abstinence. Many contemporary Christians will try to give up something that they normally indulge in. Lent was first developed in order to prepare CATECHUMENS for baptism at the Easter vigil.

Leshya *Jainism*   The psychic colour of a soul's relative purity. The malevolent colours are black, blue and grey. These colorations of the soul will lead to cruelty, lust, deceit, sloth and other vices. The benevolent colours are yellow, red and white and will lead to virtuous behaviour. The psychic colours function between the soul and the physical body and assist in the transferral of karmic particles back and forth from the centre of the being to the periphery. (*See* KARMA)

Lesson *Christianity*   The liturgical reading of the scripture that takes place in most Christian services. In the Episcopal churches it consists of three readings: one from the OLD TESTAMENT and two from the NEW TESTAMENT. The final reading is from the GOSPELS. Members of the laity may take the first two readings but a priest always makes the final reading. In Roman Catholicism and High Church Anglicism, the final reading is accompanied by incense and a procession of the priest and servers to the LECTERN.

Levites *Judaism*   The priests appointed to attend the sanctuary after its establishment by Moses. They were appointed from the tribe of Levi and developed as a wandering priesthood with little institutionalization. The Levite chose to become a priest and then wandered free of tribal affiliation searching for a local sanctuary where he could be employed. Later they became priests at the Temple in JERUSALEM.

Leviticus *Judaism*   The third of the five books of the Jewish scriptures that compose the TORAH or PENTATEUCH. It focuses on laws of ritual and purity. Leviticus means 'LEVITES' and the book details their sacred duties in the sanctuary along with rules concerning diet, purification, festivals and marriage.

Liberation Theology *Christianity*   Any theology and action that interprets Christian teachings in favour of an oppressed group or an oppressive situation. Thus Feminist or Black Theology can be regarded as a form of Liberation Theology. However, the term is more precisely used for movements established in South America in the 1960s and 1970s which declared that the church had often in the past sided with the powerful and the rich instead of the poor and the oppressed. Liberation Theology borrows heavily from Marxist ideology and practice and sees the work of the church as radical, in that it should work actively to promote social justice and the transformation of society.

Lila *Hinduism*   The divine play or sport. In VEDANTA philosophy, the cosmos is created through the *lila* of the supreme being. It also describes the involvement of the supreme being in creation. This may be used to describe God's immanence or alternatively to express a series of inexplicable events that are ascribed to divine intervention in human affairs. In the VAISHNAVA tradition, *lila* is often used to describe the events in the life of an AVATAR of VISHNU. For example, it is used to describe the teasing play of love between KRISHNA and the GOPIS who adored him.

Lilith *Judaism*   The belief that God gave ADAM a first wife before EVE, named Lilith, who was created his equal, as in the Genesis verse: *and God created man in own image, in the image of God He created him; male and female He created them* (Genesis 1:27). She was pursued by Adam's son and returned to dust. The mystical tradition states that Lilith stood before God and demanded absolute equality, pronouncing the sacred name of God that is forbidden. As a result she was made a demon to haunt mankind. It is said that Lilith tries to tempt men through the power of women and inspired the serpent to tempt Eve in the garden of EDEN.

Lin Ch'i *Buddhism*   A movement of CH'AN that emphasized the use of KUNG-AN and developed in Japan as RINZAI Zen in the twelfth and thirteenth centuries. (*See also* KOAN)

Lingam *Hinduism*   A common phallus used to worship SHIVA. It is usually a U-shaped upright stone standing in the middle of a shallow teardrop-shaped bowl that represents the female sex organs (YONI). The lingam and the yoni represent the union of SHAKTI and Shiva, the male and the female principles of divine energy. The lingam can be found throughout India in countless places, including village shrines, roadside shrines and great temples. Most Hindu temples in Britain contain a lingam, which devotees cover in milk. It was the worshipping of Shiva lingams with offerings of milk that gave rise to the simultaneous and inexplicable consumption of the milk in many Hindu temples, both in the West and in India.

Litany *Christianity*   A part of Christian liturgy first developed in the Eastern churches that aids congregational participation through several short prayers sung by a priest and consisting of a series of petitions which the congregation respond to with a KYRIE ELEISON or 'Lord have mercy'.

Liturgical Movement *Christianity*   Various movements that aimed to restore the active participation of the laity in the official worship of the church. The origins of the modern liturgical movement began in the first decades of the twentieth century amongst certain monastic orders, who were ideally suited for the widening of participation in the LITURGY, as they were primarily concerned with worship and maintained a certain degree of independence from the church.

Liturgy *Christianity*   The prescribed or formal service of worship performed publicly or communally rather than privately within the various denominations of Christianity. Liturgy is also the subject of academic study that aims to assess its origins and development over the last two thousand years. In the Eastern Church, liturgy is the term used for the Eucharist. (*See* EVENSONG; LITURGICAL MOVEMENT; OFFICES, DIVINE)

Lobh *(greed)* *Sikhism*   Sometimes associated with envy or jealousy. According to the teachings of GURU NANAK, it is one of the five enemies of the soul produced by attachment to the world that prevents salvation. They are all manifestations of HAUMAI or self-centredness and can only be overcome by obedience to the Guru's teachings, which lead to purification and then finally to God-centredness (*See also* GURMUKH; MANMUKH).

Lobha *Hinduism*   The vice of greed that along with MOHA (delusion) and KRODHA (anger) is considered to be the root of all vices.

Logos *(Greek: word)* *Christianity*   Used as a title for Jesus Christ in the fourth Gospel of John. The term 'logos' was used in number of ways in the Greek language, but metaphysically it meant the divine power by which the universe is given unity and coherence. The *logos spermaticus* was the primal word that, like a seed, germinated and gave form to primal matter. Human beings, therefore, inwardly contain the logos and express it in reason and speech. The most famous use of the term 'logos' in the context of Jesus Christ appears at the beginning of John's Gospel, where the author uses it to refer to the pre-existent word of God incarnated as Jesus Christ. (*See* JOHN, GOSPEL OF)

Loka *(the universe)* *Jainism*   One of the twelve reflections practised by ascetics in order to maintain a correct religious attitude. *Loka* refers to the belief that the human being is insignificant compared to the infinity of time and space that makes up the universe. This maintains the correct perspective of human life. (*See also* ANUPREKSAS)

Lord's Day *Christianity*   See SABBATH.

Lord's Prayer *Christianity*   The prayer taught by Jesus to his apostles at the SERMON ON THE MOUNT (Matthew 6:9–13). Christians believe that it is the model of prayer taught by Jesus for all successive generations. Christian liturgy uses the text of the prayer contained in Matthew, which is regarded as particularly sacred in that it expresses Jesus' teaching and is the prayer he suggested was acceptable to God. The words are as follows:

Our Father in heaven
Hallowed be your name
Your kingdom come
Your will be done
On earth as in heaven.
Give us today our daily bread.
Forgive us our sins
As we forgive those who sin against us.
Lead us not into temptation
But deliver us from evil.
For the kingdom, the power,
And the glory be yours for evermore.
Amen

Lord's Supper *Christianity*   See EUCHARIST.

Lot *Judaism*   The brother of ABRAHAM, as recounted in the book of GENESIS, who led his people into the wicked cities of Sodom and Gomorrah but was reluctant to leave when warned that God intended to destroy them. His wife looked back longingly on the cities and was turned into a pillar of salt.

Lotus Sutra *Buddhism*   Properly known as Saddharma Pundarika Sutra, it is one of the earliest SUTRAS and a major scripture in the MAHAYANA tradition. It describes the virtues of a BODHISATTVA, and emphasizes that all sentient beings can attain enlightenment. It was the basic text of the TI'EN T'AI school in China.

Love *Christianity*   The greatest of the three theological virtues expounded by Paul. The New Testament uses the Greek AGAPE, which means the highest form of love that sees something infinitely precious in the object of love. The highest manifestation of the love of God according to the apostle was the birth, life and death of Jesus Christ, and Jesus is the focal point of Christian love. Christ is also the beloved of God and the love between them pre-exists creation and expresses the innermost nature of the Godhead. Thus Christians believe love is the essential nature of God and it is also the correct and ultimate response of humans towards God. (*See also* FAITH; HOPE)

Low Church *Christianity*   The wing of the Church of England that represents the Protestant tradition as opposed to HIGH CHURCH and which assigns relatively little importance to the priesthood and the sacraments. (*See also* OXFORD MOVEMENT; TRACTARIANISM)

Loyola, Ignatius (1491–1556) *Christianity*   A major Roman Catholic figure of the Reformation period. He was born of a knightly family in Spain and served as a soldier. He retired from military service after receiving injuries and began to read the lives of the saints. Determined to become a soldier of Christ and the Virgin Mary, he renounced his weapons and dressed as a beggar. He then passed a year in the town of Manresa practising harsh penances and meditating on *The Imitation of Christ* by Thomas à Kempis. During this time he received a number of visions and experiences of ecstasy. After educating himself and practising his own spiritual exercises, recorded in his book, *Spiritual Exercise*, he was inspired to start a monastic order dedicated to the service of the Pope. Ten companions joined him, and in 1540, the Pope officially authorized the Society of Jesus, commonly known as the JESUITS. By the 1550s they had been entrusted with the task of combating Protestantism.

Lubavitch *Judaism*   An ultra-Orthodox group based in the USA and led by the recently deceased Lubavitcher Rebbe, a great Hasidic leader, who some followers regarded as the Messiah. The Lubavitcher are active in missionary work amongst lapsed Jews and have developed a chain of Jewish schools that combine secular and Orthodox education. They have also established student centres in American universities to promote Orthodox practice. (*See* HASIDIM)

Lucifer *(light-bearer)* *Christianity*   The Latin name for the planet Venus but also applied to the King of Babylon, who identified himself with the gods. It is used as a synonym for the Devil in which he is described as a fallen angel. This may arise from the idea of fallen pride associated with the King of Babylon. The book of Revelation states that the title should be given to Jesus Christ after his ascension and return to God in glory. (*See also* SATAN)

Luke, Gospel of *Christianity*   One of the three SYNOPTIC GOSPELS which tell of the birth, life and death of Jesus Christ and which along with St John's Gospel form the first four books of the New Testament. It was certainly written by the same author as ACTS OF THE APOSTLES and was probably the same Luke who was the companion and friend of Paul. The gospel's content suggests that the author had access to eyewitness accounts of the ministry of Jesus as well as previous written sources. The gospel includes most of Mark's Gospel and was most certainly derived from the earlier gospel's content. However, it also contains sources drawn from Matthew. It is therefore speculated that all three Synoptic

Gospels may have drawn on an earlier source. (*See also* MARK, GOSPEL OF; MATTHEW, GOSPEL OF)

Luke, St *Christianity* According to tradition, the writer of the third gospel and the ACTS OF THE APOSTLES. He is believed to have been a physician and a GENTILE, who accompanied Paul on some of his missionary journeys. (*See also* LUKE, GOSPEL OF)

Lulav *Judaism* The practice of waving palm leaves during the recital of HALLEL which takes place on the festival of SUKKOT. The practice dates back to the time of the Temple in Jerusalem, where the priests made a circumambulation of the altar waving palm leaves. (*See also* ARBA MINIM)

Lumbini *Buddhism* The birthplace of SIDDATTHA GOTTAMA, who became the Buddha. It is now situated in modern Nepal.

Luther, Martin (1483–1546) *Christianity* German Protestant reformer and key figure in the REFORMATION. Luther was an Augustinian monk who broke from the Roman Catholic Church initially over the matter of indulgences. As a professor of biblical studies at the University of Wittenberg, he had already begun to reconsider the church's doctrines concerning JUSTIFICATION. In 1517, he published his famous Ninety-Five Theses on Indulgences and went on to criticize scholasticism. In 1520, he began to argue forcibly for the reform of the Roman Catholic Church, insisting that it had departed from the teachings of the New Testament. He further developed these arguments by stating that the church had made the Gospels their servant by binding them in a complex system of sacraments and priesthood. He left the Augustinian order and married in 1525. (*See also* CALVIN, JOHN; LUTHERANISM; ZWINGLI, ULRICH)

Lutheranism *Christianity* The religious ideas developed from the thoughts of Martin LUTHER and encapsulated in the Lutheran Church, a Protestant denomination which is strong in Germany, Scandinavia and the USA. The doctrines of Lutheranism are expressed in the Lesser Catechism (1529) and the Augsberg Confession (1530). While not overtly challenging many of the doctrines of Roman Catholicism, they do insist on JUSTIFICATION by faith as the correct doctrine based on the teachings of St Paul. They also condemn the intercession of saints, monastic vows and prescribed fasting, but do not mention the more controversial issues of the priesthood of all believers, TRANSUBSTANTIATION and PURGATORY. (*See also* REFORMATION)

M

Maariv   *Judaism*   The final of the three obligatory daily prayers which is offered after nightfall. The prayer is believed to have been instituted by Jacob. Sometimes in the synagogue, the afternoon and evening prayers are combined to avoid two visits in a short period of time. The *Maariv* service consists of a few verses from the Psalms, some blessings, the SHEMA, several more blessings, the silent AMIDAH and then the ALEINU to conclude. (*See also* MINHAH; SHAHARIT)

Maccabees   *Judaism*   The Jewish family that led the rebellion against Antiochus V, Epiphanes and the Seleucids in 165 BCE under the leadership of Judas Maccabeus. The Maccabees succeeded in capturing Jerusalem and in restoring the Temple. This event is celebrated at the festival of HANUKKAH.

Machzor *(cycle of prayers)*   *Judaism*   The prayer book used only for festivals which contains prayers and the readings from the TORAH and the books of the Prophets that are prescribed for the days of the festivals. (*See also* PESACH; SHAVUOT; SUKKOT; SYNAGOGUE)

Madhhab   *Islam*   The term given to the variety of movements that form various schools of Islamic thought. It can also be applied to the four different schools of law. A *madh* is not considered to be a separate sect, as all the various schools of thought are regarded as members of the Muslim community, but rivalries between them can be strong. (*See* BARELWI; DEOBAND; HANAFI; HANBALI; JAMAAT; MALIKI; SHAFI'I; SUFI)

Madhva (1238–1317)   *Hinduism*   A dualistic Vaishnavite from south India who opposed the ADVAITA VEDANTA of SHANKARA. Madhva's doctrine of DVAITA VEDANTA directly challenges Shankara's complete identification of ATMAN and BRAHMAN. Although the atman is completely dependent on God and shares in the nature of SATCHITANANDA (truth, consciousness, bliss) that are the qualities of the divine being, individual souls remain eternally independent. The soul is therefore independent from both Brahman and the creation. The way to liberation is through total self-surrender to VISHNU, achieved through complete worship of the MURTI (image). Liberation is dependent on Vishnu's grace. However, Madhva's insistence on complete individuality of the JIVATMAN led to the possibility of separate eternal destinies. Thus he is the only famous Hindu philosopher to posit the destiny of everlasting hell. For this reason, it is sometimes suggested that he was influenced by the teachings of Christianity. Madhva was a prolific writer and commentator on scripture. His most famous work was the Brahma Sutra-bhasya, but he also wrote famous commentaries on the BHAGAVAD GITA, the UPANISHADS, the RIG VEDA and the MAHABHARATA. His revolutionary contribution to the interpretation of the relationship between Brahman and atman lies in his interpretation of TAT TVAM ASI ('You are that'), the famous statement of the Upanishads. Madhva manipulates the order of the Sanskrit to arrive at the opposite meaning – 'That you are not' – and then develops his ideas of dualism. (*See also* RAMANUJA)

Madhyaloka   *Jainism*   The quadrant of the cosmos that is reserved for humans and animals. Madhyaloka is the realm of KARMABHUMI (realm of action), where human beings can perform actions that can either lead them on the path of liberation or delude the soul so that the path to liberation is further delayed. (*See also* MANUSHYA)

Madhyamaka   *Buddhism*   School of philosophy founded by NAGARJUNA, a south Indian philosopher, in the second century BCE which asserted the middle position between realism and idealism. The school emphasized wisdom but gave little importance to DHYANA. Their aim was to annihilate the illusionary world through ruthless analysis.

Madinah / Medina / al-Madinah   *Islam*   The name given to the city of Yathrib after the Prophet migrated there from MAKKAH in 622 and is believed to have founded the first Islamic state. The invitation to come to Madinah arrived at a time of increasing persecution and completely transformed the fortunes of the fledgling community. The date of the migration from Makkah to Madinah marks the beginning of the Muslim calendar. In Madinah, the Prophet was treated with honour and regarded as the city's leader. It remains the second most important city for Muslims and contains the Prophet's mosque and his tomb. (*See also* HIJRA)

Madonna *(My lady)* *Christianity*   A term used for MARY, the mother of Jesus, especially to indicate her statues or icons. (*See also* IMMACULATE CONCEPTION; LADY, OUR)

Madrasa / Madrasah / Madrassa / Madrassah *Islam*   A school for religious study usually attached to a mosque and teaching a curriculum that extends from study of the Qur'an and Hadith through to Islamic jurisprudence, recitation, FIQH (schools of law) and sometimes logic. Muslim minorities in non-Muslim countries would probably include language study in Arabic or the vernacular language of the country of origin. The graduates of the eight-year course of study are known as ULAMA and are qualified to become imams of mosques and make judgements on issues of Islamic law. The *madrasa* system was established throughout the Muslim world by the twelfth century and in many ways contributed to the unity of the Muslim worldview and the maintenance of SHARI'A law after the collapse of the Abbasid empire and the disintegration of the caliphate after the invasion of the Mongols. (*See also* DAR AL-ULUM; DARS I NIZAMI)

Madya *Hinduism*   Alcohol; one of the five MAKARAS forbidden to orthodox Hindus but used as a religious practice by those who follow the left-hand path of Tantric or SHAKTI cults. (*See also* TANTRA)

Magadhi *Buddhism*   The language spoken by the Sakyas, the community that the Buddha was born into. Magadha was one of the principal kingdoms of north India and was adjacent to the territory of the Sakyas. (*See* SIDDATTHA GOTTAMA)

Magen David *Judaism*   The six-pointed Star or Shield of David which is used in the flag of Israel and often presented as the symbol of Judaism.

Magga (P) / Marga (S) *Buddhism*   The fourth noble truth, which tells of the path leading to the cessation of suffering which is known as the middle path or the noble eightfold path. It is known as the middle path as it avoids the two extremes of asceticism and sense gratification, both tried by SIDDATTHA GOTTAMA before achieving Buddhahood. The fourth noble truth provides the path that will lead Buddhists out of suffering. (*See also* CATTARI ARIYASACCANI; MAJJHIMA PATIPADA; SAMMA)

Maghrib / Salat al-Maghrib *Islam*   The fourth of the obligatory five-times daily prayers which is held at sunset. They can be recited from after sunset until darkness falls. (*See* ASR; FAJR; ISHA; SALAH; ZUHR

Magi *Christianity*   Three wise men who supposedly came from the east under the guidance of a star to offer the newly born Jesus Christ gifts of frankincense, gold and myrrh. Various traditions suggest that they were either kings or Zoroastrian sages. Symbolically important, they were the first GENTILES or non-

Jews to worship Jesus Christ and thus pre-empted the belief that he was a universal saviour rather than the Jewish messiah. (*See also* CHRISTMAS)

Magnificat   *Christianity*   The song of praise sung by MARY when she was greeted by her cousin Elizabeth as the mother of the Lord and contained in the first chapter of the Gospel of Luke. It is an integral part of Christian liturgy and sung in EVENSONG or VESPERS in the Western Church. It is part of morning worship in the Eastern churches. It has become an unofficial anthem of South American liberation theology, because of the implicit bias for the poor and lowly in its words:

My soul proclaims the greatness of the Lord;
My spirit rejoices in God my saviour;
For He has looked with favour on his lowly servant:
From this day all generations will call me blessed;
The Almighty has done great things for me: and holy is His name.
He has mercy on those that fear Him: in every generation.
He has filled the hungry with good things: and the rich He has sent away
  empty.
He has come to the help of His servant Israel: for He has remembered His
  promise of mercy,
The Promise He made to our fathers: to Abraham and his children forever.
(*See also* LIBERATION THEOLOGY)

Mahabba   *Islam*   The reciprocal love that exists between Allah and His creation. The ideal of the lover and the Beloved is strong in Sufism, where the lover yearns to be drawn into the flame of the divine and lose all individual identity. It is believed that at a certain stage the role is reversed and the Beloved yearns to be with His lover. During this stage God reaches out in grace towards the ardent devotee. (*See* FANA; MAHBUB, AL-; SUFI)

Mahabharata   *Hinduism*   The Sanskrit epic poem and part of the collection of SMRITI scripture that was completed around 200 CE. Containing nearly 100,000 verses, it tells of the events that led to the war between the PANDAVAS and Kauravas over ownership of a kingdom and culminated in the battle of KURUKSH-ETRA. The famous discourse between KRISHNA and ARJUNA that forms the independent scripture the BHAGAVAD GITA is a part of the Mahabharata. Like many Hindu epics, it ranges across many lifetimes showing how all the characters were inexorably led by karma throughout various rebirths to the eventual battle that took place. The Mahabharata is important, as it develops the figures of VISHNU and SHIVA more fully for the first time. However, it is Vishnu in all his forms who becomes the central figure of the text, and thus the scripture is essential to Vaishnavites and contains many of their doctrinal beliefs. The epic poem is very popular and is performed throughout India in various forms, such as theatre, dance, puppet shows, cinema and, most recently, in ninety-four episodes on television.

Mahadeva *(the great god)* *Hinduism* Although one of the well-known appellations for SHIVA, it was originally used to describe RUDRA, the ancient deity first mentioned in the RIG VEDA.

Mahakasyapa *Buddhism* The monk who received enlightenment after observing the Buddha silently holding a flower. It is believed that his direct lineage of enlightened masters led to the founding of the CH'AN and ZEN schools. (*See also* BODHIDHARMA)

Mahant *Sikhism* Commonly used in Hinduism as a title for the head of a religious sect or the senior monk in charge of an ASHRAM or religious community. Historically, the term was used in Sikhism during the period that the UDASIS were in control of Amritsar. The Udasis used the title for the appointed custodians of GURDWARAS. (*See also* SGPC)

Mahapari-nibbanasutta (P) *Buddhism* A part of the PALI CANON that provides biographical details of the Buddha's life. It is an account of the last few months of his life and the details of his passing.

Mahaparinirvana Sutra (S) *Buddhism* The MAHAYANA SUTRA, which is also an account of the death and final events of the Buddha's life. It is noteworthy for teaching that the doctrine of ANATTA was adopted by the Buddha to help destroy the lower ego self and to oppose the existence of the ATMAN or eternal higher self.

Mahapuranas *Hinduism* The eighteen PURANAS that form part of accepted SMRITI scriptures and are used by the major Hindu traditions. The bedrock of popular Hinduism, they provide the legends of the most commonly worshipped deities. The Puranas also deal with themes that form essential components of Hindu belief, such as creation myths, dissolution myths, religious observances, pilgrimage places, liberation and world cycles. Although not usually considered part of SHRUTI or Vedic literature, they are nevertheless respected, and tradition allocates their authorship to the great sage, VYASA. The major Puranas are the Vishnu Purana, Brahma Purana, Padma Purana, Agni Purana, Varaha Purana, Vamana Purana, Matsya Purana, Bhagavata Purana, Naradiya Purana, Garuda Purana, Brahmanda Purana, Brahmavaivarta Purana, Markandeya Purana, Bhavisya Purana, Shiva Purana, Linga Purana, Skanda Purana, Kurma Purana.

Maharasa *Sikhism*   A term used for spiritual nectar which is tasted as a result of perfection in YOGA. In the GURU GRANTH SAHIB it refers to the bliss experienced by the devotee in worship. (*See also* AMRIT)

Mahasanghika *(The Great Sangha)* *Buddhism*   Those who seceded from the orthodox STHAVIRAS at the Second Council held at Vesali between fifty and one hundred years after the PARINIBBANA of the Buddha. They insisted that monastic rules should be made easier, but they also differed philosophically in that they set the standards required by an ARHANT at a lower level. They also played down the idea of the Buddha's humanity and saw him as some kind of manifestation of an eternal principle.

Mahat *Hinduism*   According to SAMKHYA philosophy, *mahat* is the Great Principle that gives rise to individual existence; it is also known as BUDDHI, the primordial intellect. *Mahat* is not God, but is itself a product of the disturbance of the balance of the three GUNAS under the influence of PURUSHA. (*See also* PRAKRITI)

Mahatma *(a great soul or great-souled one)* *Hinduism*   It is a title often conferred on religious leaders or SANNYASIN monks, and was given to GANDHI in recognition of his saintly qualities. It is sometimes used to refer to the great spiritual figures in Hindu history.

Mahatmyas *Hinduism*   A passage praising the greatness of each PURANA, which usually appears at the beginning of each one as a prologue. They usually indicate the manifold blessings that will be derived from either reading the texts or just keeping a copy in the home.

Mahavakyas *Hinduism*   A great saying or aphorism from a Vedic scriptural text. The most famous is TAT TVAM ASI, or 'You are that' from the CHANDOGYA UPANISHAD, which became the foundation for the various interpretations of VEDANTA.

Mahavir *Jainism*   The twenty-fourth TIRTHANKARA and historical founder of Jainism, whose teachings form the foundation of the tradition. He was a contemporary of the Buddha, believed to have been born in 599 BCE to a royal couple from the lineage of the rulers of a tribal confederation in Bihar known as the Vajjis. In many ways his story parallels that of the Buddha, except that Mahavir asked permission of his family to become an ascetic and he followed a much more extreme path of renunciation. He attained the state of omniscience after twelve years of arduous penance and meditation. In this he had perfect knowledge of all worlds and all living beings. Aware of the suffering condition of all creatures, at the age of forty-two he determined to enter a path of teaching. He first converted eleven learned BRAHMINS, who became his first disciples. His followers became known as NIRGRANTHAS (freed from all bondage). (*See also* GANDHARAS)

Mahavratas   *Jainism*   The five major vows of the mendicant or Jain ascetic. They are non-violence, truthfulness, non-stealing, celibacy and non-attachment. (*See* ABRAHMA; ACAURYA; AHIMSA; APARIGRAHA; SATYA)

Mahayana *(the great vehicle)*   *Buddhism*   Prominent in Tibet, parts of Asia and the Far East, the Mahayana tradition emphasized the BODHISATTVA ideal and elevated compassion alongside wisdom as the foremost virtue. Buddhahood was perceived as a transcendental principle which has existed over aeons. Individual Buddhas have therefore manifested in countless forms in countless places. Consequently the emphasis moves away from the historical Buddha. Mahayana Buddhism also provided a new role for the laity either through devotional cults or the ideal of the enlightened layperson. (*See also* THERAVADA)

Mahayogi *(the great yogi)*   *Hinduism*   Usually used as a name for SHIVA, who is regarded as the ultimate renunciate and the inspiration of many SHAIVITE yogic orders. Contemporary YOGIS from the Shaivite tradition may be given the honorific of Mahayogi.

Mahbub, al-   *Islam*   The name of Allah that refers to His divine attribute of the 'beloved', the goal of the heart's aspiration to lose itself in divine love. (*See* FANA; MAHABBA)

Mahdi Al-Muntazar   *Islam*   The messianic figure who is awaited and will appear towards the end of time to lead the Muslim UMMA and restore Islam throughout the world as the first and final religion of God. He will be accompanied by ISA (Jesus). Muslims believe that he is the fulfilment of the prophecy of a messiah contained within Jewish and Christian traditions. In the SHI'A tradition, the Mahdi is believed to be the return of the last IMAM, who was taken into occultation, or removal to a divine place of safety, in order to protect him from persecution and assassination.

Mahesh Yogi Maharishi   *Hinduism*   The founder of the Transcendental Meditation Society, better known in the West as TM. Mahesh Yogi became famous in the early 1960s when he first arrived in the West from his home in Rishikesh and attracted several famous stars of the entertainment world, including the Beatles. His movement has been very successful in attracting Westerners and teaching them basic mantra meditation. Recently the followers of TM have attracted considerable publicity over their claims to teach levitation.

Mahil *(a palace)* *Sikhism*   A title of respect given to the wives of the ten Sikh GURUS.

Maimonides / Rabbi Moses ben Maimon (1135–1204)   *Judaism*
Famous philosopher, physician and codifier of Jewish law respected by both Christians and Muslims. After leaving Spain, he lived in Cairo as the court physician to the Muslim sultan of the Fatimid dynasty. Maimonides introduced Aristotelian philosophical thought to Jewish philosophy and provided Jewish rationalism with a classical foundation. He combined a systematic approach to the organization of human knowledge based on reason with the religious tradition based on revelation and the Bible. His main philosophical work was the *Guide to the Perplexed* and his brief thirteen principles of the Jewish faith have come to be regarded as creed and appear in simplified form in the liturgy of the SYNAGOGUE. Maimonides' principles of faith are as follows:

God is the Creator of the Universe
God is One
God has no body, form or likeness
God is eternal. There was never a time when He did not exist, and there will
    never be a time when He will cease to exist
One must pray only to God
God revealed Himself to the Prophets
The Torah was given by God to Moses
The Torah is eternal; God will not change the Torah, nor will He allow the
    Torah to be superseded
God knows all the thoughts and all the deeds of the people
God rewards those who keep His laws and punishes those who disobey them
God will send His Messiah to usher in a new and better world
God will revive the dead.

Maithuna *Hinduism*   Sexual intercourse outside of marriage; one of the five MAKARAS forbidden to orthodox Hindus but used as part of religious practice by those who follow the left-hand path of Tantric or SHAKTI cults. (*See also* TANTRA)

Maitreya (S) / Metteya (P) *Buddhism*   The name of the Buddha who is still to come and who has the nature of loving kindness. He is the only BODHISATTVA acknowledged by the Theravadin school as well as the MAHAYANA. He will only be reborn in the human world when the DHAMMA established by SIDDATTHA GOTTAMA is finished or worn out. (*See also* THERAVADA)

Maitri *Jainism* The condition of universal friendliness to all living beings that should be cultivated by all Jains who aspire to omniscience and liberation. It forms part of the central doctrine of AHIMSA.

Maitri (S) *Buddhism* *See* METTA.

Maitri Upanishad *Hinduism* One of the later UPANISHADS that attempts to synthesize Vedic teaching with other systems of thought and practice that had developed. One of these was YOGA, a set of mental and physical disciplines usually associated with SAMKHYA philosophy. The Maitri Upanishad uses the categories of yogic discipline such as DHYANA (meditation), DHARANA (concentration) and SAMADHI (absorption) in order to discuss liberation, or union of the self with BRAHMAN.

Majjhima Patipada *Buddhism* The middle path taught by the Buddha as the way that leads to the end of suffering. It is known as the middle path, as it avoids the two extremes of the pursuit of happiness through sensory pleasure or ascetic practices. Both of these were experienced by the Buddha and rejected as leading to suffering. The middle path is laid out and developed as the noble eightfold path, which outlines the way that Buddhists should conduct their daily lives. (*See* ARIYATTHANGIKAMAGGA; MAGGA; SAMMA)

Majlis *Islam* A gathering or assembly of Muslims usually convened for the purposes of religion. The term is also used in the SUFI tradition to describe the collection of a saint's sayings or aphorisms. When Muslims are gathered together for the remembrance of Allah through the recital of His names, it is known as *majlis adh-dhikr* (a gathering for the recollection of God). In contemporary Islam, *majlis* often takes the form of a conference with several invited in-spirational or scholarly speakers. (*See also* DHIKR; WALI)

Makaras *Hinduism* The five forbidden or taboo practices that are used by the followers of the left-hand path of TANTRA as religious or spiritual disciplines. They are drinking alcohol, eating meat, unlawful sexual intercourse, eating fish and fried rice. Left-hand Tantra reverses the normal Hindu conception of auspiciousness or purity in order to remove the problem of attachment by indulging, under controlled conditions, in the vices that normally lead to worldly attachment. The five forbidden substances would be taken after the repetition of holy mantras and under the guidance of a GURU. (*See also* MADYA; MAITHUNA; MAMSA; MATSYA; MUDRA)

Makkah / Mecca *Islam* The foremost of the holy cities for all Muslims. It is the city where the KA'ABA is situated and the direction in which all Muslims face when performing the obligatory SALAH. All Muslims are expected to attend the HAJJ or pilgrimage to the city at least once in their lives if it is financially or physically possible. The city of Makkah is associated with many key religious events in the history of the revelations believed to have been given to humanity. It is believed that Adam and Eve received God's mercy and forgiveness in the hills that surround the city. Makkah itself was founded by the miraculous appearance of the ZAMZAM spring, which saved HAJAR and ISHMAEL. The ka'aba itself is believed to have been established as a place of worship by Abraham when visiting his other family. More importantly, Muhammad was born in the city, where he began to receive the first revelations of the QUR'AN's verses. Although opposed by the city's merchants, he finally entered the city in triumph in 630 and performed the pilgrimage after first destroying the idols at the Ka'aba shrine. Makkah provides a geographical focal point for worship, which helps supply a sense of unity for Muslims everywhere and reinforces the ideal of the UMMA. (*See also* IBRAHIM)

Maktab / Maktub   *Islam*   A school where children can study the Qur'an that is usually attached to the mosque. In Britain and other Muslim minority communities, the school operates for two hours in the early evening after normal schooling has finished. Children are usually instructed by the IMAM in recitation and memorization of the Qur'an, correct performance of the rituals of the religion and basic knowledge of Islamic beliefs, practices and morality. (*See also* DAR AL-ULUM; MADRASA)

Makum Kadosh *(a holy place)*   *Judaism*   The term is generally used for the Temple and the SYNAGOGUE. (*See also* BET HA MIKDASH)

Mala   *Buddhism*   String of 108 beads used in Buddhist practices in order to remember the repetition of sacred formulas. It is similar to the function of a rosary.

Mala   *Hinduism*   A rosary or circle of stringed beads used in repeating MANTRAS, traditionally made from *tulsi* or sandalwood. The term is also used for a garland placed around the neck of a holy person or dignitary.

Malachi   *Judaism*   A prophet and a book named after him included in the Jewish scriptures. He preached against the innovations and corruptions that were creeping into temple worship after the Second Temple was completed in 516 BCE. Malachi blamed the priests and the LEVITES and appealed to Israel to obey the TORAH. (*See also* BET HA MIKDASH; NEVIIM)

Malfuzat   *Islam*   A collection of a saint's writings taken down by disciples from their experiences of being together with him informally at meals or other occasions. (*See* MANAQIB; SUFI; WALI)

Maliki *Islam*   One of the four orthodox schools of law in Sunni Islam founded by Malik ibn Anas (d.795) in Madinah and currently dominant in North and West Africa and Upper Egypt. Malik ibn Anas founded the school on the principle of relying upon living traditions practised in Madinah that were authenticated and supported by HADITH. (*See also* HANAFI; HANBALI; SHAFI'I)

Malkhut *Judaism*   According to the tradition of the KABBALAH, the last of the ten SEFIROTH that emanate from the AYN SOF. The source of God's sovereignty, it manifests itself in the material creation or realms of existence that exist below the levels of the *sefiroth*.

Mamsa *Hinduism*   Eating meat; one of the five MAKARAS forbidden to orthodox Hindus but used as a religious practice by those who follow the left-hand path of Tantric or SHAKTI cults. (*See also* TANTRA)

Man *Sikhism*   Often loosely translated as mind, it more accurately refers to the aspect of human consciousness that receives the data of sense experience and then interprets it as either thoughts or visualizations and then decides to act. According to the teachings of the Sikh gurus, it is this mental activity that needs to be controlled, as it robs human beings of their inner peace. It makes people self-willed and leads them away from God. (*See* HAUMAI)

Manaqib *Islam*   Hagiographical accounts of a saint's life or works that describe their virtues and merits. These can be combined with MALFUZAT (informal collections of their conversations) to produce larger biographical texts. (*See also* WALI)

Manas *Buddhism*   The sense that coordinates the perceptions of the other five senses to provide a complete representation of the perceived object. The *manas* corresponds to the mind, in that it is a sense that conceives as ideas and thoughts the experiences or objects perceived by the sense organs.

Manas / Man *Hinduism*   Although used in most of the six schools of orthodox Hindu philosophy, the meaning is slightly different. The BRHADARAN-YAKA UPANISHAD describes *manas* as the attached mind, and it is this meaning that is further developed in medieval BHAKTI and SANT traditions. This carries through into modern Hinduism, where it is usually used to describe the aspect of mind that can lead a person away from truth or knowledge of God. It was commonly used by medieval *bhakti sants* like KABIR and Nanak to describe the mind deluded by anger, greed, hatred, lust and attachment. In meditation, it is the *manas* that prevents the ability to experience ATMAN or BRAHMAN. ADVAITA VEDANTA refers to the sense that coordinates the perceptions of the other five senses and differentiates between subject and object, and thus holds the atman under the spell of illusion. (*See also* MAYA)

Manay / Manne   *Sikhism*   Total faith in the teachings of the Sikh Gurus. In Sikhism, the state of complete trust in the truth of the utterances of the Gurus has considerable spiritual benefits. According to the teachings of GURU NANAK, such a person is on the path to salvation and can guide others on the correct spiritual path.

Mandala   *Hinduism*   A symbolic diagram, circular in form, that represents wholeness or completeness. It is often used to represent the cosmos or the totality of SAMSARA. In some traditions, such as TANTRA, it is used as a visual meditation aid.

Mandapa   *Hinduism*   The rectangular hall usually supported by pillars that constitutes the part of a temple used by the worshippers. (*See* MANDIR)

Mandir   *Hinduism*   A Hindu temple that contains an image (MURTI) of a god or goddess. Temples in India range from huge complexes to small roadside shrines, but the traditional pattern for all larger temples is an inner sanctum containing the image, which is usually oblong or square in shape. This consecrated area is covered by a tapering tower or spire and is known as the *vimana*. The Brahmin priests will remain in this area to serve the deity and perform the various rituals. The devotees only enter this consecrated area when receiving DARSHAN (blessings) of the *murti*. This assembly area may be roofed and pillared. Larger temples may contain living quarters, kitchens, storerooms and subsidiary shrines to divine consorts or lesser deities associated with the major temple deity. Some temples can be very large and ornate, and in the south consist of concentric squares each containing deities. The main deity will occupy the central square. (*See also* GARBHA-GRIHA; SHIKHARA)

Manish *(a human being)*   *Sikhism*   In the teachings of the Sikh gurus the human being is the crown of creation and capable of union with the divine. As the vehicle of salvation and the container of the spark of God or soul, human life should not be wasted in the pursuit of temporary satisfaction and sensory pleasures. (*See* GURMUKH; MANMUKH)

Manji / Manji Sahib *(cot, seat)*   *Sikhism*   A small platform or stage upon which the GURU GRANTH SAHIB is placed in the GURDWARA. It refers to a string bed or seat used by a chief to address his followers. In 1552, GURU AMAR DAS divided the congregations of Sikhs into twenty-two territories under the authority of a leader later known as a MASSAND. These congregations were originally known as *manjis* and were used for preaching or administrative purposes.

Manjushri   *Buddhism*   A celestial Tibetan BODHISATTVA of the tenth stage where Buddhahood is achieved. Manjushri is equal in status to AVALOKITESH-WARA, the Bodhisattva of compassion. Manjushri, who is represented as a youth, is considered to be the repository of wisdom, and thus the two Bodhisattvas manifest the two principles of Mahayana Buddhism. The cult of Manjushri has reached the West, where it is practised by the New Kadampa Tradition. (*See also* KARUNA; PRAJNA)

Manmukh / Munmukh *(one who follows the mind)* *Sikhism*   In the teachings of the Gurus this refers to a human being who is self-orientated or follows the dictates of his/her desires rather than the direction of the Guru. The *manmukh* will be at the mercy of his/her ego and the victim of pride, greed, hatred, anger and lust. (*See* GURMUKH; HAUMAI; MAN)

Manne   *Sikhism*   *See* MANAY.

Manosancetanahara   *Buddhism*   One of the four AHARAS or conditions that nourish the clinging to existence that manifests in all living creatures except for the enlightened. It refers to mental volition or self-will. (*See also* KAHALINKAR-AHARA; PASSAHARA; VINNANAHARA)

Manqulat   *Islam*   Traditional sciences of studying the QUR'AN and HADITH that formed part of the DARS I NIZAMI curriculum taught in the medieval MADRASAS, where it is still maintained to this day, particularly in the Indian subcontinent. (*See also* DAR AL-ULUM; MA'QULAT)

Mantra   *Buddhism*   A sacred formula or chant, usually in Sanskrit, which can be recited verbally or visualized. The essence of a Tantric deity is contained in its mantra. The repetition of mantras can bring magical powers, prevent idle chatter and protect the mind by providing an everyday spiritual connection. The most famous Buddhist mantra is OM MANE PADME HUM used by Tibetan Buddhists. (*See also* TANTRA)

Mantra   *Hinduism*   A Sanskrit sacred formula or chant usually consisting of the names or attributes of a deity. It may also be a verse from scripture. From very early times, sound was a fundamental aspect of the Vedic sacrifice performed by BRAHMINS. Many Vedic hymns are composed of short sentences in praise of the deity, and these became well-known mantras or formulations of truth in the form of sound. In other words, it is believed that mantras bring into reality the special power of the deity through the use of spoken speech, in much the same way as the MURTI itself can work through the sense of sight. Mantras are used to facilitate worship or as a meditation practice to control the mind through their continuous repetition. A mantra may be bestowed with magical qualities that allow the desires of the devotee to be fulfilled through repetition. A mantra is usually provided by a GURU on initiation, when the disciple is instructed in the duration and number of repetitions. (*See also* MANAS)

Manu *Hinduism*   The founder of the human race or primal man and the Hindu lawgiver. He is believed to have provided the rules of conduct (DHARMA) followed in Hinduism. These are found in the 'LAWS OF MANU', and because Manu is the mythical father of the human race his ordinances are perceived as universal or natural.

Manushya *(a human being) Jainism*   Jain tradition allocates human beings to the same category as the most advanced of animals, the vertebrates, who are categorized as five-sense beings. However, human beings differ from their fellow five-sense beings in that they have the potential for high intelligence and spiritual growth leading to liberation. Jain scriptures claim that there are 303 different types of human being. Fifteen are born in KARMABHUMI (the realm of action, from which liberation can be obtained); thirty are born in the realm of pleasure (BHOGABHUMI); and fifty-six are born on islands (*antardvipa*) in the midst of the cosmos. Of these, 101 types are known as 'completed', while a further 101 are 'uncompleted'.

Mappah *(tablecloth) Judaism*   Notes added to the SHULHAN ARUKH by Rabbi Moses Isserles of Cracow that made Joseph Caro's influential compilation of the law acceptable to Ashkenazi Jews. (*See also* ASHKENAZIM)

Maqam / Maqamat *Islam*   The various stages of spiritual development leading to FANA through which a SUFI adherent can progress under the guidance of a master. The term also refers to a place where a saint has manifested his presence and can be communicated with by those seeking his guidance or spiritual blessings. (*See also* AHWAL; HAQIQA; MAZAR; WALI)

Ma'qulat *Islam*   The rational sciences of logic and philosophy which formed the other half of the DARS I NIZAMI curriculum along with MANQULAT, the study of the Qur'an and Hadith. The curriculum was taught in the medieval MADRASAS and is still maintained to this day, particularly in the Indian subcontinent. (*See also* DAR AL-ULUM)

Mar Thoma *Christianity* A Christian community in Kerala, south India, who claim that were founded by the apostle THOMAS but whose earliest existence dates back to the sixth century. The oldest Christian presence in India, originally they were NESTORIANS of Syrian origin but in 1599 united with the Roman Catholic Church. They recognize the Syrian Orthodox Patriarch of Damascus as their leader.

Mara *(Death)* *Buddhism* The Evil One or the Tempter who tried to prevent the Buddha achieving enlightenment as he sat under the BODHI TREE. In Buddhist mythology, his role is to maintain delusion and desire in order to keep beings enchained to the wheel of SAMSARA. (*See also* BODHI; SIDDATTHA GOTTAMA)

Mardana *Sikhism* The Muslim musician who accompanied GURU NANAK on many of his preaching tours and played the accompaniment to Nanak's poetical utterances. Mardana may have been Nanak's first follower, as it is known that he accompanied the Guru on his retreats to the forest to worship God when Nanak worked as a storekeeper in Sultanpur. (*See also* KIRTAN)

Marga *Buddhism* *See* MAGGA.

Marga *Hinduism* A path leading to salvation sometimes used synonymously with religion. There are three basic paths in Hinduism that incorporate the complete range of traditions within their all-embracing fold. These are KARMA YOGA, JNANA YOGA and BHAKTI YOGA; the paths of action, knowledge and devotion.

Ma'rifa *Islam* Esoteric knowledge that is arrived at by direct perception or apprehension of God, and experienced by the SUFI adherent as a result of practising the spiritual techniques of Sufism under the guidance of a qualified master. (*See also* DHIKR; FANA; HAQIQA; SHAIKH; WALI)

Mariology *Christianity* The academic study of MARY, the mother of Jesus, and her place in the divine order.

Mark, Gospel of *Christianity* One of the three SYNOPTIC GOSPELS which, along with St John's Gospel, form the first four books of the New Testament. It is ascribed to the authorship of John Mark of Jerusalem, who was companion of Peter, Barnabas and Paul. Many scholars believe it to be the forerunner of the other two Synoptic Gospels and the forerunner of the gospel style of writing. It is likely that Mark wrote down Peter's memories of the time he spent with Jesus Christ when Mark and Peter were in Rome and travelling. (*See also* GOSPEL; LUKE, GOSPEL OF; MARK, ST; MATTHEW, GOSPEL OF)

Mark, St *Christianity*   The traditionally ascribed writer of St Mark's Gospel and early Christian evangelist who travelled with Barnabas and Paul. He is also believed to have been in Rome with Peter and Paul. (*See* MARK, GOSPEL OF)

Marpa (1012–96)   *Buddhism*   The famous wealthy Tibetan layman and translator who travelled in India and received instruction from the sage Naropa. On return to Tibet, he became the master of the better-known MILAREPA, the great Tibetan yogi and poet. Marpa, Milarepa and his disciple Gampopa were responsible for founding the Kaagyu order, better known as the Red Hats.

Martyr *(Greek: witness)* *Christianity*   The term used for Christians who have suffered death through persecution. They are often venerated and regarded as intercessors as a result of their conviction that paying the price of the ultimate renunciation of their mortal life was not equal to giving up their life in Christ. This unique reverence for those who had given up their lives for their faith during the persecutions under the Roman authorities began in the second and third centuries of Christianity. By the fourth century it had blossomed into a cult of martyrs, which maintained that the martyrs were not dead but SAINTS living in the presence of the Lord. Their physical remains were often commemorated by special memorials. (*See also* FERETORY; RELICS)

Martyriology *Christianity*   The official register of Christian martyrs which contains the names, places of death, commemorative feast days and brief events from their lives. The most famous example is attributed to Usuard and forms the basis for the Roman Catholic martyriology. (*See* MARTYR)

Marwah *Islam*   *See* SAFA.

Mary, the Blessed Virgin *Christianity*   The honorific title given to the mother of Christ. The idea of her perpetual virginity was accepted from the fifth century onwards and is first mentioned in the apocryphal book of James. The Gospels themselves relate little about Mary other than the birth stories and her role in the CRUCIFIXION, where she accompanied 'the disciple that Jesus loved' at the foot of the cross. The ACTS OF THE APOSTLES states that she was devoted to prayer along with the other disciples. However, the gaps in the Gospel accounts are filled by hagiography arising from the beliefs of pious Christians over the ages. (*See also* IMMACULATE CONCEPTION; MAGNIFICAT; VIRGIN BIRTH)

Mary Magdalene, St *Christianity*   A follower of Jesus traditionally believed to have been a prostitute before he cast seven devils out of her, and who accompanied him on his evangelistic mission along with the twelve APOSTLES. She was one of the women who found Christ's empty tomb and, according to the Gospel of John, the first person granted an appearance of the resurrected Christ. (*See also* RESURRECTION)

Maryam   *Islam*   Mary, the virgin mother of ISA (Jesus), who was visited by the angel JIBRIL to announce the birth of her son. The Qur'an states that she was given to the Temple as a virgin but was accused of giving birth to an illegitimate child. Her spotless reputation was preserved by the miraculous defence of his mother by the newly born Isa. Maryam is proclaimed by the Qur'an to be the foremost of women and therefore occupies the highest status given to any woman in the tradition, higher even than Muhammad's wives.

Mashiach   *Judaism*   See MASSIACH.

Masjid *(a place of prostration)*   *Islam*   An alternative title for a MOSQUE or Muslim place of worship.

Maskilim   *Judaism*   A group of eighteenth-century Jews who upheld the principles of the Enlightenment and insisted that Jews should emerge from the ghetto mentally, spiritually and physically and combine their religious practice and belief with science, education and the arts. They were influenced by Moses Mendelssohn and the HASKALAH.

Masorah   *Judaism*   The present text of the Jewish scriptures which has been carefully preserved by the scribes. The text was the work of the Masorites, Palestinian scholars of the biblical text from around the sixth to eighth centuries. They explored the text, noting every Hebrew letter, the frequency of unusual words, parallels in the text and searched for variant readings which were highlighted in the margins. (*See* TANAKH; TORAH)

Masorites   *Judaism*   See MASORAH.

Mass   *Christianity*   A term for the EUCHARIST most commonly used by the Roman Catholic Church.

Massands   *Sikhism*   The title given to Sikh devotees of the Gurus who were appointed to administer the MANJIS from the time of GURU AMAR DAS. The position gave them the authority to collect religious tithes. The Massands abused their position under the later Gurus until they were finally deprived of any authority when GURU GOBIND SINGH brought all the Sikhs back under his direct control through the creation of the KHALSA brotherhood. (*See also* DASWAND)

Massiach / Mashiach / Moshiach / Messiah   *Judaism*   The anointed one awaited by the Jews who will bring deliverance and usher in a new era for the world. Since the destruction of the Temple, Jews have been comforted by the belief that one day God would forgive them and allow them to return to the Holy Land of ISRAEL. During this time of redemption, the whole world would be transformed into the kingdom of God and war and human conflict would disappear. The original messianic ideal apparently expressed the belief that the kingdom of Israel would be reunited as it was at the time of DAVID. The Jews began to hope for a king in the line of David who would restore the kingdom to its original glory. At the same time, prophets such as ISAIAH were beginning to speak about a future age when God's kingdom would reign on the earth. These two ideas dovetailed after the DIASPORA in 70 CE. Orthodox Jews certainly regard the Massiach as more than a political figure; the usual understanding is of a human being endowed with special spiritual powers from God. However, the Temple in Jerusalem and the Davidic kingdom of Israel will also be re-established. Human beings will live in peace and harmony with each other under obedience to God's commandments as expressed in the TORAH. This period of peace and prosperity will then be followed by the Day of Judgement.

Mata *Hinduism* Independent female DEVATAS, rather than the great goddesses of the SHAKTI tradition, traditionally found in village or rural Hinduism. They often have specialist functions associated with particular diseases, and one of the most famous is the Goddess of Smallpox, whose temple is in Varanasi. New goddess cults continue to emerge and recently a large following has appeared for Santoshi Mata, a previously little-known goddess who may have been created as a character in a popular film.

Math / Matha *Hinduism* A monastic institution where large numbers of renunciates live together. The most famous are the four *maths* founded by SHANKARA in the four quarters of India. This was the first attempt to systematize Hindu renunciates into orders similar to those in Buddhism. The four *maths* continue as orthodox forms of Hindu renunciation and their respective leaders, or Shankaracharyas are respected national religious figures. (*See also* ADVAITA VEDANTA)

Mathnawi *Islam* The famous inspired poetical work of Jalaludin RUMI (d.1273), which consists of spiritual anecdotes, ecstatic utterances and parables that explore the inner relationship of the SUFI with Allah. It is known in Iran as the 'Qur'an in Persian' and is regarded as an exposition of the esoteric meaning of the Qur'an.

Mathura *Hinduism* The ancient pilgrimage town associated with VISHNU believed to be the birthplace of KRISHNA and situated in north India near to

VRINDAVAN on the Jumna River. The original legends of Krishna place his birth at DVARKA in Gujarat. However, it is possible that the new site at Mathura could have been adopted after the discovery of Vrindavan by CAITANYA MAHAPRABHU in the fifteenth century as the site of Krishna's exile and life with the GOPIS. The temple that celebrates Krishna's birthplace shares a wall with a historic mosque and is therefore guarded by troops to avoid a similar incident to the one that occurred at the Babri mosque in AYODHYA.

Matins *Christianity* The designation for the service of morning prayer in the Church of England. Traditionally the first office of the day, it took place in the early hours of the morning and not long after midnight. After the REFORMATION, the Protestant churches created a morning prayer service by merging matins and prime. The structure of the service is similar to EVENSONG. In monastic communities in the West, matins remains the early morning prayer and consists of a hymn, psalms, lessons, the Te Deum and a collect. (*See also* OFFICES, DIVINE)

Matsya *Hinduism* The first AVATAR of VISHNU, who manifested as a giant fish to save MANU, the primordial man, from the primeval flood.

Matthew, Gospel of *Christianity* One of the three SYNOPTIC GOSPELS which, along with St John's Gospel, form the first four books of the New Testament and recount the birth, life and death of Jesus Christ. It is more concerned with the relationship between the ethical teachings of Jesus and Jewish law than the other GOSPELS. There has been controversy over the authorship of the gospel, as it contains almost the complete Gospel of Mark, who was not one of the original apostles. Scholars have debated the question of why an original eyewitness of Jesus Christ's life would rely on the account of someone who was not there in person. However, the writer of Matthew does include a large number of sayings of Jesus taken from a source that seems to be common with the author of Luke's Gospel. (*See also* LUKE, GOSPEL OF; MARK, GOSPEL OF)

Matthew, St *Christianity* One of the original twelve APOSTLES, who were chosen by Jesus Christ as his companions and first missionaries, and traditionally believed to be the writer of the first gospel. He is believed to have been a tax-collector and his gospel recounts how Jesus entered the tax office and declared that Matthew should leave and follow him. (*See also* MATTHEW, GOSPEL OF)

Matthias, St *Christianity* The apostle chosen to replace JUDAS ISCARIOT after his betrayal of Jesus Christ and subsequent suicide and to bring the number back to twelve. Little is known of Matthias' later career as an apostle, although Gnostic groups claimed to have secret teachings that originated from him and there are apocryphal works attributed to his authorship. (*See also* APOSTLE)

Matzah / Matzot *Judaism*   The unleavened bread used during the Passover when the consumption of any kind of yeast is prohibited. This refers back to the bread that was used by the Israelites in their flight from Egypt after being released from slavery. They were in such a hurry to depart that there was no time to bake any leavened bread. (*See* PESACH; SEDER)

Maulana / Mawlana / Maulvi *Islam*   A title usually reserved for Muslim religious scholars who, having completed the syllabus of a MADRASA, have gone on to become members of the ULAMA and are knowledgeable about the Qur'an, Hadith and Islamic jurisprudence. (*See also* FIQH)

Maulid / Milad an(e) Nabi *Islam*   The birthday of Muhammad celebrated on the twelfth night of Rabi'al-awwal, the third lunar month of the Muslim calendar. Even in the early reports, miraculous events were associated with the Prophet's birthday and the tradition of celebrating goes back at least as far as the FATIMID dynasty in Egypt (969–1169). It is generally observed with prayer meetings, sermons and songs in praise of the Prophet, alms giving, distribution of sweets and sometimes illumination and processions. The celebration has always been of special significance to SUFIS, but some orthodox theologians have declared the celebrations to be BID'A (innovation). It was especially criticized by the orthodox reformer, Ibn TAYMIYYA (d.1328) and continues to be dismissed by the WAHHABIS and SALAFIS. In spite of the criticism, the day of celebration is observed throughout the Muslim world, with the notable exception of Saudi Arabia.

Maulvi   *See* MAULANA.

Maundy Thursday *Christianity*   The day in the Christian liturgical year that is celebrated on the Thursday before EASTER. It commemorates the LAST SUPPER and has traditionally been used to bless holy oils. The night of Maundy Thursday is also marked by vigils to remember the prayer vigil demanded by Jesus Christ of his disciples in the garden of GETHSEMANE. (*See also* CHRISM; GOOD FRIDAY)

Mawali *(client or freedman)* *Islam*   The term applied to non-Arab Muslims when Islam first spread beyond the Arabian peninsula into Persia. Initially, the Mawali were taxed by their Arab conquerors, for which they felt resentment, as this went against the supposed equality of the Muslim community. The resentment was expressed against the UMAYYAD dynasty and was one of the factors in the empire's downfall and its replacement by the ABBASID dynasty.

Mawdudi, Maulana (1904–80)   *Islam*   A Muslim journalist and the foremost thinker and activist of the twentieth-century Islamic revival. He was born in Hyderabad, India, but moved to Lahore when the partition of India and Pakistan took place. Bitterly opposed to nationalism, democracy, socialism and secularism as Western imports into the Muslim world, he argued that Muslim nations should develop a form of governance based upon the Islamic revelation and the strict observance of Muslim law (SHARI'A). His main argument rested upon the sovereignty of Allah as central to Islam. Therefore any attempt to promote systems of government based upon the sovereignty of the people was tantamount to SHIRK, the sin of idolatry. As an activist, Mawdudi believed that the best minds of the Muslim world should be trained to form a JIHAD movement to bring about Islamic revolution. In 1941, he formed the organization JAMAAT-I ISLAMI to actualize his vision and work towards the Islamicization of the law and the state. (*See also* BANNA, HASAN AL-)

Mawlana   Islam   *See* MAULANA.

Mawlawi / Mevlevi   Islam   The SUFI order founded in Turkey and established in Konya by Jalaludin RUMI after his meeting with the wandering FAQIR, Shams al-Tabriz, in 1244. The Mawlawi TARIQAH expanded throughout the Seljuk and Ottomon empires and eventually became an influential part of the establishment as its SHAIKHS were appointed to advisory positions in the empire. However, it gained wider fame through its spiritual reputation and mystical practices, especially the use of distinctive music and dance to express and induce ecstasy. The order became famous throughout Europe as the 'whirling dervishes'.

Maya   Buddhism   The mother of the Buddha, who, according to legend, dreamed that a white elephant had entered her body through the right side when she conceived. She gave birth to the Buddha in the wooded garden of LUMBINI, near Kapilavastu. (*See also* SIDDATTHA GOTTAMA)

Maya (illusion)   Buddhism   The reality of everyday perception, which is regarded as an illusionary or limiting mode of experience of the complex and multi-faceted universe. (*See* SAMSARA)

Maya   Hinduism   Although usually translated as illusion, various schools of thought amongst Hindu sects and schools of philosophy have different understandings of the concept. While all Hindus agree that illusion is the power that prevents or obscures the vision or apprehension of ultimate reality, the nature of illusion is debated. Essentially, the debate falls into two categories: those who believe *maya* is a human creation and those who believe it is a divine creation. *Maya* can be perceived as caused by the soul identifying itself with mind and matter, thereby forgetting its true nature. Or it can be seen as the divine power that creates the universe as appearance and obscures the reality of the ultimate being. In this sense, *maya* can also mean the actual creative power of the supreme being and is then associated with SHAKTI, the female creative principle. Sometimes, Hindus will use *maya* to mean delusion rather than illusion: for example, the attraction to certain sensual pleasures may be described as *maya*. Whatever the particular interpretation, the concept of *maya* is central to understanding the Hindu worldview, as liberation from SAMSARA cannot be obtained without overcoming its illusionary power. If *maya* is a human creation, then the potential for self-liberation exists in human spiritual effort alone, but if *maya* is a divine creation, then grace will be required to be liberated. (*See also* MUKTI)

Mayin *Hinduism* The supreme being or BRAHMAN described as the originator of MAYA or illusion.

Mazar *Islam* A tomb of a holy man or woman that has become a shrine. They may range from small domed tombs close to a village, containing the body of righteous or pious Muslims, to grand edifices in large complexes that also contain a mosque, religious schools and hostels and function as centres of worship and SUFI teaching. The tombs exist throughout the Muslim world, but the most famous is the tomb of Muhammad in Madinah. Other tombs are believed to be the burial place of earlier prophets or famous Sufi saints. Millions will gather at the more famous tombs, especially on the occasion of the anniversary of the saint's death (URS). Most traditional Muslims believe that the tomb of a saint or prophet can be used as place for prayers of intercession. (*See also* DAR; ZAWIYA)

Mecca *Islam* See MAKKAH.

Medina *Islam* See MADINAH.

Meditation *Christianity* The term used in Christian spirituality to describe a discursive exercise of devout reflection on a passage of scripture in order to deepen insight and increase devotion.

Megha *Buddhism* The forerunner of the BODHISATTVA ideal believed in by Mahayana Buddhists. Megha was an ascetic who met with the previous Buddha, Dipamkara. If Megha had chosen to become an enlightened ARHANT, there would have been no SIDDATTHA GOTTAMA. Instead, Megha chose to follow the six PARAMI, or paths to perfection, and entered the way of the Bodhisattva. After many lifetimes he was reborn as Siddattha Gottama.

Megilloth *Judaism* Five of the books that belong to the section of the Jewish scripture known as Holy Writings which are read on special occasions in the synagogue. They are the Song of Songs, RUTH, LAMENTATIONS, ECCLESIASTES and ESTHER. (*See also* KETUVIM)

Mekhilta *Judaism*   The MIDRASH that deals with the book of EXODUS.

Mendicant Friars *Christianity*   Members of religious preaching orders who are forbidden to have common property. In the Middle Ages they traditionally begged for a living or even worked. They are not bound to one monastery or under the control of the episcopacy and were given considerable privileges to preach and hear confessions. (*See* DOMINICANS; FRANCISCANS)

Menelogion *Christianity*   A liturgical book arranged according to the ecclesiastical year which contains the lives of the saints and is used by the Eastern Orthodox churches.

Menorah *Judaism*   The eight-branched candelabrum, also known as the Chanukiah or Hanukiah, used at the feast of HANUKKAH and that was previously lit daily in the Temple in Jerusalem.

Messiah *(Hebrew: the anointed one)* *Christianity*   The Jews believed that God would send a descendant of David to deliver His people; this expectation was heightened by the Roman occupation and consequently contained both religious and political hope of deliverance. During Jesus' lifetime, there is no doubt that there were expectations of his being the Jewish messiah. In the preaching of the early church, Jesus is still identified with the Jewish messiah as the deliverer of his people, but after the RESURRECTION, the apostles begin to preach the message that Jesus remains the Messiah after his death as he is now enthroned in glory at the right hand of God. Gradually, the messianic hope of the early Christians shifted from the Jewish expectation of a political/religious leader who would fulfil their national hopes to a world messiah who had come to restore all humanity to God. (*See also* ATONEMENT; JESUS CHRIST; MASSIACH)

Messiah *Judaism*   See MASSIACH.

Methodism *Christianity*   A Protestant denomination that emerged as the result of the revivalist inspiration of the preaching of John Wesley (1703–91) against the general moral laxity in the working classes and the rationality of the established Church of England. Initially, Wesley had not wanted to break with the Church of England or establish separate places of worship. However, there were doctrinal differences, and after his death in 1791, the Wesleyan Methodists formed as a separate sect of NON-CONFORMIST Christianity. They were named Methodists because of their methodical practice of prayer and Bible study.

Metropolitan *Christianity*   The title given to a bishop with provincial rather than diocesan authority who has the rank of ARCHBISHOP or PRIMATE.

Metta (P) / Maitri (S) *(loving kindness)* *Buddhism*   One of the four BRAHMA VIHARAS and one of the PARAMI, or perfections, cultivated in the pursuit of Buddhahood or enlightenment, also one of the perfections of the BODHISATTVA. It is an essential aspect of Buddhism experienced in meditation whereby the practitioners produce in themselves the awareness of loving kindness and radiate it out to all sentient beings. It is said that the Buddha valued loving kindness above morality. Thus a Buddhist who feels enmity is not fulfilling one of the Buddha's central teachings. (*See also* BHAVANA; DANA; KHANTI; PANNA; SACCA; SILA; UPEKKHA; VIRIYA)

Metta Sutta *Buddhism*   A scripture that is part of the PALI CANON which describes the nature of loving kindness. (*See also* METTA)

Metteya (P) *Buddhism*   *See* MAITREYA.

Mevlevi *Islam*   *See* MAWLAWI.

Mezuzah *Judaism*   A small scroll placed on the doorposts of Jewish homes and at the entrance to the living-room which contains the first two paragraphs of the SHEMA specially written by scribes. It is contained in a small narrow case with an opening in the back which is placed on the right-hand doorpost about two-thirds of the way up. It is positioned diagonally so that the upper end inclines towards the house or room. The mezuzah is commanded in the book of Deuteronomy, which states: 'And you shall write them upon the doorposts of your house and upon your gates'. While the mezuzah functions to remind Jews that they are under God's protection and guidance, it is also simply an indicator of identity.

Mian Mir *Sikhism*   A SUFI mystic renowned for his wisdom and spiritual knowledge. He was a friend of GURU ARJAN DEV and, according to Sikh tradition, the Guru invited him to lay the foundation stone of HARMANDIR in Amritsar. The story indicates the affinity between the teachings of the Gurus and that of the Sufi masters.

Micah *Judaism*   A prophet and a book of the Jewish scriptures that is named after him. A younger contemporary of ISAIAH, he condemned the corruption and tyranny of the judges, aristocracy and false prophets in the kingdom of Judah. Micah provides prophecies that tell of the coming of the Messiah. (*See also* MASSIACH; NEVIIM)

Miccha *Buddhism* That which is false or untrue. It usually refers to wrong views or opinions that derive from an illusionary or limited understanding of the nature of reality. (*See* MAYA; SAMSARA)

Midrash *Judaism* The practice of interpretation of scripture that developed into collections of rabbinical commentaries on the Hebrew Bible. They deal with legal matters, but also expound on scriptural narrative. The difference between Midrash and MISHNAH is that the latter need not refer to scripture, as it is based on oral tradition. The early Tannaitic Midrash, written in the first two centuries CE, consist of interpretations of the books of EXODUS, LEVITICUS, NUMBERS and DEUTERONOMY. In the later Amoraic period, far freer and more far-fetched interpretations of scripture were produced that contain a compilation of hagiographic accounts of rabbinical behaviour. The best known of these collections, together with the earlier work on the TORAH, are known as Midrash Rabbah or 'the Great Midrash'. (*See also* TALMUD)

Mihrab *Islam* The niche or alcove in the wall of the MOSQUE that faces towards MAKKAH. Traditionally the IMAM stands in front of the mihrab to lead the communal prayers. (*See also* QIBLA)

Mikvah *Judaism* A special pool that must be filled with water that has been in contact with either a stream or rainwater. Tap water may be added once an amount of 'living water' has been collected. Traditionally the pool must contain a minimum of 240 gallons of water. At one time all traditional Jewish communities would have contained a bathhouse for the performance of *mikvah*, the ritual bathing. It is still used in Orthodox Judaism for the ritual cleansing of women after menstruation; the submersion of converts as a rite of passage into Judaism; by women on the eve of their marriage, and by Jews who had been in contact with anything that was considered defiling, such as a dead body. (*See* NIDDAH)

Milad an(e) Nabi *Islam* See MAULID.

Milah *Judaism* See BERIT MILAH.

Milarepa (1040–1123) *Buddhism* The disciple of MARPA who had previously been a magician. He was treated with great harshness by his master and subjected to numerous tests to expiate his bad KARMA. After six years he was initiated and passed the remainder of his life as a wandering YOGI living in caves in the Himalayas. Milarepa wrote many poems and attracted a large number of disciples. He is a beloved figure of Tibetan Buddhism.

Milendra *Buddhism*   The Greek king Menandros, who ruled over a kingdom in Bactria, now in modern Afghanistan. He was attracted to Buddhism and his discussions concerning his spiritual conflict are recorded in question-and-answer form with a monk named Nagasena. They are known as the *Milinda-Panha*, an important Pali text that is not part of the canon. The main discussion revolves around the problem of how the Buddha could have believed in rebirth without acknowledging an incarnating permanent self.

Militant, The Church *Christianity*   *See* CHURCH MILITANT, THE.

Millenarianism *Christianity*   Various groups within Christianity who empha-size a belief in an imminent thousand years of peace which will either follow the second coming of Christ or prepare the way for it. Millenarianism has a long history in Christianity which goes back to the early church, some of whose members expected an early return of the resurrected Christ, through to the Protestant Reformation, where it was represented by ANABAPTISTS and various groups of brethren. The arrival of the third Christian millennium has revived interest in millenarianism amongst some movements, but mainstream Christian churches remain cautious. (*See also* ADVENTISTS; PAROUSIA)

Mimansa / Purva Mimansa *Hinduism*   One of the six orthodox schools of philosophy that all recognize the authority of the VEDAS. Mimansa is concerned with the ritual dimension of the Vedic texts and has developed a theology based on Vedic aphorisms or ritual formulas. Those who developed Mimansa assumed without question that the brahminic or Vedic sacrifice was the means to attain all divine favours and that correct performance was essential. Consequently Mimansa continues to be concerned with DHARMA or correct performance of action. It is therefore a path for the 'twice-born' VARNAS and excludes SHUDRAS and women. The goal of Mimansa is the attainment of heaven, and originally it was not theistic, as both earth and the Vedas were deemed to be eternal. Later it developed into a theistic system probably under the influence of the various forms of VEDANTA that were so successful in gaining adherents from all classes of Hindus. The primary scripture for the Mimansa school is the Mimansa Sutra, written around 200 BCE. (*See also* DARSHAN SHASTRAS)

Mina *Islam*   A plain near MAKKAH which is included in the city's area for the performance of some of the obligatory rituals of the HAJJ. On the tenth day of the pilgrimage each pilgrim casts seven stones upon a large heap to symbolize Abraham's stoning of the devil as he tried to tempt him from sacrificing his son. The stoning ends the official pilgrimage and opens the celebration of the Great Festival or ID AL-ADHA.

Minaret   *Islam*   The tower on the MOSQUE from which the MU'ADHIN traditionally makes the prayer-call five times a day, although today this is more likely to be transmitted by a recording from a loudspeaker. The design of the minaret varies throughout the Muslim world, but the most typical is a tall, narrow circular tower with a pointed top and an opening for the *mu'adhin* near the summit.

Minas *(cunning, wicked)*   *Sikhism*   A term used by the Sikh Gurus for family members or disciples who break away and declare themselves to be Gurus without the qualifications or proper authority. Several significant religious sects have their origin as breakaway Sikh movements (*See* SRI CHAND; UDASIS)

Minbar   *Islam*   The platform or chair from which the IMAM delivers the Friday sermon or KHUTBA at JUMA prayers.

Minhah   *Judaism*   The middle of the three obligatory prayers that is recited in the afternoon. Traditionally believed to have been instituted by ISAAC, it is named after the meal offering made in the Temple in Jerusalem. The prayer is offered during the second half of the day and must take place between nine and a half and eleven and a half hours after daybreak. The service opens with Psalm 145, the half-KADDISH followed by a silent AMIDAH and confession, and ends with ALEINU. (*See also* MAARIV; SHAHARIT)

Minister   *Christianity*   A person who is officially responsible for carrying out religious functions in the church. In NON-CONFORMIST churches it is the common term used for the clergy who are not members of the priesthood as in Roman Catholicism and Anglicanism. (*See also* PRIEST)

Minyan   *Judaism*   Congregational prayer is very important in Judaism, and it is said that whenever Jews are gathered together in prayer, the SHEKHINA, the divine presence, is there amongst them. It is also written in the TALMUD that a man's prayers are heard by God only when he prays as part of a congregation. The RABBIS have agreed that a group of at least ten men is required to hold a Jewish service whenever the most sacred prayers of Judaism are recited, such as the AMIDAH or the KADDISH, and the TORAH scrolls are read. Some progressive communities now include women in the *Minyan*. (*See also* SEFER TORAH; SYNAGOGUE; TEFILLAH)

Miqat *(Place appointed)*   *Islam*   The place where pilgrims enter into the state of IHRAM or ritual purity in preparation for the HAJJ. This must be completed somewhere after departure and before entering the precincts of MAKKAH. Many pilgrims enter the state of *ihram* at the edge of the city and herald their arrival with the cry of 'LABBAIKA'.

Mirabai *Hinduism*   The most famous female devotee of northern India. She was born in 1547 and is believed to have fallen in love with KRISHNA at an early age. She betrothed herself to the deity and adorned, bathed, sang and danced to his image. Later she was married to the ruler of Chitor, a family who traditionally worshipped the Goddess. Mirabhai's continual devotions to the image of Krishna in the local temple led to mistaken rumours that she was conducting an adulterous relationship. Her husband broke into the temple only to find her singing love songs, enraptured before Krishna's image. It is believed that the Emperor Akbar travelled incognito to hear her songs of devotion. Ordered to leave the kingdom, she settled in Vrindavan, where her fame spread throughout north India. She began to identify herself with RADHA, the consort of Krishna. She eventually returned to her husband's court, but after his death, Mirabhai's mother-in-law continued to persecute her so she again retired to Vrindavan. It is believed that she died in the city by being absorbed back into Krishna's form in the temple. This form of death is a rare honour bestowed on very few of Hinduism's countless lovers of the divine. Mirabhai is remembered throughout northern India as the embodiment of devotion and her thousands of songs are still recorded by modern artistes and sung on radio as well as in congregational worship. Some traditions believe that in later life she became a disciple of the low-caste SANT master, RAVIDAS. (*See also* BHAKTI)

Mi'raj *(ladder)*   *Islam*   The term refers to the ascent of Muhammad through the heavens. The Night Journey, as it is known, is referred to in the Qur'an in SURA 17: 'Praise be He who travelled by night with his servant from the sacred mosque to the farthest sanctuary'. The earliest biography of the Prophet describes how Muhammad, accompanied by the angel JIBRIL, was taken by a heavenly mount to Jerusalem where he leads all the former prophets in prayer. After this he is taken on a mystical journey through all the levels of heaven and finally enters paradise. For SUFIS, it is this experience that marks the Prophet out as a supreme mystic and places him above Moses, who was unable to enter God's presence. The Mi'raj is celebrated annually on the twenty-seventh day of Rajab, the seventh lunar month, and like the birthday celebration, it is regarded as a day of illumination in which mosques are decorated with lamps. (*See also* BURAQ; MAULID)

Miri/Piri *Sikhism*   The important concept in Sikhism that relates to the ideal of both temporal and spiritual power being represented in the figure of the Guru. Sikhs believed that the concept originated with GURU HARGOBIND (1595–1644), who wore two swords to represent the two sources of authority. The latter Sikh

Gurus ruled as temporal leaders of the Sikh people as well as spiritual guides. The last human Guru, GURU GOBIND SINGH, exemplified the relationship between temporal and spiritual authority. (*See also* AKAL TAKHT; DEG; HARMANDIR; KHALISTAN; KHALSA)

Misals / Misls   *Sikhism*   In the eighteenth century when the Punjab was invaded three times from Afghanistan by Ahmad Shah, the Sikhs organized themselves into several independent but cooperating associations under the central control of the SARBAT KHALSA. These *misals* originally provided the Sikhs with the power to rebuff the invasion, but they were later brought under the central control of Maharaja RANJIT SINGH.

Mishkan   *Judaism*   The original travelling sanctuary used by the Jewish nomadic tribes before the building of the Temple in Jerusalem. The book of EXODUS relates how the Jews would set up the sanctuary in their encampments in the desert. It was placed in the centre in an open courtyard surrounded by a fence covered with cloth. Inside this courtyard was the Holy of Holies that contained the ark of the covenant. (*See also* ARON HAKODESH)

Mishnah   *Judaism*   The original writing down of the oral TORAH tradition that now forms part of the TALMUD. It is divided into various sections: *Zeraim*, which deals with agricultural laws; *Moed*, which is concerned with festivals and the Sabbath; *Nashim*, which deals with matters concerning women, particularly the laws of marriage; *Nezikin*, which covers legal matters such as commerce and criminal law; *Kadashim*, which deals with the sacrificial system; and *Toharot*, which is concerned with matters of ritual impurities. The writing down of the oral tradition that represented the teachings of Jewish sages throughout history was accomplished during the period from the first-century BCE through to Judah ha-Nasi's compilation in the second century CE. It is believed that the oral law was revealed to Moses and passed down through a direct line of transmission to the PHARISEES, who oversaw the beginning of the writing down of the Mishnah. In the fourth century CE, the teachings of these rabbis were collected and incorporated into the Palestinian Talmud. In the sixth century CE, the great rabbinical colleges in Babylon created the Babylonian Talmud. Both Talmuds essentially contain the Mishnah. Explanations of laws are provided, inconsistencies between interpretations are resolved and any laws that have become redundant are explained.

Mishpatim   *Judaism*   The laws in the TORAH that are considered accessible to reason or whose *raison d'être* is transparent. (*See also* MITZVAH)

Misls   *Sikhism*   See MISALS.

Missal *Christianity*   The Roman Catholic book that contains all the text and directions for performing the MASS, which was first developed in the thirteenth century in order to allow the priest to perform the sacrament alone. (*See also* BREVIARY)

Missions *Christianity*   The propagation of the Christian faith to non-Christian people by preaching the gospel. A primary task of the church since the origin of Christianity, it became linked with empire and colonialism from the sixteenth century, since when Christian mission has been associated with three world powers: Spain in the sixteenth and seventeenth centuries, Britain in the nineteenth and the USA in the twentieth. Christian mission is becoming aware of the necessity to acknowledge cultural diversity and avoid Western cultural forms when evangelizing. (*See* APOSTLE; EVANGELICAL; GOSPEL)

Mitra *Hinduism*   A Vedic god associated with the sun. He is the ruler of the day and a close associate of VARUNA, the guardian of cosmic order. He was regarded as a benefactor and close friend to human beings. (*See also* SAVITRI; SURYA)

Mitzvah / Mitzvot *(commandment)* *Judaism*   Just as TORAH refers to Jewish observance as a totality, a mitzvah refers to an individual instruction or obligation required by God of the Jews. The compilers of the TALMUD divided mitzvah into two categories: *mitzvot aseh* – the commands to perform an action; and *mitzvot lo ta'aseh* – the commands to refrain from a certain action. The aim of both kinds of commandment is to promote sanctity, and traditional Jews will recite a blessing before performing a mitzvah: *Blessed art Thou, o Lord, King of the Universe, who has sanctified us with His commandments and has commanded us to . . .* Another division of mitzvah made by rabbinical commentators is *hukkim* – those commandments that are clear or easily understood and MISHPATIM – those whose meaning is unclear and have to be accepted without understanding the rationale behind them. Of the 613 laws revealed by God to MOSES, 248 were positive and 365 were negative, but laws have also been added to the original law of Moses throughout Jewish history as specific historical events have arisen. There are also laws pertaining to worship in the Temple in Jerusalem that can no longer be followed since its destruction in 70 CE. (*See also* BET HA MIKDASH)

Moggallana *Buddhism*   One of the prominent disciples of the Buddha, who is regarded as a master of meditation and psychic powers.

Mogul / Moghul / Moghal *Islam*   One of the three great Muslim empires which lasted from the sixteenth to the nineteenth century. The Mogul dynasty was established in India in 1526 when Babar, the ruler of Afghanistan, captured

Delhi. By the reign of Akbar (1556–1605) the empire had expanded to cover most of India. Although in decline, the last effective emperor was Aurangzeb, who found himself increasingly under attack from the Marathas and the Sikhs. The empire of the Moguls lasted until 1857, when the British removed the last emperor. (*See also* OTTOMAN; SAFAVID)

Moha *(delusion, stupidity, dullness)* Buddhism   One of the three fires that have to be extinguished in order to provide the equanimity that is necessary to attain enlightenment. (*See* DOSA; RAGAS)

Moha Hinduism   Delusion. One of the three vices, along with (LOBHA) greed and (KRODHA) anger, identified as the source of all evil. *Moha* is regarded as the key to all vice, as it is believed that greed and anger arise from it. Delusion is associated with unconsciousness or ignorance, which manifests as carelessness, misjudgement, false pride and confusion. When overtaken by unconsciousness or in a condition of ignorance, the human being falls prey to the other vices through the loss of discrimination and self-control. (*See also* MAYA)

Moha *(love or attachment to the world)* Sikhism   According to the teaching of GURU NANAK it is one of the five enemies or obstacles in the way of the soul that prevent salvation. Like the other four, it is regarded as a manifestation of HAUMAI or ego-centredness.

Mohaniya Karma *(deluding karma)* Jainism   KARMA that reinforces illusion and overcomes right faith and right conduct. Consequently it is divided into two categories: faith-deluding and conduct-deluding karma. Deluding karma is the major block to revealing the true nature of the soul and once it is removed, other forms of karma are much easier to deal with. (*See also* CARITRA MOHANIYA; DARSHANA MOHANIYA)

Moharram / Muharram Islam   The first month of the lunar year in which is held the festival that marks the tragedy at KARBALA when HUSAIN, the grandson of Muhammad, was martyred in 680. This is a major occasion for SHI'A Muslims, who mark it by performing passion plays which dramatically represent Husain's suffering, renderings of grief-stricken poems and processions, in which adult males flagellate their backs to empathize with the suffering of the ultimate martyr. The occasion is also marked by most Muslims in the Indian subcontinent who, as a result of SUFI influence, hold the family of Muhammad in great regard.

Mohel Judaism   A religious person trained to perform the ritual of circumcision. Today modern surgical instruments are used. At the circumcision, the *mohel* stands before two chairs. One chair contains the child, who is held by his godfather; the other is the chair of ELIJAH, the prophet who is the guardian of Israel. The child is given to the *mohel*, who places him in Elijah's chair and makes a benediction. He is then handed back to the godfather and the ritual circumcision takes place on the godfather's lap. The *mohel* recites all the blessings throughout the ritual. (*See also* BERIT MILAH; SANDEK)

Mohenjodaro   *Hinduism*   The city excavated in the first half of the twentieth century along with HARAPPA, and originally believed to confirm the theory that the DRAVIDIAN or Harappan culture was destroyed suddenly by an invasion of the ARYANS from the northwest. The theory is now under challenge but remains speculative. The script of the two cities remains undeciphered and theories concerning religion and its relationship to the development of Hinduism rely on interpretation of discovered artefacts.

Moksha   *Hinduism*   The end goal of most forms of the Hindu spiritual quest. It refers to the release of the soul from SAMSARA, or the cycle of rebirth, and is usually translated as liberation. It can be achieved by following one of the three MARGAS or paths to liberation. The various schools of philosophy offer variations on the concept of *moksha* depending on how they regard the relationship of BRAHMAN, the absolute being, and ATMAN, the eternal in human beings. For Advaita Vedantins, liberation is the realization that Brahman and atman are identical. For most *bhakti* or devotional traditions, liberation is perceived as eternal companionship with the divine, usually as a form of Vishnu. The many SAMPRADAYAS, or sects of Hinduism, offer a vast range of methods for achieving liberation, but there is a basic distinction between those who consider liberation to be ultimately achievable only after death and those who believe that liberation is obtainable whilst alive as a human being. Release from samsara results in freedom from all suffering and the enjoyment of the qualities of Brahman described as SATCHITANANDA or truth, consciousness and bliss. (*See also* VEDANTA)

Moksha   *Jainism*   Ultimate deliverance or liberation. When all the karmic particles are shred from the soul and no more KARMA is allowed to enter the human being, the soul retains its original state of omniscience. On death it then attains liberation, as there is no karmic force to keep it in the realm of SAMSARA. It moves upwards to the summit of the cosmos, where it dwells in eternal but individual bliss, freedom and omniscience. The attainment of *moksha* is only possible for human beings in the realm of KARMABHUMI (realm of action). All other beings have to wait for the possibility of human life before being able to achieve liberation. (*See also* KEVALIN, SIDDHA)

Monarchianism   *Christianity*   A second- and third-century theological movement arising in Byzantium which believed in the unity of the Godhead and played down the idea of the Son as an independent entity. The early form of Monarchianism, developed from the ideas of Theodotus, claimed that Jesus Christ was fully human and therefore not a part of the Godhead. However, the more successful later Monarchianism developed from Noetus. This teaching claimed that it was the Father Himself who was born and there was consequently no independent being known as the Son. (*See* ARIANISM; CHRISTOLOGY; MONO-PHYSITISM; TRINITARIAN; TRINITY)

Monastery   *Christianity*   The house of a religious community containing monks, friars or nuns belonging to one of the Christian ORDERS. (*See also* ABBESS; ABBOT; CONVENT; MENDICANT FRIARS; MONK; NUN; RELIGIOUS)

Monasticism   *Christianity*   The idea of monasticism developed from the early Christian hermits who withdrew from the world and lived in the desert, but had its roots in the Christian martyrs who had considered their faith to be greater than the values of the world around them. From around the fourth century monastic communities began to develop in the East and by the end of the century had spread to the West. The basic framework of the movement was based on the idea of progression from baptism into a life in Christ to a contemplative knowledge of God achieved through renunciation, asceticism, penance, prayer, fasting and service. By the fifth century, the Order of St Benedict (480–550) had been formed and was to become the norm for all orders of Western monasticism. (*See* BENEDICTINE; CISTERCIANS; CONVENT; DOMINICANS; FRANCISCANS; MENDICANT FRIARS; MONASTERY; MONK; NUN; RELIGIOUS)

Monk   *Christianity*   A member of the laity or priesthood who lives the life of MONASTICISM according to the rule of one of the religious orders in order to achieve personal closeness to God through the vows of poverty, chastity and obedience. (*See also* MONASTERY; ORDERS; RELIGIOUS)

Monophysitism   *Christianity*   The fifth-century dissenting doctrine opposed to the views of the Council of Chalcedon (451) that asserts Christ only had one divine nature rather than the orthodox view that he was both fully human and fully divine. It is still prevalent in the eastern Mediterranean, including the Coptic, Armenian, Syrian and Abyssinian churches. (*See* ARIANISM; CHRISTOLOGY; COUNCIL; EBIONITES; NICAEA, COUNCIL OF)

Monsignor   *Christianity*   A title given in the Roman Catholic Church to a CARDINAL or any other high clerical office that is directly appointed by the POPE. (*See also* PAPACY)

Montanism *Christianity*   A second-century apocalyptic movement founded by Montanus around the year 170 and which believed in the imminence of the last days. The movement was known for its moral rigour, asceticism and refusal to compromise with society. Montanus claimed to be a prophet and the movement spread rapidly from Asia Minor to Rome, alarming the leaders of the Christian community. Its greatest convert was Tertullian, a famous early Christian writer. Montanism was eventually condemned at a number of COUNCILS. (*See* MILLENARIANISM)

Mool Mantar / Mul Mantar / Mul Mantra *Sikhism*   The first few lines of JAPJI written by GURU NANAK which form the opening verses of the GURU GRANTH SAHIB. It contains the basic statement of belief upheld by Sikhs and is regarded as the essence of the Sikh faith. It states that God is one, the eternal reality, the creator, without fear or enmity, immortal, never incarnated, self-existent and known by the grace of the Guru.

Moral Theology *Christianity*   The theological study of Christian behaviour and character first treated systematically by Thomas AQUINAS in the second section of SUMMA THEOLOGICA. In recent years attention has shifted from attempting to find systems of behaviour that are binding on all Christians to treating each case as individual but guided by the overriding principle of LOVE.

Morning Prayer *Christianity*   *See* MATINS.

Mortal Sin *Christianity*   A form of SIN that is a deliberate act of turning away from God. It is committed with clear knowledge of its consequences and full consent of the will. It will bring the punishment of eternal damnation unless repented. (*See also* ACTUAL SIN; ATONEMENT; CONFESSION; ORIGINAL SIN; PENANCE)

Mosadhamma (P) *Buddhism*   The expression used by the Buddha to describe unreality or the belief in the permanence of phenomena. (*See* MAYA; NIRVANA; SAMSARA)

Moses *Judaism*   The leader and law-giver of ISRAEL at the time of the EXODUS from Israel. Born a Jew in captivity, his parents had floated him down the River Nile where the daughter of the Pharaoh discovered him in the bulrushes. He was brought up as a prince of Egypt but had to flee after killing an Egyptian who was ill-treating a Jewish slave. God appointed him a prophet after appearing in the Burning Bush and commanded him to free the Jews from captivity. Moses received the revelation of the law on Mount Sinai after leading the people out of Egypt. Most traditional Jews believe that Moses received both the written and the oral TORAH from God and passed them both down via an unbroken chain of transmission through Joshua, the elders, the prophets and finally to the rabbis. The first five books of the Bible are known as the Books of Moses. The seventh day of the month of Adar is observed in commemoration of Moses' death.

Moshiach *Judaism*   *See* MASSIACH.

Mosque *Islam*   The building erected or used for public prayer. The name is derived from MASJID. The first mosque was built for community prayer and gatherings in MADINAH and was also Muhammad's home. Essentially, a mosque is built on an axis which points to the KA'ABA. The basic features are a hall for prayer, a pulpit for the Friday sermon, a niche to point the direction of MAKKAH and a source of water for ritual washing before prayer. However, the minimum requirement is a rectangle drawn in the sand with a niche that points to Makkah. The large mosques built by various Muslim rulers were far more elaborate and contained MINARETS, calligraphy and splendid domes. (*See also* ADHAN; MIHRAB; MINBAR; MU'ADHIN; QIBLA; SALAH; WUDU)

Mrtyu *Hinduism*   Death; in the PURANAS; Mrtyu is said to have been born from the offspring of Dharma and Adharma, who were in turn the grandchildren of BRAHMA's offspring, the primeval man or MANU. Mrtyu is still prayed to at funerals by contemporary Hindus as the Lord of Cremation.

Mu'adhin / Muezzin *Islam*   The Muslim elected to call the faithful to prayer by reciting the ADHAN. Muhammad decided that the human voice should be the distinctive mark of the Muslim call to prayer, as opposed to the bells of Christianity and the ram's horn of Judaism. He appointed BILAL, the black Ethiopian freed slave, as the first *mu'adhin*. Usually the call is made from the MINARET of the mosque, but in places where Muslims are in a minority, such as Western Europe, it may be completed in the mosque just prior to the prayer.

Mu'amala *Islam*   Outward religious duties as distinct from the obligatory rites of the religion laid down in the SHARI'A. It is also used by some Sufis to describe the outer or exoteric manifestations of Islam. (*See also* IBADAH; TARIQAH)

Mu'awiyah *Islam*   The founder of the UMAYYAD caliphate in 661 when he succeeded after the death of ALI. Mu'awiyah moved the centre of the Muslim world away from Madinah to his own power base in Damascus and designated his son as his successor to the caliphate, thereby founding a hereditary dynasty. There were many Muslims amongst the companions of Muhammad who regarded Mu'awiyah, as a usurper and a corrupter of Islamic values.

Mudda (P) / Mudra (S) *(a seal or a symbol)* *Buddhism* Ritual hand gestures that have deep symbolic significance and are associated with blessings usually related to a particular Tantric deity. (*See* TANTRA)

Mudita *Buddhism* One of the four sublime states or BRAHMA VIHARAS experienced by an advanced practitioner. *Mudita* is sympathetic joy or the experience of sharing the success and achievements of others without feelings of hostility or competitive envy at their success. (*See also* KARUNA; METTA; UPEKKHA)

Mudra *Hinduism* Eating fried rice; one of the five MAKARAS forbidden to orthodox Hindus but indulged in by those who follow the left-hand path of Tantric or SHAKTI cults. More commonly, *mudra* refers to the sophisticated symbolic language of hand gestures used in various dance forms but is also the symbolic language used in YOGA postures. Deities and representations of holy people are often depicted with their hands in various *mudras*. The most common are the *abhaya mudra*, expressing tranquillity or protection, where the hand is turned to the front with the fingers pointing upwards, and the *varada mudra*, expressing blessings, where the hand is turned to the front but the fingers point downwards. TANTRA has developed these into a very sophisticated system and they are also used extensively in some forms of Buddhism.

Muezzin *Islam* See MU'ADHIN.

Mufti *Islam* A Muslim legal scholar or lawyer, either private or public, who is able to apply interpretation of the SHARI'A to individual cases. In time large numbers of individual case laws became collections that could be used by Muslim judges in deciding cases that came before the courts. (*See also* QADI)

Mughal *Islam* See MOGUL.

Muhajir *Islam* Indian Muslims who migrated to Pakistan in 1947 at the time of the partition of the subcontinent. They see themselves as a deprived minority in modern Pakistan and have organized themselves politically to obtain equal rights.

Muhammad *(praised)* *Islam* The name of the final prophet, who was born in MAKKAH around 570. At around the age of forty he began to receive a series of revelations in which he was commanded to recite the QUR'AN, the final book of God, which contains the complete instruction that leads to submission and obedience to God's will. In 622, he departed for MADINAH, where he organized his followers into the first Muslim community, which went on to spread the message of Islam very successfully throughout the Arabian peninsula and, after

Muhammad's death, throughout the world. All Muslims acknowledge Muhammad as the final prophet of God and the exemplar of Muslim belief and practice. The SUNNA or behaviour of the Prophet is second only to the Qur'an as a divine source of guidance. However, millions of Muslims look to Muhammad as a perfect intercessor for their prayers to Allah and believe that he will also intercede for his community at the Day of Judgement. It is also traditionally believed that Muhammad is sinless and pre-existed creation as the light of Allah. In the SUFI tradition, he is the ultimate mystic or saint as well as the final prophet. The Prophet's tomb in Madinah is regarded as the second most holy shrine in Islam and is visited by millions of Muslims every year. (*See also* ISTIGHATHA; NA'T; NUR; RASUL)

Muhapatti *Jainism*   The distinct white cloth mask worn over the mouth of STHANAKAVASI monks to prevent them breathing in small organisms.

Muharjihun *(the emigrants)* *Islam*   The original Muslims, approximately 140, who elected to leave MAKKAH and depart with the Prophet to MADINAH and therefore shared in the HIJRA.

Muharram *Islam*   *See* MOHARRAM.

Mujaddid *Islam*   A devout Muslim popularly believed to renew the faith every hundred years by restoring it to its original purity. It is also believed that a special *mujaddid* appears every thousand years.

Mujahada *Islam*   One of the mainstays of the mystical or SUFI path, it refers to the ideal of striving after perfection or complete purification of the heart. It is also used to describe the mortification or penance undertaken to grapple with the unregenerate NAFS. In Sufism, *mujahada* is associated with JIHAD.

Mujahiddin *Islam*   Muslims engaged in JIHAD or armed struggle to defend Islam. The term is often used by militant Islamic groups struggling to restore Islamic law and behaviour to various Muslim nations, or those involved in freedom struggles in such countries as Afghanistan or Kashmir.

Mujawar/Mujawir *Islam*   The attendants at a shrine of a SUFI or Muslim holy man/woman. They are usually descendants of the person in the tomb, who achieve their position on a hereditary basis. They will look after the shrine and guide the pilgrims to attend in worship and petition. Often the families will control the stalls from which offerings can be purchased, and the guesthouses where pilgrims are accommodated. (*See also* DAR; MAZAR; SAJJADA NASHIN)

Mu'jiza   *Islam*   The miracles performed by Muhammad. However, most Muslims regard the revelation of the QUR'AN as the great miracle manifested through the Prophet. In recent centuries, Muslim modernists have tried to play down the vast body of traditional miracle literature associated with Muhammad, but the miracle stories still function to inspire the faithful. The Qur'an mentions three miraculous events and they are celebrated in Muslim life: the Night Journey, the Splitting of the Moon and the Opening of the Breast. (*See also* KARAMA; MI'RAJ)

Mujtahid   *Islam*   Someone versed in grammatical, legal and theological training and considered qualified to carry out IJTIHAD, or independent reasoning or initiative, to understand the right action or correct interpretation of the QUR'AN or HADITH. The medieval ULAMA 'declared the door of *ijtihad* closed', meaning that this kind of independent reasoning was no longer permissible. However, several prominent Muslim scholars through to the present day have announced themselves as *mujtahid*, including most of the leaders of the twentieth century revival movements. (*See also* IJMA)

Mukte Sikhs   *Sikhism*   The term refers to Sikhs who are prepared to sacrifice everything for their faith. Such Sikhs have given their lives in defence of other adherents of the faith and are believed to have secured their own liberation by their unselfish actions. (*See* MUKTI)

Mukti   *Hinduism*   An alternative term for liberation from the endless cycle of birth and rebirth otherwise known as MOKSHA.

Mukti   *Sikhism*   As in other Indian traditions, Sikhs believe that liberation is release from the endless cycle of birth and death. The means to liberation is devotion to God and obedience to the teachings of the GURU. For contemporary Sikhs this is contained in the GURU GRANTH SAHIB, which provides the complete teachings of the ten human Gurus.

Mul Mantra   *Sikhism*   *See* MOOL MANTAR.

Mulk   *Islam*   A form of ownership in Islamic law approximately corresponding to modern-day freehold.

Mu'min (faithful)   *Islam*   A term used for believers or practising Muslims who are perceived to have given themselves wholeheartedly in submission to Allah's will. They are considered to be at peace with themselves and creation. (*See* ISLAM)

Munafiqun   *Islam*   A term used in the Qur'an for hypocrites or those who claim they are believers but only do so in order to benefit politically or socially. Muslim revivalists sometimes use it to describe nominal Muslims who claim membership of the UMMA but do not practise their religion and its obligatory duties. (*See also* MU'MIN)

Mundaka Upanishad   *Hinduism*   One of the principal UPANISHADS that introduces the theme of higher and lower knowledge. Lower knowledge consists of the study of scripture, including the VEDAS, while higher knowledge is the direct perception or 'grasping' of the imperishable BRAHMAN.

Mundan   *Hinduism*   Head-shaving ceremony performed as a rite of passage in the first or third year of life. (*See* SAMSKAR)

Munmukh   *Sikhism*   See MANMUKH.

Muraqaba   *Islam*   A technique of contemplation commonly used in Sufism, in which a practitioner attempts to attain spiritual communion through concentration on a verse from the Qur'an, or by visualizing the form of Muhammad or one's spiritual master. The latter very often takes place at a Sufi's tomb. (*See* DHIKR; MAZAR; TARIQAH; WALI)

Murid   *Islam*   A follower or disciple of a SUFI master. The Sufi TARIQAHS (paths) are based upon the relationship between the MURSHID (spiritual director) and the MURID (aspirant). The aspirant is expected to travel in search of a master. Once found, the aspirant takes BAI'A or initiation at the hands of the master. Many prominent Sufis have had several masters before arriving at their final one. (*See also* SHAIKH)

Murji'ite   *Islam*   Early group of Muslim theologians who believed in 'postponement' or leaving punishment or rewards to Allah at the Last Day. They were opposed to the more extreme of the KHARIJITES who considered that it was right to proclaim JIHAD against unjust Muslim rulers. The basic premise of the Murji'ites is that possession of faith is sufficient over deeds in order to be defined as a Muslim. The political implications were that bad rulers had to be obeyed as they ruled by God's will. (*See also* MU'TAZILA)

Murshid   *Islam*   A Sufi master or teacher. (*See* SHAIKH; PIR)

Murti   *Hinduism*   The image of a deity used as a focus of worship either in a temple or at home. The power of the deity is believed to exist within the installed image and a temple deity is consecrated in a ceremony where life is believed to be breathed into the *murti*. Hinduism contains a vast array of deities: human, supernatural beings, animal, half-human, half-animal, all both male and female. The most important are the forms of SHIVA and VISHNU and their family members. These two deities make up the dominant traditions of Shaivism and Vaishnavism. However, Hindus generally believe that all the deities are manifestations or aspects of the one absolute being, BRAHMAN, who pervades the universe. Hindus will choose their deity according to need, caste, status or sectarian allegiance. Although the focus will be on the chosen deity, there is no denial of the others in the Hindu pantheon. Thus Hinduism cannot be strictly defined as polytheism; henotheism would be a more accurate description of *murti* worship. (*See also* SHAIVITE; VAISHNAVA)

Murugan   *Hinduism*   An ancient deity of the Tamils associated with youth, beauty and freedom that is still the object of popular worship throughout Tamil-speaking south India. According to ancient Tamil texts, he is the god of war, whose emblems are the elephant and the blue-feathered peacock. The usual form of worship involves offerings of rice and honey, but goats are also sacrificed. His temples or places of pilgrimage are usually situated on high ground. Murugan worship has been identified with the north Indian worship of SKANDA, the Aryan god of war. Since Skanda has become identified with KARTIKEYA, the multi-headed son of SHIVA, Murugan has been assimilated into Shaivism, the worship of Shiva and his family. A further assimilation has resulted in the merging of Murugan's identity with SUBRAMANIYAM.

Musa   *Islam*   The Muslim name for Moses, the prophet of Allah to whom the book known as the TAWRAH was given. Moses is regarded as the prophet who brought the revelation to the Jewish people. Their disobedience led to the coming of Jesus, whose mission was to restore the inner dimension to the Jewish law and try for the last time to guide the Jewish people to the correct observance of the Tawrah. The final revelation to Muhammad gave the responsibility to the Arab nation but was also a universal message for all humanity. (*See also* AHL AL-KITAB; NABI; RASUL)

Musafaha   *Islam*   The joining of hands between an adherent and a Sufi master which affirms discipleship and formalizes the relationship of MURID and MURSHID. The hand-clasping takes place in the initiation ceremony known as BAI'A. (*See also* PIR; SHAIKH)

Musaph   *Judaism*   An additional prayer to the obligatory three daily prayers that is recited on the Sabbath and festival days and is believed to date back to traditional practices conducted at the Temple in Jerusalem. (*See* MAARIV; MINHAH; SHAHARIT)

Musar *(instruction or reproof)* Judaism   These are ethical works that call Jews to live a better life based on God's commandments in the TORAH, the voice of conscience and social duty. During the Middle Ages many *Musar* were produced, such as Rabbi Bahya's *Duties of the Heart*. However, the *Musar* movement was founded in the nineteenth century in Lithuania by Rabbi Israel Lipkin. He introduced the idea of consistent chanting of the *Musar* literature so that it penetrated the depths of the being, without which it had little impact and the transformation of character could not take place. The *Musarists* have had considerable impact on the education of Jews in the Yeshiva of the USA and Israel.

Mushaka *Hinduism*   The rat sanctified as the mount of GANESH. There are temples in India that are sacred to rats. In VRINDAVAN, an annual procession takes place, in which an especially fattened and large rat is taken through the city as a representative of the animal's sanctity.

Mushriq *(an idolater)* Islam   The worst offence in Islam, which espouses a rigorous and strict polytheism. The term applies to someone who worships other gods alongside Allah. This person is guilty of SHIRK, the gravest sin. Christians are sometimes referred to in this way for their maintenance of the doctrine of the TRINITY, and some Muslim groups have accused other Muslims of veering towards idolatry in their respect and veneration of Muhammad. Maulana MAWDUDI accused Muslims who paid loyalty to human political systems that acknowledged the sovereignty of the people rather than the sovereignty of Allah of this sin.

Muslim (m) / Muslima (f) *Islam*   A practitioner of Islam or one who submits to Allah through obedience to the revelation and belongs to the community of Islam. It is usually used to describe someone who has either been born into the faith or converted. The minimum requirement to become a Muslim is the uttering of the SHAHADAH in front of two witnesses. The community has been divided over the definition of a Muslim. Some groups, notably the KHARIJITES and a number of contemporary revivalist movements, have attempted to define Muslim according to practice rather than birth. The traditional position is to suspend judgement, as only Allah can know the depths of the human heart. (*See also* MU'MIN)

Mustafa *('the chosen one')* Islam   A name given to Muhammad that refers to his role as the seal of the prophets and the vehicle for Allah's final revelation.

Mutakullum (U) *Islam*   A Muslim speaker or preacher who may attend the

JUMA prayers or a variety of public festivals or religious conferences. (*See also* IMAM; KHATIB; ULAMA)

Mu'tazila *(the neutralists)* *Islam* A group of MURJI'ITES who maintained neutrality in the political divisions between Ali and his opponents, as they advocated a strict predetermination that allowed for no human free will. This became pure determinism that accepted moral laxity on the grounds that everything is predetermined and it could therefore be used politically to justify corrupt regimes.

Muzdalifah *Islam* The place where the pilgrims on the HAJJ pass the night in the open after the ninth day of the pilgrimage, standing from noon to sunset listening to sermons on ARAFAT, 13 miles from MAKKAH.

N

Naam Simran   *Sikhism*   *See* NAM SIMRAN.

Nabi   *Islam*   One of the many prophets or messengers of Allah. Usually used to refer to a messenger who does not receive a revelation in the form of a book and is chosen to warn human beings of the consequences of disobedience to God's commandments and the rewards of obedience. Although the Qur'an focuses on the Jewish prophets, it acknowledges that there have been thousands of such prophets in all cultures. Those who come with a book of revelation are much more uncommon. (*See* RASUL)

Nad *(sound)*   *Sikhism*   It usually refers to the inner sound heard in deep meditation. The SANT BHAKTAS, including GURU NANAK, often write of the ecstasy of immersing themselves in the inner sound or music within. Contemporary Sikhs usually identify *nad* with SABAD and therefore view it as the revelation that originates in the words of the Sikh Gurus.

Nadhir   *Islam*   A term that describes one of the essential activities of a prophet and refers to his role as a warner of the penalties of disobedience to God's commandments and the risks of relying on anything that is not God. All prophets, whether their status is NABI or RASUL, perform the function of warning.

Nafs   *Islam*   A term used in Sufism and traditional Islam to describe the lower self, egocentricity or the base instincts and evil qualities which need to be overcome, subdued and transformed or dissolved by purification. This can be achieved by remembering Allah through DHIKR, prayer, reciting the Qur'an or any other of the requirements of Islam. Muhammad described the battle to purify the *nafs* as the greater JIHAD and beholden on every Muslim. (*See also* QALB; SUFI)

Nagar Kirtan   *Sikhism*   The public singing of the GURBANI in processions through city streets. This is usually done on the occasion of a major Sikh festival. The GURU GRANTH SAHIB heads the procession and is often accompanied by brass bands and five KHALSA Sikhs representing the PANJ PIARE.

Nagarjuna *Buddhism* Teacher who founded the MADHYAMAKA school of philosophy in the second century BCE. He was born in Maharashtra, but after becoming a monk lived in Andhra. He was a prolific writer who systemized the Perfection of Wisdom Sutra which formed the basis of the Madhyamaka school. The most radical assertion made by Nagarjuna, based on the Perfection of Wisdom Sutra, was that all things are empty or have no existence independent of external circumstances.

Nagas (S) *Buddhism* Mythical serpents which protect Buddhas and Buddhists. In Indian mythology the *nagas* are symbols of the initiates into wisdom.

Nagas *Hinduism* A collective name for various groups of renunciates, usually from the Shaivite tradition, who are famous for their lack of clothing. Some Nagas are fully naked, while others only wear a small loincloth. Their hair is worn long in locks and they cover their bodies in ash; their foreheads and limbs are usually covered in painted sectarian marks. Although Hindu renunciates are often associated with tranquillity and non-violence, the various Naga groups formed armed bands, probably in order to resist attack by Muslims. However, they have also been known to fight each other. A well-known group of Nagas is the NATH YOGIS or KANPHATA. (*See also* SHAIVITE)

Nagas *Hinduism* Mythical snake-gods who dwell in the netherworlds, and are often represented as cobras with several heads. Snakes, particularly cobras, are regarded as sacred animals. (*See* SESA)

Nahmanides *Judaism* A thirteenth-century rabbi otherwise known as Moses Ben Nahman, a kabbalist, who provided substantial exegesis of the sacred texts. He posited the idea of an eternal TORAH that was only recorded by Moses. He also disputed MAIMONIDES' emphasis on the afterlife being the immortality of the soul and preferred to emphasize the resurrection of the body. (*See also* KABBALAH; OLAM HA-BA)

Nahum *Judaism* One of the twelve 'minor' prophets and a book of the same name in the Jewish scriptures. Nahum's prophecies mainly dwell on the fate that would befall the Assyrian empire because of their cruelty. He preached that there was a divine code of righteous behaviour that all humanity had to observe and that all those nations that failed to observe it would eventually be doomed. The main brunt of his prophecy is levelled towards the Assyrian capital, Ninevah, which eventually fell in 612 BCE. (*See* NEVIIM)

Najar / Nazar   *Hinduism*   The evil eye, believed to be incurred by the envy of neighbours or supernatural beings. In village Hinduism, severe and recurring misfortune could be interpreted as some form of malevolent possession, the most common of which is the evil eye. As in most cases of possession, the cure would be sought with a local practitioner. (*See* OJHA)

Najdites   *Islam*   A sect of KHARIJITES who came to dominate Arabia until defeated by the UMAYYADS. They held a more moderate position than other Kharijite movements regarding expulsion from the community. This was probably because they had to moderate the extreme positions often associated with the movement in order to regulate territory.

Nam   *Sikhism*   The name of God, which in the teachings of the Sikh Gurus is synonymous with God. The name is central to both revelation and salvation in GURU NANAK's poetry. It is the way in which God reveals that He is immanent in both creation and His devotee's heart. Inner remembrance of the name is the sole means of salvation. In contemporary Sikhism the term is used to describe the GURBANI or compositions of the Sikh Gurus contained in the GURU GRANTH SAHIB. It can also refer to praise of God. (*See also* NAM SIMRAN; SATNAM)

Nam Japan   *Sikhism*   *See* NAM SIMRAN.

Nam Karan   *Sikhism*   The naming ceremony in which a newly born child is presented to the GURU GRANTH SAHIB at the GURDWARA. The GRANTHI will recite prayers and stanzas from the Guru Granth Sahib and drop AMRIT on the child's lips. The name is selected by opening the Guru Granth Sahib at random. The first letter of the first word becomes the initial letter for the name selected.

Nam Simran / Nam Simaran / Naam Simran / Nam Japan   *Sikhism*   Continuous remembrance of the name of God encouraged by GURU NANAK as the only means to achieve salvation. Recollection of the name reveals God's presence both within the devotee and outside in creation. In contemporary Sikhism this is achieved by reciting passages from the GURU GRANTH SAHIB. However, eventually it is necessary to achieve spontaneous continuous remembrance through unuttered meditation. (*See also* NAM)

Nama *(name)*   *Buddhism*   Used collectively for the aspects of the mind, or to describe four of the five KHANDHA with the exception of RUPA. (*See also* SKANDA; VEDANA; VINNANA)

Nama *Jainism* Body-producing KARMA that is responsible for the diversity of living beings found in the Jain cosmos. This karma determines the kind of body that one will take at rebirth. It has four varieties: human-producing, animal- or plant-producing, celestial-producing or hell-producing.

Nama Rupa *(name and form)* *Buddhism* Used as a collective term for the five KHANDHA. In the context of the *khandha*, it refers to mind and body, but it can also be used as a description of all phenomenal existence. It is also a part of the causal chain of existence arising out of VINNANA and leading to SALAYATANA. (*See also* NAMA; NIDANAS; RUPA; SAMSARA)

Namajapa *Hinduism* The remembrance of the name or names of God. Although reference to the remembrance of God's name is found in many ancient Hindu scriptures, it is the medieval BHAKTI tradition that made the practice popular amongst the masses. The great *bhakti* poets, both Shaivite and Vaishnav-ite, praise the name of God in their poems. Generally, the practice consists of the repetition of a favoured name of the deity of a particular SAMPRADAYA (sect) often aided by use of a MALA (rosary). The success of the *bhakti* tradition has led to a proliferation of divine names and the composition of litanies containing the thousand names of God. The most popular names are those associated with VISHNU, SHIVA and the DEVI. The Hindu scriptures state that to be effective, the name of God has to be the name that God acknowledges as His eternal name and therefore identical to Himself. It is stated that the remembrance or repetition of this eternal or uncreated name is the only means of salvation. Many *bhakti* and SANT poets stated that this name could only be known through association and initiation with a SATGURU (true guru). This particular belief was developed by the Sikhs into a new religion based around the *satguru* and the SATNAM. (*See also* SABAD)

Namarupa *(name and form)* *Hinduism* TULSIDAS wrote a famous passage in the RAMACHARITAMANASA in which he argues that the name of God is greater than both the absolute BRAHMAN and the various ISVARAS or AVATARS (forms or incarnations of God). Tulsidas' argument is that although Brahman, the reposi-tory of infinite truth, consciousness and bliss, dwells in all hearts, still creatures are miserable, yet by the remembrance of the name they become joyful. He goes on to argue that while avatars only save favoured devotees at a particular time or place, the remembrance of the name of God has saved countless souls since the beginning of time. Tulsidas, however, does acknowledge that name and form are one entity, and cannot be separated from each other. (*See also* NAMAJAPA; NIRGUNA BRAHMAN; SAGUNA BRAHMAN)

Namaskar *Hinduism* The typical Hindu greeting made to each other and on greeting a deity. Typically, the hands are folded together in a prayer position, the head is bowed and a greeting is made with the words *namaskar* or *namaste*; however, particular religious sects (SAMPRADAYAS) may have their own unique wording often associated with the particular name of their chosen deity.

Namaz (U)   *Islam*   Used by Muslims in the Indian subcontinent as a name for SALAH or the five-times daily obligatory prayers.

Namdev   *Hinduism*   A fourteenth-century SANT from Maharashtra, a tailor by trade, who taught that caste was not a barrier to complete devotion to God. As with most *sant* teachers, Namdev focused on remembrance of the name of God to attain salvation, taught and wrote his poetry in the vernacular and preached that God can be found within the heart of the devotee regardless of caste, creed or gender. Namdev has sixty-one poems included in the GURU GRANTH SAHIB. (*See also* NAMAJAPA)

Namdhari   *Sikhism*   A Sikh reform movement founded by Baba Balak Singh (1799–1861) during the reign of Maharaja RANJIT SINGH. The Namdharis were influential in bringing Sikhs back to the teachings of the gurus by opposing immorality, the use of drugs and alcohol, dowries, observance of caste in marriage and the forbidding of remarriage to widows. They have an ambivalent relationship with the KHALSA, as they do not accept AMRIT initiation or the supreme authority of the GURU GRANTH SAHIB. They do not believe that GURU GOBIND SINGH was the last guru and have their own continued lineage of living gurus. Namdharis are easily recognized by their distinctive dress of white *kurta*, white pyjama and white turban, which is tied straight across the forehead. They usually celebrate festivals commemorating the birthdays of their own line of gurus.

Name of Jesus   *Christianity*   St John's Gospel seems to use the idea of belief in the name as synonymous for personal commitment or faith in Jesus Christ, and generally it is used in the New Testament in reference to Christ's power and authority. The first disciples performed miracles and baptized in the name of Jesus. Devotion to the holy name became popular under the influence of the FRANCISCANS in the fifteenth century. (*See also* BAPTISM)

Nanak Panthis   *Sikhism*   The followers of GURU NANAK. Today the term is usually applied to any sect that emphasizes the teachings of Guru Nanak over the formal religious observances introduced into Sikhism by GURU GOBIND SINGH or later. They refer to Guru Nanak's teachings on the uselessness of ceremony, ritual, pilgrimage and the equality of castes. Generally, they do not feel that KHALSA allegiance is necessary and most of them do not accept the supreme authority of the GURU GRANTH SAHIB. (*See also* SAHAJDHARI)

Nandi   *Hinduism*   The bull sacred as the mount (VAHANA) of SHIVA and whose statues are found in front of the entrance to Shiva temples. Some statues of Nandi are massive.

Nankana Sahib   *Sikhism*   The contemporary name of the small town in the Punjab where GURU NANAK was born. It is now in Pakistan. (*See also* TALWANDI)

Naomi   *Judaism*   The mother-in-law of RUTH who is regarded as the ideal of the righteous convert. In Orthodox Judaism, a set of questions and answers attributed to Ruth and Naomi are used in the process of conversion. (*See also* GER)

Naqshbandi / Naqshbandiya   *Islam*   The largest of the SUFI orders and the most orthodox in their attitude to the SHARI'A. They are found throughout the Muslim world but originally came from three lines that developed in India, central Asia and Turkey. The founder was Baha'ud'din an-Naqshbandi (d.1389). However, he traced his own lineage back to Muhammad, but uniquely amongst the Sufi orders, it comes up through Abu Bakr rather than Ali. The Naqshbandi are famous for performing their DHIKR (remembrance of Allah) in silence, although it is rare to find the pure silent form today. The order was prominent in reforming and reviving Islam in the eighteenth and nineteenth centuries and remain active and influential in contemporary Muslim societies. (*See also* SILSILA; TARIQAH)

Narada   *Hinduism*   A great sage and exponent of BHAKTI (devotion). He is regarded as the foremost disciple of VISHNU and the author of the Bhakti Sutras, a scholarly exposition of the devotional tradition. There are many popular tales and legends associated with Narada as an archetypal sage and devotee of Vishnu. He seems to have complete access to all divine worlds, including the heaven of Vishnu, but some of the stories deal with his humiliation through excess pride and then salvation through Vishnu's grace. The overriding theme is the Lord's protection of his devotees.

Narada Devi   *Hinduism*   The wife of RAMAKRISHNA PARAMHANSA. She was married to him as a child and the relationship was never consummated. Narada Devi joined him at the temple in DAKSHINESHWAR in 1871 as a devotee. He regarded her as a manifestation of the Goddess but probably not in any significant sense other than his ecstatic ability to see the divine in all. However, after his death some followers began to regard her as an incarnation of the Goddess.

Narasimha   *Hinduism*   The fourth incarnation (AVATAR) of VISHNU, who manifested as half-man, half-lion to destroy the demon HIRANYA KASIPU, the father and persecutor of the child-devotee PRAHLADA.

Narayan *Hinduism* One of the most common names for invoking VISHNU. The earliest mention of Narayan in Hindu scripture is in the Satapatha Brahmana, a part of the Vedic texts, which states that Purusha Narayan performed a five-day sacrifice to become the Lord of Creation. In one of the Vedic forest texts, the Taittiriya Aranyaka, Narayan is referred to as the supreme Lord of Creation and identified with HARI, the other common appellation of Vishnu. The same text identifies Narayan with Vishnu.

Narthex *Christianity* The name given to the antechamber of the nave used by penitents and those awaiting baptism in the Eastern Orthodox churches. (*See* ORTHODOX CHURCH)

Nasik *Islam* A term used for some of the pious Muslims in the early period after the death of Muhammad who lived in MADINAH and maintained a life of humility, simplicity and asceticism based on the model of the Prophet rather than being caught up in the perceived worldliness and luxury of the UMAYYAD empire. They are sometimes seen as the forerunners of the SUFIS.

Nastika *Hinduism* Any of the unorthodox schools of Hindu philosophy that do not accept the Vedic revelation or its authority. Principally, these are considered to be Buddhism and Jainism, which went on to become religions in their own right. Sikhs also do not base authority on the teachings of the VEDAS. There were other groups in antiquity, such as the atheistic Charvakas and the extreme ascetics, the Ajivikas, that denied the Vedic revelation, but these no longer exist. (*See also* ASTIKA; DARSHAN SHASTRAS)

Na't *Islam* A song of praise in honour of Muhammad and traditionally sung in the mosque at the end of Friday prayers. There are many such prayers to the Prophet and they provide excellent examples of Muslim piety and the importance of the relationship with God's chosen final prophet. They speak of the Prophet's compassion, humility, wisdom and special closeness to God. (*See* NUR I MUHAMMADI)

Natalitia *(Greek: birthday)* *Christianity* A term used in the early Church to commemorate the deathdays of MARTYRS whose death was believed to mark their birth into eternal life. (*See also* SAINTS)

Nataraja *Hinduism* SHIVA as the Lord of the Dance who controls the movement of the cosmos and orders destruction. Nataraja is depicted as an ascetic with one head and four arms. One hand holds a small drum, maintaining the rhythm of the universe, while a second contains the fire of destruction. The other two hands are kept in the MUDRAS (symbolic gestures) of salvation and protection. He dances on the demon of ignorance and is surrounded by a circle representing an arch of flames that signifies the cycle of life or time.

Natchiketas *Hinduism*   The young Brahmin boy who is sacrificed to Death by his father in the KATHA UPANISHAD. As Death does not receive him at the gates of the otherworld, he is offered three boons after waiting for three days. As a result, a discourse takes place between Death and Natchiketas on the nature of truth. This discourse is one of the most famous in the UPANISHADS and tells of the relationship between BRAHMAN and ATMAN and how liberation can be achieved. Effectively, the Upanishad uses the literary device of making Death the teacher of the young brahmin disciple.

Nath yogis *Hinduism*   A vast variety of both renunciate and married orders of YOGIS who claim that their teachings are derived from GORAKHNATH and his guru, Matsyendranath. Many of the orders have become semi-nomadic sub-castes who survive through fortune-telling, supernatural cures, exorcisms and snake charming. (*See also* KANPHATA)

Nathan *Judaism*   The Jewish prophet who lived at the same time as DAVID. He criticized David on several occasions when the king departed from the moral code expected of a lover of God. In particular, he criticized the king for introducing the innovation of a permanent temple in Jerusalem when formerly the God of the Israelites had been worshipped by a travelling people in the desert.

Nathan, Rabbi *Judaism*   A prominent rabbi and scholar from the period of the fourth generation of TANNAIM (139–65) in Babylon after the exile from Israel by the Romans. He was a significant contributor to the development of the MISHNAH but remained in opposition to the authorities in Rome, unlike many of the fifth generation of Tannaim. (*See also* ABOT DI RABBI NATHAN)

Nathanael *Christianity*   One of the original twelve APOSTLES who were chosen by Jesus Christ as his companions and missionaries. Although mentioned in all the New Testament lists of the original twelve, nothing further is known about him. The Gospel of John tells the story of how he came to Jesus through Philip but maintained the normal Jewish scepticism towards anyone born in Nazareth. He was convinced that he had found the Jewish messiah when Jesus knew who he was without formerly meeting him.

Nativity *Christianity*   See CHRISTMAS.

Navakara mantra *Jainism*   A daily Jain salutation used as a prelude to most religious ceremonies. Jains are taught it in childhood and although commonly repeated by the congregation at temple worship, it can be repeated in silence anywhere or by anyone. It is recited in Prakrit language as follows:

> *Namo arihantanam, Namo siddhanam, Namo ayarianam, Namo uvajjhayanam, Namo loe sava sahunam, Eso panca namokaro, Savva pavapanasano, Mangalanum ca savesim, Padhamam havai mangalam.*

The English translation is:

> I venerate the enlightened souls
> I venerate the liberated souls
> I venerate the religious leaders
> I venerate the religious teachers
> I venerate all ascetics
> These fivefold venerations destroy all sins
> Of all auspicious things
> It is the most auspicious.

Navaratri *Hinduism*   An important festival to the goddess DURGA or Amba that is celebrated for nine nights in September/October. The festival commemorates the victory of the goddess over the buffalo-demon, Mahishasura, the king of demons and embodiment of ignorance and chaos. The demon-king had thrown the gods out of heaven and taken up residence there himself. Cosmic order had been thrown upside down, and Durga's victory restored DHARMA. The tenth day of the festival is known as DASSERA or victory. Sometimes the complete festival of ten days is also known as Dassera. Since the festival also coincides with RAMLILA, the re-enacting of the victory of RAMA over RAVANA, the demon-king of Sri Lanka, both are often celebrated together, especially in north India. Navaratri is an important festival for the Gujarati Hindu community in Britain, as they have strong traditions of Durga worship, but the goddess is known as Amba.

Nave *Christianity*   In traditional CHURCH architecture the nave is the main part of the church, which runs from west to east, from the front door to the SANCTUARY, and is assigned to the congregation. (*See also* ALTAR; CHANCEL)

Naya *Jainism*   A partial view of reality. Jainism believes reality to be complex and difficult to perceive in its entirety. It is permanent, eternal, omnipresent and constantly changing. Thus, with the exception of enlightened souls, neither an object nor reality can be fully comprehended by a human being. (*See* NAYAVADA)

Nayanars *Hinduism*   Sixty-three SHIVA *bhakti* teachers from south India who composed many hymns and poems in praise of the deity from the seventh to tenth centuries. As did many later medieval BHAKTI groups, the Nayanars taught that caste was irrelevant to devotion and that repetition of the name of God was the only means to salvation in the KALI YUGA (Age of Darkness). The Nayanars taught the doctrine of eternal separation from God in order to experience the fruits of the relationship of blissful devotion and the showering of divine grace. Their poems were kept in several collections that were combined in the tenth century to form the major SHAIVITE scripture of Tamil-speaking India, the Tirumurai. (*See also* ALVARS)

Nayavada *Jainism* The doctrine of NAYA that is part of the essential principle of Jainism known as relative pluralism or ANEKANTAVADA. Reality can only be comprehended from a standpoint or a different 'angle'. There are an infinite number of these standpoints, as each individual being will have his/her own. (*See also* SYADVADA)

Nazar *Hinduism* See NAJAR.

Nazarene *Christianity* Someone who comes from the town of NAZARETH. Jesus Christ is called 'Jesus the Nazarene' in the New Testament on several occasions. The Galilean people were looked down upon by the Jews of Judea and there may be a note of derision in calling Jesus a Nazarene. The Judean Jews called the first Christians Nazarenes and the Jewish/Christian movements that originated in the Jerusalem Church may have called themselves Nazarenes.

Nazareth *Christianity* The town in GALILEE where Christ was raised by Mary and Joseph and lived for around thirty years until rejected by its people. It is because of Christ's origins in Nazareth that the New Testament indicates that he was known as Jesus of Nazareth. (*See also* NAZARENE)

Nehemiah *Judaism* One of the books of the Hebrew Bible known as Holy Writings. Nehemiah was the cup-bearer of Artoxerxes, the King of Babylon. He managed to secure permission to return to Jerusalem and in 444 BCE was appointed Military Governor of Judea. He worked with EZRA to ensure that the Jewish people obeyed the TORAH and oversaw the rebuilding of the walls of the city. (*See also* KETUVIM; TANAKH)

Neilah *(closing) Judaism* The last of the five services held in the SYNAGOGUE on YOM KIPPUR. The title may refer to the closing of the gates of the Temple in Jerusalem after the evening prayers, whilst others maintain that it refers to closing of the gates of Heaven. The congregation petition God to answer their prayers and seal them in the Book of Life. The service ends with reciting the last verse of the SHEMA.

Nembutsu *Buddhism* The Japanese translation of the Chinese NIEN-FO. It describes the practice of chanting the names of the Amitabha Buddha that is central to the Pure Land schools of Buddhism. The great practitioner of Japanese Pure Land is HONEN, who is believed to have practised the *nembutsu* seventy thousand times a day. (*See also* AMIDA)

Neminatha *Jainism* The twenty-second TIRTHANKARA, who is believed to have been the cousin of KRISHNA, the Hindu AVATAR of VISHNU. A sage named Neminatha is mentioned in the MAHABHARATA and in both Rig and Arthava Vedas. This dating of the *tirthankaras* to before the birth of MAHAVIR, the historical founder of Jainism, reinforces Jain belief that their religion is the rediscovery of the eternal truth. Neminatha, like many of the Jain *tirthankaras*, is believed to have been born into a royal family somewhere near the city of Agra. He renounced the world to become a wandering ascetic after seeing the distress of the animals that had been gathered for slaughter on the occasion of his wedding. After meditating for fifty-four days he achieved omniscience and began to preach the path to liberation. It is believed that he attained final liberation at Mount Girnar in the state of Gujarat. This site remains a prominent Jain pilgrimage centre. (*See also* KEVALAJNANA)

Ner Tamid *(eternal light)* *Judaism* The lamp that is kept burning above the ARON HAKODESH in the synagogue and which represents the light that was kept in the sanctuary of the Temple in YERUSALEM.

Nestorian *Christianity* A doctrine attributed to NESTORIUS (fifth century) but probably originating with Theodore, Bishop of Mopsuestia (392–428) concerning the nature of Jesus Christ, which asserts that the divine and human aspects of Christ were independent and separate. This is opposed to orthodox Christology, which teaches that Christ was simultaneously both fully human and fully divine. After the Council of Ephesus in 431, those bishops who would not accept the orthodox view formed their own Nestorian Church, which was centred in Persia. Today, the Syrian Orthodox Church still maintains a Nestorian position.

Nestorius *Christianity* A monk from Antioch who was made Patriarch of Constantinople in 428 and immediately entered the controversy concerning the human and divine nature of Jesus Christ. He maintained the position of Theodore, Bishop of Mopsuestia (392–428), that the two aspects of Christ's nature were independent and distinct. On arrival in the capital of Christendom, he gave a sermon in which he declared 'that which is formed in a womb is not ... God' but that God was within the human nature of Christ. After 431, Nestorius was defeated by the allies of Cyril, the Patriarch of Alexandria, and retired to his monastery in Antioch. However, the issue created the first division in Christianity. (*See* NESTORIAN)

Neti, Neti *('not this, not this')* *Hinduism*   The negative term used to answer enquiries concerning the reality or nature of BRAHMAN in some of the UPANIS-HADS. As an impersonal absolute devoid of form or qualities, Brahman was considered to be indescribable and beyond the conception of the intellect. Even though Hindu sages acknowledge the ability of the human being to experience absorption directly into Brahman through various paths, they also agree that even the person who had achieved such an experience would not be able to describe it. (*See also* SAMADHI)

Netzah *(victory)* *Judaism*   According to the tradition of the KABBALAH, the eighth of the ten SEFIROTH who emanate from the AYN SOF. It is the third on the right-hand side of the Tree of Life and, along with HOD, is one of the two supports for the *sefiroth*.

Neviim *Judaism*   The books ascribed to the prophets in the Hebrew scriptures that appear in the second section. They are divided into two parts: the early prophets and the later prophets. The first part deals with the prophets Samuel, Nathan, Ahijah, Elijah, and Elisha, and consists of the books of JOSHUA, JUDGES, the two books of SAMUEL and the two books of Kings. The second part is also divided into major and minor prophets. The division is not qualitative but simply refers to the size of the books. The major prophets are ISAIAH, EZEKIEL and JEREMIAH. The twelve minor prophets are HOSEA, JOEL, AMOS, OBADIAH, JONAH, MICAH, NAHUM, HABAKKUK, ZEPHANIAH, HAGGAI, ZECHARIAH and MALACHI. In the Hebrew Bible the last twelve are considered as one book because of the brevity of the material. In Judaism, the prophets are the carriers of revelation; they are human beings called upon by God to be His messengers. They preached in God's name, moved by His spirit, and called upon the people to obey God's law. They also warned of the consequences of disobedience. (*See also* TANAKH; TORAH)

New Testament *Christianity*   The collection of twenty-seven books written after the death of Jesus Christ which form the distinctively Christian part of the canon of scripture known as the BIBLE. The New Testament provides the scriptural affirmation of the new covenant that replaces the old Jewish covenant given to Moses through the salvation offered by faith in Jesus Christ. Just as the OLD TESTAMENT records the history of God's revelation through the prophets, the New Testament records the final revelation through the incarnation of the Son of God. The twenty-seven books are divided into the four GOSPELS; the ACTS OF THE APOSTLES; twenty-one letters written by the apostles and the book of

Revelation. Although the earliest books were the letters written by Paul some-where between 48 and 60 CE, the New Testament is organized chronologically according to when the events described took place. The central message of the New Testament is salvation. In the New Testament, God himself is the saviour through the mediation of Jesus Christ. Salvation is through God's grace calling forth the human response of faith and obedience to his will. (*See also* REVE-LATION, BOOK OF)

Nhavana *Jainism*   A holy water that is applied to the forehead and eyebrows by Jain worshippers. It is also spread on places that Jains wish to purify. The 'water' is first used to clean the images in the temple and is made up of a mixture of water, milk, curds, ghee and sugar. It is also believed to cure many ailments.

Nibbana (P) *Buddhism*   *See* NIRVANA.

Nicaea, Council of *Christianity*   The first ecumenical council called by CONSTANTINE, the first Christian emperor of the Roman empire, in 325 to resolve the destabilizing controversies caused by various understandings of Christ's human and divine nature, especially the Arian heresy. The Council, composed of members from throughout the Christian world, asserted the orthodox position laid out in the NICENE CREED that Christ is both fully human and fully divine. (*See also* ARIANISM)

Nicene Creed *Christianity*   The fullest version of the CREED, which contains strong statements concerning the divinity of Christ and his unity with God, such as 'God from God' and 'being of one substance with the Father'. It was compiled to resist a number of Christological heresies that existed in the fourth-century church and provide believers with a statement of orthodox belief. (*See also* APOSTLES' CREED; CHRISTOLOGY; HERESY; NICAEA, COUNCIL OF)

Nichiren *Buddhism*   A form of Japanese Buddhism that is popular in the West. It is unusual in that it advocates worldly success and devotees chant '*namu myoho renge kyo*' in order to fulfil personal desires. The movement actively recruits, is not ascetic and has a lay approach to Buddhism. The main character-istics are faith in the chanting of the mantra written in a form of a mandala originally by Nichiren Daishonin, a thirteenth-century priest.

Nicholas, St *Christianity*   The Bishop of Myra who is reputed to have participated in the Council of Nicaea in 325. He is the patron saint of sailors, children and Russia. It is in his role as the patron saint of children that he is best known as Santa Claus or Father CHRISTMAS.

Nicodemus *Christianity*   The devout Jew, described as a PHARISEE and member of the SANHEDRIN, who came to Jesus secretly at night and provoked the famous discourse on spiritual rebirth found in John 3:1–15. He protested against the condemnation of Christ and it is believed that he later helped in the burial of Jesus. (*See also* CRUCIFIXION)

Nidanas (P) *Buddhism*   The causal chain that describes the way in which being or individual existence takes place. Each *nidana* or link is mutually dependent and expresses the process taught by the Buddha 'that arising, this becomes; this ceasing to be, that ceases to be'. Therefore, all things arise and exist due to the presence of something else, and cease to exist once these conditions are removed. The twelve *nidanas* are the links in the chain. The root cause is ignorance, which gives rise to constructing activities, followed by consciousness, mind and body, the six senses, sensory stimulation, feeling, craving, grasping, existence, birth, ageing and death. (*See* AVIDYA; BHAVA; JARAMARANA; JATI; NAMA RUPA; PATICCA-SAMUPPADA; PHASSA; SALAYASAMUDAYA; TANA; UPADANA; VEDANA; VINNANA)

Niddah *(she who is separated)* *Judaism*   The laws contained in the Torah regarding the separation of women during menstruation and after giving birth. In Orthodox Judaism, a woman in this condition may not sleep with her husband or attend the synagogue. The rabbis interpreted the law to state that a woman remains unclean for seven days after the flow of blood has stopped. After childbirth, she is impure for fourteen days after the birth of a boy and twenty-one days after the birth of a girl. After the period of impurity, she attends the ritual bath. (*See* MIKVAH)

Nien-fo (Ch) *Buddhism*   The recitation of the AMIDA Buddha's name as a loving expression of receiving his grace to enter the Pure Land or celestial realm where the Buddha teaches. (*See also* NEMBUTSU)

Nifaq *Islam*   One of the great sins, and a term for hypocrisy or pretended belief in the Qur'an which is devoid of real faith. The condition of hypocrisy is much criticized in the Qur'an.

Nigoda *Jainism*   *See* EKENDRIYA.

Nigura *Sikhism*   Someone who is without a GURU. In Sikhism the guidance and grace of the Guru is essential to salvation. Since the time of GURU GOBIND SINGH, the last of the human Gurus, Sikhs have been expected to attend the GURDWARA in order to listen to the wisdom of the Guru embodied in the GURU GRANTH SAHIB.

Nihang *(free from care)* *Sikhism* It indicates someone who is humble or without pride. The title of *nihang* is given to AKALI Sikhs.

Nihilianism *Christianity* The doctrine that the human nature of Christ was nothing and that his essential being was contained only in the Godhead. It was condemned as heresy in the twelfth century. (*See* CHRISTOLOGY)

Nij Thav *Sikhism* The original home or place where all human beings belong. In the teachings of the Sikh Gurus, it refers to the presence of God within the human heart. The sense of coming home takes place when the individual finds the presence of God through meditation on the name of God. (*See* NAM)

Nikaya *Buddhism* A collection of five sets of discourses and texts, also known as Agamas, that form the SUTTA PITAKA, the second of the three baskets of scripture that make up the PALI CANON. They are Digha Nikaya, Majjhima Nikaya, Samyutta Nikaya, Anguttara Nikaya and Khuddaka Nikaya.

Niranjan *Sikhism* Used in the GURU GRANTH SAHIB to denote the divine essence. It refers to the formless God who is untouched by MAYA or illusion. Sikhs believe that God is both with and without qualities. *Niranjan* refers to the absolute essence that is beyond all attributes or qualities. (*See also* NIRANKAR; NIRGUNA; SAGUNA)

Nirankar *Sikhism* Used in the GURU GRANTH SAHIB to indicate that God is formless. Sikhs do accept that God is personal but cannot be represented by any form such as a MURTI or image. Both the NIRGUNA and SAGUNA aspects of God are without form. (*See also* NIRANJAN)

Nirankari *Sikhism* A Sikh sect founded by Baba Dayal Singh in 1845. After partition in 1947, the Nirankaris moved to India from the newly created Pakistan, leaving behind their centres in that country. The Nirankaris accept the GURU GRANTH SAHIB but also have a line of human gurus who have succeeded Baba Dayal Singh. They return to the teachings of GURU NANAK as the source of pure Sikh practice and doctrine. Regarded as strictly orthodox Sikhs, they are not to be confused with the SANT NIRANKARIS.

Nirbhau *(fearless)* *Sikhism* One of the lines of the MOOL MANTAR, which ascribes to God the quality of being without fear. All created beings experience fear, so fearlessness is a quality of God alone. Those who serve God and become His devotees are given the quality of God's fearlessness.

Nirgranthas *Jainism* The ancient name for those who followed the Jain path to liberation at the time of MAHAVIR. It means those who are freed from all the bonds of this world. (*See also* KEVALAJNANA; SANGHA)

Nirguna *Hinduism* Formless, without attributes or qualities. The doctrine of the formless, impersonal BRAHMAN was most fully formulated in the teachings of ADVAITA VEDANTA by SHANKARA. The basic division in the medieval BHAKTI tradition is between those who worship through a form of God or ISVARA, and those who worship the formless God. (*See also* NAMA RUPA; SAGUNA; SANT)

Nirguna Bhakti *Hinduism* A term used to describe intense devotion to the formless God without the worship of an ISVARA or an AVATAR. This tradition, often classified as SANT, developed in north India during the medieval period and is represented by such figures as KABIR and GURU NANAK. It is often suggested that such devotion to a formless God developed under the influence of Islam, but the teachings are already existent within Hinduism and found in the UPANISHADS. However, the application of qualities to the formless BRAHMAN provided opportunities for synthesis with Islam, especially the SUFI tradition.

Nirguna Brahman *Hinduism* The term for the formless BRAHMAN without attributes or qualities. However, even the formless Brahman is usually described as SATCHITANANDA (truth, consciousness, bliss). The main division in Hindu religious thought concerns the order of divine emanation. While those who promote the form of God as supreme, for example VAISHNAVA sects, do not deny the formlessness of Brahman, they perceive the formless as an emanation of the eternal form. Practitioners of ADVAITA VEDANTA do not deny the forms of the divine but rather see them as temporary manifestations of the formless. The debate between these two schools can at times become heated. (*See also* RAMA-NUJA; SHANKARA)

Nirjara *(shedding)* *Jainism* One of the twelve reflections practised by ascetics in order to maintain a correct religious attitude. *Nirjara* refers to the belief that KARMA can be removed by the practice of austerities and penances (*See also* ANUPREKSAS; TAPAS)

Nirmalas *Sikhism* A sect of Sikh renunciates or celibate SADHUS who trace their origin to GURU GOBIND SINGH and are rivals of the AKALIS. They have accepted the AMRIT PAHUL initiation and are KESDHARIS, but they also accept the teachings of orthodox Hindu scriptures.

Nirmanakaya (S) *(transformation or appearance body)* *Buddhism* One of the three bodies of the Buddha according to MAHAYANA doctrine. The *nirmana-kaya* refers to the physical body which the Buddha uses to appear in the world in order to help suffering beings. It also applies to apparitions or visions of the Buddha that may appear in dreams. (*See also* DHARMAKARA; SAMBHOGAKAYA; TRIPIKAYA)

Nirodha *Buddhism*   The third of the four noble truths taught by the Buddha which refers to extinction or cessation of desire and brings to an end all suffering. It will also bring to an end all finite existence as experienced on the wheel of SAMSARA. It therefore equates with NIRVANA as the ultimate goal of Buddhism and is attainable through the noble eightfold path. (*See also* CATTARI ARIYASACCANI)

Nirvair *(without enmity)*   *Sikhism*   One of the lines of the MOOL MANTAR, which attributes to God the quality of being without any sense of resentment or need for vengeance. It is not possible for God to have enemies, as He has no rivals.

Nirvana (S) / Nibbana (P) *Buddhism*   The indescribable state of ultimate peace or bliss achieved by the enlightened and the supreme goal of all sentient beings. It indicates the blowing out or extinction of the self and the annihilation of all KARMA. It is the only way to end the continuous cycle of birth and rebirth on the wheel of SAMSARA. (*See also* ARHANT; BODHISATTVA; BUDDHA)

Nirvana *Hinduism*   The cessation of the wheel of existence and the end of SAMSARA. More common in Buddhism, but sometimes used in Hinduism to describe MOKSHA or MUKTI.

Nirvana *Jainism*   Used in Jainism to describe the death of an enlightened Jain, which is followed by MOKSHA or liberation.

Nirvana Sutra *Buddhism*   A partisan MAHAYANA text written around 200–400 which is critical of the THERAVADA school and claims that Buddha gave a secret teaching before his death. The Sutra claims that anyone insulting the Mahayana tradition is destined for extreme punishment.

Nishan Sahib *Sikhism*   The Sikh flag which is always flown outside a GURDWARA. Its colour should be either saffron or blue and the flagpole itself is covered in saffron cloth. The pennant contains the KHANDA, the symbol of Sikhism. Very often, Sikhs coming to worship will touch the foot of the *Nishan Sahib* in respect as they enter the gurdwara. On the festival of BAISAKHI, the coverings of the flag are changed as part of the religious ritual and celebration.

Nishkam karma *Hinduism*   The practice of performing action without concern for its results. In this way, the BHAGAVAD GITA claims that it is possible to maintain complete tranquillity without physical renunciation. The teachings of the Bhagavad Gita define renunciation of the fruits of action as KARMA MARGA, leading to liberation through absence of desire when performing actions. (*See also* KARMA)

Nit nem *Sikhism* The daily recitation of specified prayers taken from compositions in the GURU GRANTH SAHIB. There are five BANI which should be read every morning: the JAPJI, composed by GURU NANAK; the Jap Sahib; Mukh Vak Saviyas and Chaupai, composed by GURU GOBIND SINGH; and finally the Anand Sahib, composed by GURU AMAR DAS. The Nit nem also includes the evening prayers; the Rahras and the ARDAS and the final prayer before sleeping: the SOHILA. These prayers are considered compulsory for the KHALSA brotherhood. Nit nems are published in Amritsar as prayer books for Sikhs and include some explanatory chapters on Sikh doctrine.

Niyama *Hinduism* The second of the eight stages on the path to liberation as defined by the YOGA school of philosophy. *Niyama* refers to full observance of the rules associated with DHARMA and devotion to the Lord. In particular, it refers to cultivating the observance of purity, contentment, austerity, study and dedicating one's actions to the Lord.

Niyyah *(intention)* *Islam* The statement of intent that must precede all ritual acts in Islam. Before WUDU, the ritual bathing, a Muslim repeats, 'I make the ritual intention of legal purification'. When standing to perform prayer, again a similar formula is followed: 'I stand facing the QIBLA, and raising my hands to the level of my ears, I say: "I make my intention to perform the two prostrations of the prescribed prayer-rite"'. There is also a tradition that extends the *niyyah* to the condition of the Muslim's heart as he walks to the mosque. The idea of *niyyah* is to ensure that the heart is engaged in religious practice and that the worshipper is not merely going through the motions. (*See also* SALAH)

Noachide Laws *Judaism* The seven laws that form the foundation of a just human society. They were revealed by God to NOAH at the end of the flood and form part of the covenant made between God and Noah. The seven laws are usually depicted as:
1. To worship only the one God and to renounce all idol worship.
2. To live a moral life and not commit adultery or incest.
3. To live as a useful member of society and not commit murder.
4. To be honest and not steal.
5. To have respect for God and not blaspheme.

6. To provide courts of law and a system of justice to maintain society.
7. To be kind to animals and to refrain from cruelty.

Noah *Judaism* The patriarch chosen by God to save a remnant of the people and a sample of all the earth's creatures during the great flood. This is achieved by the building of a great ark. Noah is regarded as the father of all people born after the flood, and the revelation made to him is for all humanity rather than only the Jewish people. One of the three covenants was made with Noah, but unlike the other two, it is not exclusive to the Jews. (*See* BERIT; NOACHIDE LAWS)

Non-conformist *Christianity* Protestant denominations that separated from the Church of England during the period of the Civil War and the Restoration in the seventeenth century. The term is generally used to describe Protestant movements that have broken away from or dissented from the state Church of England. These would include BAPTISTS, English PRESBYTERIANS, CONGREGA-TIONALISTS and Methodists. (*See also* CALVINISM; METHODISM; PURITANS)

Noor *Islam* *See* NUR.

Noor e Muhammadi *Islam* *See* NUR I MUHAMMADI.

Novice *Christianity* A probationary member of a monastic community who is expected to observe the vows of the respective order but can leave without incurring any penalty before taking the final vows to become a MONK or NUN. (*See also* FRIAR; OBLATE)

Nubuwwa *Islam* The concept of the pre-eternal lamp of prophethood which is exemplified and perfectly manifested in Muhammad, as opposed to the physical appearance of the prophethood as manifested in the historical figure of the final prophet. (*See* NUR I MUHAMMADI; RISALA)

Numbers *Judaism* The fourth of the five books of the TORAH or PENTATEUCH which tells of the wanderings in the wilderness after liberation from slavery in Egypt. The title refers to the numbering of the people that was carried out in the wilderness.

Nun *Christianity* A female member of a monastic community who has undertaken the vows of chastity, poverty and obedience. (*See* MONK; NOVICE; OBLATE; RELIGIOUS)

Nunc Dimittis *Christianity* The Song of Simeon from Luke 2:29–32 used in Christian evening liturgy and funerals. Roman Catholics sing it at COMPLINE,

Anglicans at EVENSONG, whereas Eastern Orthodox churches sing it at VESPERS. (*See also* CANTICLE)

Nuncio   *Christianity*   An ambassador or diplomatic representative of the VATICAN, the independent city-state which is the administrative and ecclesiastical centre of Roman Catholicism and home of the POPE.

Nuptial Mass   *Christianity*   The Roman Catholic Mass held at weddings which includes the celebration and blessing of the marriage itself. (*See also* SACRAMENT)

Nur / Noor   *Islam*   The primordial light of Allah. (*See* NUR I MUHAMMADI)

Nur i Muhammadi / Noor e Muhammadi   *Islam*   A SUFI and SHI'A doctrine which acknowledges that Muhammad has a primordial existence as an emanation of God's light which pre-existed creation. This primordial pre-creation light from which all prophets, angels, saints and ordinary human beings were created passed down unimpaired into the final prophet. The Shi'a believe that this process continues into the direct bloodline through ALI and FATIMA and down through the imamate. (*See also* BASHAR; NUBUWWA)

Nyasa   *Hinduism*   A Tantric mental concentration using mantras that is believed to place or 'project' certain divine powers or deities into parts of the body of the practitioner. (*See* TANTRA)

Nyaya   *Hinduism*   One of the six orthodox schools of Hindu philosophy that acknowledge the authority of the VEDAS. Its basic text is the Nyaya Sutra attributed to Gotama, the supposed founder of the tradition, somewhere between 200 BCE and 200 CE. Nyaya lays stress on the rational analysis of logical arguments and regards knowledge or right reasoning as the key to liberation. Ignorance is seen as the cause of suffering and bondage to the wheel of SAMSARA. Nyaya was not originally a theistic system but only accepted the idea of God at a later date under the influence of Shaivism. The Nyaya school remains strong in the state of Bengal. (*See also* ASTIKA; DARSHAN SHASTRAS)

O

Obadiah   *Judaism*   One of the twelve minor prophets and a book of the same name in the Jewish scriptures. The book consists of only one chapter, which rails against the people of Edom for handing over fugitive Jews to the Babylonians after the invasion of Nebuchadnezzar in 586 BCE. (*See* NEVIIM)

Obedience   *Christianity*   One of three vows undertaken by a RELIGIOUS, a member of a monastic community. Absolute obedience is only due to God; whereas obedience to humans is limited by authority and conscience. Generally, in a monastic community obedience will be maintained through the rules of the individual ORDER.

Oblate   *Christianity*   Members of the laity who live in close connection to a religious or monastic ORDER but do not take the full vows of poverty, chastity and obedience. It is often used by novitiates as preparation for entry into the order, but some individuals remain oblates throughout their lives. The term was originally used in the Middle Ages for children offered to the service of God by being dedicated to a monastery and brought up by the monks. (*See also* NOVICE; RELIGIOUS)

Oblations   *Christianity*   The technical term that is applied both to the offering of the consecrated bread and wine used in the EUCHARIST and to any gift brought by the congregation to the service for use by the clergy or given to charity.

Occasional offices   *Christianity*   The term used in the Book of Common Prayer to describe offices or prayer-rites that are held on a particular occasion rather than as part of daily worship, such as visitation of the sick or baptism (*See* OFFICES, DIVINE)

Offertory   *Christianity*   The procession that brings the elements of bread and wine as an offering from the congregation to the PRIEST so that it may be consecrated at the altar and participated in by the communicants at the EU-CHARIST. (*See also* CONSECRATION; HOST)

Offices, Divine   *Christianity*   The daily prayer which is supposed to be performed seven times in a day by priests and RELIGIOUS and was introduced in the fifth century. Their arrangement was fixed by St Benedict in the sixth century and consists of LAUDS, prime, terce, sext, none, VESPERS and COMPLINE. Each office is made up of psalms, hymns, lessons, antiphons, prayers and responses. At the Reformation, Protestant churches replaced them with two daily offices of morning and evening prayer. (*See also* EVENSONG; MATINS)

Ojha   *Hinduism*   A non-BRAHMIN village priest who functions as a shaman. He/she will be consulted in order to deal with possession by ghosts, demons, the evil eye and other supernatural beings that are believed to be the cause of human misfortune. (*See also* BHUT; NAJAR)

Olam ha-ba   *Judaism*   Belief in the afterlife. Judaism refers to the world beyond this life in two ways: the immortality of the soul and the resurrection of the body. Traditionally, the Jewish belief in the afterlife is connected with the coming of the Messiah. After his kingdom on earth, the dead will be resurrected. However, NAHMANIDES believed that the resurrected bodies would live for ever, albeit refined. MAIMONIDES argued that only the soul was immortal, so eventually even the resurrected bodies would die. The mystical tradition affirms a blissful eternity spent in proximity to God. There is very little in the Bible to affirm an afterlife and Judaism has been called a 'this-worldly' religion that focuses on a Godly and just life here on earth. (*See also* GEHENNA)

Old Catholics   *Christianity*   A collection of small national churches in Holland, Germany, Austria, Switzerland and Croatia that have separated themselves from the Roman Catholic Church after objecting to the doctrine of papal INFALLIBILITY introduced in 1870 at VATICAN COUNCIL I. Ordination is received from the Jansenist church of Utrecht.

Old Testament   *Christianity*   The portion of the canon of scripture that Christians share with Judaism, which consists of the thirty-nine books of Hebrew scripture. Christians view the text differently from Jews, in that they see the NEW TESTAMENT as the fulfilment of the Jewish scriptures. The Old Testament is often used as a prophetic preparation for the coming of Jesus Christ. An Old Testament reading takes place in Christian services and there is also extensive use of the PSALMS in Christian worship. (*See also* TANAKH)

Olives, Mount of   *Christianity*   The highest point of a range of hills just outside the walls of eastern Jerusalem. The base of the mount contains the garden of GETHSEMANE, where Jesus Christ and his disciples passed the night before his arrest. The Mount of Olives is traditionally believed to be the site of Jesus Christ's ascension into heaven and at the summit there is a Muslim shrine believed to contain his footprints.

Om *Hinduism* *See* AUM.

Om mane padme hum *Buddhism* The most famous MANTRA used in Tibetan Tantric Buddhism. Literally it means 'Hail to the Jewel in the Lotus' and its popularity in Tibet is indisputable. All classes of Buddhists recite it, inscribe it on flags, paint it on walls and enclose it in turning prayer-wheels. It functions as a symbolic and condensed expression of the path to enlightenment. (*See also* TANTRA)

Oneg Shabbat *(the delight of the Sabbath)* *Judaism* The positive aspects of the weekly SHABBAT, in which Jews attempt to rediscover the peace and tranquillity of God by having a day that combines festivity and spirituality. The expression comes from a verse in Isaiah (58:13): 'And call the Sabbath a delight'.

Opus Dei *(Latin: the work of God)* *Christianity* A powerful conservative Roman Catholic organization founded in Spain in 1928 to promote the application of Christian morality to daily living. The organization is traditional Spanish Catholicism at its most conservative and functions to combat liberal Catholicism, particularly LIBERATION THEOLOGY in South America.

Oratory *Christianity* A term used generically for a place of worship other than the parish church. However, most oratories are more likely to be the place of worship used by the Oratorians, a Roman Catholic congregation of priests who live in a community but do not take the monastic vows of poverty, chastity and obedience. Cardinal Newman introduced them into Britain in 1848.

Order *Christianity* A monastic community of monks, friars or nuns such as the FRANCISCANS, DOMINICANS or BENEDICTINES living under a set rule. Also the division of the priesthood into three hierarchical categories of BISHOP, PRIEST and DEACON. (*See also* CARMELITES)

Orders *Christianity* The term used for the divine calling or vocation believed to come from God to an individual about to be ordained into the priesthood in the Episcopal churches. The sacramental service of ordination into the priesthood is known as the Sacrament of Orders. (*See* PRIEST; SACRAMENT)

Ordination   *Christianity*   The SACRAMENT performed by a bishop in the Episcopal churches which provides entry to the priesthood. The service of ordination always takes place in the context of the EUCHARIST and includes the laying-on of hands by a bishop and the repetition of a special prayer known as the Ordination prayer. Traditionally, the candidate for priesthood was a baptized and confirmed male of good moral character who had felt the vocation from God to be a priest. Recently, the Church of England has joined the rest of the Anglican Communion in extending ordination to women. (*See also* ORDERS)

Orientation   *Christianity*   The traditional method of construction used in church architecture that ensures that the longer axis leading up the NAVE to the SANCTUARY always runs from east to west.

Origen (185–254)   *Christianity*   One of the church fathers and an early influential theologian who provided the foundations for Eastern Christian thought. There are some doubts about his orthodoxy, as he believed that creation was eternal and the divinity of the Son was somehow less than that of the Father, but he developed the important notion of a distinction between the surface meaning of scripture and allegorical interpretation, leading to deeper spiritual understanding. He also adopted the theological position of universalism, which asserts that all creatures will eventually be saved by a loving God. (*See* ARIANISM; ORIGENISM; UNIVERSALISM)

Origenism   *Christianity*   The group of theological speculations attributed to ORIGEN, in particular the pre-existence of souls and the denial of the identity between the mortal and the resurrected body. Origen's ideas were condemned as heretical at the Council of Alexandria in 400 and after a renaisssance in the fifth and sixth centuries were once again refuted at the Second Council of Constantinople in 553.

Original sin   *Christianity*   The state of sin which humankind has inherited from the fall of ADAM and EVE and which means that all human beings are born in the state of sin and separated from God. Human nature is therefore flawed or corrupted and requires the intervention of God to attain salvation and reconciliation. The theology of original sin was fully developed by St Augustine of Hippo in the fourth and fifth centuries CE and came under considerable criticism from Enlightenment thinkers, who saw it as an obstacle to human social and political development. In the orthodox Christian tradition, infant baptism is perceived as the remission of the inheritance of original sin. (*See also* AUGUSTINE OF HIPPO, ST; PELAGIANS)

Orthodox   *Christianity*   The term used to define right belief as opposed to

HERESY. Generally debates concerning right doctrine took place at a series of councils. Those adhering to non-orthodox belief were likely to find themselves treated as sects and even excommunicated from the church. However, since the rise of denominations, orthodoxy is more likely to describe conformity to the creeds sanctioned by the ecumenical councils. (*See also* EXCOMMUNICATION)

Orthodox Church   *Christianity*   The appellation for the Eastern Church, which is formed of several independent national churches, including the original Eastern patriarchates who are in communion with the patriarchate of Constantinople. The Orthodox Church developed from the Christianity of the Byzantine empire, but gradually became independent churches with the rise of nation-states in Europe. The Byzantine Church had experienced its first schism arising from Monophysite and NESTORIAN disputes in the fifth and sixth centuries, but a greater split occurred with the separation of Christianity into the Orthodox and Roman Catholic Church in 1054. The Orthodox churches believe in seven SACRAMENTS or 'mysteries', BAPTISM is by full immersion and children participate in Communion from a young age. The most distinctive aspects of Orthodoxy are the LITURGY and the extensive use of ICONS. Monastic communities are influential, and although parish priests are allowed to marry, bishops are selected from the monastic communities. (*See also* MONOPHYSITISM)

Orthodox Judaism   *Judaism*   The term used for traditional Jews who observe both the written and oral law in its entirety, particularly ritual laws. They implicitly believe that the TORAH is the revealed word of God and cannot be tampered with by human interference. Orthodox was originally coined by the REFORM movement as a term of reproach but was adopted by those who were criticized as backward looking as a form of pride in their conservative stance.

Ottoman   *Islam*   The Ottoman empire was built upon the Mongol–Turkish inheritance of Genghis Khan and his successors. In 1453, Mehmet II resided over the fall of Constantinople and the old Christian Byzantine empire. He established his capital Istanbul on the old site of Constantinople and provided a major Muslim force on the borders of Europe and Asia. The Ottomans combined a warrior tradition with Islam's message of universal conversion and religious struggle. At its peak the empire extended throughout the Middle East, North Africa and into Eastern Europe. After two centuries of struggle with Europe, they were finally thwarted at the battle of Lepanto in 1571. By the 1600s, the Ottoman empire was at its peak. Istanbul had a population of over half a million and was an international centre of Muslim culture. The empire finally came to an end after World War II when Turkey emerged as a new nation. (*See* MOGUL; SAFAVID)

Oxford Movement   *Christianity*   An Anglican movement of the nineteenth century determined to restore HIGH CHURCH principles which began in Oxford. The leaders were John Henry Newman (1801–90), Richard Froude (1803–36), Edward Pusey (1800–82) and John Keble (1792–1866). In spite of some conversions to Roman Catholicism, most notably John Newman, the majority stayed in the Church of England, where they had considerable influence on liturgy and ceremonial. They were responsible for the restoration of monastic life to the Church of England. (*See also* ANGLO-CATHOLIC; TRACTARIANISM)

P

Paasban (U) *Islam* A social work programme developed by Islamic revivalist movements such as JAMAAT-I ISLAMI that reflects their ideology that there is no differentiation between religion and politics in Islam. As their overriding goal is the establishment of an Islamic state, they are also registered as political parties. Increasingly they have organized themselves into productive welfare movements.

Pabbaja (P) / Pravrajya (S) *(going forth)* *Buddhism* Renunciation of the world. It is the admission of the desire to become a monk made to the SANGHA undertaken before formal training begins. (*See also* BHIKKU; SAMANERA)

Pac Khand / Pach Khand *Sikhism* The five stages or realms taught by GURU NANAK, which are passed through on the journey to salvation. (*See also* DHARAM KHAND; GYAN KHAND; KARAM KHAND; SAC KHAND; SARAM KHAND)

Paccaya *Buddhism* The essential requirements of life required by a monk which should only be received as gifts given by the laity. (*See also* DANA)

Padmasana *Buddhism* The lotus position commonly used for meditation. It is a cross-legged position in which both ankles are placed on the thigh of the opposite leg.

Padmasana *Hinduism* The lotus position, which is believed to be the best posture for meditation. Originally, the YOGA SUTRAS of PATANJALI recommended that postures for meditation (ASANA) should be comfortable and relaxed, but a variety of more complex positions developed. The most famous is the *padmasana* and there are many depictions of Hindu gods and sages seated cross-legged, their feet placed sole upwards on the opposite thigh. (*See also* YOGA)

Padre *Christianity* A popular designation of a CHAPLAIN to the armed forces. It is sometimes used to describe a priest.

Pagdi / Pagri   *Sikhism*   The distinctive turban is one of the common markers of Sikh identity. However, it is not essential dress for Sikhs, although KHALSA Sikhs are required to wear a turban to cover their uncut hair. A child who has been initiated, or who comes from an initiated family, is expected to wear the turban as soon as he is able to tie one himself. This is usually around the tenth birthday. The first turban-tying is usually celebrated within the family. The colour of turbans is not usually significant, except that orange may indicate allegiance to the KHALISTAN movement and white is often associated with the NAMDHARIS.

Pali   *Buddhism*   The scriptural and liturgical language of THERAVADA Buddhism. Although now a dead language, it is one of the most important languages for the preservation of the DHAMMA. It was introduced in Sri Lanka by Theravadins for the formal writing down of the *dhamma* in the first century BCE. (*See also* PALI CANON)

Pali Canon   *Buddhism*   The formal canon of scripture for the THERAVADA Buddhists compiled in Sri Lanka at the Fourth Council held at the Aloka Cave. It is divided into three PITAKAS or 'baskets' known as VINAYA, SUTTA PITAKA and ABHIDHAMMA. (*See also* TIPITAKA)

Pall   *Christianity*   A cloth that is spread over a coffin at the funeral but also used to describe the small cloth that covers the CHALICE at the EUCHARIST.

Palla   *Sikhism*   The scarf that is given and accepted during the wedding ceremony. During the ceremony, one end is held by the bridegroom whilst the other is held by the bride. (*See* ANAND)

Palm Sunday   *Christianity*   The Sunday before EASTER which celebrates Christ's triumphant entry into Jerusalem. Often the worship will be accompanied by a procession around the outside or inside of the church.

Panca Namaskara   *Jainism*   The most basic Jain prayer which states, 'I bow to the enlightened souls; I bow to the liberated souls; I bow to religious leaders; I bow to religious teachers; I bow to all the monks in the world.' (*See* NAVAKARA MANTRA)

Pancasila   *Buddhism*   The five rules or precepts binding on all Buddhists. They are avoidance of killing or even sanctioning the destruction of a living being; abstention from taking anything that is not given; avoidance of unlawful sexual intercourse; abstention from falsehood; and finally abstention from alcohol or other intoxicants.

Pancayat   *Hinduism*   A traditional Hindu village council or caste assembly that functions to enforce caste regulations and resolve disagreements between caste members. Although Hinduism has no established criteria for orthodoxy that can be reinforced through a central authority, the leaders of the *pancayats* have traditionally maintained caste orthodoxy and morality, sometimes enforcing this through the imposition of penances or even expulsion from the community. (*See* JATI)

Pancgavya   *Hinduism*   The mixture of the five products (milk, yoghurt, butter, dung and urine) of the cow, an animal considered to be highly sacred, and used as purification against ritual pollution. (*See* PAP)

Panchamas *(the fifth group)*   *Hinduism*   A term for the castes outside of the four VARNAS. (*See also* HARIJANS)

Panchatantra   *Hinduism*   A scripture consisting of a collection of fables, mainly all animal stories with a moral. The animals are depicted with virtues such as wisdom and loyalty.

Panchen Lama (T)   *Buddhism*   The second highest rank after the DALAI LAMA in the Gelugpa school of Tibetan Buddhism. As with the Dalai Lama, on the death of the incumbent, the new Panchen Lama is searched for in the body of a small child. He is believed to be the manifestation of AMIDA Buddha.

Pandavas   *Hinduism*   Five brothers whose conflict over the ownership of their kingdom with their cousins, the Kauravas, culminated in the battle of KURUKSHETRA. Their story is told in the great epic, the MAHABHARATA. The two principal brothers are YUDHISHTHIRA, the eldest, whose sense of justice is so revered that he sometimes identified with Dharmraj, the King of Righteousness, and ARJUNA, the youngest. Arjuna becomes associated with devotion to KRISHNA, as he is chosen to receive the great revelation of the BHAGAVAD GITA and the vision of Krishna's cosmic form.

Pandit   *Hinduism*   A title for a member of the BRAHMIN caste who performs a priestly function but specializes in the study and interpretation of scriptures and ancient texts of law and philosophy. The term *pandit* is commonly used as a title for a learned man or a priest.

Pangat   *Sikhism*   A group of people sitting in a row in order to be served food. This is the traditional way of receiving food at the free kitchens in the GURDWARA and the term is often used interchangeably with LANGAR.

Panj Bania   *Sikhism*   The five sacred texts that form the basic liturgy of Sikhs. They are: the JAPJI of Guru Nanak; the Jap Sahib of Guru Gobind Singh; the ten Tav Prasad Savaye of Guru Gobind Singh; the ROHILLAS or evening prayer; the KIRTAN SOHILA or bedtime prayer.

Panj Isanan *(five limbs)*   *Sikhism*   Although ritual ablution is not an essential within Sikhism, in practice Sikhs wash the face, hands and feet before reciting the GURBANI from the GURU GRANTH SAHIB.

Panj kakke   *Sikhism*   The five Ks or symbols of membership of the KHALSA believed by Sikhs to have been initiated by GURU GOBIND SINGH at Anandpur in 1699. Although several symbolic meanings are given to the five Ks, the real reason why most Sikhs adhere to them is that in doing so they remain obedient to the instructions of the last human guru. (*See also* KACCHA; KANGHA; KARA; KES; KIRPAN)

Panj Parshad   *Sikhism*   The five kinds of sanctified food that can be distributed to the congregation of a GURDWARA. They are KARAH PARSHAD, PATASES, *gur* (molasses), *ilachi* (cardamoms) and fruit.

Panj Piare / Panj Pyare *(the five loved ones)*   *Sikhism*   The five Sikhs traditionally believed to have belonged to different castes to represent equality, who committed themselves to GURU GOBIND SINGH's call for dedication and thus founded the KHALSA brotherhood with him in 1699. They are Bhai Daya Singh, a KSHATRIYA; Bhai Dharam Singh, a farmer; Bhai Himat Singh, a washerman; Bhai Mokhan Singh, a tailor; and Bhai Sahib Singh, a barber. Five Khalsa Sikhs represent them at every Khalsa initiation ceremony. (*See also* AMRIT PAHUL)

Panj Takht   *Sikhism*   The five centres of Sikh authority. Each one is connected with key events in the lives of the Gurus. They are:
1. The AKAL TAKHT, which was built by GURU HARGOBIND opposite the HARMANDIR in AMRITSAR. It represents the *miri* (temporal authority) as opposed to the *piri* (spiritual authority) of Harmandir.
2. The *Takht Patna Sahib*, which marks the birthplace of GURU GOBIND SINGH.
3. The *Takht Kesgarh Sahib*, Anandpur, which marks the place where the KHALSA was created in 1699.
4. The *Takht Sri Huzur Sahib*, where Guru Gobind Singh was cremated.
5. The *Takht Sri Damdama Sahib*, where Guru Gobind Singh dictated the final version of the GURU GRANTH SAHIB.

The head of a *takht* has the authority to issue HUKAM NAMAS, which are binding on all Sikhs. (*See also* JATHEDAR; MIRI/PIRI)

Panj Tat *Sikhism* The five elements, which according to the GURU GRANTH SAHIB are the constituents of all creation. They are fire, earth, water, air and space.

Panjab *Sikhism* *See* PUNJAB.

Panjabi *Sikhism* *See* PUNJABI.

Panna (P) / Prajna (S) *Buddhism* Wisdom or discernment. It refers to understanding the true nature of things, which leads to the freedom from bondage to SAMSARA and eventual NIRVANA. Wisdom and meditation (DHYANA) are the two highest virtues of Buddhism and the mainstays of the DHAMMA. The state of *panna* or wisdom exists outside time and duality and its cultivation is one of the six PARAMIT which, according to MAHAYANA traditions, lead to the state of BODHISATTVA. Wisdom and compassion are the two pillars of the Mahayana tradition. (*See also* MANJUSHRI)

Panth *(the path or way)* *Sikhism* It can be used to describe all the followers of a teaching originating from a Guru. In this context it can be used to describe the full Sikh community as the community that accepts the teachings of GURU NANAK. It can also be used for the total community that accepts the GURU GRANTH SAHIB as the final Guru of the Sikhs. The KHALSA brotherhood is also known as the Khalsa Panth.

Pap / Papa *Hinduism* Sometimes translated as sin but more accurately as moral or natural evil. In Hindu texts, the term can be used to describe those who are ritually impure because they consciously persist in performing impure actions or because they are unfortunate enough to have been born into a ritually impure caste or even as a woman. This is attributed to wrongdoing in previous lives. A third meaning describes people who are wrongdoers in the more conventional sense of performing morally wrong actions or leading others into immorality. Strictly speaking, the best translation of *pap* as used in Sanskrit scriptures is 'demerit', a state caused by poor observance of traditional rituals. However, in common parlance, more and more Hindus are beginning to use it to refer to immorality. The opposite of *pap* is PUNYA (merit) and it is necessary to understand both in order to grasp the full concept.

Papacy *Christianity* The doctrinal and administrative office of the POPE which is the central organization and leadership of the Roman Catholic Church. The authority of the Pope is believed to derive from the apostle Peter who led the Roman Church before his martyrdom. Catholicism believes that Peter was the first Pope and that there is an unbroken line to the present day. (*See also* APOSTOLIC SUCCESSION; CARDINAL; COLLEGE; INFALLIBILITY; VATICAN)

Parables *(Greek: analogy)* *Christianity* 'Putting things side by side' or allegorical teaching, or the utilization of analogy that Jesus Christ used to convey spiritual truths. Many parables are attributed to Jesus in the GOSPEL accounts and they usually recount short descriptive stories or develop similes in order to illustrate a single truth or answer a question.

Paraclete *Christianity* See HOLY SPIRIT.

Paradise *Christianity* See HEAVEN.

Parama brahma *Jainism* The supreme being. Unlike Hinduism, Jainism does not accept a god as creator or sovereign lord of the cosmos. Therefore the term usually refers to the principle of AHIMSA. The liberated sage or SIDDHA would have developed qualities that are considered godlike. Dominant amongst these would be compassion and harmlessness towards all beings.

Paramanu *Jainism* The smallest indivisible unit of matter that is the equivalent of the atom. These units join with others to form aggregates of matter (PUDGALA SKANDA). The *paramanu* are indestructible and eternal. (*See also* PUDGALA)

Paramartha-satya *Buddhism* The ultimate truth. Some MAHAYANA Buddhists, for example, regard the Buddha nature as the ultimate form of the truth. NAGARJUNA, the founder of the MADHYAMAKA school, declared that on the level of *paramartha-satya*, the conventional world did not exist and it is only on the plain of the conditioned world that the teachings of the Buddha exist.

Paramatman *Jainism* The highest soul or supreme soul. Unlike Hinduism, Jainism does not accept a god as creator or sovereign lord of the cosmos. Therefore the term *paramatman* refers to the liberated soul that develops godlike qualities of compassion, eternal bliss and omniscience. This state was attained by the JINAS and TIRTHANKARAS and is the final quest of all Jains. (*See also* KEVALIN; MOKSHA; SIDDHA)

Parami (P) / Paramita (S) *Buddhism* A perfection or virtue. One of the attainments necessary for Buddhahood. It consists of the highest possible development of DANA, SILA, KSHANTI, VIRIYA, DHYANA and PANNA. These are regarded as the six stages of spiritual perfection required by a BODHISATTVA on the journey to Buddhahood.

Parashurama   *Hinduism*   The seventh AVATAR of VISHNU or RAMA of the Axe who incarnated to protect BRAHMINS from the tyranny of unjust KSHATRIYAS (warriors). It is said that Vishnu manifested in human form as the son of a brahmin but lived the lifestyle of a kshatriya in order to rescue the brahmin caste from complete domination. In the RAMAYANA of TULSIDAS, he appears when Rama breaks the SHIVA's bow to win the hand of SITA in marriage. Parashurama is infuriated that the bow has been broken by two members of the kshatriya caste but is humiliated verbally by Rama and his brother, LAKSHMAN. This presents the odd dilemma of the seventh avatar being admonished by the eighth. However, Rama is a true or ideal kshatriya who protects the brahmins. As an incarnation of DHARMA, he is outraged by the mixing of VARNA functions manifested in Parashurama. The story demonstrates that a new age has arrived where brahmins no longer need to fear kshatriya domination. Parashurama, however, becomes the forerunner and prototype of martial renunciate sects in Hinduism. (*See also* NAGAS)

Parasparopagraho jivanam   *Jainism*   The Jain doctrine of the interdependence of souls which is summed up in the expression 'all living things depend upon one another'. It is this doctrine that has led to the contemporary Jain concern with environmental and ecological issues. Daily prayer rituals offer friendship to all living beings, but the doctrine is fully put into practice through the central belief in AHIMSA.

Paratantra   *Hinduism*   The DVAITA VEDANTA doctrine taught by MADHVA that all worldly things depend for their activity on God.

Parchar / Prachar *(preaching)*   *Sikhism*   Originally intended to indicate the spreading of the message of the Gurus, but as Sikhism is no longer a missionary faith it refers to a religious sermon or any activity that promotes the KHALSA brotherhood.

Pardon   *Christianity*   *See* INDULGENCES.

Parev / Pareve / Parvah   *Judaism*   A part of the KASHRUT or Jewish dietary laws. It refers to neutral foods that are neither milk nor meat. Fruit would be an example. (*See also* KOSHER)

Parigraha   *Jainism*   Possession or ownership. The desire for ownership or possession of material objects is contrary to the Jain doctrine of non-possessiveness. Someone who is too attached to worldly pleasures is regarded as a practitioner of 'cruel meditation'. One aspect of this state is taking pleasure in guarding wealth and property. This state of being includes both the desire to amass possessions and the fear of losing them. (*See* APARIGRAHA)

Parigraha tyaga pratima   *Jainism*   One of the eleven stages of spiritual progress in a lay Jain's evolution. It is the stage of possessory renunciation, non-possessiveness or renunciation of ownership. This is the final stage before withdrawing for an ascetic life and involves getting rid of all possessions except for clothes, food and shelter. (*See* APARIGRAHA; PARIGRAHA; PRATIMA)

Parikrama   *Hinduism*   A special pilgrimage around a sacred city that takes pilgrims on a prescribed route that visits all the holy places and important temples. (*See* PRAVRAJYA)

Parinibbana (P) / Parinirvana (S)   *Buddhism*   Final and complete NIRVANA achieved on the death of a Buddha, after which there is no more rebirth.

Parisad   *Buddhism*   The four categories of Buddhists which make up the complete community. It comprises the order of the SANGHA (monks, nuns) and male and female laity. (*See also* BHIKKU; BHIKKUNI)

Parisaha jaya   *Jainism*   The twenty-two 'afflictional victories' that are part of the Jain ascetic's practice to ensure that KARMA does not continue to enter the soul and hinder the path to liberation. The victories over affliction refer to the hardships that have to be endured by the ascetic with patience, forbearance and cheerfulness. These hardships are: hunger, thirst, cold, heat, absence of pleasure, insect bites, disagreeable surroundings, sexual restraint, physical tiredness, physical discomfort arising from meditation postures, sleeping or resting on hard ground, disease, being unable to wash, and, finally, mental discomfort arising from censure, criticism, insult, disrespect, lack of appreciation and the persistence of his/her own mental and spiritual shortcomings. (*See also* ANUPREKSAS; GUPTI; KEVALAJNANA; SADHU; SAMITI; SAMVARA)

Parish   *Christianity*   An ecclesiastical, pastoral and administrative area under the control of a Church of England clergyman. Several parishes will form one DIOCESE under the control of a bishop. All the inhabitants of that area are entitled to his/her spiritual care and assistance. (*See also* INCUMBENT; VICAR)

Parivraka   *Hinduism*   A Hindu pilgrim. (*See* PRAVRAJYA)

Parkarma *(to go round)*   *Sikhism*   The practice of circumambulating a sacred pool usually contained in the historic GURDWARAS. The devotees go around in a clockwise direction until they reach the entrance to the main shrine. It is customary to take a bath in the pool.

Parmesha *(the supreme Lord)* *Sikhism*   A title used by the Sikh Gurus to describe the supreme being or God.

Parokhet *Judaism*   The curtain hung in front of the ark (ARON HAKODESH) in a synagogue that represents the veil hung over the original ark as described in Exodus 26: 31–3.

Parousia *(presence or arrival)* *Christianity*   The expected return or the second coming of Jesus Christ, in which he will announce the last days and the final judgement by God of humanity. According to the Book of Revelation this will be marked by a gigantic struggle between the forces of good and evil and a series of portents, natural disasters, plagues and wars. In the final confrontation between Christ and the forces of Satan, Christ will triumph and herald a thousand years of peace and righteousness. (*See* ARMAGEDDON; REVELATION, BOOK OF)

Parshad *Sikhism*   See PRASAD.

Parshat / Parshiot *Judaism*   The passages of the TORAH that are apportioned for each reading in the SYNAGOGUE throughout the Jewish year. At each section a member of the congregation will recite a blessing and provide the reading in Hebrew from the Torah scrolls and offer a final blessing at the end of the section. (*See also* ALIYAH)

Parshvanatha *Jainism*   The twenty-third TIRTHANKARA, who preceded MAHAVIR. He is believed to have lived in the ninth century BCE, two hundred and fifty years before Mahavir. Parshvanatha follows the usual Jain pattern associated with *tirthankaras* of complete renunciation from a noble and wealthy family. His parents are believed to have been rulers of Varanasi. Jains also believe that the followers of Parshvanatha were numerous at the time of Mahavir, and that Buddha was a follower of a descendant of Parshvanatha whilst a practising ascetic before achieving enlightenment. The mountain where Parshvanatha achieved final liberation remains an important site of Jain pilgrimage.

Parson *Christianity*   Sometimes used in the Church of England to describe any member of the clergy, originally it had the same meaning as rector, or a clergyman who had full rights over a benefice. (*See* PRIEST; VICAR)

Parvah *Judaism*   See PAREV.

Parvati *Hinduism*   One of the forms of Mahadevi, the Goddess and principal consort of SHIVA. She is the goddess of the Himalayas and also known as UMA or Devi. The PURANAS and the RAMACHARITAMANASA of TULSIDAS provide a rich source of legends regarding the relationship of Shiva and Parvati, and his other consorts are usually considered to be her incarnations. In TANTRA she is identified with SHAKTI, the cosmic female power, and is considered to be so close to Shiva that they are inseparable as one composite being. She is also regarded as the mother of GANESH, the elephant-headed god who is popularly worshipped throughout India.

Paschal *Christianity*   Referring to the PASSOVER or EASTER.

Paschal Lamb *Christianity*   The lamb sacrificed at the Jewish feast of Passover and by analogy used to refer to Christ's sacrificial role remembered at EASTER. (*See* LAMB OF GOD)

Passahara *Buddhism*   One of the four AHARAS or nourishments which feed the conditions that keep a being in the wheel of SAMSARA. *Passahara* refers to the contact of the sense organs with the external world.

Passion *Christianity*   The redemptive suffering of Jesus Christ which took place in the final week of his life and is celebrated in the Christian festival of EASTER. (*See also* ATONEMENT; CRUCIFIXION; HOLY WEEK; REDEMPTION; RESURRECTION)

Passover *Judaism*   See PESACH.

Patal *Sikhism*   Regions that are believed to be under the earth. It also refers to those people who reside in the nether regions. There are believed to be countless realms of this kind.

Patanjali *Hinduism*   The reputed author of the YOGA SUTRAS and founder of the YOGA school of philosophy, one of the six Hindu orthodox schools, somewhere around the second century BCE.

Patases *Sikhism*   The sugar crystals that are diluted in water and stirred with a sword to create AMRIT and used in the KHALSA initiation ceremony. (*See also* AMRIT PAHUL)

Paten *Christianity*   The dish that holds the bread during the EUCHARIST. (*See also* CHALICE; HOST)

Paternoster *Christianity*   The Latin title of the LORD'S PRAYER which is taken from the first two words, 'Our Father'.

Paticca-samuppada (P) / Pratitya-samutpada (S) *Buddhism*   The causal chain of existence. The causal sequence of the wheel of life, or twelve distinct links in the chain of causation which are all interdependent. As the wheel of life is a cycle, there is no primal cause, although it is recognized that ignorance is the first link in the chain. The Buddha taught that failure to understand the nature of the causal chain of existence resulted in deep, almost impenetrable, entanglement in SAMSARA. (*See also* NIDANAS)

Patimokkha (P) / Pratimoksha (S) *Buddhism*   The code of monastic rules contained in the VINAYA PITAKA which are binding on all members of the SANGHA. They are traditionally chanted by monastic communities at each full moon. While there are 227 variant versions in the THERAVADA tradition, the differences only apply to the minor rules concerning etiquette.

Patit *(fallen ones)* *Sikhism*   Members of the community who are deemed to have given up the Sikh way of life. It refers particularly to those who have fallen away from the KHALSA by cutting their hair or breaking the prohibitions against tobacco, adultery or eating HALAL meat.

Patriarch *Christianity*   The title given to the heads of the various Eastern Orthodox churches which is derived from the old title used for the bishops of the five principal SEES in the Christian world. The Patriarch of Constantinople is regarded as the titular head, but each patriarch is the actual leader of a nationally autonomous church within Orthodoxy. (*See also* ORTHODOX CHURCH)

Patristics *Christianity*   The period of the church fathers lasting from 100 to 451, or the theological study of their writings and the distinctive doctrines that developed during the period, especially regarding CHRISTOLOGY.

Patron saint *Christianity*   A SAINT who has been chosen as the intercessor or guardian of a particular person, organization or place.

Paul, St *Christianity*   The apostle who was most influential in the development of early Christianity through spreading the message of Jesus to the GENTILES. Born a Jew and possibly brought up as a PHARISEE in Tarsus, he had initially fiercely opposed the first Christians and was present as a sympathizer at the stoning of STEPHEN, the first Christian martyr. After seeing a vision of the risen Christ on the road to Damascus, he converted to Christianity. He believed that Jewish law should not be imposed on non-Jewish Christians and embarked on a number of missionary tours around the Mediterranean world culminating in his visit to Rome, where he was imprisoned for two years. Paul's contribution to the development of Christianity is documented in the ACTS OF THE APOSTLES and in the EPISTLES he wrote to several of the early Christian communities to inspire their faith, resolve their problems and correct doctrinal errors. These form some of the earliest contributions to the New Testament. (*See also* COLOSSIANS; CORINTHIANS; EPHESIANS; PHILIPPIANS; ROMANS; THESSALONIANS; TIMOTHY AND TITUS)

Pax *Christianity* See KISS OF PEACE.

Peculiar *Christianity* An ecclesiastical centre in the Church of England that is not under the authority of the bishop in charge of the diocese. The two notable peculiars in Britain are WESTMINSTER ABBEY and St George's Chapel in Windsor, which are both under the direct authority of the sovereign. (*See also* WINDSOR, ST GEORGE'S CHAPEL)

Pelagians *Christianity* Followers of the British monk Pelagius based in Rome who opposed the doctrine of ORIGINAL SIN and PREDESTINATION as taught by St AUGUSTINE OF HIPPO. Pelagius argued that human beings have complete free will and the power to reject or accept the Gospels without the added weight of original sin to contend with. He used grace to signify the natural human capacities already given by God which, if used effectively, are sufficient to save humanity from sin.

Penal substitution *Christianity* A Protestant doctrine that Christ was the sinless victim punished in the place of sinful humanity. Thus he was a substitute who sacrificed his own self as ATONEMENT for those who had been elected by God for salvation. (*See also* REDEMPTION; SATISFACTION)

Penance *Christianity* One of the seven SACRAMENTS recognized by the Roman Catholic Church. The penance is given by the priest, known as a penitentiary, at CONFESSION before the pronouncement of ABSOLUTION.

Penitentiary *Christianity* See PENANCE.

Pentateuch *Judaism* The first five books of the Hebrew scriptures: GENESIS, EXODUS, DEUTERONOMY, LEVITICUS and NUMBERS, known as the Books of Moses. (*See also* SEPTUAGINT; TORAH)

Pentecost *Christianity* The festival that commemorates the day when the APOSTLES received the gift of the HOLY SPIRIT and spoke in tongues. After this occasion, which is described in the ACTS OF THE APOSTLES, they began to preach and perform miracles in the name of Jesus. The festival takes place in May on the Sunday that falls on the final or fiftieth day of Easter. (*See also* GLOSSOLALIA; PENTECOSTALISTS)

Pentecostalists   *Christianity*   A modern religious movement which received its impetus from a series of revivalist meetings led by the black preacher William Seymour (d.1923) in Los Angeles in 1906. The movement, which is now interdenominational, believes it is possible for Christians to receive the same experience as the APOSTLES during the original Pentecostal event. They give particular emphasis to GLOSSOLALIA, prophecy, healing and exorcism. There are specific Pentecostal churches which flourish amongst the African-Caribbean migrant communities in Britain and other black-led churches. The Pentecostal churches that call themselves the Assemblies of God are predominantly white, whereas the Churches of God in Christ are mainly black. The movement is now spreading to many parts of the world and can be found in North and South America, Asia, Africa and Europe. (*See also* PENTECOST)

Pesach / Pessah   *Judaism*   The spring festival held in the month of Adar after PURIM that celebrates the EXODUS from Egypt and is regarded as the national birthday of the foundation of the Jewish people. The festival is known as Passover, to commemorate the biblical account of the destruction of the first-born of Egypt that did not affect the children of Israel, as promised by God. The angels literally passed over them. The significant feature of the festival is the SEDER meal which is ritually eaten according to the instructions contained in the HAGADAH. The festival is observed for eight days (seven in Israel) and each day has its own sequence of events. On the first day, the TORAH reading is from the book of Exodus and tells the story of the origins of the festival, the death of the first-born and the flight from Egypt; the second day is the same as the first, but the reading concerns the foundation of the Jewish festivals as instituted in the Torah. From the third day the songs of praise in the SYNAGOGUE are shortened in order to remember the suffering of the Egyptians, as the Jews are commanded to be a compassionate people. On the Sabbath, known as HOL HA-MOED, the Torah reading introduces God's thirteen attributes of mercy and the Song of Songs is read, with the emphasis on spring and renewal. On the seventh day the Torah reading recounts the drowning of the Egyptians in the Red Sea. (*See also* SEUDATH MITZVAH)

Peta (P) / Preta (S) *(the hungry ghosts)*   *Buddhism*   One of the six types of being who inhabit the three realms in Buddhist cosmology. They are the shades of the dead or disembodied spirits who inhabit the realms of hell. They are still within the realm of KAMADHATU, the realm of desire, and it is traditional in some forms of Mahayana Buddhism to give them some of the offerings provided at PUJA. They are often depicted with bloated stomachs and tiny mouths, which represents their insatiable desires. After an interminable period of purgatory, they are released to continue on the wheel of SAMSARA. In Buddhism, a period in hell cannot last longer than the KAMMA, which brought it about.

Peter, Epistles of St   *Christianity*   There are the two letters ascribed to St Peter which are included in the books of the New Testament. Addressing a wide audience, the first dwells upon the themes of persecution, whilst the second is concerned with refuting false teachers. There is more doubt concerning the authorship of the second epistle, as the style of language is different to the first. Peter's contribution to the New Testament goes beyond the two epistles, as it is likely that Mark based his Gospel on Peter's first-hand accounts of travelling with Jesus Christ. (*See* EPISTLES; MARK, ST; PETER, ST)

Peter, St   *Christianity*   A Galilean fisherman and one of the original twelve APOSTLES who were chosen by Jesus Christ as his companions and first mission-aries and regarded as the foremost amongst their number. He is known as the Prince of the Apostles and his name is always written first in any list of Jesus' original disciples. He is believed to be buried in St Peter's in Rome, where he probably died during the persecution of Christians by Nero. The Roman Catholic Church regards him as the first Pope, based on the belief that he was the first Bishop of Rome. His original name was Simon and it is believed that Jesus renamed him Peter (*petros* – a rock). He was present at the TRANSFIGURATION and although famous for his three denials of Christ at the time of the CRUCIFIX-ION, he undertook the leadership of the disciples after Jesus' ASCENSION. He was instrumental in bringing the message of Jesus to non-Jews and after several missionary tours helped develop the fledgling church in Rome. (*See also* PETER, EPISTLES OF ST)

Pew   *Christianity*   Fixed wooden benches known as pews were probably introduced into the NAVE of Western churches sometime in the medieval period as a concession to the old and sick, but are now the usual form of seating for the congregation.

Pharisees   *Christianity*   The founders of rabbinical Judaism and strict upholders of the TORAH who were criticized by Jesus for their purely external conformity to the law and subsequent self-righteousness. (*See also* PHARISEES; SADDUCEES)

Pharisees   *Judaism*   The founders of modern rabbinical Judaism, this important Jewish movement was formed in the second century BCE and was known for its strict observance of the Torah. They differ from the SADDUCEES, their great rivals, in the great emphasis they place on the oral tradition as well as the written Torah. This unwritten corpus of traditional lore was known as the 'tradition of the fathers' and became part of Jewish discourse and interpretation, used to formulate law. The other major difference between the Pharisees and the Sadducees is the acknowledgement by the former of an afterlife, whether it be heaven or hell.

Phassa *Buddhism*   The sense of touch which is the strongest of the six sense organs. The sixth link in the causal chain of existence, it is dependent on SALAYATANA and gives rise to VEDANA. (*See also* NIDANAS)

Philemon, Epistle to *Christianity*   A letter written by Paul whilst imprisoned requesting the release of the Christian, Onesimus, from his owner Philemon. Onesimus had been converted by Paul after meeting the apostle in prison. (*See* EPISTLES; PAUL, ST)

Philip *Christianity*   One of the original twelve APOSTLES who were chosen by Jesus Christ as his companions and first missionaries. He was from the town of Bethsaida and is placed fifth amongst the twelve in the Gospel lists of the disciples. He is mentioned in the New Testament on three occasions: he asks Jesus if he can have a vision of the Father; brings Greeks to him; and expresses his inability to deal with the lack of food at the miracle of the feeding of the five thousand.

Phillipians, Epistle to the *Christianity*   One of books of the New Testament, which consists of Paul's letter to the church in Philippi that he had established as the first Christian community in Europe. It refers to Paul's imprisonment and was probably written during his two-year spell of captivity in Rome. The purpose of the letter seems to have been to introduce Timothy to the church as a future missionary. While Paul does address a number of doctrinal issues and issues a rebuttal of Gnostic influence, on the whole the tone of the letter is one of personal exhortation and encouragement outlining Paul's own hopes for himself and his future plans. (*See* EPISTLES; PAUL, ST)

Pidyon Ha-Ben *Judaism*   A ritual ceremony performed when the first child is a son and not born into a Kohen or Levi lineage. The rite goes back to the belief that God had originally intended all the first-born males to be His priests but that this was overturned when they joined in with the worship of the golden calf after release from Egypt. Consequently their birthright was given to the tribe of Levi, who refrained from idol worship. As a result, the first-born males have to be released from this obligation in a ceremony that takes place thirty days after birth. The child is brought on a pillow by his mother up to a table laid with HALLAH and a KIDDUSH cup. His father stands at the table ready to hand over five silver coins to a Kohen, a member of the priestly caste, who stands facing him. A dialogue then takes place between the father and the Kohen, in which the child is ransomed to free him of his obligation to become a priest. The ceremony ends with a MITZVAH meal. Some non-Orthodox Jews perform the ceremony for all children as a mark of gratitude for the gift of a first child. (*See also* LEVITES)

Pikei Avot / Pirke Avoth *(sayings of the fathers)* Judaism   Part of the MISHNAH, which contains the ethical teachings of the rabbinical sages.

Pikuakh Nefesh *Judaism*   The permitted setting aside of certain laws (HALAKHAH) if by doing so it is possible to save a life.

Pinchi *Jainism*   A broom of peacock feathers used by Jain monks to sweep the earth around them to ensure that they do not accidentally destroy life. It is one of the three possessions allowed to the DIGAMBARA sect of monks, the other two being a wooden food bowl and scripture. (*See also* MUHAPATTI)

Pinda *Hinduism*   An offering of ten balls of cooked rice prepared on the eleventh day of the funeral period which are believed to assist the deceased in finding a new and better rebirth. They are also prepared and given to guests and BRAHMIN priests at the auspicious SHRADDHA ceremony which takes place a year after the death and thereafter annually.

Pipal *Hinduism*   A sacred tree often used by renunciate monks to meditate under or as a site of a shrine. The leaves are also used in religious rituals as offerings to deities.

Pir (U) *Islam*   The Indian subcontinent term for a Muslim saint or a SUFI teacher, also used in Iran and Turkey. The equivalent of the title 'SHAIKH', used throughout the rest of the Arab-speaking Muslim world. (*See also* PIRBHAI)

Pirbhai (U) *Islam*   An Indian subcontinent term for a fellow-follower of a PIR or co-members of a SUFI TARIQAH. The influence of Sufism is so widespread in certain parts of India, such as the Punjab, that to be described as BE-PIR (without a *pir*) is tantamount to describing someone as godless.

Pirit *Buddhism*   A Sri Lankan charm or ceremony used in popular or rural Buddhism which protects from evil.

Pirke Avoth *Judaism*   See PIKEI AVOT.

Pirzada (U) / Pirzade (P) *Islam*   *See* SAJJADA NASHIN)

Pitaka *(basket)* *Buddhism*   Used to refer to the three collections of scripture which make up the PALI CANON. (*See also* ABHIDHAMMA; SUTTA PITAKA; TIPI-TAKA; VINAYA)

Piyyutim *Judaism*   Liturgical poetry written by medieval poets for special occasions, such as Jewish festivals, which may be added to prayers so long as the established framework of ritual prayer is not changed. (*See* TEFILLAH)

Plainsong *Christianity*   The traditional liturgical music of the Roman Catholic Mass also known as the Gregorian chant. It does not require any accompaniment by a musical instrument. It is rarely used since the liturgical changes of VATICAN COUNCIL II except by some monastic orders.

Pogrom *Judaism*   Organized persecutions of Jews, particularly those that took place in Eastern Europe and Russia from the Middle Ages through to the nineteenth century. The systematic and periodic persecution of Jewish communities that culminated in the Holocaust. (*See* SHOAH)

Pontifex Maximus *(Latin: the supreme priest)* *Christianity*   One of the titles of the POPE.

Pontifical *Christianity*   The prayer book used in the Western Church which contains the prayers and ceremonies for rites performed by a bishop, such as CONFIRMATION and ORDINATION. A revised edition was produced by the Roman Catholic Church at the VATICAN COUNCIL II in 1962.

Pontius Pilate *Christianity*   The fifth Roman Governor (*praefectus*) of Judea, who presided over the CRUCIFIXION of Christ. The New Testament seems to indicate that he was more concerned with displeasing the emperor with the possibility of unrest in Judea than pleasing the SANHEDRIN, whose decisions he had the power to overrule. (*See also* BARABBAS)

Poor Clares *Christianity*   Strict and austere enclosed contemplative order of nuns founded by St CLARE (1194–1253) and St FRANCIS OF ASSISI as the female branch of the FRANCISCANS sometime between 1212 and 1214. Their nunnery at the church of St Damian in Assisi was the only one founded by St Francis himself, although others were founded in central Italy soon after the saint's death.

Pope *Christianity*   The title given to the chief bishop of the Roman Catholic Church. Also known as the vicar of Christ. (*See* PAPACY)

Popery *Christianity* A hostile Protestant term for the doctrines and practices of the Roman Catholic Church. (*See* PAPACY; POPE; ROMAN CATHOLIC)

Posan *Buddhism* Sri Lankan festival held on the full moon in June that celebrates the arrival of Buddhism brought to the island by the Venerable Malinda.

Postulant *Christianity* The preliminary stage of being tested before becoming a novitiate of a religious or monastic order. (*See* NOVICE; RELIGIOUS)

Prachar *Sikhism* *See* PARCHAR.

Pradakshina *Hinduism* The common practice of circumambulating a shrine, keeping the shrine always on the right. (*See* DARSHAN; MANDIR; MURTI)

Pradakshina patha *Hinduism* A path around the deity that facilitates the circumambulation of pilgrims or worshippers. (*See* PRADAKSHINA)

Prahlada *Hinduism* A legendary child devoted to VISHNU. He was the son of a demon-king named HIRANYA KASIPU, who thought that he was the supreme power in the world. Prahlada refused to acknowledge his father as the supreme power and instead worshipped Vishnu. Consequently he suffered extreme persecution, but would never renounce his faith. Vishnu eventually incarnated in a lion/man (NARASIMHA) form and destroyed Prahlada's father. The devotion of Prahlada is remembered in the HOLI festival.

Praina *Jainism* Wisdom. The ability to be able to perceive things as they are rather than be deluded by the impact of KARMA. It is a natural quality of the soul which manifests as the practices of Jainism and allows the soul to move closer to its natural state of omniscience. (*See also* JIVA; KEVALIN)

Prajapati *Hinduism* In the ancient Vedic tradition, where the brahminic sacrificial ritual is described as the creator and preserver of the cosmic order, Prajapati is known as the Lord of Generation. The RIG VEDA identifies Prajapati with PURUSHA, the cosmic entity that creates the universe through a cosmic sacrificial act. Prajapati is then restored to life by AGNI, the god of fire. This restoration of Prajapati echoes the stages of the fire sacrifice, so important in brahminic ritual. The myth of Prajapati therefore provides an archetypal version of the most important Vedic ritual. (*See also* BRAHMIN; HAVAN)

Prajna (S) *Buddhism* *See* PANNA.

Prakirnakas *Jainism* Miscellaneous sacred texts which are not part of the primary or secondary canon. They are concerned with preparation for a holy death and with certain aspects of ascetic life. They contain many of the ritual hymns. There are ten *prakirnakas: catuhsarana, aturapratyakhyana, bhaktaparijna, samthara, tandulavaicarika, candravedhyaka, devendrastava, ganitavidya, mahap-ratyakhyana* and *virastava*.

Prakriti *Hinduism* The basic substance of being or primordial matter which exists as latent energy but when empowered by contact with PURUSHA (the life essence or spirit) gives rise to the differentiated material world which is experienced through the mind and senses. *Prakriti* consists of three GUNAS: RAJAS, TAMAS and SATTVA, which exist in an infinite variety of combinations to form all created beings. However, *prakriti* does not of itself contain consciousness, which is only a quality of *purusha*. Once united with consciousness, experience is possible. However, mental and moral faculties are the creation of the *gunas* intermixing and are part of *prakriti*, not *purusha*. This dualistic theory to explain animate and inanimate creation through two interwoven and eternal forces, known as *purusha* and *prakriti*, was first used by the non-theistic SAMKHYA school of philosophy, but is now common throughout Hinduism, even in theistic systems.

Pramanas *Buddhism* The logical intellectual pursuit to discover valid sources of knowledge to engage in philosophical debate with non-Buddhist opponents which became a part of the standard syllabus in Buddhist universities.

Prana *Hinduism* The breath of life that supports all other life functions. While there is an ode to the breath of life in the RIG VEDA, later philosophical and yogic systems suggest that there are several vital functions or breaths. Many yogic systems are based on breathing or breath control. Certainly by the time of the UPANISHADS, concentration on the breath as a means of controlling the senses was a well-developed system. (*See also* PRANAYAMA)

Pranam *Hinduism* Prostration or obeisance to a deity, a guru or even a respected elder. The physical action varies from simply folding hands and bowing the head to lying completely prostrate on the ground. More commonly, devotees may kneel with their heads on the ground. It is also common to touch or even kiss the feet of a holy person or an image. (*See* NAMASKAR)

Pranatipata-viramana *Jainism* One of the Jain virtues that will help overcome the four passions of anger, pride, greed and deceit and therefore aid in the removal of KARMA. It is the virtue of non-injury, which means living one's life in such a way as to cause minimum harm to living beings. It is closely connected to the central doctrine of AHIMSA.

Pranayama *(breath restraint)* *Hinduism*   Various ancient methods of controlling the breath are used in Hinduism either to control the mind or achieve spiritual states. The most common is slow, deep breathing through the nose, in which the inhaling and exhaling is increasingly prolonged until the breathing is hardly existent. It is claimed that some YOGIS can suspend their breath completely. Other methods of *pranayama* involve suppression of the breath, different rhythms of breathing and sometimes violent inhalations or exhalations. All *pranayama* systems are designed to assist mind control and single-minded concentration, hopefully leading to the desired state of ego-loss known as SAMADHI. The main object of *pranayama* is PRATYAHARA or withdrawal of the senses inwards and away from the outer world. *Pranayama* is the fourth stage of the path of YOGA as explained in the classical texts of the school. (*See also* PRANA)

Pranidhana   *Buddhism*   The vow to achieve Buddhahood which, along with the six perfections (PARAMIS), is considered by some MAHAYANA schools to be a prerequisite to entering on the path followed by a BODHISATTVA.

Prasad / Parshad   *Sikhism*   The sacred food given out to all participants in worship at the GURDWARA. It is made of wheat flour, sugar and water, which ensures that even the poorest member of the congregation will be able to contribute. There are also four other legitimate foods that can be used as *parshad*. (*See also* KARAH PARSHAD; PANJ PARSHAD)

Prasada   *Hinduism*   Food offered to a deity or a guru, which is then considered to be consecrated and is shared out amongst the devotees. In temple worship the *prasada* is usually offered to the devotees after the ceremony of ARTI at the conclusion of the ritual or PUJA (worship). *Prasada* is offered to the deity in two ways: devotees will bring offerings with them, which are then distributed; also the deity is offered food by the priests at the normal times of eating. This is also distributed or eaten by the priests themselves. *Prasada* can refer to the blessings or grace of the divinity which is also considered to be a gift from the divine. (*See also* MURTI)

Prasrabdhi   *Buddhism*   A refined state of purely mental spiritual happiness in which the practitioner is absorbed in bliss with little awareness of physical surroundings. It is one of the seven stages on the road to enlightenment. (*See* PRITI; SAMADHI; SMRITI; UPEKKHA; VIRIYA)

Pratikramana   *Jainism*   One of the six daily duties that should be practised by all devout Jains. It refers to the practice of penitential retreats in which the Jain devotee performs a ritual of confession for transgressions made in the previous twenty-four hours. (*See* AVASYIKAS)

Pratima   *Jainism*   The eleven rules or stages that gradually lead to liberation for a lay Jain. Although they form a large collection of rules and ethical behaviour, they can correctly be called stages, as they progress towards renunciation and asceticism as lived by the monks and nuns. The eleven stages are: the stage of right faith, vows, equanimity, specific fasting, renouncing food containing life, renunciation of eating at night, celibacy, occupational renunciation, possessory renunciation, withdrawal and renouncing food. (*See* ANUMATI TYAGA PRATIMA; ARAMBHA SAMARAMBA TYAGA PRATIMA; BRAHMACARYA PRATIMA; DARSHANA PRATIMA; PARIGRAHA TYAGA PRATIMA; PROSADHOPAVASA PRATIMA; RATRI BHO-JANA TYAGA PRATIMA; SACCITTA TYAGA PRATIMA; SAMAYIKA PRATIMA; UDDISTA TYAGA PRATIMA; VRATA PRATIMA)

Pratimoksha (S)   *Buddhism*   *See* PATIMOKKHA.

Pratitya-samutpada (S)   *Buddhism*   *See* PATICCA-SAMUPPADA.

Pratyahara   *Hinduism*   Explained in the YOGA SUTRAS as withdrawal of the senses from their objects or the state of being where the senses no longer have contact with the outer world. This is a desired state in most meditation systems. The achievement of *pratyahara* is the fifth stage of the path of YOGA as explained in the classical texts of the school. (*See also* PATANJALI; PRANAYAMA; SAMADHI)

Pratyakhyana   *Jainism*   The renunciation of food, drink and comfort that is one of the six daily duties expected of lay Jains. Although the complete renunciation of these activities is possible in the Jain practice of 'sacred death', this remains a rigidly controlled activity. In practice, the lay Jain would observe a variety of fasts and partial renunciations as prescribed in the eleven PRATIMAS. (*See also* AVASYIKAS; SALLEKHANA)

Pratyekabuddha   *Buddhism*   A term for an awakened human being who achieves enlightenment independently like the Buddha but who chooses not to teach. (*See* ARHANT; BODHISATTVA)

Pravachan   *Hinduism*   A type of religious lecture based on recitation and interpretation of passages from any scripture.

Pravrajya (S)   *Buddhism*   *See* PABBAJA.

Pravrajya (S) *Hinduism* Sanskrit for a pilgrimage. The spiritual map of India contains countless pilgrimage sites that range from local shrines to all-India sites visited by millions annually. Many Hindus embark on a pilgrimage, abandoning their normal everyday life for a period of time to seek moral and spiritual benefits from a sacred space. There are many famous pilgrimage towns and sites on riverbanks and some pilgrimages link various sites. Such pilgrimages may take three months and involve the pilgrim in hundreds of miles of travelling. The more difficult the pilgrimage, the more merit is acquired by the pilgrim. (*See* PARIKRAMA; PRADAKSHINA)

Pravrajya *Jainism* Renunciation. Physical, mental and verbal self-restraint is considered essential in Jainism in order to remove all traces of KARMA so that liberation can be obtained. The practice of non-injury to all beings, when coupled with Jain belief that even plants and animals possess souls, also tends to lead towards renunciation and withdrawal. Jain monks are arguably the most austere and stringent on the Indian subcontinent. SVETAMBARA Jains accept that lay Jains can gradually work towards complete withdrawal through the PRATIMAS or stages, but DIGAMBARAS believe only complete renunciates can obtain liberation. Their monks renounce clothing and only possess three objects: a peacock feather to use as a broom to remove small creatures in their path, a wooden begging bowl and scripture. (*See also* AHIMSA)

Prayascitta *(penance)* *Jainism* Jain scriptures state that without penance it is not possible to follow right conduct. When seeking spiritual advice, a Jain should be ready to accept the possibility that penances will be set. They can include confession, austerities, extra meditation or, for ascetics, demotion or expulsion from the order. Penance is considered to be one of the six internal austerities. (*See* TAPAS)

Prayer *Christianity* Christian prayer shares with other world religions prayers of petition, adoration, invocation, thanksgiving and penitence. Prayer may be offered in private individual devotion or in set liturgical forms which are congregational. Prayer may also be vocal or silent. In silent prayer the individual attempts to ascend mentally and emotionally to God, and various disciplines have been developed by the monastic orders to help achieve this. This has given rise to a number of Christian mystics. The distinct aspects of Christian prayer arise from the atoning role of Jesus Christ, who provides the deepest evidence of the personal and intimate relationship which God has with His creation. It is Christ who has provided the JUSTIFICATION that makes it possible to move closer to God, and many prayers are made through his intercession. (*See also* ATONEMENT; EUCHARIST; EVENSONG; LITURGY; LORD'S PRAYER; MATINS; MEDITATION; OFFICES, DIVINE)

Predestination *Christianity* The doctrine usually associated with John CALVIN, which asserts that God in his omniscience has determined the fate of all creatures, and therefore eternal damnation or eternal reward has already been decided for each individual. While the problem of predestination arises out of free will and omnipotence, Augustine saw it as a matter of grace. He argued that salvation does not come as a reward for good actions, as all human beings are under the sway of sin. Only grace can set human beings free, but this is not conferred on everybody. Therefore only some were predestined to be saved. The doctrine of predestination remains associated with movements that arose out of CALVINISM. (*See also* AUGUSTINE OF HIPPO, ST; ORIGINAL SIN; PRESBYTERIAN)

Prelate *Christianity* A term used for members of the clergy who have attained high rank. In the Church of England it is reserved for BISHOPS. (*See also* ARCHBISHOP; CARDINAL; POPE)

Presbyter *Christianity* The elders of the PRESBYTERIAN churches modelled upon the earliest form of Christian organization in Palestine, which was in turn based upon the Jewish synagogues. (*See also* PRESBYTERY)

Presbyterian *Christianity* The churches established from the doctrines of John CALVIN and based upon his model of organization imposed in Geneva. The first Presbyterian churches were established by John KNOX in 1560, when the Scottish parliament accepted a Calvinist confession of faith as the creed of the realm. The term Presbyterian is based upon 'PRESBYTERS', or councils of elders, who administered the churches established by Paul. The Presbyterian churches reject the episcopalian authority of bishops and priests and elect a hierarchy of courts represented by ministers and elders. The courts function first at the local or KIRK level, but the ultimate authority is the General Assembly. There are Presbyterian churches in Scotland, England, Hungary, France, Holland, Northern Ireland, Switzerland and the USA. (*See also* PAUL, ST; PRESBYTERY)

Presbytery *Christianity* The Presbyterian church court that has authority over a number of KIRKS or churches and is responsible for public worship and the appointment of ministers. The term is also applied to the SANCTUARY or area of a church beyond the choir and to the residence of a Roman Catholic priest. (*See also* PRESBYTER; PRESBYTERIAN)

Preta (S) *Buddhism* See PETA.

Preta *Hinduism* From the day of death to around two to three weeks later, the deceased person is considered to be a ghost *(preta)*. The correct rituals have to be performed by relatives to build up the soul so that it can leave the earth and move on to its next existence. For a variety of reasons a soul can remain earthbound as a ghost, particularly if the correct rituals are not performed. In this case, the *preta* or ghost is likely to cause problems, especially for relatives, until exorcized by an expert in the art. (*See* OJHA; PINDA; SHRADDHA)

Priest *Christianity* The institution of clergy existing in the Episcopal churches which derives its authority from the APOSTOLIC SUCCESSION from Jesus Christ (who is the culmination of Jewish priesthood, in that his sacrifice reconciles humanity to God) down through the APOSTLES to an unbroken chain of BISHOPS. Priesthood in Christianity derives its authority from God and confers the supernatural function to consecrate the HOST, celebrate the EUCHARIST, provide ABSOLUTION of sin in CONFESSION and minister all the remaining SACRAMENTS. The Protestant reformers would reject the supernatural elements of the priest-hood as unbiblical and promote instead the ideal of a 'priesthood of all believers'. (*See also* CONSECRATION; MINISTER)

Primate *Christianity* The senior BISHOP who is the overall authority of a national church or people. The POPE is the primate of the Roman Catholic Church, whereas the ARCHBISHOP of Canterbury is the primate of All England.

Prior / Prioress *Christianity* The title given to the head of a mendicant community or a monk/nun who deputizes for the ABBOT or ABBESS takes charge of a subsidiary or satellite house dependent on the abbey. (*See also* MENDICANT FRIARS; MONASTERY; ORDER)

Priory *Christianity* The community under the authority of a PRIOR/PRIORESS.

Priti *Buddhism* A release of ecstatic energy which fills the practitioner with rapture. It is considered to be the fourth of the seven stages towards enlighten-ment. It follows VIRIYA and leads on to PRASRABDHI once the experience has settled down and its emotional aspects have quietened. (*See also* SAMADHI; UPEKKHA)

Profession, Religious *Christianity* The taking of the vows of chastity, poverty and obedience that occurs at the end of a novitiate period and functions as the entry to full monastic life in a religious ORDER. (*See also* MONK; NOVICE; NUN; RELIGIOUS)

Propitiation *Christianity* See ATONEMENT.

Prosadhopavasa pratima *Jainism* Fourth of the eleven stages of spiritual progress in a lay Jain's evolution. In this stage the lay Jain fasts regularly, at least twice a month, while maintaining regular prayer, study of scriptures, listening to discourses and practising meditation. (*See* PRATIMA)

Protestant   *Christianity*   The term originated in the protest against the decision of the Diet of Speyer to end the toleration of Lutheranism in Germany in 1529 and has become associated with the REFORMATION and all those Christians since then who have broken away from the beliefs and practices of the Roman Catholic Church. The essential characteristics of Protestantism are the rejection of priesthood in favour of the 'priesthood of all believers', the acceptance of the Bible as the only source of revealed truth and JUSTIFICATION by faith alone. The hearing of the word has also been given priority over sacramental practice. (*See also* CALVIN, JOHN; LUTHER, MARTIN; SACRAMENT; ZWINGLI, ULRICH)

Prothesis   *Christianity*   A table or altar in the Eastern Orthodox churches where the preparation of the bread and wine to be used in the EUCHARIST takes place. (*See also* LITURGY; ORTHODOX CHURCH)

Protomartyr   *Christianity*   The title given to the first MARTYR of any Christian nation. (*See also* STEPHEN)

Proverbs   *Judaism*   A book of the Jewish scriptures that appears in the section known as Holy Writings. They stress the importance of wisdom and provide maxims for right conduct in daily life. Attributed to SOLOMON, they are regarded as proof of his reputed wisdom. (*See also* KETUVIM)

Psalms   *Judaism*   Of the one hundred and fifty psalms, Jews believe that seventy-three were written by DAVID. The psalms were sung in the Temple in Jerusalem by the Levites until its destruction by the Romans. For example, fifteen psalms were sung on the festival of Succoth and one psalm introduced the daily morning sacrifice. Today psalms are used in daily prayer and on some occasions in the synagogue. (*See also* PSALMS, BOOK OF)

Psalms, Book of   *Christianity*   The Jewish psalms have been used in Christian public and private devotions since very early times, and certainly by the second century were regularly included in Christian liturgy. They form an essential part of the regular divine offices and are sung in morning and evening prayer. The book which contains the psalms and their place in the liturgical year is known as a psalter. (*See* OFFICES, DIVINE; PSALMS)

Psalter   *Christianity*   See PSALMS, BOOK OF.

Pudgala *Jainism*   Matter. The domain from whence KARMA is collected. Matter is the corporeal aspect of AJIVA or non-living substance. It is made up of single or indivisible particles that come together to form aggregates of matter. These aggregates are constantly forming, changing, disintegrating and separating. Matter has the four primary characteristics of touch, taste, smell and colour. The soul (JIVA) uses matter to form the body and the organs of sense that are able to perceive the characteristics of matter depending upon the number of senses that the individual being possesses. (*See also* PARAMANU; PUDGALA SKANDA)

Pudgala Skanda *Jainism*   The collection of matter which encases and traps a soul. Jainism contains an early attempt to explain the universe atomically. Single particles (PARAMANU) come together to form *skandas* or multiple particles. These aggregates of matter encase the soul. Although every individual soul is encased within matter, it is KARMA that is ultimately binding. Karma itself is formed of subtle aggregates of matter. (*See also* PUDGALA)

Pudgalavadin (S) / Puggalavadin (P) *(Personalists)*   *Buddhism*   The second group of Buddhists to break away from the STHAVIRA. They challenged the doctrine of ANATTA by asserting that there existed a very subtle transcendental self only experienced by Buddhas. This, they claimed, was ultimate reality and should not be confused with the false self-identification accurately diagnosed by the Buddha.

Puja (S) *(worship)*   *Buddhism*   In contrast to theistic religions where God or gods are worshipped, the Buddhist is expected to take control of his/her own spiritual progress by following the DHAMMA. However, for most Buddhists the central focus of their ceremony is usually an image of the Buddha. They will make offerings of flowers and incense to the Buddha as a mark of respect and to express their gratitude. Whilst performing this ritual the following traditional *puja* is recited: 'With these flowers I do homage to the Buddha. And through this merit may there be release. Even as these flowers fade, so does my body move towards old age and death'. (*See also* PRATIMA)

Puja *Hinduism*   Hindu worship. All rituals and ceremonies of worship are generically called *puja*, but the term is commonly used to describe rituals performed to a deity or a guru either in the home or at the temple. Individuals will visit a temple or shrine and offer flowers, fruit, money, rice, grains and prayers to the MURTI (deity). In the home, families will perform *puja* in a small shrine maintained in the house. This could take place twice a day, but more often occurs in the morning. When *puja* is performed congregationally at a temple, a BRAHMIN priest will usually oversee the event and lead the prayers. The priest himself will perform specialist *pujas* to the *murtis* in his temple, particularly at dawn and night-time. The *murtis* are awoken with special ceremonies and offerings. At night they are put to sleep. Most Hindu worship involves ARTI, a ceremony where a tray containing small lighted GHEE candles is swung in front of the deity to the accompaniment of a specific hymn. (*See also* DARSHAN; MANDIR)

Puja *Jainism* Worship or veneration. The most common form of *puja* practised by Jains is directed towards the consecrated images of JINAS or TIRTHANKARAS (the liberated teachers and founders of Jainism). Jain *puja* consists of the recitation of the NAVAKARA MANTRA and the names of the *tirthankaras*; songs of praise directed towards the *tirthankaras'* achievements; listening to recitation of scripture; bowing and making offerings to the images. The full ritual of temple worship takes place in three stages (AGRA PUJA, ANGA PUJA, CAITYA VANDANA), but many will only perform the first stage before beginning each day's activities. The daily *puja* is also accompanied by regular fasting and trying to adopt an attitude of equanimity. Jain teaching states that *puja* involving images is only necessary for the first eight of the fourteen stages leading to liberation. The last six require direct meditation on the soul.

Pujari *Hinduism* Sometimes used to describe a village BRAHMIN priest, but more accurately employed as the title for a brahmin who conducts the worship at a temple or shrine and is mainly concerned with performance of ritual. (*See also* PANDIT; PUROHIT)

Pujaris *Jainism* Temple employees who take care of the images and lead the daily worship. They rarely receive any formal training and their knowledge of Jainism is often negligible compared to that of the monks and nuns. (*See* PUJA)

Pulpit *Christianity* A raised stand of stone or wood, traditionally placed on the north side of the NAVE, from which the priest or preacher delivers the sermon.

Punjab / Panjab *(Land of the Five Rivers)* *Sikhism* The province of India in which Sikhism began. As Sikhism is interwoven with PUNJABI culture, a Sikh sometimes has difficulties in differentiating between ethnic and religious identity. It remains to be seen whether future generations of Sikhs born outside of the Punjab disassociate the religion from the culture of the province.

Punjabi / Panjabi *Sikhism* The language spoken in the PUNJAB and also the common language of Sikh worship regardless of geographical location. The GURU GRANTH SAHIB is always recited in its original language, and although translations exist, it would be inconceivable to install a translation in the

GURDWARA. The tie of religious language links the community firmly to its ancestral roots in the Punjab. (*See also* GURMUKHI)

Punna (P) / Punya (S)   *Buddhism*   A meritorious act of ethical or moral behaviour bringing with it a reward either in this life or the next. Accumulation of merit is considered essential to attain enlightenment and five of the six PARAMIS, or perfections, are involved with ethical action.

Punya   *Hinduism*   An action that brings merit either in this life or the next. Although contemporary Hindus are beginning to use the term to mean wrong or immoral actions, it was not originally understood in the context of morality. Demerit was brought about by faulty or incorrect performance of ritual. This was then extended to include the incorrect performance of caste duties or failure to observe DHARMA. (*See also* PAP)

Punya   *Jainism*   As in Hinduism or Buddhism, this refers to actions that are meritorious and bring with them karmic reward in either this life or the next. Jainism does not categorize meritorious actions on the basis of caste as in Hinduism. In this respect, it is closer to Buddhism, in that it categorizes actions on the basis of whether they will take one closer to liberation or enlightenment. However, in Jainism, even good actions such as charity or kindness accrue karmic particles. These will eventually hinder liberation even though they will bring beneficial consequences to the individual. In Jainism, good actions do not balance out bad actions. All karmic consequences have to be experienced eventually. The ideal is to achieve the state where there is no KARMA. The ideal merit-causing action would be one that increases the longing and capacity to achieve liberation. (*See also* KEVALAJNANA)

Purakh *(a conscious being)*   *Sikhism*   God is the ultimate conscious being who, as the source of the life-force, is also the originator of consciousness. Human beings can become more conscious as they align themselves with the essence of God within. In this context, the Sikh GURUS could also be described as conscious beings.

Puranas   *Hinduism*   A series of scriptures that form part of the SMRITI collection. They are epic poems and stories that chronicle the sagas of various gods and recount the myths of creation. They contain many of Hinduism's best-known religious stories and many of the correct forms of worship for different deities. Traditionally, there are eighteen – six each for SHIVA, VISHNU and BRAHMA. The Puranas are first mentioned in the Arthava Veda, but the majority of them were written in the first millennium CE, the product of the development of theistic traditions during that period. (*See also* MAHAPURANAS)

Purdah *Islam*   The term used generally to describe the veiling and seclusion of women. Usually, the women of the family will have their own quarters in the household and will not appear before men who are not close relatives. They are not required to attend the mosque for prayer but may pray at home. The degree of purdah will vary from culture to culture and household to household. Traditionally, Muslim women encountered a greater degree of purdah in the cities, as village life necessitated that they performed an economic role in the fields. Often middle-class urban men would demonstrate their own status by maintaining strict purdah on their womenfolk. However, this is increasingly under pressure from the changing economic situations in many Muslim nations where women are entering paid employment. (*See* HIJAB)

Purgatory *Christianity*   The Roman Catholic belief in a temporary place or state where believers who have died in a state of grace may receive the punishment for their venial as opposed to mortal sins. The pain of purgatory is relieved by the expectation of salvation and the granting of the BEATIFIC VISION following temporary punishment. Purgatory can also be relieved by the prayers of the faithful and the offering up of the REQUIEM MASS. (*See also* HELL)

Puri *Hinduism*   The city in Orissa where the famous worship of JAGANNATH, a form of Krishna, takes place.

Purim *Judaism*   A spring festival held in the month of Adar (1 February–18 March) that remembers the success of ESTHER in preventing the massacre of Persian Jews as recounted in the book of Esther. On the eve of the festival, traditional Jews will attend the SYNAGOGUE, still fasting from the one day fast known as the 'Fast of Esther'. Two plates are kept at the entrance to the synagogue; one for a silver coin and the other for an offering to the poor. The TORAH reading will include the Book of Esther. The children attending the synagogue will shake rattles every time the name of Haman, the wicked vizier, is mentioned. At dinner and throughout the day special pastries known as *Haman-taschen* or 'Haman's hats' are eaten. During the morning synagogue service, verses from the MEGILLOTH are recited and afterwards gifts of food are exchanged by the congregation. A special banquet takes place in the afternoon where much drinking of alcohol is permitted. In Israel, children will go from house to house in fancy dress.

Puritans *Christianity*   Exponents of a form of pronounced English Protestantism associated with the doctrines of CALVINISM, who attempted to reform the Elizabethan and Stuart Church of England by attacking church ornamentation and the institution of the episcopacy. They were successful during the English revolution of 1642, but the term disappeared after the proliferation of NON-

CONFORMIST sects at the Restoration of Charles II. However, the Puritan movement was transplanted to North America in the seventeenth century. (*See also* CALVIN, JOHN; PRESBYTERIAN; PROTESTANT)

Purohit   *Hinduism*   A BRAHMIN who functions as a family priest. He might conduct rituals and ceremonies for a number of families. (*See also* PANDIT; PUJARI)

Purusha   *Hinduism*   The term *purusha* is used in the RIG VEDA for the primordial man or cosmic being whose sacrifice brings into existence the world. In SAMKHYA philosophy it is one of the two eternal components of all existence. PRAKRITI is changeable nature, while *purusha* is the unchangeable spirit. There is a difference of opinion as to whether the *purusha* is singular or plural. Some sects argue that there are many *purushas* and the way to liberation is to free the *purusha* from *prakriti* by the intellectual grasp of the true nature of *prakriti* and the denial of sense perception. Jain doctrines of liberation are very similar to the Samkhya philosophy. Once the *purusha* is liberated it exists in perfect and eternal isolation. For those who believe in one universal *purusha*, the goal remains to free oneself of *prakriti*. (*See also* KEVALIN; PRAJAPATI)

Purva Mimansa   *Hinduism*   See MIMANSA.

Purvas   *Jainism*   The fourteen scriptural texts known as the pre-canon which are believed to have originated at the time of the first TIRTHANKARA. These texts, once believed to have been lost, are incorporated into the primary canon, the twelfth text of which contains a synopsis of their teaching. (*See also* AGAMA; ANGAS)

Pushkar   *Hinduism*   A small pilgrimage town in Rajasthan sacred to BRAHMA. Although possessing many temples surrounding a small lake, Pushkar is famous for containing the only Brahma temple in India. The lake is holy, as it is believed to have been the place where Brahma and SARASWATI manifested on a lotus flower.

Pushti Marga   *Hinduism*   A large devotional sect founded by VALLABHA (1481–1533). It has several million followers in northern India and many places of worship. Pushti Marga places great emphasis on the grace of God, which cannot be deserved or won even though the devotee is committed to a spiritual life. Surrender of possessions and self to the guru are essential for salvation, and service performed through pure and selfless love is emphasized. The way is open to all, including women and low-caste Hindus, but family life is extolled over and above renunciation. Pushti Marga, in common with other BHAKTI (devotional) movements, emphasizes the eternal enjoyment of God rather than MOKSHA (liberation) as the supreme goal of life. The GOPIS, the beloved companions of Krishna, are regarded as the ideal of devotion. (*See also* SANT)

Pyx *Christianity*   A small gold or silver box used by a priest to carry the consecrated HOST when visiting the sick. (*See also* EUCHARIST)

Q *Christianity* The symbol given to the hypothetical text that is believed by some scholars to be a common source for passages in the Gospels of St Matthew and St Luke, which show remarkable similarity to but differ from St Mark's Gospel. (*See* SYNOPTIC GOSPELS)

Qadar *Islam* The total control of Allah over destiny, or the fulfilment of events which provides Islam with a strong sense of predestination. There were several debates in the first two centuries of Muslim history regarding the relationship between free will and predestination. These were finally resolved by al-Ashari. (*See* QADARITES; ASHARI, ABU'L HASAN AL-)

Qadarites *Islam* An early theological group who maintained that human beings had control over their own destinies and the power to determine events. The Qadarites' justification for their position was that since Allah had allocated rewards and punishments for human actions, God became a tyrant if He assumed total control of these actions. The counter-arguments revolved around God's omniscience. The ASHARITE position of compromise eventually became orthodoxy. (*See also* KALAM)

Qadi *Islam* The title of a Muslim judge who administers the SHARI'A or Islamic law. The ideal qadi is a man who is qualified in Muslim law but also pious in religious devotion. Islamic law states that he must treat all citizens equally, granting them the right to a personal appearance before him. All defendants have the privilege of taking an oath, and the qadi has an obligation to award *hadd* (deterrent) punishments if the crime is proved beyond the shadow of a doubt.

Qadiani *Islam* *See* AHMADIYA.

Qadiriya / Qadiriyya *Islam* A SUFI order believed to have been founded by Abdul Qadir GILANI and passed on through his sons. However, the TARIQAH (order) never achieved the universal acclaim given to its founder by Sufis throughout the Muslim world. In many areas it remained a small local order, spreading relatively late into India (sixteenth century) and Turkey (seventeenth century). Some Western scholars have cast doubt on whether Abdul Qadir Gilani was a Sufi at all, and point out that he was an orthodox Hanbali ALIM who did not introduce anything innovatory into Muslim life. Even Muslim commentators point out that he was known for his orthodoxy, sermons and courses on religious instruction but that he did not promote Sufi teachings. But there is no doubt that after his death, he became known as the foremost of all Sufis, and the *tariqah* is proud to be associated with him as its founder.

Qalandari   *Islam*   A type of Sufism often associated with wandering FAQIRS who have little contact with the established TARIQAHS where disciples gather around a teacher (SHAIKH). While Qalandaris may have received initiation from a shaikh, they pass their lives moving from place to place, often maintaining celibacy. Their spiritual focus is on the inner experience of the ecstatic heart, and they often reject both social norms and the outer observances of Islam such as prayer and fasting.

Qalb   *Islam*   The heart or the spiritual centre of human beings where God can be perceived. In SUFI theosophy, the heart is made unclean by the activities of the NAFS. The most common metaphor for the heart is the mirror. A dirty mirror cannot reflect the truth, but the heart purified by the unbroken remembrance of Allah becomes a clear mirror which reflects the face of the divine beloved. (*See also* DHIKR)

Qari'ah   *Islam*   The preaching of the last day or the Day of Judgement that is so prominent in the early revelations of the Qur'an. The Makkan revelations seem to suggest that such a day is close. It is described as the Day of Separation, the Day of the Reckoning, the Calamity, the Smiting. Muslims believe that it is impossible to determine when the time will come, but it is a terrible summons that will usher the final retribution of God upon the sins of the human race.

Qawwali (U)   *Islam*   A form of devotional singing in veneration of Muhammad, Ali and several famous Sufi masters popular in the Indian subcontinent. The singing is associated with the CHISHTI Sufi order, the largest in the subcontinent, and believed to have been introduced by their founder Mu'inuddin chishti as a means to promote Islam to the Hindu population when he realized how much they used music in their religious life. The *qawwalis* are used as the main form of DHIKR (remembrance of Allah) by followers of the order, and large gatherings can generate considerable fervour. *Qawwali* music has been popularized by professional musicians, such as Nusrat Fateh Ali Khan, reaching an international audience from all religious communities. (*See also* CHISHTI, MU'INUDDIN)

Qibla / Qiblah   *Islam*   The direction that all Muslims face when in prayer. The *qibla* marks the axis towards the KA'ABA in MAKKAH and every mosque must contain a niche to indicate the right direction to face. Kenneth Cragg has described Muslims as 'the People of the Point', in that the focus of all the various communities around the world is on one geographical point. (*See also* MIHRAB)

Qiyas   *Islam*   A legal principle introduced by ABU HANIFA to deduce the correct interpretation of Islamic law by the process of applying the QUR'AN and the HADITH to new situations by the use of analogical deduction. Although the Qur'an may not, for example, mention travel by car, certain laws may be developed by looking at what the text says about utilizing whatever means of travel are available at the time and then applying a deductive process to arrive at a Qur'anic interpretation of the new situation. (*See also* IJMA; IJTIHAD; RA'Y; SHARI'A)

Quakers   *Christianity*   See RELIGIOUS SOCIETY OF FRIENDS.

Quinque Viae   *Christianity*   The five arguments used by St Thomas AQUINAS to demonstrate rationally the existence of God. They are as follows:
1. The argument that everything that moves must be caused by something else. There must eventually be a prime mover from which all motion begins.
2. All effects must be traced back to a single cause.
3. The world contains contingent beings who are not essential. It is necessary to explain why they exist. God is the necessary being that explains our existence.
4. There must be an origin to the human values of truth, goodness and nobility.
5. The world shows evidence of order and design which must be attributable to an intelligent creator.

Qumran   *Christianity*   The site of the caves near the Dead Sea where the first of the DEAD SEA SCROLLS was found in 1947. (*See also* ESSENES)

Quo vadis *('Where are you going?')*   *Christianity*   According to legend, this is the question asked by Peter when he met Christ on the road after fleeing from Rome and martyrdom. Christ is believed to have replied that he was on his way to be crucified again. Peter returned to Rome, where he was martyred. (*See* PETER, ST)

Qur'an *Islam* The final revelation of Allah to humanity and believed to be God's speech or the word of God. Muslims believe that since the Qur'an is God's own words to humanity, it must also be eternal, as anything associated with God must exist for eternity. Although other revelations were given to Christians and Jews, it is believed that they corrupted their holy books. Muslims, however, believe that the Qur'an has been kept in the pure form revealed to Muhammad by the angel Jibril and recited by him to the first Muslims. It was collected by them and transcribed to become the sacred book of Islam at the time of the third caliph, Umar. As the book is literally the speech of God, it is not only the meaning which is important. The actual Arabic words are imbued with sacredness and potency and will confer blessings if recited, even if the reciter does not understand them. The recitation is so important that all mosques will train young boys to remember parts of the Qur'an by rote. The most proficient are able to recite the entire text and are called upon to perform recitals at various public occasions. (*See* AHL AL-KITAB; KITAB)

Quraysh / Quraish *Islam* The ruling clan or tribe in MAKKAH at the time of the Prophet who had benefited from the new-found merchant wealth and derived considerable income from the pilgrims who came to worship the idols installed in the KA'ABA. Muhammad was a lesser member of the tribe, whose message of monotheism they opposed, fearing that it would impact on their incomes. Although defeated and discredited by the success of the Muslims, they were able to re-establish their position in Arab society after his death. They became one of the forces that influenced the political dynamics of the new Arab empire, and after the death of ALI, the fourth caliph, re-emerged as the leaders of the UMAYYAD dynasty under MU'AWIYAH.

Qush *Islam* The missionary tours undertaken by the international proselytizing movement known as TABLIGH-I JAMAAT, which was founded by Muhammad Ilyas in India. Volunteers influenced by the movement set aside up to six months in a year for preaching tours, where they join with a party and target a particular Muslim area. The group will stay in the local mosque and preach. Members of the group will go from house to house, encouraging the occupiers to attend the mosque and join the prayers. The movement preaches the simple message of a return to prayer and obedience to the basics of Islam infused with strong piety.

Qutb *(axis)* *Islam* In the theosophy of Sufism, the head of an invisible hierarchy of saints upon whom the order of the universe depends. The imperative mood of direct mystical knowledge of God leads to the belief that the *qutb* periodically manifests to a chosen group of elite mystics and directs the activities of all the AWLIYA (SUFI masters) both alive and dead. This ideal of a master of masters in the mystical tradition, who corresponds to the role of Muhammad as the ultimate and final prophet, goes back in Muslim history at least until the ninth century. Ibn ARABI wrote the most developed theosophy of the *qutb*. It is generally accepted by most Sufi orders that Abdul Qadir GILANI was a manifestation of the *qutb*, but rivalry between the orders leads disciples often to proclaim their own master as possessing such illustrious credentials. (*See also* SHAIKH; WALI)

Qutb, Sayyid *Islam* Qutb was the successor to Hasan AL-BANNA, after his death in 1949, as the new leader of the IKHWAN (Islamic Brotherhood) in Egypt. Sayyid Qutb was executed in 1965 for political activities affirming the need for an Islamic state in Egypt as opposed to the modern nation-state. Qutb's ideas are very similar to those of Maulana MAWDUDI of the Indian subcontinent. (*See also* JAMAAT-I ISLAMI)

Qutbah *Islam* See KHUTBA.

R

Rabbi *(my master)* *Judaism*   The title given to an authorized Jewish teacher who has been trained and examined in Jewish religious law. They are the religious leaders of the Jewish people and, historically, have provided the textual interpretations and commentaries on the Jewish scripture that provide the manuals for correct Jewish practice. (*See* SYNAGOGUE)

Rabbi Moses ben Maimon *Judaism*   *See* MAIMONIDES.

Rabbi Schlomo ben Yitzhak *Judaism*   *See* RASHI, RABBI.

Rabi'a *Islam*   *See* ADAWIYA, RABI'A AL-.

Rachel *Judaism*   The wife of the patriarch, JACOB, whose father he served for seven years in order to win her hand. After Rachel's father tricked him into marrying her sister LEAH, Jacob served for another seven years, finally winning the hand of Rachel.

Radha *Hinduism*   The consort of KRISHNA first mentioned in the Vishnu and Bhagavada PURANA. The Vishnu Purana contains the stories of Krishna's exile amongst the cowherds of Vrindavan known as the GOPIS. The Bhagavad Purana develops these tales and introduces Radha as Krishna's favourite *gopi* and eventual consort. Many of medieval India's poets took up the theme of the love between Krishna and Radha as a great symbol of BHAKTI, or divine love. Radha came to be perceived as the ideal devotee and as an incarnation of the benign form of the goddess SRI or LAKSHMI, the eternal consort of VISHNU. In the fifteenth century, CAITANYA MAHAPRABHU, a Bengali BRAHMIN, ecstatic with the love of the divine, created a form of Krishna worship based on dance and devotional music. He often impersonated Radha in order to identify with her perfect love for Krishna. There are some VAISHNAVA movements that believe Caitanya to be the incarnation of both Radha and Krishna.

Radhakrishnan (1888–1975)   *Hinduism*   President of India from 1962 to 1967 and one of the most influential figures in the renaissance of Hinduism that took place in the nineteenth and twentieth centuries. Radhakrishnan was not a renunciate or a creator of a new Hindu movement but an academic professor of philosophy. He had been deeply influenced by VIVEKANANDA and his attempts to portray Hinduism as a creditable and reasonable intellectual tradition based on the ideas of VEDANTA philosophy. Radhakrishnan became the foremost apologist for Hinduism and developed a rational view of his own tradition based on his understandings of Vedanta and the influence of Western rationalism and science.

Radhasoamis   *Hinduism*   A contemporary movement that has its roots in mid-nineteenth-century Agra with the teachings of Shiv Dayal Singh. The movement can be considered as a modern form of the north Indian SANT tradition, influenced by the NIRGUNA BHAKTI (devotion to the formless God) of KABIR and the early Sikh gurus, especially NANAK. However, in common with other contemporary Hindu movements, it borrows from the universalism of figures such as RAMAKRISHNA and the eclecticism inherent within popular Hinduism. After Shiv Dayal Singh's death, the movement splintered into at least twenty organizations. The most successful flourished in the PUNJAB under the leadership of a succession of masters from Sikh background who claim direct descent from Shiv Dayal Singh. Their headquarters is a large ASHRAM on the banks of the River Beas, known as Satsang Beas. The Radhasoami movement has prospered in India and has major branches consisting of ashrams and hospitals throughout the country. Satsang Beas has attracted followers from outside the Hindu community, especially amongst Sikhs and Western spiritual seekers. (*See also* SANT MAT)

Ragas *(passion, greed or uncontrolled lust)*   *Buddhism*   One of the three fires that have to be extinguished in order to achieve enlightenment. (*See* DOSA; MOHA)

Ragi   *Sikhism*   Musicians who sing extracts from the GURU GRANTH SAHIB in the GURDWARA. Traditionally there are three musicians, who play the harmonium, the tabla (drum) and a stringed instrument. One of them will sing the KIRTAN and sometimes expound on their meaning.

Rahit / Rehat   *Sikhism*   The obligations required of the Sikh. The primary one, according to the teaching of the Gurus, is to remember God constantly. However, more detailed codes of conduct were issued by the followers of the Gurus. KHALSA Sikhs are bound by a separate code of conduct to which they swear allegiance on initiation. (*See also* RAHIT MARYADA; RAHIT NAMA)

Rahit Maryada / Rehat Maryada   *Sikhism*   The ethical code or code of discipline undertaken by KHALSA Sikhs as part of their initiation into the brotherhood. It is believed to originate in the teachings of GURU GOBIND SINGH, although it was not finally issued until 1915. It is based on the RAHIT NAMA, which were collected and compiled by the Sikh reform movement, the SINGH SABHA. (*See also* RAHIT)

Rahit Nama *Sikhism* The code of conduct attributed to the Gurus is found in the GURU GRANTH SAHIB. However, later followers of the Gurus compiled most of the Rahit Nama and the earliest is attributed to a follower of GURU GOBIND SINGH. Most of the codes of conduct were drawn up in the post-Guru period of Sikhism. (*See also* RAHIT MARYADA)

Rahma li-l'alamin *(a mercy to the worlds)* *Islam* The Qur'an's description of Muhammad which provides Muslims with the special sense that Muhammad is unique amongst the messengers of God and opens up the possibility of veneration and piety directed towards the Prophet that has always been the hallmark of traditional Islam. (*See* RASUL; USWA HASANA)

Rahula *(fetter)* *Buddhism* The son of SIDDATTHA GOTTAMA who was born shortly before his father set out to seek enlightenment. He is believed to have entered the SANGHA at the age of fifteen.

Raja Yoga *Hinduism* The royal or supreme YOGA described as the path of self-control performed to comprehend reality or the self through direct experience. Although spoken about by KRISHNA in the BHAGAVAD GITA, Raja Yoga was fully defined as a system by PATANJALI in the YOGA SUTRAS. He describes yoga as the 'cessation of all changes of consciousness' and outlines an eightfold path that constitutes a fully developed meditation discipline. The stages of the path are abstention or self-control, observance of the rules of devotion, posture, breath control, sense control, fixed concentration and complete single-mindedness. (*See also* ASANA; DHARANA; DHYANA; NIYAMA; PRANAYAMA; PRATYAHARA; SAMADHI; YAMA)

Rajas *Hinduism* One of the three GUNAS or qualities that combine in varying proportions to form all created beings and material entities. *Rajas* denotes the quality of energy or activity sometimes translated as passion. In inanimate objects, *rajas* would provide energy or movement. It would be more manifest in the energetic forces of nature such as wind or fire. In the human being, *rajas* manifests as a passionate nature and is the source of emotions such as anger, hatred, ambition, pride and sexual desire. Some VAISHNAVA traditions have classified foods according to the predominant *guna*. Some foods, such as onions and garlic, for example, are believed to create sexual passion and anger, However, *rajas* can be a positive force when restrained by DHARMA and can be utilized for the service of the society in the warrior caste (KSHATRIYA), for example. However, it is considered an obstacle to spiritual enlightenment, and its influence on human nature would have to be overcome to secure liberation (MOKSHA) or final release from SAMSARA. (*See also* PRAKRITI; RAJASIK; SATTVA; TAMAS)

Rajasik   *Hinduism*   Either someone whose nature is dominated by RAJAS, the GUNA that promotes anger and lust, or the typology of food that promotes those qualities in a human being.

Rak'ah   *Islam*   A unit of the obligatory prayer, or SALAH, which is made up of a set ritual recitation, standing, bowing and two prostrations. A minimum number of *rak'ahs* is required to complete the communal prayer, but individuals may perform extra units both before and after that event.

Rakhi   *Hinduism*   An amulet made of silk or cotton thread which is placed on the wrist to give protection and increase the bond of mutual love. It is tied by the groom on the left wrist of the bride at Hindu weddings. (*See* RAKSHA BANDHAN)

Raksha   *Hinduism*   Manifestations of supernatural beings who live in celestial or demonic realms. While they possess powers that would be considered miraculous to human beings, they are not divine. They are part of the world of SAMSARA and will be subject to death and rebirth even though their lifespans are very long.

Raksha Bandhan   *Hinduism*   The festival in which women tie RAKHIS onto their brothers' wrists in order to express the bond of love and demonstrate their appreciation for the protection a brother offers.

Ram Mohan Roy (1772–1833)   *Hinduism*   Born in Bengal, Ram Mohan Roy was originally influenced by Muslim monotheism and the monistic interpretation of the UPANISHADS taught by ADVAITA VEDANTA. He studied English and went on to develop a strong interest in European philosophy and religious ideas. He accepted the common critique of Hinduism current amongst the British in India that Hinduism was a degenerate version of a once-great philosophical tradition. He wanted to reform Hinduism in the light of European Christian thought and knowledge, and embarked on a campaign to restore the Vedic tradition as the original form of Hindu monotheism. In response to Christian missionary criticism of Hinduism as a polytheistic idol-worshipping religion steeped in superstitious practices, he founded the BRAHMO SAMAJ, first known as the British India Unitarian Association, to propagate a Hinduism based on the philosophical ideas of the Upanishads. The movement is one of the first of the reform movements that are sometimes called neo-Hinduism and was the forerunner of contemporary Hindu ideas based on rational interpretation of VEDANTA. (*See also* DAYANANDA, SWAMI; RADHAKRISHNAN; VIVEKANANDA, SWAMI)

Rama   *Hinduism*   Along with Krishna, one of the two most commonly worshipped AVATARS of VISHNU, especially popular in north India. Rama is the hero of the RAMAYANA and believed to be the manifestation of DHARMA. He was born as the son of King DASARATHA, an aged ruler of the kingdom of Kosala, who had performed sacrifices in order to produce sons. Vishnu agreed to manifest partially in all the king's three offspring by his three wives but to incarnate completely as Rama, the fourth son. The story of Rama is told in several versions of the great epic, the Ramayana, but the two most famous ones are the original Sanskrit version attributed to VALMIKI and the later medieval version by TULSIDAS, correctly known as the RAMACHARITAMANASA. (*See also* SITA)

Ramacharitamanasa   *Hinduism*   A Hindi version of the RAMAYANA written by the sixteenth-century BHAKTI poet and saint, TULSIDAS, that was able to reach the common people in a way that the Sanskrit version by VALMIKI could not achieve. Tulsidas wrote the work in Varanasi in the late sixteenth century. While the storyline is basically the same as Valmiki's version, the major difference is the emphasis on devotion which is apparent throughout the text. Although the book acknowledges the orthodox BRAHMIN tradition asserted in the Ramayana, it introduces the universal possibility of salvation to women, outcastes and low castes. This is achieved by remembrance of God's true name. In this respect, the work is highly influenced by the *bhakti* and SANT traditions which were so popular in medieval north India. Tulsidas' version of the epic is extremely popular throughout northern India and has influenced religious life immensely. The famous RAMLILA performances are all based on the Ramacharitamanasa and the text is recited throughout Hindi-speaking north India.

Ramadan / Ramazan (U)   *Islam*   The ninth month of the Muslim year which is observed as a fast lasting from sunrise to sunset. The fast is one of the five pillars of Islam and during this period Muslims should abstain from food, water and sexual activity. The fast is commanded by Allah in the Qur'an and is therefore obligatory for all adult Muslims unless they are ill or menstruating. In such circumstances it is permissible to make up the period of the fast at a later date. The period of Ramadan includes some of the holiest occasions of the Muslim year, such as the Night of Power which marks the first revelation of the Qur'an to Muhammad. The fast ends with the festival of ID AL-FITR. The month of Ramadan is a period of intense religious activity, and many Muslims who are not usually observant will attend the mosque and perform their prayers five times a day. While the fast provides an opportunity to reflect on religious matters and pass a month in prayer, it is also considered as a means of creating empathy for the poor and needy in the community. (*See also* ITIKAF; LAYLAT UL-QADR)

Ramakrishna Mission   *Hinduism*   When RAMAKRISHNA died in 1886, he had not founded a sect or society or even written a book, but his closest followers were dedicated in promoting his teachings throughout India and the world. In order to achieve this aim the Ramakrishna Mission was founded by VIVEKAN-ANDA, a close disciple of the saint. Today, with its headquarters in Calcutta, there are branches of the Ramakrishna Mission throughout India. Typically a centre or ASHRAM of the mission will include a library, hostel, hospital and prayer or meditation hall. Usually, the meditation hall contains murals of all the great figures of the world's religions in accord with Ramakrishna's teachings that all religions are pathways to God. The central focus of worship is a statue of the saint himself surrounded by the normal paraphernalia of Hindu temple worship. Vivekananda established several branches of the Ramakrishna Mission in the West, but they are often registered as the Vedanta Society. His missionary activity in the Western world was the forerunner for the explosion of interest in oriental philosophy and spiritual practices in the 1960s and 1970s.

Ramakrishna Paramhansa (1836–86)   *Hinduism*   A Hindu mystic often associated with the nineteenth-century reform and revival of Hinduism. He was born in a small village in Bengal but followed his brother to Calcutta, where he eventually became the priest at the Kali temple at DAKSHINESHWAR. Although he began as a devotee of the Goddess, during his life he achieved an extraordinary range of personal experiences of the divine. Throughout his life he practised intense meditation and prayer and experienced visions and unitative states of God-awareness. He followed a variety of Hindu paths, or SADHANAS, under the guidance of various teachers who visited Dakshineshwar. He practised TANTRA, VEDANTA and Vaishnavite traditions of deep devotion to an ISVARA (personal form) of Vishnu. He also looked at Muslim and Christian teachings and received visions of Muhammad and Jesus. Such deep experiences prompted him to teach that all the main religions can lead to God. He began to attract a group of disciples, including undergraduates from Calcutta University. After his death many of them formed a renunciate order and began the RAMAKRISHNA MISSION. His most famous disciple, Swami VIVEKANANDA, took the message out of India to North America and Europe. The significance of Ramakrishna in the development of contemporary Hinduism cannot be overestimated. He united the traditional Hinduism, especially that of the ecstatic saint figure drunk on the love of God, to the new rational forms of Hinduism that were developing in India under the influence of Western rationalism and Christianity. The idea that all religions lead to God because they are all variations of the SANATAN DHARMA (eternal truth) is now endemic amongst Hindus. Ramakrishna is regarded by millions of Hindus as a contemporary incarnation of the divine.

Ramana Maharshi (1879–1950)   *Hinduism*   Another of the significant modern Hindu mystics who contributed to the development of contemporary Hinduism and the promotion of Advaita teachings in the West. Ramana Maharshi was born in south India and at the age of seventeen underwent a deep experience in which his sense of body consciousness dissolved leaving him with an intuitive feeling of identification with the inner eternal spirit. The impact of this experience never left him and shortly after he took up residence as a renunciate at the local pilgrimage site at Arunachala. He was deeply influenced by ADVAITA VEDANTA and visitors to the sacred mountain were asked to consider the question 'who are you?' He eventually attracted thousands of visitors, many of whom became disciples. He was visited by Paul Brunton, the orientalist, who went on to write many books on Hindu spirituality and helped to prepare the soil for the explosion of interest in Eastern spirituality in the West during the 1960s and 1970s.

Ramananda   *Hinduism*   A fourteenth-century Vaishnavite who is believed to have been a direct spiritual descendent of RAMANUJA. Ramananda worshipped God in the form of the Vishnu AVATAR, RAMA. In common with many of the north Indian medieval BHAKTI (devotion) figures, he allowed everyone, including women and low-caste members, to become his followers. His most famous disciple is believed to have been KABIR. Today, the Ramananda movement is one of the biggest SAMPRADAYAS (sects) in northern India. Known as the Sri Sampradaya, its headquarters are in AYODHYA, the pilgrimage city associated with Rama. The followers, known as Ramanandis, worship Rama and SITA and there are several hundred centres throughout India. Mostly poor, uneducated people known for the fervour of their devotion, they tattoo the name of Rama on their skin and adopt the suffix of '*dasa*' (servant or slave) to their names.

Ramanuja (d.1137)   *Hinduism*   A Hindu philosopher and BRAHMIN who opposed the ADVAITA VEDANTA philosophy of SHANKARA. Objecting to Shankara's basic premise that BRAHMAN and ATMAN are identical, he posited the view that the God and devotee were separate in order that the central relationship of loving worship could take place. He was a great devotee of VISHNU and maintained that God, souls and the world are all real, but that the last two depend completely on God. The created universe is regarded as the body of God rather than illusion (MAYA). Ramanuja wrote extensive commentaries on Vedanta Sutra, UPANISHADS and the BHAGAVAD GITA. His interpretation of the Bhagavad emphasizes monotheism and personal devotion rather than Shankara's monism. Consequently Ramanuja can be considered the philosopher *par excellence* of the

BHAKTI (devotional) tradition, although, unlike the later *bhakti* movement of medieval Hinduism, he did not advocate universalism. Ramanuja's school of Vedanta is known as VISHISHTADVAITA, or Qualified Non-Dualism. After his death, his followers divided into two main schools, known as the cat (*marjara*) and monkey (*markata*). The former developed in south India and taught that the devotee was completely dependent on God's grace for spiritual development, just as the kitten is carried by the mother cat. The latter developed in north India and advocated that the devotee developed by spiritual effort, just as the infant monkey clings on to the mother when she travels. (*See also* VAISHNAVA)

Ramayana *Hinduism*   The Sanskrit version of the great epic which recounts the saga of RAMA and SITA. It is attributed to the sage VALMIKI and was written somewhere between 400 and 300 BCE. Although the Ramayana is essentially Vaishnavite (worship of Vishnu) in its doctrine, it contains strong elements of the SHAIVITE (worship of Shiva) tradition and represents the move towards eclecticism so dominant in modern Hinduism. The Ramayana consists of seven books (*kandas*), although some scholars have argued that the first and last are later additions to the narrative. It recounts the adventures of Rama, the incarnation of Vishnu, from his birth to his exile from his father's kingdom. It goes on to explore his wandering in the jungle with his wife, Sita, and brother, Lakshman, during which Rama assists BRAHMINS and sages from their persecution by demons. Sita is kidnapped by the demon-king, RAVANA, and the Ramayana goes on to recount his search of his wife, the war with Ravana and the eventual triumphant return to AYODHYA. Rama is considered to be the AVATAR (incarnation) and is the personification of DHARMA. Consequently, the original Ramayana represents orthodox brahminical tradition, but later versions, such as the RAMA-CHARITAMANASA, incorporate the more revolutionary teachings of the BHAKTI (devotional) tradition that subvert the brahmin hegemony of the religious teachings of Hinduism. (*See also* HANUMAN; TULSIDAS)

Ramazan (U) *Islam*   See RAMADAN.

Ramgharia *Sikhism*   A subgroup within Sikhism belonging to the carpenter caste (*tarkhans*). They claim to originate from the Ramgarhia MISAL and to be the builders of the Ram Garh fort near Amritsar. The Ramgharias often have their own GURDWARAS, although they participate with all other Sikhs on major festivals and religious occasions. Many of them migrated to East Africa as skilled labour for the British. They came to Britain after the expulsion of Indians from Uganda and Kenya as part of the process of the Africanization of newly independent nations. Their impact on British Sikhism has been significant. As skilled craftsmen with a long historical tradition of building a community as migrants, they have transformed the Sikh population in Britain. (*See also* JAT)

Ramlila   *Hinduism*   A popular festival in north India that incorporates DASSERA, replacing NAVARATRI, and celebrates the victory of RAMA over RAVANA, the demon-king of Sri Lanka. The festival usually lasts for several days, during which Rama's story, as recounted in the RAMAYANA, is acted out. The festival ends with the burning of effigies of Ravana combined with large firework displays. The most elaborate form of Ramlila takes place in Varanasi and lasts for one month. The Maharaja of Varanasi traditionally still attends the complete festival and at the culmination of Rama's triumphant return, the whole town of Ramnagar, near Varanasi, is turned into AYODHYA. (*See also* RAMACHARITAMANASA)

Ramnavami / Ramnavmi   *Hinduism*   The birthday celebration of RAMA, which is particularly prevalent in north India, where the worship of Rama is very strong. (*See also* RAMAYANA; RAMLILA)

Ranjit Singh (1780–1839)   *Sikhism*   The Maharaja of the Punjab who was originally the head of the Sukarchakia misal. By 1820 he was the effective ruler of the Punjab and his territory stretched from the Sutlej to the Indus rivers. His kingdom is considered by Sikhs to be a golden age in their history, and the movements for a separate Sikh state in the Punjab, renamed KHALISTAN, perceive his kingdom as a role model and an inspiration.

Ransom   *Christianity*   A term applied to the death of Jesus Christ which derived from the Greek custom of being able to buy the freedom of a slave. The term suggests that Jesus' death bought humanity its freedom from enslavement to sin. (*See* RECONCILIATION; REDEMPTION)

Ranters   *Christianity*   One of the Protestant sects of the seventeenth century that, like the Quakers, appealed to inner experience of the individual as opposed to priesthood, scripture and creed. (*See also* RELIGIOUS SOCIETY OF FRIENDS)

Rasa   *Hinduism*   A scale of devotional feeling developed in GAUDIYA VAISH-NAVISM, an intensely emotional form of KRISHNA worship. Traditionally there are nine *rasas* that can be experienced by the devotee. The idea is to subsume a variety of human emotions into single-minded devotion to Krishna as the object of all human feeling. The emotions that are transformed are: erotic love, laughter, compassion and pain, anger, frustration, fear, admiration and tranquillity.

Rasalila   *Hinduism*   The dance performed by the GOPIS, the cowherd devotees of KRISHNA, in the forests of VRINDAVAN. It is said that each *gopi* longed to dance with Krishna personally. He obliged by manifesting in a separate form for each one. The *rasalila* is performed by Hindu dancers in various parts of India. (*See also* RADHA)

Rashi, Rabbi (1045–1105) *Judaism*   Otherwise known as Rabbi Schlomo ben Yitzhak, a leading commentator on the TORAH and TALMUD whose work is considered indispensable in understanding the Torah. He provides commentary not only on passages, but also on individual phrases and separate words.

Rashidun *Islam*   See AL-KHALIFA-UR-RASHIDUN.

Rasul *Islam*   A prophet or messenger of Allah who is sent with a book of revelation. While the Qur'an acknowledges that there are thousands of messengers from God, only a few are blessed to receive God's revelation and the detailed commandments about how to live a life of submission and obedience. This revelation is given in the form of a holy book that contains the specifics of how to live a life of closeness to God through obedience. A *rasul* is the human vehicle chosen to receive the revelation, live an exemplary life based on its tenets and preach its message to others. Most prominent amongst these are Abraham, Moses, David, Jesus and the final messenger, Muhammad. (*See* DIN; NABI; NADHIR; RISALA; SHARI'A; WAHY)

Ratnasambhava (*The Jewel-Born One*) *Buddhism*   One of the five main celestial Buddhas, known as Dhyani Buddhas, venerated in Tibetan Tantric traditions. (*See* TANTRA; YIDAM)

Ratnatraya *Jainism*   The three jewels of right faith, right knowledge and right conduct, often symbolized by three dots, which are the foundation of the Jain tradition. It is this path of purification that is believed to lead to complete liberation of the soul from the bondage of KARMA. The goal is achieved by following the three jewels and does not require the intervention or grace of a divine being. (*See also* SAMYAK CARITRA; SAMYAK DARSHANA; SAMYAK JNANA)

Ratri bhojana tyaga pratima *Jainism*   Sixth of the eleven stages of spiritual progress in a lay Jain's evolution. During this stage the lay Jain renounces eating or drinking after sunset. This helps towards the development of complete AHIMSA, as it avoids harming minute nocturnal creatures. (*See also* PRATIMA)

Ravana *Hinduism*   The many-headed demon-king of Sri Lanka who kidnapped SITA, the faithful wife of RAMA, the human AVATAR of VISHNU. A large part of the saga of Rama is taken up with his search for Sita and the eventual war with Ravana. Ravana is extremely powerful due to austerities practised in a previous life and almost defeats Rama and his allies. It is believed by some devotional movements that Ravana was, in fact, a great devotee, as he was obsessed with Rama. This corresponds with the devotee's aim never to forget the name of the Lord. Rama's triumph over Ravana can also be seen symbolically as the triumph of the soul over evil. The many-headed Ravana may represent the endless desires of the human mind that have to be overcome before liberation or salvation can be achieved. (*See also* RAMAYANA)

Ravidas   *Sikhism*   A well-known north Indian mystic of the SANT tradition who belonged to the *chamar* (cobbler) caste. He was born in the Hindu city of Varanasi, where he attracted many followers through his teachings promoting love of God and self-surrender. Like GURU NANAK and KABIR he extolled NAM SIMRAN as the only practice that can liberate human beings. Sikhs acknowledge the life and teachings of Ravidas by including his poems in the GURU GRANTH SAHIB. Today, many Hindu and Sikh *chamars* belong to the Ravidasis, the followers of Ravidas. Their temples are known as GURDWARAS, where they also install the Guru Granth Sahib. Many of their practices are indistinguishable from Sikh religious practices.

Ra'y   *Islam*   The process of utilizing expert private opinion in interpreting the QUR'AN and SUNNA of the Prophet in order to form jurisprudence. There has been considerable debate as to the freedom of scholars and the limitations that need to be imposed on such activity. (*See also* FIQH; IJMA; IJTIHAD; QIYAS)

Real Presence   *Christianity*   The belief in the actual presence of the body and blood of Christ in the bread and wine used in the EUCHARIST. (*See also* CONSUBSTANTIATION; TRANSUBSTANTIATION)

Rebbe *(rabbi)*   *Judaism*   The respectful but affectionate title used by Hasidic Jews for their religious leaders or *zadeks*. (*See* HASIDIM; ZADDIKIM)

Receptionism   *Christianity*   A doctrine concerning the EUCHARIST which states that while the bread and wine are unchanged, the body and blood of Jesus enter the participant during the SACRAMENT. (*See also* CONSUBSTANTIATION; TRANSUBSTANTIATION)

Reconciliation   *Christianity*   There are four passages in the New Testament (Romans 5:10; 2 Corinthians 5:18; Ephesians 2:11 and Colossians 1:19) that perceive Jesus Christ as an offering or sacrifice to bridge the gap between sinful humankind and God. The theme of reconciliation is important, as it heals the enmity that had existed between human beings and their creator since the fall of Adam and Eve had left all humanity with the legacy of ORIGINAL SIN. The reconciliation offered by the sacrifice of Jesus Christ was the new covenant or

REVELATION that made forgiveness of sin possible. In the Roman Catholic Church, the sacrament of confession is also known as reconciliation. (*See also* RANSOM)

Redaction criticism *Christianity*   The study of the Bible that seeks to explore the editorial processes which linked earlier and later texts. (*See* FORM CRITICISM)

Redemption / Salvation *Christianity*   The theological idea that God has freed human beings from their bondage to sin and death through incarnating as Jesus Christ. However, redemption goes beyond mere deliverance and is bound up with the idea of RANSOM or sacrifice. For example, in the Gospel of Mark (10:45) the writer speaks of Christ as being 'a ransom for many'. The Bible usually provides allegories for redemption that indicate a payment or price for deliverance. The death of Christ is regarded as the payment for the release of all human beings from the bondage of sin. (*See also* RECONCILIATION; REVELATION)

Reform *Judaism*   The Reform movement originated in nineteenth-century Germany from the questioning of traditional Judaism that arose as a result of the challenge posed by Western society and developments in science, education and technology. German Jews were concerned about the numbers who were leaving the practice of their faith as a result of the influence of contemporary cultural thinking. The reformers felt that while Judaism had much to offer, it had to come to terms with the modern world. Originally the pace of reform was slow and resulted only in minor changes, such as prayers in the vernacular language. The basic tenet of the Reform Jews is that while the ethical laws of Judaism are eternal and immutable, the ritual laws can be adapted to modern life and even replaced altogether. Consequently, the traditions of divorce, dietary laws, the role of women, dress, synagogue practices and even the maintenance of the Sabbath have all come under scrutiny. The Reform tradition came to prominence in the USA and Western Europe. (*See* ORTHODOX JUDAISM)

Reformation *Christianity*   The term used to describe a sixteenth-century Western European reform movement focused around individuals such as Martin LUTHER, Ulrich ZWINGLI and John CALVIN that led to the creation of the Protestant churches. It is traditionally believed to date from the protests made by Luther against perceived corruptions in the Roman Catholic Church in 1517. However, earlier movements, such as the ANABAPTISTS, had called for a return to the simplicity and piety of the primitive church. Although the reformers were concerned with the moral, theological and institutional reform of the church, the actual agenda varied from country to country.

Reformed Churches *Christianity*   The Protestant churches that are historically associated with the doctrines of CALVIN and ZWINGLI as opposed to LUTHER. (*See also* CALVINISM; NON-CONFORMIST; PREDESTINATION; PRESBYTERIAN)

Regeneration   *Christianity*   The theological idea that all creation is renewed through the incarnation of God in Jesus Christ. However, the individual partici-pates fully in this through the transformation that takes place in accepting Jesus Christ. This transformation is seen as a new birth in which sin is no longer in control. The HOLY SPIRIT guides the newly transformed human being. This spiritual rebirth is closely linked to BAPTISM, and the New Testament writers suggest that the sacrament is capable of initiating the transformative process. (*See also* REDEMPTION)

Regular   *Christianity*   Members of the priesthood who are also bound by the vows of a religious order and live in a religious community such as the BENEDICTINES or the JESUITS. (*See also* RELIGIOUS)

Rehat   *Sikhism*   See RAHIT.

Rehat Maryada   *Sikhism*   See RAHIT MARYADA.

Relics   *Christianity*   The venerated remains of SAINTS, or material objects that have been in contact with them, that are used as objects of devotion after their death. They are usually kept in a church, shrine or place of pilgrimage. (*See also* FERETORY; RELIQUARY)

Religious   *Christianity*   A proper term for a member of a religious ORDER or monastic community such as a MONK, FRIAR or NUN. They may be categorized into active and contemplative communities; hermits or members of a community; mendicants or cloistered. Most religious are lay members of the church, but it is possible for male religious to be priests. Recently, the nuns of the Church of England have also been able to join the priesthood. (*See also* NOVICE; OBLATE; ORDER; REGULAR)

Religious Society of Friends   *Christianity*   Founded in the seventeenth century by George Fox, the Society is also known as the Quakers. The central doctrine is the presence of inner light or the direct working of Christ in the soul. It is this which leads to their rejection of the SACRAMENTS, the ministry and all set forms of worship. In worship the congregation usually sits in silence unless any member is moved by the spirit to speak. Quakers are pacifists and renowned for their religious tolerance and involvement in charitable activities that espouse ecological or environmental issues.

Reliquary *Christianity*   A container used to hold the RELICS of a SAINT. (*See also* FERETORY)

Repentance *Christianity*   The condemnation of SIN by the individual who has committed it, and the subsequent return to dependence on and obedience towards God. The New Testament suggests a state of remorse followed by transformation is required. In Christian theology repentance and forgiveness are only possible because of the RECONCILIATION made possible through the sacrifice of Jesus Christ on the cross. In Christian practice, repentance usually consists of remorse, CONFESSION and an act of reparation which involves transformation. (*See also* RANSOM)

Reprobation *Christianity*   The belief maintained by some Christians, especially Calvinist-influenced Protestants who believe in PREDESTINATION, that unrepentant sinners are condemned to eternal damnation. (*See also* REPENTANCE; SIN)

Requiem Mass *Christianity*   The service of the MASS or EUCHARIST offered for the dead which precedes the funeral. (*See also* SACRAMENT)

Reredos *Christianity*   Any kind of decoration placed above and behind the ALTAR in a church, such as murals, painted wooden panels or wall paintings. (*See also* SANCTUARY)

Responsa *Judaism*   See SHEELOT U-TESHUVOT.

Resurrection *Christianity*   The faith in the resurrection or the rising from the dead attributed to Jesus Christ is central to Christian belief. The Gospels indicate the importance of the resurrection by the amount of coverage they give to the incidents leading up to Jesus' death. They clearly state that Jesus Christ was crucified, died, was placed in the tomb and then on the third day rose again from the dead. Over a period of time, Jesus then appeared to his disciples in the flesh. The resurrection not only restored the disciples to faith and provided the impetus for the spread of early Christianity; it formulated the Christian doctrine that Jesus had been finally victorious over death and confirmed his victory over sin. Death had been the punishment for sin meted out to Adam and Eve as a consequence of the fall. The resurrection also contains the promise of resurrection for all believers at the final Day of Judgement. The newly restored eternal life of Christ provides the possibility for a new life in Christ given by grace to a believing Christian. (*See* CRUCIFIXION; RANSOM; RECONCILIATION; REDEMPTION)

Revelation *Christianity*   One of the central themes of Christian theology is the faith in the self-disclosure of God made throughout human history. The principal sources of the history of revelation are the OLD and NEW TESTAMENTS. It is generally agreed that human beings utilizing their own faculties are unable to comprehend the mystery of the divine and therefore require knowledge of God, which comes from what He has revealed and the process by which this takes place. Protestant denominations generally believe that all revelation is contained in the Bible, whereas Roman Catholics believe that it is also contained in the unbroken tradition of the church itself. (*See also* JESUS CHRIST)

Revelation, Book of *Christianity* The last book of the New Testament, attributed to the apostle John, which consists of a series of apocalyptic visions concerning the end of time. The book is written in an intensely symbolic style that is difficult for the modern reader to interpret. A major influence on Christian millennial movements, the book relates the events that will take place when God finally intervenes in a catastrophic way to bring about His will. The book tells of the second coming of Christ, the final war with the forces of evil and the eventual triumph of God before the Day of Judgement. (*See* MILLENARIANISM)

Reverend *Christianity* A title of respect applied to Christian clergy since the fifteenth century and used as the correct prefix in correspondence.

Revivalism *Christianity* An EVANGELICAL type of worship based on public rallies, where great fervour is exhibited often stimulated by preaching and prayer. The meetings are marked by the practice of calling up members of the audience either to testify to being touched by the Holy Spirit or to affirm their renewal of Christian faith. (*See also* METHODISM)

Riba *Islam* The Muslim understanding of usury, which is forbidden in the Qur'an. Muslim law generally interprets this to mean the making of gain without due return. Thus a distinction is made between usury and profit. The legitimate return for wealth is usually perceived to be one in which the investor is personally involved in the enterprise and does not seek a guaranteed return for investment. Thus, for example, Muslims should not invest on stock exchanges, where investors are not involved in the enterprises that make use of their capital.

Rida *Islam* The state of grace in which a person is able to declare from the bottom of the heart that he/she finds satisfaction only in God. This deep satisfaction has been a hallmark of Muslim piety and manifested amongst the countless WALIS or friends of God, usually known as SUFIS. In this state of being, whatever manifests is the will of God and is therefore accepted and embraced. (*See also* ISLAM)

Rig Veda *Hinduism*   The major SHRUTI text and to orthodox Hindus, the most sacred and ancient of the Hindu scriptures. It was probably composed around 1500 BCE, but Hindus believe its Sanskrit hymns and sacred formulas to be eternal and revealed to ancient RISHIS (sages) in their meditation. Although there are many strands to the Rig Veda, its central theme is the sacrificial fire ceremony performed by the BRAHMINS to maintain cosmic order (RTA). The Rig Veda sees the original sacrifice performed by the gods as the primal cause of creation. The text is still essentially the preserve of the brahmin caste, who used its sacred formulas for their rituals, ceremonies and Hindu rites of passage. It is studied and interpreted in the MIMANSA school of orthodox philosophy so that the brahmins are versed in the correct performance of ritual. (*See also* VEDA)

Rinzai *Buddhism*   A large sect of ZEN and the first school to arrive from China. It was introduced to Japan by the monk Eisai (1141–1215) and emphasized the use of KOAN in its teaching. The Rinzai school was adopted by the Samurai rulers and assisted in the spread of Chinese culture within the ruling classes of Japan.

Risabhdeva *Jainism*   The first TIRTHANKARA of Jainism believed to have lived in the third epoch of the current half-cycle. These cycles cover vast periods of time and the birth of Risabhdeva is therefore pre-historical. The third epoch is a period in which human life is characterized more by unhappiness than happiness and in which social problems are beginning to emerge. Jains believe that the first *tirthankara* was a powerful monarch who established the rules of social, political and economic life so that people knew how to live with each other. For example, he is believed to have established social organization by introducing the Hindu VARNA system but based on occupation rather than birth. As with the other Jain *tirthankaras*, Risabhdeva eventually renounced the world and lived as a teaching ascetic. (*See also* AVARSARPINI; UTSARPINI)

Risala / Risalah *Islam*   The office of the prophethood. (*See* RASUL)

Rishi *Hinduism*   One of the ancient seers or sages of the ARYAN civilization who are believed to have received the original revelation of the VEDAS in their meditation. They are still traditionally propitiated by the BRAHMIN priests.

Rishonim *(The Early Ones)* *Judaism*   The writers of the earlier codes of law that preceded the setting down of the authoritative SHULHAN ARUKH written by Rabbi CARO (1488–1575). They are considered to have more authority than the later commentators, who can only overrule a decision made by one of them if it is possible to find another *Rishon* to support the new interpretation or addition. (*See also* AHARONIM)

Rissho Kosei-Kai   *Buddhism*   A Japanese religious movement that focuses upon the LOTUS SUTRA, founded in 1938 by Niwano Nikkyo (b.1906) and Nagamuna Myoko (1889–1957). The early emphasis was on faith healing by chanting from the Lotus Sutra. After 1957, the movement changed its emphasis from healing physical ailments to the discovery of the eternal Buddha as revealed in the Lotus Sutra. (*See also* SOKA GAKKAI)

Ritam   *Hinduism*   *See* RTA.

Ritsu   *Buddhism*   A Japanese Buddhist sect begun in 754 by Ganjin and his followers, who had arrived in Japan to perform the proper ceremonies for ordination into the SANGHA. The sect that developed was primarily concerned with carrying out the teachings of the VINAYA PITAKA, the code of discipline that governs the life of monks.

Rohillas   *Sikhism*   The evening prayer usually performed by devout Sikhs at sunset when a day's work has been completed and before taking the evening meal. The prayer consists of the repetition of a selection of verses from the GURU GRANTH SAHIB which are placed second after the JAPJI in the book's composition. These verses are attributed to GURU NANAK, GURU RAM DAS and GURU ARJAN DEV. The verses are followed by the Anand, a poem which describes the joy of a devotee who has achieved mystic union with God. The prayer closes with the Mundavani, the words which appear as the finale to the Guru Granth Sahib. (*See also* SOHILA)

Roman Catholic   *Christianity*   That part of Christianity which gives its allegiance to the Bishop of Rome or the POPE, as opposed to Orthodox or Protestant traditions. The Roman Catholic tradition presents itself as a hierarchical organization of bishops and priests with the Pope at its head, in which the mysteries of the church are mediated to the lay members through seven sacraments which can only be delivered through the priesthood. The centre of Roman Catholic worship is the liturgy of the MASS and attendance is obligatory on all Sundays. The church also consists of several large monastic orders and lay congregations which seek to combine contemplative life with the rigours of working in the world. (*See also* CARDINAL; SAINT; VATICAN)

Romans, Epistle to the   *Christianity*   The longest of the letters of Paul which forms one of the books of the New Testament. It was written just before the apostle completed his work in the eastern Mediterranean and turned his attention towards the West and his forthcoming visit to ROME. Paul provides his reasons for visiting Rome and outlines the reasons why God rejected Israel and brought salvation to the GENTILES. As a Roman citizen, Paul was aware of the importance of the young church at the heart of the Roman empire and this influenced his reasons for writing the EPISTLE. (*See also* PAUL, ST)

Rome *Christianity*   By the time of Paul's ministry, there was already a fledgling Christian community in the heart of the Roman empire. Paul passed two years in Rome and by the second century of Christian history a tradition had developed that Peter had been martyred there. Certainly, by the time of Nero, Roman accounts indicate that there were many Christians in the city, and it later became the centre of the Christian Church until CONSTANTINE moved his capital to Constantinople in 330. In the seventh century relationships between the church in the East and the church in Rome deteriorated and eventually they divided, leaving Rome as the centre of Western Christianity and the capital of the Holy Roman Empire until the founding of the Protestant churches. (*See also* ROMAN CATHOLIC; ROMANS, EPISTLE TO THE)

Rosary *Christianity*   The most common method of popular devotion, in which prayers are counted on beads in order to assist the memory. The most important prayer associated with the rosary is the devotion to the fifteen mysteries arranged in groups of five which articulate the essential events in the life of Jesus Christ and his mother. Each item in the rosary is formed of one LORD'S PRAYER, which precedes ten Hail Marys followed by the Gloria Patri. Every five decades of Hail Marys, known as a chaplet, is preceded by the APOSTLES' CREED. (*See also* CONFESSION)

Rosh Hashanah / Rosh Ha-Shanah *Judaism*   The festival of the Jewish New Year which remembers God's act of creating the world. It is followed by the Ten Days of Penitence which culminate in the Day of Atonement (YOM KIPPUR) and thus it marks the beginning of the most sacred part of the Jewish religious calendar. It is believed that all human beings will pass before God on the New Year and that the Book of Judgement is updated and sealed on Yom Kippur, ten days later. In the SYNAGOGUE, the ark curtain, the reading desk and the TORAH scroll mantles are all decked in white and the RABBI, cantor and the blower of the SHOFAR are all dressed in white robes. The shofar is blown thirty times at three places within the ceremony and the service consists of the MUSAPH, *Malkhuyyot* and ZIKHRONOT and specific readings from the three sections of the Bible, the Torah, the NEVIIM and the KETUVIM. The Torah readings are primarily concerned with the binding of ISAAC. In the home a piece of bread is dipped in honey and eaten. This is followed by an apple, and a prayer that the year ahead will be sweet.

Rosh Hodesh *(the head of the month)* *Judaism*   A minor festival that occurs at the beginning of each Jewish month. There is no work prohibition and the festival is celebrated in the SYNAGOGUE by a reading of the HALLEL and the TORAH. Four people are called up for the reading, and then the festive prayer or MUSAPH is recited to bless the following month. Traditionally, the holiday is regarded as honouring women for their superior piety.

Rta / Ritam *Hinduism*   The Vedic concept of cosmic law, guarded by the two gods, VARUNA and MITRA, that maintains all existence. Human order (DHARMA) was also considered to be part of *rta* and consequently anyone who broke the ordinances of society was guilty of violating the cosmic order. From this concept developed the law of dharma and KARMA. Although dharma is now associated with moral law, the central concern of the VEDAS was the maintenance of cosmic order through the correct performance of sacrificial ritual. The intricate codes of moral law associated with caste observances developed later and was formulated in the LAWS OF MANU.

Ruah ha-kodesh *Judaism*   The holy spirit of God that is bestowed upon the righteous or pious person who has attained various stages of progress in his/her spiritual life through his/her own efforts and love for God. The holy spirit is the gift of holiness or saintliness.

Rudra *Hinduism*   A minor deity of the RIG VEDA who is the father of the Maruts, the storm gods. Rudra was feared for his destructive powers and control over the forces of nature. Consequently, he was held in awe and was given the title 'siva' (auspicious), 'samkara' (beneficent), 'sambhu' (benign) in the YAJUR VEDA. In other ancient texts, he is called 'Hara' (the destroyer). He was believed to bestow healing and offer protection against the forces of nature. By the time that the SVETASVATARA UPANISHAD had been written, Rudra was identified with BRAHMAN in a more personal form. The Upanishad is essentially theistic and advocates the path of salvation through devotion to the personal God identified as Rudra or SHIVA. Thus the ancient storm deity of the Vedas developed into Shiva, the personal manifestation of Brahman, the supreme spirit and ruler of the world and the human self, and probably the most popularly worshipped deity in Hinduism. (*See also* SHAIVITE)

Rumi, Jalaludin (1207–73) *Islam*   A famous mystic and SUFI who founded the MAWLAWI order commonly known as the 'whirling dervishes'. Originally from Balkh in modern Afghanistan, Rumi's family settled in Konya, now in Turkey, escaping from wars and disturbance. His father was a Sufi whose teachings were accepted in Konya. It is said that Rumi himself was a great scholar of Muslim jurisprudence and may have studied Sufism under al-Tirmidhi. However, it was Rumi's meeting with the wandering FAQIR, Shams al-Tabriz, that completely transformed his life. The love between the two has become the exemplar of the relationship between disciple and master. After his master's tragic death, Rumi continued to attract disciples, and the city of Konya became famous as the centre of the growing Sufi order. Rumi was known for his ecstatic movement to celebrate his experience of Allah and it was this that developed into the unique practice of the Mawlawi TARIQAH. Rumi's magnificent collection of poetry, known as the Mathnawi, is famous throughout the Muslim world but especially in Iran, where it is regarded as a spiritual commentary on the Qur'an.

Rupa *(form)* *Buddhism* As physical form it is the first of the five KHANDHA, but it is also used to describe the realm of form as opposed to the formless realms. (*See also* ARUPADHATU; NAMA RUPA; RUPADHATU)

Rupadhatu / Rupaloka *Buddhism* The realm of form that constitutes the middle section of the three layers that make up the world system in Buddhist cosmology. (*See* ARUPADHATU; KAMADHATU)

Rural dean *Christianity* The title for a priest in the Church of England who is in charge of a group of parishes and appointed by the BISHOP of the DIOCESE.

Ruth *Judaism* A book of the Bible that belongs in the section known as Holy Writings. It tells the story of Ruth of the Moabites who loved a Jew named Boaz, whom she met in the fields during the harvest season. Ruth is regarded as the ideal for the perfect convert. The answers that she gave to the questions posed by her mother-in-law, NAOMI, remain the test for the Jewish convert in Orthodoxy. The book of Ruth is read during the festival of SHAVUOT. (*See also* GER)

Sabad / Shabad / Shabd *(the divine word)* *Sikhism* *Sabad* carries several meanings according to the context in which it is being used. In contemporary Sikhism it refers to hymns from the GURU GRANTH SAHIB, which are believed to be the word of the Guru, since they are both the teachings of the human Gurus and the content of the last and final Guru, the Guru Granth Sahib. In the teachings of the Gurus, the Word is used to describe an aspect of the divine which pre-exists creation, brings creation into existence and exists within creation. It is the true and eternal form of the Guru and the reality of the immanent divine. Very often the word is used interchangeably with the name of God. (*See also* NAM; SATGURU; SATNAM)

Sabbatarianism *Christianity* Certain Christian movements that observe the SABBATH very strictly and argue that its laws should be followed on the basis of Old Testament restrictions, or alternatively advocate strict observance of the Sabbath nationally. Particularly strong in Britain's puritan traditions, while they have influenced the observance of Sunday nationally, this influence has been growing progressively weaker since the nineteenth century. (*See also* SHABBAT)

Sabbath / Lord's Day *Christianity* The early church maintained the Jewish Sabbath, which celebrates the seventh day when God rested from the act of creation. However, as Christianity spread to the Gentile world, this was changed to Sunday to coincide with the day of Jesus Christ's resurrection from the dead. Christians use it as a day of worship and religious education for children. There are some Christians, however, who maintain that no work should be done on the Sabbath unless it is an act of goodness or charity. (*See* SABBATARIANISM; SHABBAT; SUNDAY SCHOOLS)

Sabda Brahman *Hinduism* The supreme being, the formless BRAHMAN, in the form of sound. This primeval, uncreated sound is regarded as the medium between the formless Brahman and the material world. Some yogis and spiritual practitioners claim to be able to hear this sound in their meditations. The idea of an unstruck sound has given rise to the important concept of MANTRA meditation in Hindu religious traditions. (*See* AUM; SABAD)

Sabr *Islam* The spiritual quality of patience and fortitude in adversity that leads to endurance. In Muslim spirituality, this state of being develops through trust in God and the knowledge that everything, even adversity, is Allah's inscrutable will. It is expressed in the phrase, *Al-hamdu lillahi 'ala kulli hal* or 'Praise be to God under all conditions'. (*See* HAMD)

Sac / Sach *(truth)* *Sikhism* One of the six forms of immanent divine expression and the essence of Sikh teaching. It stands for God, who is the eternal and unchangeable reality, but it also refers to the teachings of the Gurus. One who has pursued the path revealed by the Gurus would come closer to truth and develop the qualities of a truthful human being such as the virtues of compassion, humility and honesty. (*See* SATGURU; SATNAM; SATSANG)

Sac Khand / Sach Khand *Sikhism* According to the teachings of GURU NANAK, the final stage or realm experienced on the path to salvation. This is the culmination of the human journey when one sees the reality of the creation as through the eyes of God. The soul joins with God in the realm of eternal bliss and experiences timelessness. The term is also used to describe the room put aside in the GURDWARA to house the copies of the GURU GRANTH SAHIB. The room is furnished as a personal bedroom and reflects the status of the book as the last living Guru of the Sikhs. (*See also* KHAND)

Sacca (P) / Satya (S) *Buddhism* Used for both absolute and relative truth, it usually refers to the four noble truths. (*See* CATTARI ARIYASACCANI)

Saccitta tyaga pratima *Jainism* The fifth of the eleven vows or stages undertaken by the lay Jain on the path to liberation. This PRATIMA refers to dietary restrictions such as giving up all roots and tubers, green leaves and shoots. Unboiled water is also forbidden. The diet undertaken is the same as that usually eaten only by renunciate monks. (*See also* ARAMBHA SAMARAMBA TYAGA PRATIMA; BRAHMACARYA PRATIMA; DARSHANA PRATIMA; PARIGRAHA TYAGA PRATIMA; PROSADHOPAVASA PRATIMA; RATRI BHOJANA TYAGA PRATIMA; SAMAYIKA PRATIMA; UDDISTA TYAGA PRATIMA; VRATA PRATIMA)

Sach *Sikhism* See SAC.

Sach Khand *Sikhism* See SAC KHAND.

Sacha Padshah *(The True Emperor)* *Sikhism*   The term was first used to describe GURU ARJAN DEV and denotes the ruler of the spiritual realm who can provide the guidance for the soul to achieve salvation. The expression may have been used by the Sikhs to contrast the Guru with the temporal power of the Moghul emperor. (*See also* MIRI/PIRI)

Sacrament *Christianity*   Certain rites of the church which are defined as an outward, visible sign ordained by Christ of an inward spiritual blessing. Thus for the Roman Catholic Church, the seven sacraments of BAPTISM, CONFIRMATION, matrimony, ORDERS, EUCHARIST, PENANCE and UNCTION are the main ways in which the presence of God manifests itself in the church. However, the Protestant churches argue that the New Testament only refers to two sacraments: baptism and the Eucharist.

Sacramentals *Christianity*   Certain religious practices which, according to Roman Catholicism, are similar to the seven SACRAMENTS but not as important, as they do not carry the grace of God. However, they help to make daily life sacred and carry spiritual effects. They include the sign of the cross and the reciting of grace at meals.

Sacred College *Christianity*   See COLLEGE.

Sacred Heart *Christianity*   Devotion to the physical heart of Jesus, often followed by mystics, that originated in the medieval period. In the Roman Catholic Church, such devotion is observed on the Friday after Corpus Christi, the feast that commemorates the institution of the EUCHARIST on the Thursday after Trinity Sunday.

Sacristan *Christianity*   An alternative title for a SEXTON or an official who has responsibility for the contents of the SACRISTY, namely the vestments and the vessels used in the EUCHARIST.

Sacristy *Christianity*   A room for housing the vessels used in the EUCHARIST and used as a changing room by the clergy. (*See also* SACRISTAN; VESTRY)

Sadaqah *Islam*   A good deed or voluntary payment of charity that is independent and extra to the obligatory payment of ZAKAH.

Saddha (S) *(confidence or faith)* *Buddhism*   *Saddha* does not refer to faith in the sense of belief in the teachings of the Buddha. The Buddhist should ideally experience or understand rather than merely believe; consequently *saddha* is more correctly translated as confidence or conviction born out of experience rather than belief. However, many Buddhists do have an element of faith in the three jewels: that is the BUDDHA, the DHAMMA and the SANGHA.

Saddharma Pundarika Sutra (S) *('Sutra of the Lotus of the Good Law')*
Buddhism An important MAHAYANA text commonly known as the LOTUS SUTRA. It was written in India in the second century CE in Sanskrit and claims to be the teaching of the transcendent Buddha, who is depicted as exultant on a Himalayan mountain top. It teaches the identification of the transcendent Buddha with the historical Buddha through proclaiming the doctrine that the Buddha's birth and life was a skilful device undertaken to teach the DHAMMA to humanity.

Saddhu *Hinduism* See SADHU.

Sadducees *Christianity* A Jewish sect at the time of Jesus who were opposed to the PHARISEES. They were influential in Jerusalem and at the Temple, where many of them were members of the SANHEDRIN. The Gospels present them as opposing Jesus and his disciples very vigorously, and they are depicted as proud, arrogant and rigid in their application of Jewish law.

Sadducees *Judaism* Conservative priests and their followers who became prominent in the first centuries BCE and CE in Israel. They believed only in the written law and denied the oral law, and were opposed to the idea of any kind of afterlife. (*See* OLAM HA-BA; PHARISEES; TORAH)

Sadhana *Buddhism* Spiritual practices or disciplines, usually meditations concerned with visualizations of BODHISATTVAS, BUDDHAS and MANDALAS, all used in Tibetan Tantric traditions. (*See also* YIDAM)

Sadhana / Sadhan *Hinduism* The spiritual practice or discipline followed by an adherent of a particular path believed to lead to liberation or salvation. A GURU usually teaches this to his disciple through an initiation. (*See* DIKSA)

Sadhanamala *Buddhism* Tantric collections of SADHANAS devoted to visualization exercises and incorporating MANDALAS many of which contain BUDDHAS and BODHISATTVAS in the centre.

Sadhsangat / Sangat *Sikhism* Commonly used to describe an assembly or congregation of Sikhs usually gathered for worship. When Sikhs gather inside the GURDWARA, in the presence of the GURU GRANTH SAHIB and sing KIRTAN, it is believed that their individual consciousness is united to the divine. The Sikh Gurus were more explicit in linking the *sadhsangat* to the benefits of keeping the company of those who were wholeheartedly committed to the Path of Salvation through obedience to the Guru's teaching. (*See also* SATSANG)

Sadhu / Saddhu   *Hinduism*   A wandering holy man or woman who has renounced the life of a lay Hindu. They may be part of a sectarian movement or an individual, but their lifestyle should embrace celibacy, homelessness, SADHANA and minimum possessions. They will gather at pilgrimage places in their distinctive saffron robes, often with long matted hair or shaved heads. The sectarian orders of sadhus generally maintain ASHRAMS, where they can stay and practise their spiritual disciplines or preach to lay members and visitors. The practices of sadhus reflect the breadth and depth of Hinduism, but some are known for their ascetic lifestyles and practice of austerities. (*See also* SANNYASIN)

Sadhu   *Jainism*   Although the term is used throughout all Indian communities for a wandering mendicant, it is specifically used by Jains to describe the order of male monks. The monastic order was founded by MAHAVIR and continues to the present day. Jain monks are renowned for their asceticism, but they are also traditionally great scholars. Generally, the monks and nuns teach Jain beliefs and practices to the laity of the SANGHA. The ascetics maintain the five great vows (MAHAVRATAS) of AHIMSA (harmlessness), SATYA (truthfulness), ACAURYA (non-stealing), BRAHMACARYA (celibacy) and APARIGRAHA (non-possession) in order to seek liberation. The monks and nuns are allowed very few possessions. DIGAMBARA monks go naked and are allowed only a begging bowl, a peacock feather (to use as a broom to avoid destroying insects) and a scripture. SVETAMBARA monks are allowed the fourteen possessions considered necessary to maintain their religious life. These include: a two-piece white cotton robe, a shoulder cloth, a shawl, a mat, a sheet, a cloth to cover the mouth when speaking, a broom of soft woollen threads, a rosary, a wooden plate and water bowl, and scriptural texts. In Jainism, the ascetic path is considered the most appropriate path to shred KARMA and achieve liberation. It is a life of absolute renunciation, in which many of the penances and austerities are maintained to ensure adherence to ahimsa.

Sadhvi   *Jainism*   A SVETAMBARA nun. The DIGAMBARA sect of Jainism does not allow women to become full nuns, as it believes that they must be reborn as men before attaining liberation. However, MAHAVIR established his order of ascetic monks for both male and female followers, and the numerically dominant Svetambara sect maintain the tradition of female ascetics. The nuns follow the same ascetic lifestyle as the monks and are very active in the Jain community. Jain nuns outnumber the monks by two to one. (*See also* SADHU; SANGHA)

Safa   *Islam*   One of the two hills in MAKKAH which are now inside the precincts of the Grand Mosque. The two hills (Marwah and Safa) are said to be the location of HAJAR's desperate search for water in order to save her child, ISHMAEL, from dying of thirst. She ran back and forth between the two hills pleading for God's mercy and intervention. The miraculous appearance of the ZAMZAM spring not only saved Hajar and Ishmael but also ensured Makkah's location as a place for caravans to stop *en route* through the desert. Pilgrims on the annual HAJJ re-enact Hajar's desperation by running back and forth between the two hills.

Safavid   *Islam*   The Safavid dynasty or empire in Persia lasted from 1501 to 1722. The Safavids began as a revivalist SUFI order in the thirteenth century but were transformed by the time they came to power into a religio-political movement that combined SHI'A doctrines of the messianic return of the IMAM with a call for armed struggle against other Muslim regimes. In 1501, Ishmael, who claimed to be a descendant of the Shi'a imams, conquered Tabriz and declared himself the Shah of Iran. He built an empire comprising modern-day Iran to the east of the OTTOMANS, and declared Shi'a Islam as its official religion. The shah considered himself to be both the religious and temporal leader, both emperor and messianic messenger. The shahs ruled as the 'Shadow of God on Earth', and all other religious beliefs were suppressed. Iran's Sufi past, with its veneration of saints, was exchanged for the key figures in Shia's past, such as the family of Ali and the imams. The Safavid empire reached its peak under Shah Abbas (1588–1629), who embarked upon an ambitious programme of state building, including a major construction programme supported by endowments. (*See also* MOGUL)

Saguna *(with form or qualities)*   *Hinduism*   Used to describe the qualities or aspects of the divine. Hindu philosophy has been divided over the question of whether the absolute reality has qualities or form. It can be argued that most of the early schools of philosophy were non-theistic and therefore did not see the absolute as having qualities, but later theistic movements merged the pantheon of deities into a henotheistic umbrella where each individual worshipper chose his or her own deity as a manifestation of the supreme being. This personal theism resulted in the impersonal absolute acquiring a host of personal qualities and manifestations. (*See* ISVARA; NIRGUNA BRAHMAN; SAGUNA BRAHMAN)

Saguna Bhakti   *Hinduism*   Devotion to one of the forms of the divine acknowledged in Hinduism or alternatively worship of a living or deceased Guru as a manifestation of the divine. (*See also* BHAKTI; ISVARA; SAGUNA; SAGUNA BRAHMAN)

Saguna Brahman / Sagunam Brahman   *Hinduism*   BRAHMAN or the supreme being endowed with form or qualities and becoming the personal God or ISVARA. It is usually acknowledged that Brahman contains the qualities of SAT (truth), CHIT (consciousness) and ANANDA (bliss) but is otherwise impersonal. Dedicated adherents of certain practices may find Brahman as their own inner-most reality (ATMAN) but most BHAKTI-orientated movements go further and apply to Brahman attributes such as love, grace and compassion. The term SAGUNA is also used to transform the incarnations (AVATARS) of the supreme being into animal or human form in order to perform a saving act. The images of these avatars maintained in temples are believed to be enlivened by the presence of the actual deity. Thus a devotee who focuses on a MURTI or temple deity may also believe that he/she worships God with form and attributes. There are arguments between various Hindu movements over whether the form or the formless appears first as the ultimate reality. Many Vaishnavite movements argue that their chosen VISHNU *isvara* pre-exists the formless God, who is perceived to be an infinite emanation of the radiant form of God. (*See also* NIRGUNA BRAHMAN; SATCHITANANDA; VAISHNAVA)

Sahaba *Islam* The companions of the Prophet Muhammad who became the first Muslims and his loyal and devoted followers. The *sahaba* not only provide a role model for Muslim piety but also are important for ensuring the authenticity of accounts of Muhammad's words and deeds as transmitted through the HADITH. Each hadith must have a chain of transmission that goes back to one of the companions in order to be considered authentic. (*See also* ISNAD)

Sahaj *Sikhism* The state of oneness with God when the devotee experiences absolute joy, tranquillity, natural goodness and love for God. This is the condition of a devotee who has attained salvation through the grace of the Guru. (*See* JIVAN MUKT)

Sahajayana *Buddhism* A Tantric path associated with the figure of VAJRAYANA, which extols the discovery of inner bliss achieved through yogic practices. It is associated with eighty-four SIDDHAS, or accomplished YOGIS, who travelled the countryside between the ninth and the twelfth centuries performing Tantric rituals. (*See also* TANTRA)

Sahajdhari *(slow adopter)* *Sikhism* The collective term for Sikhs who are not members of the KHALSA. They believe in the teachings of the ten Gurus and recite the GURBANI, but not necessarily maintain the five Ks. Some of the Sahajdhari Sikhs belong to sectarian movements that focus on the teachings of GURU NANAK rather than the more formalized Sikhism of GURU GOBIND SINGH. (*See also* NANAK PANTHIS)

Sahasrara *Hinduism*   The ultimate CHAKRA (power centre) situated at the top of the inside of the skull and generally symbolized in Hindu sacred art as the thousand-petalled lotus. The YOGI performs various practices designed to raise the female KUNDALINI energy located at the base of the spine, which then travels up through the SUSHUMNA psychic canal through the various chakras until it unites in SAMADHI with the SHIVA energy stored in the *sahasraha*. (*See also* TANTRA)

Sahih al-Bukhari *Islam*   The title of the collection of HADITH compiled by Muhammad Ibn Ishmael al-Bukhari (810–70). This is one of the six collections of Muhammad's deeds and sayings that is described as authentic or sound. Al-Bukhari's collection of over seven thousand hadith is regarded as next only to the Qur'an in authority. In some places, the whole of Bukhari's *sahih* was read out publicly during the month of RAMADAN.

Sahih Muslim *Islam*   The title of the collection of HADITH compiled by Abul Husayn Muslim ibn al-Hajjaj (d.875). This is one of the six collections of hadith that is described as authentic or sound. It is considered to be second only to the collection compiled by al-Bukhari. (*See also* SAHIH AL-BUKHARI)

Saibhang *Sikhism*   One of the attributes of God described in the MOOL MANTAR. It refers to the self-existence or self-effulgence of God. The supreme being is not dependent on anything else.

Saicho (J) *Buddhism*   The founder of the TENDAI school of Japanese Buddhism. As a young monk in 788 CE, he was dissatisfied with the corruption of his monastery and left to establish a new community strictly based upon the rules of the Vinaya Sutta. He studied CH'AN, VINAYA and T'IEN T'AI in China, and on his return to Japan created a single system from all the elements, including Shinto, which became known as Tendai.

Saijojo (J) *Buddhism*   The fifth and highest form of ZEN believed to be the culmination of all Buddhist Zen paths and the one practised by the Buddhas themselves.

Saiksya-dharmas *Buddhism*   Part of the PATIMOKKHA based on the VINAYA PITAKA regulations for monastic life, which outline the minor rules concerning etiquette.

Saint *Christianity*   The term used in early Christianity to denote things or people that were set apart as hallowed or consecrated to God. It is derived from the Latin *sanctus*, which is in turn a translation of the Greek *hagios*. It was first used in a Christian context by St Paul when he addressed the Christian communities as saints. Paul was referring to every member of the community being sacred or consecrated to God as the new Israel called to sanctity and God's service. Later the term was applied individually to the martyrs who died in God's service. Gradually, the term 'saint' was applied to special individuals such as bishops or monks. From this developed its present-day usage as a title of honour conferred on an individual who has lived a life of devotion to Christ to a degree that marks them out amongst their fellow Christians. The Roman Catholic Church employs an official process known as CANONIZATION, in which the individual is investigated and awarded sainthood by the Pope. (*See also* APOSTLE; BEATIFICATION)

Saint Paul's Cathedral   *Christianity*   A church in London originally built in 607. It was burned down in 1666 in the Fire of London and rebuilt by Sir Christopher Wren. It is often used for official and some state occasions.

Saint Peter's, Rome   *Christianity*   The original church is believed to have been built on the site of Peter's crucifixion in ROME, but the present building is sixteenth century. It is the apostle's traditional burial place and the public face of the VATICAN. It stands at the end of St Peter's Square where the Pope traditionally blesses the faithful from a balcony. (*See also* PETER, ST)

Saints, Devotion to   *Christianity*   The practice of venerating and calling upon saints for intercession which remains a strong element of Roman Catholic worship. During the first thousand years of Christian history, the veneration of departed Christians was mainly reserved for martyrs, but the medieval period saw a marked increase in the belief in and demand for miracles which was centred in a cult of saints. Devotees began to pray to saints to intervene miraculously in their own lives, and miracles became the proof of sainthood. The veneration of saints' RELICS became increasingly popular and they were placed in church altars as well as in their own shrines and basilicas. As the number of saints proliferated, so did saints' feast days and the assigning of special roles to particular individuals. (*See* ALL SAINTS' DAY; FERETORY; PATRON SAINT; RELIQUARY)

Saiyid   *Islam*   *See* SAYYID.

Sajjada nashin *(he who sits on the mat)*   *Islam*   The term used to describe the ancestral successors to a PIR or saint from the SUFI tradition, also known as Pirzada. Many traditional Muslims believe that the bloodline endows the descendants of a holy man with innate spirituality. Very often, the *sajjada nashin* will function as the hereditary leaders of the saint's order and custodians of his tomb and shrine. (*See also* DAR; MAZAR; SILSILA; TARIQAH)

Sakrdagamin *(the once-returner)* *Buddhism*   A stage on the journey to enlightenment in which the practitioner will only have one more rebirth, during which he/she will attain the goal of NIRVANA. (*See also* SAMYOJANA)

Sakti *Hinduism*   See SHAKTI.

Sakyamuni (P) / Shakyamuni (S) *(the sage of the Sakyas)* *Buddhism*   The Sakyas were the tribe of the Buddha. One of the titles given to the historical Buddha. (*See* SIDDATTHA GOTTAMA)

Salaam *Islam*   See AS-SALAMU-ALAYKUM.

Salafi *Islam*   Movement founded by Muhammad ABDUH (d.1905) which influenced nationalist groups in North Africa and was essentially a group of back-to-basics or fundamentalist reformers opposed to traditional Islam, especially Sufism. The Salafi view of Muhammad is essentially influenced by rational and humanitarian ideals meeting the Muslim world from Europe in the nineteenth and twentieth centuries. While the prophet is regarded as the founder of a virtuous community and a moral leader who transformed Arab society, the mystical and devotional emphasis of the medieval period is criticized. In the late twentieth century, new forms of Salafi thinking developed with a much more aggressive stance towards traditional Muslims.

Salagram *Hinduism*   See SHALAGRAM.

Salah / Salat *Islam*   The second pillar of Islam or the five-times daily prayer believed by Muslims to be prescribed by Allah as the correct form of worship. Western scholars note that the prayer-rite is not mentioned in the Qur'an and was gradually developed by Muslims. However, Muslim commentators are clear that the distinctive movements and recitals were used by Muhammad and passed on to his companions. The movement consists of three positions: standing, bowing and prostrating. The whole sequence of the three positions and the words that are repeated is known as a RAK'AH. Each one of the five prayer occasions may contain several *rak'ahs*, although two is the minimum when praying formally behind the imam. Worshippers can perform individual prayers both before and after the formal prayer. The prayers follow the ADHAN, or prayer-call, that is traditionally made from the minaret of the mosque, and Muslims are required to wash ritually before the prayer (WUDU). When the prayer begins, the congregation stands in lines or rows, shoulder to shoulder. The five occasions of prayer are as follows:

Salat al-FAJR, performed between dawn and sunrise.

Salat al-ZUHR, performed immediately after noon.

Salat al-'ASR, performed in the late afternoon.

Salat al-MAGHRIB, performed immediately after sunset.

Salat al-'ISHA, performed in the night, but not later than midnight.

There are also two optional prayers performed by Muhammad and very devout Muslims. These are *Salat al-Lail*, performed in the night between midnight and dawn; and *Salat al-Duha*, performed between dawn and the noon prayer.

Salawat sharifa *Islam*   Countless formulas that bless Muhammad and his family and which are known as *darud-i sharif* in the subcontinent. These are particularly emphasized by the SUFI tradition, but millions of traditional Muslims sing or chant them, sometimes after morning and sunset prayers. Many are used as intercessionary prayers and it is generally believed that intercession is not possible without first calling blessings upon the Prophet. The most common form of blessing is *salla allahu alaihi wa sallam* ('God bless him and give him peace'), which is uttered every time a pious Muslim mentions the Prophet's name. (*See also* DU'A; ISTIGHATHA; SHAFA'A)

Salayatana *Buddhism*   The six organs of sense and their functions which form one of the NIDANAS in the causal chain of existence. The *salayatanas* are dependent upon the NAMA RUPA, and the PHASSA is in turn dependent upon the *salayatanas*.

Salik *Islam*   The second stage of SUFI discipleship known as the journeyer or pilgrim. In this context it refers not to outward pilgrimage but spiritual travelling to attain proximity to Allah. However, as a stage of progress, it refers to the need for the seeker of truth to travel in search of an enlightened master or SHAIKH who can provide the guidance required to develop the seeker's innate capacity to come closer to God through purification of the heart. (*See* NAFS; QALB; TARIQAH)

Sallekhana *Jainism*   The sacred death ritual unique to Jainism in which the adherent fasts to death. This practice is normally undertaken by someone who feels that they are soon to die and takes place under stringent conditions, as Jains are completely opposed to suicide. Jain tradition allows for a follower to choose how to die if he/she is aware that death is imminent. It is essential to have the permission of one's family, and an ascetic guides the ritual. It consists of several stages: obtaining the required permission and taking the vow to fast to death; time passed in penitential retreat, study of scripture and meditation; the renunciation of all sense pleasures; silent recitations of the NAVAKARA MANTRA.

Sometimes the practitioner, if a lay Jain, will take the five vows (MAHAVRATA) of the ascetic. The conditions for fasting to death are as follows: extreme danger such as captivity or torture; acute famine, where acceptable food is not available; extreme old age which inhibits religious observance and physical well-being; terminal illness or fatal injury; and astrological prediction of imminent death. Usually the sacred death ritual is only undertaken by Jain ascetics.

Salvation   *Christianity*   See REDEMPTION.

Salvation Army   *Christianity*   An international Protestant Christian organization for evangelical work founded by William Booth in 1865. Its individual members are sometimes referred to as Salvationists. Organized on a military basis, it is well known for its uniformed evangelists who play in brass bands and participate in social work amongst the poor and needy. They are unusual amongst Christian movements in that they do not accept any sacraments.

Salvationist   *Christianity*   See SALVATION ARMY.

Sama *(hearing)*   *Islam*   The term used to describe listening to music as a spiritual discipline in some SUFI orders, notably the CHISHTI. It is also the term used for the Dervish or MAWLAWI turning ceremony commonly described as a mystical dance. Early commentators describe Sufi gatherings using music and rhythmical movements to induce ecstasy. Although there has been considerable debate regarding the lawfulness of music, it is generally considered that the human voice aided by drums is permissible. (*See also* DHIKR; JALALUDIN; RUMI)

Sama Veda   *Hinduism*   The VEDA that arranges the verses of the RIG VEDA into a form that can be chanted in ritual worship by the *udgatar* (the priest who chants at the Vedic sacrifice). (*See also* YAJNA)

Samad *(eternal)*   *Islam*   One of the ninety-nine names of Allah that describe His attributes. *Samad* is commonly chanted in DHIKR gatherings.

Samadhi   *Buddhism*   The last stage of the noble eightfold path before NIRVANA. It is used to describe intense concentration in meditation, which leads to awareness of reality or a state of equanimity where the condition of duality caused by thought can no longer disturb the surface of the Ocean of Truth. In this state the distinctions between subject, object and their relationship is transcended. (*See also* DHYANA)

Samadhi   *Hinduism*   The condition of single-minded focus on the object of meditation to the degree that subject–object consciousness is completely lost, resulting in a state of awareness that experiences complete oneness. In Tantric YOGA, *samadhi* results from the union of the KUNDALINI with the SAHASRARA, but SADHANAS (spiritual disciplines) may teach MANTRA meditation or breath techniques. In theistic traditions of Hinduism, *samadhi* is understood to be complete absorption into the experience of the divine usually discovered within. In this state all sense of individual self and ego are lost. Whatever the difference in regard to theistic or non-theistic traditions, *samadhi* is perceived to be, above all, the state of unitive consciousness. It is generally believed that the person who achieves *samadhi* is liberated from bondage to the cycle of birth and death, although some sects believe that final release can only be achieved after death. (*See also* TANTRA)

Samanas (m) / Samani (f)   *Jainism*   A recently developed semi-ascetic movement created by the TERAPANTHI sect of Jainism. They are allowed to use modern transport, travel abroad and cook for themselves. This has allowed the Samanas and Samanis the opportunity to visit Jain communities outside India and promote the tradition's teachings.

Samanera   *Buddhism*   A novice who keeps the precepts but has not yet been ordained as a monk. (*See* BHIKKU)

Samaritans   *Judaism*   The inhabitants of Samaria who are regarded with intense suspicion and dislike by the Jews. The Samaritans built their own temple on Mount Gerizim. There remains a small community in modern Israel which is monotheistic and accepts only the prophethood of Moses.

Samasvatsari   *Jainism*   The annual festival held by most Jain sects in the monsoon season in which all Jains are expected to make confession of any wrong-doing and plead for forgiveness from monks, preceptors, friends and family. Letters are written to all acquaintances not attending the festival for the same purpose. Finally, the participant extends his/her own forgivenness to all beings and asks to be forgiven by them. The ideal is to return to the condition of universal friendship and goodwill. (*See also* PRATIKRAMANA)

Samatha   *Buddhism*   A state of concentrated calmness in which the attention is focused exclusively on a single object as a meditation aid. When the attention is fully focused SAMADHI can be achieved. Meditations which produce calmness or tranquillity are contrasted with VIPASSANA, where a cognitive transformation is sought.

Samatva   *Jainism*   Sense of kinship and equality with all living beings that arises from the awareness of the Jain philosophical doctrine of PARASPAROPA-

GRAHO JIVANAM, or 'all living beings depend upon each other'. This ideal arises out of the central Jain belief in AHIMSA and led to many Jain initiatives in ecology and environmental issues in the twentieth century.

Samayika pratima   *Jainism*   Equanimity or dispassion. One of the eleven stages of spiritual progress required of the lay Jain and an important virtue that prevents Jains falling under the sway of passion that can lead to thoughts, words and actions that accrue KARMA and hinder liberation. *Samayika* can be achieved by the important Jain practice of meditating for 48 minutes three times a day. This practice is one of the six essential daily duties (AVASYIKAS) and is undertaken to achieve mental calm. It can be performed in the home or temple and consists of sitting in various yogic postures whilst reciting sacred sutras and meditating. (*See also* PRATIMA)

Sambhogakaya   *Buddhism*   One of the three bodies of the Buddha according to the MAHAYANA tradition. It refers to the subtle body of bliss which appears to BODHISATTVAS when they commune with the truth in the celestial realm. (*See also* DHAMMAKAYA; NIRMANAKAYA)

Samdhya   *Hinduism*   The morning prayer observed by millions of practising Hindus that takes place from just before sunrise and ends when the sun's disc is fully above the horizon. While the main prayer is the GAYATRI MANTRA, repeated several times, various sects may have their own versions and some BRAHMIN priests use a longer form of the prayer that contains verses from the PURANAS and a ritual to drive away evil.

Samiti   *Jainism*   Self-regulation or carefulness. The 'carefulnesses' exist in order to prevent Jain ascetics from performing accidental harm to living creatures and thus accruing KARMA. There are five *samitis*: carefulness in walking; carefulness in speech; carefulness in eating; carefulness in picking and placing; carefulness in urinating and defecating. Although these apply to ascetics, lay Jains are expected to maintain care in their actions to avoid accidental harm to life-forms. (*See also* ADANA-NIKSEPA SAMITI; BHASA SAMITI; ESANA SAMITI; IRYA SAMITI; UTSARGA SAMITI)

Samjna (S) / Sanna (P)   *Buddhism*   Perception or the awareness of sensation. The third of the five KHANDHA or elements which make up the nature of all beings or forms of life.

Samkalpaja-himsa   *Jainism*   The worst form of violence (HIMSA). Premeditated violence carries with it the largest influx of KARMA and should be avoided at all costs by a practising Jain. All violence is to be avoided, but intentional violence will cause more harm to the soul of the aggressor than to the victim. (*See also* AHIMSA; VIRODHI-HIMSA)

Samkhya / Sankhya *Hinduism* One of the six orthodox schools of philosophy possibly founded in the seventh century BCE; however, its teachings are found in the Samkhya Karika, attributed to Isvarakrishna, which was probably written at a later date, somewhere between the fourth and second centuries BCE. *Samkhya* philosophy is essentially non-theistic and views the cosmos as made up of two eternally existing energies known as PURUSHA and PRAKRITI. *Prakriti* consists of twenty-four kinds of energy and matter that include mental experiences in a state of constant flux. The twenty-fifth category is *purusha*, the individual, but eternal, changeless spirit. The aim of *Samkhya* is to bring about self-identification with the *purusha* and release it from the bondage of *prakriti*. The *purusha* then lives in eternal but blissful self-being. The YOGA school of philosophy is associated with *Samkhya* as its practical application. Yoga, however, accepts a supreme *purusha*, or ISVARA, who assists the practitioner as the focus for meditation. (*See also* DARSHANSHASTRAS)

Samkirtana *Hinduism* See KIRTAN.

Samma (P) / Samyak (S) *(supreme or true)* *Buddhism* The summit of achievement. While it can refer to the highest point that an individual is capable of reaching, it can also be used to describe each step of the noble eightfold path. It can also refer to the Buddha and to enlightenment. (*See* ARIYATTHANGIKA-MAGGA; MAJJHIMA PATIPADA)

Samma ajiva *(right livelihood)* *Buddhism* The fifth of the eight noble truths, which recommends Buddhists to refrain from any occupation that will cause harm to others, such as trading in arms, intoxicants, poisons, slaughter of animals and cheating. (*See* ARIYATTHANGIKAMAGGA; MAJJHIMA PATIPADA)

Samma ditthi *(right understanding)* *Buddhism* The first of the eight noble truths, which refers to the understanding required to enter upon the path to enlightenment. Essentially this requires grasping the meaning and the significance of the four noble truths taught by the Buddha in his first sermon at Varanasi. (*See* ARIYATTHANGIKAMAGGA; CATTARI ARIYASACCANI; MAJJHIMA PATIPADA)

Samma kammanta *(right action)* *Buddhism* The fourth of the eight noble truths, which aims to promote correct moral and ethical conduct. It recommends abstention from dishonesty, violence, sexual misconduct and all forms of dishonourable behaviour. (*See* ARIYATTHANGIKAMAGGA; CATTARI ARIYASACCANI; MAJJHIMA PATIPADA)

Samma samadhi *(right concentration)* *Buddhism*   The last of the eight noble truths, which is concerned with meditation, in which the practitioner passes through the four stages of DHYANA to the level of perfect equanimity. (*See also* ARIYATTHANGIKAMAGGA; CATTARI ARIYASACCANI; MAJJHIMA PATIPADA; NIRVANA; SAMADHI)

Samma sankappa *(right thought)* *Buddhism*   The second of the eight noble truths, which is concerned with maintaining positive and beneficial thoughts, which lead to detachment, compassion and non-violence, and avoiding negative thoughts, which lead to selfish desire, ill-will, hatred and anger. (*See* ARIYATTHANGIKAMAGGA; CATTARI ARIYASACCANI; MAJJHIMA PATIPADA)

Samma sati *(right mindfulness)* *Buddhism*   The seventh of the eight noble truths, which recommends to the practitioner awareness of the activities of the mind, body and sensations. Particularly associated with this is meditation upon the breath to develop self-awareness and concentration. (*See* ARIYATTHANGIKAMAGGA; CATTARI ARIYASACCANI; KAYA; MAJJHIMA PATIPADA; VEDANA)

Samma vaca *(right speech)* *Buddhism*   The third of the eight noble truths, which is concerned with abstention from telling lies and indulging in any backbiting, gossip and slander that will create hatred, violence, anger or any kind of disharmony between individuals or communities. Abusive language is also shunned and generally the practitioner should maintain speech that is friendly, benevolent and promotes the DHAMMA. (*See also* ARIYATTHANGIKAMAGGA; CATTARI ARIYASACCANI; MAJJHIMA PATIPADA)

Samma vayama *(right effort)* *Buddhism*   The sixth of the eight noble truths, which promotes the will to maintain the practice of the DHAMMA through preventing negative states of mind from arising and to encourage the development of positive and beneficial states of mind. (*See also* ARIYATTHANGIKAMAGGA; CATTARI ARIYASACCANI; MAJJHIMA PATIPADA)

Samnyasin *Hinduism*   *See* SANNYASIN.

Sampradaya *Hinduism*   The correct term for the countless sects that exist within the framework of Hinduism. Although the three foremost divisions of Hindu belief and practice are VAISHNAVA (Vishnu worship), SHAIVITE (Shiva worship) and SHAKTI (Goddess worship), these are not sects, as each one contains many sects within the tradition. Hindu sects are usually the result of individual spiritual teachers (GURUS) and developed historically after the founder's death. They each contain a distinct set of beliefs and practices but maintain the central themes of SAMSARA (cycle of birth and death), KARMA (law of action and reaction) and MUKTI (liberation). Hindu sects are rarely exclusive and followers may well belong to other forms of Hindu practice. Sects continue to develop, as Hinduism remains a living tradition that produces many holy men and women.

Samsara *(continuing, becoming)* *Buddhism*   Daily life, the world of continuous flux in which all humans live or the state of transmigration on the wheel of life in which all beings revolve, coming again and again until achieving NIRVANA. All life which is dependent upon something else for its existence or which consists of an aggregate of various components is in the realm of samsara. In the MAHAYANA school, nirvana and samsara are two aspects of one reality, which is ultimate non-duality.

Samsara / Sansara *Hinduism*   It is a central belief in all Indian traditions that all beings are caught in an endless ocean of continuous rebirths or an eternal process of coming and going from one life to another, which only ceases when the soul achieves liberation or MUKTI. Samsara refers not only to the process of endless birth and death but also to the worlds where rebirth is possible. This includes the worlds of animals, humans, demons, gods and demi-gods. Rebirth can take place in any of the countless forms that inhabit these realms. The inner world of the mind is also included in samsara, as it is created or formed. In general, samsara is everything that is created, survives for a duration and then decays or dies; it is the process of endless change as opposed to BRAHMAN or ATMAN, the changeless reality that lies behind and within samsara. (*See also* KARMA)

Samsara *Jainism*   The cycle of rebirths or worldly existence. There is little difference between Jain concepts of samsara and other Indian traditions. Jains believe that all souls are trapped in matter through the weight of karmic influx arising out of actions performed over countless lifetimes. Thus the cycle of birth, death and rebirth continues until the soul is free from all KARMA. The essential difference between Jain views of samsara and those of Buddhism and Hinduism is that unlike Buddhism, Jains believe in an eternal soul but do not accept union of the soul with an absolute reality (BRAHMAN) as in Hinduism. (*See also* JIVA; KEVALAJNANA)

Samskar / Samskara / Sanskar *Hinduism*   Rites of passage or life-cycle rituals that mark a new stage in life. There are a total of sixteen that begin before birth with conception and continue after death, but not all Hindus observe them all. The most important are birth, naming, first haircut, receiving the sacred thread, betrothal and marriage, taking vows of renunciation, death and rites for the dead. The rules for the performance of *samskars* are written down in the

Grihya Sutras composed in the last few centuries BCE. (*See* SHRADDHA; UPANAYANA)

Samskara (S) / Sankhara (P)   *Buddhism*   The second link or NIDANA in the causal chain of existence and the fourth of the five KHANDHAS or elements/ aggregates that make up human nature. It is used to describe the intellectual faculties or, more generally, all the contents of mind. However, in the causal chain of existence, the *samskaras* arise from ignorance (AVIDYA), and, in turn, give rise to consciousness (VINNANA). In this sense it applies to volitional activities which lead to the desire or longing for life. It is also used in a much more general sense to refer to all mental and physical phenomena which are conditioned or compounded.

Samudaya / Tanha (P) / Trishna (S)   *Buddhism*   The second of the four noble truths taught by the Buddha in his first sermon at Sarnath. Having first identified DUKKHA, or suffering, as the first noble truth, the Buddha explains that it has a cause variously translated as thirst, craving or desire. *Samudaya*, or the thirst for life, is also one of the NIDANAS or links in the causal chain of existence. It depends on VEDANA and, in turn, is depended upon by UPADANA. (*See also* PATICCA-SAMUPPADA)

Samuel   *Judaism*   Two books of the Jewish scriptures that come in the first part of the section known as the Prophets where the early prophets are recorded. The books of Samuel recount the life of the prophet of the same name and the rise of the monarchy from the appointment of SAUL as Israel's first king through to the reign of his successor, DAVID. (*See also* NEVIIM)

Samvara   *Jainism*   Stopping the process of KARMA or the influx of karma. This is essential in order to progress on the path of liberation. Jains can prevent karma accruing by several processes that are part of the Jain religious discipline. This includes the observance of: three guards; five types of carefulness; ten virtues; twelve reflections; twenty-two victories over affliction; and five types of right conduct. (*See also* ANUPREKSAS; CARITRA MOHANIYA; DHARMA; GUPTI; KEVALAJNANA; PARISAHA JAYA; SAMITI)

Samyak (S)   *Buddhism*   See SAMMA.

Samyak Caritra *(right conduct)*   *Jainism*   One of three jewels that constitute the threefold path of Jainism, which when followed leads to liberation from the bondage of KARMA. Although right conduct is listed as the third jewel, Jainism attaches great importance to it. Right conduct is based upon right knowledge. It is achieved through non-violence, truthfulness, non-stealing, sexual purity and non-possession, the five major vows of Jainism. Right conduct is divided into two categories: perfect or unqualified conduct, which is sought by ascetics who have renounced worldly ties; and partial or qualified conduct, which should be observed by lay Jains. There is no difference in the rules of discipline or the substance of the vows. The latter form of conduct takes into account the difference in lifestyle of ascetics and laity. (*See also* ANUVRATAS; MAHAVRATAS; SAMYAK DARSHANA; SAMYAK JNANA)

Samyak Darshana *(right faith)* *Jainism* One of three jewels that constitute the threefold path of Jainism, which when followed leads to liberation from the bondage of KARMA. Right faith is understood to be insight into truth or seeing things from the right viewpoint. Jain scriptures state that the Jain with right faith should have the following aspects: be free of doubt concerning Jain teachings; be detached from the things of this world; have respect for the body as the vehicle of liberation; avoid religious beliefs and practices that are erroneous or superstitious; protect Jainism from criticism by observing a high degree of spirituality and respecting the pious; be steadfast in one's convictions and observe right knowledge and right conduct; have respect and affection for the pious and righteous followers of the Jain tradition; observe Jain conduct by demonstrating its values and teachings. (*See also* SAMYAK CARITRA; SAMYAK JNANA)

Samyak Jnana *(right knowledge)* *Jainism* One of three jewels that constitute the threefold path of Jainism, which when followed leads to liberation from the bondage of KARMA. Right knowledge involves true perception of the nature of the world and the role of humans within it. While Jain scriptures acknowledge that any kind of knowledge that facilitates spiritual development is beneficial, they stress that right knowledge should be complete, based upon experience, study of scripture and without exaggeration or falsehood. There are five types of knowledge described in Jainism. They are sensory knowledge, scriptural knowledge, clairvoyant knowledge, telepathic knowledge and omniscient knowledge. Although the first four are present in enlightened souls, it is the fifth that marks out the culmination of the Jain quest. Omniscience is full and perfect knowledge of both material and non-material entities. It is not limited by time or space and is possessed by all souls when the karmic particles have been removed. Jains believe that the acquisition of this kind of knowledge is the goal of human life. In practice, it is scriptural knowledge that becomes the focus of samyak jnana, and Jains are expected to study sacred texts with devotion, understanding and an open mind. (*See also* KEVALAJNANA; SAMYAK CARITRA; SAMYAK DARSHANA)

Samyasin *Hinduism* See SANNYASIN.

Samyojana *Buddhism* A number of fetters that have to be broken by the successful practitioner in order to be free from suffering. There are nine altogether: belief in separate selfhood, sceptical doubt, blind attachment to rules and regulations, sexual desire, desire for physical existence, desire for celestial existence, conceit, restlessness and ignorance. (*See* NIRVANA; SAMSARA)

Sanatan Dharma *(the eternal religion)   Hinduism*   Many Hindus prefer the Sanskrit term 'sanatan dharma' to describe their religious practice and belief. It is believed that the original form of Hinduism was in the pre-existent VEDAS and was revealed to several sages known as RISHI. However, as Hindus believe in an endless cycle of creation and destruction, the Vedas are given again to human beings at the beginning of each cycle of creation. Other Hindus use the term to describe the end goal (of oneness with BRAHMAN, the absolute reality) as the eternal quest of all living beings.

Sanctification *Christianity*   The process by which a believer is made holy by following the teachings and actions of Jesus Christ or participating in the SACRAMENTS. It refers to an inward process that gradually takes place and effects a change of character leading to an outward life of virtue and godliness. Paul talks of sanctification as the gift of new life made possible by faith in Jesus Christ. (*See also* JUSTIFICATION; REDEMPTION)

Sanctuary *Christianity*   In the Old Testament it refers to a place set apart for the worship of God. The highest Jewish sanctuary was the Temple in Jerusalem. In Christianity, the term applies to the most sacred part of church, which contains the ALTAR and the choir stalls and lies beyond the NAVE at the eastern end of the church.

Sandek *Judaism*   The godfather allocated by the parents to a male child and who accompanies him to his circumcision when eight days old. The godfather has the honour of holding the child after the benedictions and during the actual operation. The godparents are also appointed to function as counsellors to the child throughout their lives. (*See* BERIT MILAH)

Sangat *Sikhism*   See SADHSANGAT.

Sangatia *Sikhism*   The term used at the time of the first Gurus to describe a leader of a Sikh community or congregation selected from the devout ones amongst them. (*See* SADHSANGAT)

Sangha *Buddhism*   The assembly of monks and nuns in THERAVADA but often used to denote all the community in Mahayana Buddhism. The order of monks was founded by Buddha, and is probably the oldest in the world. The

Sangha is one of the three refuges of the Buddhist. No oaths are taken on entry to the Sangha and the BHIKKU is free to leave the order at any time. In many Buddhist countries it is customary to enter the Sangha for a temporary retreat from the world. (*See also* BHIKKUNI)

Sangha *Hinduism*   An assembly of sages or holy men and women who have come together to worship God. In BHAKTI (devotional) movements, the Sangha would usually come together to hear discourses praising God or to take part in congregational singing. (*See also* KIRTAN; SATSANG)

Sangha *Jainism*   The totality of the Jain community made up of male ascetics (SADHUS), female ascetics (SADHVIS), male laity and female laity. Although the sangha has overall authority, in practice, the ascetics guide the Saity on spiritual matters, while committees of laity oversee other activities. Overall leadership of the community is handed over to the most capable monks (ACARYAS). This follows the practice of MAHAVIR, the historical founder of Jainism, who appointed the responsibility of guidance of the Sangha to his eleven principal monks.

Sangha Yatra *Jainism*   The traditional Jain custom of taking part in pilgrimage by walking barefoot to the sacred site. The pilgrim should observe five additional rules: refrain from carnal or sensual pleasure; avoid sleeping in a bed; partake of food only once a day; avoid eating raw or green vegetables; and maintain a vow of righteousness. A family will usually sponsor a Sangha pilgrim and will perform special acts of worship and charity during the period of the pilgrimage. The custom of Sangha Yatra has been re-established in recent times. (*See* YATRA)

Sanhedrin *Christianity*   The supreme court and council of the Jews that met in Jerusalem. Several of the early Christians found themselves on trial by the Sanhedrin including Peter, John and Paul. The council was also involved in the decision to stone Stephen to death. However, they are most remembered in Christianity as presiding over the trial of Jesus Christ and pronouncing his death sentence for the charge of blasphemy. (*See* CRUCIFIXION)

Sanhedrin *Judaism*   The highest Jewish court that met in Jerusalem. It ceased to function sometime around 425 CE. Its rabbis were instrumental in developing and interpreting the MISHNAH, and until its disbanding they were responsible for determining the Jewish lunar calendar. As soon as the new moon rose, they dispatched messengers throughout the land of Israel to announce the date. They also made the decision to celebrate the festivals over two days to accommodate the DIASPORA communities who could not be informed by the messengers. The practice of a two-day celebration is still observed. (*See also* YOMTOV SHENI)

Sanjog *Sikhism*   The state of union with God or the state of all people who place themselves under the will of God rather than the control of their own ego (*vinjog*). These two polarities are in opposition to each other in the Sikh view of human existence and salvation. (*See* GURMUKH; MAN; MANMUKH)

Sankhara (P) *Buddhism*   *See* SAMSKARA.

Sankhya *Hinduism*   *See* SAMKHYA.

Sanna (P) *Buddhism*   *See* SAMJNA.

Sannyasin / Samyasin / Samnyasin / sennyasin *Hinduism*   A man or woman who has completely cut all ties with the world and renounced worldly affairs. In classical Hinduism this is regarded as the fourth and final stage of life that should be entered by individuals who are born into the 'twice-born' VARNAS. It is, however, possible to become a *sannyasin* at any stage of one's life and take up the life of a wandering monk. *Sannyasins* may belong to large orders founded by particular individuals or they can be solitary wanderers. They are expected to follow some kind of SADHANA (spiritual discipline) that will allow them to focus only on the goal of liberation. The *sannyasin* is the only individual who is regarded as being outside caste and its duties. (*See also* ASHRAMA; MUKTI; SADHU)

Sansara *Hinduism*   *See* SAMSARA.

Sanskar *Hinduism*   *See* SAMSKAR.

Sanskrit *Hinduism*   The classical language of the ARYANS used to write many of the ancient Hindu and Buddhist scriptures. It is still used in ritual worship and studied by the BRAHMIN priests.

Sansthana vicaya *Jainism*   The fourth type of virtuous meditation practised by Jain ascetics, in which they focus on the universe in order to increase the feeling of detachment from the world. In this meditation, Jains can reflect upon the nature of the body and the reality of worldly status, repeat various MANTRAS and reflect upon the ideal life of the TIRTHANKARAS. (*See also* VICAYA)

Sant *Sikhism*   The term used to describe collectively the north Indian devotional movements that date from the medieval period. The *sants* criticized the outward forms of religion and emphasized the inner experience and guidance of the SATGURU. Sikhism acknowledges their teachings by including the poems of several prominent *sants* in the GURU GRANTH SAHIB. The term is also used to describe a Sikh spiritual leader with a personal following. In this way, the problem of using the controversial term GURU can be avoided. The followers of Sikh *sants* display all the behaviour of discipleship, but the *sants* themselves acknowledge the authority of the Guru Granth Sahib.

Sant Mat *(the path of the sants)*   *Hinduism*   Increasingly, since the medieval period, India has produced holy men and women who have preached in vernacular languages, often using song and poetry, a message that God is to be found within the heart of the devotee. The SANTS were opposed to caste distinction, gender inequality and even religious differences on the grounds of their conviction that God was the inner reality of all. They were also iconoclasts and often criticized the exoteric emphasis of both Hinduism and Islam. Some go as far as to state that all the outer phenomena of religion – rituals, ceremonies, austerities, fasting, pilgrimage, etc. – are of no consequence in achieving direct experiential knowledge of God. The *sants* promoted a threefold path that leads to experiential devotion: SATGURU, SATSANG and SATNAM. The first was the necessity of meeting a true guru who could show how to experience the divine within. The second encouraged the followers of the path to meet and share in their experiences through song and preaching; the last advocated the constant re-membrance of the true name of God as the only spiritual practice to bear fruit in the Age of Darkness. Famous *sants* are KABIR, NAMDEV, SURDAS, TULSIDAS and the Sikh gurus. (*See also* GURU NANAK; NIRGUNA BHAKTI)

Sant Nirankaris   *Sikhism*   Although it is not exactly correct to define the Sant Nirankaris as Sikh, since their membership consists of Hindus and Western adherents, they arose out the NIRANKARI movement founded in 1845 by Baba Dayal Singh to promote the true teachings of GURU NANAK. The Sant Nirankaris were founded in the 1930s by Buta Singh, but they gained a large following under the leadership of his son, Avtar Singh. Avtar Singh wrote the Avtar Bani and the Yug Purush, which are now regarded as the two scriptures of the movement. The movement has an uneasy relationship with orthodox Sikhism, as it maintains a lineage of living Gurus and does not acknowledge the guruship of the GURU GRANTH SAHIB.

Sant Sipahi *(saint/warrior)*   *Sikhism*   One who combines the spirituality of a true devotee with the courage of a warrior. This is the ideal of Sikhism, especially since the creation of the KHALSA of GURU GOBIND SINGH in 1699. Many of the outer symbols of the Khalsa signal the fact that both sets of qualities are combined in the brotherhood. For example, long uncut hair was traditionally worn only by renunciate holy men or Rajput warriors.

Santa Sophia   *Christianity*   One of the most famous churches in Eastern Christianity built in Constantinople by the Emperor Justinian in 538. In 1453 it was converted into a mosque but is now a museum in the city of Istanbul. However, both Christians and Muslims are allowed to pray in separated parts of the building.

Sanusi / Sanusiya / Sanusiyya *Islam*   A reform SUFI order popular in North Africa, it was founded by Muhammad ibn Ali as-Sanusi (1787–1859). The founder preached to the tribes of the Sahara a form of Sufism that focused on DHIKR but played down the emotional excesses criticized by the WAHHABIS and SALAFIS. The movement succeeded through its adaptation of Sufi lodges, or ZAWIYAS, to the nomadic people of the desert. Each lodge contained a complex of buildings that included a mosque, school, retreat cells, guest blocks and residences for students constructed around an inner courtyard and a well. A wall that could be defended if necessary encompassed the complete structure. The surrounding land was cultivated. The *zawiya* was regarded as belonging to the tribe whose territory it inhabited. (*See also* TARIQAH)

Saram Khand *Sikhism*   According to the teachings of GURU NANAK, the third of the five stages or realms which are experienced on the journey to salvation. *Saram Khand* refers to the realm of grace. It follows from the realm of effort and indicates that God's grace takes over from the efforts of the devotee. In this stage, the devotee is filled by the power of God, whose presence manifests in the heart. The devotees' spiritual experience comes from God's gift rather than their achievement. (*See also* KHAND)

Sarana *(protection or shelter)* *Buddhism*   Seeking the protection or refuge of the Buddha, the DHAMMA and the SANGHA. The declaration of taking the Three Refuges. (*See also* TISARANA)

Saraswati *Hinduism*   The consort of BRAHMA and the goddess of learning, the arts and the power of knowledge. In temples, her MURTI (image) is depicted as a white-skinned woman with two arms, one of which is holding a stringed instrument known as the *veena*. She rides upon a peacock.

Sarbat Khalsa *Sikhism*   The term used for the entire body of the Sikh people. When the tenth and final human Guru died, he maintained that the Sikhs should henceforth be led by the GURU GRANTH SAHIB (the sacred writings of the Gurus) and the decisions of the GURU PANTH (Sikh community). In the eighteenth century, the Punjab was divided into twelve separate Sikh territories (MISALS), each with its own leader. These leaders would come together in Amritsar on the festive occasions of Vaisakhi (April) and DIVALI (November) to make decisions that concerned the entire Sikh community. These decisions were made in front of the open Guru Granth Sahib, as it was believed that the eternal

Guru was present amongst them. The decisions reached were known as GURMATA or the Guru's decisions. The last Sarbat Khalsa was held in 1805. (*See also* KHALSA; RANJIT SINGH; SINGH SABHA)

Sarvastivadins *Buddhism*   One of the schools of early Buddhism that split away from the STHAVIRA school around about the time of the reign of Ashoka in the third century BCE. The school dominated north Indian Buddhism for nearly a thousand years and had a profound influence on the spread of Buddhism to China. It paved the way for later Mahayanan doctrines of the Buddha and created the famous Wheel of Life consisting of the six realms of existence and the twelve-linked causal chain of existence (NIDANAS).

Sashtra *Jainism*   A popular Jain appellation for their collection of scriptures. (*See also* AGAMAS)

Sat *(truth)* *Hinduism*   One of the three attributes or qualities of BRAHMAN according to VEDANTA. It refers to changelessness or existence. The UPANISHADS explained that behind the changing phenomena of the universe was an unchanging reality that gave existence out of itself to all individual beings. This eternal being was *sat*, because when everything else had passed away, the existence of Brahman would remain. Thus it was truth, the real. (*See also* ANANDA; ATMAN; CHIT; SATCHITANANDA)

Sat Purush *Sikhism*   A completely spiritual realm containing only the presence of the formless God. It is the first emanation or manifestation of the formless being and the destination of those who have achieved salvation. (*See* NIRANKAR; SAC KHAND)

Sat Sri Akal *Sikhism*   The Sikh greeting to each other when they meet. The approximate translation is 'Truth is timeless or immortal'.

Sat Yuga *Hinduism*   See KRTA YUGA.

Satan *(Hebrew: the accuser)* *Christianity*   Also known as the Devil. The leader of the spirits or chief of the devils who are opposed to God. He is traditionally believed to be a fallen angel. In the Old Testament, Satan occasionally appears as a figure who is always perverting, corrupting or working against the best interests of human beings. However, in the New Testament, he is identified with the personification of evil and is always hostile to God and his purposes. The Gospel writers Matthew and Luke recount that Satan tempted Jesus Christ during his forty-day retreat at the commencement of his ministry. The New Testament presents the history of humanity as a war between the forces of good, loyal to

God, and the forces of evil led by Satan. The final overthrow of Satan's dominion on earth began with Christ's death and resurrection and will be completed at the second coming of Jesus Christ. (*See* LUCIFER; PAROUSIA; TEMPTATION)

Satan *(Hebrew: the accuser) Judaism*   Although he plays that role in the book of Job, generally Judaism does not assign a prominent role to the idea of a personification of evil, even though the belief in demons and a hell realm has existed in Jewish folk tradition. The separate existence of an all-powerful demonic force would undermine the central tenet of Jewish monotheism.

Satchitananda *Hinduism*   In Vedantic philosophy, the name that describes all three essential attributes of BRAHMAN, the supreme being, namely truth (SAT), consciousness (CHIT) and joy (ANANDA). The ATMAN (the individual soul) also shares in the nature of Brahman and therefore has the same three qualities, just as a spark has the same qualities as the fire, or a drop of water has the same qualities as the ocean. (*See also* VEDANTA)

Satguru *(the true teacher) Sikhism*   Used in Sikhism either as a name for God or to describe the ten human Gurus. It generally refers to a holy man who has the commission from God, or the teacher before him, to reveal the inner path which leads to the discovery of God dwelling within the human being. The term is commonly used in the poetry of the Sikh Gurus and other north Indian SANTS. (*See also* SATNAM)

Sati *Buddhism*   Mindfulness or awareness required in order to achieve success in meditation. (*See* DHYANA; SAMMA SATI)

Sati / Suttee *Hinduism*   The outlawed practice of widows immolating themselves on the funeral pyres of their dead husbands. There are countless village shrines commemorating to those who successfully followed their husbands into death.

Satisfaction *Christianity*   A theological doctrine linked to Anselm of Canterbury (d.1109). It proposes that the death of Christ was offered to God as an ATONEMENT to make amends for the affront of human sin. Anselm argued that God had originally meant human beings to be righteous creations capable of eternal life. However, such a state is dependent on obedience. Human disobedience led to a state of sin, which has to be atoned in order to restore human beings to righteousness. As human beings were not themselves capable of providing the satisfaction, or atonement price, a 'God-man' was necessary. The incarnation of Jesus Christ provides both the ability and the will to pay the atonement price. (*See also* CRUCIFIXION; REDEMPTION; RESURRECTION)

Satkaryavada *Hinduism*   A theory of KARMA, the law of cause and effect, held by the SAMKHYA school of philosophy, which states that the effect will always be identical to the cause. This idea is generally believed by the majority of Hindus.

Satnam *Sikhism*   Often used by the Sikh Gurus as synonymous with God. It refers to the true name of God which is revealed by the SATGURU to his followers. SAT refers to that which is constant or unchangeable. The SANT teachers all spoke of a name of God which pre-existed creation and which could be discovered by seekers of truth within themselves. The tongue or the mind does not repeat it but it is self-repeated in the inner rhythm of life. (*See also* SABAD; NAM)

Satori (J) *(awakening)* *Buddhism*   The term used in ZEN Buddhism to describe a state of being where differentiation and duality are overcome. It may range from an intuitive flash or momentary experience to complete NIRVANA. It marks the beginning of the Zen path, as no awareness of the reality of Zen could exist prior to *satori*. Various Zen traditions utilize different methods to arrive at *satori*.

Satsang *(company of truth)* *Hinduism*   A term commonly used by the SANTS and the followers of the BHAKTI tradition. While TULSIDAS describes *satsang* as a genuine enthusiasm to listen to the praises of God, the term has entered the common parlance of Hinduism and can be used to describe the gathering of devotees to partake in KIRTAN (communal devotional singing), the discourse of a guru to disciples or any kind of religious public gathering.

Satsang *(the true company)* *Sikhism*   In contemporary Sikhism it is interpreted as attending congregational worship or listening to spiritual discourse. The SATGURUS of the SANT tradition, including the Sikh Gurus, taught that *satsang* was essential on the path to true knowledge of God. In their poetry it refers to keeping the company of the holy or those who have committed their life to the path of surrender to God. The presence of the *Satguru* himself would be regarded as the ultimate manifestation of *satsang*. For most contemporary Sikhs this would be found in the presence of the GURU GRANTH SAHIB, although there are Sikh movements which still have living human *Satgurus*.

Satta (P) / Sattva (S) *(being or existence)* *Buddhism*   It describes the six kinds of living being who exist in the three realms or planes of existence. (*See* ARUPADHATU; KAMADHATU; RUPADHATU)

Sattva / Sattwa *Hinduism*   According to SAMKHYA philosophy, *sattva* is one of the three GUNAS or qualities of nature that, in infinite variations, form PRAKRITI or primordial matter. *Sattva* is the quality of harmony, balance or goodness; sometimes it is translated as brightness. A wise person tries to cultivate the quality of *sattva* through harmonious living, peacefulness, meditation and a vegetarian diet consisting of fresh fruit, vegetables and dairy products. While the qualities that arise from a more *sattvic* nature will not in themselves lead to closer proximity to BRAHMAN or PURUSHA (the absolute reality), they will increase the desire for knowledge of Brahman and a life of devotion. (*See also* RAJAS; TAMAS)

Satya (S) *Buddhism* See SACCA.

Satya *(truthfulness) Jainism* Unlike Hinduism, which generally uses *satya* to describe the eternal and absolute reality of BRAHMAN, Jains use it to refer to the virtue of truthfulness. *Satya* is one of the five major vows (MAHAVRATAS) binding on Jain ascetics and adapted for Jain laity in the five lesser vows (ANUVRATAS). AHIMSA, the doctrine of non-harmfulness, demands that Jains should be non-violent in thought, word and deed. Consequently Jains are expected to be careful in their speech to avoid intentional or accidental violence to any fellow-creature. In practice, this would mean avoiding backbiting, gossip, lying, breach of trust, betraying confidences or speaking angrily. *Satya* also involves the communication of right knowledge or inspiring fellow-Jains towards right faith or right conduct. (*See also* SAMYAK CARITRA; SAMYAK DARSHANA; SAMYAK JNANA)

Satyagraha *(soul-force or truth-force) Hinduism* Mahatma GANDHI's philosophy of non-violent action used so successfully against the British in the independence movement. Gandhi insisted that India would first have to conquer herself through self-restraint and a return to the moral values of the Hindu scriptures and sages before it would be possible to remove the British. He set out to establish the example that the rest of India should follow. The independence movement therefore had a moral and religious dimension to its political ambitions.

Saul *Judaism* The first king of Israel around the year 1050 BCE. It is usually suggested that the pressure to become a monarchy arose from the warlike excursions of the Philistines who could not be defeated by tribal alliances. It was the loss of the ark to the Philistines at the battle of Aphek, where the forces of Israel were defeated, that finally led to calls for a king. Saul had proven his military and charismatic qualities in fighting the Ammonites and the people asked the prophet Samuel to anoint him as a king. (*See* DAVID; SOLOMON)

Saum / Sawm *Islam* Fasting and abstinence from just before dawn until sunset that is performed during the month of RAMADAN. The observance of the fasting is binding on all adult Muslims save for the aged, the sick, menstruating and pregnant women, nursing mothers and travellers. However, it is expected that those who are able to observe the fast but are prevented by changeable circumstances, such as travelling or menstruation, should make up the period of fasting as soon as possible after the month of Ramadan.

Savitri *Hinduism*   A woman who represents the ideal of motherhood. Her story is recorded in the MAHABHARATA. The daughter of a barren king who had prayed for a child to the goddess of the same name, she grew up to be so virtuous and beautiful that all men were intimidated by her, and she could not find a husband. Eventually, she fell in love with Satyavit, the son of a blind king, who had been brought up in a forest hermitage. However, Satyavit only had a year to live. At the time of his impending death, Savitri fasted and performed penance. When YAMA, the god of death, came to escort Satyavit's soul from its body, Savitri followed the god and would not leave. He offered to grant her any wish except her husband's life. She succeeded in retrieving Satyavit's father's sight and his lost kingdom. Eventually she tricked Yama by asking for sons for herself. When the god agreed, she persuaded him to release her husband or, otherwise, she would lose her virtue. Savitri is regarded as the ideal wife and daughter and the model of resolution.

Savoraim *(expounders)* *Judaism*   The term used for the rabbinical commentators who contributed to the Babylonian TALMUD after the Muslims conquered Babylon in the tenth century. There were two famous schools at Sura and Pumpedita. The leaders were known as GEONIM and the first qualification was to know the Talmud by heart. They are partly responsible for the Babylonian Talmud becoming the authoritative version in Jewish life. (*See also* AMORAIM)

Sawm *Islam*   See SAUM.

Sayogakevalin *Jainism*   The thirteenth of the fourteen stages of spiritual progress towards liberation from all bondage to KARMA. The *sayogakevalin* has attained the ultimate state of omniscience but is still embodied and active in this world. This is due to GHATI KARMA, which still remains although all AGHATIYA KARMA has been removed. (*See also* KEVALAJNANA; SIDDHA)

Sayyid / Saiyid *Islam*   A title of respect given to descendants of Muhammad, especially through his grandsons, HUSAIN and HASAN. Although the respect and veneration given to the prophet's bloodline is universal, it is more emphasized in the SHI'A tradition. However, SUNNI Muslims also regard the descendants of the Prophet with respect and the SUFIS have always venerated to the Prophet's family. Al-Hallaj, the great Sufi mystic, declared that 'God has not created anything that is dearer to him than Muhammad and his family.' (*See also* ALI)

Scholasticism   *Christianity*   A particular approach to Christian theology associated with the medieval period in which the use of the intellect is advocated to understand revealed truth through philosophical or theological speculation. Scholasticism is not a movement but a system of organizing knowledge by making fine distinctions. The most influential user of scholasticism to provide a body of theology was Thomas AQUINAS.

Second Adam   *Christianity*   A title for Jesus Christ used by Paul which refers to Christ's role as the leader of redeemed humanity, as opposed to ADAM, who was responsible for the fall. (*See also* ATONEMENT; REDEMPTION; SIN)

Second Coming   *Christianity*   *See* PAROUSIA.

Seder   *Judaism*   The home-based ritual meal maintained at the Passover festival which has been celebrated since the night before the EXODUS from Egypt. It is one of the most important events in the Jewish religious calendar. The story of the escape from Egypt, as described in the book of Exodus, is told to Jewish children, who ask a number of set questions to further their understanding of the occasion. The meal consists of three MATZAHS (unleavened bread) that represent the food of slavery and bitter herbs that represent the pain endured by the Jews in captivity. The herbs are dipped into condiments and *haroset* (a creamy sauce made of apples, nuts, cinnamon and a little wine). The condiments remind the participants that they are a free people but also remind them of the tears that have been shed in Egypt before their release. The *haroset* serves as symbol of the mortar used to construct the buildings of Egypt and also of the fruits of spring and thus hope. The other foods on the Seder plate are a roasted shank bone of lamb and a roasted egg, which served to remind the participants of the ancient sacrifice that took place at the Temple in Jerusalem at Passover. Neither of these can be eaten. Four cups of wine are also drunk that represent the fourfold promise of salvation made by God in Exodus 6:6–7. A fifth cup of wine is kept but not drunk. It is symbolically poured for the prophet Elijah, who is due to herald the coming of the Messiah. Traditionally, the Seder meal is eaten in a reclining position. (*See also* MASSIACH; PESACH)

See   *Christianity*   The official throne of a bishop which is normally kept in a CATHEDRAL and which denotes the bishop's authority over a diocese. (*See also* ENTHRONIZATION; HOLY SEE)

Seera (T)   *Islam*   *See* SIRA.

Sefardim   *Judaism*   *See* SEPHARDIM.

Sefer Torah *Judaism*   The scrolls that contain the five books of the TORAH handwritten on parchment. Traditionally the scrolls are made of leather taken from an animal that Jews are allowed to eat. A special type of black ink is used and lines are ruled so that the Hebrew letters remain straight. The scribes who write the sacred script take about one year to complete one scroll. However, if any letter that is part of a divine name is written incorrectly, the scroll becomes unfit for use and the particular column has to be removed and buried. There are specific requirements for the text, such as writing certain letters with a crown or a dot above them, and some letters are written larger than others. The scrolls are kept in the ark in the SYNAGOGUE and read in the services. (*See also* SIMCHAT TORAH)

Sefiroth *Judaism*   The ten attributes or emanations of the divine Essence of God (AYN SOF) which join the celestial to the material world according to Jewish mysticism. They are sometimes depicted in visual form as the Tree of Life. They are *keter* (crown), which is at the top of the Tree. The left-hand descending branch contains BINAH (understanding), GEVURAH (power) and HOD (splendour). Parallel to these on the right-hand branch are HOKHMAH (wisdom), HESED (loving kindness) and NETZAH (victory). Descending straight down from *keter* are TIFERET (beauty), YESOD (foundation) and finally MALKHUT (kingdom of God). This divine hierarchy is reflected in life on earth, with the *sefiroth* on the left-hand side representing God's sternness, whilst those on the right express His mercy. Although we cannot comprehend the *ayn sof*, we can perceive the *sefiroth* at work in the creation and in human life.

Seminary *Christianity*   Theological colleges for the training of the priesthood maintained by both the Roman Catholic and Anglican churches. (*See* PRIEST)

Sennyasin *Hinduism*   *See* SANNYASIN.

Sephardim / Sefardim *Judaism*   The Spanish Jews, including those who originated from around the Mediterranean or Middle East, as opposed to the ASHKENAZIM or German Jews. This twofold division of the Jewish people has existed for at least one thousand years.

Septuagesima *Christianity*   The third Sunday before LENT and the seventh before EASTER celebrated in the Church of England's liturgical year.

Septuagint *Judaism*   The Greek version of the Hebrew scriptures produced by the Jews of Alexandria around 2,000 years ago. (*See* PENTATEUCH; TORAH)

Sermon on the Mount *Christianity*   The famous discourse of Jesus described in Chapter 5 of Matthew's Gospel which provides the basis of Christian ethics. (*See* BEATITUDES; LORD'S PRAYER)

Server *Christianity* One who assists the priest at the EUCHARIST by making the responses, washing the hands of the celebrant and bringing the HOST to the altar.

Sesa *(remainder)* *Hinduism* The thousand-headed snake, also known as *Ananta* (endless), upon which VISHNU, the cosmic preserver, sleeps and observes the cycles of successive creation and destruction.

Sesshin (J) *Buddhism* An intensive or extended period of ZEN meditation practice held in a RINZAI monastery. The monks can pass up to one week practising meditation in the daytime and meeting with their teacher in the evening.

Seudath Mitzvah *(The Feast of Unleavened Bread)* *Judaism* An alternative name for the feast of Passover that refers to the unleavened bread prepared by the people of Israel before their rapid departure from slavery in Egypt. (*See* SEDER; PESACH)

Seung Sahn (b.1927) *Buddhism* The founder of the Kwan Um school of Korean Buddhism famous for his teaching of the 'don't know mind' who has opened more than fifty affiliated groups throughout Europe and North America.

Seva *Hinduism* The act of selfless service performed either on behalf of humanity or dedicated to the divine. Very often such service will be performed by devotees to living holy persons or gurus by spreading the teachings or helping to maintain them physically so that they can concentrate on their spiritual activities. Service can also be carried out by cleaning or performing simple manual tasks in a sacred place such as a shrine, temple or ASHRAM. (*See also* DAN; MAN)

Seven churches *Christianity* The seven early communities of Christians in Asia Minor which are addressed in the book of Revelation in the New Testament. They are Ephesus, Smyrna, Pergamum, Thyatira, Sardis, Philadelphia and Laodicea. (*See* REVELATION, BOOK OF)

Seven deadly sins *Christianity* The seven sins of pride, anger, lust, envy, gluttony, sloth and covetousness that can damn the human soul to an eternity of separation from the presence of God. (*See* SIN)

Seven sacraments   *Christianity*   See SACRAMENT.

Seven virtues   *Christianity*   The qualities of FAITH, HOPE, LOVE, fortitude, temperance, justice and prudence whose cultivation is considered to be the ideal for human life. (*See also* SEVEN DEADLY SINS)

Seventh Day Adventists   *Christianity*   A group of Protestant ADVENTISTS who formed in 1863 and who observe adult baptism, temperance and maintain the SABBATH from sunset on Friday until sunset on Saturday.

Sewapanthis   *Sikhism*   A sect of Sikh renunciates founded by the followers of Kanhaya Lal, a disciple of GURU TEGH BAHADUR and GURU GOBIND SINGH. At the seige of Anandpur, he tended the wounded of both sides. It is believed that he was commissioned to preach by Guru Gobind Singh. The followers are also known as Nanak Shahis.

Sexagesima   *Christianity*   The second Sunday before LENT and the sixth before EASTER celebrated in the Church of England's liturgical year.

Sexton   *Christianity*   A Church of England lay official appointed by the parish council and responsible for grave-digging, bell-ringing and cleaning the church. (*See* SACRISTAN)

SGPC   *Sikhism*   The initials of the Shiromani Gurdwara Prabandhak Committee, whose headquarters are in Amritsar. Since the 1925 Gurdwara Act, the Committee has been responsible for the taking care of the historical GURDWARAS of Sikhism. There are 140 elected members and fifteen appointed members, including the four heads of the *takhts*, or seats of religious authority, and the Head GRANTHI of HARMANDIR. The Committee is increasingly responsible for the decisions that govern gurdwaras throughout the world. (*See also* AKAL TAKHT)

Shaatnez   *Judaism*   See SHATNEZ.

Shabad   *Sikhism*   See SABAD.

Shabbat / Shabbos   *Judaism*   The day of rest and renewal that is dedicated to the remembrance of God. It begins at sunset on Friday and finishes at nightfall on Saturday. The Sabbath day remembers the verses of Genesis where God ceased the activity of creation and then sanctified the seventh day. The day provides the opportunity for the practising Jew to appreciate the sanctification of time by ceasing all work and therefore experiencing time as a simple gift of God. Rabbis have declared that the observation of the Sabbath is the equivalent to observing the whole TORAH and that if all Jews were to observe one Sabbath correctly, the Messiah would return. The observation of the Sabbath is the fourth of the Ten Commandments, and it is believed that the beauty of the Sabbath pours out into the rest of the week. There are seven kinds of prohibited work that have been developed into thirty-nine prohibitions. These are:

1. The growing and preparation of food.
2. The manufacture and preparation of clothing.
3. Any work with leather or writing.
4. Provision of shelter
5. Lighting or extinguishing fire.
6. The completion of work already begun before the Sabbath.
7. Transportation.

On the morning of the Sabbath, devout Jews attend the SYNAGOGUE in order to hear readings from the Torah and to remember the moment of revelation. This is also the time that a BAR MITZVAH might take place. The meal that follows is similar to the meal that takes place on the Friday evening. Although the Sabbath afternoon is a time for relaxation, this ends with another visit to the synagogue, where the first section of the following week's Torah reading will begin. The third meal then takes place but this time without the KIDDUSH. The regular evening service at the synagogue takes place but ends with the recitation of the HAVDALAH to bring the Sabbath to a solemn conclusion at nightfall. This is also to be done at home by those not attending the synagogue. (*See also* EREV SHABBAT)

Shabd *Sikhism* *See* SABAD.

Shafa'a *(intercession)* *Islam* Although the countless Sufi saints are believed to be able to intercede on behalf of the petitioner to Allah, the prime intercessor for Muslims is Muhammad, the final prophet. Millions of Muslims pray to Allah through the intercession of Muhammad and even ask for forgiveness of their sins by invoking his name as Allah's favoured beloved. It is generally believed by most Muslims that the Prophet will mediate and intercede on their behalf at the Day of Judgement. (*See also* DU'A; ISTIGHATHA; TAWASSUL)

Shafi'i *Islam* One of the four schools of jurisprudence named after its founder, Muhammad ibn Idris al-Shafi'i (d.820) and based in Cairo and Baghdad. Al-Shafi'i was instrumental in developing the principles of Islamic jurisprudence, in which the verbal tradition of the HADITH took precedence over customary tradition. (*See also* HANAFI; HANBALI; MALIKI)

Shahadah *Islam* The proclamation that 'there is no god but God, and Muhammad is His prophet' (*la ilaha illa allah, muhammadun rasulu 'llah*) which forms the basis of the Muslim confession of faith. This is the first pillar of Islam, also known as the *kalima*, and its utterance is the only requirement for becoming a Muslim. The *shahadah* is a covenant between the Muslim and Allah which opens the doors of paradise, and Muslims hope to recite it as their last words before death. It is regarded as protection against evil and a means of forgiveness of sins. The first part of the *shahadah* is continuously repeated as a means of spiritual discipline and remembrance of God by most of the Sufi orders. (*See also* DHIKR; SHAHID; TARIQAH)

Shaharit *Judaism* The morning prayer and the first of the three obligatory daily prayers in which traditional Jews wear the TALLIT and TEFILLIN. God is thanked for the new day and psalms are recited in order to attune with the divine. The public worship consists of various blessings, the SHEMA and the AMIDAH. On some days the TORAH is also read and on festival days the MUSAPH is added. (*See also* MAARIV; MINHAH)

Shahid *(a witness)* *Islam* Every Muslim is a witness to the oneness of Allah and finality of Muhammad as the seal of the prophets. This is testified through the SHAHADAH and the obligation to promote Islam. However, the term has become inextricably linked with martyrdom as the ultimate testimony of faith. While martyrdom should not be sought intentionally, as that could be tantamount to suicide, the martyr's place in paradise is secured. It is believed that the martyr, defined as one who dies when involved in JIHAD, finds immediate rest in paradise and does not have to wait until the final Day of Judgement. (*See also* DA'WA)

Shahid-Ganj *Sikhism* This term is used to describe several Sikh shrines. It refers to a place where a Sikh has laid down his/her life for the faith.

Shaikh / Sheikh *Islam* A title given to an old or respected man, but often denoting a saint or spiritual master in the SUFI tradition. (*See also* PIR; WALI)

Shaikh al-Hadith *Islam* The title bestowed upon the senior teacher of the HADITH in a Muslim religious school or DAR AL-ULUM. (*See also* MADRASA)

Shaikh Farid / Shakar Ganj (1173–1265) *Sikhism* A SUFI saint who has four of his poems included in the GURU GRANTH SAHIB, thus indicating the close affinity between the teachings of the Sufis and the north Indian SANTS.

Shaitan / Shaytan *(rebellious, proud)* *Islam* The term used for the devil who tries to lure human beings away from the path of righteousness. *Shaitan* is perceived as a hidden whisperer in the hearts of all human beings, but is personified as a fallen angel who, out of pride, refused to bow to Adam. He was cast out from the company of angels and swore to divert all human beings from God's ordinances in order to prove that they were unworthy of the honour of being Allah's representatives on earth. (*See also* IBLIS; KHALIFA)

Shaiva Agamas *Hinduism*   A group of twenty-eight scriptures held to be sacred by the followers of SHAIVA SIDDHANTA. The first was probably written around the sixth century BCE. They teach the worship of the ultimate being in the form of SHIVA and teach the different ways to liberation, in relation to Shiva as divine reality.

Shaiva Siddhanta *Hinduism*   An ancient and still vigorous tradition of SHIVA worship that is strong in Tamil-speaking India. The followers of Shaiva Siddhanta regard Shiva as the ultimate reality, the origin and end of all things. The tradition acknowledges a sacred canon made up of the VEDAS, the UPANIS-HADS, the SHAIVA AGAMAS, twelve Tirumura that contain devotional poetry and fourteen Meykanta Sastras, medieval theological works. The theology of the tradition centres around three concepts: *pati* (God in the form of Shiva), *pashu* (the soul) and *pasha* (fetters). The soul is kept in bondage by *pasha* and may only be released by the love of Shiva, who is an immanent and transcendent personal God full of boundless bliss and intelligence. He is the creator, preserver, destroyer and also personal saviour to his devotees. All other deities are under his control and he is immanent in creation as SHAKTI, his creative power, which is known as the Goddess. The practices of the tradition include various rituals, YOGA and personal discipline. At the highest level a GURU is required. In the state of final liberation, the soul remains individual but lives in state of pure bliss and devotion to Shiva. It is therefore possible to speak about salvation rather than liberation in this context.

Shaivite *Hinduism*   The worship of SHIVA and his family, which, along with VAISHNAVA (worship of Vishnu and his forms) and the worship of the Goddess, represents one of the largest constituents of Hinduism. Generally speaking, the family of Shiva consists of PARVATI, his wife and consort, and their two sons, GANESH and KARTIKEYA. The Shaivite tradition comprises hundreds of sects, some of which are made up of renunciates who regard Shiva as the ultimate ascetic. (*See also* SHAIVA SIDDHANTA; TANTRA)

Shakar Ganj *Sikhism*   See SHAIKH FARID.

Shakta *Hinduism*   One who worships the Goddess in any one of her countless forms or, more specifically, someone who follows the path of TANTRA. (*See also* SHAKTI)

Shakta Agamas *Hinduism*   A group of scriptures held to be sacred by the followers of TANTRA. They teach the worship of spiritual power in the form of the Divine Mother or Goddess. (*See also* SHAKTI)

Shakti / Sakti *Hinduism*   The active energy or power of the divine that is manifest in creation. It is usually associated with the power of the Goddess as present in nature or with PRAKRITI, the primordial matter described in SAMKHYA philosophy. Sometimes she is identified with MAYA, the veiling power that hides BRAHMAN from the individual human soul. Shakti is also used to describe the path of devotion to the forms of the Goddess or universal Mother as opposed to Vaishnavism or Shaivism, the worship of Vishnu or Shiva. There is a vast variety of forms of the Goddess. Many of them are consorts of major Hindu deities or AVATARS. Principal amongst these are SRI, LAKSHMI, SITA, RADHA, SARASWATI, DURGA and PARVATI. Other goddesses exist as independent from any male; the most important amongst these is KALI.

Shakyamuni *Buddhism*   See SAKYAMUNI.

Shalagram / Salagram *Hinduism*   A smooth tubular stone containing an ammonite fossil with spiral markings on the inside, particularly revered by the devotees of VISHNU. It is one of the symbols of Vishnu and the inner markings are believed to be representations of his discus. It is kept wrapped in a cloth and ritually bathed. The water is then drunk to remove sins and impurities. (*See also* VAISHNAVA)

Shalosh Seudoth *(The Day of Delight)* *Judaism*   A phrase taken from the Book of Isaiah 58:13 to describe the Jewish Sabbath. (*See* SHABBAT)

Shalwar kamis (U) *Islam*   The distinctive long tunic and baggy trousers worn by both male and female Muslims in the subcontinent, especially the PUNJAB. Many Muslims of subcontinent origin who have settled in the West regard the *shalwar kamis* as obligatory dress when attending the mosque even if they wear Western dress as everyday clothing. This has given a symbolic aspect to a mode of dress that is only customary in the subcontinent.

Shankara (788–820) *Hindu*   A Hindu sage and philosopher famed for his development of ADVAITA VEDANTA, in which he propounded the belief that ATMAN and BRAHMAN are identical. Born in Kerala in south India, he renounced the world to become a SANNYASIN at the age of eighteen. He is well known for engaging his philosophical opponents in debate, and Hindus believe that he was responsible for the decline in Indian Buddhism and the revival of Vedic Hinduism. While this belief certainly exaggerates the role of Shankara, there is no doubt that he was a formidable philosopher and reformer. In his short lifetime he wrote several books and commentaries, and also succeeded in organizing Hindu renunciates into four orders, each established in respective headquarters in the north, south, east and west of India. These four orders remain dominant amongst Hindu renunciates and the four centres are now led by hereditary leaders, known as Shankaracharyas, who are still major Hindu religious leaders.

Shanti *Hinduism* The condition of inner peace that is felt in meditation, worship or the presence of the divine. It is also believed that *shanti* can be felt in sacred places or in the quietness of nature.

Shari'a / Shari'ah *Islam* Islamic law as based upon the revelation laid out in the QUR'AN and SUNNA of Muhammad and interpreted by the founders of the four Muslim schools of law (HANAFI, HANBALI, SHAFI'I and MALIKI). One of the central tenets of Islam is that Allah is sovereign over everything and therefore only God has the right to determine the correct course of action for human beings. Shari'a indicates the path to be followed and literally means 'the way to the watering place'. Justice is central to the message of the Qur'an and in Muslim terms indicates actions that should be performed and those that are forbidden by Allah's ordinances. In the two hundred years following Muhammad's death, various Muslim commentators developed a comprehensive system of right and wrong actions based upon the revelation in the Qur'an and the precedents set by the Prophet's deeds and actions. Local customs were thoroughly investigated insofar as they complied with the injunctions implicit in the revelation. During this period a comprehensive system of law based on Allah's commandments was worked out and became the norm and the ideal for Muslim societies. Islamic family law, criminal justice, business and trade obligations, and rules of warfare were all developed on the basis of revelation. This gave rise to a unique form of government in which rulers were considered not to be lawmakers and custodians of divine law. Debates still rage in the Muslim world as to whether an Islamic state is the only vehicle for the correct maintenance of Islamic law. (*See also* FIQH)

Shashthi *Hinduism* The universal Mother or Goddess in the form of the protector of children, commonly worshipped by women in their homes. (*See* SHAKTI)

Shatnez / Shaatnez *Judaism* Clothes that contain a forbidden mixture of wool and linen and should not be worn by Orthodox Jews.

Shavuot *Judaism* The Feast of Weeks celebrated fifty days after Passover on the sixth and seventh day of Sivan and also known as the Festival of the Wheat

Harvest and the Day of the First Fruits. The two-day festival (one day in Israel) remembers the revelation of the law to Moses on Mount Sinai, although it probably originated as a harvest celebration. There are no special rituals and ceremonies, as it believed that it is impossible to express the greatness of the revelation. However, it is customary to eat dishes made from dairy products. In recent times it has become the custom to decorate the SYNAGOGUE with plants and flowers, which reflects the original harvest festival. Some traditional Jews will pass the night in the synagogue studying the TORAH. The synagogue service consists of prayers and poems that reflect both the revelation and the beneficence of nature. The reading from the Torah will include the passage that contains the Ten Commandments. The book of RUTH is read on the second day. (*See also* BERIT; PESACH; SUKKOT)

Shaytan *Islam*   *See* SHAITAN.

Shechita / Shehitah *Judaism*   The ritual killing of animals that is carried out in accordance with the Jewish laws concerning food. Traditionally, the killing had to be performed by a skilled specialist who knew the religious law. Since the blood has to be removed from the meat, the animal's throat is slit and the blood allowed to drain. (*See* KASHRUT; KOSHER)

Sheelot u-Teshuvot *Judaism*   A form of Jewish religious literature that appeared in the period of the SAVORAIM, the rabbinical commentators in Babylon at the time of the Muslim invasion from the tenth century. Various questions on matters of law were put to the GEONIM, the heads of the Talmudic schools in Babylon, who provided answers often based on consensus. The decisions were based on their knowledge of the MISHNAH and the TALMUD and often there was fierce debate from other experts who disagreed. Many collections of these questions and answers were written down and became known as responsa literature or *Sheelot u-Teshuvot*.

Sheikh *Islam*   *See* SHAIKH.

Shekhina / Shekhinah *Judaism*   The presence of God that is immanent in His creation. It is said that whenever Jews pray together the *shekhina* is present with them. It is also manifest within the heart of the pious Jew. Rabbis have described the *shekhina* as the glory of God, referred to as light. It is believed to be the manifestation of God that appears at the time of prophecy and revelation. Medieval rabbis have argued that in the passages of the Bible where God is described in anthropomorphic terms, it is the *shekhina* that is being described.

Sheloshim *Judaism*   The period of thirty days of mourning that begins with the burial of a close relative. In the case of a parent it is extended to one full year. During this period the male mourner may not cut his hair or beard, attend festivities or marry. In the case of the death of a parent, the children attend the SYNAGOGUE every day for a year, both in the morning and in the evening, and recite the KADDISH. During this period the mourners do not visit the grave until the end of the year, when the tombstone is laid. (*See also* ANINUT; SHIVAH; YAHRZEIT)

Shem ha-Gedolim *(Names of the Great)* *Judaism*   A book written by Rabbi Azulai (1724–1806) in Jerusalem that outlines the lives and works of great RABBIS.

Shema *Judaism*   Three passages from the book of Deuteronomy in the Bible that begin '*Hear O Israel: the Lord our God, the Lord is One!*'. This affirmation of monotheism and election is recited at the time of morning and evening prayer and is written inside the MEZUZAH that are fixed to the doorposts of Jewish homes. They are also contained in the TEFILLIN that are strapped on the body during prayer. They have become virtually the article or essence of the Jewish faith and many devout Jews will utter them as their last words before death. The full rendering is as follows:

> *Hear O Israel: the Lord our God, the Lord is One!*
> *Blessed be His glorious Kingdom for ever and ever!*
> *Love you then the Lord your God*
> *With all your heart, with all your soul, with all your might!*
> *Take to heart these words, which I command you this day,*
> *Impress them upon your children*
> *By speaking about them*
> *When you sit in your home and when you walk by the way,*
> *When you lie down and when you rise up;*
> *Bind them as a sign upon your hand*
> *And let them serve as frontlets between your eyes,*
> *Inscribe them on the doorposts of your house*
> *And upon your gates.*

(*See also* BERIT; TEFILLAH)

Shemini Atzerat *Judaism*   The final two days of the feast of SUKKOT are the Eighth Day of Assembly (*Shemini Atzerat*) and SIMCHAT TORAH, but in Israel both festivals are held on one day. At the Day of Assembly prayers are recited for rain.

Shemoneh Esre *Judaism*   *See* AMIDAH.

Sheol   *Judaism*   *See* GEHENNA.

Shi'a / Shi'ah / Shi'at Ali   *Islam*   The first division amongst Muslims after the death of Muhammad and the most important schism in Islam. The Shi'a believe in the succession of the direct descendants of Muhammad through the line of ALI rather than the caliphate. This is known as the Imamate. The IMAMS are considered to be infallible bearers of esoteric wisdom who have direct spiritual contact with Muhammad. They are the source of authority upon which Shi'a theology rests. The tradition has a strong passion motive originating in the violent death of HUSAIN, the Prophet's grandson, at Kerbala at the hands of the ruling UMAYYAD dynasty. As a result of persecution and the passion motive, the Shi'a have developed a strong cult of martyrdom. The emphasis on living, charismatic leaders has resulted in several divisions over leadership taking place amongst the Shi'a. The Twelver Shi'as, who believe in the succession of twelve imams beginning with Ali, are the dominant form of Islam in Iran and the largest Shi'a group. The next most prominent are the ISHMAELIS or Seveners. The other main group is the Zaidis, but Shi'a has also given birth to non-Muslim religious movements: namely, the Ba'hai and the Druse. (*See also* AYATOLLAH; HASAN; ZAID)

Shi'at Ali *(The Party of Ali)*   *Islam*   *See* SHI'A.

Shikan taza (J) *(only sitting)*   *Buddhism*   A SOTO ZEN practice which refers to concentrated thought or a period of quiet reflective meditation.

Shikhara   *Hinduism*   The traditional tower or spire built on top of the shrine room in a Hindu temple. (*See* GARBHA-GRIHA; MANDIR)

Shin shu (J)   *Buddhism*   A Japanese version of Pure Land Buddhism founded by Shinran Shonin (1173–1262) and one of the largest schools of Buddhism in Japan. Also known as the Shin sect, it allows the marriage of priests. The *shin shu* doctrine teaches that faith alone in the AMIDA Buddha is sufficient.

Shingon (J)   *Buddhism*   A sect of esoteric (Tantric) Buddhism introduced into Japan by Kobo Daishi (774–835). It is a syncretistic movement that believes that all religions are the expression of self-realization towards Buddhahood. The universe is regarded as the manifestation of the ultimate reality personified in Vairocana Buddha.

Shirk *(association)*   *Islam*   The sin of idolatry or regarding anything as equal to or a partner to Allah. This is a serious or cardinal sin in Islam and is used for any serious deviation from the worship of one God. Christians are accused of *shirk* because they have provided Jesus with a status equal to God which is far above his role as a prophet or messenger of God. Contemporary debates concerning *shirk* have revolved around various ideologies such as democracy or socialism, that are based on the sovereignty of the people rather than the sovereignty of Allah. Some Muslim groups have accused traditional Muslims, influenced by Sufism, of raising the status of MUHAMMAD to a divine personality considered close to the Christian view of Christ. (*See* ISA; WAHHABI)

Shishah Sedarim   *Judaism*   The arrangement of the MISHNAH into six sections known as 'orders'. They are *Zeraim, Moed, Nashim, Nezikin, Kadashim* and *Tohorot*, which deal with, respectively, agricultural laws, laws pertaining to the Sabbath and festivals, marriage laws and issues concerning women, commercial and criminal law, sacred laws, especially those dealing with sacrifice, and laws of ritual purity.

Shitala Mata   *Hinduism*   The goddess of smallpox or epidemic diseases. She is generally worshipped in the villages, although there is a famous temple in Varanasi. Regarded as unmarried and full of hot anger, her victims are cured by propitiating her through animal sacrifice and cooling rituals.

Shiva / Siva *(the auspicious or gentle)*   *Hinduism*   Sometimes regarded as part of the triad or triune God, BRAHMA, VISHNU and SHIVA. In this context he represents the destructive power in the constant process of change. He is also seen as the great YOGI and is regarded highly by many SADHUS. Many Hindus regard Shiva as the ultimate reality in himself, and his sects constitute the vast variety that make up the SHAIVITE tradition. The cult of Shiva is very ancient, and it is speculated that it goes back to the pre-ARYAN cultures of northern India, particularly the Indus Valley civilizations. Although Shiva is unknown by name in the VEDAS, the storm-god, RUDRA, has many of his attributes. Shiva is first used in the UPANISHADS to describe the personal form of the impersonal BRAHMAN, the ultimate reality. The PURANAS describe Shiva in greater detail and contain many images of the God: from a fierce deity, associated with death and time, who wears skulls and snakes around his body and lives in cremation grounds, to the chaste renunciate who eventually marries PARVATI and produces two children. He is also depicted as NATARAJA, the Lord of the Cosmic Dance. While some Shaivite texts mention AVATARS (incarnations) of Shiva, it is the south Indian devotional tradition, SHAIVA SIDDHANTA, that eventually elevates the god to the position of Supreme God of all Creation. (*See also* SHAIVA)

Shiva / Shivah   *Judaism*   The first seven days of deepest mourning following the death of a close relative that takes place immediately after the funeral. Traditionally, the mourner returns home and covers all mirrors and lights a lamp in honour of the dead person. The mourner removes leather shoes and sits on the ground or uses a low stool. It is forbidden to cut the hair, shave or indulge in sexual relations. Even study of the TORAH ceases. However, comfort is available from relatives and friends: the first meal after the funeral is made by close friends and is traditionally eggs or lentils, the symbols of mourning. A service takes place in the house every morning and evening. (*See also* ANINUT; SHELOSHIM; SHIVAH)

Shivaratri *Hinduism* Festival celebrated in honour of SHIVA held every February and March.

Shoah *Judaism* The systematic genocide of six million Jews by the Nazi regime during World War II.

Shofar *Judaism* The ram's horn which has been used on special religious occasions since biblical times. It is said to have accompanied the revelation on Mount Sinai and was blown at the start of battle or after victory. It is also said that the shofar will sound on the coming of the Messiah. It is also blown at the Jewish New Year (ROSH HASHANAH) and at the end of YOM KIPPUR.

Shojo (J) *Buddhism* The third type of the five types of ZEN. This refers to HINAYANA or 'lesser vehicle' Zen, which is concerned with one's peace of mind. Believed by practitioners of the other forms of Zen to accommodate the inner needs of the individual, it remains indifferent to the needs of others and thus echoes the critique of the THERAVADA school of Buddhism by the Mahayana.

Shraddha / Sraddha *Hinduism* An important religious ceremony which is the final rite of passage in Hinduism. Food is offered to the poor and sick, and visiting BRAHMINS are given food and coins. The ritual is in memory of departed ancestors and takes place a year after the death of a close relative. It is the duty of the male descendants to maintain the memory of departed ancestors through twice-yearly *shraddhas*: one on the anniversary of the death; and the other during the waning moon at the end of the rainy season, which is known as the fortnight of the ancestors. (*See also* SAMSKAR)

Shramana *Jainism* A monk who does not follow one of the six orthodox schools of Hindu philosophy that are based on the VEDAS. This term is specifically used by Jains to describe their monks and nuns. However, the term is also applicable to Buddhist monks. (*See also* DARSHANA)

Shri / Sri *(illustrious)* *Hinduism* Used as a title of respect preceding the name of a deity or holy man/woman. The feminine form is *shrimati*.

Shruti / Sruti / Srti *(that which is heard)* *Hinduism* Applicable to the revealed scriptures, the VEDAS, BRAHMANAS, ARANYAKAS and UPANISHADS, which are believed to have no human authors, but are eternal revelations, breathed out by God at the beginning of each cycle of creation. 'Heard' by sages in their meditation, they were passed on orally.

Shudra *Hinduism* The fourth and lowest of the four VARNAS which refers to the labouring castes of Hindu DHARMA. According to the Vedas they were born from the feet of the sacrificed PURUSHA. It was believed that the Shudra caste was created by the gods for those human beings who needed to atone for sins and be reborn into a lower manifestation of human life. It is the only *varna* that is not allowed to take the initiation into the sacred thread in order to become 'twice-born'. (*See also* DVIJA)

Shukr *Islam* Gratitude or thankfulness, which is the only correct response to the divine. Islam is characterized by a strong mood of gratitude, which is manifested in many of its prominent spiritual figures, especially the SUFI tradition. Gratitude is considered the virtue of the purified heart and is not regarded as part of a bargain with God for answering human prayers for material well-being. It has sometimes been seen as a guarantee against loss of grace, but generally speaking it is perceived as its own reward for giving Allah His due and brings with it spiritual satisfaction, joy and a light heart. (*See also* HAMD; SABR)

Shulhan Arukh *(the set table)* *Judaism* The authoritative code of Jewish law as elaborated by Joseph CARO (1488–1575). During the period of the GEONIM (the heads of the schools of law in Babylon), from the time of the rise of Islam to the eleventh century, it had become the custom to provide answers to questions posed by Jews concerning points of law. These generated vast written collections known as responsa. It became necessary to organize the responsa into a systematic collection. The authoritative collections are the *Shulhan Arukh* and the MISHNAH. The *Shulhan Arukh* is divided into four sections as follows: *The Path of Life*, which deals with worship and festivals; *The Teacher of Knowledge*, which is concerned with ethics, charitable duties, dietary laws and mourning; *The Stone of Help*, which deals with marriage; and *The Breastplate of Judgement*, which covers civil law. (*See also* SAVORAIM; SHEELOT U-TESHUVOT)

Shunyatta / Sunyatta *Buddhism* The Mahayana concept of emptiness, based on the unreality of the causal chain of existence, which overcomes the delusive quality of mind that thinks of things as separate and self-sustaining. Awareness of *shunyatta* removes delusion and helps create compassion. (*See* KARUNA)

Shura *(a council)* *Islam* A consultative body of Muslims presiding over religious and worldly affairs and responsible for the maintenance of Muslim law. It is prescribed by the Qur'an as the model of leadership. (*See* SHARI'A)

Shushan Purim *Judaism* The celebration on the feast of PURIM on the fifteenth day of the month of Adar (February–March) instead of the usual fourteenth day. This is a requirement for cities with ancient walls dating back to the time of Joshua, such as Jerusalem. It is celebrated in remembrance of the Jews of Shushan, who began to fight on the fourteenth day and achieved victory on the fifteenth day.

Shvayambhu *Hinduism* *See* SVAYAMBHU.

Siddattha Gottama (P) / Siddhartha Gautama (S) / Gotama (P) / Gautama (S) *(wish-fulfilled* or *he whose purpose has been completed)* *Buddhism* The personal name of the historical BUDDHA. Although there are thousands of legends told in Buddhism concerning the countless lives of the Buddha leading up to his final enlightenment, the actual historical figure was born in the sixth century BCE in the small republic of Sakya, now in the modern state of Nepal. His father was the ruler of the Sakyas and according to the legend Siddattha was married at sixteen and maintained in his palace with every conceivable luxury. This was undertaken by his father, who was afraid that his son would fulfil the prophecy made at his birth to renounce the world. At the age of nineteen, after witnessing an old man, a sick person and dead body, the young prince set out in pursuit of enlightenment and liberation from suffering. For many years he pursued a life of extreme asceticism but could not find satisfaction. Finally, he achieved enlightenment after meditating under the BODHI TREE situated in Bodh-gaya, also in the modern Indian state of Bihar. The Buddha decided to teach in order to alleviate the suffering of his fellow-beings, and for forty-five years travelled around northern India in the company of his monks and nuns teaching the practical path to release from the suffering caused by bondage to SAMSARA. (*See also* BODHI; CATTARI ARIYASACCANI; MAGGA; NIRVANA; SAKYAMUNI; SAMMA)

Siddha *Buddhism* A group of wandering ascetic YOGIS, traditionally eighty-four, who practised Tantric rituals sometime from the ninth to twelfth centuries and followed the cult of the VAJRAYANA. They were against the formalism of the monastic orders and the ritualistic emphasis of traditional Buddhism. They were certainly influenced by converts from Hindu Tantric systems. (*See also* SAHAJAYANA; TANTRA)

Siddha *Hinduism* Legendary holy men with special powers who are believed to live in the high Himalayas as immortals. The term is also used to describe

YOGIS who are believed to have achieved exceptional supernatural powers, in particular those of the NATH tradition founded by GORAKHNATH. (*See also* SIDDHI)

Siddha *Jainism* One who has achieved the fourteenth or final stage of liberation, in which they have achieved omniscience and destroyed all KARMA. On death the soul rises to the summit of the universe where it eternally enjoys perfect bliss, knowledge, freedom from karmic bondage, infinite energy, perfect conduct and non-corporeality. It is only the completely liberated who are no longer embodied in SAMSARA who are referred to as *siddhas*. This category of being includes the TIRTHANKARAS and JINAS. (*See also* KEVALAJNANA; SAYOGAKEVALIN)

Siddha *Sikhism* Eighty-four legendary sages who achieved the state of absolute bliss and immortality whilst meditating in the Himalayan regions. They are mentioned in the JANAM SAKHI, where they are often confused with the NATH YOGIS. GURU GOBIND SINGH claims to have been meditating in the Himalayas when the order came for him to take birth in the world in order to restore the true religion. This would suggest that he identified himself with these legendary sages, and many Sikhs acknowledge them.

Siddhartha Gautama (S) *Buddhism* *See* SIDDATTHA GOTTAMA.

Siddhi *Hinduism* Supernatural powers, such as levitation, invisibility, flying, omniscience, appearing simultaneously in different places, withholding breath, curing the sick or raising the dead, or walking on water, that are believed to arise from the practice of YOGA or austerities. Many of Hinduism's holy men and women, particularly those of the BHAKTI or SANT tradition, have criticized the motivation of those who practise disciplines to achieve these kind of powers. They argue that the true devotee of God or the adherent trying to achieve liberation should ignore such powers. (*See also* SIDDHA)

Siddhi *Jainism* Powers or accomplishments. Jainism rejects the attainment of psychic powers to achieve any kind of worldly attainment or status, as this will only add to one's KARMA. It is believed that while one who practises the spiritual disciplines of the Jain path attains certain powers, these should only be utilized in the pursuit of removing karma. Omniscients are believed to have exceptional powers, but the DIGAMBARA and SVETAMBARA differ on this. Digambaras believe that those who have attained omniscience no longer require food and drink, while Svetambaras consider that such souls retain normal human characteristics but are endowed with exceptional wisdom and compassion. (*See also* KEVALA-JNANA; SIDDHA)

Siddhi / Sidhi *Sikhism*   Normally used to describe the occult or psychic powers achieved by YOGIS. However, these were forbidden in the teachings of the Sikh Gurus. As a consequence the term has taken on a unique Sikh meaning and refers to those who have united their individual consciousness to the supreme being through continuous remembrance of His name. (*See also* NAM; NAM SIMRAN; SIDDHA)

Siddur *Judaism*   The daily prayer book which contains the order of service held in the SYNAGOGUE. The first written arrangement of Jewish liturgy was made by Rabbi Amram (d.875), one of the GEONIM of Sura. However, the essentials of the synagogue service were probably known from around the sixth century. (*See also* SHEMA)

Sifra *Judaism*   The exposition of the book of LEVITICUS, also known as Torah Kohanim, that is one of the three writings that form the MIDRASH. (*See also* MEKHILTA; SIFRE)

Sifre *Judaism*   The exposition of the books of Numbers and Deuteronomy that is one of the three writings that form the MIDRASH. (*See also* MEKHILTA; SIFRA)

Sign of the Cross *Christianity*   An important Christian blessing made by bringing the right hand from the forehead to the breast and then from shoulder to shoulder. It is used to sanctify and bless various occasions and as a sign of recognition during periods of persecution.

Sikh *(student, disciple)* *Sikhism*   Originally used by GURU NANAK as the title for his disciples, who could have been either Hindu or Muslim. Gradually, as the disciples of the Gurus began to take on a distinct religious identity, it became the term used for anyone who believed in the teachings of the ten Gurus and the GURU GRANTH SAHIB. There is also an ethnic connotation, in that it is used for anyone born to a Sikh family. (*See also* KHALSA; NANAK PANTHIS; SAHAJDHARI)

Siksavratas / Sikshavratas *(educative vows)* *Jainism*   These are the four vows of spiritual discipline undertaken by devout lay Jains: equanimity; specific fasting; limiting consumables and non-consumables and, finally, hospitality. The vow of equanimity requires lay Jains to devote their time to three periods of 48-minute meditation every day (SAMAYIKA PRATIMA). The second vow of specific fasting (*prosadhopavasa*) is a form of limited asceticism and requires fasting for twelve hours at regular intervals in a month. The third vow limits the use of consumable goods such as food and non-consumables such as possessions (*bhogapabhogaparimana*). The final vow (ATITHI SAMVIBHAGA) requires taking care of ascetics and the needy before looking after one's own needs. These vows allow the lay Jain to move towards the renunciation characteristic of the ideal ascetic life through temporary periods of retreat marked by abstinence (*desavakasika*). (*See also* ANUVRATAS; GUNAVRATAS; MAHAVRATAS; VRATAS).

Sila *Buddhism* It can mean either character or habitual behaviour, or morality or moral precepts. *Sila* is embodied in the eightfold noble path in the practices of right action, right speech and right effort. The ethical teachings of the Buddha were embodied in the five universal precepts binding on all Buddhists and the enlarged code of conduct for monks known as the PATIMOKKHA. The most comprehensive listing of moral and ethical codes is contained in the ten ethical precepts or *dasakusalakarmapatha*. It lists the following codes of behaviour: non-violence and compassion towards all creatures; avoidance of anything that is not given and the cultivation of generosity; abstention from sexual misconduct and contentment; maintenance of right speech; avoidance of greed and possessiveness and the cultivation of tranquillity; avoidance of anger and hatred and the abandonment of false views. (*See also* PANCASILA)

Silsila / Silsilah *Islam* The sequence of SUFI masters that must reach back in an unbroken chain to Muhammad. All the *silsilas* come through Muhammad to his son-in-law, ALI, except for the NAQSHBANDIS, who trace their spiritual lineage through ABU BAKR. Each Sufi order (TARIQAH) will have a *silsila*, which provides the order with legitimacy and ensures that the follower feels secure in the discipline. Through the line of SHAIKHS, the blessing of the Prophet and all the former masters is received through the living master. Most Sufi orders will recite the lineage after evening prayer or the weekly JUMA prayers held on a Friday. (*See also* BAI'A; MURID)

Simchat Torah / Simhat Torah *(rejoicing in the Torah) Judaism* The ninth day and completion of the festival of SUKKOT, and the day on which the annual cycle of TORAH readings is completed and begins anew. It is a happy occasion in which the Torah scrolls are removed from the ark in the synagogue and carried around in procession by the congregation. Thirteen-year-old boys are called to read from the Torah together with an adult, who recites the blessing. (*See also* SEFER TORAH)

Simon Peter *Christianity* See PETER, ST.

Simran / Simaran *(remembrance) Sikhism* The continuous remembrance of God which, according to the teachings of the Gurus, is achieved through remembrance of the name of God. This usurps in priority remembrance of precious things or persons which leads to attachment and sorrow at parting. (*See* NAM SIMRAN)

Sin *Christianity*   Sin, sometimes referred to as formal sin, is an intentional act of rebellion or disobedience against the known will of God and a falling away from the moral condition of righteousness in which the human race was created. Death, punishment in HELL and the denial of God's presence are the penalties of sin. The state of sin is the human condition and ruling principle of human life since the fall of Adam and Eve, and consequently human beings are in need of transformation or regeneration, which becomes possible through the death and resurrection of Jesus Christ. (*See also* ATONEMENT; HEAVEN; REDEMPTION; SATAN; SATISFACTION)

Singh *(lion)* *Sikhism*   Many of the Rajput or ruling castes of northern India maintained the name Singh. Since 1699, it has been given to Sikh males upon initiation into the KHALSA through the AMRIT ceremony. While not all Sikhs are called Singh, increasingly there are those who adopt the name without taking the Khalsa initiation. (*See also* AMRIT PAHUL; KAUR)

Singh Sabha *Sikhism*   A term used either for an organization of Sikhs belonging to the KHALSA brotherhood or, alternatively, an assembly or organization of Sikhs for prayer. The Singh Sabha organization was founded in 1873 with the intention of revitalizing Sikhism and publishing literature on Sikh religion and history. (*See also* TAT KHALSA)

Sira/Sirat / Seera/Seerat *Islam*   Biographical writings concerned with the exemplary behaviour of Muhammad. The most respected, and the source for all later versions, were those written by Ibn Ishaq (d.768) and Ibn Hisham (d.830) based on early stories of Muhammad's deeds, the poems of Hassan ibn Thabit and accounts of Muhammad's military struggles with the opponents of Islam. They contain numerous legends constructed around a strong kernel of factual material. In the early twentieth century countless biographies of the Prophet were written and this renewed interest in the historical Muhammad became known as the Sirat movement. (*See* HADITH)

Sis Ganj Sahib *Sikhism*   The GURDWARA and shrine in Chandni Chowk, Old Delhi, which commemorates the martyrdom of the ninth Guru, GURU TEGH BAHADUR, on 11 November 1675. The place where the Guru was imprisoned by the Moghuls is also situated on the site of the shrine.

Sisters of Mercy *Christianity*   A name commonly used for a member of a religious community engaged in nursing or other social activities on behalf of the poor and the sick. (*See* MENDICANT FRIARS; NUNS; RELIGIOUS)

Sita   *Hinduism*   The consort of RAMA and daughter of Raja JANAK who was kidnapped by RAVANA, the demon-king of Sri Lanka. The RAMAYANA describes Sita's wedding to Rama, her journeys with him in exile, her kidnap by Ravana and her single-minded chaste devotion to her husband and Lord when in captivity in Sri Lanka. Eventually Rama and the monkeys fight Ravana and destroy him. Sita is released and returns in triumph to Ayodhya with her husband. She is regarded as the exemplar of the perfect wife.

Siva   *Hinduism*   *See* SHIVA.

Skanda *(aggregate or bundle)*   *Buddhism*   A technical term for the five constituents that comprise the physical mental being. They consist of RUPA, or physical being; VEDANA, or feeling; SAMJNA, or perception; SAMSKARA, or mental activities; and VINNANA, or consciousness. Since all these aggregates are impermanent and subject to dissolution, attachment to them will bring suffering. Their impermanence is usually taken to mean that Buddha rejected the concept of a permanent soul or ATMAN. (*See also* ANATTA)

Skanda   *Hinduism*   The ancient Vedic god of war who is assimilated into the family of Shiva as one of his two sons. Skanda is also identified with KARTIKEYA, MURUGAN and SUBRAMANIYAM.

Skandhaka   *Buddhism*   The second part of the VINAYA PITAKA, which provides the details of the rules for communal monastic life as opposed to the rules governing the behaviour of individual monks and nuns. They deal with initiation into the community, dress codes, training, retreats, resolution of disputes and punishment for infringement of the rules. (*See also* PATIMOKKHA)

Smartas   *Hinduism*   The followers of Shankara who worshipped both Vishnu and Shiva. They attempted to reconcile sectarian differences through a monistic view of existence. It is also used to describe BRAHMINS who follow a strict orthodox interpretation of SMRITI or scripture. (*See also* SHAIVITE; VAISHNAVA)

Smriti   *Buddhism*   The first of the seven stages that lead to enlightenment, it refers to mindfulness or being aware of the activities of the body, mind and sensations. It is embodied the noble truth of right mindfulness. (*See also* PRASRABDHI; PRITI; SAMADHI; SAMMA SATI; UPEKKHA; VIRIYA)

Smriti *(that which is remembered)*   *Hinduism*   The term used for all scripture that is not in the Vedic canon, or SHRUTI. *Smriti* refers to tradition and usually relates to the PURANAS, including the two great epics, the RAMAYANA and MAHABHARATA. Very often, *smriti* scripture is perceived as the blessings of God upon all human beings, as the teachings bring Hinduism to everyone regardless of gender and caste. They are therefore less exclusive than the Vedic texts, which are restricted to the top three VARNAS. (*See also* VEDA)

Sobernorst *Christianity*   A theological concept of the Eastern ORTHODOX CHURCHES which states that while there is a unity of many individuals within the community of the church, each individual maintains full freedom and personal integrity.

Society of Friends *Christianity*   See RELIGIOUS SOCIETY OF FRIENDS.

Sodar *(that door)* *Sikhism*   The most important of ten hymns contained in the GURU GRANTH SAHIB which are recited as the evening prayer by devout Sikhs. (*See also* ROHILLAS; PANJ BANIA)

Sohila / Sohilla / Suhela *Sikhism*   A song of praise that begins on page 12 of the GURU GRANTH SAHIB, which devout Sikhs recite as bedtime prayer before sleep. It is regarded as one of the five compulsory prayers of the Sikh liturgy. (*See also* PANJ BANIA)

Soka Gakkai (J) *Buddhism*   A modern Japanese movement founded in 1931 and based on the teachings of NICHIREN Buddhism (1253 CE). Twice a day the followers chant *Namu-myoho-renge-kyo* in front of the mandala scroll originally written by Nichiren. Chanting can be used to fulfil worldly desires, which may appear paradoxical when one considers the teachings of the Buddha. Under the name of Nichiren Shoshu, the school has attracted many young people and media stars in the West.

Solifidianism *Christianity*   The doctrine of JUSTIFICATION by faith alone asserted by the Protestant reformers.

Solomon *Judaism*   The son of DAVID and king of ISRAEL. He developed the absolute monarchy begun by David and brought about economic, social and cultural changes to Hebrew society. The kingdom was divided into twelve provinces under the control of the central state situated in Jerusalem. The state of Israel became rich and powerful and took part in the diplomatic life of the Middle East. Solomon married the daughters of surrounding rulers, including the Pharaoh. Trade and cultural exchanges also took place with the surrounding area and the Temple and palace in Jerusalem reflect the influence of Phoenician architecture. Some leaders were disturbed by the new wealth and the outside cultural influences, and after Solomon's death the kingdom divided into two. However, Solomon is usually regarded as a repository of wisdom and the author of the Song of Songs and the book of ECCLESIASTES, eventually accepted as part of the Jewish canon of scripture.

Soma *Hinduism* The unknown intoxicant used by the BRAHMINS in the ritual sacrifice of the VEDAS. It was believed that the god INDRA used the substance and was intoxicated by it. By taking the juice of the soma plant, the participant shared in the experience of the gods. The soma was drunk as a libation but like AGNI, the god of fire, was believed to be a god in its own right. There was also a soma ritual, where the juice was pressed from the sacred plant and interpreted as the death of the god. Life was given back to the men who participated in the ritual drinking of the juice. The ritual was therefore sacrificial. (*See also* YAJNA)

Son of God *Christianity* The title given to Christ denoting the majesty of his divinity and referring to his role as the second aspect of the TRINITY. It points to the belief that God incarnated in human form as Jesus Christ, which is fully explored in the LOGOS principle described in John's Gospel. (*See also* SON OF MAN)

Son of Man *Christianity* A title that Jesus Christ gave to himself. It is difficult to ascertain the origins of the term, but traditionally it is used to describe Christ's humanity and the HUMILITY of the INCARNATION. It is also used to denote the universal nature of Christ's mission. (*See also* SON OF GOD)

Soteriology *Christianity* The branch of theology that deals with salvation. In Christianity it is concerned with the fall of humankind and sin, grace and eternal life, the redemptive role of God in human history and the ATONEMENT in Christ. (*See also* PAROUSIA; REDEMPTION; RESURRECTION)

Soto (J) *Buddhism* A ZEN sect introduced into Japan by DOGEN (1200–54). It advocates ZAZEN or 'just sitting' meditation. As opposed to RINZAI, it became popular amongst the peasantry and as a result developed a number of popular rituals for rites of passage.

Spirit *Christianity* See HOLY SPIRIT.

Sraddha *Hinduism* See SHRADDHA.

Sramanas *(strivers)* *Buddhism* The term used to describe the groups of wandering ascetics such as those joined by the Buddha in his search for enlightenment. (*See also* SIDDATTHA GOTTAMA; SRAMANAS)

Sramanas *Hinduism* Non-BRAHMIN teachers of the Upanishadic period who attracted many followers by their practice of austerity and meditation rather than the performance of ritual sacrifices. (*See also* UPANISHADS)

Sravaka *Jainism* The term used to describe Jain laity as opposed to the monks. Although asceticism and renunciation are considered essential for liberation, the laity plays a prominent part in Jainism. The doctrine of the interdependence of all beings has ensured a close relationship between the laity and the renunciate ascetics, who perform duties for each other. SVETAMBARA Jains differ from the DIGAMBARAS in that they believe it is possible for lay Jains to work towards liberation in progressive stages. (*See also* PRATIMA; SADHU; SADHVI; SANGHA)

Sri *Hinduism* The archetypal goddess and consort of VISHNU, who may have been worshipped independently before being absorbed into VAISHNAVA tradition. In later medieval Vaishnavism, Sri is identified with all the consorts of the AVATARS of Vishnu, but RAMANUJA taught that she is the primeval GURU, the saving grace of God, who appears in the form of the guru, endowing that person with compassion and selfless love for humanity. South Indian Vaishnavism is often known as Sri-Vaishnavism because of the prominent role of the goddess. (*See also* SHAKTI; SHRI)

Sri Chand *Sikhism* The eldest son of GURU NANAK born in 1494. Sri Chand is said to have lived a life of celibacy and asceticism. He was angry that his father did not nominate him to succeed in the guruship. However, his piety and renunciation won him many followers in the Punjab and a sect formed which acknowledged him to be their leader and the rightful successor of the Guru. (*See also* UDASIS)

Srimad Bhagavatum *Hinduism* Also known as the Bhagavata Purana, it tells of the exploits of KRISHNA, especially the popular mythology of the child Krishna and the time he passed as a cowherd with the GOPIS. An important work for the devotees of Krishna, it attempts to reconcile the BHAKTI cult with the high philosophy and ritual of the VEDAS. It is an important scripture for the devotees of ISKCON. (*See also* BHAGAVAD GITA)

Srotapani *Buddhism* The first stage on the journey to enlightenment known as 'stream-entry' and indicative that there are only seven more births left in the human or celestial realms before NIRVANA is achieved. (*See also* ARHANT; BODHISATTVA; SAKRDAGAMIN)

Srti / Sruti   *Hinduism*   *See* SHRUTI.

Srutamayi Prajna   *Buddhism*   Wisdom or understanding that comes from discerning or interpreting the meaning of scripture as opposed to the higher wisdom that is attained by direct experience. (*See also* PANNA)

State prayers   *Christianity*   Prayers recited in Britain, and included amongst the intercessionary prayers, for the sovereign and the royal family. (*See* CHURCH OF ENGLAND)

Stations of the Cross   *Christianity*   A series of fourteen places on the Via Dolorosa in JERUSALEM, which is supposed to be the route that Jesus Christ took on his way from trial to CRUCIFIXION. The stages present the various episodes in the death of Christ based on biblical and non-biblical sources, and it remains a popular form of devotion for pilgrims to visit and meditate upon each station. From the Middle Ages, pilgrims who could not afford to visit the Holy Land adopted the custom of circumambulating their parish churches, where depictions of the stations of the cross would be displayed as statues in stained glass windows.

Stephen, St   *Christianity*   One of the seven men appointed by the APOSTLES as the first DEACONS with the duty of looking after the distribution of alms to the poor and deprived in the early Christian communities. He was also a fervent missionary and preacher of the Gospels. As a Hellenistic Jew, he was brought before the SANHEDRIN on the charge of blasphemy. He boldly denounced the Council as the murderers of the MESSIAH and announced that he saw Jesus at the right hand of God. He was sentenced to death by stoning and thus became the first Christian martyr. Stephen is important, because his death speech was the first clear articulation of the universal application of the Christian message and his death was probably one of the factors in the conversion of PAUL, who was present at the stoning.

Sthanakavasi   *Jainism*   A sub-sect of SVETAMBARA Jains who reject the worship of images. They first appeared in the fifteenth century CE as followers of the Lonka sect. They do not worship in temples where images are installed but have their own prayer-halls known as *sthanaks*. In most respects there is little difference between the Sthanakavasis and other Svetambaras. They do not, however, attend pilgrimages and they accept a smaller canon of scripture. (*See also* TERAPANTHIS)

Sthavara *(immobile souls)* *Jainism* In the Jain categorization of living beings, these are beings who only possess the sense of touch. There are five types of one-sense or immobile soul beings. They are earth-bodied, such as precious stones and minerals; water-bodied, such as dew, water, fog and rain; fire-bodied, such as flames, lightning and fire; air-bodied, such as wind and gases; and vegetable-bodied, such as root vegetables, leaves, fruits, grains and flowers. (*See* TRASA)

Sthavira / Sthaviravada (S) *Buddhism* An early school of Buddhist tradition whose teachers considered themselves to be the strict guardians of tradition. They came into existence as a result of the first schism in Buddhist history, which took place at the Second Council between fifty and one hundred years after the Buddha's death. The creation of Sthavira and MAHASANGHIKA schools began the basic division in Buddhism between MAHAYANA and THERAVADA. However, it should be remembered that the contemporary Theravadin school was not Sthavira but one of several schools that came into existence resulting from divisions within the Sthavira. (*See also* SARVASTIVADINS)

Sthvira *Jainism* A title given to a Jain ascetic responsible for the religious discipline of other monks. (*See* ACARYA; SADHU)

Stigmata *Christianity* The apparent miraculous manifestation of the wounds of Jesus Christ in the hands and feet of a worshipper either as invisible sites of pain or visible areas of bleeding. Stigmata can also appear around the head, where the crown of thorns was placed on Christ, or on the back and shoulders, where he was scourged. The first stigmatization in Christianity is attributed to St FRANCIS OF ASSISI.

Stupa (S) / Thupa (P) *Buddhism* A reliquary mound containing the ashes or relics of an important religious personage or monuments commemorating events in the life of the Buddha. They are dome-shaped and constructed on a rectangular platform. Some of them are extremely large, whilst others are very small.

Subha *(beautiful, or that which is beautiful)* *Buddhism* Some Buddhists believe that a momentary enlightenment can be achieved through loss of self, attained by an appreciation of beauty or contemplation of great beauty. The Buddha did not deny the beauty of the world, but was aware that attachment to the ephemeral would result in eventual suffering. (*See* DUKKHA)

Subhah *Islam* A string of beads used to count the names of Allah during recitation, especially used by Sufis when performing DHIKR but common amongst many traditional Muslims.

Submersion *Christianity*   The type of BAPTISM involves completely covering the body in water usually associated with adult baptism. Some Protestant denominations insist upon a baptism in which the believer enters a pool and is completely submerged. (*See also* BELIEVER'S BAPTISM; BAPTISTS)

Subordinationism *Christianity*   An early Christological argument that existed in the first three centuries of Christian history and asserts that the Son is under the Father and the Holy Spirit is under the dominion of the Father and the Son. (*See* ARIANISM; CHRISTOLOGY; FILIOQUE; NICAEA, COUNCIL OF; TRINITY; TRINITARIAN)

Subramaniyam *Hinduism*   The Aryanized form of the Tamil god, MURUGAN, worshipped in Sri Lanka and the Tamil parts of south India. (*See also* SKANDA)

Succoth *Judaism*   See SUKKOT.

Suddhodana *Buddhism*   The ruler of the Sakya tribe and the father of SIDDATTHA GOTTAMA, the future Buddha. It is Suddhodana who tried to prevent his son from experiencing any suffering by creating a palace of luxury for the young prince. The intention was to avoid a prophecy in which his son would renounce the world to become a wandering ascetic.

Sudra *Hinduism*   The lowest of the four VARNAS. They are not 'twice-born' and therefore have no access to the sacred thread or the Vedic scriptures. They are expected to engage in servile occupations and to serve the three higher varnas. It has been theorized that they are the descendants of the people conquered by the ARYANS, but whatever their origins, they have suffered through their low position in Hindu society and are regarded as ritually polluting by the higher castes. (*See also* HARIJANS)

Sufi *Islam*   A practitioner of Sufism, which is sometimes defined as Muslim mysticism, Sufism is a systemized method of bringing the practitioner into an alignment or correspondence with Allah, which is portrayed in terms of union or communion with the unity of the one God. By the end of the ninth century Sufis had developed both the doctrine and the methodology of the path to mystical union. The Sufi experience of union led to a profound understanding of the nature of divinity and the human being, and brought about a unique understanding of TAUHID (oneness of Allah) not accessible to the orthodox, who simply followed the outer teachings of Islam. The development of Sufism affirmed the need for a spiritual teacher who could guide the MURID (disciple) through various spiritual disciplines based on repetition of the names of Allah, and leading through successive internal stages to purification of the heart and eventual loss of self into the unity of Allah. These lineages of masters developed into well-established orders that remain influential in contemporary Islam. In spite of criticism from several neo-revivalist movements, Sufism remains a viable force in the Muslim world and claims to represent the beliefs of the majority of traditional Muslims. (*See also* DHIKR; NAFS; QALB; SHAIKH; TARIQAH; TASSAWUF)

Suhela *Sikhism* See SOHILA.

Sujata *Buddhism* The milkmaid who nourished the Buddha back to health after he had failed to find enlightenment through the practice of extreme austerity. According to some accounts of the legend, she was the first to introduce him to the idea of the middle way by providing the example of a sitar string that is either too loose or too tight. (*See* MAGGA; SIDDATTHA GOTTAMA)

Sukhavati *Buddhism* Paradise as described by Pure Land Buddhists of the JODO and SHIN SHU schools in Japan. It is the 'Pure Land' of the AMIDA Buddha.

Sukkah *Judaism* A temporary shelter of foliage constructed by Jewish families in which meals are eaten during the festival of SUKKOT. The booths are three-sided structures covered with foliage or any matter that grows from the soil. They are decorated with hangings and pictures. The *sukkah* are constructed to recall the temporary dwellings built by the Jews whilst wandering in the Sinai desert after release from Egypt. It is also stated that they should remind the Jews of the transience of all things.

Sukkot / Sukkoth / Succoth *Judaism* One of the three important festivals celebrated in Judaism and known as the Feast of Tabernacles. It is held for eight days (seven in Israel) during the month of Tishrie (6 September–4 October) a few days after YOM KIPPUR. The festival remembers the care taken by God during the wandering after release from bondage in Egypt and contains two distinctive ceremonies. The first is the making and waving of four interwoven branches of the palm, citron, myrtle and willow known as the ARBA MINIM. The second is the creation of SUKKAH. The festival includes the three sacred days of HOSHANA RABBA, SHEMINI ATZERAT and SIMCHAT TORAH.

Summa Theologica *Christianity* The principal theological work of Thomas AQUINAS (1225–74). It is divided into three parts which deal with, respectively, God the creator, the restoration of humanity to God and, finally, the means by which the individual can bring about the salvation of humanity through joining the work of Christ. The work develops a systematic theology of the relationship between faith and reason and arguments for the divinity of Christ. (*See also* SCHOLASTICISM)

Sunday   *Christianity*   *See* SABBATH.

Sunday schools   *Christianity*   Schools for providing religious instruction to children founded in 1780 by Robert Raikes (1735–1811). Originally, the schools provided both religious instruction and education in reading, writing and arithmetic with paid teachers. But as full-time public education was introduced, the secular curriculum disappeared and the teachers became voluntary members drawn from the local PARISH. Sunday schools continue to educate children into the fundamentals of Christian life in Britain and they are organized on a parish basis.

Suniai *(to listen)*   *Sikhism*   The term used to describe the experience that results from attentive listening to the GURBANI or the verses of the GURU GRANTH SAHIB with faith and devotion. (*See also* SATSANG)

Sunna (P) / Sunya (S)   *Buddhism*   The emptiness of all existence or the doctrine that nothing exists in itself, as taught by some early schools of Buddhism. It means the Void of Emptiness and implies the denial of all conceptual constructions in relation to ultimate reality. (*See* SHUNYATTA)

Sunna / Sunnah *(the beaten path)*   *Islam*   The exemplary practices, customs and traditions of the Prophet as recorded in the HADITH and SIRA and used as the model for Muslim behaviour and custom. The Sunna is regarded as the second authoritative source after the Qur'an.

Sunni   *Islam*   The vast majority of Muslims who believe in the successorship of the caliphs rather than the imamate. They are the largest group within Islam and are the majority population in most Muslim nations, with the exception of Iraq and Iran. However, there are debates within the Sunni community as to its constitution. Both traditional Muslims influenced by the teachings of the SUFIS and new revivalist movements such as the WAHHABIS and the SALAFIS claim to be the genuine Sunni community to the exclusion of their opponents. (*See also* AHL AS-SUNNA WA JAMAAT; IMAM; KHALIFA; SHI'A)

Sunyatta   *Buddhism*   *See* SHUNYATTA.

Supatra dana   *Jainism*   One of the ways of giving charity that form part of the six daily duties maintained by Jain laity. *Supatra dana* refers to giving food and books to ascetics in order to assist their physical and spiritual well-being. (*See* DANA)

Superior *Christianity*   The title frequently used for the head of a religious order, for example Mother Superior. (*See* ABBESS; ABBOT; GENERAL; RELIGIOUS)

Sura / Surah *Islam*   The divisions of the QUR'AN into chapters consisting of AYAT or verses written in blank verse, each one given a title that indicates the theme covered. They are arranged in order of size rather than chronology, with the longest appearing first. Various debates have taken place concerning the chronology of the suras as to whether they were revealed in MAKKAH or MADINAH. Generally speaking, the less legalistic, shorter suras were revealed in Makkah.

Surdas (1483–1563) *Sikhism*   The authentic details of Surdas' life are not known, but he was a blind Vaishnavite SANT and a prolific writer of devotional poetry in the Hindi language. Six of his poems were included in the final composition of the GURU GRANTH SAHIB. (*See also* VAISHNAVA)

Surplice *Christianity*   A loose white garment with wide sleeves that is placed over a CASSOCK and worn by both clergy and some lay participants, such as choir members and servers, and used in liturgical worship.

Surya *Hinduism*   The god of the sun. Many Hindus offer their prayers to the rising sun at the time of their ritual morning prayers.

Sushumna *Hinduism*   The psychic channel that is believed to run from the base of the spine to the top of the head, connecting all the CHAKRAS or centres of energy. It is along the *sushumna* channel that the KUNDALINI energy travels when raised by YOGA and other spiritual practices. (*See also* TANTRA)

Sutra (S) / Sutta (P) *(a thread)* *Buddhism*   A collection of aphorisms on a single theme. A common form of Buddhist scripture which is written in the form of a dialogue or discourse between the Buddha and a disciple or seeker. (*See* SUTTA PITAKA)

Sutra *Hinduism*   A collection of scriptures based on a theme usually attributed to one author and often regarded as the sourcebook for a particular sect or school of philosophy. Usually they are written in a very condensed form as aphorisms. There are many such collections in Hinduism as well as Buddhism.

Sutta Pitaka (P) / Sutra Pitaka (S) *Buddhism*   The second of the three baskets of scripture in the PALI CANON which contains the dialogues or discourses of the Buddha. There are over 17,000 *suttas* that describe the teaching output of the Buddha over forty-five years. Each *sutta* has an introduction which describes the circumstances in the Buddha's life which preceded the teaching. They are all introduced by the testimony of Buddha's closest disciple, Ananda, reassuring the adherent that he was a witness to the event. However, many of the *suttas* were certainly compiled after the Buddha's death. (*See also* TIPITAKA)

Suttee *Hinduism*   See SATI.

Svadhyaya *(self-study)* *Jainism*   This consists of the study of scriptures in order to acquire right knowledge. It can also refer to the application of the teachings to one's own circumstances and disseminating the teachings to others. It is one of the six internal austerities and six daily duties observed by devout lay Jains. (*See* TAPAS)

Svantantra *Hinduism*   A doctrine taught by MADHVA that only God is autonomous. Only the activity of God is truly independent. All other beings are dependent. (*See also* DVAITA VEDANTA)

Svayambhu / Shvayambhu *(self-existent)* *Hinduism*   This term for the supreme being is used in the UPANISHADS. It is derived from *sva* meaning 'the self' and refers to the belief that only BRAHMAN is self-existent, whereas all other beings are dependent. (*See also* ATMAN)

Svetaketu *Hinduism*   The son of the BRAHMIN in the CHANDOGYA UPANISHAD who is the recipient of the famous teaching that is associated with the unity of ATMAN and BRAHMAN. While the son has returned full of pride in his knowledge, he has never experienced the reality of Brahman. His father teaches him in a series of comparisons that lead to the message of TAT TVAM ASI ('You are that').

Svetambara *(the white-clad)* *Jainism*   The numerically dominant form of Jainism found primarily in northern and western India. The name originates from the monks, who unlike the DIGAMBARA ascetics who do not wear clothing, dress in simple white cotton robes. There is little difference in doctrine or practice amongst the laity of the two sects, even though there are some minor differences amongst the ascetics. The Svetambara acknowledge a larger canon of scripture; accept that both men and women can attain liberation; depict their images of TIRTHANKARAS wearing clothing and jewellery; and allow more possessions to the monks. The Svetambara are divided into several sects, but the principal division is between those that accept image worship and those that do not. (*See also* SADHU; STHANAKAVASI; SVETAMBARA MURTIPUJAKA)

Svetambara Murtipujaka *Jainism*   From the earliest periods of Jain history there is evidence that many worshipped images. Today, the majority are image worshippers. With the exception of STHANAKAVASIS, SVETAMBARA Jains offer flowers, sandalwood paste, jewelled ornaments and decorative clothes to the images of the TIRTHANKARAS. As with Hindus, rice, fruit, sweets and incense are offered during PUJA, but Jains cover their mouths when washing or touching the images. (*See also* DIGAMBARA)

Svetasvatara Upanishad   *Hinduism*   One of the principal UPANISHADS considered a revelation by the followers of SHIVA, as it presents a fully developed treatise on Shiva worship or BHAKTI.

Swami   *Hinduism*   An honorific title applied to a renunciate monk or SANNYASIN. It is derived from *Goswami* (one who has complete control over the senses).

Swaminarayan   *Hinduism*   A large sect of the VAISHNAVA tradition strong in the state of Gujarat and introduced into Britain and other countries where Gujaratis have migrated. The first custom-designed Hindu temple in Neasden, London, was built by the Swaminarayan movement. The movement was founded by Swami Sahajananda (1781–1830), who joined an order of ascetics believed to be the descendants of RAMANUJA. Sahajananda went on to found his own order consisting of around 2,000 ascetics. The movement spread throughout Gujarat. The teachings combine Vaishnavism with strict ethical principles and adopt a reform line on issues such as widow immolation, animal sacrifice and female infanticide. Lay Hindus are appointed as administrators of temples and maintain lineages through the male line. Unlike some BHAKTI movements, the Swaminarayan movement is traditional in regard to the maintenance of strict caste differentials.

Swaraj *(home rule)*   *Hinduism*   The object of GANDHI'S SATYAGRAHA campaign against the British raj.

Swastika   *Hinduism*   An ancient Indian symbol of good fortune that is commonly drawn in red dye or made up of flower petals for various rituals or festivities. The four arms signify the four directions (space), the stages in the life-cycle (time) and the four VEDAS (knowledge). It is more significantly used as a symbol in Jainism.

Swastika   *Jainism*   One of the traditional symbols of the Jain tradition. The four spokes of the cross represent the wheel of eternal rebirth into four forms of life: human, animal, celestial and infernal. This cycle can only end with liberation. Jain devotees will often create swastikas from rice grains and offer them to the images of the TIRTHANKARAS. (*See also* PUJA)

Syadvada *(the relativity of truths)* *Jainism*   In the Jain theory of knowledge this refers to tentativeness in the description of things and is part of the important doctrine of ANEKANTAVADA. Generally, it is used in the context of religious pluralism and instils Jainism with a tolerance of other faiths and sects within its own tradition. It is asserted that any viewpoint cannot be absolute, as it is only a partial perspective of reality based upon a particular standpoint. Only someone possessed with KEVALAJNANA would be able to transcend a relative perspective of reality. (*See also* NAYAVADA)

Synagogue *Judaism*   The Jewish meeting place for communal prayer, instruction and social activities that probably became prominent after the destruction of the Second Temple by the Romans in 70 CE. The Talmudic rabbis insisted that for certain occasions, such as the repetition of the KADDISH, the KEDUSHAH, the AMIDAH and the readings from the TORAH scrolls, a MINYAN of ten adult male Jews was required. They also stated that communal prayer was more important than individual prayer. For both these reason the synagogue came to play a central role in Jewish worship. The architectural rules for the sacred space are simple: the building should contain an ark in the east wall to contain the Torah scrolls, and there should be a raised platform from which the Torah can be read. The building should also have windows. Everything else is at the discretion of the congregation and the architect. (*See also* ARON HAKODESH, BIMAH; BET HA MIDRASH; BET HA TEFILLAH; SEFER TORAH)

Synod *Christianity*   A term that can be used to refer to a COUNCIL or to the system of government used by the CHURCH OF ENGLAND comprising a House of Bishops, a House of Clergy and a House of Laity. The three houses deal with matters of doctrine, ligurgy and administration.

Synoptic Gospels *Christianity*   A term applied the GOSPELS of Matthew, Mark and Luke and their presentation of the life of Jesus, as contrasted with the portrayal that appears in the Gospel of St John. Synoptic means having a common viewpoint, and arguments have taken place amongst scholars as to whether Mark or Matthew is the original gospel. Others argue that there was a common original oral or written source for the Synoptic Gospels. (*See also* MATTHEW, GOSPEL OF; MARK, GOSPEL OF; LUKE, GOSPEL OF; NEW TESTAMENT)

Tabernacle *Christianity* A container for the vessels and the consecrated elements of bread and wine that is usually kept on the ALTAR in a side chapel and marked by a lit candle. Normally only used by Roman Catholic and Eastern churches. (*See also* EUCHARIST)

Tabligh-i Jamaat *Islam* An organization founded in the late 1920s by Muhammad Ilyas, a graduate of DEOBAND in northern India. Unlike the Deoband members, Ilyas did not consider it necessary to belong to the professional ULAMA in order to reform Islam. Tabligh-i Jamaat is a grassroots movement aimed at inspiring religious renewal. There is no central administrative structure and the key activity is coordinated voluntary commitment to participate in preaching teams. These teams, comprising between three and ten members, go out to Muslim communities to inspire renewed commitment to prayer and mosque attendance. They sleep in the local mosque and invite local Muslims to their meetings. The teams strongly emphasize humility and prayer and encourage others by their example. Those who are inspired by them are formed into new preaching teams. In this way the circle of preachers has gradually increased throughout the Muslim world.

Tachanun *Judaism* Part of the traditional funeral arrangements, in which the washing and clothing of the dead is performed by the HEVRAH KADISHAH, a local body of Jews who serve the dying and the dead. (*See also* TAHARAH; TAKHRIKHIM)

Tafsir *(explanation)* *Islam* The science of interpretation or exegesis of the QUR'AN through commentary. Muslim commentators have considered that the best explanation of the Qur'an is contained in the Qur'an itself, as Allah would not have made the final revelation too obscure for human beings to comprehend. One part of the Qur'an will provide clarification for another part. However, one famous exegesist of the Qur'an, Dehlavi, noted three conditions that should be adhered to when engaging in commentary:

1. Every word should be explained by providing its real meaning and its roots in the Arabic language.
2. Everything should be explained in the context of the revelation as a whole.
3. The interpretation should not be contrary to the understanding of Muhammad's companions (*sahaba*) who witnessed the revelation.

(*See also* HADITH)

Tag *Hinduism* One who renounces the world or practises TYAGA. (*See also* SANNYASIN)

Tagore, Devendranath (1817–1905) *Hinduism* He took over the leadership of the BRAHMO SAMAJ from RAM MOHAN ROY. He changed Roy's emphasis on Upanishadic monism to a more universal form of theism under the influence of the Western-educated middle-class young Hindus who were joining the organization. Under his leadership the Brahmo Samaj adopted a stance of active social reform to improve the conditions of India's poor.

Taharah *Judaism* The washing of the body that takes place before the dressing in preparation for the funeral. This function is traditionally carried out by the HEVRAH KADISHAH, a local body of Jews who serve the dying and the dead. The body is washed in lukewarm water through a sheet placed on top of it. The nails are cut and the hair is groomed. (*See also* TACHANUN; TAKHRIKHIM; TUMAH)

Tahiyya *Islam* A greeting made in the prayer-rite in which the worshipper states the following: 'salutations and blessings and ascriptions of goodness belong to God. Peace be to you, O prophet, and the mercy of God and His blessings. Peace be to us and to the righteous worshippers of God'. (*See* AS-SALAMU-ALAYKUM; SALAH)

Tahrif *Islam* The doctrine that the scriptures of the Jews and Christians, although true revelations of the divine word given to the respective prophets, Moses, David and Jesus, were corrupted or changed by later generations of followers. (*See* AHL AL-KITAB; INJIL; TAWRAH)

Taittiriya Upanishad *Hinduism* One of the principal UPANISHADS. The Upanishad is cited by Vaishnavites to support the path of devotion to a personal God. It contains references to *bhajananda* (devotional bliss) and *svarupananda* (the bliss of the Lord's form) that can be used to provide ancient doctrinal evidence of the SAGUNA BHAKTI (devotion to form) path. The Upanishad also contains examples of ethical behaviour.

Taize *Christianity* An ecumenical monastic community founded in southern France in 1940 and famous for its work in promoting Christian unity and attracting young Christians. The monks wear ordinary clothing and only perform three offices a day instead of the customary seven. (*See* OFFICES, DIVINE)

Tajdid *Islam* The idea that faithful believers periodically renew Islam in order to maintain the purity of the final revelation. Many Muslims believe that every century sees the birth of a reformer who is sent to restore the faith, regenerate the community and prevent any drift away from the revelation caused by human error or ignorance. Many new revivalist movements since the twentieth century have been concerned with *tajdid*: they often use it as a critique of the Muslim establishment and a call to purge Islam of foreign or cultural accretions. (*See* ISLAH; MUJADDID)

Takhrikhim *Judaism* Traditional Jewish garments in which the dead are buried. After washing, the body is dressed in a white cap, shirt, trousers, linen shoes and the *kittel* worn on YOM KIPPUR, and wrapped in a white shroud. Finally a TALLIT is placed in the coffin resting over the deceased person's shoulders, as worn in life. (*See also* HEVRAH KADISHAH; TACHANUN; TAHARAH)

Talbiya *Islam* *See* LABBAIKA.

Tallit / Tallith *Judaism* A four-cornered white prayer-shawl with fringes worn by Orthodox men at morning prayers and on the Day of Atonement (YOM KIPPUR). It is also placed in the coffin over the shoulders of the corpse. The tallit is seen as a robe of responsibility that marks the Jew out as someone who is accountable in every action, whether in the home or at work. It allows the Jew to remember his special relationship with God. There is no restriction in the size of a tallit, but it should be white and possess four corners, each of which must have a fringe or tassel. One of the tassels should be blue. (*See also* ATTARAH; ZIZIT)

Tallith katan *Judaism* *See* ARBA KANFOT.

Talmud *Judaism* The main source of Jewish law. It contains the MISHNAH and the GEMARA. The former is a collection of the oral law compiled by the second century CE. The latter comprises rabbinical commentaries on the Mishnah written between 200 and 500. By the first half of the fourth century, Jewish scholars had collected together the teachings of generations of rabbis who had lived in the great centres of study in Palestine. This work became known as the

Palestinian Talmud. However, parallel developments had taken place in Babylon with the opening of several influential schools of learning. As the institutions in Israel went into decline, the Babylonian schools took over and produced their own collections of interpretations of the Mishnah. This is known as the Babylonian Talmud. The Talmud goes further than the Mishnah, in that it contains debates between rabbis, theology, philosophy and ethics. (*See also* TORAH)

Talwandi *Sikhism*   Now known as Nankana Sahib, it is the town where GURU NANAK, the founder of Sikhism, was born. It is situated about 30 miles southwest of Lahore and has been in Pakistan since Partition in 1947. Sikhs are allowed across the border of India and Pakistan to visit Nankana.

Tamas *Hinduism*   One of the three GUNAS or qualities that make up PRAKRITI (nature). *Tamas* is usually translated as 'dullness' or 'inertia'. It is often regarded as the lowest of the three *gunas* and its influence in human nature results in sloth and gluttony. Certain foods are described as best avoided because they generate a *tamasic* nature. These are foods that are not fresh or are produced by allowing decaying or fermentation processes to take place. (*See also* RAJAS; SATTVA)

Tanakh / Tenakh *Judaism*   The twenty-four books of the Jewish scriptures which together form the TORAH, NEVIIM and KETUVIM. There is a hierarchy of sanctity associated with the books: the five books that compose the Torah are the most sacred, as they are the direct revelation of God to Moses and provide the law that binds Jews to God in a holy covenant; the books that compose the writings of the prophets (neviim) are next in order of sacredness; while the books known as Holy Writings (ketuvim) are believed to have been written through inspiration rather than revelation.

Tandava *Hinduism*   One of the dances of NATARAJA, a form of SHIVA. It is a cosmic dance that brings with it world destruction. A legend states that the first dance of Shiva took place at the famous Shaivite pilgrimage centre in south India at Cidambaram.

Tanha (P) *Buddhism*   *See* SAMUDAYA.

Tankhah *Sikhism*   The reinstatement into the KHALSA community of a Sikh who has broken his vows undertaken at the AMRIT initiation and contained in the RAHIT MARYADA. Traditionally a Sikh in this position was asked to perform a religious penance, such as the recitation of additional prayers or to perform service in the community. Afterwards they would be allowed to renew their vows and re-enter the Khalsa brotherhood by going through a new *amrit* ceremony. (*See also* AMRIT PAHUL; PATIT; TANKHAIAH)

Tankhaiah *(a bought man)* Sikhism   The term derives from Sikhs who were persuaded by gifts of cash or land to give their loyalty to the Muslim rulers. It is now used to describe a KHALSA Sikh who has infringed the code of ethics contained in the RAHIT MARYADA. (*See also* TANKHAH)

Tannaim Judaism   The term used for the rabbinical commentators on the Jewish scriptures who lived before 200 CE prior to the editing of the MISHNAH. The same term is also used for the agreed conditions that traditionally were drawn up when a Jewish couple entered their formal engagement to be married. (*See also* AMORAIM)

Tantra Buddhism   A form of Mahayana Buddhism which spread from India to Tibet and then to China. Tibetan Tantric texts are believed to have been revealed by the Buddha as an elite esoteric discipline available only to initiates. The practitioner of Tantra must have a qualified teacher, who initiates the disciple into various practices for the attainment of Buddhahood. Traditionally these involved the use of MANTRAS and MANDALAS for aid in meditation. However, the Tantric scriptures are believed to be magical. They contain spells, descriptions of divinities and instructions concerning ritual. (*See also* DHARANA)

Tantra Hinduism   A series of scriptures written in the form of a dialogue between SHIVA and his consort, PARVATI, which describe a variety of practices, leading to release through union. Tantra has been developed into a unique path leading to liberation, in which the Goddess is the supreme deity. According to Tantra philosophy, BRAHMAN could not create, as it is a neutral absolute, so Shiva and SHAKTI were produced as the two eternal principles of the cosmos. Shakti (the female power) is the active principle that is capable of bringing liberation, whereas Shiva is the cause of bondage. Shakti is the life power of the universe and is identified with PRAKRITI. The worship in Tantra consists of several overlapping paths. Devotion to Shiva is found amongst many Tantric followers, but the unique practices begin with the worship of the Goddess. This is known as the right-handed path (*dakshinakara*). Two other paths have generated considerable interest: the first is the left-handed path (*vamacara*), where the initiate is guided through spiritual disciplines that involve the use of forbidden or taboo objects (MAKARAS) such as drugs, sex and meat. The second is the path of KUNDALINI YOGA, where certain meditation techniques are used to activate the *kundalini* (serpent power), which is the form of Shakti lying dormant in the human body. The Shakti power rises up through certain centres of energy (CHAKRAS) until it reaches the top of the head. Here it unites with the Shiva power and SAMADHI (union) takes place.

Tanzih Islam   The important concept of Allah's transcendence, which is linked to the central Muslim doctrine of TAUHID (divine unity and uniqueness). There has been continuous debate concerning lines in the Qur'an that describe Allah having qualities that could be allocated to created beings and seem to anthropomorphize the absolute transcendence of Allah. Generally, Muslims accept that Allah's attributes, such as power, knowledge and will, are equally absolute. (*See also* TANZIL)

Tanzil *Islam*   The term used to describe the descent of the revelation from Allah to Muhammad through the angel JIBRIL. It is derived from the Arabic TANZIH (transcendent) and suggests a reaching out or descent of the almighty omniscient Allah to His human creation through the revelation of His eternal word. (*See also* QUR'AN; WAHY)

Tapas *(heat)*   *Hinduism*   The term usually refers to the various forms of austerity practised by ascetics in order to build up their spiritual power. The identification of spiritual power with heat and austerity probably developed from the ancient Vedic correspondence of the heat generated by the sacrificial fire and the heat produced by the efforts of the BRAHMIN performing the sacrifice. Tapas was associated, therefore, with the power of the gods, but could be reproduced by the priests either in ritual activity or in devotional fervour. The RISHIS who had received the VEDAS direct from the gods were also believed to possess *tapas*, and later Hinduism formulated a variety of techniques to develop the power within. Generally, the creation of *tapas* became associated with renunciation and austerity. (*See also* AGNI; HAVAN)

Tapas *Jainism*   Austerities practised to free the soul from KARMA. Jains believe that while the threefold path of right faith, right knowledge and right conduct can stop any further influx of karma, it is not able to remove karma that has been carried over from previous lives. Even the pious take on new karma from their present speech, thoughts and actions. It is therefore necessary to remove karma at a faster rate than it is accrued. Thus it is necessary to perform austerities that will control the demands of the senses. There are six external austerities practised by Jains: fasting; eating less than one needs; limiting the food that one eats according to the rules of AHIMSA; abstention from pleasurable food; resisting temptation; and mortification of the body. In addition to these external austerities there are also six internal austerities: penance, reverence, service, self-study, detachment and meditation. (*See also* DHYANA; PRAYASCITTA; SVADHYAYA; VAIYAVRITRA; VINAYA; VYUTSARGA)

Taqlid *Islam*   The principle of strict adherence to the established doctrines of the four schools of Islamic law that has been blamed by some revivalist movements for producing stagnation and petrification in the Muslim world. It is perceived as promoting conservatism, traditionalism and uncritical veneration. (*See* FIQH; IJTIHAD)

Taqrirat al-rasul   *Islam*   The preaching of Muhammad. Collected from the recollections of his companions and contained in the HADITH collections, these form the second most authoritative source for Muslims to follow after the Qur'an. (*See also* IJMA)

Taqwa   *Islam*   Self-protection or fear of God. A religious attitude of fear and awe arising from an overwhelming Muslim belief in an all-powerful, omnipresent God who has commanded submission to his will and who will pass judgement on all on the last day. (*See* ALLAH; IHSAN)

Tariki (J)   *Buddhism*   Reliance on powers outside oneself or seeking salvation from outside assistance. Used by Pure Land Buddhists to describe salvation through faith and devotion to the personification of the absolute manifested in the AMIDA Buddha. (*See also* JIRIKI; JODO; SOTO)

Tariqah / Tariqa *(the way)*   *Islam*   A term used to describe the inner path of purification that parallels the maintenance of SHARI'A (Islamic law) and according to SUFIS constitutes the correct or complete practice of Islam. In order to follow the esoteric or inner path, it is considered necessary to have a guide who has walked the path himself. The paths of individual guidance have developed into Sufi orders, some of which are international and contain millions of adherents. Some of the most famous of these schools of guidance along the Sufi path are the NAQSHBANDI, QADIRIYA, MAWLAWI and Alawiya. Many may be regional or confined to a smaller locality. The organization is generally based around a group of followers studying under the guidance of an individual SHAIKH or master. Each *tariqah* is known for variations on the discipline used for self-purification. (*See also* DHIKR; MURID; TASSAWUF)

Tasdiq   *Islam*   The QUR'AN as confirmation of all the earlier revelations of Allah given to the previous messengers such as Adam, Abraham, Moses and Jesus. The Qur'an is both a new revelation and a repetition of the essentials contained in the earlier books. Thus Islam is both new in its inception and a continuation of God's one true religion. (*See also* DIN; NABI; RASUL; TANZIL; WAHY)

Tashlikh   *Judaism*   A traditional prayer of repentance observed on the afternoon of ROSH HASHANAH in which the people should pray by a riverbank.

Tasliya   *Islam*   The common practice in prayer and on other occasions to call down blessings upon Muhammad. The most common form is used whenever a Muslim mentions the Prophet's name. There is also a blessing called for in the prayer-rite and in the call to prayer. (*See* ADHAN; SALAH)

Tassawuf *Islam*   The preferred term for the spiritual or esoteric path of Islam commonly referred to as Sufism. It is generally used to describe the process of inner purification required in order to be a practising Muslim. The person who follows the inner path of purifying the heart through the remembrance of Allah as well as the outer forms of Islam is known as a SUFI or practitioner of *tassawuf*. (*See also* DHIKR; TARIQAH; TAZKIYAT AL-NAFS)

Tat Khalsa *Sikhism*   A term used to describe a Sikh who adheres to the teachings of GURU GOBIND SINGH. A variety of reform movements that have arisen in Sikhism since the period of the last guru have asserted a return to pure KHALSA principles as the only Sikh orthodoxy. These groups are often described as *tat khalsa*. The term is sometimes used to define the movement for an independent Sikh kingdom of KHALISTAN based on Khalsa sovereignty.

Tat tvam asi *('You are that')*   *Hinduism*   This Sanskrit phrase is found in the CHANDOGYA UPANISHAD and different interpretations of its meaning form the foundation of the various types of VEDANTA philosophy. SHANKARA used it to justify his claim that BRAHMAN and ATMAN are identical. MADHVA argued that Shankara had not rendered the meaning correctly and that the true translation was *'That you are not'*. In this way he used it to support his dualistic philosophy, or DVAITA VEDANTA, which argues that the soul and God are distinct and separate. RAMANUJA took up an intermediate position but still essentially saw a distinction between the subject and the object in the phrase, rather than Shankara's more monistic interpretation. (*See also* ADVAITA VEDANTA; VISHISH-TADVAITA VEDANTA)

Tathagata (S) *Buddhism*   A title to describe the BUDDHA used by both his followers and himself. The meaning is probably something like 'one who has arrived' or 'one who has realized suchness' (TATHAHA). Other interpretations suggest that it means 'one who has come and gone'.

Tathaha (S) *(suchness)* *Buddhism*   Used by Mahayana Buddhists to describe the ultimate and unconditional nature of all things. It has to be found on the path to enlightenment, but it cannot be discovered by searching, nor can it be lost, as one is never separate from it. (*See* DHAMMAKAYA; SHUNYATTA; SUNNA)

Tauhid / Tawhid *Islam*   The belief in the oneness and uniqueness of God. This is the central doctrine of Islam and leads to its assertion of uncompromising monotheism. *Tauhid* has two components: first, it contains the idea of Allah's total uniqueness or otherness from His creation. He cannot be compared with anything that is known or created. This doctrine of absolute transcendence gave rise to many theological questions in Islam, such as free will, predestination, moral accountability, self-sufficiency and the problem of creation. This position left the divine as essentially unknowable and inscrutable. Any apparent contradiction can only be resolved in God's knowledge of His own being. On the other hand, there have been those who have concentrated more on the oneness of God and the close relationship between worshipper and worshipped, creation and creator. Many Muslim mystics have explained creation in emanationist or panentheistic or even pantheistic terms and asserted the oneness of everything encompassed within Allah's being. Although arguable by Qur'anic exegesis, this has not sat comfortably with many orthodox theologians, who have preferred to emphasize transcendence over immanence. (*See* SUFI; TANZIH)

Tawaf *Islam* The practice of circumambulating the KA'ABA in MAKKAH seven times performed by all Muslims when undertaking either the HAJJ or the UMRAH.

Tawassul *(seeking a means)* *Islam* Any means which can be used by a Muslim to come closer to Allah and surrender to His will. Many traditional Muslims regard seeking assistance from Muhammad through his intercession as the most valuable form of *tawassul*. (*See* DHIKR; ISTIGHATHA; SHAFA'A)

Ta'widh / Ta'wiz *Islam* Amulets or bracelets containing verses of the Qur'an given to cure diseases or protect from ill fortune. These are often handed out by the descendants of famous mystics (SUFIS) who maintain their shrine centres or tombs. Some Muslims are highly opposed to the practice and see it as a folk superstition that has entered into Islam. However, it is undeniably true that countless millions of Muslims, especially in rural areas, maintain the practice. (*See also* BARAKA; MAZAR; SAJJADA NASHIN)

Ta'wil *Islam* A form of TAFSIR that provides an allegorical rather than a literal exegesis of the QUR'AN. It results in philosophical or mystical understanding and posits the view that the Qur'an has an esoteric or hidden meaning. It is the usual form of *tafsir* used by SUFIS.

Tawrah *Islam* The Arabic for the TORAH or the book given to the Prophet Musa (Moses) by Allah. It is one of the four sacred books revealed to a messenger containing the sacred law. The three earlier books have all been superseded by the final revelation contained in the QUR'AN. (*See also* INJIL; ZABUR)

Taymiyya, Taqi al-Din ibn (1263–1328) *Islam* A Muslim scholar who is frequently used as the inspiration for neo-orthodox movements since the twentieth century such as the WAHHABIS and SALAFIS. However, Ibn Taymiyya was less orthodox than these latter groups and was not as anti-Sufi as they claim. He was opposed only to those Sufis who flaunted obedience to Islamic law on the grounds that their personal inner experience negated the outer practices of Islam. In fact, Ibn Taymiyya demonstrated a remarkable degree of open-mindedness to all opinions and often made remarks such as 'the truth does not belong to one party exclusively but is divided among all groups'. He reinstated into Muslim theology the doctrine that human power and divine will are not mutually exclusive.

Tazkiyat al-nafs   *Islam*   The term used in the Qur'an to describe the process of inner purification or struggle against the ego, the part of the human psyche that refuses to submit to Allah. (*See* NAFS; QALB; TASSAWUF)

Techinah   *Judaism*   A prayer-book used by Orthodox Jews, and written in Yiddish especially for women, that provides instructions on how to pray.

Tefillah / Tefila   *Judaism*   The term for all Jewish prayer and meditation. Prayer is regarded as a communication from the heart overflowing into words. They may be calls for forgiveness, repentance or petition. In Judaism, while individual prayer is important, communal prayer has precedence, as the community in prayer is a microcosm of the covenant between God and His chosen people. After the ritual communal prayer, Jews may offer their individual petitions. Prayers may be in any language, but Hebrew is regarded as the holy tongue or sacred language. The prayer is structured and there is a fixed liturgy for the three-times daily prayer. The set prayers require the Orthodox Jew to don the TALLIT and the TEFILLIN.

Tefillin / Tephillin / T'filin   *Judaism*   Small leather boxes or phylacteries that contain four passages from the TORAH (Exodus 13:1–10; 11–16; Deuteronomy 6:4–9; 11:13–21) that place emphasis on the unity of God, divine rule and redemption from Egypt. One is tied to the forehead and the other to the forearm of Jewish men when they recite the morning prayers. The commandment in the Torah to wear the *tefillin* is regarded as one of the three outward signs of Judaism along with the MEZUZAH and the TALLIT. (*See also* TEFILLAH)

Tehillim   *Judaism*   The Hebrew term for the book of PSALMS, one of the books of the Hebrew scriptures that forms part of the Holy Writings (KETUVIM). The Psalms are sung to music in the SYNAGOGUE on many occasions in the Jewish religious calendar. Most of the songs express the glory of God, ask for forgiveness and mercy and extol the qualities of God. Of the 150 Psalms, 73 are attributed to David.

Temperance *Christianity*   The control of passion and sense pleasure which is regarded as one of the four cardinal virtues in Christianity. The need for self-control is associated with the Christian belief that the body is the temple of the HOLY SPIRIT. In the nineteenth century a number of Christian organizations, especially associated with Methodism, sprung up to counter the abuse of alcohol amongst the British working classes. These were known as Temperance Societies.

Templars *Christianity*   A military order also known as the Knights Templars or Knights of the Temple founded by Hugo de Payens in 1119 and so named because it was bequeathed land near the site of the old Jewish Temple in Jerusalem. Bernard de Clairvaux created a rule for them based on the CISTERCIANS and they were popular throughout Western Christianity. Their remit was to protect the pilgrims *en route* to the Holy Land, defend the Holy Land and to fight with infidels. During the twelfth and thirteenth centuries they had considerable influence in Europe as a result of the CRUSADES, and they became the greatest landowners in Europe. The end of the Crusades brought about their suppression and eventual destruction in the early fourteenth century. (*See also* HOSPITALLERS)

Temple *Judaism*   See BET HA MIKDASH.

Temptation *Christianity*   The incitement to SIN, which is the consequence of free will but also carries connotations of testing or trial by God with the benevolent intention of improving character or Godly qualities. In the New Testament, trials or temptations can be both the work of God or SATAN. Temptations are Satan's work but God's too, and although temptations form part of God's will, the desire to fall prey to sin belongs to the human being. Temptation in itself is not sin, and only becomes so when the human being gives in and performs the particular act. (*See also* ATONEMENT; ORIGINAL SIN; TEMPTATION OF CHRIST)

Temptation of Christ *Christianity*   The unsuccessful attempt by SATAN to corrupt Christ after his forty-day vigil in the desert described in two of the gospels (Matthew 4:1; Luke 22:28). The temptations were essentially concerned with Christ using the spiritual power given to him for worldly ambitions and temporal power. Christ, although tempted, remained sinless and provided the example for his disciples to resist TEMPTATION.

Tenakh *Judaism*   See TANAKH.

Tendai (J) *Buddhism* A syncretic school of Buddhism introduced into Japan from China by SAICHO (767–822). It considers the LOTUS SUTRA to be the ultimate and final teachings of the Buddha. (*See also* TI'EN T'AI)

Tephillin *Judaism* See TEFILLIN.

Terapanthis *Jainism* A sub-sect of STHANAKAVASI Jains founded by Muni Bhikhanji in 1760. The Terapanthis do not worship images and are organized around the leadership of a single ACARYA. They are considered a reform movement who observe the basic teachings of Jainism. They do not construct monasteries and focus on meditation and scriptural interpretation. Their most famous achievement is the foundation of the Jain Vishva Bharati University to promote AHIMSA in its widest sense. Terapanthi ascetics are unique, in that they regularly visit the West to promote Jainism. (*See also* SAMANAS)

Teresa of Avila, St (1515–82) *Christianity* A Spanish CARMELITE nun and well-known mystic who, along with her disciple, St John of the Cross (1542–91), provided the example of a life of pious, self-renouncing contemplation expressed through silent prayer that resulted in ecstatic inner union with God. Together they reformed the Carmelite order in Spain and provided a monastic model that united active and contemplative orders. She is famous for her efforts to provide a methodology to the mystical path by describing the various states that exist between discursive meditation and ecstasy. These can be found in her two books, *The Way of Perfection* and *The Interior Castle*.

Tertiary *Christianity* The 'third order' or Order of Penitence first created by the FRANCISCANS in the twelfth century and extended to all the mendicant orders. It allows membership to certain religious communities but does not involve withdrawal from the world. Both men and women can be employed in normal occupations and live a semi-monastic life of prayer, fasting, pacifism and worship. (*See also* DOMINICANS; MENDICANT FRIARS)

Teshuvah *(return)* *Judaism* Repentance or returning to God which is considered to be a daily obligation by devout Jews. The action of repentance should consist of remorse, confession and correction. Words of repentance are part of the three daily prayers. There is also a season of the year put aside for repentance which begins at the month of Ellul (8 August–6 September) with the daily blowing of the SHOFAR. Several days before the feast of ROSH HASHANAH in the following month of Tishrie, penitential prayers begin. The week after Rosh Hashanah is known as the Days of Repentance but it is YOM KIPPUR, or the Day of Atonement, that is most associated with the act of repentance.

Tevilah *Judaism*   The full immersion into water in the presence of a rabbinical court that is required by Jewish law as part of the ritual of conversion and followed by Orthodox Jews. (*See* GER; MIKVAH)

T'filin *Judaism*   *See* TEFILLIN.

Theosophy   An influential movement for the development of New Age religion and non-Christian new religious movements of the twentieth century. Theosophy refers to intuitive knowledge of the divine and includes a number of movements that advocate pantheistic ideas and natural mysticism as part of their teachings. The Theosophical Society was founded by Madame Blavatsky and Col. H. Olcott in Madras in 1875. Later, the two founders were joined by Annie Besant. The society believes in reincarnation and the brotherhood of humanity regardless of race and creed. The movement's understanding of the divine is influenced by ADVAITA VEDANTA and Neoplatonism. (*See also* KRISHNAMURTI)

Theotokos *(Greek: the God-bearer)*   *Christianity*   A title given to MARY, the Mother of Jesus.

Theravada (P) *(Way of the Elders)*   *Buddhism*   A principal school of Buddhism established by Mahinda in around 247 BCE in Sri Lanka and south-east Asia as a result of a mission dispatched by ASOKA. Originally a sub-sect of the dominant STHAVIRA school, its form of Buddhism gradually prevailed. Today, the Theravada school is the only remaining school of the original eighteen HINAYANA schools. It claims to preserve the Buddha's teachings in their pure form transmitted through the collection of scripture known as the PALI CANON. (*See also* MAHAYANA)

Thessalonians, Epistles to the   *Christianity*   Two New Testament books that were originally written as letters by St Paul to the church in Thessalonica. Important documents, they provide insights into the Christian faith only twenty years after Jesus Christ's death. Paul had been in Thessalonica preaching in 50 CE but had left to avoid persecution after making a number of converts. Timothy had been sent back to confirm the converts in their new faith by further teaching. He had reported back to Paul on the strength of the fledgling church but indicated problems with ethical teachings about sexuality and eschatological concerns regarding the status of dead Christians at the Day of Resurrection. The letters were written to answer their concerns and express Paul's joy at their maintenance of the faith. (*See* EPISTLES; PAUL, ST; TIMOTHY, ST)

Thirty-Nine Articles   *Christianity*   Short summaries of Protestant dogmatic tenets used by the CHURCH OF ENGLAND to formulate its doctrinal position. They were first published in 1563, but received their final form in 1571. Since 1875, newly ordained clergy are required to affirm the doctrines formally by giving a general assent to the beliefs enshrined in the Thirty-Nine Articles, but in practice little attempt is made to enforce them.

Thomas, St *Christianity*   One of the original twelve APOSTLES who were chosen by Jesus Christ as his companions and missionaries. While he appears in the Gospel of St John on several occasions, he is famous for doubting the RESURRECTION of Jesus Christ by asking to feel the wounds inflicted by the CRUCIFIXION after missing the first appearance of Jesus to his disciples. This has given rise to the saying 'Doubting Thomas'. Some traditions believe that he spread Christianity to Persia and India, and some forms of Christianity in south India call themselves the Marthoma Church as they believe it was founded by the apostle.

Thomism *Christianity*   The systemized philosophical and theological study of the doctrines of Thomas AQUINAS. (*See also* SCHOLASTICISM)

Thupa (P) *Buddhism*   *See* STUPA.

Thurible *Christianity*   A container attached to chains that is carried by the THURIFER in traditional Christian processions, ceremonies and services, and which is swung back and forth and used for the ritual burning of incense.

Thurifer *Christianity*   *See* THURIBLE.

Ti'en T'ai (Ch) *Buddhism*   Chinese school of Buddhism founded by Chih-i (538–97) which was later introduced into Japan, where it is known as TENDAI. It gives ultimate status to the LOTUS SUTRA and teaches that all things partake of a single organic unity. Therefore all things partake of the Buddha nature, as they are manifestations of the one mind.

Tiferet *(beauty)* *Judaism*   According to the tradition of the KABBALAH, the sixth of the ten SEFIROTH that emanate from the AYN SOF. The second in the central trunk of the Tree of Life, it is the harmonizing principle between love and power, an essential balance that is required for the world to exist.

Tikkun Olam / Tikun *Judaism*   Care for the world or stewardship of the earth. In traditional Judaism this would arise from the words in GENESIS, indicating that mankind has been entrusted with stewardship over all the plants and animals. The mystical tradition has posited the idea that *tikkun* is a task of cosmic repair that restores the creation to harmony with God. This may be achieved by maintaining all of God's commandments. (*See also* KABBALAH; TORAH)

Tilak   *Hinduism*   The caste or sect marks that are placed upon the forehead or other parts of the body using coloured powders or sandalwood paste. These vary from sect to sect and caste to caste. VAISHNAVAS traditionally paint their marks vertically, whereas those used by the SHAIVITES are horizontal. Married women generally place a small dot on their forehead above the nose. Tilaks are often placed on the forehead during temple worship.

Timothy, St   *Christianity*   A friend and companion of St Paul who may have been converted by him on the first missionary journey and who accompanied the apostle on his second missionary journey. Timothy was entrusted with several important lone missions, including Thessalonica, where he was able to encourage the persecuted Christians, and then to Corinth. He accompanied Paul to Corinth, Ephesus and Jerusalem. He is last mentioned in Ephesus, where he was entrusted with the task of combating false teachers and the supervision of public worship. (*See also* PAUL, ST; THESSALONIANS, EPISTLES TO THE; TIMOTHY AND TITUS, STS, EPISTLES TO)

Timothy and Titus, Sts, Epistles to   *Christianity*   Three New Testament books believed to have been written as pastoral letters by Paul, of which two are addressed to Timothy and one to Titus. There have been some disputes concerning their authorship. While the content of the letters deals with the ecclesiastical organization of the early church, they were probably written by the apostle to encourage and teach two of his closest and most trusted companions, whom he probably perceived as the next generation to continue his missionary activities. (*See* EPISTLES; PAUL, ST; TIMOTHY, ST; TITUS, ST)

Tipitaka (P) / Tripitaka (S) *(The Three Baskets)*   *Buddhism*   The PALI CANON of Buddhist scriptures accepted by the THERAVADA school. It is divided into three main parts consisting of the VINAYA PITAKA, SUTTA PITAKA and ABIDHAMMA PITAKA. (*See also* PITAKA)

Tiratana (P) / Tisatana (P) / Triratna (S)   *Buddhism*   The triple refuge in the Buddha, the DHAMMA and the SANGHA which is referred to as the three jewels and is the foundation of Buddhism. Swearing allegiance or faith in the three refuges marks the initiation into becoming a Buddhist. (*See also* SARANA; TISARANA)

Tirtha   *Hinduism*   The basic offering of water made to the temple deities and given out to the worshippers who have come to perform PUJA (ritual worship).

The water is sometimes taken from a holy river, and can be kept in the family shrine at home. The water of the River Ganges is considered to be especially sacred. Devout Hindus desire water from the Ganges to pass their lips at the moment of death. (*See also* PRASAD)

Tirtha *(a ford or a place to cross a river)* *Jainism*   Used to describe the crossing from this existence to the place of liberation (KEVALIN). This crossing is revealed to the Jain by the teachings and example of the TIRTHANKARAS. It is also sometimes used as a name for the Jain community. (*See also* SANGHA)

Tirtha-ksetras *Jainism*   A designated place of pilgrimage for DIGAMBARA Jains. (*See* YATRA)

Tirthankara *(a ford-maker)* *Jainism*   The title used for the twenty-four great spiritual teachers and liberated souls who are born throughout each half of a cycle of time and commit their lives to preaching the path to liberation. The first *tirthankara* of the present half-cycle was RISABHDEVA, while MAHAVIR, the founder of historical Jainism, was the last. The *tirthankaras* do not directly succeed each other and vast periods of time can pass without such a world teacher. The twentieth *tirthankara*, Munisuvrata, is said to have been a contemporary of RAMA, the Hindu AVATAR of VISHNU, whilst the twenty-second, NEMINATHA, is believed to have been a cousin of Krishna. The twenty-four *tirthankaras* of the current half-cycle of time are Risabhdeva, Ajita, Sambhava, Abhinandana, Sumati, Padmaprabha, Suparsva, Candraprabha, Suvidhi, Sitala, Sreyansa, Vasupujya, Vimala, Ananta, Dharma, Shanti, Kunthu, Ara, Malli, Munisuvrata, Naminatha, Neminatha, PARSHVANATHA and Mahavir. Jains do not worship God or gods but venerate the *tirthankaras* for their achievements, example and teachings. Images of the *tirthankaras* are present in most Jain temples and Jain pilgrimage places celebrate key events in their lives. (*See also* JINA)

Tiruvembavai *Hinduism*   A famous collection of Tamil hymns to the Goddess which form part of the Tiruvasagam (hymns to Shiva). The songs are sung during the festival to Minakshi, a south Indian form of the Goddess.

Tisarana (P) / Trisarana (S) *Buddhism*   A technical term for the 'Three Refuges' that refers to the actual vow made in the ceremony in which one formally agrees to become a Buddhist. It involves repeating 'I go to refuge in the Buddha, I go to refuge in the Dharma, I go to refuge in the Sangha' three times. (*See* BUDDHA; DHAMMA; SANGHA; SARANA; TIRATANA)

Tisatana (P) *Buddhism*   See TIRATANA.

Tishah B'Av *Judaism* A fast day held on the ninth day of Av (9 July–7 August) known as 'the black fast' as it commemorates the destruction of the Temple. The fast lasts from evening to evening and begins with a mourning meal of eggs and bread dipped in ashes. Leather shoes are removed until the fast is completed. The synagogue is dimly lit and the worship performed as if the congregation were in mourning. The book of Lamentations is read at the service. On the second day participants are not permitted to wash; the TORAH reading is taken from Deuteronomy, after which the congregation sing dirges until noon that recount all the tragedies that have befallen the Jewish people. With the rising of the moon and appearance of the stars, the fast ends. (*See also* BET HA MIKDASH)

Titus, St *Christianity* A trusted companion of St Paul and early church missionary who accompanied Paul and Barnabus to Jerusalem at the time of the Gentile controversy. He acted as a reconciler between Paul and the church in Corinth. He was in Crete with Paul and later church tradition describes how, in advanced old age, he was bishop of the island. (*See* PAUL, ST; TIMOTHY AND TITUS, STS, EPISTLES TO)

Tobit *Judaism* A central figure in a Jewish apocryphal book of the same name. (*See* APOCRYPHA)

Toladot *Judaism* The specific actions that are forbidden on the SHABBAT under the heading of each of the thirty-nine categories of labour known as AB.

Tona / Tuna *Hinduism* Magic practices of popular Hinduism used by villagers to cause pain or disaster to those they hold grudges against. It would be necessary to use exorcism carried out by a local expert to remove the spells. (*See* OJHA)

Tonsure *Christianity* The distinctive style of shaving the centre of the head traditionally associated with MONKS and FRIARS. Most orders now follow their own customs according to choice.

Torah *Judaism* The term used for the first five books of the Jewish scriptures which incorporate the law of God provided in the revelation given to Moses. The books are GENESIS, EXODUS, DEUTERONOMY, LEVITICUS and NUMBERS. However, the rabbis have written extensive commentaries and interpretations that include the concept of an oral TORAH that was passed on to Moses but not written down, in which God fully explained the written Torah. The term *Torah* is therefore enlarged to include the written Torah, the other books of the Jewish scriptures, the MISHNAH and the TALMUD. In other words, the full canopy of Jewish teaching, the complete picture of God's commandments as elaborated and understood through Jewish history. (*See also* SEFER TORAH)

Torah Kohanim   *Judaism*   See SIFRA.

Totka   *Hinduism*   Magic rituals carried out by a village priest in order to free a victim of possession by ghosts or the evil eye. (*See* BHUT; OJHA)

Tra-Mudra *(three symbols)*   *Sikhism*   Although GURU GOBIND SINGH created five Ks as symbols of the KHALSA brotherhood, KES (uncut hair), KACCHA (loose underwear) and the KIRPAN (sword) are known as the *tra-mudra*. (*See also* PANJ KAKKE)

Tractarianism   *Christianity*   The name given to the early development of the OXFORD MOVEMENT, so called because of their successful use of leaflets or tracts. From 1832 John Henry Newman (1801–90) began publishing his famous *Tracts for the Times*. Overall, ninety tracts were published by Newman and the other leaders of the Oxford Movement, Richard Froude (1803–36), John Keble (1792–1866) and Edward Pusey (1800–82). Increasingly the *Tracts* reflected doctrines and practices that were identified as primitive Christianity but were also popularly associated with Roman Catholicism. (*See also* HIGH CHURCH)

Tradition   *Christianity*   In the early church, tradition was used to describe the continuous revelation from God to His people through a succession of prophets and apostles. The challenge of GNOSTICISM led the early generations of Christian leaders to define tradition as the act of handing down a carefully preserved expression of the teachings contained in the canon of scripture, which ensures that the teachings of the church in any one generation or period of time is the same GOSPEL proclaimed from the time of the Apostles. Thus tradition now refers to the accumulated wisdom and experience of the church throughout its history. The Roman Catholic position has always been that tradition and scripture have equal authority, whereas Protestants focused on scripture alone. (*See also* APOSTOLIC SUCCESSION)

Transfiguration   *Christianity*   The term used to describe the event recorded by the Synoptic Gospel writers in which Jesus Christ appears as the Lord in full glory accompanied by the Jewish prophets Moses and Elijah, and witnessed by his three closest disciples, Peter, John and James (Matthew 17:1–8; Mark 9:2–8; Luke 9:28–36). They accompanied Jesus up to the summit of a mountain, where they witnessed his transformation; the Gospels record that a voice spoke from a cloud proclaiming Christ's Sonship and divine authority. The transfiguration functions to affirm Christ's divinity and demonstrates how he fulfils the revelation made earlier by God through the Jewish prophets. It also looks forward to the RESURRECTION and ASCENSION.

Transubstantiation   *Christianity*   The traditional doctrine associated with the Roman Catholic position that asserts that the elements of bread and wine used in the EUCHARIST are transformed into the body and blood of Jesus Christ at the time of CONSECRATION. The doctrine rests upon Thomas Aquinas's interpretation of Aristotle's distinction between accident and substance. The substance of a thing is its real nature, whereas its accidents are its outward appearances. Therefore, the doctrine of transubstantiation is able to posit that while the accidents of bread and wine remain the same, the substance is transformed by the Eucharistic rite. (*See also* CONSUBSTANTIATION)

Trappists   *Christianity*   A reform movement of the CISTERCIAN religious order founded in 1662 and properly known as the Cistercians of the Strict Observance. It is renowned for its austerity and silence.

Trasa *(mobile souls)*   *Jainism*   In the Jain categorization of living beings there are two kinds, mobile and immobile (STHAVARA). Mobile souls are those creatures with two or more senses. These include two-sense beings (touch and taste), such as worms and sea molluscs; three-sense beings (touch, taste, smell), such as ants and snails; four-sense beings (touch, taste, smell, sight), such as bees, butterflies, scorpions and most insects; five-sense beings (touch, taste, smell, sight, hearing), such as mammals, reptiles, birds, fish, amphibians. Five-sense beings are further classified: human beings, some animals and the occupants of celestial and hellish worlds are considered to be five-sense beings endowed with mind.

Trefa   *Judaism*   Food that is forbidden to Jews by their dietary laws and is not KOSHER.

Trent, Council of (1545–63)   *Christianity*   A council called by the Roman Catholic Church to counter the REFORMATION and develop a theological response to the challenge of Martin LUTHER. It also attempted to re-establish the church through a renewal of spiritual discipline and moral life. The reforming process conducted at the Council became known as the Counter-Reformation. The church clarified and reformed its position on JUSTIFICATION, SACRAMENTS, the relationship between scripture and TRADITION and reviewed the behaviour of clergy, ecclesiastical discipline, religious education and missionary activity.

Treta Yuga   *Hinduism*   The second of the four ages that form the cycle of one round of creation or one day of BRAHMA. Increasing deterioration characterizes these ages. However, the *treta* age is still relatively close to the original golden age and is marked by the prevalence of wisdom in human beings. Since human lifespan decreases by one-quarter in each age from an ideal of four hundred years, so in the Treta Yuga, human beings are believed to live for three hundred years. (*See also* YUGA)

Triguna *Hinduism*   The three GUNAS; SATTVA; RAJAS and TAMAS.

Trika *Hinduism*   A form of Tantric shaivism once common in Kashmir. It advocated a form of monism similar to the teachings of SHANKARA. Only a few Trika teachers remain alive today in Kashmir. (*See also* SHAIVITE; TANTRA)

Trikaya *Buddhism*   The Mahayana doctrine of the three bodies of the Buddha or aspects of Buddha nature. They are (i) the eternal teaching or essence; (ii) the historical Buddha; (iii) the transcendental Buddha. (*See* DHAMMAKAYA; NIRMAN-AKAYA; SAMBHOGAKAYA)

Triloka *(three worlds)* *Hinduism*   The Vedic division of the cosmos into three worlds: the worlds of the gods, the ancestors and, finally, human beings. Each is assigned eleven gods to look over them. All the worlds are part of SAMSARA, where the soul can be reborn. Although the lifespans of the gods, for example, might be vast, even they will eventually die and continue on the cycle of life until final release or liberation. (*See also* BRAHMAN; MUKTI)

Trimarga *Hinduism*   The three paths to liberation considered the main vehicles for Hindu spiritual practice. They are KARMA YOGA, JNANA YOGA and BHAKTI YOGA. (*See also* MARGA)

Trimurti *Hinduism*   The three principal deities, BRAHMA, VISHNU and SHIVA, who are said to control the three activities of creation, preservation and destruction which are inherent within the created cosmos. The visual form of the Trimurti is represented as three heads in one composite deity. Contemporary Hindus, having had contact with Christianity, sometimes refer to this triad god as a trinity, but the texts that describe the Trimurti as three aspects of one God are usually loyal to a particular tradition that only worships one of the deities. They are, therefore, attempts to indicate that their particular ISVARA (personal Lord) is superior to and incorporates the other two, rather than any effort to create systematic monotheism.

Trinitarian *Christianity*   The doctrine of the TRINITY, or a person who believes in the doctrine. The Trinitarian position is one of the main markers of Christian orthodoxy, although there are differences of doctrine between the Western and

Eastern churches. The basis of the doctrine resides in the belief that the three aspects of the Trinity should be regarded as possessing equal divinity and equal status. The co-equality of the Father and the Son was established at the Council of Nicaea. The Eastern churches have focused attention on the relationship by considering how the three aspects may be experienced in the life of a Christian. The Western position is more theological. (*See also* BINITARIANISM; UNITARIANISM)

Trinity   *Christianity*   The doctrine maintained by all mainstream forms of Christianity in which there are three persons within the Godhead – Father, Son and HOLY SPIRIT. All three are equally divine and have the same status. Two distinctive positions were to develop in regard to understanding the Trinity. The Eastern Church focused on considering the different ways in which the Father, Son and Holy Spirit were experienced, emphasizing the function of each independent aspect of the Godhead. The Western Church focused on the unity of the Godhead and perceived the Trinity as relational. The original development of the doctrine arose out of early Christian debate concerning the divinity of Jesus Christ. This growing belief in Christ's divinity necessitated understanding his relationship to the creator God. At a later date the concept of unity was extended to include the Holy Spirit. (*See also* CHRISTOLOGY; FILIOQUE; HOMOIOUSIOS; NICAEA, COUNCIL OF; TRINITARIAN; UNITARIANISM)

Trinity Sunday   *Christianity*   One of the holy days marked out in the Christian liturgical calendar. It marks the transition between the first six months, known as the half-year of Christ, and the second six months, known as the half-year of the church. It is celebrated on the first Sunday after Pentecost or Whitsun and is dedicated to the TRINITY. (*See also* TRINITARIAN)

Tripikaya   *Buddhism*   A MAHAYANA term used to refer to the three forms of the Buddha: NIRMANAKAYA, the inner Buddha or personification of the DHAMMA shared in by all living beings; DHAMMAKAYA, the physical manifestation of the historical Buddha; and SAMBHOGAKAYA, the subtle body of bliss.

Tripitaka (S)   *Buddhism*   *See* TIPITAKA.

Triratna (S)   *Buddhism*   *See* TIRATANA.

Trisarana (S)   *Buddhism*   *See* TISARANA.

Trishna (S)   *Buddhism*   *See* SAMUDAYA.

Trividya *(three knowledges)* *Hinduism* The knowledge contained in the three VEDAS.

Tukaram (1598–1649) *Hinduism* One of the four great saints deemed to have died without leaving their physical bodies on earth. The others were KABIR, MIRABAI and CAITANYA. Tukaram was a seventeenth-century VAISHNAVA poet-saint from the state of Maharashtra. While the saint did not begin a SAMPRADAYA, or movement, today there is a lay group known as the Varkaris who claim to be descendants of his original followers. Images of Tukaram are found in many Hindu temples in Britain, especially those established by East African migrants of Gujarati origin. (*See also* BHAKTI; SANT)

Tulasi / Tulsi *Hinduism* A variety of basil tree which is sacred to the devotees of VISHNU or those follow the VAISHNAVA tradition of BHAKTI (devotion). The plant is a symbol of Vishnu and the wood is often used to make the prayer-beads used by Vaishnavas to count the names of God whilst chanting.

Tulku (T) *(emanation)* *Buddhism* A term used in several ways by Tibetan Buddhism: (i) a reincarnated Lama who is found by a rigorous process of recognition as a small child and raised to fulfil the function he/she was believed to have performed in the last life; (ii) the appearance in the world of a Buddha who has refused NIRVANA in order to assist suffering beings; (iii) the use of a human body by a spiritual power. (*See also* BODHISATTVA; DALAI LAMA; NIRMAN-AKAYA; PANCHEN LAMA)

Tulsidas (1532–1623) *Hinduism* The most influential of the medieval saints of the north Indian BHAKTI tradition. He was a devotee of Rama and rewrote the RAMAYANA in Hindi so that the common people would have access to the tale. His version is different to VALMIKI's, in that it incorporates the teaching of the *bhakti* tradition. Known as the RAMACHARITAMANASA, it is widely read and loved in north India. Tulsidas taught and wrote in the cities of Ayodhya and Varanasi, where there is a temple dedicated to him that has the complete *Ramacharitaman-asa* written on its walls.

Tumah *Judaism* The condition of impurity of a dead Jewish body that makes it unclean for those who touch it or live in the same house where the body is kept. In Orthodox Jewry, a member of the Kohen (hereditary descendants of the temple priesthood) may not attend the cemetery or be a member of the HEVRAH KADISHAH, the professional body that takes care of the dead and dying. (*See also* TAHARAH)

Tuna *Hinduism* See TONA.

Turiya   *Hinduism*   The fourth state of consciousness identified by the Upani-shads. All conscious living beings are believed to experience the three states of waking consciousness, dreaming and deep sleep. Only enlightened humans such as YOGIS can experience the fourth state of being. *Turiya* occurs when conscious-ness becomes completely absorbed in itself rather than the objects of the senses or the movements of the mind. This state is achieved by deep meditation combined with a virtuous life. *Turiya* is indescribable, but is experienced as complete freedom, peace and joy arising from awareness of the self alone. (*See also* MUKTI; SAMADHI; SATCHITANANDA)

Tyaga   *Hinduism*   Originally associated with the Vedic sacrifice, it referred to the importance of the sacrificer relinquishing attachment to the object being sacrificed. As the renunciate ascetic traditions developed in Hinduism, *tyaga* became associated with being detached from the world or living a renunciate's life. However, it is possible to practise *tyaga* as a lay Hindu by detaching oneself from the idea of ownership and remaining dispassionate when confronted with worldly success or adversity. (*See* TAG; KARMA MARGA)

Tzedak   *Judaism*   A just or righteous person who loves God and his TORAH and practises good deeds. According to Judaism, the aspiration to be a *tzedak* should be the goal of all Jews. (*See also* TZEDAKAH)

Tzedakah   *Judaism*   The striving to be a righteous person by acquiring such virtues as truthfulness, uprightness, piety, honesty and justice. The most effective way to practise *tzedakah* would be to obey the TORAH through a single-minded love of God. In popular usage the term refers to an act of charity. Jews are famous for their charitable acts, but they should be performed with joyfulness and with respect for the recipient. (*See also* TZEDAK)

Tzizit / Tzittzit   *Judaism*   See ZIZIT.

Tzom Gedaliah   *Judaism*   The day that follows ROSH HASHANAH and is used as a fast to commemorate Gedaliah, a pious Jew murdered by his fellow Jews after being appointed governor of Judah by the Babylonians. The fast is used to reinforce the ethical teaching that one should not blame others for one's own misfortunes, but instead use them as an occasion to examine oneself.

Udasis *(solitary ones)* *Sikhism*   The first breakaway sect in Sikhism came about from a difference over the succession of spiritual authority from GURU NANAK. Sri Chand, the elder son of Guru Nanak, was accepted as Guru by some of his father's followers instead of GURU ANGAD DEV. Embracing a life of renunciation, they therefore became known as Udasis. They continue to be an ascetic order that gives special reverence to the ADI GRANTH and Guru Nanak. The rituals of worship conform to the usual temple practices of Hinduism such as ARTI. During the eighteenth century, Udasis gained control of HARMANDIR in Amritsar and many of the historical GURDWARAS of Sikhism. This situation continued until the passing of the Gurdwara Act by the British gave control back to the KHALSA.

Uddista tyaga pratima *Jainism*   The eleventh or final stage undertaken by the lay Jain on the path to liberation. At this stage the lay Jain renounces all food and lodging prepared for him/her by the family and leaves home to live in a temple or special accommodation prepared for renunciates. (*See also* ANUMATI TYAGA PRATIMA; ARAMBHA SAMARAMBA TYAGA PRATIMA; BRAHMACARYA PRATIMA; DARSHANA PRATIMA; PARIGRAHA TYAGA PRATIMA; PRATIMA; PROSADHO-PAVASA PRATIMA; RATRI BHOJANA TYAGA PRATIMA; SACCITTA TYAGA PRATIMA; SAMAYIKA PRATIMA; VRATA PRATIMA)

Udgatri *Hinduism*   A priest who sang the sacred formulas from the VEDAS at the fire sacrifice ritual. (*See also* HAVAN; RIG VEDA)

Udgitha *Hinduism*   An ancient Vedic term for the sacred MANTRA 'AUM' as sung by the UDGATRI BRAHMIN.

Uhud *Islam*   A famous battle fought in 625 by Muhammad and the first Muslims of MAKKAH and MADINAH against their opponents in Makkah. The battle came after the famous victory at BADR, but the outcome almost went against the Muslims. It was attributed to a lack of discipline, and the Qur'an rebuked the Muslims for loss of faith and declared that their near defeat was a chastisement from God. The battle of Uhud seriously challenged the doctrine of Manifest Success confirmed at Badr. In a sense the two battles set the pattern of Muslim history. Worldly or political success is seen as a sign of Allah's favour, while failure is explained as a loss of faith arising in divine displeasure. Consequently Muslims have responded to political decline with religious revival.

Ulama / Ulema *Islam* Religious scholars of Islamic law and jurisprudence who have graduated from a MADRASA. In the first centuries of Islam, the *ulama* created and controlled the system of education and developed the curricula to realize their own spiritual and intellectual goals. Through this they were successful in bringing a stability and cohesion to the community, reinforced by dogmatic theology and an all-embracing legal system. In recent history, however, the *ulama* have been blamed for stifling creativity and holding to a medieval mindset that has blocked the development of the Muslim world. Many of the new revivalist movements in Islam, with their powerful political agendas, are anti-*ulama*. (*See also* FIQH; IKHWAN, SHARI'A; JAMAAT-I ISLAMI)

Uma *Hinduism* One of the principal names of the Goddess and consort of SHIVA. As Uma she lives in the mountains, especially the Himalayas, where she is the daughter of Himachal, the king of the Himalayas. TULSIDAS recounts the legend of how Shiva awoke from thousands of years of deep meditation in order to meet Uma and marry her. She is considered in his account to be a later reincarnation of PARVATI, who seeks to be reunited with her Lord. This story may be an attempt to resolve the various consorts of Shiva into one single entity.

Umam *Islam* Plural of UMMA.

Umar ibn ul-Khattab *Islam* The second caliph of Islam from 634 to 644 and known as one of the four righteously guided caliphs and a father-in-law of Muhammad. During Umar's rule, the Arabs significantly expanded outwards and conquered Jerusalem. The new territories were administered effectively and the tax system helped create the wealth that provided for the extensive expansion at the time of the UMAYYADS. Muslims regard Umar as a man of great piety as well as an able ruler, and countless stories are told of his wisdom and humility. (*See also* ABU BAKR; AL-KHALIFA-UR-RASHIDUN; ALI; UTHMAN)

Umayyad / Ummayad *Islam* First Arab Muslim dynasty founded in 661 after the death of the fourth righteously guided caliph, ALI. The Umayyad dynasty was founded by MU'AWIYAH, who moved the capital of the new Arab empire from MADINAH to his own stronghold in Damascus. There are questions concerning the Umayyad's conviction towards Islam. While they maintained the caliphal form of rule and accepted the SHARI'A law as the basis of the constitution, most of the caliphs lived in moral laxity and the Arab state was used as a foundation for the pursuit of personal power. The religious leadership in Madinah remained deeply dissatisfied with the condition of the empire and focused on personal piety and the study of religious sciences such as the HADITH and law. The Umayyad dynasty was superseded by the ABBASIDS in 750. (*See also* KHARIJITE; SHI'A)

Umm al-Kitab *Islam* The primordial prototype of the QUR'AN that pre-existed the revelation to Muhammad. In early Muslim history, various groups disputed whether the Qur'an was eternal. It was eventually decided that the Qur'an must have pre-existed with Allah, as it was the prototype of revelation and the ultimate form of God's word.

Umma / Ummah *(plural umam)* *Islam* The universal community of Muslims that incorporates the totality of all who profess the faith regardless of nationality, ethnicity, class or gender. It is the only community to which a Muslim belongs simply by virtue of being a Muslim. The ideal of the *umma* is of a community bound together in the beliefs and practices of Islam to worship Allah through submission to the revelation conveyed to humanity through the Prophet Muhammad. The purpose of the *umma* is to act as a witness for Allah through the example of obedient worship and the relation of one member to another. It represents the ideal organization responsible for upholding the true faith and instructing humanity in the revealed way of God as contained in the Qur'an and the SUNNA of the Prophet. Despite the ideal held by many Muslims of a single, divinely revealed and united Islam, there have been, and continue to be, diverse interpretations of the religion and considerable challenges from nationalism, ethnicity and secularism. It is debatable whether the ideal of the *umma* has ever actually existed in reality after Muhammad's death except as a powerful symbol of cohesion. (*See also* KITAB; RASUL; SHARI'A)

Ummah Wusta *Islam* The ideal or model Muslim community that according to the Qur'an replaces the Jewish and Christian communities that had lost their way and corrupted their revelations. Throughout Muslim history various religious factions would declare themselves as the model Muslim community within the wider context of Muslim society. (*See* AHL AL-KITAB; JAMAAT; UMMA)

Ummayad *Islam* See UMAYYAD.

Ummi *(unlettered)* *Islam* The important doctrine that Muhammad was not able to read or write. Although some Western orientalists have challenged the idea that a merchant would have been illiterate, the belief is important to

Muslims, as it supports the idea that Muhammad could not have been the author of the QUR'AN and assists in proclaiming the miracle of the book as the literal word of Allah.

Umrah   *Islam*   The lesser pilgrimage to MAKKAH which Muslims can perform at any time of the year, as opposed to the HAJJ, which must be performed in the correct month.

Unbhav Nagar *(the city without fear)*   *Sikhism*   The realm of truth or the court of God, where the surrendered servants of the divine remain for ever in God's presence. It is not a location but a state of eternal bliss. (*See* SAC KHAND; VAIKUNTH)

Unction   *Christianity*   One of the seven SACRAMENTS observed by Roman Catholicism and Eastern Orthodoxy in which a sick or dying person is anointed with oil by a priest. While Roman Catholics generally perform the sacrament when it is believed that there is no hope of recovery, in Eastern Orthodoxy it is used for healing. Anointing with oil is also used in Britain to bless the monarch at a coronation ceremony.

Unitarianism   *Christianity*   A type of Christian thought and religious practice that rejects the doctrine of the Trinity and the divinity of Jesus Christ. The first organized communities appeared in the sixteenth century in Poland, Hungary and England. The first Unitarian denomination was founded in Britain in 1773 as a breakaway from the Church of England. In the USA, Unitarianism dates back to the late eighteenth century. Contemporary Unitarianism is divided between those who follow traditional non-conformist Protestant Christianity but reject Trinitarianism as non-biblical and those who espouse a pluralist position drawing upon inspiration from many of the world's religious and spiritual figures. (*See* REFORMATION; TRINITARIAN)

United Reformed Church   *Christianity*   A Protestant denomination formed in Britain by the union of CONGREGATIONALISTS and English PRESBYTERIANS in 1972.

Universalism   *Christianity*   The theological position that all people will eventually achieve salvation regardless of whether they have accepted the Christian proclamation of redemption through Jesus Christ. This position arises from the belief that a God of Love could not allow evil to triumph. The earliest exponent was ORIGEN, one of the early Church fathers.

Upadana   *Buddhism*   The ninth NIDANA or link in the causal chain of existence which maintains the wheel of SAMSARA. Referring to attachment or clinging to life, it depends on SAMUDAYA and gives rise to BHAVA.

Upadesha *Hinduism* A rite of the initiation of a disciple into a religious order or sect under the direction of a guru. Usually it refers to some kind of religious or spiritual instruction rather than the ritual aspects of initiation. (*See* SAMPRADAYA)

Upadihyaya *Jainism* A title given to a Jain monk responsible for organizing education and who teaches scripture to other monks. (*See* ACARYA; SADHU)

Upanayana *Hinduism* One of the most important of the Hindu life-cycle rituals (SAMSKARAS) that takes place traditionally during the eighth year of a BRAHMIN boy, the eleventh of a KSHATRIYA and the twelfth of a VAISHYA. It is the ceremony that marks the investing of the sacred thread to the members of the three 'twice-born' VARNAS and the beginning of the life-stage when the child becomes responsible for his own actions and can be punished for infringements of DHARMA. Traditionally it also marked the beginning of the stage when learning began at the feet of the GURU, but today very few Hindu boys will leave home or change schools. However, it is still a significant ceremony, as it represents the first occasion when the Hindu child can take part in a religious ceremony in his own right.

Upangas *(extra limbs)* *Jainism* The twelve scriptures that make up the secondary canon of Jain scriptures. They elaborate on the teachings of the TIRTHANKARAS and were written by ascetics in the later periods of Jain history. Supplementing the primary canon, they deal with such subjects as astrology, cosmology, biology and history. The twelve books are: Aupapatika Sutra, Raja-prasniya, Jivabhigama Sutra, Prajnapana Sutra, Surya Prajnapti, Jambudvipa Prajnapti, Candra Prajnapti, Nirayavalika, Kalpavatamsika, Puspika, Puspaculika and Vrisnidasa. (*See also* AGAMA – JAINISM; ANGAS)

Upanishads / Upanisads *('to sit near')* *Hinduism* An important collection of 108 scriptures which reflect on the inner teachings of the VEDAS and were probably written somewhere between 800 and 400 BCE. The early Upanishads are considered to be part of the SHRUTI or Vedic canon, and are known as VEDANTA or the culmination of the Vedas, in that they deal with speculative philosophical issues concerning the relationship between ATMAN and BRAHMAN and the way to achieve final release from suffering caused by the chains of bondage to SAMSARA. They are written in the form of a discourse between an enlightened guru and a disciple often tracing their lineage back to family traditions that were important in the maintenance of Vedic ritual. Although the Upanishads could be described as mystical in their content, they also contain many references to the Vedic ritual tradition. The main Upanishads have been, and remain, extremely influential and provide the basis of the various forms of Vedanta philosophy; however, they are respected as Vedic literature by most variations of Hinduism. (*See also* BRHAD-ARANYAKA; CHANDOGYA; KATHA; SVETASVATARA; TAITTIRIYA)

Upasaka (m) / Upasika (f)   *Buddhism*   Buddhists who maintain the five precepts at all times whilst living in the world rather than retiring to a monastery or convent. (*See* PANCASILA)

Upasakadasa   *Jainism*   The seventh book of the twelve primary canons of Jain scripture which deals with the deeds of pious lay Jains and recounts tales of their heroism in defeating evil. (*See* AGAMA – JAINISM; ANGAS)

Upavedas   *Hinduism*   Supplementary texts to the VEDAS that deal with non-religious knowledge such as the Arthaveda, the science of statecraft; GANDHARVA VEDA, the science of music and the arts; Dharusveda, the art of archery and warfare; and the AYURVEDA, the science of medicine.

Upaya *(skilful means)*   *Buddhism*   In Mahayana Buddhism it refers to a practical means used to achieve a spiritual goal. However, once the goal has been achieved, the means should be put aside to avoid attachment. It is sometimes used to refer to any meditation on loving awareness that is employed to overcome anger. (*See* ANUPREKSAS)

Upayoga   *Jainism*   Conscious activity that will lead towards liberation. It is one of the basic characteristics of the soul that begins to manifest increasingly as karmic influx is stopped. All living creatures possess conscious activity to some degree, and it can never be completely obliterated by KARMA. It manifests itself as knowledge and perception and provides the door through which the individual can turn towards the path to liberation. (*See also* CETANA; DARSHANA; JNANA; KEVALAJNANA)

Upekkha (P) / Upeksa (S)   *Buddhism*   The BRAHMA VIHARA of equanimity or complete evenness of mind in the face of all the diversity of experience.

Uposatha   *Buddhism*   Certain days of the month that are based on the lunar cycle. From early times they were recognized by the SANGHA (community of monks) as a time to participate in special events like expounding or listening to the DHAMMA or maintaining fasts. Most Buddhist countries still uphold them and they are utilized by monks for fasting or public confession.

Urf *Islam*   Customary law or known practices of a society that are recognized by all the schools of Islamic law as long as they do not contradict the *Qur'an* or the SUNNA of the Prophet. If a contradiction does arise, then Islamic law prevails and the Muslims of that society are forbidden to follow the practices. The ability to combine SHARI'A with *urf* has given Muslim society a great deal of flexibility as it has moved around the world through conquest or migration.

Urs *(wedding)* *Islam*   An anniversary of a WALI's death which is regarded as celebrating their union with God. All Sufi TARIQAHS will maintain an *urs* to the founder of their order and it will feature as one of the main celebrations of the liturgical year. Some *urs* celebrations in the Indian subcontinent can attract millions of pilgrims to the saint's shrine. (*See also* DAR; MAZAR)

Uswa hasana *(the beautiful model)* *Islam*   The description of Muhammad as the ideal embodiment of the Qur'anic revelation and the exemplar for all Muslims to follow. The Qur'an states: *to obey him is to obey God* (4:80). For this reason the SUNNA of the Prophet sits next to the Qur'an as a source of inspiration and direction for Muslims. (*See also* ADAB)

Uthman *Islam*   The third caliph of Islam from 644 to 656 and known as one of the four righteously guided caliphs and a companion of Muhammad. Uthman compiled the authoritative version of the QUR'AN and ordered the destruction of alternative versions. Uthman was an old man by the time he inherited the caliphate, and it is debatable whether he had the ability to rule the expanding empire with the expertise of ABU BAKR and UMAR. Charges of nepotism were widespread. In June 656 he was assassinated by the son of Abu Bakr and a group of insurgents who had been part of an uprising supported by the followers of ALI. Thus Uthman became the first of the caliphs to die at the hands of Muslims.

Utsarga samiti *(carefulness in calls of nature)* *Jainism*   One of the five 'carefulnesses' or precautions undertaken by Jain ascetics to prevent accidental harm to living creatures. It refers to controlled codes of behaviour when defecating or urinating that limit damage to small organisms or insects. (*See* SAMITI)

Utsarpini *Jainism*   Jain cosmology divides time into cycles that consist of several epochs. Every cycle is divided into two halves, each marked by the advent of a TIRTHANKARA. The *utsarpini* is the ascending half-cycle characterized by an increase in spirituality. The round of cycles is endless, as creation is regarded as eternal. (*See also* AVARSARPINI)

Uttara Mimansa *Hinduism* The name given to the various forms of VEDANTA as opposed to the ritualistic Purva Mimansa. (*See also* MIMANSA)

Uttradhyayana Sutra *Jainism* The final sermon of MAHAVIR, the historical founder of Jainism, given over a non-stop period of thirty-six hours prior to his death. The scripture that reproduces this sermon contains the fundamentals of Mahavir's teachings.

Vaak *Sikhism*   See VAK.

Vac *Hinduism*   The Hindu concept of sacred speech or the correct utterance of the sacred word. The Vedic sacrifice was accompanied by the repetition of verses from either the RIG VEDA or YAJUR VEDA. Without correct pronunciation and rhythm of the appropriate words, the sacrifice would be deemed invalid. The vibrations of the sacred words connected the human to the divine. The idea of divine speech is picked up again in the BHAKTI or devotional tradition, where the discourses or poetry of a BHAKTA master were considered to be SATSANG (company of truth). The words had a power beyond their message and were capable of connecting the listeners to the experience of the divine. (*See also* VEDAS; YAJNA)

Vahana *Hinduism*   The vehicle or mount of Hindu deities often worshipped as minor gods in their own right. Famous *vahana* are NANDI, the bull of Shiva; the rat that is ridden by GANESH; and GARUDA, the king of the birds who is ridden by Vishnu.

Vaikunth / Baikunth *Sikhism*   The term used in Sikhism to connote heaven or paradise. It is not perceived as a place but rather a state of being in which the devotee achieves perfect peace and tranquillity. The company of the holy or the SADHSANGAT is often described as Vaikunth. (*See also* SAC KHAND; UNBHAV NAGAR)

Vaikuntha *Hinduism*   The heavenly realm of VISHNU, where he eternally resides seated upon SESA, the thousand-headed snake. According to RAMANUJA and other Vaishnavites, the liberated souls of devotees live there, eternally experiencing the DARSHAN of their Lord. It is, however, common for Hindus to believe that their chosen ISVARA (personal god) dwells in his own heaven, where those who are committed to virtue and remembrance of the deity's name will also reside. (*See also* VAISHNAVA)

Vairagya *Hinduism*   The quality of dispassion that leads to renunciation. It is the experience of detachment from worldly pleasures that leads to outer renunciation and to some Hindus adopting SANNYASIN (renunciate) lifestyles. However, the quality of dispassion is valued highly in lay Hindus as a sign of spiritual progress and leads to inner detachment or renunciation. Some Hindu movements believe that the only true renunciation is inner as opposed to outer.

Vairagya *Jainism*   Aversion to the world that arises from understanding its true nature and the real condition of all living beings. Such aversion leads to renunciation but it should not be as a reaction to emotional crises. Thus, in Jainism, novice monks are checked for their motivations. A genuine longing for liberation and freedom from the bondage of KARMA coupled with an understanding of AHIMSA would be perceived as real *vairagya*. (*See also* KEVALAJNANA; SADHU)

Vaisakha (S) *Buddhism*   See WESAK.

Vaisakhi *Sikhism*   See BAISAKHI.

Vaiseshika *Hinduism*   One of the six orthodox schools of philosophy whose origins are attributed to Kanada in the third century BCE. Its two most important texts are the Vaiseshika Sutras, possibly written by Kanada himself, and the later text, the Dasapadartha Sastra, probably written around the sixth century CE. The Vaiseshika and the NYAYA schools are increasingly fuelling scholars' interest, as they show the formation of early Indian attempts to systematize and develop logic. In this sense, the Vaiseshika is more traditionally a school of philosophy, as understood in Western terms, than the other DARSHAN SHASTRAS (right views). Salvation is explained as a cognitive process of the recognition of reality rather than intuitive or experiential. Vaiseshika taught that the elements are composed of atoms or infinitely small indivisible parts, and acknowledges the division of the cosmos into the eternal constant and the eternally changeable. The former consists of earth, fire, water, air, ether, time, space and mind and various volitions and qualities. The existence of the ATMAN is inferred from various vital signs, such as breathing, love of life and animation.

Vaishnava / Vaisnava *Hinduism*   A Hindu who is devoted to VISHNU or one of his AVATARS (incarnations). Vaishnavism, in all its forms, constitutes one of the three major divisions in Hindu worship along with the SHAIVITE and Goddess traditions. Vaishnavism is one of the great traditions of Hindu theism and has been popularly promoted through the two epics, the MAHABHARATA and the RAMAYANA, and also the ecstatic devotional activities of countless saints, particularly of the medieval period, who utilized the human forms of Vishnu as their personal focus on the divine. In this way, Vaishnavite traditions have been influential in promoting Hinduism as a religion that worships one God in many forms. Through the activities of these countless saints and their followers, Vaishnavism is divided into countless sects that maintain a variety of belief and practice, but the tradition has been given a coherent theology through the work of figures such as RAMANUJA and MADHVA, who link Vaishnavism to schools of VEDANTA. (*See also* BHAKTI; KRISHNA)

Vaishya / Vaisya   *Hinduism*   The third of the four VARNAS which is traditionally made up of farmers and merchants. They are the last of the three 'twice-born' classes, and in Vedic literature are given the duties of protecting cattle, cultivation of land, trade, commerce and performing sacrifice. They are, therefore, the managers and implementers of the economic system and provide the support for the society so that DHARMA can be maintained. In the VEDAS, it is stated that they are born from the thighs of the cosmic person (PURUSHA). (*See also* DVIJA)

Vaiyavitra *(service)*   *Jainism*   Performing service in the form of good works, charity or freely given assistance to those who are worthy of being a recipient. This could be the poor or needy, or people respected for their spiritual or religious life. It is considered one of the six internal austerities. (*See* TAPAS)

Vajja (P) / Vrajya (S)   *Buddhism*   Actions that produce bad results and which should therefore be avoided in order to prevent the possibility of undesirable rebirth. (*See* KARMA SAMSARA)

Vajrayana *(Diamond Vehicle)*   *Buddhism*   A distinct esoteric teaching that originated between the third and seventh centuries in India and Tibet. It is more commonly known as TANTRA. The name derives from the deity Vajrayana (the adamantine vehicle) who utilizes the symbol of the thunderbolt, the weapon used by the Indian god INDRA. The tradition is heavily dependent on the use of mantra and borrows extensively from SHAIVITE traditions in which sexual union is the paradigm for spiritual union. Emptiness and bliss in union and loss of self become the practitioner's goal. (*See also* SIDDHA)

Vak / Vaak   *Sikhism*   *See* HUKAM.

Valentine, St   *Christianity*   St Valentine's Day (14 February) was originally associated with a Christian martyr of that name. The association with romantic love probably derives from a seasonal pagan festival held in February.

Vallabha (1481–1533) *Hinduism*   A Hindu reformer and Vaishnavite who taught the monistic doctrine of identity between ATMAN and BRAHMAN in order to advocate the supremacy of KRISHNA, whom he perceived as the personification of Brahman. Vallabha advocated lay life as the ideal vehicle for worshipping God and was opposed to renunciation. As with many of medieval BHAKTAS, he was opposed to caste or gender restriction in the worship of God. He founded the PUSHTI MARGA, which he regarded as superior to the other paths to the divine such as the traditional schools of KARMA, JNANA or BHAKTI. *Pushti* refers to the grace of the divine that is given to the devotee as a gift but cannot be influenced by any action that the devotee carries out.

Valmiki *Hinduism*   The author of the original Sanskrit version of the RAMAYANA. According to legend, Valmiki began his life as a brigand but was transformed by a meeting with a forest sage who became his GURU. He performed penance and meditation in order to seek forgiveness for his earlier crimes. Whilst in unbroken meditation, during which ants built their hill over his body, the story of RAMA in Sanskrit poetic form was revealed to him.

Vamana *Hinduism*   The fourth AVATAR (manifestation) of VISHNU as a dwarf. The story states that Bali, the ruler of the earth, offered a sacrifice to which hundreds of lesser kings and rulers were invited. Each was offered a boon as custom dictated. Vishnu manifested as the dwarf, Vamana, and asked to be given an area of land that he could cover in three steps. The king agreed. The dwarf grew to a huge size and covered the earth in one step and the cosmos with his second, which left nowhere for his third. The king offered his head for Vamana's third step and acknowledged the supremacy of Vishnu as the Lord of the Universe. One of the principal PURANAS is named the Vamana Purana.

Vanaprastha *Hinduism*   The third of the four stages of life that compose VARNASHRAMDHARMA and should be ideally followed by the 'twice-born' VARNAS. It literally means 'forest-dweller' and it indicates a withdrawal from the duties of the world prior to complete renunciation in preparation for death. Ancient Hindu literature mentions that elderly couples would set up a new home on the outskirts of a village and dedicate their activities to the pursuit of MOKSHA (liberation). In modern India, very few follow the custom literally, but many elderly couples try to develop a lifestyle that allows more time for the worship of God once their children have attained adulthood. (*See also* ASHRAMA)

Vanaprasthi *(a forest-dweller)* *Hinduism*   The term denotes someone in the third stage of life. (*See* VANAPRASTHA)

Vand chhakna *(charity)* *Sikhism*   The sharing of time, money and resources with the poor or less fortunate is part of the central teachings of GURU NANAK, the founder of Sikhism. Sikhs who undertake the initiation into the KHALSA brotherhood promise to donate 10 per cent of their income to either religious or charitable causes.

Varaha *Hinduism*   The fourth AVATAR of VISHNU, who manifested as a giant boar to lift the earth from the universal flood waters and thus save it from destruction.

Varanasi *Buddhism*   Although the most sacred of the Hindu pilgrimage cities, Varanasi is also famous for the delivery of the first sermon of the Buddha after he attained enlightenment, in which he spoke of the four noble truths and the noble eightfold path. The city still contains the deerpark of Sarnath, a Buddhist pilgrimage centre said to be the site of the sermon and one of the locations for an offshoot of the BODHI TREE.

Varanasi *Hinduism*   A city on the banks of the GANGA (Ganges) River, also known as Kashi or Benares. It is one of the holiest of pilgrimage sites and an ancient seat of learning. The university is one of the oldest in the world and still trains BRAHMIN priests. The city is sacred to SHIVA and it is believed that he roams the streets at night looking for the souls of those about to die so that he may liberate them. As a consequence, many Hindus come to Varanasi believing that to die in the city ensures liberation. Two of the GHATS that lead down to the river are used for funerals and it is said that the pyres have not ceased to burn for thousands of years. The city's riverfront is one of the most distinctive sights in the world, where thousands of pilgrims bathe and perform religious rites in front of ancient palaces and temples.

Varna *(colour)* *Hinduism*   The four classes or principal divisions of Hindu society: namely, BRAHMIN, KSHATRIYA, VAISHYA and SHUDRA. The first three are denoted 'twice-born' and may take part in the sacred thread ceremony (UPAN-AYANA). Many Hindus believe that the varnas were established at the creation of the world and are therefore immutable. This ideal of the varnas is supported by the fourfold division of the cosmic man (PURUSHA) described in the RIG VEDA. Others believe that they denote natural divisions of labour according to archetypal human character. This opens up a debate on whether one is a member of a varna by birth or quality. Most Hindus retain the idea of membership by birth and do not marry out of varna. It should not be confused with caste or JATI, which refers to numerous subdivisions within each of the four varnas. (*See also* VARNASHRAMDHARMA)

Varnashrama *Hinduism*　The four VARNAS and the four stages of life that should ideally be followed throughout the life of a Hindu born into one of the three 'twice-born' varnas. (*See also* VARNASHRAMDHARMA)

Varnashramdharma *Hinduism*　The ancient Vedic system believed to be divinely ordained, whereby society is divided into four VARNAS (BRAHMIN, KSHATRIYA, VAISHYA, SHUDRA) and four stages of life or ASHRAMAS (BRAHMA-CHARYA, GRIHASTHA, VANAPRASTHA and SANNYASIN), where each has specific duties to be performed. (*See also* DHARMA)

Varsha Pratipada *(the day of creation)* *Hinduism*　Usually celebrated as New Year's Day in Hindu India.

Varuna *Hinduism*　An important deity in early ARYAN civilization. Mentioned in the VEDAS as the god responsible for physical and moral order (RTA), he is also the sky god and the king of the universe. In the RIG VEDA he is next in importance after INDRA and AGNI, but he is rarely mentioned in modern Hinduism except in parts of the Vedic sacrifice performed by BRAHMINS at rites of passage. It is argued by some scholars that Varuna was superseded by VISHNU.

Vasudeva *Hinduism*　One of the names of VISHNU particularly associated with KRISHNA, who is often called Vasudeva Krishna. Vasudeva is filled with the six divine qualities: knowledge, strength, lordship, heroism, power and splendour.

Vatican *Christianity*　A self-governing state or Apostolic See situated in the city of Rome which functions as the residence of the POPE and the administrative centre of the Roman Catholic Church.

Vatican Council I (1869–70) *Christianity*　An important council, as it tackled the question of the POPE's authority and declared INFALLIBILITY to be a tenet of the Catholic faith. It clearly maintained the principle of infallibility but only on the occasions when the Pope is defining doctrine on a matter of faith or morality. However, it was considered a defeat by church liberals who wanted to maintain authority in the Council of Bishops.

Vatican Council II (1962–5) *Christianity*　The famous reforming council held by Pope John XXIII, and otherwise known as the Twenty-First Ecumenical Council, was called to modernize the teachings, discipline, liturgy and organ-ization of the church with a view to the eventual unity of all denominations, or, at least, closer cooperation with the ecumenical movement. The main changes were the use of the vernacular instead of Latin in the Mass, greater participation of the laity, an acknowledgement of modern biblical scholarship and increased participation in ECUMENISM.

Vayu *Hinduism*   The Vedic god of the wind sometimes associated with INDRA and also known as the god of the spirit. According to the RIG VEDA, he was born from the breath of the cosmic sacrifice of the primal being. (*See also* MADHVA)

Veda *(knowledge)* *Hinduism*   The earliest body of scriptures written somewhere between 1500 and 800 BCE but passed down as an oral tradition. The Vedas are believed to have been revealed to fully enlightened sages known as RISHIS and consist of the following texts, which are all regarded as SHRUTI: Rig Veda, which mostly contains hymns to gods associated with the sacrifice and cosmic order; Yajur Veda, which contains MANTRAS and ritual formulas for use in the sacrifice; Sama Veda, which contains chanting instructions for the sacrifice; and the Atharva Veda, which contains practices of popular folk Hinduism such as spells and exorcism of spirits. There are three other categories of text that are considered to belong to the Vedic canon: BRAHMANAS, which contain commentaries written upon the four Vedas by priests; ARANYAKAS, which contain secret or mystical interpretations of the Vedic rituals; and UPANISHADS, which contain speculative interpretation concerning the relationship of human beings, the universe and supreme reality.

Vedana *Buddhism*   Sense perception or feeling. It is the second of the five KHANDHA which make up life on the material plane. It is also the seventh link, or NIDANA, in the causal chain of existence dependent on PHASSA and giving rise to SAMUDAYA.

Vedangas *Hinduism*   A branch of explanatory literature used to provide Brahmin students with the means to interpret the RIG VEDA and use it correctly in ritual. The Vedangas consist of Siksha, which deals with correct pronunciation; Jyotisa, which teaches astrology and astronomy; Chanda, which focuses on explanation of the verse metres; Kalpa, which deals with correct performance of ritual; Vyakarana, the study of grammar and Nirukta, which provides an etymology of rare words. (*See also* VEDA)

Vedanta *(end of the Vedas)* *Hinduism*   One of the six schools of orthodox philosophy that is based on the teaching of the UPANISHADS and therefore considered to be the culmination of Vedic teaching. It could be argued that Vedanta is the most influential of the schools of philosophy, as it provides intellectual coherence to the teachings of the BHAKTI movement through the ideas of RAMANUJA and MADHVA. SHANKARA'S ADVAITA VEDANTA is the exception, as it was opposed by the above two Vaishnavite figures. The three main proponents disagree over the relationship between BRAHMAN, ATMAN and creation. Their respective schools of Vedanta are called: Advaita Vedanta, VISHISHTADVAITA VEDANTA, DVAITA VEDANTA. Advaita Vedanta has been very influential on the intellectual classes of modern Hinduism and even influenced some nineteenth-century Western philosophers.

Venerable *Christianity* The title given to someone in the Roman Catholic Church after BEATIFICATION. It is also the official title given to an ARCHDEACON in the Church of England.

Venial Sin *Christianity* In Roman Catholic doctrine it describes a sinful act that does not remove the sinner from the receipt of the grace of God or lead to eternal damnation like a MORTAL SIN. However, it can still result in a period of PURGATORY unless confessed and forgiven. (*See also* SIN)

Verger *Christianity* The lay official who takes care of the interior of a church.

Vesak / Vesakha / Vesakka *Buddhism* See WESAK.

Vespers *Christianity* The evening prayer office celebrated along with MATINS (morning prayer) from the first centuries of Christianity. While the daily offices were maintained in the cathedrals and monasteries in the Middle Ages, it was the Lutheran Reformation that brought them back as daily congregational worship. The evening office usually consists of a minimum of two or three psalms, the ANTIPHON, LESSON, MAGNIFICAT, COLLECT, LITANY and BENEDICAMUS. (*See also* OFFICES, DIVINE)

Vestments *Christianity* The distinctive historic dress consisting of a knee-length SURPLICE, full-length CASSOCK and stole worn by the clergy when participating in worship. Roman Catholics and Anglo-Catholics vary the colours of the vestments based upon the liturgical year. Non-conformist Protestants traditionally only wear a cassock and gown in black and white throughout the year. Some Protestant movements may not wear vestments, as they associate them with priesthood. (*See also* COPE)

Vestry *Christianity* A room in a church where the VESTMENTS and ritual objects required in public worship are kept when not in use. The clergy use it as a dressing room before and after worship. (*See also* EUCHARIST)

Via Dolorosa *Christianity* The road through Jerusalem that Christ is believed to have taken on his way to CRUCIFIXION after leaving the judgement hall of PONTIUS PILATE. It is a major place of pilgrimage for Christians, as it contains the fourteen STATIONS OF THE CROSS or sites of major incidents that took place on the route to crucifixion. Pilgrims will recite prayers and meditate on each incident.

Viaticum *(Latin: provision for a journey)* *Christianity*   The final Communion given to those considered about to die in order to provide the spiritual sustenance for the journey to the afterlife. (*See also* EUCHARIST; UNCTION)

Vibhuti *Hinduism*   Used by PATANJALI to describe the miraculous powers that can be attained from the practice of YOGA, *vibhuti* also refers to the sacred ash from the sacrificial fire that can be smeared on the body or imbibed as a magical potion to cure diseases or fulfil boons and prayers. The practice of using *vibhuti* is strong in certain SHAIVITE traditions, where ascetics also daub their entire bodies with ash.

Vicar *Christianity*   The title given to a parish PRIEST in the Church of England. The title 'the Vicar of Christ' is also given to the POPE.

Vicar of Christ *Christianity*   *See* POPE.

Vicaya *Jainism*   Four types of virtuous meditation to be practised by Jains in order to facilitate liberation. They are: reflection on the teachings of the JINAS (AJNA VICAYA); reflection on overcoming passions (APAYA VICAYA); reflection on karmic consequences (VIPAKA VICAYA); and reflection on the universe (SANSTHANA VICAYA). Ideally these meditations need to be practised under the guidance of a teacher.

Vidya *Hinduism*   Used to describe spiritual knowledge or wisdom. It is used by the proponents of ADVAITA VEDANTA to refer to the experiential knowledge of the unity of BRAHMAN and ATMAN. From the time of the UPANISHADS onwards, a variety of systems have differentiated between the eternal reality and the endlessly changing SAMSARA. The Upanishads and later scriptures posit the existence of both the eternal and the changing existing side by side within the human being, who alone has the capacity to disengage from the changing phenomena and identify completely with the changeless and eternal reality. This can be achieved whilst alive. If this process occurs, liberation is certain after death. The process of gaining knowledge of one's being as both eternal and changing but increasingly identifying with the eternal is known as *Vidya*. (*See also* MOKSHA)

Vigil *Christianity*   Periods of prayer that go on through the night and usually end with EUCHARIST in the morning. Although common in the early Church, they were abolished in the 1969 calendar of the Roman Catholic Church. The only remaining vigil in the Christian calendar takes place at EASTER, traditionally on MAUNDY THURSDAY, the night before Good Friday, and commemorates the vigil in the garden of GETHSEMANE when the disciples accompanied Jesus on the night before his arrest.

Vihara *(a dwelling place) Buddhism*   Originally used to describe houses that were donated to the Buddha for his use, it is now employed as a term for a monastery or place of retreat. It can also be used to describe a stage in the spiritual life. (*See* BRAHMA VIHARAS)

Vijay Dashmi *Hinduism*   Another name for the festival of DASSERA. (*See also* NAVARATRI)

Vinaya *Buddhism*   The list of rules and regulations governing the life of monks and nuns contained in the first basket of scriptures in the PALI CANON. (*See also* VINAYA PITAKA)

Vinaya *(reverence) Jainism*   Reverence in Jainism consists of respect for those who merit it in thought, speech and actions. Generally this is given to those who seek spiritual liberation or have obtained liberation. However, Jainism would acknowledge that a humble attitude is conducive to discovering any kind of knowledge. Reverence can also be devotion to penance and is one of the six internal austerities. (*See* TAPAS)

Vinaya Pitaka *Buddhism*   The first of the three baskets of scriptures that form the TIPITAKA. They contain rules for establishing and governing the SANGHA. In these can also be found the regulations governing the lives of monks and nuns. (*See also* ABHIDHAMMA PITAKA; PATIMOKKHA; PITAKA; SUTTA PITAKA)

Vinnana (P) / Vijnana (S) *Buddhism*   Individual consciousness or conscious thought. It is the fifth of the five KHANDHA which make up life on the material plane. It also refers to the third link, or NIDANA, in the causal chain of existence which is dependent upon the SAMSKARA and gives rise to NAMA RUPA.

Vinnanahara *(consciousness) Buddhism*   One of the four causes or conditions that are believed to be essential for the existence and continuity of all beings. (*See* AHARA)

Vipaka *Jainism*   Retribution that comes as a result of bad deeds or accrued KARMA. (*See also* VIPAKA SUTRA; VIPAKA VICAYA)

Vipaka Sutra *Jainism*   The eleventh canon of Jain scripture (ANGAS) which deals with the law of KARMA and describes the results of various good and bad actions.

Vipaka vicaya *Jainism*   One of the four virtuous meditations aimed at understanding the causes and consequences of accruing KARMA in this life or previous lives. In particular, reflection on karmic consequences allows Jains to think about the impact their actions have on other living beings. (*See also* VICAYA)

Vipassana (P) / Vipashyana (S) *Buddhism*   Insight into the true nature of things. Also used to describe certain forms of meditation used by Buddhists that achieve such insight. It is *vipassana* that leads to the realization of the ultimate truth or NIRVANA. In *vipassana* meditation, which could be described as uniquely Buddhist, the practitioner focuses on achieving an insightful awareness of the processes of ANICCA, ANATTA and DUKKHA that form the essence of SAMSARA. (*See also* DHYANA)

Virgin Birth *Christianity*   The doctrine that states that Christ was miraculously conceived of the Virgin Mary through the power of the HOLY SPIRIT and without a human father. While Protestants believe only in a virginal conception, Roman Catholics maintain that the birth itself was a miraculous event which left Mary intact. This supports the Catholic doctrine that insists that Mary remained a virgin throughout her life. The virgin birth is based upon the Gospel accounts in Matthew and Luke. Since the second half of the twentieth century it has come under increasing attack from liberal theologians but still remains orthodox Christian doctrine.

Virgin Mary *Christianity*   See MARY, THE BLESSED VIRGIN.

Viriya (P) / Virya (S) *Buddhism*   Energy or exertion applied to the practice of the DHAMMA which corresponds to the noble truth of right effort. One of the six virtues necessary to attain Buddhahood. (*See also* PARAMI; SAMMA VAYAMA)

Virodhi-himsa *Jainism*   The focus on AHIMSA (non-injury to all beings) requires a categorization of HIMSA (violence) in order that Jains can know the cause of the maximum karmic influx that will hinder liberation. Virodhi-himsa is injury done to other living beings in self-defence and brings less karmic influx than premeditated violence. (*See also* SAMKALPAJA-HIMSA)

Virtualism *Christianity* One of the several doctrines formulated to explain the relationship between the Eucharistic bread and wine and the body and blood of Christ. The doctrine of virtualism states that the bread and wine are not changed into the body and blood of Jesus Christ by act of CONSECRATION, but that the faithful participating in the rite receive the body and blood of Christ through the agency of the bread and wine. (*See also* CONSUBSTANTIATION; HOST; TRANSUBSTANTIATION)

Vishishtadvaita Vedanta *Hinduism* The school of VEDANTA founded by RAMANUJA in opposition to Shankara's philosophy of unqualified non-dualism. Ramanuja argued that there was a distinct difference between God, the soul and creation. Consequently, the most important relationship is that between worshipped and worshipper.

Vishnu *Hinduism* One of the most important gods in the Hindu pantheon. Part of the TRIMURTI with BRAHMA and SHIVA, he is the aspect of the supreme being that is concerned with preservation of creation and righteousness. Consequently, it is Vishnu who manifests as the AVATAR in order to preserve SANATAN DHARMA, or the eternal religion. Traditionally there are ten avatars of Vishnu from the beginning of this cycle of creation. Five are non-human: they are MATSYA, the fish; EKASRINGA, the unicorn; KURMA, the tortoise; VARAHA, the boar; NARASIMHA, the man-lion. Five are human: they are Vamana, Parasurama, Rama, Krishna and the future avatar, Kalki. However, many Hindus add their own favoured saint to the list of Vishnu avatars, and millions include Buddha and Jesus; the most popularly worshipped avatars of Vishnu are the universal saviour figures: Rama and Krishna. Vishnu is regarded by the countless sects of the VAISHNAVA tradition as the cause of all existence, but he differs from BRAHMAN in that he is a personal saviour God full of grace and compassion for his devotees. The roots of Vishnu worship are found in the earliest scriptures of Hindu tradition and may even be pre-ARYAN.

Vishva Parishad / Vishwa Parisad *Hinduism* The Hindu Worldwide Fellowship founded in Bombay in 1964 as a religious organization with the intentions of promoting a unified version of Hinduism that brings all the sects together with an articulate set of beliefs and practices. The movement is often perceived to be the religious arm of the political RSS (Rastriya Svayam-Sevak Singh). Both movements have been criticized for inciting inter-communal violence and are an anti-Muslim and Christian presence in India. The two movements are represented in Indian party politics by the BJP (Bharatiya Janata Party).

Vishvakarma / Vishwakarma *Hinduism* First mentioned in the VEDAS as the Father-God who has made all things, he is now more often associated with particular castes, especially smiths, as the god of architecture who has designed the universe. His image is usually that of a venerable old man with a long white beard whose four arms hold design instruments. In Britain, many Hindu temples contain the image of Vishvakarma, which probably reflects the number of Hindus from East Africa who were originally recruited from the artisan castes of India in the nineteenth century as indented labour.

Vishvamitra / Vishwamitra   *Hinduism*   One of the Vedic sages and leader of the Bharata clan mentioned in the Rig Veda who probably lived somewhere between 2609–2293 BCE. Tradition states that he was born into a KSHATRIYA (warrior) family but through the performance of austerities received a boon from VISHNU that allowed him to change his caste to BRAHMIN. In the RAMAYANA, written by TULSIDAS, he is the sage who takes RAMA and his brother away from the kingdom of AYODHYA in order to destroy various demons who were interfering with the religious practices of the forest hermits. (*See also* RAMACHARITAMANASA)

Visitation of the Sick   *Christianity*   The duty of a priest to ensure that prayers, blessing, confession and Mass are available to those unable to attend public worship through ill health. (*See* UNCTION; VIATICUM)

Viveha   *Hinduism*   The SAMSKARA (life-cycle rite) of marriage. This is an important event in the Hindu life-cycle, as it marks the passage from the BRAHMACHARYA (celibate student) to GRIHASTHA (householder) stages of life. These are part of VARNASHRAMDHARMA, which is considered to be the ideal pattern of life for the first three VARNAS ('twice-born' castes). The wedding ceremony is based on the ancient fire-sacrifice and is performed by BRAHMINS. The bride and groom circumambulate the fire whilst making offerings and their vows to each other. The wife will generally leave her family and move in with her husband's family, where she will be subject to the household leadership of the mother-in-law. Marriages are generally arranged within caste boundaries and are the union of two families. However, traditional ancient Hindu law acknowledged certain kinds of love marriage. Today, the system of traditional arranged marriages within caste is under severe pressure from urbanization and globalization.

Viveka   *Hinduism*   The important quality of discrimination. Most Indian traditions see the human condition in terms of the dichotomy of knowledge/ignorance rather than sin/redemption. Thus the ability to differentiate truth from falsehood or reality from illusion, the real from the unreal, is crucial for making any progress towards liberation or enlightenment. (*See* MUKTI; NIRVANA; SAMSARA)

Vivekananda, Swami (1863–1902) *Hindu*   Famous disciple of RAMAK-
RISHNA and founder of the RAMAKRISHNA MISSION. Although Ramakrishna was
himself opposed to any kind of organizational activity, Vivekananda went on to
become the most successful reformer of contemporary Hinduism. In 1893,
Vivekananda departed India to attend the World Parliament of Religions in
Chicago. He continued to tour the USA and Europe promoting a Vedantic view
of Hinduism that emphasized philosophy and experience of the divine. His
championing of Hinduism abroad helped bring a new self-confidence to Hindus,
while the Ramakrishna Mission contributed to the development of a Hindu social
conscience, organizing schools, colleges, hospitals, hostels and relief organizations.

Voluntarism   *Christianity*   The theological position posited by William of
Ockham, a medieval theologian, which states that God was not under any
obligation to reward good deeds. He argued that the position contended by
Thomas AQUINAS, in which God recognized the value of an action, limited the
freedom of the divine will.

Vrajya (S)   *Buddhism*   *See* VAJJA.

Vrata pratima *(the stage of vows)*   *Jainism*   The second of the eleven stages
that allow lay Jains to move gradually towards liberation. During this stage, the
lay Jain maintains twelve vows that allow more progress towards the ultimate
goal. While many of the vows are concerned with fasting and penance, one is to
carry out the Jain 'sacred death'. (*See* ANUVRATAS; SALLEKHANA; VRATAS)

Vratas *(a vow)*   *Hinduism*   An important element of Hindu religious practice.
Vows are made to bring blessings for new initiatives or to transform an existing
situation by enlisting divine assistance. They may also be made by ascetics in
order to increase their TAPAS and bring them supernatural powers. Common
vows are made to gods by pilgrims in order to secure divine intercession to deal
with life problems. Vows often involve fasting or giving up certain foods,
practising austerities, renouncing various sense pleasures for a duration or going
on pilgrimages under specified conditions.

Vratas   *Jainism*   The religious vows maintained by Jains in order to pursue a
path that takes them closer to liberation. They are divided into five MAHAVRATAS,
observed by the ascetic community, and five ANUVRATAS, observed by Jain laity,
that are modifications adapted to suit lay life. In addition to these vows there are
also other *vratas*, such as GUNAVRATAS and SIKSAVRATAS, that are practised by
devout lay Jains.

Vrindavan   *Hinduism*   A famous pilgrimage city in north India associated with KRISHNA's childhood and youth. The AVATAR of VISHNU is believed to have passed time in the area of Vrindavan after his exile. It is also believed to be the site of Krishna's various LILAS or divine play with the GOPIS (cowherds). The city is the centre of the Bengali tradition of Krishna devotion which originated with CAITANYA MAHAPRABHU and his followers. It is likely that it was unknown as a site of Krishna worship until discovered by the Bengali medieval saint on his travels throughout India. Today it is one of the most important centres of pilgrimage in India. (*See also* GAUDIYA VAISHNAVISM)

Vulgate *Christianity*   The Latin version of the Bible translated by St Jerome from 382 onwards. When the various books came to be collected into a single volume it became known as the Vulgate. Although it was influential in the Middle Ages, Erasmus' edition of the Greek NEW TESTAMENT in 1516 allowed for direct comparison and highlighted several major errors in the Latin translation.

Vyakhya Prajnapti *Jainism*   See BHAGAVATI SUTRA.

Vyasa *Hinduism*   A famous sage and devotee of VISHNU who is credited with writing the original text of the MAHABHARATA, including the BHAGAVAD GITA. Tradition states that Vyasa dictated the great epic to the god GANESH. Vyasa is also considered to be the author of the MAHAPURANAS. The accreditation of such popular texts to an elevated sage with a status similar to that of the RISHIS who composed the VEDAS may have been a device to gain authenticity for popular new, as opposed to Brahmanic, texts.

Vyutsarga *(detachment)* *Jainism*   This refers to renunciation of external possessions such as property and wealth or internal possessions such as the passions pride, anger and greed. *Vyutsarga* is closely related to the fifth of the five great vows, APARIGRAHA. It is also considered one of the six internal austerities. (*See also* TAPAS)

Wahguru *('Hail guru')* Sikhism The exclamation of faith in the Guru. The lengthened form of '*Waheguru Ji Ka Khalsa, Waheguru Ji Ka Fateh*' ('the KHALSA belongs to God, victory belongs to God') has become a greeting of the Khalsa brotherhood. The RAHIT MARYADA states that any Sikh who is greeted in this way must respond identically. Many Sikhs actually use *wahguru* as a form of MANTRA and perceive it to be NAM SIMRAN.

Wahhabi *Islam* Follower of the movement founded by Muhammad ibn 'Abd al-Wahhab (1703–87) in Arabia. Muhammad al-Wahhab was inspired by the puritanical teachings of Ibn TAYMIYYA and launched a campaign to restore Islam to a form that was stripped of all accretions arising from culture, tradition or mysticism. He opposed the traditional beliefs in saint veneration, reliance upon intercessionary prayers, the visiting of tombs and the elevation of Muhammad to semi-divine status. He advocated a return to the basics of SHARI'A but supported the right of individual Muslim scholars to go directly to the Qur'an and HADITH to interpret and understand the revelation. Consequently he was opposed to the ULAMA, who insisted on their sole right to interpret according to FIQH. Muhammad al-Wahhab aligned himself with the House of Saud, and together they created the modern state of Saudi Arabia. The term 'Wahhabi' is used generically to describe any movement that supports purification of the faith through stripping away cultural accretions, including the traditions of Sufism, and also believes in the right of independent individual judgement taken directly from the Qur'an and the SUNNA of the Prophet. (*See also* AHL AS-SUNNA WA JAMAAT; DEOBAND; IJTIHAD)

Wahy *Islam* The state of receptivity or openness in which Muhammad received and communicated the revelation of the QUR'AN. It is said that such outer signs as physical limpness, swooning and ecstasy accompanied the appearance of a Qur'anic utterance. Essentially there are two, sometimes conflicting, views expressed by Muslims. The first articulates the view that the prophet is merely an ordinary human being who is chosen to hear, understand and communicate. However, many Muslim scholars, including al-Ghazali, argue that the messengers are special people endowed with a religious sensitivity. They are given special gifts to receive the revelation and pass it on to others. Those who advance in religion are able to enter into an experience in which they share in the Prophet's understanding of revelation. (*See also* RASUL; TANZIL)

Wali *(a friend of God, plural awliya)* *Islam*   Often used to describe those who are believed to have come close to Allah through their constant remembrance and piety. Although the thousands of SUFIS who have lived such lives are often called saints in translation, the term *awliya* is an accurate description of their relationship to Allah in Muslim terms. A *wali* is believed to possess BARAKA or the ability to bless and intervene on the behalf of the petitioner to Allah. Therefore it is believed that places where he lived or died are still inhabited by his spirit and may be used as retreats to develop a closeness to the divine. His successors are also believed to embody his spiritual power and this has given rise to the SILSILA that maintains a Sufi order or TARIQAH. (*See also* MAZAR)

Wali, al- *Islam*   One of the ninety-nine names of Allah that describes His closeness to human beings, in that He walks alongside them and will give protection and shelter. (*See* WALI)

Waliallah, Shah (1703–62) *Islam*   A NAQSHBANDI Sufi mystic and scholar who lived in Delhi. A prolific writer and theologian who attempted to reconcile the differences between the esoteric and the exoteric traditions of Islam by reconciling the SHARI'A (law) to the TARIQAH (Sufi orders). This was especially important in the Indian subcontinent, where any form of mysticism was likely to become influenced by Hindu practices and ideas. Shah Waliallah reformed the Naqshbandi *tariqah* and virtually all subcontinental Muslim strands can demonstrate their lineage back to the influence of the SHAIKH and his sons. The school of DEOBAND arose from the influence of his successors.

Walsingham *Christianity*   An important eleventh-century shrine in Norfolk which was a replica of the Holy House in Nazareth. Although it was destroyed in 1538, Roman Catholics and Anglicans have revived the pilgrimage and today its popularity is undiminished based on a reputation for healing.

Wasila *Islam*   A vast liturgical literature of prayers of mediation. In traditional mosques the prayer-call will be followed with a prayer of mediation addressed to Muhammad. *Wasila* describes the honourable position of a man of influence who has proximity to a monarch. He may be called upon for assistance because of his special access to the ruler. It is believed that prayers that bless Muhammad can be used to gain access to Allah. (*See* SHAFA'A)

Watan *(fatherland)* *Islam* The term used to describe one's country in Arab nationalism. The appeal of national patriotism exists in some tension with the Islamic ideal of UMMA (community) united through the revelation and the leadership of Muhammad. Various Muslim revivalists such as Maulana MAWDUDI and Hasan al-BANNA have argued that loyalty to the nation runs the risk of supplanting Allah's sovereignty unless the state is an Islamic one.

Wataniyah / Wataniyyah *Islam* Patriotism. (*See* WATAN)

Watch Tower Bible and Tract Society *Christianity* See JEHOVAH'S WITNESSES.

Wazifa *Islam* A term used by followers of a SUFI order to describe the daily office that is given to them by the SHAIKH at the time of initiation. (*See also* BAI'A; DHIKR; MURID; TARIQAH)

Wesak / Vaisakha / Vesak / Vesakha / Vesakka *(sin)* *Buddhism* Buddha Day. The Sinhalese name of the festival held on the full moon between April and May which celebrates the birth, death and enlightenment of the Buddha. Japanese ZEN schools only celebrate the birth of the Buddha on 8 April.

Wesley, Charles (1707–88) *Christianity* The brother of John WESLEY and an early Methodist. Charles received his experience of awakening to the spirit and personal salvation through the forgiveness of sins only a few days apart from his brother John, the founder of METHODISM. Although an inspired preacher, he is particularly famous for his hymn writing.

Wesley, John (1703–91) *Christianity* The founder of METHODISM. He was ordained as a priest in the Church of England but came under the influence of the Moravians after visiting North America. The Moravians espoused a belief in personal salvation through Jesus Christ. In 1738, along with his brother Charles, he received a transforming experience. On finding the doors of the churches closed to him whenever he preached 'enthusiasm', he began a prolific ministry preaching outdoors, especially to the working classes. There are many accounts of the emotional and physical effects of his preaching on the audience. Although preferring to remain in the Church of England, he inspired a movement of lay preachers that followed in his footsteps and gradually the new denomination of Methodism evolved.

Wesleyan Methodists   *Christianity*   *See* METHODISM.

Westminster Abbey   *Christianity*   The present church was completed in 1540 on the site of a Benedictine abbey founded in the thirteenth century. The Abbey is a Royal Peculiar, which means that it is independent of any diocese and under the direct jurisdiction of the British monarch. It has been the site of royal coronations since William I. The Abbey's association with the state and state occasions has given it a unique place in the national life of Britain. (*See* CHURCH OF ENGLAND; WINDSOR, ST GEORGE'S CHAPEL)

Westminster Assembly   *Christianity*   An assembly of 121 clergymen and 30 laymen chosen to advise Parliament on the government and creed of the national church in England after the abolition of the episcopacy in 1643. (*See* WESTMINSTER CONFESSION)

Westminster Cathedral   *Christianity*   The nineteenth-century cathedral of the Roman Catholic Archbishop of Westminster who is the leading Roman Catholic primate in Britain.

Westminster Confession   *Christianity*   The profession of the PRESBYTERIAN faith drawn up by the WESTMINSTER ASSEMBLY in 1646 and approved by Parliament in 1648. It remained in force until the restoration of the monarchy and the episcopacy in 1660. The Confession remains the definitive statement of Presbyterian doctrine for the English-speaking world.

White Friars   *Christianity*   A name given to the CARMELITE friars after their distinctive white cloaks.

White Monks   *Christianity*   A name for the CISTERCIAN monks who wear a habit of undyed wool.

Whitsunday   *Christianity*   The feast day that celebrates the descent of the Holy Spirit to the APOSTLES at the Jewish feast of PENTECOST. Traditionally it is celebrated on a Sunday, the fiftieth day after Easter. It is regarded as the second most important Christian feast after Easter. (*See also* GLOSSOLALIA)

Windsor, St George's Chapel   *Christianity*   The royal chapel inside Windsor Castle, one of the main residences of the British monarch, who is the titular head of the CHURCH OF ENGLAND. It has the status of a Royal Peculiar, a parish or place of worship exempt from diocesan authority and under the direct jurisdiction of the monarch. (*See also* WESTMINSTER ABBEY)

Wird *Islam*   *See* HIZB.

Word of God *Christianity*   *See* LOGOS.

World Council of Churches *Christianity*   An organization established in 1948, originally consisting of 145 denominations from 44 nations, to bring Christian denominations together to discuss matters of faith and practice. While the Council has no authority over individual members, it is the practical expression of the ecumenical movement. Today it has over 200 participating denominations and the organization has resulted in a closer understanding among the varieties of Christian churches. However, the 'basis' for membership that was adopted ('the World Council of Churches is a fellowship of Churches which take our Lord Jesus Christ as God and Saviour') has become a measure of Christian orthodoxy and has led to some Christian sects being excluded. (*See* ECUMENISM)

Wudu / Wuzu *Islam*   The ritual ablution that is performed before SALAH. The hands, forearms and legs below the knee are washed, whilst the face, mouth and nose are rinsed. While this ritual cleansing may take place at home, every mosque traditionally contains running water so that *wudu* may be performed before prayer. If water is not available, sand or clean earth may be used as a lesser substitute. (*See also* NIYYAH)

Wujud *Islam*   Allah as pure being or the All of All rather than a being. This is an important concept for Muslim mystics (SUFIS), as human beings also share in being. It is argued that the spirit is a part of God's being and therefore that union is possible. *Wujud* is also used to describe the state of oneness attained by a Sufi in the ecstasy of losing all external consciousness. Ibn ARABI declared the doctrine of unity (*wahdat al-wujud*) which stated that all things pre-exist as ideas in the knowledge of God, whence they emanate and eventually return. This statement gave credence to the Sufi quest. (*See also* TARIQAH)

X

Xavier, St Francis (1506–52)   *Christianity*   One of the original JESUITS and a successful missionary. In 1534 he vowed to follow in the footsteps of Christ by spreading the gospel to non-Christians. He made his headquarters in Goa, from where he travelled on missionary activities to Sri Lanka and Japan. His tomb can be found in Goa.

Yad   *Judaism*   A pointer held in the hand when reading from the TORAH in the SYNAGOGUE. Any damage to the Torah scrolls makes them *patul* or unusable. Thus, every care is taken to avoid damaging the text, and for this reason the readers do not mark their place in the text with their fingers as this may cause smudging of the ink.

Yadavas   *Hinduism*   The north Indian tribe mentioned in several scriptures to which KRISHNA was born as a prince.

Yahadut   *Judaism*   The religion of the Jewish people known as Judaism that believes in one God who has chosen Israel by giving the people His TORAH so that they may be an example to humanity, and so that the presence of God may be amongst humanity. As a consequence of its covenant with God to obey His law as revealed in the Torah, the emphasis of Judaism is on orthopraxy rather than orthodoxy, but belief also plays an important role. (*See also* YEHUDIM)

Yahrzeit   *Judaism*   The anniversary of a parent's death. A candle is lit from evening to evening and the offspring of the dead may fast on the day. They would be expected to visit the synagogue, recite the KADDISH and spend some time in study of the TORAH. The graves of the departed are visited, when prayers will be recited and a small stone is left on the grave by the visitor. (*See also* ANINUT; SHELOSHIM; SHIVA; YIZKOR)

Yahweh   *Judaism*   The name given to the God that is not expressible and usually depicted as YHWH if it needs to be written. This name has not been spoken since the Exile and is usually substituted by other names such as ADONAI.

Yahya ben Zakariya   *Islam*   The Muslim name for JOHN THE BAPTIST, believed to be the prophet of God who preceded Jesus. (*See also* ISA; RASUL)

Yajamana *Hinduism*   The person who commissions a Vedic ritual to be performed and a participant in the ceremony. (*See* BRAHMIN; YAJNA)

Yajna *Hinduism*   Originally used to describe the two kinds of ancient Vedic sacrifice performed by BRAHMINS. The first kind of *yajna* was a public ceremonial event consisting of the sacrifice of a grain, an animal and the SOMA rituals. The second form of *yajna* was performed for a specific purpose on a special occasion in order to achieve certain ends, such as extra merit leading to immortality, victory in battle, the birth of a child, good health, long life, prosperity or cure from disease. Offering sacrifices were part of the world order (DHARMA) and maintained cosmic order (RTA). Millions of *yajnas* are still performed, especially in the latter category above. Public sacrifices are much more rare. The *yajna*, properly performed, is more powerful than the DEVA (god), who is obliged to obey the power of the sacrifice. Although various *yajnas* may take diverse forms, they must have the common elements of sacrificial materials; the mental attitude of non-attachment to the items sacrificed; a god (MURTI), who is addressed as the recipient of the sacrifice; a MANTRA or sacred formula that has power over the god; and the brahmin priests required to perform the ceremony. (*See also* HAVAN)

Yajnavalkya *Hinduism*   A sage who teaches the path to liberation in the BRHADARANYAKA UPANISHAD. Yajnavalkya's teaching represents a major shift away from the ritualism of the VEDAS to an analysis of the physical and psychological states of humankind. In the process, he defines the nature of the self and distinguishes between the lower self, made up of PRAKRITI, and the higher self, or ATMAN, which he posits is identical to the ultimate and cosmic reality, BRAHMAN. Yajnavalkya purports that it is the knowledge of the higher self that leads to liberation or the end of the cycle of the rebirth. (*See also* ADVAITA VEDANTA; UPANISHADS)

Yajur Veda *Hinduism*   One of the four VEDAS that provides the formulas and the precise form of the ceremonies for sacred rituals performed by BRAHMIN priests.

Yaksha (m) / Yakshi (f) *Jainism*   In Jain mythology beings who are born in celestial realms as a result of good KARMA established in previous lives. These beings live for thousands of years in great splendour. They are able to answer the prayers of supplicants and sometimes make visits to assist those who need their guidance. They often appear on earth to herald the birth of a TIRTHANKARA.

Yama *Hinduism*   The god of death and final arbiter of rebirth decided by the weight of KARMA or deeds performed whilst alive. Yama appears in several famous stories concerning victory over death, the two best known being those of SAVITRI and NATCHIKETAS. Yama is also used to describe the first stage of spiritual development for a student of the YOGA school in which abstention or self-control of the senses is advocated.

Yamim Noraim *Judaism* The ten days of repentance in the month of Tishrie (6 September–4 October) that begin with ROSH HASHANAH and end with YOM KIPPUR and are considered the most sacred in the Jewish calendar. It is a time for forgiveness and repentance both before God and one's fellow human beings.

Yamulkah *Judaism* The Yiddish term for the small skullcap worn by Jewish men. (*See* KIPPAH)

Yamuna / Jamuna *Hinduism* A sacred river to Hindus and a tributary of the GANGA associated with KRISHNA, as it flows through the pilgrimage town of VRINDAVAN. It is also associated with the famous twelve-yearly celebration of the festival of KUMBHA MELA, held at Allahabad, where the Yamuna meets the Ganga.

Yantra (S) *Buddhism* A mystical diagram conceived in meditation and used to aid concentration in Tibetan Buddhism. Whereas a MANTRA is spoken and TANTRA is performed, a YANTRA is seen. (*See also* MANDALA)

Yantra *Hinduism* A symmetrical geometrical diagram such as a MANDALA used in TANTRA as a visual form of meditation or as a symbol in certain rituals. The typical design of a *yantra* is an outer square with gateways containing a design of concentric circles and triangles and an innermost design of arcs that forms the petals of a lotus. Everything leads to the centre of the diagram. Different parts of the *yantra* represent different aspects of the Goddess. The initiate uses the *yantra* to project through the gates and then identify with various aspects of the Goddess until the centre is reached, where complete identification can take place. Whereas a MANTRA is spoken and TANTRA is performed, Yantra is visualized or seen.

Yaquta baida *(white chrysolite)* *Islam* A description of the light or innermost reality that Allah creates from Himself at the beginning of creation, and which is often known as the light of Muhammad. (*See* HAQQ; NUR; NUR I MUHAMMADI)

Yasoda *Hinduism* The foster mother of KRISHNA during the period that he was exiled from AYODHYA and lived amongst the cowherds of VRINDAVAN. (*See also* GOPIS)

Yathrib *Islam*   *See* MADINAH.

Yatra *Hinduism*   Hindu pilgrimage. (*See* PRAVRAJYA)

Yatra *Jainism*   Pilgrimage. There are many places of pilgrimage throughout India associated with Jain tradition. These sites are called YATRA-DHARMAS by Svetambara Jains and TIRTHA-KSETRAS by Digambara Jains. Generally the important pilgrimage places are associated with events in the lives of *tirthankaras* and other saints, especially the place of their final liberation. Famous pilgrimage places are Satrunjay, a temple city of over three thousand shrines; Sammet Sikhara, believed to be the place of liberation for twenty *tirthankaras*; Girnar, the place of liberation for the twenty-second *tirthankara* and many Jain saints; and Pavapuri, place of liberation for MAHAVIR. (*See also* SANGHA YATRA; YATRANIKA)

Yatra-dharmas *Jainism*   A designated place of pilgrimage for Svetambara Jains. (*See* YATRA)

Yatranika *Jainism*   The ritual of triple pilgrimage that is one of the eleven duties of lay Jains to be performed annually or at least once in a lifetime. The pilgrimage consists of taking part in PUJAS and festivals that venerate the TIRTHANKARAS; chariot processions and temple festivities; and pilgrimage to important Jain sacred sites. (*See also* YATRA)

Yawm ad-din *Islam*   The Day of Judgement when all human beings will be called before the throne of Allah for final recompense. There will be a physical resurrection of the dead. It is generally believed that the People of the Book (Jews, Christians and Muslims) will be judged as communities behind their respective prophets. However, after the final balancing of the books, all human souls will eventually find their way to paradise through God's overriding infinite mercy and compassion. The judgement will be based on records kept by various angels who have accompanied each human being throughout their lives and to the grave, where it is believed that the balancing of the final judgement continues. Muslims in the grave receive the fruits of ongoing good actions that they performed in their lifetimes, such as introducing someone to Islam or building a well from which all can benefit. The Day of Judgement is described in the Qur'an as a violent and terrifying event, out of which God finally appears surrounded by angels. (*See* SHAFA'A)

Yehudim *Judaism*   The Hebrew term for a Jew. Jewishness is traditionally defined by matrilineal descent: that is, a child of a Jewish mother is a Jew. However, this is complicated by two factors: in 1983, the Central Conference of American Rabbis, a REFORM gathering, determined that a child of either a Jewish mother or a Jewish father can be deemed a Jew if brought up in an environment that led to identification with the Jewish people; second, it is possible to convert to Judaism. The important point here is that Jewishness is not defined by religiosity; however, Judaism is the religion of the Jewish people. (*See also* YAHADUT)

Yerusalem *Judaism*   Yerusalem or Jerusalem is the geographical focus of the Jewish people, expressed in one of the psalms of DAVID as 'if I forget thee, O Jerusalem, may my right hand lose its cunning' (137:5). Jews pray facing in the direction of the city and ask God to rebuild it in its ancient glory from the time of David and Solomon. A similar prayer is recited after every meal, and YOM KIPPUR and PESACH have long been celebrated in diaspora by the climax of 'next year Yerusalem'.

Yeshiva / Yeshivah *Judaism*   A college for the study of the TORAH and the TALMUD. Although Jewish males had always engaged in study of the Torah under the guidance of their rabbis, in the nineteenth century, organized colleges appeared in Eastern Europe which allowed progression through the various stages of study. Secular study was not permitted and some students spent a lifetime in study of Torah, Talmud and HALAKHAH.

Yesod *(foundation)* *Judaism*   According to the tradition of the KABBALAH, the ninth of the ten SEFIROTH that emanate from the AYN SOF. It is the third in the central trunk of the Tree of Life and is the means by which God's light flows into the MALKHUT and then into creation.

Yidam *Buddhism*   A personal deity matched to the disciple's nature or psychological profile used in the VAJRAYANA tradition of Buddhism as visualizations in meditation. They can be male or female and possess a number of different qualities that are matched to the disciple's spiritual needs. They are believed to be manifestations of the SAMBHOGAKAYA.

Yiddish *Judaism*   The constructed language made up of German, Russian and other East European languages used by the ASHKENAZIM in the DIASPORA and still spoken by many Orthodox Jews even in Israel. Hebrew is maintained as a sacred language, although it is spoken by most other Israelis. (*See also* IVRIT)

Yihud *Judaism*   In Orthodox Jewish weddings, the practice of taking the couple to a room in the building and leaving them alone. The door of the room will be guarded by the witnesses to the marriage. The announcement is made to the guests that the couple are breaking their fast, but the reason is so that the marriage can be consummated, thereby fulfilling one of the three ways of entering a marriage contract. (*See* KETUBAH)

Yihus   *Judaism*   Achieving distinction. Although this could be obtained by distinguished ancestry or right marriage, the correct way to obtain distinction was through one's lifestyle as a practising Jew. The Jew who gave to charity, studied the TORAH, fulfilled all his/her religious duties and brought up children in the knowledge and practice of the Torah was considered to possess Yihus. In this way the community in exile was able to combat any forces that weakened or diluted the practice of Judaism.

Yisrael   *Judaism*   See ISRAEL.

Yizkor   *Judaism*   A special memorial service observed on the final day of the pilgrimage festivals (PESACH, SHAVUOT, SUKKOT) and YOM KIPPUR in order to remember the recently departed in front of the congregation. (*See also* YAHRZEIT)

Yoga   *Hinduism*   Yoga is popularized as a system of physical exercises and mental relaxation, but it is primarily varieties of HATHA YOGA that are taught. The term yoga is used in a variety of ways in contemporary Hinduism. It describes methods of self-control and discipline that have a spiritual dimension and also union of the soul and the supreme reality or a method that promotes that experience; it is also one of the six orthodox schools of Hindu philosophy. The school of Yoga was founded by PATANJALI in the first centuries CE in an attempt to organize a coherent system of practice out of a vast variety of techniques and methods. The philosophy of the school is based on SAMKHYA and provides a coherent system of practice. Yoga is based on an eightfold path to direct the practitioner from awareness of the external world to a focus on the inner. The first five stages attempt to remove the external causes of mental distraction. The first two, YAMA (restraint) and NIYAMA (observance), provide the moral basis for the discipline and help to control unruly emotions. The next three provide the physical environment or discipline for the practitioner. They are ASANA (posture), PRANAYAMA (breath control) and PRATYAHARA (control of the senses). The final three stages are concerned with the increasing ability to control the movement of the mind. DHARANA focuses the mind on one object of meditation; DHYANA is the state when the mind achieves the ability to remain in a focused state of concentration without distraction. The final state of SAMADHI is achieved when subject/object consciousness is lost and there is only the experience of meditation. (*See also* YOGA SUTRAS)

Yoga Sutras   *Hinduism*   A scripture written by PATANJALI, probably in the first centuries CE, that provided a systematic exposition and elaboration of the path of YOGA as a means of release from the bondage of SAMSARA. The bare essentials of the philosophical school of Yoga are laid out in short but concentrated aphorisms that begin with a definition of yoga as the system of mind control. Complete cessation of all mental activity is defined as the goal of yoga, in which consciousness rests in itself without any awareness of external or mental distraction. Thus consciousness is liberated from PRAKRITI (primordial matter) and the influence of the GUNAS. The Yoga Sutras describe an eightfold path that enables the yoga practitioner to move from internal to external consciousness. (*See also* SAMKHYA)

Yogacara *Buddhism*   A school of philosophy founded by Asanga (310–90), who is believed to have received the teachings direct from MAITREYA, the future Buddha. It propounds the idea that only consciousness is real and emphasizes the practice of meditation. (*See also* CITTAMATRA)

Yogananda, Paramhansa *Hinduism*   A twentieth-century Hindu SANNY-ASIN (monk) who travelled to the USA and Britain and founded the Yoga Fellowship of California. He is more famous for the influence of his book, *Autobiography of a Yogi*. There is no doubt that it helped promote the teachings of Hinduism in the West, especially amongst members of the 1960s counter-culture.

Yogi *Hinduism*   A practitioner of the disciplines of YOGA.

Yom Ha-Atzmaut *Judaism*   The day set aside to celebrate the founding of the modern state of ISRAEL or Independence Day. It is celebrated on 14 May.

Yom Hashoah *Judaism*   The day which is set aside to commemorate the SHOAH, and to remember the six million Jewish martyrs who were massacred by the Nazi regime in Germany. It is held on the twenty-seventh day of the month of Nissan that falls between mid-March and mid-April.

Yom Kippur *Judaism*   The Day of Atonement that occurs ten days after ROSH HASHANAH, the New Year. The ten days in between are known as the Days of Penitence and are used to re-examine one's life. This period culminates in Yom Kippur, the most solemn of the Jewish holy days, which is maintained by fasting and refraining from sexual intercourse. The ark is draped in white and traditionally many of the congregation at the SYNAGOGUE will also wear white. Although it is a time to ask for God's forgiveness, it is not only a confession of sin but also a day of reconciliation between God and His people. The vigil begins on the eve of Yom Kippur, and the evening service is the only time when everyone wears the TALLIT. After the arrival of the TORAH scrolls, the cantor will chant the KOL

NIDREI three times. The Yom Kippur service consists of confessions in the morning with readings from the Torah followed by the HAFTARAH, the reading from the book of Prophets taken from Isaiah, where the motivations for fasting are revealed; the MUSAPH, the extra service only performed on festival days; and the second Torah reading. The *musaph* prayer service will include a memorial to Jewish martyrs and recently dead friends and relatives. The concluding prayer, known as the NEILAH, is only performed on this occasion and is recited with great fervour. During the evening service, the emphasis is on reaffirmation of faith and ends with a blast of the SHOFAR.

Yom Kippur Katan *Judaism*   A miniature form of YOM KIPPUR introduced by the mystics of Safat to purge the soul of arrogance and pride that is celebrated in the synagogue before the feast of the new moon. (*See also* ROSH HODESH)

Yomtov *(days of celebration)* *Judaism*   This term is used collectively to describe the Jewish festivals that always commemorate great events in Jewish history. The principal festivals are PESACH, SHAVUOT, SUKKOT, YOM KIPPUR, HANUKKAH, PURIM and ROSH HASHANAH.

Yomtov Sheni *Judaism*   The practice of observing a second holy day when only one is prescribed in the TORAH. This has become normal observance, except in the case of YOM KIPPUR, when the rabbis ruled that two days' fasting would be too arduous. The idea of observing a second day arose out of uncertainty about a festival's beginning when communities in DIASPORA were far removed from the decisions that were being made in the SANHEDRIN in Jerusalem.

Yoni *Hinduism*   A representation of the female sex organ and symbol of SHAKTI (the power of the Goddess) that complements the LINGAM (a common phallus symbol associated with SHIVA). It is usually formed as a circular construction with a rim that drains away the liquid offerings of milk and water made by worshippers to the Shiva lingam that is set in the middle of the yoni.

York *Christianity*   One of the oldest Christian communities in Britain and the site of the present York Minster built in the thirteenth century. While a Bishop of York is mentioned as far back as 314, the struggle for pre-eminence with CANTERBURY began in the eleventh century. It was decided by Pope Innocent VI (1352–62) that the Archbishop of Canterbury should be the leading primate in Britain. The Archbishop of York remains the second highest prelate in the Church of England after the Archbishop of Canterbury.

Yudhishthira *Hinduism*   The eldest of the PANDAVA brothers known for his sense of righteousness. He was trapped into a gambling contest with his cousins, the Kauravas, who cheated. As a consequence, the Pandavas lost their kingdom and were forced into exile. So began the sequence of events that led to the battle of KURUKSHETRA as described in the MAHABHARATA. (*See also* ARJUNA; KRISHNA)

Yuga *Hinduism*   An age or extended period of time that together form one cycle of creation. After the completion of each age, the creation is dissolved back into primal reality, from where it is re-created to begin another cycle of existence. There are four such ages, which are differentiated by the degree of spirituality they exhibit. They are KRTA YUGA or SAT YUGA (1,728,000 years), TRETA YUGA (1,296,000 years), DVAPARA YUGA (864,000 years) and finally KALI YUGA (age of darkness), which lasts for 432,000 years. The *kali yuga* is the current age and will end with the coming of KALKI, the tenth avatar of Vishnu.

Zabur *Islam* The Arabic for the book of Psalms which is one of the four revealed scriptures given by Allah to a chosen messenger. It was revealed to the Prophet DAWUD. (*See also* INJIL TAWRAH; QUR'AN)

Zaddikim *(righteous ones)* *Judaism* The leaders of the HASIDIM who are believed to be in a state of closeness or proximity to God at all times. The Hasidic Jew is expected to find a *zaddik* or REBBE to act as a guide and a counsellor in order to bring him closer to the divine. There are several famous dynasties of *zaddiks*, such as the Lubovitch, Sotmar, Ger and Bobov, who have passed on their leadership for several generations. The *zaddiks* have produced over 3,000 works that supplement the traditional Jewish canon of scripture.

Zafar-Nama *Sikhism* A letter written by GURU GOBIND SINGH to the Moghul emperor Aurangzeb in 1705. An important historical document, it demonstrates the political relations between Sikhs and both Hindu and Muslim rulers. It admonishes the emperor for being guilty of fratricide and religious persecution.

Zaid, ibn Ali *Islam* A grandson of HUSAIN who is claimed as the fifth IMAM of the SHI'A community by a breakaway movement who became known as the Zaidis. They rebelled against the UMAYYAD and ABBASID dynasties and founded their own dynasty on the Caspian Sea in 864. Another Zaidi state was founded in the Yemen in 893 and lasted until 1963. Zaidi Shi'a Muslims can still be found in the Yemen. (*See also* ISHMAELI)

Zakah / Zakat *Islam* The third of the five pillars of Islam is the annual payment of welfare obligatory on all Muslims. In the Qur'an, the obligation to give charity is often linked with prayer as the dual priorities of submission to God. *Zakah* ensures that Islam remains a communal religion with an emphasis on social responsibility and economic justice. The proportion of income that should go to *zakah* has ranged from culture to culture, as have the collection mechanisms. The general rule for the proportion of wealth given in *zakah* is that it should be one-fortieth of one's extra income over and above that required to maintain a reasonable standard of living. Very often it is collected in the mosques, whose committees ensure that the money goes to worthy Muslim causes. (*See* HAJJ; RAMADAN; SADAQAH; SALAH; SHAHADAH)

Zakat ul-Fitr   *Islam*   The customary almsgiving observed at the end of the month of fasting or RAMADAN. (*See also* ZAKAH)

Zalama   *Islam*   To sin in the sense of self-wrongdoing. Muhammad often began his prayers with 'I have wronged myself'. It is typical of Muslim private devotion to ask for forgiveness of such sins, which are usually associated with hubris or pride. (*See* DU'A)

Zamzam   *Islam*   The name of the spring that miraculously appeared to save HAJAR and ISHMAEL in answer to Hajar's prayers for God's assistance. The discovery of the spring allowed MAKKAH to develop as a stopping-off point for merchant caravans. The well was supposed to have been filled in by invaders as a punishment for idol worship in the city, but was rediscovered by a devout monotheist who was an ancestor of Muhammad. The spring is believed to be the well adjacent to the KA'ABA and is bathed in by the pilgrims who attend the HAJJ.

Zawiya / Zawiyah *(a corner)*   *Islam*   It can be used to describe a small mosque, a tomb of a holy man, a cell used by a SUFI for retreat or a small Sufi community sharing the same spiritual discipline. It is most commonly used in North Africa to describe the centre of a Sufi order. (*See also* DAR; TARIQAH)

Zazen (J) *(Zen sitting)*   *Buddhism*   ZEN Buddhist forms of sitting meditation usually practised in the lotus position. The meditation sessions normally take place in the ZENDO. (*See also* SESSHIN)

Zechariah / Zachariah / Zacharias   *Christianity*   A Jewish priest and husband of Elizabeth. He received a visitation from an angel announcing that he would have a son in his old age. Later his wife gave birth to JOHN THE BAPTIST, the prophet who foretold the coming of Jesus Christ.

Zechariah   *Judaism*   One of the twelve minor prophets and a book of the Bible of the same name. Zechariah prophesied and preached around 520 BCE. He was a contemporary of HAGGAI and emphasized spiritual and righteous living over and above material power such as wealth or physical prowess. (*See also* NEVIIM)

Zeman Herutenu *(the season of our freedom)* *Judaism*   One of the names given to the festival of Passover (PESACH). It refers to the deliverance of the Hebrew tribes from slavery in Egypt through the intervention of God and their eventual emergence as a separate nation with their own land in ISRAEL. (*See also* BERIT)

Zen (J) *Buddhism*   A type of Mahayana Buddhism developed in China, where it is known as CH'AN, and then transported to Japan. It emphasizes meditation, direct experience and enlightenment without dependence on scriptures or external authority, although usually a master is required. The essence of Zen is described in the famous words attributed to its founder BODHIDHARMA: *A special transmission outside of the scriptures; no dependence on words or letters; Direct pointing to the soul of man; Seeing into one's nature, and the attainment of Buddhahood.* The term is derived from the Sanskrit 'DHYANA', meaning intense or ecstatic concentration, although it is important to acknowledge that the path of Zen is about realizing the Buddha nature in everyday life. In order to accomplish this goal there are several different schools of Zen Buddhism.

Zendo (J) *Buddhism*   A hall usually in a separate building within the grounds of a monastery used by ZEN Buddhist monks for meditation and sleeping. (*See also* ZAZEN)

Zenga (J) *Buddhism*   Ink drawings that indicate the spirit of ZEN by attempting to capture the essence of the eternal now.

Zenji (J) *Buddhism*   The title of respect used for a teacher of ZEN. Zen Buddhism considers that the guidance of an enlightened master is an essential requirement to attain realization of the Buddha nature.

Zephaniah *Judaism*   One of the twelve minor prophets and a book of the Jewish scriptures of the same name. A contemporary of JEREMIAH, he warned the people that the time of final judgement by God was inevitable and therefore to display humility and live a righteous life. (*See also* NEVIIM)

Zhikr *Islam*   See DHIKR.

Zikhron Teruah *Judaism*   The reference to the memorial blowing of a ram's horn (SHOFAR) in the book of LEVITICUS in the Bible that is repeated annually on the feast of the Jewish New Year. (*See also* ROSH HASHANAH)

Zikhronot *Judaism*   A proclamation that God is the Master of Absolute

Remembrance and Judge of the Universe that is made on the feast of ROSH HASHANAH, the Jewish New Year. (*See also* MUSAPH)

Zimmi *Islam*　　See DHIMMI.

Zion *Christianity*　　The name of the ancient citadel of JERUSALEM that became synonymous for Jerusalem itself. It is used by some Christian denominations to denote the heavenly city of God.

Zionism *Judaism*　　The movement founded by Theodore Hertzl in 1897 to establish a Jewish state in Palestine. Although Jews in the DIASPORA had always prayed to return to Jerusalem, the hope of return was bound up with messianic expectations. Increasingly, under the pressure of anti-Semitism in Eastern Europe and Russia, non-religious groups began to campaign for a Jewish homeland as the only solution to persecution. At the end of the nineteenth century the first Zionist Congress was held, after which their leaders began a campaign to persuade the British authorities to hand over Palestine to the Jews. After World War II the creation of a Jewish state became the approved policy of the United Nations. Eventually, the Zionists achieved their aim in 1948. However, there has always been conflict with Orthodox Jews, who believe that ISRAEL should be a religious state implementing the TORAH (Jewish law) in its entirety.

Ziporah *Judaism*　　The wife of the prophet MOSES, and daughter of JETHRO, the priest of Midian.

Ziyarat *Islam*　　A religious event in which a tomb of a deceased holy man, SUFI or IMAM is visited, usually in order to petition the divine through the saint's ability to intervene. The petitions are typically pragmatic, such as helping in a family problem, curing sickness or infertility. (*See also* DAR; MAZAR)

Zizit / Tzizit / Tzittzit *Judaism*　　The fringes are required on the four borders of Jewish garments according to the instructions in the TORAH. Today, Orthodox Jews retain the fringes of wool or silk on each of the four corners of their prayer shawls. It is also used for the fringed undervest worn by Orthodox males. (*See also* ARBA KANFOT)

Zohar *Judaism*　　The most important text of Jewish mysticism, sometimes called the Bible of the KABBALAH, written in the thirteenth century and attributed to Moses de Leon of Spain. This work has been highly influential on later scholars and mystics of the kabbalah tradition, especially those of the Safat school in Palestine. A verse-by-verse commentary on the five books of the PENTATEUCH written in Aramaic, it attempts to provide a deeper allegorical understanding that reveals the nature of God.

Zorowar Singh *Sikhism* One of the sons of GURU GOBIND SINGH, the last human Guru of the Sikhs. He was captured with his younger brother by the Muslim forces after becoming separated from his father. Both sons refused to convert to Islam and were bricked up alive in a wall in 1704.

Zuhr / Salat al-Zuhr *Islam* The second of the five obligatory daily prayers which can be performed from soon after midday until the afternoon. (*See* ASR; FAJR; ISHA; MAGHRIB; SALAH)

Zwingli, Ulrich (1484–1531) *Christianity* One of the key figures of the REFORMATION, although not as prominent as LUTHER or CALVIN. He initiated Protestant reform in Switzerland by rejecting the authority of the Pope, clerical celibacy and the sacrifice of the Mass. He developed a symbolic interpretation of the Eucharist in which Christ is not considered to be actually present. The term 'Zwinglian' became associated with the belief that the Communion was only a memorial of Christ's death. (*See also* CONSUBSTANTIATION; TRANSUBSTANTIATION)